Introduction

This collection of readings reflects a significant change in the study of human development and behavior during the past decade. The change has not yet, and may never, become the norm, but it has significantly altered and enriched our understanding of the forces that shape the development of the human being.

The nature of the change is reflected in a superficial sign. Ten years ago, it would have been difficult to find research literature with a rigorous study that was not couched in terms of S and E. S was of course the subject, and E the experimenter. The latter, and often the former, had or needed no further identity—no name, no age, no sex, no role in life other than to participate in an experiment that ended on the same day, or even in the same hour, in which it began.

By and large, the participants in the experiments and investigations cited in this volume have lost their anonymity. They are not merely passive strangers, but active and familiar agents who play significant roles in each other's lives as family members, friends, pupils, teachers, and fellow workers. They come from particular segments of society and share common experiences. Indeed, the experiments in which they participate, whether made by man or nature, often continue over a period of days, weeks, or months—or, on occasion, even a lifetime. And these experiments are conducted not only in the laboratory, but also in the setting in which the activities under investigation normally occur, such as the home, play group, school, or community. In short, the new approach combines rigorous scientific method with what might be called *ecological validity*—the study of the developing person in the contexts in which he lives.

This same orientation characterizes the course out of which these readings have emerged. They are the product of two decades of experience in teaching a large beginning class on "The Development of Human Behavior." In addition to being an introduction to two fields (Human Development and Psychology), the course serves undergraduate and graduate students from many disciplines as a general introduction to behavioral science.

This broad perspective is reflected in the selection of readings, which draw not only on psychological research, but also on studies from biology, human genetics, sociology, and anthropology. The principal focus of concern is the interplay of biological factors, human interaction, social structures, and cultural forces in shaping the individual. Thus we have selected articles which document specific influences—biological and social—on the process of development. Special emphasis is given to the implications of science for social policy, and in turn, to the manner in which social policy shapes, and sometimes stifles, scientific endeavor.

Some of these readings, like the articles of Spitz, and Skodak and Skeels, have stood the test of a quarter of a century of discussion; others are as yet untried, having been published only in the past year or specially written for this volume. But we commend them all to our readers as invitations to scientific inquiry and adventure in understanding the process of human development.

The editor wishes to acknowledge the outstanding contribution of one of his graduate students, Maureen Mahoney, in evaluating manuscripts and preparing them for publication. In the last frenzied days of editing, another graduate student, James Garbarino, aided immeasurably in our task and wrote a much needed note on major gaps in our knowledge of the effects of television on parent-child interaction. In addition, four undergraduate students, Elizabeth Bernstein, Dana Friedman, Wendy Michel, and Linda Rifkin, contributed in the search for articles. Finally, the one who not only typed the manuscript but also made it possible for the rest of us to function was Carmela Mondelli. Thanks are due to all of them; also to Roger Williams and the staff of Dryden Press for their resourcefulness and patience; and, above all, to the authors represented in these pages for making the real contribution—first in research, and now in teaching.

Contents

Part One
Scientific Method in the Study of Human Behavior

Whatever the subject matter, the aims and methods of science are fundamentally the same—to formulate and verify general principles through the joint application of logic and objective, controlled observation. Science begins with a question and proceeds to a tentative answer. This tentative answer is referred to as a hypothesis. A hypothesis is usually derived from observation, theory, or a combination of both.

But, while there are no restrictions on the source of a hypothesis, there are rather rigorous technical requirements on the form that a hypothesis must take and on the conditions that must be met if the hypothesis is to be considered as verified or, more properly, as not rejected. Unfortunately, these technical matters are typically presented in abstract terms, without reference to concrete research problems. This is particularly true in discussions of the structure of hypotheses, the logic of verification, and the problems of measurement in the study of human behavior. For this reason, a special chapter has been written to deal with these topics. In addition, an introduction to statistics and research design prepared by Professor Donald Hebb for his own introductory text on psychology has been included.

1.1   The Structure and Verification of Hypothesis

Urie Bronfenbrenner
Cornell University

What is a Hypothesis?

The scientific process begins with the asking of a question about the nature of objective reality. The scientist then tries to obtain an answer to his questions through observing, classifying, and relating what he sees. He tries to arrive at tentative answers. Such tentative answers are called *hypotheses*.

Actually, in science, the term *hypothesis* is used with several different meanings. If we seek a general definition, one that encompasses all uses of the term, we can say that *a hypothesis is any supposition about a fact.*

Let us examine what forms such suppositions may take.

Forms of Hypotheses

Some years ago, Dr. Louis DiCarlo, then the director of a speech clinic in Syracuse, New York, was surprised by the unexpectedly high proportion of cases of cleft palate coming from certain sparsely populated counties in upstate New York. He was so struck by the phenomenon that he reported it to the district office of the U. S. Public Health Service directed by Dr. John Gentry. Gentry responded by doing what public health physicians have done for decades; he started putting up pins on a map, in this instance a map of New York State, one pin for each case, not only of cleft palate, but of all reported congenital malformations (which are deformities present at birth). When all the pins were in place, they made a pattern that Gentry found familiar. Where had he seen it before? After some effort, he remembered. It was in a geology course, on a map of igneous rock formations in New York State. Igneous rocks are those that were originally extracted from within the earth's surface. They are found in mountainous areas and glacial deposits. What is more, some of these rocks emit natural radiation, and, as Gentry knew, radiation had been suspected as a possible source of cleft palate and other deformities present at birth.

In short, Gentry had arrived at a hypothesis about DeCarlo's original observation. He had a "supposition about a fact." Indeed, he had several. In his published paper, Gentry (1959) investigated a series of hypotheses. Let us examine three of them:

1. Igneous rocks are radioactive.
2. Rates of congential malformation are higher among residents of mountain areas than of plains and valleys.
3. An increase in the amount of natural radiation increases the rate of congenital malformation in the population living in the area.

Each of these three statements is a supposition about a fact, but the propositions differ in kind. To begin with, note how the first statement can be distinguished from the other two. The latter both postulate a relation between variation in one factor and variation in another, whereas the former involves no variation at all; it merely claims the presence of a particular characteristic in a class of objects, in this case of radioactivity in igneous rocks. A supposition that simply postulates the presence of a phenomenon we shall refer to as an *attributive* hypothesis. It merely asserts that a particular entity or event exists and can be observed. Witness the following examples:

1. In 1869, Mendelyev (1869), using his periodic table as a basis, predicted the existence of three then-unknown elements and specified their properties. The elements were subsequently discovered and found to have precisely the properties Mendelyev had attributed to them.
2. In 1929, the German psychiatrist, Hans Berger (1930), found evidence for the hypothesis that the human brain exhibited constant electrical activity, even during sleep.
3. In 1956, the Swedish biologists, Tjio and Levan (1956), using a new method for handling cells, obtained photographic evidence that the normal number of chromosomes in man was not 48, as had been thought previously, but 46. This hypothesis was subsequently confirmed by numerous investigators.
4. For over a quarter of a century, the American psychologist, J. B. Rhine (1964) has claimed validity for the hypothesis of *extrasensory perception*—the ability to receive information without benefit of the known physical senses (for example, thought transference, clairvoyance, etc.). Although much evidence has been adduced in support of the phenomena, most psychologists remain unconvinced, because of flaws in the methods used (for a critical review, see Gerden, 1962).

If we now turn our attention to hypotheses involving two variables, we observe a difference in the two examples given from Gentry's research. Strictly speaking, the first simply posits a statistical relationship between two variables, rate of congenital malformation on the one hand, geographical environment on the other. In contrast, the last proposition explicitly goes beyond a merely statistical association in claiming a cause and effect relationship: natural radiation is presumed to contribute to the development of congenital malformations.

To distinguish one kind of statement from the other, we shall designate the first as an *associative hypothesis,* and the second as a *casual hypothesis.* In other words, an *associative* hypothesis is one that stipulates a statistical relationship between two variables without explicitly asserting that one of these variables influences the other. *A causal* hypothesis does add this

additional specification; it asserts that variation in one factor produces variation in the other.

It is true that many associative hypotheses, when proved correct, add weight to an existing causal hypothesis, or suggest a new explanatory principle. We have an instance of the latter when confirmation of the purely geographical hypothesis proposed by DiCarlo led Gentry (1959) to identify natural radiation as a possible cause of congenital malformation.

But the associative hypothesis may not imply or suggest any explanations at all; it may merely call attention to a phenomenon to be explained. Consider, for example, the hypothesis proposed by Bronfenbrenner (1958) that over recent decades child rearing practices in the United States have become more permissive. Certainly one cannot conclude that the sheer passage of time makes successive generations more lenient in bringing up their children. We are left with the question as to what factors lead parents to treat their own children differently from the way in which they themselves were treated. In reply to this question Bronfenbrenner suggests that one explanation is to be found in the changing pattern of advice given to parents in successive editions of such widely read publications as the Children's Bureau bulletin on Infant Care (1951) and Benjamin Spock's pocketbook on the same subject (1957).

The foregoing example illustrates the nature and uses of the associative hypothesis. What this type of hypothesis does is to raise the question of a possible pattern among the variables observed. If the presence of the pattern is confirmed, this fact in time may serve one of three purposes: call attention to a new research problem, suggest a new causal hypothesis for investigation, or provide evidence in support or rejection of an already existing one.

The Causal Hypothesis Analyzed.

We have said that a causal hypothesis differs from a purely associative one in stipulating a cause-and-effect relationship. What do we mean by this term?

The answer to this question turns out to be rather complex. We may begin with a formal definition. A cause-and-effect relationship exists when *a change in one variable is a necessary or sufficient condition to produce a given effect on another variable.*

Independent and dependent variables.

Let us now look at the definition in greater detail. Notice first of all that the hypothesis postulates a relation between two factors, one which produces the change, the other the one in which the change is produced. The first, the one that produces the change, is called the *independent* or *antecedent* variable. The other, the one that is changed, is called the *dependent* or *consequent* variable, because it hangs (depends) on the

independent variable and follows from it. Thus in Gentry's causal hypothesis the amount of natural radiation is the independent variable, the rate of congenital malformation the dependent variable.

Usually, the causal hypothesis is a one-way street. It works in only one direction. For example, changing the amount of natural radiation increases congenital malformation, but a change in the malformation rate, say by medical intervention, cannot have the slightest effect on the radioactivity of the rocks. But there can be causal relationships which operate in both directions. Contemporary theories of interpersonal relations (Homans, 1950; Heider, 1958; Newcomb, 1953) contain many hypotheses of this character. For example: the more similar two people are, the more likely they are to have positive feelings toward one another. But the process also operates in the reverse direction: the more two people like each other, the more they take on each other's characteristics. In other words, in this particular instance, independent and dependent variables are interchangeable. For this and other reasons, statements of causal hypotheses can be deceptive and may require careful analysis to ascertain which variable is which.

A helpful device in this connection is to conduct a hypothetical experiment in your mind—what the German psychologists call a Gedanken Experiment, a "thought experiment." Try changing each of the variables, and see what happens to the other one. If a change in A leads to a change in B, then A is an independent variable and B dependent. Conversely, if A varies with the change in B, it is A which is the dependent variable. If both change, we have what may be called a *reciprocal* causal relationship.

This does not mean, however, that a directional relationship, in which a change in one variable is followed by a change in the other, necessarily implies cause and effect. A case in point is provided by Bronfenbrenner's hypothesis, already cited, that over the past twenty-five years American child rearing practices have become more permissive. Clearly, it is the practices that have changed with time, rather than the reverse. In other words, the passage of time is the independent variable, parental behavior the dependent. But one cannot regard time as the factor which makes successive generations more lenient.

Necessary and sufficient conditions.

This brings us to the main feature which distinguishes the causal hypothesis from its purely associative counterpart: the former always stipulates that one variable actually *influences* the other. This requirement may take two different forms, specified in the definition by the terms "necessary" or "sufficient." What do each of these terms mean?

Necessary means that *the effect cannot occur except under the* specified condition. For example, the disease process known as tuberculosis cannot occur in animal or man in the absence of a creature known as *Microbacter-*

ium tuberculosis, the bacterium which we say "causes" the illness. It is a *necessary* condition.

Although the tubercular bacillus is necessary for the development of the disease, it is quite possible for a person to be a carrier of this baccillus and yet be perfectly healthy, because the human organism develops antibodies which keep the bacillus under control. In other words, the bacillus is a necessary condition, but not a *sufficient* one. A sufficient condition is one that produces a given effect: for example, stick a healthy baby with a pin, and it cries. Of course inflicting pain is not the only condition that will make a baby cry. He will also cry if deprived of food. But sticking him with a pin will do the job. It is a *sufficient* condition.

An example of a less obvious sufficient condition is provided by a study conducted by Rheingold, Gewirtz, and Ross (1959) at the National Institutes of Health. These investigators were interested in what it takes to make a baby vocalize more—that is, make more sounds. They showed that the rate of vocalizing among three-month-old infants could be increased markedly by such simple actions on the part of the adult as touching the baby's abdomen with the finger every time the infant made a sound, smiling at it, and clucking at it ("tsk, tsk, tsk") in return. When the adult experimenter reacted in this way, the baby's vocalization rate just about doubled. None of these things was *necessary* to make the baby vocalize more, but they were *sufficient*.

Notice that in actual practice, a sufficient condition may not produce the given effect in every case. A baby will not vocalize every time an adult touches, smiles, or makes noises at it. It may be tired, fearful, or simply distracted by some other event. Nor will an infant cry every time it is stuck with a pin; it may have a bad case of laryngitis, the pin may not hit a pain spot, or the baby may be crying already. In other words, something can interfere.

To put it in another way, a given phenomenon can occur only under certain *boundary conditions*. These boundary conditions are of two kinds. First, all *necessary* conditions to make possible variation in the dependent variable must be satisfied. Thus a baby cannot cry without a functioning voice box (larynx); it cannot smile if the facial nerve is injured; it can do neither if it is seriously ill or exhausted. In other words, a sufficient condition cannot be effective until all necessary conditions are met. But even if all necessary conditions for producing the effect are satisfied, the infant may not be able to perceive the stimulus, and hence not make the response. He may not hear the "tsk, tsk", see the smiling face, or feel the touch or the pin because the stimulus doesn't hit a functioning touch receptor. These are conditions that must be met—not for the effect to occur in the dependent variable (a blind, deaf, or tactilely insensitive baby may be perfectly able to smile and cry) but for the independent variable to be functional in producing the effect. In other words, we are dealing here with a class of variables

which limit not the dependent variables but the *relation* between the independent and dependent variables. To distinguish such requirements from what we have called necessary conditions—those that apply to the dependent variable itself—we shall refer to them as *contingent* conditions. Given an independent variable x and a dependent variable y, a contingent condition is one that is not necessary to produce a given effect in y but is required *for x* to produce the given effect in y. Boundary conditions, then, include all necessary and contingent conditions.

We are now in a position to offer a definition of a sufficient condition: *within a given set of boundary conditions, x is a sufficient condition if a change in x produces a change in y.*

Interrelation of the Three Types of Hypotheses.

A causal hypothesis, then, is one that stipulates one variable as a necessary or sufficient condition for another. Note also that the causal hypothesis always implies an associative hypothesis as well, since a necessary or sufficient condition inevitably produces a statistical relationship between independent and dependent variables. Finally, an associative hypothesis assumes that each of its components is an observable phenomenon; in other words, it implies two attributive hypotheses. In short, the three types of hypotheses fall into a nested arrangement, like a set of Russian dolls, with the causal hypothesis containing the associative hypothesis, and the associative containing two attributive hypotheses.

If one asks whether there exists still a higher order construct encompassing more than one causal hypothesis, the answer is of course found in the concept of a *theory*. Although this term has no rigorous definition or use, it usually refers to a body of interrelated hypotheses such as Freudian theory, learning theory, dissonance theory, or role theory, all of which have been employed in the attempt to understand the development of human behavior.

As we shall see, the hierarchical structure of the causal hypothesis dictates the steps to be followed in proving a cause-and-effect relationship. The investigator begins by specifying a procedure for observing each of the separate variables in the investigation. By demonstrating that such observations can be made, he in effect confirms the attributive hypothesis for each factor. He then proceeds to demonstrate a statistical association between two of the variables under circumstances which require such an association to be the product of a cause-and-effect relationship.

We turn next to an examination of the principles and procedures involved in the process of hypothesis testing.

II. The Logic of Verification

In our discussion we shall focus attention on the causal hypothesis since, as we have seen, this incorporates all other types as well. Given our

definition of a cause and effect relationship, the task of verification becomes that of demonstrating that a given condition is necessary or sufficient. As we shall see, the proof begins somewhat differently for the two cases, but ends with a similar exacting requirement.

The logic of demonstrating a cause and effect relationship.

Let us begin with the case of a necessary condition. Since necessary means that the dependent variable (B) cannot occur without the independent variable (A), one must show first of all that all possible instances of (B) are preceded or accompanied by (A). The situation with a sufficient condition involves a different requirement. Here variation in one factor must produce a given effect on the other. In other words, a change in A must be followed by the specified effect in B.

Now let us suppose that one or the other of the above requirements is fulfilled. Does this mean that a necessary condition has in fact been demonstrated in the one case, and a sufficient condition in the other? Unfortunately not. If that were all there was to it, the work of the scientist would be much easier than it is, and much less interesting.

The inadequacy of either of the above demonstrations is brought home by the tale of a man who obviously understood exactly what he was doing. This chap discovered that every time he drank a highball of scotch and ginger ale, he became drunk. The next time he tried gin and ginger ale and got the same effect. Then he experimented with rye and ginger ale and you know what happened. What to do? "Aha'," he said, "I know what does it." And the next time he eliminated the ginger ale.

This example shows that, to demonstrate a necessary or sufficient condition, it is not enough to show the required kind of relationship between the independent variable A and the dependent variable B. One must also establish that no other factor X is functioning as an independent variable. For if it is, then the results are *confounded*; that is, one cannot separate the effect of A from the effect of X. And if X is actually responsible for the effect, then A is neither necessary nor sufficient.

Demonstrating that a given effect is produced by A, and not by some other factor, can turn out to be a fairly complicated task, especially if people in general—and scientists in particular—are sure they already know what the necessary or sufficient condition is.

The Goldberger story

To show how complicated it can be, let us look at the case history of a hypothesis that is all inclusive, since it postulates a condition which is both necessary and sufficient at the same time. The case history begins back in the early 1900's.[1] At that time they were having trouble down in the South —in Virginia, South Carolina, Mississippi, and Georgia. It was a different

kind of trouble. But they did what they so often do when there is trouble in the South; they sent a man from Washington. This mans name was Joseph Goldberger.

In the period 1900 to 1914, 100,000 people died every year in the American South from a disease called *pellagra*. In Italian, pellagra means "rough skin," one of the symptoms of the disease.

Other symtoms, which come on gradually, include running sores, foul odor, vomiting, diarrhea, terrible pain, nervous and mental disturbances, and finally that ultimate symptom—death.

In 1912, just before Goldberger was sent down from Washington, a top medical commission had surveyed all the available evidence and had concluded that pellagra was "a specific infectious disease communicable from person to person by means at present unknown."

Goldberger got off the train at Spartanberg, South Carolina, where there was a pellagra hospital. As an investigator he saw his first task as one of observing. Pellagra cases were everywhere; not only in the hospital but all round the countryside. Goldberger saw emaciated bodies, sallow sunken faces, cases of insanity.

But he noticed other things too. It was cotton country. In the mill towns and villages everyone was trying to live by cotton, and not succeeding. Families were attempting to survive on fifteen dollars a week, and they looked it. If they paid the rent and bought the barest necessities in clothes, there wasn't half enough left for food. And it was the same in Georgia, in Florida, Alabama and Virginia.

In fact, you can still see it—not the pellagra, but the poverty. And it still takes its toll, both physically and psychologically.

But back to Goldberger. As he visited hospitals and institutions, he noticed a strange thing: none of the nurses, attendants or other employees, who were in daily contact with the pellagra cases, had ever developed the disease.

He also observed that in an orphanage he visited, there were virtually no pellagra cases below the age of six or above the age of twelve, but in the middle group, practically all the children had pellagra.

Goldberger knew that he had run onto a critical natural experiment. He was hot on the trail of a hypothesis.

In the institutional setting, it didn't take him very long to find what he was looking for. It had to do with food.

1.   The middle group ate only the regular institutional diet.
2.   The little ones got a regular milk supplement.
3.   The older group supplemented their diet by foraging on their own.

And what did the regular institutional menu consist of? Traditional Southern dishes—but low cost ones—biscuits, hominy grits, corn mush, syrup, molasses, gravy, sowbelly. Plenty to eat, but no milk, no eggs, no butter, no meat—in short, no animal proteins.

It would seem he had found the answer. All that remained was to publish it to the world. But Goldberger didn't. Instead, he went to another institution with lots of pellagra cases, instituted dietary changes, and the pellagra went away. Just like that.

Then Goldberger published. And what was the reaction? Leaders of the medical profession were unconvinced. Goldberger had not found the agent of contagion, and "as is well known, pellagra is a contagious disease."

So Goldberger decided to do an experiment that would be convincing. He would show that he could produce pellagra in healthy human beings. But he needed volunteers. So he went to the Governor of Mississippi with a request. Would the Governor grant pardons to 12 convicts with long-term sentences in state prison if they volunteered to stay in Goldberger's experiment for six months. The risk: pellagra, the gain: freedom.

The Governor of Mississippi was an understanding man, Goldberger got his volunteers—twelve enterprising fellows—embezzlers, highwaymen, murderers—and in the best of health.

When the experiment started, the volunteers were sure they had a good thing going. Instead of the regular prison fare, they were being given special meals—and what meals! The food was well cooked, tasted fine, an every man got all he wanted. For breakfast there was: biscuits, fried mush, syrup. For dinner: corn bread, cabbage, sweet potatoes, grits. For supper: rice, gravy, fried mush, coffee with sugar.

Eighty additional convicts, who were designated as a control group, lived under the same conditions as the volunteers—except for diet.

After a few weeks, the volunteers began to doubt that they had made such a fine bargain. They began to feel queer—headache, stomach ache, dizziness. By the fifth month, the skin began to scale, and all the classical symptoms of pellagra were present.

The convicts were pardoned, released, and offered a cure, but they were too frightened to take it. Goldberger hastened to report his findings at a meeting of public health experts in Washington. At the meeting, the Chairman had some remarks to make. He said he wished "to enunciate certain beliefs concerning pellagra, these beliefs being backed by research done by good American citizens such as Siler, Garrison, and MacNeal." The Chairman then went on to state that pellagra was "a specific infectious disease, communicable from person to person by unknown means."

In short, Goldberger's argument was unconvincing in the light of prevailing views. How did Goldberger react? With another experiment. He recognized that he had not yet proved his point. He still had a requirement to fulfill. He had built a case for his own independent variable—diet, but he had

not shown that another independent variable, X, had not infuenced the results. Specifically, he had not dealt with the accepted explanation for pellagra, and for virtually all the other diseases known at that time—contagion. He hadn't really answered the principal argument of his opponents.

Goldberger set out to eliminate the contagion hypothesis once and for all. This is how he did it.

He drew an ounce of blood from a pellagra patient suffering an acute attack. A colleague then injected five cubic centimeters of the patient's blood into Goldberger's shoulder. In addition, secretions from the patient's nose and throat were swabbed into Goldberger's nose and throat. Finally, he selected two patients—one with scaling sores and the other with diarrhea. He scraped the scales from the sores, mixed the scales with four cubic centimeters of urine from the same patients, added an equal amount of liquid feces, and rolled the mixture into little dough balls by the addition of a few pinches of flour. The pills were then taken voluntarily by him, by his assistants and by his wife. Publication of the experiment was withheld for five months to make sure that there were no delayed effects. The report mentioned no names. It simply spoke of 15 men and a housewife.

The experiment made its point. Finally, the "infectionists" were silenced. Years after Goldberger's death the substance contained in animal protein necessary to prevent pellagra was named Vitamin G. But the name didn't stick. Personal tribute had to give way to scientific progress. In 1936, the critical substance was identified morespecifically as nicotinic acid.

Proof as a psychological problem.

As Goldberger's experience demonstrates, the process of proof may demand more than satisfying logical requirements. It may also necessitate overcoming psychological barriers. Verification does not take place in a vacuum; it occurs in the minds of men. The human mind is not always capable of seeing objectively, let alone thinking objectively. Both perception and thought can be distorted by conviction and desire. Nor are scientists any more immune to such distortions than other men. The medical scientists who heard and read Goldberger's reports were neither stupid nor evil. They simply *knew* that pellagra was a contagious disease, and—what is more important—they knew this was the opinion of the "best authorities."

Since one does not have to be a social scientist to regard himself or be regarded by others as an authority on problems of human behavior, the researcher in this sphere frequently finds himself confronted with a task of psychologoical as well as logical persuasion.

Some principles of verification.

Nevertheless, it is logic that lies at the heart of the matter. To make explicit the principles involved, let us analyze the steps in the argument as exemplified in Goldberger's work.

What was Goldberger's line of reasoning? Where did he begin?

First he established that every case of pellagra he observed ate a certain diet; persons not eating the diet never contracted pellagra.

In other words, Goldberger showed that two variables were related statistically. He confirmed what we have called an associative hypothesis.

What does this demonstration accomplish?

Does it prove a necessary condition? He had shown every case of pellagra had eaten the same kind of diet.

Could some other factor have accounted for the same results?

Yes, contagion—through infected food; through sewage.

Does his demonstration prove a sufficient condition? He had shown that a difference in diet was related to pellagra, but could some other factor have accounted for the same results? Again the answer is yes. The food could have been infected. This brings us to our first principle.

Principle I

A causal hypothesis is not proved so long as an alternative hypothesis can be offered to explain the same findings.

In other words, no causal hypothesis can be regarded as confirmed until all plausible alternative hypotheses have been eliminated. This requirement points up a critical limitation of any purely associative hypothesis, such as the one we have just been considering. The demonstration that a particular kind of association exists of course does not eliminate the possibility that this association is the product of some third factor. This is one of the reasons why—

Principle II

The demonstration that a particular kind of association between two variables exists cannot, by itself, prove that one of these variables is a necessary of sufficient condition for the other.

So what did Goldberger's first step accomplish? Could he draw any inferences from it at all?

What was his associative hypothesis? Was it simply that diet and pellagra tend to occur together?

Suppose Goldberger had found the following:

	Percent pellagra cases
Eating diet	85%
Not eating diet	5%

Do we have an association? Yes.
Do we have a necessary condition? No.

Putting the matter more generally—in establishing a necessary condition, *all* positive instances of the dependent variable must be associated with *presence* of the independent variable. There can be no exceptions.

And Goldberger didn't find any. The actual percentage among those not eating diet was zero.

So the results for an associative hypothesis can be useful after all. They can be used to *disprove* a hypothesis about a necessary condition. We may put this as a general principle.

Principle III

Results for a hypothesis of association can disprove a hypothesis of necessity so long as there is even a single case in which the dependent variable occurs without the independent variable.

Can results for a hypothesis of association disprove a hypothesis of sufficient condition as well?

The answer to this question turns out to be somewhat more complicated. To demonstrate the point, we must take a different example. Suppose that instead of working with pellagra, Goldberger had been working with a still unsolved mystery, the common cold, and was investigating the hypothesis that exposure to damp weather increases susceptibility. In studying case records of visits to general practitioners by persons complaining of colds, he finds the following:

	% of all patients with colds
Persons working mainly indoors (businessmen, secretaries, etc.)	50%
Persons working mainly outdoors (laborers, policemen, etc.)	50%

In other words, no association. Does this mean that exposure to dampness does not increase susceptibility to colds? No.

Persons working outdoors may be healthier.

Persons working indoors may take their complaints to a doctor more often.

Principle IV

A negative result for a hypothesis of association cannot, by itself, disprove a hypothesis of sufficiency, since it does not eliminate the possibility that an association in fact exists but is counteracted by some third factor.

Since results for a purely associative hypothesis can neither prove nor disprove that a variable is a sufficient condition, do they have any utility at all in investigating hypotheses of sufficiency?

Did it make any difference to Gentry that the association between congenital malformation and rock formations came out as it did?

Of course; the association suggested that he was on the right track.

Since an association between two variables can imply a possible causal relation—

Principle V

A positive result for an associative hypothesis increases the probability that the implied causal hypothesis can be sustained; a negative result decreases that probability, eliminating it completely in the case of a hypothesis of necessity.

In view of the above principle, tests of associative hypotheses are very useful in the early stages of research, not only to narrow down the independent variables that are to become the foci of further investigation, but also tentatively to identify or eliminate other factors that may have to be controlled in order to establish the hypothesis in question.

We had just identified one such factor in relation to the first step in Goldberger's investigation; namely, we pointed out that the observed association between diet and pellagra did not rule out the possibility of contagion.

Let us now eliminate that possibility and see where we stand then.

Suppose Goldberger had done both the first step and the last; that is, he

a. showed an association between diet and pellagra, with all cases of pellagra eating a deficient diet,

b. showed by his experiment that pellagra was not contagious.

Would he have proved his hypothesis?

Remember: A hypothesis is not proved until no alternative hypothesis can be given to explain the observed findings.

Can an alternative explanation be offered?

Who were the people who ate the deficient diet? Poor cotton workers. What about the following possibilities:

1. Contact with some poison associated with processing cotton.
2. Excessive exposure to sunlight.
3. Exposure to natural radiation.
4. Exposure to extremes of temperatures.

Notice that in the groups that Goldberger studied these are factors that were associated with eating a deficient diet—that is, with the independent variable of the hypothesis.

Does this mean that you have to rule out any factor that happens to be associated with the independent variable of the hypothesis?

What about the evil eye? Some people think you can get sick from being given the evil eye. And poor people are more likely to have such beliefs than the well-to-do and well-educated.

Is it necessary to rule out the evil eye as a possible influence?'

No. Because there is no scientific basis for believing that an evil eye could have such an effect.

So what alternatives hypotheses do you have to rule out? Any and all? When must a variable be considered as a potentially confounding factor?

Principle VI

In testing a hypothesis, a variable must be considered as a potentially confounding factor when it is associated with the independent variable of the hypothesis, and scientific ground exists for believing that the variable in question could influence the dependent variable.

Poison encountered either in the course of cotton processing or—more important—simply in the diet eaten by poor families, would satisfy both of the above conditions. And in Goldberger's time, perhaps so could exposure to dampness, sunlight, or extremes of temperature.

How would one rule out the possibility that such factors could explain the observed results?

Would one have to disprove each of them the way Goldberger did with contagion?

That would have been an awful lot of work. Did Goldberger do all that? No, he didn't.

Then Goldberger didn't prove his case after all? We have all been taken in—and so have all the scientists—then and today.

What did Goldberger do that eliminated all of these alternative hypotheses—and some others as well—at one fell swoop?

He supplemented the diet of pellagra cases with animal proteins and the pellagra disappeared.

Notice that this procedure immediately eliminates the possibility that poison, climate, sleep, etc. could influence the results. Since the same individuals are involved throughout, and they remain in the same environment, all of the above variables—and a host of others—are held constant. Only one factor is allowed to vary—the independent variable of the hypothesis—change in diet. If, under the circumstances, the dependent variable then also changes, the change can be attributable only to the independent variable.

We have just illustrated the fundamental principle for verifying causal hypotheses.

Principle VII

To establish a cause-and-effect relationship, one demonstrates that variable x has an effect on variable y by allowing x to vary, holding constant other sources of variation for y, and then showing that y varies in a specified fashion as a function of the variation in x.

There are a number of different methods for varying x while holding constant other sources of variation for y; these are discussed in textbooks on experimental design. One more step remains to complete our examination of principles of verification as illustrated by Goldberger's classic investigation.

Suppose Goldberger had carried out only the second and the last steps of his research. That is, he had shown that

Step 2.   Supplementing the diet of pellagra cases with animal proteins made the pellagra disappear

Step 4.   Pellagra could not be contracted through contagion.

Are these two steps enough to prove that deficient diet is a necessary condition for pellagra?

To prove a hypothesis of necessity you have to show two things:

1.   that without the independent variable (diet), the effect cannot take place.

Has this been shown? Yes.

2.   and that no other independent variable can explain the obtained results.

Does any alternative explanation remain? Note that contagion was eliminated by the experiment in Step 4. Such things as amount of sleep, exposure to sunlight, natural radiation, etc. are held constant by having the same individuals be sick and well in the same environment.

In other words, the combination of Step 2 and Step 4 has established the hypothesis of necessity.

What about the hypothesis of sufficiency. Do Steps 2 and 4 confirm that as well?

To prove a hypothesis of sufficiency, one has to demonstrate that a change in the independent variable A produces a given effect B, and that no other independent variable can explain the obtained results. Thus far we have shown only that diet A is a necessary condition for producing pellagra and that a normal diet is sufficient to cure pellagra. What we still have to do is prove that diet A is sufficient to produce pellagra. How to do it?

By means of Goldberger's experiment producing pellagra in convict volunteers. Other variables were controlled by feeding a comparable group in the same institution on a normal diet.

Here change in A produces the effect in question. And no alternative hypothesis remains.

Quod erat demonstrandum!

Taken together, the results of Goldberger's three experiments "prove" his hypothesis. By producing pellagra through the removal of animal protein from the diet, by curing pellagra through adding this same ingredient to the diet, and by showing that pellagra was not transmitted through contagion, Goldberger established that the necessary and sufficient condition for pella-

gra is absence of animal proteins in the diet. The cause of the disease—what medical scientists call its etiology—was now fully known.

The problem of levels of analysis

But was it really? Perhaps a medical scientist would be satisfied, but what about a chemist?

After all, subsequent investigation showed that pellagra was actually caused not by protein deficiency in general but by the absence in the diet of a specific chemical substance knoyn as nicotinic acid.

And if biological hypotheses have to be reduced to chemical ones, what about psychological explanations, or sociological ones—must each be reduced ultimately to the level of charged particles?

Clearly not. The scientists is free to choose the level of analysis at which he wishes to work. His independent and dependent variables may be at the same or at different levels. The only restriction upon him is that he may not claim conclusions beyond the levels at which he has worked, although his results may suggest new problems and hypotheses at these other levels.

Thus we shall find students of human behavior working at different levels of analysis. Some attempt to relate the behavior of the individual to its physiological and even chemical substrata. Others seek to explain the actions and attitudes of one person as a function of the behavior of others acting individually or in concert as groups, communities, and societies.

But at whatever level the causal hypothesis is couched, the logic of proof remains the same. We may summarize this logic by offering a paradox: *the process of proof is actually one of disproof.* The scientist never really demonstrates that a hypothesis is true; what he does is to eliminate all other possible explanations. In sum, scientific truth is established by default.

III The Measurement of Variables

We have examined the *logic* of science—the principles involved in formulating and testing hypotheses. What about the method? How does one translate the logic into actual research operations?

Operational Definition

Since variables constitute the building blocks of every hypothesis, the first step calls for expressing these variables in some concrete form, in terms of some operation which enables the investigator to determine a change, or lack of change, in the variable in question. Thus, Goldberger had to serve some way of knowing when the subjects in his experiments developed pellagra and when they were cured of this affliction. For this purpose, he used as an index the symptoms of the disease, primarily the appearance of

the characteristic rash for which the condition was named. In other words, the measure of the dependent variable in his hypothesis was simply the diagnosis made by a physician as to whether pellagra was present or absent. Similarly, Goldberger's independent variable was defined by presence or absence of animal proteins in the diet fed to his research subjects.

Of course, we are often interested in intermediate points between complete absence and full development of a variable. For example, as his measure of the relative degree of congenital malformation in a given area, Gentry used the rate of such cases per thousand births as determined from entries in the infants' birth and death certificates of abnormalities observed by the attending physician.

In science, the procedure one employs to determine the degree to which a particular variable is present is called *operational definition*. It is also referred to as *indexing* or just plain *measuring*.

Scales of Measurement

As the foregoing examples illustrate, measuring always involves specification of the category into which a particular observation falls. Categories may differ from each other in one of two ways, in quality or in quantity. Examples of the former are classifications of disease, nationality, occupation, or sex. When a system of classification is based on qualitative distinctions without any implication of order among the categories, we refer to such a system as a *nominal scale*. In a nominal scale, the classes differ by name and not by number; that is, they do not fall into any fixed sequence.

Where the categories do fall into a regular order, but the interval between steps is not fixed in terms of a constant unit of measurement, we speak of an *ordinal scale*. The most simple example of an ordinal scale is a ranking. Ranks, however, have the disadvantage that their significance depends on the number of persons ranked. Thus the student ranking 10th in a class of 10 is clearly not comparable to one who ranks 10th in a class of 100. For this reason, distributions of ordinal position are often broken up into divisions with an equal number of cases in each division. Thus one speaks of a measurement in the top *quartile* (upper fourth of all the cases), *decile* (tenth) or *percentile* (hundredth). All of these are examples of ordinal scales.

The chief limitation of ordinal measurements is that the distance between successive ordinal positions may not be equal (e.g., the difference between the tallest and the second tallest may not be the same as that between the second tallest and third tallest). It is of course much more convenient when the units of measurement are stable. When this condition is satisfied we have what is called an *interval scale*, illustrated by the common thermometer. Notice that the location of the zero point on such a scale is usually quite arbitrary; on an ordinary thermometer, zero does not mean the absence of

any temperature at all. It is for this reason that one cannot say that a temperature of 40° C is twice as hot as 20° C. To be able to make such proportional statements, it is necessary to have an absolute zero point, as in measurements of weight, time, and distance. When an interval scale has this property it is referred to as a *ratio scale*. The scale of cardinal numbers— the one we use to count a series of objects—is of course a ratio scale.

Except for their use in counting people or frequencies of an event, ratio scales are a rarity in the behavioral sciences, since it is difficult to establish an absolute zero point for psychological characteristics. It is usually possible, however, to construct interval scales for most aspects of human behavior. This is fortunate, since the interval scale has many advantages for scientific work. In particular, because of its equally-spaced intervals, it permits the calculation of stable indices which summarize the characteristics of a whole series of measurements.

But before considering how and for what purpose measurements themselves can be manipulated and summarized, we must confront a prior problem regarding their basic soundness.

The Problem of Validity

Whenever one undertakes to translate theoretical variables into concrete indices, one must take into account an omnipresent danger—the danger of mistranslation. The index may not be *measuring what it is supposed to measure*. In scientific terminology, it may not be *valid*. For example, in measuring brain waves, the meter may be plugged into the wrong circuit, with the result that what is being recorded is not the perturbations of electric current in the brain but in the overhead light fixture.

The foregoing example may not be so outlandish as it may seem. In the age of computers, the possibility that one set of data has been substituted for another is hardly negligible. Take the experience of the writer of these lines. A dozen years ago, in a Presidential address (Bronfenbrenner, 1958), I reported some fascinating findings on the effects of different types of parental treatment on the behavior of the child. The results were rather complex, some seemingly contradictory, but I managed to show how they all really fitted together into a single theory. It was rather impressive.

Unfortunately, at the next convention of the American Psychological Association a year later I had to present the same material again to much the same audience (Bronfenbrenner, 1959). I was able to assure my listeners, however, that no one would be bored. You see, through a misunderstanding at the computing center, the signs on all the computations had been reversed, so every relationship that I had reported a year before was in fact exactly backwards. In my second address, I had to set everything right side up. And of course, I came up with a new theory that fitted the "new" results, but somehow it was not so impressive any more.

Here, then, was an instance in which the measurements as they were being used, were completely *invalid*. The more typical case, however, is that of partial validity—the index reflects the variable in question plus other factors as well, which may account for much if not most of the variation. For example, years ago, before the French psychologists Binet and Simon (1905) invented an "objective method" for testing functional intelligence, the evaluation of a child's mental ability was made simply by asking some adult who knew him—usually the teacher—to make a judgment. We know now that although teachers' judgments show a positive relation to more objective measures of the child's intellectual performance, they are also influenced by other factors such as the child's social class level, how he behaves in school, or—perhaps most importantly—the degree to which the teacher likes him. To the extent that these other factors affect the teacher's judgment, her evaluation of the child's mental ability is an invalid index.

Of course, so-called objective measures—such as paper-and-pencil tests with predetermined scoring schemes—also present problems of validity. For example, group tests that purport to measure intelligence, or achievement in a particular subject like history, biology, or even mathematics, may actually be measuring little more than speed of reading. Another source of confounding arises with paper-and-pencil tests of personality, for there the respondent often gives not the real answer but what he thinks he ought to say—the socially desirable response.

There are various ways for getting around such difficulties more or less satisfactorily, but these are technical problems which need not concern us at the moment. The point we wish to make here is that the investigator must always consider the issue of validity with respect to each of the variables included in his investigation and provide some evidence that the procedures he is using—his operational definitions—do in fact measure what they are supposed to measure.

Validation against an outside criterion.

How does one establish that his methods of measurement are valid? When the author was himself a student, this question was simply answered. To show that your technique was valid, you simply tested it against some *external criterion* presumed to measure the same variable. This outside criterion usually took the form of a judgment by a person or persons deemed to be experts on the phenomenon in question. For example, the Stanford-Binet, the best and most widely used individual test of intelligence,[2] was originally validated against teachers' judgments. In other words, to see whether the test was measuring what it was supposed to, Lewis M. Terman, the famous Stanford psychologist, examined the degree of correspondence between the results of the test and the ratings of each child's intelligence made by his classroom teacher. There was a positive relationship

between the two sets of measures, but there were also some exceptions. Some pupils whom the teachers rated high in intelligence turned out low on the test and *vice versa*. Which measure was right? We know now that the Stanford-Binet is usually a more valid measure of intellectual performance than a teacher's rating, but this could not be determined simply from the degree of association between two measures where the validity of each was in question.

The foregoing consideration points to the principal limitation of the *outside criterion* method for evaluating validity; namely, the method is limited by the *validity* of the outside criterion. This approach, therefore, is most applicable in those situations where a valid criterion already exists. But then why develop a new method? Actually, there may be very good reason to do so. The existing valid method may be excellent but expensive of time and resources. The Stanford-Binet is a case in point. It can only be given to one child at a time, requires a trained examiner, and takes anywhere from thirty minutes to an hour and a half to administer. In contrast, group tests of intelligence can be given to an entire classroom within a specified period of time by persons without a high degree of specialized training. Such group tests are invariably validated against the Stanford-Binet as an external criterion.

But what if the outside criterion is itself of inadequate validity, or at least of poorer validity than is desired of the new instrument? Does testing against the outside criterion then have any utility at all? Clearly yes, provided this criterion is believed to have *some* validity, for, then, as in the case of teachers' ratings, it provides some reassurance that the investigator is on the right track. But equally clearly, additional evidence of validity is required, especially in those instances where no external criterion is available, as would occur when the variable was being measured for the first time. How can one establish the validity of a measuring technique without relying on some external index of the variable in question?

Construct Validity

The answer to the foregoing question is suggested by the following fact. The ability of the Stanford-Binet to predict school grades was also offered as evidence for its validity. The argument ran as follows: since intelligence is necessary for academic achievement, there should be a positive relation between measures of intelligence and measures of achievement. Since scores on the Stanford-Binet show such a positive association, this fact is *consistent with* the position that the Stanford-Binet does in fact measure intellectual capacity. Notice that, taken by itself, the existence of the expected relationship does not *prove* the validity of the measure of intelligence, it is merely *consistent* with the presence of such validity. But if one could identify a variety of such expected relationships, and if all of these expectations were

in fact fulfilled, this would obviously increase the probability that the index was actually measuring what it was presumed to measure.

Here we have the guiding principle of the process known as *construct validation*. It may be stated somewhat more formally in the following terms: *a measure has construct validity if it shows a pattern of relationships with other variables that is to be expected from a theoretical analysis of the phenomenon.*

To make clear what is implied by this definition let us take an example of construct validation carried out by Richard Christie and his associates (Christie, 1964; Geis, Christie, and Nelson, 1963; Geis, 1964; Geis and Christie, 1965; Christie and Geis, 1968; Christie and Geis, 1970) at Columbia University. These investigators posit the wide prevalence in contemporary American society of a personality trait which they call Machiavellianism. The origin and nature of this characteristic are described in the following excerpt.

> Since the publication of *The Prince* in 1532, the name of its author has come to designate the use of guile, deceit, and opportunism in interpersonal relations. These behaviors are usually conceived as accompanied by congruent perceptual and attitudinal personality dispositions, characteristically including a dispassionate readiness to expect and detect human weaknesses, failings, and foibles, and the willingness to exploit them. More generally, a Machiavellian is one who views and evaluates others impersonally and amorally in terms of their usefulness for his own purposes. The Machiavellian would thus appear to correspond to the ideal type—or steretoype of the "operator" or "manipulator."
>
> Whatever the labels applied, the syndrome of impersonal, manipulative attitudes and behavior is socially significant. As society becomes more and more organized, increasing proportions of interpersonal contacts become impersonal and means-oriented. As major activity in all areas of society is increasingly conducted by organizations, the ability to influence, direct, and use others effectively becomes increasingly valuable. (Geis, *et al.*, 1963)

To measure the Machiavellian syndrome, Christie and his colleagues have developed a questionnaire of 20 items, of which the following are examples.

Never tell anyone the real reason you did something unless it is useful to do so.

The biggest difference between most criminals and other people is that the criminals are stupid enough to get caught.

Most men forget more easily the death of their father than the loss of their property.

*One should take action only when sure it is morally right. It is safest to

assume that all people have a vicious streak and it will come out when they are given a chance.

*Barnum was wrong when he said that there's a sucker born every minute.

The respondent indicates his degree of agreement with each item on a seven point scale ranging from "strongly disagree" to "strongly agree." Starred items are scored in the opposite direction. The measure of Machiavellianism is the sum of the person's score across all 20 items.

How is the validity of such a scale to be established? Clearly an external criterion is hard to come by. This is particularly true of what might be thought of as the ideal validating index—obtaining Machiavelli's own responses to the items (although some would not deny the ultimate availability of this criterion to the originators of the scale!). The authors themselves have sought to demonstrate validity by testing and confirming a variety of hypotheses about differences between high and low scorers. Here are some of them:

1. When given an opportunity to deceive others in an experimental situation, high scorers were much more active than low scorers in thinking up and carrying out activities which confused, annoyed, and frustrated the other person.

2. In a sample of Washington lobbyists, high scorers spent more time contacting and entertaining Congressmen than low scorers. The high scorers also had more clients.

3. In group discussions, high scorers were more persuasive than low scorers.

4. In a sample of Hungarian immigrants, high scorers adapted to the American way of life more quickly than low scorers.

5. In an experimental game requiring convincing a partner to join in a coalition at a loss to the partner, high scorers generally won, low scorers lost.

6. In a sample of medical students, high scorers were more likely to choose psychiatry over surgery as a specialty.

7. The more ambiguous the rules in an experimental game, the more likely high scorers were to win it.

8. Mach (short for Machianvelli) score tended to be unrelated to amount of education, socioeconomic status, or level of intelligence.

9. When high and low scorers played strategy games over a period of time, the high scorers tended to win in the early stages, but low scorers won in the final stages. The investigators interpreted these results as supporting the hypothesis that "honesty is the best policy—in the long run."

10. When shown slides of past contestants in the Miss Rheingold contest, high scorers were more successful in selecting the winners for each year than were low scorers.
11. Persons reaching 21 years of age after 1942 had higher Mach scores than those attaining their maturity before that date. In other words, the tendency toward Machiavellianism has increased since World War II.
12. High scores on the Mach scale were associated with a history of disrupted relationships in childhood (parents separated or divorced, many moves from one location to another.)
13. "Graduate students in social psychology are more in tune with Machiavelli than any other aggregate of subjects yet tested." (Christie 1964, p. 14)

Note the following characteristics of this set of findings.

A. The variables with which the Mach score shows positive (Hypotheses 1-8. 10-12), negative (Hypothesis 9), and no relationships (Hypothesis 8) are those for which such relationships would be expected, given a valid measure of Machiavellianism as theoretically defined.
B. The hypotheses involve Machiavellianism both as an independent (Hypotheses 1-8, 9-10), and as a dependent variable (Hypotheses 8, 11, 12).
C. Since the presence of a statistical association can serve as corroborative but not as conclusive evidence for verifying a hypothesis (see preceding section), the data submitted include not only evidence of appropriate statistical relations (Hypotheses 2, 4, 6, 7, 8, 10-13), but also relevant results of controlled experiments (Hypotheses 1, 3, 5, 7, 9).
D. Since a laboratory situation necessarily leaves out aspects of the "real world" in which behavior occurs, validating hypotheses involve events outside the laboratory (Hypotheses 2, 4, 6, 8, 10-13) as well as controlled experiments.

As we see from the foregoing analysis, construct validation involves demonstrating that the antecedents, consequents, and correlates of the variable under consideration are consistent with the presumed nature of that variable. In a sentence, *construction validation involves testing the theory associated with the construct*—the body of interrelated hypotheses involving the variable in question. Confirmation of this set of hypotheses constitutes evidence that the operational definition of the variable does represent what it is supposed to represent, that the variable in question does exist and can be measured. In short, construct validation is a method for confirming what we have called a single variable hypothesis.

Notice that the confirmation is accomplished by taking advantage of the

hierarchical, nested structure of a theory and its component causal hypotheses. Specifically, where a set of causal hypotheses have in common a particular variable, either as an independent or dependent factor, then confirmation of these hypotheses is also a validation of their component elements, including the single variable hypothesis about the existence of the focal variable.

Does this mean that every operational definition must be validated in this comprehensive fashion? If so, this would mean that no measurement could be considered valid until a whole body of hypotheses involving that variable have been confirmed. Actually, this is necessary only in those instances where the operational definition is only remotely or indirectly related to the theoretical variable. Such a state of affairs is likely to occur in two kinds of situations. The first, illustrated by Christie's concept of Machiavellianism as a personality trait, involves a characteristic which is not accessible to direct observation but is inferred as a *hypothetical construct*. Hence the term "construct validity."

A second circumstance in which construct validation is indicated occurs when a theoretical variable could be measured directly, but for reasons of economy the investigator makes use of some indirect index relatively removed from the original phenomenon but more quickly and cheaply obtained. A case in point is provided by Gentry's research (1959). Here the independent variable, natural radiation, could have been measured directly, through the use of portable Geiger counters, but the cost of carrying out a radiological survey for the entire state would have been prohibitive. In its place, Gentry ingeniously employed the far cheaper alternative of utilizing already available geological survey maps of rock formations. But since his index is indirect, he is under obligation to establish its validity. This he does by demonstrating a chain of relationships as follows:

1. He cites laboratory studies showing that igneous rocks exhibit higher radioactivity than sedimentary rocks.
2. For the few sections of the state where direct field studies of rate of natural radiation had been made, he shows that areas with higher rates are those containing greater concentration of igneous rocks (eg., the Adirondacks).
3. Finally, he shows that the rate of congenital malformation is highest among persons who live in areas with the greatest concentration of igneous rocks and whose way of life involves close contact with rocky soil (e.g., obtaining drinking water from wells and springs).

Notice that where an outside criterion exists, (as in this instance) construct validation includes testing the index against the outside criterion (i.e., laboratory measurement of radioactivity of rock specimens). But, as before, evidence is presented for the validity of the measure outside the laboratory

as well. Finally, the ultimate validation of the construct is supplied by confirmation of the causal relationships involving that construct.

The Dangers of Face Validity.

But what if the existence of the theoretical variable is not in doubt and its operational definition is fairly direct rather than inferential? For example, suppose the independent variable in our hypothesis is the sex of the child and the dependent variable "crying." Obviously, one does not need to confirm a complete theory of genetics to be sure that one child is a boy or another a girl. Nor does one need to demonstrate the causes or consequences of crying to be assured that Mary or Johnny is shedding tears. Under such circumstances, a variable is said to have *face validity*; that is, the validity of the operational definition is regarded as self-evident.

But even though the validity seems self-evident, it is good practice not to take it for granted but to consider possible sources of confounding. Suppose, for example, that in testing for a sex difference in susceptibility to crying among nursery school children, the dependent variable is measured by the amount of time per hour that each child is observed to be in tears. The problem with such an index becomes readily apparent when we examine the kinds of activities engaged in by boys and girls in the nursery playroom or out of doors: the boys are at greater risk to physical injury with the result that they may actually cry more than the girls busily playing in the doll corner. In other words, for the measure of crying to be valid, one must control for the degree of instigation in the environment.

The foregoing example illustrates how the problem of validity becomes part of the more general problem of experimental design—that is controlling for the influence of confounding variables. Such sources of confounding variables are readily overlooked when the face validity of an index is taken for granted. The index may indeed reflect the theoretical variable in question, but one or more extraneous variables as well.

Systematic and Variable Errors.

To the extent that a measurement is only partially valid, it is said to be in error. There are two kinds of errors, *systematic* and *random*. A systematic error is one that deviates in one direction more than in another. For example, in a special validating study of the measure of his dependent variable, Gentry found that entries of congential malformation in birth certificates actually underestimated the true rate of such defects in the population. This fact was established by visiting the family of every nth child born in a given region and obtaining more direct information about the presence or absence of congenital defect. The rate of congenital malformation compiled on this basis turned out to be three times as high as that obtained from looking at birth and death certificates. In other words, the

information on certificates was often incomplete, producing a systematic underestimate.

The second type of error is illustrated by the following example. The following are estimates of John Jones' height by five of his classmates who observe him as he stands at the front of the class:

5′6″, 5′8″, 5′4″, 4′11″, 5′8″—Jone's height actually is 5′4½″ This is very close to the average of the above estimates, which equals 5′5″. The estimates are obviously in error, but not in any systematic way. The chance of an error in one direction is just about as great as in the other. Errors of this type are known as *variable* or *random* errors and they reflect the degree of precision of the measuring instrument.

It would be easy to increase this precision by using a measuring tape in place of the naked eye, but even so, some degree of variability in successive measurements of the same thing would remain.

Reliability

The extent to which a measuring procedure is free of such random variability, *the degree to which it yields stable or consistent results in measuring the same thing, is referred to as the reliability of the measure.* Reliability, then, is a special form of validity reflecting the extent to which a measuring technique is free of random variation or uncontrolled wobble. Notice that if an index is completely valid, it must also be completely reliable, since a totally valid measure must be completely free of error, random as well as systematic. A reliable measure, however, is not necessarily valid. For example, at one time it was thought that head size was directly related to mental ability; the larger the head, the more intelligent the person. It is, of course, possible to obtain highly reliable measures of the circumference of the skull, precise to the fraction of a centimeter, but as indices of mental capacity, such exact measurements have virtually no validity.

Reliability is obviously a relative matter, one measuring procedure being more precise than another. For this reason, it is useful to have an index of the degree of reliability of a given measuring procedure. The most direct index would be some indication of the size of the random variations obtained when the same thing is measured several times. For example, in the case of the five estimates of John Jones' height, one could index the extent to which these estimates vary around their average or mean value of 5′5″. For this purpose we need a measure of *dispersion or spread*. The most commonly used index of this type is called the *standard deviation*, designated by the Greek letter σ (sigma).

When applied to a distribution of errors in measurement, as is the case in assessing reliability, the index is referred to as a *standard error*, abbreviated as S. E. The standard deviation of a distribution, when extended on either side of the mean, will include about two-thirds of all the observations.

A standard deviation is always expressed in the same units as were employed in making the original measurement. Thus, the standard error in estimating heights would be expressed in inches, that of an intelligence test in I.Q. points, of an achievement test in grade levels, etc. Obviously, it would be desirable to be able to compare the relative reliability of different measuring instruments irrespective of what they were measuring, to be able to determine, for example, whether an intelligence scale is more or less reliable than a personality test being used in the same research. Such comparability becomes possible through the use of a statistic called a *correlation coefficient,* designated by the letter r, which measures the degree of association between two sets of measurements; for example, height and weight. The correlation coefficient varies in magnitude from -1.00 to $+1.00$. A value of $+1.00$ indicates a perfect and direct association between two variables. The higher the one, the higher the other, with perfect prediction between. A correlation of -1.00 also implies perfect predictability, but in an inverse relationship; as one variable gets bigger, the other gets smaller. A correlation of zero means no association predictability between the two variables. Most observed correlations range somewhere between these two extremes. For example, the correlation between height and weight is about .40.[2]

The correlation coefficient can also be used to measure the extent of correspondence between two sets of measures of the same variable; for example, two versions, or forms, of a test. When used for this purpose, the correlation coefficient is referred to as a *reliability coefficient,* for it measures the consistency of a given measuring instrument when applied more than once to the same set of phenomenon. For example, the reliability of a test may be assessed by giving it twice to the same group. This is called "test-retest" reliability. Such a procedure of course, has the disadvantage that the person's responses the second time may be influenced by memory, thus producing an artificial consistency between the results of the two administrations. To avoid this artifact, the same test may be divided into two parts (for example, odd-numbered items *vs* even numbered) and observing the correspondence between them; this is called "split-half reliability." Individually administered measuring instruments, such as the Stanford-Binet, often have reliability coefficients in the .90's. Group administered techniques typically have lower reliabilities, ranging from .40 to .60.

The measurement of variables is a necessary step in the testing of a hypothesis, but not a sufficient one. The process of proof, which, as we have already seen, is actually a process of disproof requires the use of an appropriate strategy of analysis, involving statistical methods and research design. These matters are discussed in the next chapter.

Notes

[1] The account which follows is condensed from Parsons, P. "Joseph Goldberger and Pellagra" in *Trail to Light*. New York: Bobbs-Merrill, 1943.

[2] In recent years, serious questions have been raised about the validity of this instrument when applied to persons from a different social and cultural background from that of the predominantly white, middle class samples for whom the rank was originally developed.

[3] The correlation coefficient should not be interpreted as a percent. It is simply a number varying between -1.00 and $+1.00$.

References

Bechtoldt, H. P. Construct validity: a critique. *American Psychologist,* 1959, *5,* (14), 619-629.

Berger, H. Ueber das Elektroenkephalogramm des Menschens, *Archiv fur Psychologie and Neurologie,* 1930, *40,* 160-179.

Binet, A. and Simon, T. Methodes nouvelles pour le diagnostic du niveau intellectuel des anormaux. *Annee Pschologique,* 1905, 191-244.

Bronfenbrenner, U. Family structure and development. Presidential Address to the Division of Development Psychology, September, 1958.

Bronfenbrenner, U. Socialization and social class through time and space. In E. E. Maccoby: T. M. Newcomb, and E. L. Hartley (Eds.) *Readings in social psychology.* New York: Henry Holt and Co., 1958. Pp. 400-425.

Bronfenbrenner, U. Parental behavior and adolescent responsibility: a reorientation. Paper presented at the annual meeting of the American Psychological Association, September, 1959.

Christie, R. The prevalence of Machiavellian orientations. Paper presented at the annual meeting of the American Psychological Association, September 7, 1964.

Christie, R. and Geis, F. Some consequences of taking Machiavelli seriously. In Borgatta, E. F. and W. W. Lambert, (Eds.), *Handbook of Personality Theory and Research.* Chicago: Rand McNally, 1968, 959-973.

Christie, R. and Geis, F. *Studies in Machiavellianism.* New York: Academic Press, 1970.

Cronbach, L. J. and Meehl, P. E. Construct validity in psychological tests. *Psychological Bulletin,* 1965, *52,* 281-302.

Geis, F. Machiavellianism and the manipulation of ones fellow man. Paper presented at the annual meeting of the American Psychological Association, Los Angeles, 1964.

Geis, F. and Christie, R. Machiavellianism and the tactics of manipulation. Paper presented at the annual meeting of the American Psychological Association, Chicago, 1965.

Geis, F., Christie, R., and Nelson, C. Some Machiavellian manipulations. Unpublished paper, Department of Psychology, Columbia University, 1963.

Gentry, J. T. An epidemiological study of congenital malformations in New York State. *American Journal of Public Health,* 1959, *49,* (4), 1-22.

Gerden, E. A review of psychokinesis. *Psychol. Bull.,* 1962, *59.* 353-388.

Grollman, A. *Functional Pathology of Disease,* Second Edition. New York: McGraw-Hill, 1963, 172-176.

This is an account of present day knowledge about pellagra and the chemistry of its effects.

Heider, F. *The Psychology of Interpersonal Relations.* New York: John Wiley, 1958.

Homans, G. C. *The Human Group.* New York: Harcourt, Brace, 1950.

Mendelyev, D. I. The principles of chemistry. Translated from the Russian (5th ed.) by George Kamensky. New York: Longmans, Green, 1891.

Newcomb, F. An approach to the study of communicative acts. *Psychological Review,* 1953, *60,* 393-404.

Parsons, R. P. "Joseph Goldberger and Pellagra. In *Trail to Light.* New York: Bobbs-Merrill, 1943. Also reprinted in Rapport, S. and H. Wright, *Great Adventures in Medicine.* New York: Dial Press, 1952, 586-604.

Rheingold, H. L., Gewirtz, J. L., & Ross, Helen W. Social conditioning of vocalizations in the infant. *J. Comp. Physiol. Psychol.,* 1959, *52,* 68-73.

Rhine, J. B. *Extrasensory perception.* Boston: Humphries, 1964.

Spock, B. *Baby and Child Care.* New York: Pocket Books, 1957.

Terris, Milton. *Goldberger on Pellagra.* Baton Rouge: Louisiana State Press, 1964.

This is the most recent and complete account of Goldberger's pursuit on pellagra including original reports by him and his critics.

Tjio, J. H. and Levan. The chromosome number of man. *Hereditas,* 1956, *42,* 1-6.

United States Children's Bureau. Infant care. (Rev. Ed.) Washington: United States Government Printing Office, 1951.

1.2   Interlude on Statistics and the Control Group

Donald Hebb

At some point in his introduction to psychology the student must be told something about statistics. It is not necessary for him to learn how to calculate standard deviations and correlation coefficients until he does research of his own, but he must know what such things are and how they are used if he is to understand the research of others. A large part of psychology must otherwise be taken on faith, which is no way to become a scientist.

All scientific measurement is subject to error, and it is important to be able to estimate the probable extent of such error. Also, when predicting a specific event on the basis of preceding observations or when drawing conclusions about a general class of phenomena from experience with a limited number of them, one is dealing not in certainties but in probabilities. To evaluate such probabilities we use statistics, which makes statistics an essential part of the science method.

The difference between biological and physical science is not that one is inexact, the other exact. Instead, the difference is in degree of exactness, this being related to the number of variables which must be dealt with simultaneously and the extent to which they can be controlled. In general, the biological sciences must deal with larger errors than the physical sciences; but this is not uniformly true, as the student will see if he considers the accuracy of meteorological prediction or if he comprehends the meaning of the fact that the structural engineer very often considers it necessary to use a safety factor of two or three hundred per cent. The statistical principles used in dealing with error in measurement, or in prediction and generalization, are the same whether the errors are large or small. Statistics is not a means of confusing issues that would otherwise be clear, nor a substitute for obtaining clear answers, but a means of checking and controlling hasty conclusions by providing an estimate of the error to which a conclusion is subject.

Statistical method has been highly developed mathematically, and is usually presented to the student in mathematical terms. Essentially, however, it is a way of thinking, which very often involves no computations and no use of formulas. It has two functions: describing empirical data, permitting one to see a mass of facts as a whole; and, secondly, providing the rules

From Donald O. Hebb; *A Textbook of Psychology*. Philadelphia, W. B. Saunders Co., 1966. By permission.

for inference and generalization from a limited set of observations to a larger universe of which one has observed only a part. It is sometimes said that science is not interested in the unique event. This is certainly not true. If the sun turned a mottled green for 30 seconds, just once, then returned to its usual sunny disposition and remained so with no sign of further upset, we can imagine what a commotion would be stirred up in astronomical circles. But it is true that the scientist is inverately concerned with general classes of events, with regularities in repeated observations, and the unique event may be considered of interest because it implies the existence of a *class* of possible events.

The scientist persistently generalizes from the seen to the unseen. When he draws a conclusion from an experiment his statement concerns more than the specific objects or events that were part of the experiment. He observes that 43 specific chicks, fed a particular drug, grow faster on the average than 43 other specific chicks not fed the drug; he reports this as a fact, but his conclusion is the inference that *all* chicks would grow faster under certain conditions. (As we will see shortly, what he says is, "The difference between the means is statistically significant"; and this statement distinguishes between the fact of a faster average growth for his particular chicks—this is a fact, there is no argument about it—and the inference about the growth of all chicks in such conditions. When a difference is found to be "significant," it implies a generalized conclusion.) When I measure the rate of learning of laboratory rats in a particular set of circumstances, my concern is not primarily with those particular rats, but the way in which rats in general, or mammals or vertebrates in general, learn.

This inference from the particular to the general is of course not peculiar to science; it is a fundamental feature of human thought, and so too is the other (the descriptive) function of statistics. Consequently, statistical thinking is of interest in two ways: to help the student understand how research is made more precise and controlled; and also as a feature of human thought that has intrinsic interest psychologically, something from which we can learn about the thought process.

If for example the student has come to the conclusion that men are taller than women, not restricting his statement to the specific men and women that he has seen personally, he has made a statistical inference. If he has ever taken an average, he has made a statistical description. If he has even, without any adding up of quantities and dividing by the number of cases, concluded that the average day in July is warmer than the average day in June, or has estimated how high the temperature may go in August, he has made a statistical summary from his own past experience (which is necessarily limited), and has gone on to generalize, with an implied prediction about what is going to happen next year and the year after.

Statistical Conclusions without Computation

If the present chapter is not an example of statistics without tears, it may be that at least fewer tears will be shed than usually. A good deal of analysis of data can be done by simply arranging them in an orderly way (especially in graphic form). The object here is to show the student how to think statistically, and perhaps he will succeed better this way than if he were given an elaborate set of mechanical computations to carry out, which sometimes act as a substitute for understanding.

First, two conceptions about which it is quite important to be clear: The scientist works with a *sample* from which he draws conclusions about a *population* or *universe*. The sample is a sample set of the items making up the population. It is one's collection of facts or observations, the empirical data available to work with, their number of course being finite and often rather small. The population is not necessarily a population of people or animals—this is another scientific figure of speech—but usually comprises events or properties of objects or events; in an experimental science a population is characteristically hypothetical and indefinitely large. The sample is a set of properties or events that have actually been observed; the population or universe includes all the properties or events in this class (i.e., of the same kind) that could have been observed in the past or that may conceivably be observed in the future. To illustrate:

An astrophysicist investigating shooting stars wants to know what they are composed of. He manages to find, let us say, fifty meteorites and determines their composition. This is his sample. The population in which he is interested however will include future meteorites and past ones which were not recovered. He may go on to draw conclusions about the bodies in space that hit other planets, thus going even farther beyond his facts—but going beyond the facts is of the essence, in the scientific method.

A psychologist breeds rats selectively for maze learning ability, mating with each other those that do well and those that do poorly. After several generations of such selection he finds that the descendants of the good learners always do better than descendants of the poor learners. He has tested perhaps 20 rats of the sixth generation in each strain, bright and dull. He has therefore a sample of 20 animals from each of two infinitely large populations: namely, rats with heredities determined in certain ways. Apart from his two samples, these populations do not exist in actuality, for no one else has bred animals in this way. But this does not prevent him from concluding that future samples will show the same difference that he has found. This means that he is talking about learning ability in two indefinitely large, hypothetical populations of *all rats that will be, or might be, obtained by the breeding operations that he has carried out.* No one really cares,

scientifically, about the maze learning of a particular rat, apart from its implications for larger questions. The question here concerns the relation of heredity to the learning ability, or intelligence, of rats in general and of mammals, including man, in general. Drawing such conclusions about hypothetical populations, making such generalizations, is certainly subject to error; but we must generalize, and there are statistical methods for evaluating the inevitable error.

Table 1
Frequency Distribution of Error Scores by 31 Rats in a Maze Test

Interval	Frequency
0–4	1
5–9	2
10–14	3
15–19	9
20–24	7
25–29	5
30–34	3
35–39	1

The first step in all this is to describe the sample. Consider for example the error scores that were made by 31 rats in a simple maze problem: 27 9 13 32 23 16 18 21 15 24 23 19 19 4 29 22 33 7 30 17 26 17 10 22 17 16 36 27 22 12 26. Each number gives the total errors for an individual rat. The properties of the sample become easier to see merely by rearranging in order: 4 7 9 10 12 13 15 16 16 17 17 17 18 19 19 21 22 22 22 23 23 24 26 26 27 27 29 30 32 33 36. The highest and lowest values, or the range of values, are evident at a glance, and the *median* value, 21, can be found by counting to the mid-point in the series from either end (if there were an even number of scores the median would be halfway between the two middle scores). The distribution of values becomes clearer from the next step, which is to group the scores by larger steps as shown in Table 1 or to represent the same grouping as in Figure 1. With this change some detail is lost—one no longer sees what the lower limit of error is, for example; it could be anything from 0 to 4, whereas in the raw data it was 4. But we now see clearly the bunching of scores near the middle; we see that the distribution of scores is approximately symmetrical, and we can estimate the *mean* directly. The mean is the "average" of elementary arithmetic, the sum of the quantities divided by their number. (Technically, there are several averages, of which the arithmetic mean is one.) By inspection, the mean is found a little above the dividing line between 15-19 and 20-24—that is, above 19.5. (By actual computation from the raw scores it is 20.4.)

Figure 1.
Histogram showing the errors made by 31 rats in a maze test (Table 3).
One rat made errors in the 0-4 range, two rats made errors in the 5-9 range, and so on.

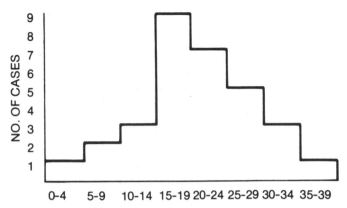

Two values here are of primary interest: the central tendency and the degree of dispersion or variability. The central tendency is the average, the single representative value which, if you must report a single value, best stands for the whole set of values concerned. The meaning of "best" here differs according to circumstances, but for most psychological experiments the mean or (less often) the median is used. As soon as we have this central value, however, the next step is to ask how much the single cases differ from it. How variable are the values in the sample. Here also there are several ways in which the answer may be given, but we shall consider only two: the *range* and the *standard deviation,* or SD.

"Range" is easily determined simply by inspection of the highest and lowest values. Often it gives a sufficient description of the degree of variability. In an experiment comparing the intelligence of dogs and rats, for example, the score for rats ranged from 5 to 20, for dogs from 24 to 27, in a test in which 27 was a perfect score. For the purposes of the experiment in question no further analysis was needed: the superiority of the dog was evident.

However, range is apt to be unsatisfactory as an index of the amount of variability, because it is determined by the two most extreme cases only and does not tell us much about the less extreme ones. In the experiment referred to, for example, one exceptionally stupid dog might have made a score of 12: then the range for dogs would be 12 to 27, and this fact would not tell one that almost all dogs make scores over 20. A more stable index —less susceptible to being deflected by one individual subject—is provided by the standard deviation. To find the SD one must do some computing (it is the square root of the average of the squares of deviations from the

Figure 2.

Histogram for heights of 8585 men. (From K. J. Holzinger, Statistical Methods for Students in Education, Ginn.)

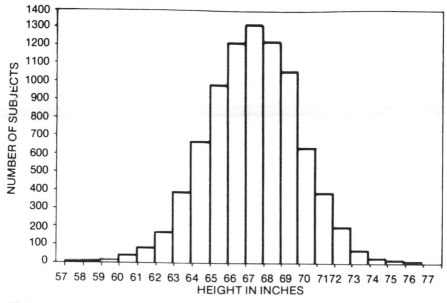

Figure 3.

Normal probability curve, showing the frequencies with which certain deviations from the mean occur.

Sigma (σ) stands for SD, or standard deviation; 68.2% of all cases fall within 1 SD of the mean, 95.4% within 2 SD (68.2 plus 13.6 plus 13.6), and so forth.

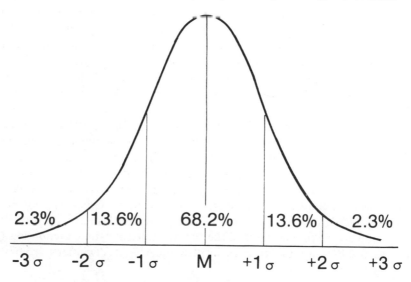

mean), but this is not necessary in order to understand how the value is used.

It is generally used in conjunction with what mathematicians call the *normal probability curve*. Distributions which are approximately symmetrical and bell-shaped, as in Figure 2, and which as the number of cases increases come closer and closer to the smooth curve of Figure 3, are frequently found with biological measures such as men's heights or weights. The smooth curve applies only to an infinitely large population an idealized conception. A finite number of cases, even as large a number as that presented in Figure 2, can only approximate it; and when we have a small number, as in Figure 1, the irregularities loom large. But Figure 1 is about as close to the smooth curve as we could expect for a sample of this size, and we can assume that it is a sample from an infinitely large population to which the normal probability curve, the idealized distribution of Figure 3, applies.

In that case, the standard deviation has certain quantitative properties shown in the figure. About two-thirds (68 per cent) of all values will fall within 1 SD of the mean value; one-sixth fall more than 1 SD below, and one-sixth more than 1 SD above the mean. About 2.3 per cent fall more than 2 SD above (or below) the mean, and 0.1 per cent more than 3 SD's above.

For example: consider adult IQ's on a particular test with a mean of 100 . . . and an SD of 15 (approximately what is given by existing tests). If these values hold for the general population, and if IQ's are normally distributed, we know without being given any further information that about a sixth of the population have IQ's above 115, or that a man with an IQ of 135 is in approximately the top 2 per cent of the population. If it is said that all students who do well in college have IQ's above 115 (as it has been; the accuracy of the statement does not matter for our present purposes), it is implied that no more than one-sixth of the population could do well in college, as things stand at present. It is usually considered that IQ 70 is the dividing line between those who can assume control of their own lives and those who cannot (between "normal" and "mentally defective"). Since intelligence tests are subject to error, a test score should not be the sole basis of judging such a question in the individual case; but statistically, for the general population, it is implied by this definition that about 2.3 per cent of the population are mental defectives.

Now let us look more closely at the inference from sample to population. Suppose that we want to know how tall the average male college student is. Having searched out and measured 20 of these rare creatures, we find their mean height to be 69.8 inches. Is this the value we are looking for? We know that men differ in height, so we cannot just measure one, or two or three. We need a large group; is 20 large enough? We track down 20 more

and measure them, and this time we get a mean of 70.3 inches. Three more groups of 20 give means of 70.1, 67.7 and 71.6. *The means of samples are variable too.* We pool the five groups and get a mean for the 100 men: 69.9. But another group of 100 would give us still another mean. The larger the samples the less variable their means will be, but the variability will not disappear. We cannot get a final, precise answer, and we must try another approach.

We first get as large a sample as is practical. The mean of this sample is the best estimate of the mean of the universe from which the sample is drawn. In the example just discussed, our best estimate of the mean height of all college men is 69.9 inches. Next we determine the variability of values in the sample, and from it estimate the variability in the universe.

Now we can look at our estimates critically, and ask how far off they are likely to be. We can ask, for example: could the true value be as low as 69.5 inches? We have a sample of 100 heights with a mean value of 69.9; is it probable that such a sample could be drawn at random from a population with a mean of 69.5? Mathematically, it is possible to determine exactly how often this would happen. It turns out to be, let us say, once in 25 times. The probability that the true value is as low as 69.5 therefore is only one in 25, or 4 per cent; it can be concluded with reasonable certainty that the true value is higher than this. Could the true value be 69.6, if it is not 69.5? The probability of this degree of error in our estimate can also be determined. We cannot ever say what the true value *is*; but we can determine the probability that it differs from the estimate by a specified value, or that it lies within a specified range. With these fictitious data we might be able to say, for example, that there is a 50 per cent probability that the true value lies between 69.7 and 70.1; a 90 per cent probability that it lies between 69.6 and 70.2; and so on.

Now for scientific purposes it is customary to emphasize two levels of probability in asking such questions: the 5 per cent and 1 per cent levels. In the example just used, we may say that the mean obtained differs *significantly* from 69.5 *at the 5 per cent level.* In other words: the difference can be given some weight, since a chance difference as great as this would be found less than 5 per cent of the time. (The student must remember, however, that the chance difference at this level of significance does occur—once in 20 experimental determinations.) For a higher degree of confidence the 1 per cent level is adopted, with a 1-in-100 chance of being wrong. When one encounters the statement that a difference is "significant" it signifies, by common convention, that the probability is at least 19 to 1 against this being due to the operations of chance in obtaining our sample; "highly significant" may be considered to mean that the probability is 99 to 1 against. Alternatively, one may say that a difference is "significant at the 5 per cent level," or at the 1 per cent level.

Summarizing: we can never say what, precisely, is the true value of the mean of the universe from which a sample is drawn. But we can, with the proper computations, determine the probability that it differs from our *estimate* by more than any given amount. Also, we can state limits within which it must lie, with a probability of 20 to 1 or 100 to 1—or if we wish, 1000 to 1.

No one can do more. Improved methods of measurement and larger samples cut down the size of probable error but do not abolish it. They decrease the uncertainty range within which the true value lies, but do not decrease it to zero.

Restating Matters, with Some Further (Improbable) Examples

Statistics asks the student to think in a new way about the meaning of averages and related matters. He is used to thinking that we know—or could determine—the *exact* value for the height of the average man, or the income of the average family. Is this not the sort of thing the census does for us? If it is impractical to do it for all men, considering some of the out-of-way places in the world, why should it be impossible to obtain a precise value for the mean height of all adult male Americans, or Indonesians, or Greeks? But as we will see in a moment, precision in this sense is chimerical. The scientific use of statistics really does ask for a new way of thinking, which though inherently simple is at first hard to achieve. It is unlikely that the preceding pages have fully conveyed this point of view, so the purpose of the present section is to restate it with some bizarre examples that may help to make it intelligible.

Let us see why it is chimerical to ask for an exact figure for the mean height of American male adults. First, there is the fact that *every* measurement has its probable error. Next, any biological population is not static but changing. A number of American males die daily, and a number reach the twenty-first birthday that marks adult status. If we are really to have a precise figure for the whole population and not a sample (however large), we must fix on some date and hour—say 12 noon, July 1, in the year following the decision to undertake the project—and with the aid of 10 or 12 million assistants we get everyone measured within a few minutes of the hour, including all those on their sickbeds, aloft in airplanes, at sea or abroad.

Now, assuming that we could succeed in this improbable undertaking, we must recognize that the mean we obtain will be out of date by July 2; in fact, well before the necessary computations could be completed. The net result of all this labor would therefore be, at best, a precise value for the population at a particular time in the past, not the present. To apply it to the present at once involves an element of estimation. We cannot treat

census figures for this or any other aspects of the average man as precise factual values, independent of inference; they are estimates—from very large samples it is true and with correspondingly small deviations from the "true" value—but still estimates that are subject to error. For most purposes we will thus be better off if we recognize this fact in the first place, and frankly use a sampling-and-inference method.

Now another improbable example, which may help us in understanding the logic of this method. Let us suppose that an explorer who has penetrated to some fastness in the mountains of Mexico, where no one has been before as far as he knows, discovers and traps a single specimen of an elephant 10 inches high at the shoulder. He has seen no others, nor heard of any. What information has he about the species, the population from which his sample of one has been drawn? His best estimate of the mean height of the species is 10 inches; but having only one in his sample he has no basis for estimating variability and thus no basis for saying how far off his guess about the average height might be.

Even with a single specimen, however, he is bound to have formed some idea of the size of other members of the species, and there are some conclusions that can be drawn quite logically. He can rule out the hypothesis, for example, that the mean of the population is 40 inches, the standard deviation 12. This situation is shown roughly by the larger curve, diagram *A*, Figure 4. He can also rule out the hypothesis that the mean is 15 SD 2 (smaller curve, diagram *A*). Both hypotheses imply that the first animal he happened to encounter is one of the very smallest—2½ SD's away from the mean. The probability that this would happen is well below the 5 per cent level. Similarly, he can rule out the hypothesis that the mean height is 6 inches, standard deviation 1.5 (diagram *B*, Fig. 4). Many hypotheses cannot be ruled out, but some can be.

His most probable hypothesis is represented by one of the curves of diagram *C*: some distribution centered about a mean of 10 inches. The different curves in diagram *C* are meant to show that, with a single specimen, nothing is known about variability and so the SD may be large (considerable spread in the curve) or small (little spread). As *D* shows, these curves may be shifted somewhat to left or right and still represent tenable hypotheses, as long as the given sample value, 10 inches, remains in the central part of the curve.

When 4 more animals are captured, giving values of 9.6, 9.7, 9.8, 10.0, and 10.1 inches, an estimate of variability can be made—it is small—and now the distance becomes smaller by which the curve can be shifted to left or right and still represent a tenable hypothesis. The point for the student to get from this example is that we can quite freely form hypotheses about the population, after seeing a sample from it, but then proceed to test them rigorously. The elaborate machinery of statistics, the formulas and computa-

Figure 4.
**Possible hypotheses about the heights of a new species of pygmy elephants,
given a sample of one, 10 in. high.**
 Diagram A: two hypotheses, (1) that the mean for the species is 40 in., SD 12 in.
(larger curve, to the right); and (2) that the mean is 15 in., SD 2 in. (smaller curve).
B: mean 6, SD 1.5, and so forth; see text.

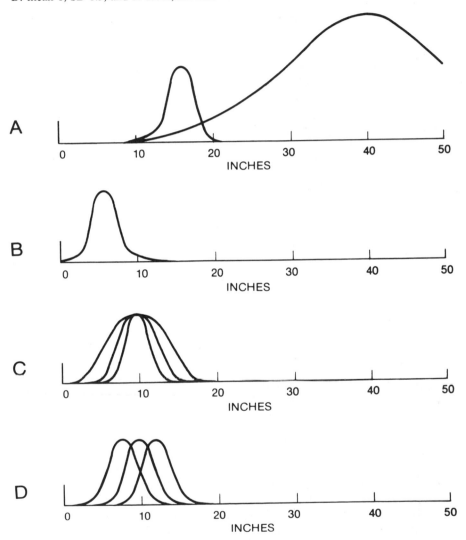

tions omitted in this book, make it possible to state precisely what the
probability would be of getting a known sample from any given hypothetical
population. If the probability is low we disregard that hypothesis (but

cannot rule it out absolutely and finally, for the very improbable sometimes happens).

However, this process cannot pick out, from among those hypothetical populations which might reasonably have produced our sample *the* one correct hypothesis. The larger the sample, the more we can narrow the zone within which probable answers lie, but we are always left with an uncertainty range, even if small. This is represented in principle by diagram *D*, Figure 64.

To be epigrammatic, science works not with absolute truth but with a probable error. Its goal is to reduce error to a minimum, only. The scientist *thinks* in terms of truth when he sets up a hypothesis for testing, for what he says in effect is: Let us suppose that the true mean has such-and-such a value; if so, what would be found in a sample? But the result, the only conclusion that can be justified, is that the "true" value has a thus-and-so probability of lying within such-and-such a range of possible values.

Comparing Two Values

Now a different but related case: the comparison of values and the determination of significant differences between samples.

Take first a familiar case, the comparison of the heights of men and women. Suppose that we have two samples, 100 in each, of the heights of college men and women. The two means are 69.9 and 65.4 inches. Are men taller than women? That is, if we had the mean of all men's heights would it differ from the mean of all women's?

We attack the question by saying, assume that the heights of men and women are *not* different. This is the *null hypothesis*. It amounts to assuming that the two samples of heights come from the same population. Now we can ask, what is the probability that we would draw from the same population two samples like these, with means that differ as much? We know that any two samples from the same population will give different means, just by chance; is that what has happened in this case? But the answer here might well be that two such different samples could come from the same population less than one in a thousand times; it is thus very unlikely that the null hypothesis is true. We therefore reject it. This in turn means that we conclude that men and women differ in height. The usual way of reporting such a result is to say that "the difference between the means is significant" (or in this case, of course, very highly significant).

This method of analysis might be applied in an experiment as follows. We want to know whether the frontal part of the brain is more important for maze learning than the occipital part. We remove equal amounts of brain tissue, on the average, from two groups of rats. Those with frontal damage make, let us say, a mean of 42.1 errors; those with occipital damage, 55.7

errors. Our two samples are certainly different, but is the difference significant? We apply the null hypothesis, assume that there is no difference in the means of *all* rats with such frontal lesions and *all* with such occipital lesions, and see how often two such samples would be drawn from a single population. The variability in our two groups is great, indicating a wide "spread" in the curve representing the parent population (Fig. 4), and this implies that the uncertainty range is rather great. As a result, computation shows that our two samples might be obtained from a single population about 20 times in 100. The difference is far from the 5 per cent level of significance, so we cannot reject the null hypothesis. We have not yet established the proposition that occipital damage is worse than frontal damage in its effect on maze running.

The student should keep in mind, however, that the odds still favor the proposition; by increasing the size of the samples, and thus decreasing the uncertainty range—the amount by which the means may vary—a further experiment might find a significant difference after all.

In the preceding examples we have dealt with measurements and normally distributed values. One is not limited to measurability, and normal distributions, in statistical thinking. Suppose we are interested in the relation of wildness to heredity in rats. We bring up 20 rats from an albino laboratory strain and 20 from a wild gray strain, all separated from the mother at weaning and brought up singly in identical cages. Heroically, the experimenter reaches into each cage when the occupant has reached 70 days of age, and picks up the animal once. He counts the bites received: 1 bite from the albinos, 13 from the grays. There are methods of computation (e.g., chi-square, which need not be described here) that make it possible to determine that this result is highly improbable on the assumption that biting rats are equally likely to occur with either heredity. The result is therefore highly significant. We reject the null hypothesis (that there is no difference in the frequency of biters in the two universes, all hypothetical albinos and all hypothetical grays, brought up in this particular way). Rejecting the null hypothesis is equivalent to concluding that there is a relation between heredity and wildness. Here we treat biting as an index of wildness, but the procedure does not measure wildness in the individual animal, and we have no idea whether it is normally distributed.

The Control Group

The experiment just considered brings us to the use of the control group. In the physical sciences it may often be possible to hold constant all but one of the factors that might affect the outcome of an experiment; this one, the "independent variable," is changed systematically, and the experimenter observes the effects in the "dependent variable." In a study of the pressure

of the atmosphere, for example, the independent variable may be height above sea level; the dependent variable is the height of a column of mercury in a barometric tube. Other influences that might affect the outcome are eliminated or kept constant: temperature, contaminating substances in the mercury, movement of the surrounding air, and so forth. In the biological sciences one can only approach this ideal procedure; and only too often fundamental questions have gone unanswered because it was not possible to get anywhere near it. In psychological research there are two great difficulties which frequently demand the use of control groups as a substitute for the ideal procedure.

One is that taking a psychological test usually changes the subject; a later test does not give the same result because of *practice effect*—the subject as we say "remembers" the first test. The second difficulty is that we are dealing with extraordinarily complex material; after we have used up our first sample of the material (the first subject or group of subjects) we cannot get a second that is identical with the first, because animals and men differ in many ways which we cannot identify before beginning an experiment.

Suppose for example that we want to find out whether removing the frontal lobes of a monkey's brain affects his ability to learn a visual discrimination. In an ideal procedure we would measure his learning ability, remove the frontal lobes, and measure his learning ability again. But in reality the second measurement is disturbed by memory of the first. We must measure learning ability by the number of trials, or the number of errors made, in achieving the discrimination. In the second measurement there will almost certainly be a practice effect, and we do not know how great it will be. Next best, in a slightly less ideal world, we would obtain two monkeys identical in all respects; we would remove the frontal lobes from one, have both learn the task under identical conditions, and see how much faster the normal monkey learned, compared to the one operated on. But in practice we cannot find two identical subjects, animal or human. (Identical twins are identical with respect to heredity, but it is impossible that everything that has happened since birth which might affect them psychologically is exactly the same. Also, of course, there are not many of them.) Thus we are driven to the comparison of two *groups,* large enough, we hope, that the kind of individual differences that may occur will average out; if the original learning capacity of two subjects is not identical, the average for two groups is likely to differ much less, and the probable degree of difference can be dealt with statistically.

The ideal cases referred to, however, should be kept in mind, for they tell us what we are trying to achieve by the use of the control group. In the frontal-lobe question referred to, what we would like to do is measure the

learning ability of the same monkey with and without his frontal lobes, with the second measurement not being affected by the first. This is impractical. So is the hope of finding two identical monkeys; but it is not impractical to find two groups which, if they are large enough, will be much more similar, as groups, than two individual monkeys. Our choice of a control group, then, is a matter of choosing animals which are as much like the animals in the experimental group as possible, in every way that affects visual learning.

The experiment may then proceed in one of two ways. First, we can operate on one group, and test both. We compare the mean scores of the operates and of the normal control subjects, and see whether they differ significantly. Statistics at this point enables us to evaluate the probability that the difference we have found is due simply to accidental differences in our two groups, treating them as two samples in the way already described. The second procedure would be to test both groups, operate on one, test both groups again, and see whether the increases in score by the normals (due to practice effect) are significantly greater than the increases by the operates (though the experiment might come out with a still clearer result, the mormals all showing increases and the operates all showing losses).

The principle is clear: make your control group like the experimental group in every way that would affect the outcome of the experiment, except for the one variable in which you are interested. The pitfalls and gins besetting the path of the investigator on this point mainly consist of not recognizing a variable that affects the results. If one is picking rats out of a colony cage, and puts the first 10 into the experimental group, the second 10 into the control group, one overlooks the possibility that the most easily-caught animals, or the ones that come to the front of the cage and allow themselves to be picked up, are tamer than the others; and this difference is likely to affect any experimental result. The easiest solution is to put no. 1 into the first group, no. 2 into the second, no. 3 into the first, and so on. (There are also more sophisticated ways of doing this by the use of random numbers assigned to the animals, but we need not go into them.)

Again, in clinical investigations one does not have the choice of one's "experimental" group, and one perforce must try to find a similar control group. This is usually difficult. The clinical group (corresponding to the experimental group of the laboratory) generally includes people of all sorts of occupations, rural as well as urban, educated and uneducated, old and young. It is difficult indeed to persuade a group of similar persons, who are not ill and have no reason to take tests, to give up the time to act as subjects —especially since they are apt to view any psychological test with suspicion. But if one wants to know whether removal of the human frontal lobe affects intelligence, and if the clinical group with frontal lobe operation has a mean age of 40 and a mean of 8 years' schooling, for example, one must make

one's comparisons with a group that is similar in these respects, as intelligence test scores vary with amount of schooling and with advancing age.

Correlations

Correlation is the degree of relation between two variables. A *coefficient of correlation* is a quantitative statement thereof. It is even more time-consuming to compute than the quantitative values we have been dealing with so far, but—once more—the student's aim here should be to understand it, instead of memorizing a formula and methods of computation.

Correlation coefficients range from plus 1 to minus 1; plus 1 represents a perfect relation between the two variables, high values accompanying high values, intermediate values accompanying intermediate values, and so on. Minus 1 *also* represents a perfect relation, though it is reversed: the highest score on X goes with the lowest one on Y, next highest on X with the next lowest on Y, and so on. The relation is perfect in this sense. Once you knew what a man got on test X you would also know what he got, or will get, on Y. Finally, a correlation of zero means no relation at all: here a high score on the first test might go with a high, a medium, or a low score on the second.

To see better what is meant, consider Figure 5. Tests A and B (first of the three diagrams) have a zero correlation. Knowing what a man has made on test A tells us nothing about what he will make on test B. Now consider tests P and Q (second diagram). These two are perfectly and positively

Figure 5.
Correlations of zero, plus one and minus one.

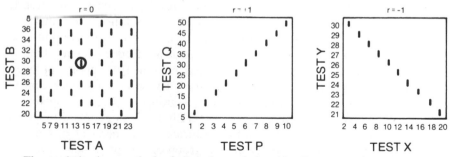

The symbol α is a particular index of correlation (the Pearson product-moment coefficient). Each mark represents a single subject's scores on the two tests being correlated. In the first diagram, for example, the encircled mark is for a subject who made 12 on the first test (test A) and 31 on the second (B).

related (perhaps we may note that such perfection simply does not occur in psychology). If we know a child's score on P we do not have to give Q; the two tests correlate 1.00, so the second score can be determined as soon as

the first is known. Similarly with tests X and Y, though now the relation is negative; if a subject makes a poor score on X we can predict, without further testing, that he will make a good score on Y.

These, however, are only the extreme cases. One thing the student needs to know is the degree of relation, roughly, that is represented by such correlation coefficients as 0.30, 0.50, 0.70, and 0.90. In general, one may say that the relation is not nearly as close as one of these figures makes it sound. The first, 0.30, represents a barely discernible relation. A correlation of 0.70 is not 70 per cent correspondence, or agreement 7 times out of 10, but 49 per cent; a correlation of 0.90 represents 81 per cent correspondence. In psychology, because we must often deal with coefficients below 0.60, it is common to speak of one above this value as representing "a high correlation." But this is misleading, and it would be better to reserve the term for coefficients above 0.90.

All this has more meaning for the student if expressed graphically. Figure 6 shows a plot of two sets of scores, on parallel forms of the same test, in which the correlation is 0.93. It is reasonable to speak of this as a high correlation, but let us see how close the correspondence really is. The vertical lines in the second diagram of Figure 6, on each side of the 17–18 value on the base line, contain the entries for all subjects who made 17 or 18 on the first form of the test. On the second test, these subjects made scores ranging from the 15–16 bracket to the 21–22 bracket. (From the raw data it could be seen that one man who made 18 on the first test made 15 on the second; another who made 18 on the first made 22 instead, on the second.) Evidently no very close prediction of the second score is possible, despite the correlation of 0.93.

Figure 7 shows a somewhat lower correlation, 0.72. A comparison of Figures 6 and 7 shows clearly that the thickness of the diagonal band made by the entries on such a correlation plot is the essential factor in predicting the second score from the first. With a high correlation we have a thin band; when the vertical lines are drawn, as in Figure 6, only a short segment from the diagonal band is enclosed, which means that the amount of variation in the second test is small—and prediction is good. When the correlation is lower, the band is broader and prediction is poor. In the perfect case, the correlation in the second diagram of Figure 5, the band would have no width whatever (all the points plotted fall on a single straight line), and prediction is perfect.

This graphical analysis is of course rough, and there are much more exact ways of dealing with the predictions that can be made, and their degree of error. But it is still true here, as elsewhere, that a good deal can be learned about complex data by simple inspection, and there is no other way that is as good for conveying the fundamental meaning of a correlation coefficient, high or low.

Figure 6.
A correlation of 0.93 (left) and the accuracy with which prediction of a second score (on form L of the test) can be made from a first (on form K of the same test).

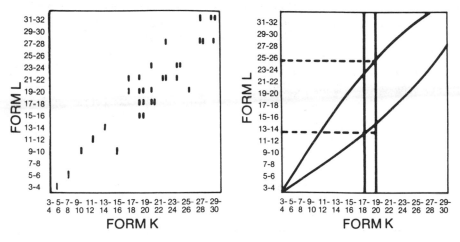

Even with as high a correlation as this, the accuracy is not great; on the right is shown the roughly drawn "envelope" enclosing the entries. The vertical lines enclose the entries which represent scores of 17 or 18 on form K; the width of the envelope at this point determines how much variability may be expected in the scores on form L—roughly, from 13 to 24.

Figure 7.
Distribution of scores illustrating a correlation of 0.72.

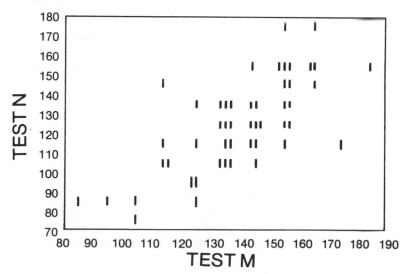

With a correlation, it is clear that we are always dealing with a casual connection. The connection may be very indirect, however, and a correlation, in and of itself, does not tell us what causes what. If *A* and *B* are correlated, *A* may cause *B*, *B* may cause *A*, both may be caused by an outside factor *C*, or there may be a mixture of these relations. It is known, for example, that intelligence-test scores are correlated with years of schooling—but we cannot leap to the conclusion that one's IQ is determined by one's education. The relation may be just the opposite—those who have not the intelligence to do well in school tend to leave earlier than others, which means that intelligence affects amount of schooling. A more important factor may be that intelligent parents tend (1) to have intelligent children, and (2) to encourage their children to keep on at school. In this case, the parent is the outside factor, *C*, that determines the level both of *A* (intelligence) and of *B* (schooling); *A* and *B* could thus be correlated without one's causing the other.

Intelligence in the growing child is known, for example, to be correlated with length of the big toe. This old joke might well be remembered by the student; the statement is quite true, for as a child grows his capacity for solving problems increases at the same time that his bones are growing in length, and the two therefore show a significant correlation. This may help the student to see that, though a correlation shows a causal relation *somewhere*, it does not necessarily mean that one of the two things correlated causes the other.

Summary:

Statistics is a fundamental feature of the scientific method; it is concerned with evaluating the errors which must occur in any measurement, or in generalizing from known data (a sample) to the larger class of values or events to which the data belong (a population or universe). The elaborate mathematical methods of statistics increase the exactness with which the estimate of error is made, but they are not the essence of the matter; graphical methods, and simple inspection, are often sufficient for a particular problem in which results are relatively clear-cut. (Some scientists say they make no use of statistics; what they really mean is that inspection is sufficient for their purposes, without formal computations.)

The first step of analysis is a description of the available data, the sample. Two values are of primary importance: a measure of central tendency, and a measure of dispersion. Central tendency is a single representative value, an average; there are several kinds of averages, of which the most important is the (arithmetic) mean. Dispersion is the extent to which individual cases deviate from the average; one index of it is the range, but a more useful one is the standard deviation, of SD. This is particularly so when we are dealing

with the "normal probability distribution," the symmetrical bell-shaped curve frequently found with biological data.

Given the mean and the SD, we can then ask how probable it is that our sample has come from any given hypothetical population. If the probability is low, we reject the conclusion that the sample has come from that population. For scientific purposes, it is customary to work with two levels of "significance" (i.e., of probability) in drawing such conclusions: the 5 per cent level (when it is reasonably sure that the sample has not come from that population) and the 1 per cent level (still surer).

To determine whether an experimental treatment of some sort has had an effect on a group of subjects, we use essentially the same method. We have an experimental group and a control group, the latter treated in exactly the same way as the experimental group except for the one treatment in whose effects we are interested. What we ask is whether the two samples, the data from the two groups, could have come from the same population. That is, we make the null hypothesis: we assume that the treatment did *not* have an effect. (The difference between our two groups may have occurred by chance since any two samples from the same population are likely to differ.) Statistics allows us to determine just how probable such a result would be—how often we would get, from the same population, two samples as different as these two. If the probability is below 5 per cent, we reject the null hypothesis: that is, we conclude that the treatment did have an effect. The chance of being wrong in this conclusion, of course, is 1 in 20; if we wish to be more certain to avoid a wrong conclusion, we may use the 1 per cent level instead.

Correlation is the degree of relation between two variables; a coefficient of correlation is a quantitative measure of the relation, ranging from plus 1 to minus 1. Graphical analysis is very useful here as well, especially since calculating the coefficient may be very laborious.

When two variables are correlated, there is a causal relation, but from the correlation alone one cannot determine what causes what: *A* may cause *B, B* may cause *A,* or they may share a common cause, *C.*

Notes

Further details on the statistical method and its use in psychology are provided in a number of books on "psychological satistics" or "the design of experiments." To find one suitable for his purposes, the student should consult his instructor, for such books vary in extent to which they go into fine detail. However, two generally useful texts are: G. A. Ferguson, *Statistical Analysis in Psychology and Education,* McGraw-Hill, and Q. McNemar, *Psychological Statistics,* Wiley. A valuable preparation for the detailed discussions contained in these books will be found in the programmed-learning text by C. McCollough and L. Van Atta, *Introduction to Descriptive Statistics and Correlation,* McGraw-Hill.

Part Two
Nature with Nurture

The articles in this section all speak to the same vital principle: namely, heredity and environment never operate in isolation from each other. With respect to human development, neither factor can exert an influence without the other. This point is beautifully illustrated in the initial presentation by Freedman of a series of researches growing out of a study undertaken when he was still a student. What originally appeared as an elegant demonstration of the impact of different training methods on the development of "conscience" in puppies turned out to be critically mediated by genetic predispositions. The fact that analogous effects have been reported for man and attributed primarily to differential patterns of child rearing serves as a reminder that, for human young as well, patterns of indulgence vs. discipline work on a genetic base.

Along the same line, at a time when observed psychological differences between the sexes are being criticized as products of discriminatory child rearing practices, Madigan's ingenious demonstration of the persistence of sex differences in men and women exposed to highly similar ways of life raises the possibility of innate foundations for psychological differences between the sexes.

Following this, the impact on psychological development of hereditary factors at the cellular level is reflected in studies of chromosomal anomalies summarized by Valenti.

Finally, the intricate question of the interplay between genetic and social factors in the development of human ability is examined in four articles. It is in this area that the critical relation between science and social policy is

most clearly apparent. Skodak and Skeels' pioneering study of the impact of true vs. foster mothers on the development of children adopted in the first six months of life presents a classic example of the difficulties of gaining acceptance for a new idea before its time. One of the first studies to demonstrate how an enriched environment can enhance intellectual capacity, this research ironically continues to be cited in support of the opposite conclusion.

A similarly unwarranted genetic bias, with even more serious social consequences, is analyzed and demolished by Scarr-Salapatek in her critique of the thesis of innate race differences in intelligence—a thesis promulgated in recent years by Jensen, Herrnstein, Eysenck, and others. The role of environmental factors in accounting for differences in measured intelligence of black and white childen is then demonstrated by Willerman and his colleagues in their ingenious analysis of offspring from interracial matings. It turns out that the child's IQ is depressed only when the mother is black and not the father, a phenomenon completely incompatible with a genetic theory of racial inferiority.

Finally, Bronfenbrenner takes on the major thesis of Jensen and others that intelligence is primarily determined by genetic factors; from a review of the evidence, he concludes that the argument for an 80 percent genetic effect is contradicted by the data, which in fact testify to the power of the environment in enabling the developing child to realize his genetic potential.

2.1   The Origins of Social Behavior

Daniel G. Freedman

The studies that form the basis of this article had their origin on the campus of Brandeis University, near Boston, Massachusetts, in 1953. In the winter of that year the campus mascot, a motley bitch with what looked like a beagle and dachshund background, gave birth to a litter of four. We were not sure who the father was. As graduate students in the newly formed graduate school Norbett Mintz and I had sufficient time to 'play around' and we had the happy notion that puppies might prove enjoyable experimental subjects—as indeed they did.

In considering what we might do with the puppies we had two previous studies in mind. The first was that of J. P. Scott and M. Marston at Bar Harbor who, in 1950, had suggested that three to eight weeks of age was a critical period in the social development of puppies. Although this was little more than an impression then, it had subsequently turned out to be largely correct within the breeds studied. Secondly, John Whiting, a psychoanalytically orientated anthropologist, had been working with adult dogs and had developed a test to measure their 'conscience'. This was assessed by the extent to which they remained obedient in the absence of the handler. The test was attractively simple and merely involved a person punishing a dog for eating food that had been forbidden him. The person then left the room and, watching through a one way glass, recorded the amount of time the animal stayed away from the forbidden food. In this way the extent to which punishment was 'incorporated' received a quantitative score.

Our chore became one of using this information in a meaningful study of development, and when the idea finally came to us it seemed the most natural study possible. As clinical psychologists, Mintz and I were aware of the work of the child psychiatrist, David Levy. As a result of his extensive experience with behaviour disorders in children, Levy had hypothesized that extreme permissiveness on the part of parents could lead to a psychiatric condition called psychopathy. This is characterized by an abnormal inability to inhibit one's impulses. These people are asocial in that their own desires and wishes always take precedence over those of others. Levy found that in many families which produced such individuals the parents allowed themselves to become complete slaves to the tyrannical wilfullness of the child.

With Levy's work in mind we carried out the following study. Two puppies were to act as 'control'. One was given to a family which we

Reprinted from *Science Journal*, 1967, *3*, 69-73, by permission.

decided was typically 'middle class'—in other words, a home in which the puppy would receive plenty of affection, but would also be restricted to certain areas, prevented from biting, be housebroken and so on. A second puppy was raised separately in a room by itself, save for the few minutes each day it took to put food in and take the old bowls out. As for the 'psychopathic' puppies, Mintz and I decided to enlist the aid of the boys in the dormitories of which we were proctors. The puppies were to have complete freedom in the dormitory. Urine and faeces were to be cleaned up after them. If they wished to climb on someone's bed or lap, they were to be helped up. If they wished to get off, they were helped off. If they wished to sleep in someone's bed, they were allowed that. (If they nipped an ear in bed, one was allowed to duck under the covers.) They were not to be punished for any offense. Since the study was to last only six weeks (from three to nine weeks of age), all the students agreed to co-operate.

At nine weeks we had two distinctly different groups of dogs, and this was nicely shown by the 'incorporation of punishment' test. Beginning at the ninth week of age and continuing for eight consecutive days we administered the test devised by Whiting. We placed each pup, which had not been fed for at least four hours, in a room with a bowl of meat at its centre. When the pup attempted to eat, the experimenter hit it on the rump with a newspaper and shouted, "No". After the experimenter left the room, the time to eat was recorded. In this early version of the test the experimenter rushed back in and punished the pup each time it ate.

We found that whereas the home reared dog averaged 37.5 minutes and the isolate 9.5 minutes between each transgression, the permissively reared pups averaged a lightning 2.2 minutes. By the eighth day of testing, in fact, the permissively reared pups managed to eat all the meat before the tester had a chance to leave the room. He would smack the pup only to have it immediately circle back through his legs for another bite. This happened so fast that we could not measure the time between transgressions accurately and consequently we over estimated the time between transgressions in the seventh and eighth test sessions.

The subsequent history of these two pups was not a happy one. Although people were initially taken with them because of their uninhibited friskiness, they were passed from home to home as each owner found something else to complain about. They seemed to have become untrainable.

The isolate's behaviour was typical of pups raised in this fashion. She was hyperexcitable and initiated contacts only to run off when a hand was reached out or when another pup tried to play with her. After the fourth session of testing, however, she calmed down somewhat and was able to learn what was demanded of her. We are happy to report that she subsequently became a beloved and loving pet, and we could not help but reflect that a dog with no experiences with people may be preferable to one with the wrong experiences.

Having become completely captured by the study, we decided to try another experiment. David Levy had postulated that a second class of psychopaths are formed by extreme cruelty or great emotional deprivation in childhood. With this second hypothesis in mind, we raised a beagle from four to nine weeks of age under conditions in which all his contacts with people were negative. Each time he tried to make contact he was either ignored or pushed aside, and it is not surprising that he developed a rather depressed, fearful personality. True to Levy's hypothesis, his performance on the test was like that of the over-indulged puppies, although the average time between transgressions was higher: 8.14 minutes. Again the controls were a home reared littermate and a littermate kept in isolation. Both quickly learned to stay away from the food and averaged one transgression each 31.13 minutes. Thus once again Levy's hypothesis, developed from studies of problem children, appeared to hold when applied to puppies.

It was clearly time to do these studies on a larger scale and in a systematic and repeatable fashion, and I proposed such a project for my PhD thesis. After interesting Paul Scott, Chairman of the Divison of Behaviour Studies at the Jackson Laboratories, Bar Harbor, Maine, it was arranged that the work be done there.

In the Bar Harbor study, eight litters of four pups each were used. They included two litters each of Shetland sheepdogs, basenjis, wire-haired fox terriers and beagles. Following weaning at three weeks of age, each litter of four was divided into two pairs which were equated as closely as possible on the basis of sex, weight, activity, vocalizations, maturation of eyes and ears, and reactivity to a startling stimulus. Thereafter, each member of one pair was indulged and each member of the second pair was disciplined. However, because of the numbers involved, this treatment could be given only during two daily 15 minute periods, again from the third to the eighth week of age.

Indulgence consisted of encouraging a pup in any activity it initiated, such as play, aggression and climbing on the supine handler. As before, these pups were never punished. By contrast, the disciplined pups were at first restrained in the experimenter's lap and were later taught to sit, to stay, and to come upon command. When still older they were trained to follow on a leash. I handled all the pups and tested them individually; they lived with the identically treated littermate in isolation boxes the remainder of the time.

A revised punishment test was initiated at eight weeks of age. As before, when the pup ate meat from a bowl he was punished with a swat on the rump and a shout of, "No!" After three minutes the experimenter left the room and, observing through a one way glass, recorded the time that elapsed before the pup again at.e This time the experimenter did not return to the room until the allotted ten minutes were up.

The first breed that went through this experimental rearing and testing was a basenji litter. By the fourth day of testing all basenjis tended to eat soon after the experimenter left the room, the method of rearing having little

effect. This was most discouraging, since we had failed to duplicate the results of the pilot experiment, but we decided to carry on.

The second group was a Shetland sheepdog litter and they were equally disappointing, except this time all tended to refuse the food. At least one thing was clear at this point: the breed of dog was a major factor to consider. Second litters of basenjis and of Shetland sheepdogs from our inbred stocks bore this out, for they performed much like the first litters.

The next breed which became available was a beagle litter. We found that their behaviour depended upon the way they were reared but, paradoxically, in a direction opposite to our pilot studies. A second beagle litter, from the same mating, performed excatly the same way and so did the two litters of wire-haired fox terriers.

The conditions of rearing were continued over a second period, when the pups were 11 to 15 weeks of age, and all tests were readministered with essentially the same results. At this point we were so fascinated by breed differences that we postponed thinking about the contradictions to our pilot work. Our question now was how could the breed characteristics explain the differences in performance?

It was clear that, during training, beagles and wire-haired terriers were strongly orientated to the experimenter and sought contact with him continuously. Basenjis, by contrast, were interested in all phases of the environment and often ignored the experimenter in favour of inanimate objects. Shetland sheep dogs showed yet another pattern; all became fearful of physical contact with the experimenter and tended to maintain distance from him. Thus the two breeds that were highly attracted to the experimenter showed behavioural differences as a result of the mode of rearing, whereas the breeds that exhibited aloofness (basenjis) and excessive timidity (Shetland sheep dogs) did not. Apparently it was the strong constitutional attraction combined with indulgent treatment that enhanced the effectiveness of later punishment.

It should be noted that basenjis and Shetland sheep dogs were not entirely unaffected by the differential treatment. The scores of all indulged animals were significantly different from those of their disciplined counterparts on five of ten tests administered. In general, these tests indicated that the indulged pups were more active, more vocal, less timid (although more easily inhibited with punishment), and more attracted to people than the disciplined pups.

We now had to reconcile the findings of the pilot studies at Brandeis and the major study at Bar Harbor. In the first we found that over-indulged rearing in the dormitories led to 'psychopathic' performance, but in the Bar Harbor work the disciplined animals of all breeds tended to be more disobedient, although this was true of the Shetland sheep dogs and basenjis over only the first three days of testing.

To recapitulate the pilot studies, a regimen of affection and freedom and no discipline produced hyper-active, disobedient pups. A regimen of discipline and no affection likewise produced a disobedient pup, albeit within a depressed and fearful personality. Actually, none of the Bar Harbor findings contradict these 'rules'.

In the Bar Harbor studies the permissive group was given free reign to express affection, to investigate and to bite, but each time they were returned to their boxes they were under enforced control; as their cries to get out attested. On thinking it over, it became clear that they were treated much like normal home reared dogs in that restrictions were regularly imposed on their freedom. We therefore changed their official title from 'over indulged,' to 'indulged', although this was still not a complete description.

The disciplined group, on the other hand, received considerably less affection than do home reared dogs and, in addition, few dogs at home have so much demanded of them at so early an age. When we had initially planned the study we called this group 'normal', but very early we changed to the word 'disciplined.' It was clear that in terms of affection and play they were a *deprived* group and that 'disciplined' was only partially descriptive of the treatment they received.

It was in this way that we attempted to resolve the contradiction between the Bar Harbor results and the Brandeis pilot studies and, setting aside any genetic factors for the moment, the general hypothesis still appeared viable: dogs who did not 'incorporate' punishment were those reared under conditions of excessive freedom *vis-a-vis* humans or, conversely, under conditions in which human contacts were largely negative. It is of interest that some of the great trainers of field trial champions, such as Tetzloff and Spandet of the Danish Kennel Club, stress the importance of basing discipline on deeply affectionate relationships between trainer and dog. . . .

References

Freedman, D. G. An Ethological Approach to the Genetical Study of Human Behaviour (in *Methods and Goals in Human Behaviour Genetics, Academic Press, New York, 1965*)

Freedman,, D. G., King, J. A. and Elliott, O. Critical Period in the Social Development of Dogs *(Science. 331, 1016-1017. 1961)*

Levy, D. M., The Deprived and the Indulged Forms of Psychopathic Behaviour *(American Journal of Orothopsychiatry, 21, 250-254, 1951)*

Melzack, R. The Genesis of Emotional Behavior: An Experimental Study of the Dog *(Journal of Comparative Physiology and Psychology, 47, 166-168)*

Scott. J. P. and Marston Mary, Critical Periods Affecting the Development of Normal and Maladjusted Social Behaviour of Puppies *(Journal of Genetic Psychology, 77, 26-60, 1950)*

Juel-Nielsen N. Individual and Environment *(Acta Psychiatrica Scandinavica, Supplementum 183, Copenhagen, 1965)*

Newman, H. H., Freeman, F. N., and Holzinger, K. J., *(University of Chicago Press, Chicago. 1937)*

Shields, J. Monozygotic Twins Brought up Apart and Together *(Oxford University Press, London, 1962)*

2.2   Are Sex Mortality Differentials Biologically Caused?

Francis C. Madigan, S. J.
University of North Carolina

Several previous studies by demographers have drawn attention to the continuous divergence of male and female expectations of life in this country since 1900. Wiehl in 1938 pointed out the widening gap between the sexes, suggested the need for research into the causes, and called for medical specialization in care for men just as gynecologists have specialized in care of women.[1] Yerushalmy in a sex and age investigation of our population composition showed the striking increases which had occurred in the percentage of women among the older people of our country during the period from the census of 1920 to that of 1940.[2] More recently, Bowerman has produced new data which prove that the gap has continued to widen rather than to narrow.[3]

In 1900, the white women of this country enjoyed but a 2.85 year advantage over comparable males in expectation of life at birth. By 1950, this female advantage had doubled to 5.8 years, and the national abridged tables for 1954 show a difference of 6.2 years.

Why have men not profited from the better conditions of this century to the same extent as women? What are the chances that their days of life can be prolonged to equal those of the female sex?

Such questions raise further ones. Are these differentials in rates of dying chiefly reflections of the greater sociocultural pressures and strains which our culture lays upon male shoulders? Or are the differentials rather to be associated mainly with biological factors related to sex? If the former is the

Reprinted from the *Millbank Memorial Fund Quarterly*, 1957 (April), *35*, No. 2, 202-223, by permission of the Millbank Memorial Fund.

case, then probably little can be done to enable men to enjoy a life as long as women's. Short of a profound cultural revolution in our society, it appears that men must continue to experience greater stresses. However, if sex-linked biological factors principally underlie the differentials, the prognosis is more hopeful. It seems likely in this case that medical research can isolate the factors responsible for greater female viability, and use this knowledge to advantage in the treatment of middle-aged and old men, assuming of course that this can be done without disturbing psychological balance or causing observable physical reactions.

A quickening of interest in the problem of the diverging death trends of our men and women has occurred during the past few years and has resulted in a rather large amount of journal literature upon the question. However, most of this has been descriptive and speculative rather than analytic and research-oriented. The present article reports upon the results of a study which has attempted to shed some light upon the problem through the tools of demographic research.

Research Design

There seems to be no question that the differentials between the sexes in perinatal and infant mortality are due to biological rather than to sociocultural factors.[4] Accordingly, this study is concerned only with that part of the life from age fifteen onwards.

The design chosen was that of the "ex post facto experiment." Thus the problem was one of finding a male group and a female group in which cultural stresses and strains had been so standardized between sexes that one could observe the operation of biological factors in comparative isolation.

The subjects chosen for study were teachers and personnel of administrative staffs of Roman Catholic religious Brotherhoods and Sisterhoods engaged in educational work. Communities of these which operated hospitals were eliminated from the universe, and in communities actually studied the life records of Brothers and Sisters devoting their energies to household and manual duties were discarded as were those of infirmarians and nurses (who are in charge not of extern patients but of sick members).

Also eliminated from consideration were the records of those who had served in foreign missions, those who had been married before entrance into religious life, the foreign-born, the non-white, and those who had entered into the religious community on or after their twenty-seventh birthday. The reason for all these eliminations was the imposition of controls that would yield as homogeneous a group of subjects as possible.

While in the general public single men are more given to dissipation than single women, a life of dissipation is equally out of the question for both sexes in religious communities. Moreover, Brothers are not subject to

military service after their entrance into religious life. Further, the daily regime of Brothers and Sisters is extremely similar as regards time for sleep, work, study, and recreation, and with respect to diet, housing, and medical care. (However, the life of the young Sisters seems to be slightly more stressful.)

It must be admitted that the Brothers are more likely to smoke and take an occasional drink. Only recently have Sisters been permitted to smoke and only in a limited number of communities. An important factor that is not controlled because of the absence of relevant data is the relative incidence of obesity or of overeating within each sex group. However, it may be observed that Sisters do not have the same motives for slimness found among their sex in the general public.

Such control of sociocultural factors, it was assumed, would permit the desired operation of biological factors working in comparative isolation. Five highly significant sources of differential stress between the sexes had been eliminated: (1) male service in the armed forces; (1) greater male liberty to dissipate; (3) the dissimilar roles of husband and wife; (4) male employment in hazardous and life-shortening occupations; and (5) the employment of men and women in diverse occupations. Other sources of differential sociocultural stress also appear to have been eliminated or greatly curtailed. Maternal mortality, of course, had also been excluded by the very nature of the female group under observation.[5]

Health requirements suitable for the teaching occupation were demanded of candidates for entrance into the religious life by both Brothers and Sisters during the entire period of observation. Such screening was based upon personal knowledge of the candidate's past health, his or her condition at time of entrance, and the person's health record during the one or more years of trial before the first vows are pronounced. It appears that Sisters required a medical examination by a physician earlier and more widely than the Brothers. This requirement seems to have become the common practice by about 1930.

Since stable death rates were desired, a large number of years of exposure to risk of dying was needed. Because the number of religious persons, especially of Brothers, was limited, the person-year of life was chosen as the unit of study, and the period of observation was extended from January 1, 1900 to December 31, 1954.

Sampling lists of all teaching communities of Brothers and Sisters in the United States were prepared from various editions of THE OFFICIAL CATHOLIC DIRECTORY[6] A sample of twenty-two Brothers' communities and of fifty-three Sisters' communities was drawn by probability sampling from these lists. In terms of members living in 1927, which we treated as the mid-year of the study, the sample of Brothers comprised 100 per cent of the Brothers' universe, while that of the Sisters included 59.3 per cent of the Sisters' universe. The response from these communities was good with twenty

communities of Brothers cooperating, representing more than 98 per cent of the Brothers' membership as measured in terms of 1927, and with forty-one communities of Sisters cooperating, representing 83.9 per cent of the membership in the Sisters' sample as measured, again, in terms of 1927.

In each of these communities life records were collected for the full membership of Brothers and Sisters since January 1, 1900, with the exception of persons who had not persevered for some part of three calendar years in the community. (The person-years in religious life of these latter were estimated on a sample basis.) All deaths were recorded, even if such death had occurred within the calendar year of entrance. When eliminations had been made according to the "experimental" controls described above, this left 9,813 life records of Brothers and 32,041 for Sisters.

In studying the literature, it had appeared to us that the greater weight of expert opinion lay on the side favoring biological factors as the principal causes for the sex differentials in the death rates. Accordingly, the research hypotheses were framed from this point of view and were expressed as follows:

1. Given two groups of American adults, one all male, the other all female, both drawn from the universe of healthy, native white persons in the United States who have reached age fifteen: if both groups are subjected to closely similar sociocultural stresses and strains over a long period of time, the female group will continue to show significantly more favorable death rates than the males.

2. The mortality differentials between the two experimental groups will not differ significantly from the patterns exhibited by the national population, or else will show increased female superiority.

While these hypotheses assume for testing purposes that biological factors linked with sex chiefly underlie women's pervasive advantage in length of life, and that the differing amounts of sociocultural stress borne by men and women have little relation to this female advantage, neither hypothesis should be misinterpreted to mean that social strains and pressures are believed to be unimportant in the chain of events which leads to an individual's death. In fact, evidence is strong that social strains may play a leading role in the deaths of both sexes. Rather, proper interpretation of these hypotheses understands them to mean that, other things being equal, the same objective stresses and strains upon equal numbers of men and women will lead to the deaths of more men than women during a given period of time.

Methodology

From the life records of these Sisters and Brothers age-specific death rates by ten year age groups were worked out for each decade, 1900-1950, and for the five years, 1950-1954, as well as for the entire period, 1900-1954.

Ratios were formed by dividing the death rates of Brothers by those of American native white males, and the rates of Sisters by the corresponding females.

Theoretical Model

On the assumption that the Brothers and Sisters studied constitute a group in which sociocultural stresses have been very greatly standardized between sexes, what results would indicate that such sociocultural factors are chiefly responsible for the differentials in mortality trends of American men and women? On the other hand, what results would point to biological factors as being the chief agents?

If the death rates of the Brothers should prove to have been lower than those of males of the general public, while Sisters exhibited death rates approximately equivalent to those of Brothers, the sociocultural hypothesis would be confirmed. For this would show that the variation in death rates of each sex is closely associated with variations in the amount of sociocultural stresses undergone.

On the other hand, this null hypothesis would be rejected and the biological hypothesis strengthened if the differences between the death rates of Brothers and Sisters should remain rather similar to the differentials found between death rates of men and women of the general public.

However, two points need emphasis here. The first concerns the Brothers. No matter which hypothesis is actually closer to the truth, Brothers should have experienced death rates somewhat lower than those of white males of the general public, at least at ages under forty-five. First of all, they presumably suffer accident rates—especially motor vehicle accident rates— far below those of white males of the same age. Secondly, they would not have been exposed to the disabilities often resulting from military service (except Brothers who had been in service before entrance, none of whom would have been admitted to religious life if they had shown serious disability). Thirdly, their occupation, teaching, seems to be less stressful and dangerous than that of the average white male outside religious life. Finally, they have not carried on their shoulders the worries of a husband or a father about the security of his family.

The second point relates to the Sisters. Young Sisters at least (those up to about age 40) lead a life which appears more stressful than that of the average female in the general public. They teach long hours, and work on college and graduate degrees during their spare time. Most of them do not have a summer vacation but rather attend classes, teach catechism, take parish censuses, or participate in other activities.

Accordingly, even if sociocultural factors should be only of slight importance in relation to the observed sex mortality differentials of the general public, one would still not anticipate finding that young Sisters, at least, had

experienced greater gains over females of the general public in mortality rates than Brothers had made over the corresponding males. Thus if Sisters have experienced significantly lower death rates than Brothers, and if at the same time the gains they made over females of the general public were not much smaller than those made by Brothers over the males, this would constitute strong evidence for rejecting the second null hypothesis. This hypothesis states that although biological factors may prove more important than sociocultural stresses, nevertheless sociocultural stresses still will be found to play an important part in the total effeet of differential sex mortality.

Findings

Results confirm both research hypotheses and indicate (1) that biological factors are *more* important than sociocultural pressures and strains in relation to the differential sex death rates; and (2) that the greater sociocultural stresses associated with the male role in our society play only a small and unimportant part in producing the differentials between male and female death rates.

Analysis of Results by Expectation of Life

In general, life expectations of Brothers at all ages but the oldest (where the frequencies were very small) proved to be considerably greater than those of white males of the general public.[7] Such a result was to have been anticipated under either biological or sociocultural hypotheses.

The important point, however, is that Sisters' expectations of life did not in general recede from the favored position of white females. Rather, they too usually made gains over these females. In thirty-eight cases Sisters had greater expectations of life than these white females, whereas the latter had greater expectations in only four cases.

Moreover, in these culturally standardized groups, Sisters' and Brothers' expectations of life did not tend to vary about the same means, but Sisters consistently exhibited greater expectations of life, and Brothers shorter expectations. Only seven times in the abridged life tables did Brothers enjoy longer expectations of life, while Sisters were favored in this manner thirty-three times. It is noteworthy that most of the Brothers' advantage came at ages 15-34 when they would be favored by accident rates, and in the years 1900-1919 when young Sisters appear to have had extremely high rates of tuberculosis.[8]

Comprehension of these results is aided by studying expectation of life at age 15, which summarizes results for the entire period of religious life from entrance until death; and expectation of life at age 45, which summarizes the experience for middle and old age only. This latter expectation is

particularly important, in fact is crucial in this research design, because if social pressures were the main reason for the differentials in death rates of men and women in our general public, then at ages 45 and above in these standardized groups Brothers' and Sisters' death rates should show great convergence. For in the general public it is during the years from 45 to 65 that men seem to undergo greatest social strains and pressures. Accordingly, one would expect such pressures to exert an ever greater cumulative weight and to exact an increasing toll in the years following age 45. Therefore, on the hypothesis of sociocultural causation, standardization of such pressures ought to result in Brothers' and Sisters' death rates which vary about the same averages for each age group.

Figures 1 and 2 make it abundantly clear that such convergence has not occurred at the middle and older ages, and they also show that even at age 15 the expectations have favored Sisters without exception from the third decade onwards. A comparison of the two figures also makes it evident that the Brothers' chief period of advantage was between ages 15 and 44.

The trends over time are important, too, for the consistency of the trend lines at age 15 minimizes the probability that Sisters' advantages after 1919 are due to chance factors, while the consistent upward secular trend of Sisters at age 45 and the fluctuation of Brothers' expectations around a mean of about 27.5 years of remaining life, appears even more cogent.

Are these differences between Brothers' and Sisters' expectations of life statistically significant? If so, the null hypothesis that sociocultural factors are the chief reasons for the differentials between male and female death rates may be rejected.

In order to make this test, the data for the entire period of observation were pooled.

Such pooling gave more stable death rates; they were based on totals of 788 deaths and 130,863 person-years of life for Brothers, and of 6,144 deaths and 718,435 person-years of life for Sisters.

When expectations of life at age 15 and age 45 were tested, the advantages of Sisters in both cases proved significant at beyond the .001 level. Thus the first research hypothesis, that biological factors mainly underlie the differential death rates, was supported. It is interesting to note in this connection that the ratios showing Sisters' advantages became larger at each successive age interval—exactly the opposite of what would be expected under the sociocultural hypothesis. A somewhat similar trend appears in the ratios for the national population.

Analysis of Results by Age-Specific Death Rates[9]

We now turn our attention to the second research hypothesis, that not only are sociocultural pressures less important than biological factors in

**Fig. 1. Expectations of life in years at age 15, Brothers and Sisters,
1900—1954.**

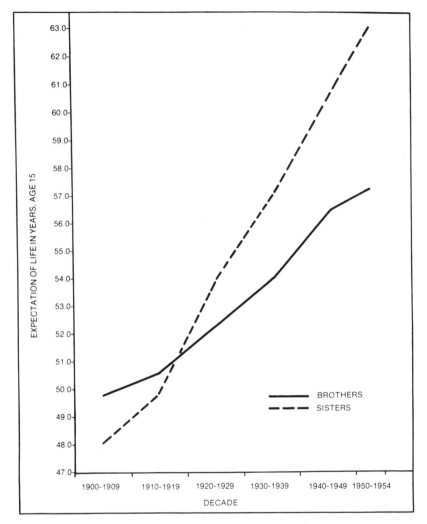

relation to the mortality differentials of the sexes, but they are of comparatively small importance in this respect. This hypothesis was examined by
means of age-specific death rates.

A point of interest in these death rates, is the spatial location of rates
which favor Brothers over Sisters. 77 per cent of all rates unfavorable to
Sisters are found within early ages during the period 1900-1939. On the
other hand, Sisters showed a clear advantage from age 45 upwards in all
decades, and at all ages after 1939.

Fig. 2. Expectations of life in years at age 45, Brothers and Sisters, 1900—1954.

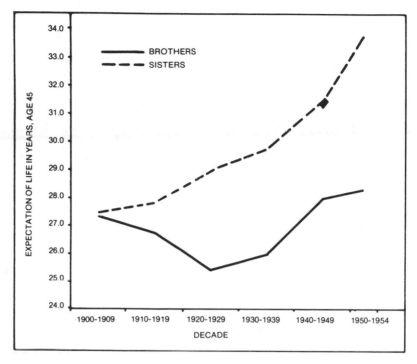

This finding supports the conclusion already reached in studying expectations of life that sociocultural pressures are not the main factors underlying sex differences in death rates, because it shows that Sisters enjoyed more favorable rates than Brothers at the crucial middle and older ages. It also indicates that Sisters' death rates at ages under 45 in the period 1900-1939 were anomalous. Analysis of the table for these ages and years makes it clear that Sisters' rates therein were at times exceptionally high. Since social pressures and degenerative diseases would hardly cause such high death rates between ages 15 and 24, and between ages 25 and 34, the conclusion seems warranted that some infectious or contagious disease or diseases plagued young Sisters in the early part of this century with unusually lethal effects.

A number of reasons suggest that this disease was tuberculosis. First, there was the greater difficulty of detecting incipient cases during the first quarter of the century in the medical examination required of candidates for admission, due to the less frequent use of X-ray pictures. Even in 1936, according to Dr. Frost, a large proportion of tubercular cases in the general public were not discovered until they had reached an advanced stage.[10] We

may be fairly sure that the same would be true among Sisters in regard to those incipient cases of tuberculosis which had escaped detection at time of entrance. Secondly, the dangers of infection would be multiplied by the close life of the Sisters among themselves in the Convent, and the lack of general understanding then prevalent of prophylactic methods to prevent the spread of the germ. "Age and prior exposure bring no such immunity against tuberculosis as they establish against many of the acute infections."[11]

Again, the highest tuberculosis mortality of cohorts of birth appears to occur between ages 20-29.[12] Moreover, it has been a fairly common observation that females between ages 10 and about 29 show higher susceptibility to tuberculosis than males of these ages, so much so, indeed, that in 1929 Sydenstricker called such women "relatively neglected groups" and found their death rates from tuberculosis were 59 per cent higher than the male rate at 10-14 years of age, 106 per cent higher at 15-29 years, and 43 per cent higher at 20-24 years.[13]

Finally, Fecher's work[14] as well as the British experience of 1930-1932[15] makes it evident that Catholic Sisters and nuns aged 15 to 34 years during the period 1900-1932 had rates of tuberculosis which were unusually high and which were far above the rates for single women. Single women at these ages generally showed rates higher than those of married women or of males. Dr. Taylor found similar results among Sisters in three American communities she studied from their foundation in the last century up through 1953.[16]

Ratios were formed by dividing Brothers' death rates by those of native white males, and Sisters' death rates by those of native white females. In order not to bias the comparison, each ratio was weighted by the number of person-years out of the total that Brothers or Sisters had lived in the particular decade-age-group, and thus average weighted ratios were formed for ages 15-44, ages 15 and above, and ages 45 and above.

These average ratios show whether Brothers made greater gains over native white males than Sisters made over native white females and vice versa. Thus they permit comparison of the differences of patterns between sexes in death rates for the "experimental" groups and for the national population. Where the ratios are equal, this shows that the patterns between sexes of the national groups are perfectly reflected in the differential rates of Brothers and Sisters. However, where male ratios are lower, this indicates tha Brothers have made greater gains, and that there has been convergence between death rates of Brothers and Sisters, when these are measured from the positions of male and female of the national population. On the other hand, where female ratios are lower, it indicates Sisters have made greater gains, and that there has been divergence.

We may again ask, what results would lead to the non-rejection of the second null hypothesis, that sociocultural factors are of more than small

importance in effecting the sex differences in mortality rates? Taking into account the lower accident rates of younger Brothers, and the less hazardous and stressful occupation in which they are engaged in comparison with that of the average native white male, as well as the fact that young Sisters are probably under greater stresses than the average native white female, non-rejection of the null hypothesis would call for large divergences from the patterns of the general public which would (a) be particularly manifested during the crucial middle and old-age periods of life, and (b) which would be in the direction of convergence between Brothers and Sisters' death rates, rather than in the direction of greater divergence.

The results shown in Table 1 do not present a picture of convergence of Sisters' death rates towards Brothers nor divergence from the general public pattern of superior female death rates at the middle and the old ages. An examination of this table reveals that Sisters exhibited as much superiority over Brothers at these ages as females over males of the general public. Almost all comparative gains of Brothers occurred at ages 15-44, a period in which it is difficult to believe that the underlying causation could have been influenced much by social stress and strain. Rather the difference, particularly in the last fifteen years of observation, appears due to gains of Brothers over native white males in lower death rates from motor vehicle and other types of accidents, on the one hand, and on the other to high death rates from infectious disease such as tuberculosis among Sisters in the first quarter of this century.

Tests of significance were made by weighted analyses of variance upon each of the values shown in Table 1[17] Brothers' ratios proved significantly lower than Sisters at ages 15-44 in the 1900, 1910, and 1950 decades, and for the period 1900-1954 (at .05 for each period, except 1910-19 when the difference was significant at .001). In the decades 1920, 1930, and 1940 the differences were not significant.

At all ages, 15 and above, Brothers' ratios proved significantly lower in the 1910, and the 1930 decades, as well as in the period 1900-1954. (The level of significance was .01 except for 1930 when it stood at .05.)

At ages 45 and above, no differences were significant within decades, but the Sisters' lower ratio for the entire period 1900-1954 was significant at the .01 level.

Since there were no large departures among Brothers and Sisters at the middle and older ages from the patterns of female superiority observed in the general public and since, in fact, at these ages Sisters' ratios were generally somewhat lower, the null hypothesis was rejected and the research hypothesis, that sociocultural pressures made only small contributions to the differential mortality rates of the sexes, was supported. Because of the nature of the tests, it was not possible to set any precise level of probability for this ejection of the null hypothesis.

Table 1
Average weighted ratios of Brothers death rates to death rates of
United States' native white males, and of Sisters' death rates to death rates
of United States' native white females, for ages 15-44, [1]5 and all ages over,
and 45 and all all ages over, 1900-1954.[1]

Group	1900–09	1910–19	1920–29	1930–39	1940–49	1950–54	1900–54	Ages
Brothers[2]	.94	.84	.73	.36	.44	.36	.61	15–44
Sisters	1.26	1.18	.97	.80	.55	.44	.96	
Brothers	.97	.85	.77	.45	.50	.44	.66	15 and
Sisters	1.18	1.09	.93	.83	.66	.56	.92	Over
Brothers	1.13	.87	.96	1.00	.83	.84	.92	45 and
Sisters	.85	.86	.82	.90	.85	.71	.84	Over

[1]The United States rates for 1950-1954 used were for the white rather than the native white population.

[2]"Brothers" was used here as a shorthand expression for the death rates of Brothers divided by the death rates of United States native white males and weighted according to the number of person years of exposure; similarly "Sisters."
Source: The Differential Mortality of the Sexes, pp. 169-171, and p. 173.

Evaluation of Results

The finding that biological factors played by far the chief part in differentiating the death rates of members of the universe studied is very important. Since these members were native white Americans of sufficient health to be admitted into religious communities engaged in the active occupation of teaching, the results point to the operation of similar biological factors as the chief agents in the differential death rates of the two sexes of the American general public.

An interesting lead for further research is the notable, even spectacular improvement of young Sisters under observation from the early to the late years of the study. From showing the poorest records of the four populations compared in the period 1900-1909, they improved rapidly to exhibit by far the best mortality records for the years after 1939. This suggests the hypothesis that *under conditions of equal stress* women may be no more resistant to the *infectious* and *contagious* diseases than men—perhaps even less so—and that the gains which women have been making over men in this century may be chiefly bound up with a greater constitutional resistance to the *degenerative* diseases. This would account for the remarkable improvement of young Sisters vis-a-vis the other three populations, because of the spectacular advances made during this century in controlling the ravages of the infectious and contagious diseases. If this hypothesis is borne out by

further research, one might then say that the growing advantage of American women over men is a function of the transition from conditions when infectious and contagious diseases were the main causes of death to conditions wherein the degenerative diseases play this role.

Of course, an alternative hypothesis is possible. There may have been some hidden selection of Sisters in the earlier quarter of the century which operated at a much reduced degree in the second quarter. What this selection would be is obscure. None of the convents took in girls to "let them die in the religious life." Nor was the ascetical life of the Sisters apparently more rigorous than that of the Brothers, although both regimes were more severe at the start of the century than they are now. Further, the physical examination of candidates for admission seems to have been more careful than that of the Brothers rather than less painstaking.[18]

The continuing phase of this study should allow some test of these hypotheses, as well as the hypothesis that the chief reason for the poor showing of young Sisters during the first quarter century was tuberculosis. However, it is hoped that the results of the present study will stimulate further research by other interested parties, including both replications of the present study among other matched groups of men and women, and medical research, first, into causes of death which carry off more men than women when social stress differentials have been minimized, and secondly, into specific biological factors which may be associated with the longer life of women. Such studies may advance the date when our men can enjoy an average lifetime as long as that of women.

Notes

[1] Wichl, Dorothy G.: Sex Differences in Mortality in the United States. Milbank Memorial Fund *Quarterly,* April, 1938, XVI, pp. 145-55.

[2]Yerushalmy, Jacob: The Age-Sex Composition of the Population Resulting from Natality and Mortality Conditions. Milbank Memorial Fund *Quarterly*, January, 1943, XXI, pp. 37-63.

[3]Bowerman, Walter G.: Annuity Mortality. *Actuarial Society of America: Transactions,* 1950, II, pp. 76-102.

[4]The most pertinent and forceful of the many studies showing the existence of these differentials is that of Sam Shapiro: The influence of Weight, Sex, and Plurality on Neonatal Loss in the United States. *American Journal of Public Health and the Nation's Health,* 1954, XLIV pp. 1142-1153.

[5]A detailed discussion of the research design will be found in a previous article by Rupert B. Vance and Francis C. Madigan, S.J.: Differential Mortality and the "Style of Life" of Men and Women: Research Design. TRENDS AND DIFFERENTIALS IN MORTALITY. 1955 Annual Conference of Milbank Memorial Fund. New York, Milbank Memorial Fund, 1956, pp. 150-163. A later and more comprehensive treatment is also available in the writer's unpublished doctoral dissertation available in the University of North Carolina Library: The Differential Mortality of the Sexes,

1900-1954: Cultural and Biological Factors in the Diverging Life Chances of American Men and Women. University of North Carolina, Chapel Hill, 1956.

6 THE OFFICIAL CATHOLIC DIRECTORY. Milwaukee, Wiltzius and Company, 1900-1911. New York, Kenedy and Son, 1912-1955.

7When comparing Brothers' expectations with those of males of the general public, one must bear in mind that a small part of the Brothers' advantage is a statistical artifact. In the first four decades, for the age group 85 years and above, the central death rate used for the life tables of both Brothers and Sisters was the United States native white rate as common to both sexes. This device was employed because of the paucity of Brothers at these ages, and because of the desire to hold constant death rates of Brothers and Sisters at previous ages, while still finishing off the tables. A similar procedure was used in the first two decades for ages 75-84. Stable Brothers' rates—if they had been obtainable—would probably have been nearer those of native white males than the rates for both sexes taken together. On the other hand, Sisters' expectations were somewhat deflated, since in general at these ages the actual rates of Sisters were more favorable than the native white rates not specific for sex.

8See footnotes 10-15.

9The fractions upon which these rates were based will be found in the writer's dissertation. The Differential Mortality, pp. 225-253.

10 Frost, Wade ampton: How Much Control of Tuberculosis. In PAPERS of WADE HAMPTON FROST, M.D. Ed., Kenneth F. Maxcy, M.D. New York, Commonwealth Fund, 1941, p. 607.

11 Frost, Wade Hampton: The Age Selection of Mortality from Tuberculosis in Successive Decades. In PAPERS OF WADE HAMPTON FROST, p. 594. of Dr. Frost to Dr. Sydenstricker, quoted.)

12Ibid., American Journal of Hygiene, 1939, xxx, Sec. A, p. 91, footnote (in letter of Dr. Frost to Dr. Syndestricker, quoted.)

13 Sydenstricker, Edgar: Tuberculosis Among Relatively Neglected Groups. TRANSACTIONS OF THE NATIONAL TUBERCULOSIS ASSOCIATION, 1929, xxv, p. 268.

14 Fecher, Constantine J.: THE LONGEVITY OF MEMBERS OF CATHOLIC RELIGIOUS SISTERHOODS. Washington: Catholic University of America, 1927, pp. 42-44. Fecher is at present bringing his interesting study up to date.

15 Registrar General's Office, THE REGISTRAR GENERAL'S DECENNIAL SUPPLEMENT, ENGLAND AND WALES, 1931. Part IIa. Occupational Mortality. London, His Majesty's Stationery Office, 1938, Table 4c, p. 303.

16 It is the writer's understanding that Dr. Ruth Taylor and Mr. Ben Carroll of the National Institutes of Health expect to publish these results in the near future.

17The Method of Fitting Constants was used to obtain adjusted sums of squares for sex and for age. Cf. Snedecor, George W.: STATISTICAL METHODS. Ames, Iowa, Collegiate Press, 1946, pp 296-99.

18The writer learned these facts from a questionnaire which he circulated among the communities in his sample after the results had become available.

2.3 The Child: His Right to be Normal

Carlo Valenti, M.D.

In his new classic of modern biology, *The Person in the Womb,* Dr. N. J. Berrill makes this, among other, declarations:

> If a human right exists at all, it is the right to be born with normal body and mind, with the prospect of developing further to fulfillment. If this is to be denied, then life and conscience are mockery and a chance should be made for another throw of the ovarian dice.

In accord with this philosophy, I draw attention to some favorable prospects for "another throw."

About one in fifty babies is born with a greater or lesser degree of abnormality inherited from its parents. These weaknesses, more than 500 of them severe enough to be classified as diseases (diabetes, for example), are ordered by the genes carried on the chromosomes. No one has ever seen a gene, but we can identify chromosomes under the microscope. Every normal person has a complement of forty-six of them, paired in twenty-three sets. One of the twenty-three pairs determines sex. The determination is made by chance and occurs as follows.

The female sex chromosomes are paired XX. In any division of the germ cell in preparation for mating with a male sperm, the female half of the marriage will therefore always be X.

The male sex chromosomes are paired XY. When the division of this germ cell occurs, the sperm may be X or it may be Y.

When a female egg is penetrated by an X sperm, the nuclei of the egg and the sperm will fuse XX and the offspring will be female.

When a female egg is penetrated by a Y sperm, the offspring will be XY, or male.

The choice is simple when everything goes well in the reproductive process. However, faulty working of the ovaries or testes sometimes produces fertilized XXX eggs (super-females, not always fertile), XXYs (outwardly male, but without sperm), XOs (outwardly female, but without ovaries and therefore without eggs), XXXXYs (typically defective mentally), and XYYs (typically defective mentally, often aggressive to a criminal extent).

The other twenty-two pairs of chromosomes suffer displacements when parents bring together certain genetic characteristics. The results can be very sad. For example, the chromosome pairs numbered 13-14-15 are catalogued by the letter D. Pairs No. 21 and 22 are catalogued by the letter G.

Sometimes one chromosome of these two pairs is displaced in what is called

Reprinted from *Saturday Review,* Dec. 7, 1968, 75-78, by permission of the author and Saturday Review, Inc. Copyright © 1968 Saturday Review, Inc.

a D/G translocation. What happens is that one of the No. 21 pair crosses over to and joins up with one of the No. 15 pair, riding piggyback as it were and giving that one No. 15 a lopsided appearance.

The person who bears this particular pattern of chromosomes is a balanced carrier for Mongolism. We say "balanced" because the total amount of genetic material on the chromosome is normal, although the number of chromosomes is only forty-five. But the chromosomal pattern is thrown off balance when the balanced carrier's offspring inherits the lopsided chromosome from the carrier along with a 21 from the carrier and a 21 from the other parent. The total inheritance then in three 21s, two in the normal position and one on the lopsided chromosome. The three 21s doom their possessor to Mongolism.

Why focus on the Mongoloid?

A Mongoloid child—in medical terms, he is a victim of "Down's syndrome"—has folded eyes and a flat-rooted nose (the Mongolian-like features from which the popular name of the anomaly derives), small head, fissured protruding tongue, pecularities in the lines of the palms of the hands and the soles of the feet, retarded intellectual development ranging from idiocy to a maximum prospective mental age of seven years.

Once given life, a Mongoloid is a poignant burden on its parents. For the Mongoloid appeals to all human instincts for companionship. He is cheerful, friendly, imitative, with a good memory for music and for details of situations he has experienced. A Mongoloid's life expectancy averages ten years—a decade of hopelessness in most cases necessarily spent in a special institution.

Now it has been known for more than a dozen years that before a child is in finished form to leave his mother's womb the chromosomes of the prospective individual can be sampled and analyzed for aberrations. Dr. Fritz Fuchs, Danish-born chief of obstetrics and gynecology at Cornell University Medical College in New York, was able to pioneer such work in his native country because of the liberality of Denmark's laws governing therapeutic abortion.

The method developed by Dr. Fuchs and others is to obtain cells from the amniotic fluid, which is the stuff that every developing fetus floats in. Although the fetus derives almost all of its nourishment from rapidly pulsing blood fed from the placenta by way of the umbilical cord, the fetus before twelve weeks have passed by begins to swallow the amniotic fluid and excrete the fluid through its kidneys and bladder. In growing, the fetus sheds its skin gradually as we living persons shed ours, and other cells are dislodged from the mouth, bronchi, trachea, kidney, and bladder in the course of the swallowing and excreting. The fluid carrying all these cells must be sampled through the wall of the pregnant woman's abdomen by means of a hollow needle similar to those used to draw blood from a vein.

Where the needle enters the womb is of critical importance; if the wrong

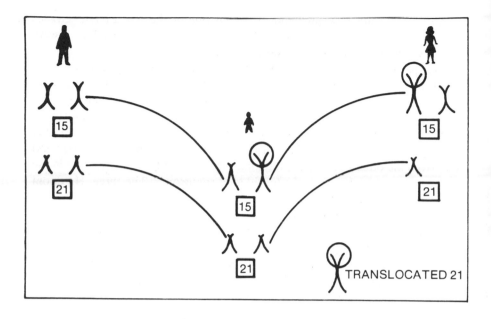

How Mongolism is transmitted through a "balanced carrier" to an offspring is demonstrated above. Only two of the twenty-three sets of chromosomes— the No. 15s and the No. 21s—are shown. Note that whereas the father has the normal 21 pair, the mother has one 21 in its normal place and the other upside down on the lopsided No. 15. When chance deals the child the lopsided 15, he has three 21s and is doomed. Palm prints and sole prints of Mongoloid child are below.

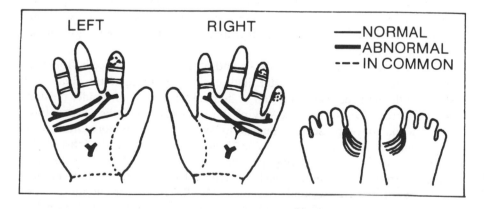

—Sketches by Doug Anderson, following Carlo Valenti, M.D.

site were to be chosen, the placenta could be punctured or the fetus itself impaled. Either event could produce serious consequence.

To assure a safe choice, the exact location of the placenta and the floating head of the fetus is determined in the same way that submarines are located when afloat in sea water—that is, by sonar or echo-sounding. The method is feasible as early as the fourteenth week of pregnancy. A tiny portable gun that fires sound waves at very high speeds is moved across the prospective parent's abdomen in sweeps proceeding successively downward until the entire belly has been scanned. A pattern similar to that seen on a radar screen emerges. With it as a guide, the entry point of the amniocentesis needle is fixed.

After a sample of the amniotic fluid has been removed through the needle, the sample is spun in a centrifuge. The liquid part of the sample is then discarded. A pellet of cells remains. In this pellet is the knowledge we seek.

Two groups of investigators have reported varying success in culturing the cells on nutritive media they have independently developed. Their techniques, described in the medical literature, did not yield good results in our obstetrics and gynecology laboratory here at State University of New York's Downstate Medical Center in Brooklyn. So Edward J. Schutta, Tehila Kehaty, and myself have worked out a culturing method of our own and with it have obtained twenty successes in twenty-four trials. All our failures occurred where the amount of amniotic fluid used was below a certain level. The twenty successful cell cultures yielded seventeen chromosome analyses, or karyotypes. The three failures apparently were due to bacterial contamination.

Two to six weeks of growth are required before the culture is ready to be karyotyped—that is, placed on a glass laboratory slide, dried. stained. and examined microscopically to determine the chromosome pattern.

Last April, a Boston medical colleague familiar with our work referred to us a twenty-nine-year-old mother from Massachusetts who was sixteen weeks pregnant. She knew her grandfather, her mother, her brother, and herself to be balanced carries of the D/G chomosomal translocation. That is, all four were outwardly normal and healthy, but each carried within himself only one No. 21 chromosome in its normal pairing, while the other 21 was grated onto one of the No. 15 chromosome pair. In short, although not themselves Mongoloid, three generations of the family carried the genetic threat of Mongolism.

The young New Englander had already experienced a spontaneous abortion, borne a daughter who was also a balanced carrier of the D/G chromosomal translocation, and borne a Mongoloid son who had lived for five months. She wanted another child, and sought our assurance that it would be normal. With the support of her husband, an engineer by profession, she requested a cytogenetic diagnosis on the unborn baby.

Amniocentesis was performed after a sonar sounding on April 15. The amount of amniotic fluid obtained proved inadequate for optimum cell growth. Amniocentesis was performed again on April 29, luxuriant cell cultures were available within two weeks, and satisfactory chromosome preparations were ready for analysis on May 21. The karyotypes showed a male pattern with the D/G chromosomal translocation characteristic of Mongolism. Our hospital's abortion committee authorized a therapeutic interruption of pregnancy on the grounds that, since Mongolism was certain, failure to interrupt could subject the young mother to unjustifiable psychiatric trauma. Notice of the therapeutic abortion was posted routinely on the staff bulletin boards, and the abortion was done on May 31. Autopsy findings and palmprint and soleprint patterns were consistent with our cytogenetic diagnosis.

The young woman who volunteered for this experience recovered and returned to her New England home within forty-eight hours. She is still eager for another child if she can have a healthy one. She has requested application of amniocentesis to all future pregnancies.

This woman now has a chance for "another throw of the ovarian dice," as Dr. Berrill put it. The British medical journal, *Lancet*, published news of her case in the form of a letter from Schutta, Kehaty, and myself. It may not be sensational news because D/G chromosomal translocations accounts for only 2 per cent of all Mongoloid children. But to the individual women involved, it is a promise of release from fear and guilt.

Furthermore, the potential benefits of amniocentesis and karyotyping are applicable to the much greater percentage of Mongolism caused by trisomies. In these there are forty-seven chromosomes, including three No. 21s which appears as triplets in the place of the normal 21 pair (as opposed to the pair of 21s and the 21 contained in the lopsided chromosome of the D/G Mongoloids).

Trisomies are related to aging. Human eggs spoil with time just as other eggs do. Every woman's supply of eggs has been nested in her ovaries since well before she herself was born. All else being equal, she begins releasing them, at the rate of one a month (except during pregnancy and subsequent nursing), when she is about thirteen years old, and continues the process for the forty-odd years that intervene before menopause. Overall, the chance of an American woman giving birth to a Mongoloid child is one in 680. To age twenty-five, the chance is one in 2,000; after age forty-five, one in fifty.

Our laboratory has made cytogenetic diagnoses of two women who feared their pregnancies might produce Mongoloid infants. One of these women was thirty-six years old, the other thirty-seven. Amniocentesis and karyotyping showed no chromosomal aberrations.

The potential of prenatal study of fetal cells obtained by amniocentesis is far greater than we have yet been able to explore. Three broad areas are open to investigation. In the first, a smear of the fetal cells can be made

immediately after the cells are collected from the amniotic fluid. The smear shows presence or absence of the sex chromatin body (a condensation of nuclear material), which only female cells possess. The sex of the unborn child can thus be identified and sex-linked hereditary diseases, such as hemophilia and muscular dystrophy, can be diagnosed in the fetus. More than ten years ago, Dr. Fuchs in Denmark demonstrated the value of the technique by screening hemophilic pregnancies and interrupting those that would have resulted in male babies. Only males actually develop hemophilia; females carry the disease without being afflicted by it.

The second field of study of cells obtained by amniocentesis is the analysis of their chromosome complement, as illustrated by the case of the young woman patient described above. Advanced maternal age can cause a number of chromosomal errors in addition to the error that results in Mongolism. Anguish for the mothers involved can be avoided in some cases by interruption of pregnancy. The number of such cases is at the moment still uncertain. The certainty is that in the present state of knowledge we cannot correct chromosomal errors. In the future, however, we may be able to correct the effect of the errors by refining our methods, by applying the principle that each effect is due to a particular enzyme and that each enzyme is ordered by a particular gene. One step in the refinement is to map the locations of the genes on the chromosomes of man, as has already been done with the mouse.

The third area of endeavor in intrauterine medicine (treatment of the fetus in the uterus) is analysis of enzymes produced by the fetal cells that are taken from the amniotic fluid. There are hereditary diseases in which deficiency of given enzymes is known in the adult. Detection of the same deficiencies in the fetal cells may permit diagnosis of diseases in the unborn baby and possibly correction of the deficiencies and thus prevention of the diseases.

For example, one of the signs of Mongolism is flaccid muscles at birth. If the body of a Mongoloid baby is laid prone on the palm of the hand, the baby's head and limbs will flop downward like those of a rag doll. The weakness of the muscles has been attributed to absence of a chemical which can be made only in the presence of a particular enzyme. According to prevailing genetic theory, this enzyme must be missing from Mongoloid cells and the absence must be related to the existence in the cells of three No. 21 chromosomes instead of the normal pair of 21s.

In an English experiment, a chemical named 5-hydroxytryptophan was administered to fourteen Mongoloid babies ranging from a few days to four months in age. Within one to seven weeks later, normal muscle tone was restored to thirteen of these babies, who became able to raise their heads, arms, and legs. Clearly, a missing something had been supplied and had countracted at least some part of the effect of the abnormal set of three No. 21 chromosomes.

The English researchers were careful to point out that there is yet no evidence that their treatment will improve the mental development of Mongoloid babies. It is conceivable, however, that if Mongolism were diagnosed sufficiently early in the development of the fetus and if the missing chemical could be administered then, the effect on the child might be remarkable.

A great many scientists the world over are now studying enzyme deficiencies in hereditary diseases in the adult human. As their reservoir of knowledge grows, the potential of amniocentesis widens proportionately.

A major determinant of the ultimate effectiveness of intrauterine medicine will be the public attitude on abortion. At present, the laws of many states do not allow therapeutic abortion on genetic grounds. Genetic grounds are habitually constructed as empirical statistical evaluations. Chromosomal analysis is not statistical but is direct and specific evidence of abnormality. As physicians, legislators, and the people come to understand the distinction, they will surely see that the law cannot be interpreted to exclude abortion based on chromosomal analysis. For a law that would compel a mother to give birth to a baby certain to be severely defective would be cruel and uncivilized.

2.4   A Follow-Up Study of One Hundred Adopted Children

Marie Skodak
Harold M. Skeels
Iowa Child Welfare Research Station, State University of Iowa

A. Historical Background

. . . This report constitutes a final chapter in a long range study in which the same group of adopted children have had intelligence tests on four occasions. . . .

The foster homes into which the children described in this study were placed became available through a number of sources. The child-placing programs of the State Board of Control and the Iowa Children's Home

Excerpted, adapted and reprinted from *The Journal of Genetic Psychology*, 1949, *75,* 85-125, by permission of the authors and The Journal Press.

Society were well known throughout the state since the majority of agency placements were made through them. Both organizations had travelling workers, assigned to certain areas whose duties included: (*a*) The supervision of children placed in wage, free, and adoptive homes to insure proper care, protection, education, and home relationships. (*b*) The evaluation of homes and foster families for children in terms of financial resources, physical set-up, attitudes toward children, future demands on children. (*c*) The development of community interest in child care, adoption, and placement.

Parents interested in adoption would write directly to the state office, the institution, agency, or one of the field workers. The application blanks contained only the minimum information regarding the type of child desired, the family's financial and vocational status, and the names of at least three references. The field worker would then visit the home, interview the applicants, evaluate the physical and emotional resources and the possible future demands with regard to education and vocation. References were contacted by mail, phone, or visit. The degree of investigation varied. Families who were well known or who were manifestly capable were accepted with less scrutiny than families in more modest circumstances or where there were questions regarding the present or future adequacy of the home. It is not known what proportion of applicants were rejected, but in many cases families were dissuaded from completing an application if it seemed unlikely that a child would be placed with them.

On the whole the foster families were above the average of their communities in economic security and educational and cultural status. They were highly regarded by the town's business, professional, and religious leaders and usually had demonstrated a long-time interest in children through church or community activities.

The placement procedure in both organizations was essentially similar. In the state agency after the application was accepted the family was placed on the waiting list and their name was considered at the monthly staff meetings when assignments were made. At these case conferences, attended by the head of the Children's Division, the superintendent of the institution, the psychologists, and head nurse, the available babies and available homes were discussed. Factors in the assignment included religion, sex, age, color or complexion, physique, medical history, and report of the family background. Pre-placement psychological examinations were not available for the children in this study. In many instances the information about the child's family background was so meager that it was of little or no value. The primary factors in matching were the stipulations of the foster parents regarding religion, sex, and hair color in that order.

This method of placement of children from relatively inferior socio-economic backgrounds into substantial homes thus provided the setting for the study. Perusal of the child's social history as recorded in the institution and

comparison with the field's agent's pre-placement evaluation of the adopting home was disheartening. It did not seem possible that children with such meager possibilities, as projected from the intellectual, academic, and occupational attainments of their parents, could measure up to the demands of cultured, educated parents. Yet careful examination of one child after another showed none of the retardation or misplacement which might have been anticipated. Following a preliminary survey of results (24) it was decided that a follow-up study was imperative, and the cooperation of the foster parents was solicited and received.

B. Description of the Sample

In general there are three levels of society from which children for adoptive placements originate. It is believed that children from culturally, socially, and educationally superior homes tend to be placed among relatives or in adoptive homes through various private sources. Because of the extreme difficulty of identifying and locating such placements, no studies have been made of the subsequent development or adjustment of these children nor is the exact number of these children known to official agencies. At what may be described as the second socio-economic level, the children tend to become the charges of private or semi-private child caring or placing agencies. Many of these children's aid and protective societies exercise considerable control over their intake. Policies may, for instance, preclude the acceptance of children of mentally defective parents, or of other children who may be judged "unplaceable" or in need of care which that particular organization does not feel equipped to offer. These organizations tend to draw from the various middle economic classes but also have a fair number of children from extremely ineffective homes as the study by Roe and Burks indicates (21). The third group of children from the lowest socio-economic levels are usually known to various public welfare agencies. The public agencies, in contrast to the private ones, are usually obligated to accept all children committed to their care and naturally receive children no other agency feels able to accept. There is no doubt that the general social, vocational, and adjustment level of the parents of children committed to public agency care is substantially below that of children who become wards of private agencies or who are adopted through private channels.

It is necessary to differentiate between observations regarding the natural families of infants committed for care and the natural families of preschool or older children. All studies which have published reports on the education of the true parents of children placed in foster homes agree that the true parents of the older children are more apt to be inadequate, unstable, retarded, unemployed, in other words, less competent by any criterion of measurement which has been used. The social factors behind this difference are not difficult to identify. The youngest children, the infants, are primarily

illegitimate children. In the first place, their parents are relatively younger. While parents-out-of-wedlock show various signs of emotional instability, the psychoses, alcoholism, and cumulating effects of maladjustment characterizing the parents of older dependent children have not yet indelibly affixed themselves. With the rest of their generation, the younger parents enjoy higher educational opportunities together with the dubious benefits of being "lifted" from grade to grade on the basis of physical size rather than academic accomplishment. Vocationally it is understandable that an 18-year-old youth is a farm hand or truck driver's helper, while an adult of 40 on the same job is prima facie scored well down on the scale of occupational success. The young illegitimate parents have not had the accumulating frustration of economic deprivation, children in unwanted numbers, and the growing weight of community disapproval of their inefficient way of living. For many it is the first, and often the only, social transgression and after this experience many, perhaps even the majority of illegitimate parents, go on to establish secure, socially acceptable homes and families. A study of what happens to illegitimate parents who decide to establish a family together, as compared to those who release their child, may shed some interesting light on the factors which operate to produce the poorer histories among the older children as compared to the younger. There is a significant socio-economic difference between the parents of the younger and older groups of children who become dependent. It does not necessarily follow, however, that this difference is genetically determined.

1. Subjects of This Study

The criteria for inclusion in this study were as follows: (a) The child was placed in an adoptive home under the age of six months. (b) The child had been given an intelligence test prior to November, 1936, and after one year's residence in the adoptive home. (c) Some information, though of variable amount and reliability, existed concerning the natural and adoptive parents. (d) The child was white, of North European background (it so happened that no children of South European, Latin, or other social backgrounds met the other criteria either).

In this study all of the children were received for care as infants. The Iowa Soldiers' Orphan's Home, identified as the public agency, was the placing agency in 76 per cent of the cases and the Iowa Children's Home Society, a state-wide, private, non-sectarian organization placed 21 per cent. The remaining three children were privately placed and were included because they were available and met the criteria set up for the other children.

It was earlier pointed out (26) that 96.6 per cent of the 319 children committed to the two agencies under the age of six months between 1933-1937, were placed in adoptive homes. In only four cases was the child withheld from adoptive placement because of poor family history. The

remaining seven had serious health problems. Since the majority of the children originally in the study had been placed during this period, and the remainder had been placed earlier during a time when the policies regarding family background had been even more lenient, it was concluded that the children in the study were representative of all those placed by these organizations.

During 1934-36, when the mental testing program was coördinated for the two agencies, and 1933-37 for the public agency alone, it was found that 90 per cent of the children placed under six months of age had been given at least one intelligence test. The mean *IQ* of this group was 119, slightly above the mean *IQ* of 116 achieved by the members of the follow-up group on the first examination during the same calendar years.

It was evident that the group of children who constituted the first sample were representative of the available children since there was no systematic withholding of numbers of children because of poor histories, nor was there a group with lower initial intelligence test scores who were excluded from the study.

In the first follow-up report (25), out of a total of 180 children who met the criteria of age at placement, race and date of examination, it was possible to retest 152 children during 1937-38. On the third examination 139 children were seen during 1940-41 (26) and the fourth and final visit in 1946 resulted in the present sample of 100. The major factor in the reduction of the size of the sample has been time and expense. The families, all originally in Iowa, are now scattered over many states and Canada. To locate and visit the 100 children in the 10 weeks available for the study, it was necessary to drive over 12,000 miles even though accurate addresses were available and careful preliminary arrangements had been made with planned appointments acceptable for the parents and the child. . . .

Comparisons were made between the continuous group of 100 and those who dropped out at the various retest points. Systematic selection which would influence the character of the final group of 100 is not evident from the comparisons between the mean *IQ*'s of the group at the various re-examination periods. The standard deviations for all means are large, ranging from 11.9 to 17.2, and none of the differences is statistically significant.

It may be concluded that this group of 100 children is probably representative of the total group placed by these agencies at comparable ages, and that conclusions based on the pattern of mental development of these children are probably applicable to others with similar experience and social backgrounds and placed under similar circumstances into comparable homes.

2. *Test Techniques*

The purpose throughout the study was to secure the most reliable and

valid measure of the child's intellectual ability at the time of examination. On first examination the children ranged from 11 months to six years in age with 78 per cent of the children between one and three years. Four children had been placed at a few days of age and were tested shortly before the expiration of the one-year observation period. The 1916 Stanford-Binet was suitable for use with the 19 per cent over three years of age and was occasionally used with younger children who were obviously accelerated in mental development. The Kuhlman Binet was routinely used with all children under three years, and occasionally as a clinical supplement with some children over three.

The re-examinations were begun in 1936 when the Revised Stanford-Binet was not generally available and the 1916 revision was consequently used. In this series of tests, although 17 per cent of the children were under 3-0 years of age, they were all over 2-6 and sufficiently accelerated to make the 1916 Stanford-Binet a usable test. Therefore, all test scores reported for the second examination were based on the 1916 revision.

When the third examination was scheduled in 1939-40, the question of "best test" was raised. From the standpoint of fatigue and future rapport, it seemed advisable to limit the number of tests given and the 1916 revision was again selected. Survey of the literature (7, 14, 18) showed that between 5 and 11 years, the ages of these children at the third examination, the results of the 1916 and 1937 scales were most nearly identical. Not only had the 1916 test been used in the earlier examinations, but it also had been used in examinations of the mothers and a few of the fathers of the children. Direct comparisons of test scores were thus made possible without getting into the knotty problems of comparability of standardization of the different revisions. The problems of such a long-time research underscore the need for an intelligence test which results in comparable scores at all ages.

When the fourth and last examination was scheduled in 1946, the children were between 11 and 17 years of age. In view of the problems surrounding the 1916 revision at these ages, it was decided to impose on the good nature of the subjects and give both the 1916 revision and Form L of the 1937 revision. This set up a program involving approximately two hours, often a great deal more, if there was marked scatter on either or both tests. Since there are a number of overlapping items, these were given and scored simultaneously. The 1916 revision was completed first and the 1937, Form L, second. Whatever advantage of practise effect there might have been, was judged to be cancelled by fatigue. Every effort was made to keep the interest and effort of the examinees at an optimum level. No subject refused to take the tests after an appointment was made and only two were openly antagonistic in typical adolescent behavior. Even these were persuaded to cooperate and no greater compliment to the intrinsic interests of the tests can be made than to say that in spite of themselves even these reluctant subjects became interested and made scores consistent with their earlier test results and their current school placements.

All of the third and fourth tests, and all but five or six of the first two tests were given in the foster homes. This made it possible to observe the relationships between child and parents, the fluctuation in family economic and cultural status over the 13-year period, and to sample the child's behavior in the home situation. A cordial relationship developed between the parents and the examiners as a result of these repeated visits. The first examination was usually a highly emotional experience for the parents, who understood that the psychologist's word was final in approving or disapproving the completion of adoption. In a sense this was even more crucial than the court action since as one parent stated "we were taking an examination in parenthood. Our success was shown by the results in our child." The majority of the families, located in areas where clinics and psychologists were not available but who were familiar with these resources through reading and the radio, availed themselves of the opportunity to discuss various child rearing problems. As would be anticipated, the character of the problems changed with age, and on the fourth visit dealt with problems of adolescence, vocational choices, educational plans, emancipation from the home, etc. There seemed to be no problem which was unique to this group of children as compared to any other group of similar age. The problem of information concerning their own adoption had been well solved by nearly all the families. Surprisingly enough two families had still not "told," but other evidence indicated that these children probably guessed. In two or three instances there had been community problems in which, despite the efforts of the foster parents, the children had had a very difficult adjustment to the adoptive status.

All the parents were aware of the research nature of the re-tests and were, on the whole, proud of the distinction. Through their contribution they felt they could facilitate early placement of children in adoptive homes and provide reassurance to families uncertain about adoption.

Relationships between the children and the examiners were more casual. Some of the children recalled the examiner's visits from one occasion to the next, and when they did, it was in terms of the fun of playing games with an unusually agreeable person. An explanation was made to all participants during the fourth examination following the general pattern that:

> When you were a younger boy, you were a member of a group of boys and girls all over the state who were given tests like this. We wanted to find out how well children could do different sorts of things, how well they could remember, figure things out and so on. Now that they are older, we would like to see how much they have changed and in what way. The tests are a little like a quiz program on the radio and most people find them rather fun.

In a few instances the question was raised as to whether children who were

not adopted were also tested and the subjects were assured that children in many places also took similar tests. Two of the participants, one, the oldest subject, who had completed one year in college, and one a superior high school senior with decided research interests, were familiar with the published reports of the study and cooperated delightfully.

C. Mental Development of the Children

All of the children had been seen on four occasions and a few for various reasons had been given additional tests. In these cases the test given at an age nearest the mean age for the group was selected for use in the major comparisons. The mean age at first examination was *2 years 2 months,* at second examination *4 years 3 months,* at third examination *7 years 0 months* and at fourth examination *13 years 6 months.*

The group included 60 girls and 40 boys. The range, median, and mean ages for both sexes were essentially the same.

Ages and results may be summarized for the 100 children as given in Table 1—The mean *IQ* of this group of children has remained above the average for the general population throughout early childhood, school age, and into adolescence. It would be generally accepted that if major changes in intellectual functioning occur after this age, they probably result from psychiatric and emotional problems rather than from developmental abnormalities. . . .

Table 1

Test	Age	Mean IQ	SD	Range	Median
I	2 yrs. 2 mo.	117	13.6	80-154	118
II	4 yrs. 3 mo.	112	13.8	85-149	111
III	7 yrs. 0 mo.	115	13.2	80-149	114
IV (1916)	13 yrs. 6 mo.	107	14.4	65-144	107
IV (1937)	13 yrs. 6 mo.	117	15.5	70-154	117

Repeated cross section analysis of the general trend of *IQ's* where tests are distributed by age shows that the group has consistently achieved a higher average mental age than would be found in a representative sampling of the total child population of the same age. Detailed statistical analysis of this material is not possible since every test for each child is presented, including some which are not used in the major comparisons. While fluctuations do occur, accentuated by the small numbers of cases at single age levels, the findings are essentially the same as in the earlier reports. The mean *IQ* of this group has remained consistently above the average of the population as a whole at each age level.

Rather wide fluctuations in *IQ* between tests were found throughout the entire period. The general trend is toward losses when the first test is taken as the basis of comparison, as the mean *IQ* on succeeding tests would indicate. Since the total number of cases is 100, the percentages may be computed automatically and only the actual number of cases is given in the table.

These results, together with the correlations reported later, are consistent with findings from other studies (3, 4, 13, 23), which show that *IQ* fluctuations of considerable magnitude are found among children who live with their own parents. The greater the time span between tests the greater the probability of wide difference between successive test scores. . . .

D. Relationships between Mental Development of Adopted Children and Characteristics of Their Foster Parents

1. *Occupational Level*

In the selection of foster homes all agencies give preference to families who not only have sufficient financial resources to assure adequate care for the child, but who show signs of culture, refinement, and intellectual and emotional understanding of the needs of children and the special problems of adoption.

The occupational level of foster families reflects this initial selection and has remained consistently well above the average for the general population. Table 2 shows the foster father and the true father occupations compared

Table 2
Distributions of True and Foster Father Occupations

Occupational classification	General U. S. population employed males, 1930 Per cent	True fathers		Foster fathers	
		Number	Per cent	Number	Per cent
I. Professional	3.1	2	2.7	14	14.0
II. Semiprofessional and managerial	5.2	3	4.1	17	17.0
III. Skilled trades	15.0	9	12.3	27	27.0
IV. Farmers	15.3	5	6.8	29	29.0
V. Semiskilled	30.6	10	13.7	8	8.0
VI. Slightly skilled	11.3	9	12.3	5	5.0
VII. Day laborers	19.5	35	48.0		
Number	100.0	73		100	
Mean	4.8	6.47		2.85	
Median	5	6		3	
Standard deviation	1.5	1.77		1.33	

with the occupational distribution of the population as a whole, based on the 1930 census and classified according to Goodenough's seven-point scale (9). Figures for the 1940 census are not directly comparable because of differences in classification method, particularly in the clerical, sales, skilled, and slightly skilled occupations.

In 1940 in the U. S. as a whole, 4.4 per cent of employed males were in professional occupations. In Iowa they constituted 3.7 per cent of the employed population while 14 per cent of the foster fathers were so employed. Although only 14 per cent of employed U. S. males are farm proprietors or managers, 29.5 per cent of Iowa men and 29 per cent of the foster fathers are so employed, thus farmers were adequately represented. In the U. S. approximately 17 per cent of men and in Iowa 19 per cent are unskilled laborers. None of the foster fathers, but 48 per cent of the natural fathers are so classified.

Further comparison between the figures for the foster parents, the general population, and the data for 73 true fathers for whom occupational information was available shows that the foster fathers are not only above the average of the population with a mean scale score of 2.85 as against 4.8 for the U. S. as a whole, but are conspicuously above the mean for the true fathers. The latter are, in addition, well below the mean for the total population with an average scale score of 6.47, equivalent to the status of an unskilled or very slightly skilled workman. The children whose natural parents, as a group, come from one extreme of the population were placed in foster homes representing the opposite extreme in occupational status.

Observation of the homes over the 13-year period showed that, although they were above the average in culture, resources, and financial security at the time the child was placed, they were, on the whole, even more prosperous at the end of the study. Only two fathers had been in military service, one as a professional man and one as a non-commissioned draftee. While some had benefited from high war wages, others on fixed incomes had been at a slight disadvantage. The general economic prosperity of 1945-47 was evident in most cases. . . .

Relationships between the child's *IQ* and foster father's occupation are obscured because the personal qualities, the cultural opportunities and intellectual stimulation of the homes are not directly reflected by the occupational classification of the families. The opportunities of many of the farm (Class IV) and skilled trades (Class III) homes exceeded some of the teachers', physicians', and managerial homes (Classes I and II). The results, however, show persistent slight differences in favor of homes in the upper three categories. Comparisons for all years except the first two are based on the 1916 Stanford-Binet. Since all available test scores were utilized and the number of cases at any year is small, detailed analysis is not attempted.

It can be concluded that, on the whole, children in homes in the higher

occupational categories tend to have somewhat higher mean *IQ*'s at all ages. However, all the children, including those in homes of lesser occupational levels, are above the mean for the total population at all age levels where the number of cases is sufficient to warrant consideration.

2. *Education*

The distribution of educational attainment of the natural and foster parents is shown in Table 3. The average school attainment of the foster parents as recorded on the application record and verified in 1946 showed that mean and median attainment for the foster parents was high school graduation, with 15 per cent having completed college. According to the 1940 census figures the median education for native Iowans in a comparable age group (35-44 years of age in 1940) was 8.8 for males and 9.3 for females. In general, urban populations have an average of one more year of education than rural populations.

Table 3
Distribution of True and Foster Parent Education

School attainment	True fathers No.	True mothers No.	Foster fathers No.	Foster mothers No.
Number	59	92	100	100
Mean	10.05	9.80	12.09	12.31
Median	10.57	9.78	12.13	12.56
SD	2.73	2.31	3.54	2.89

The educational status of the true parents is significantly below that of the foster parents and is below the average of a comparable age group for the state. The 1940 census showed that native Iowans 25-34 years of age had a mean education of 10.2 for the males and 11.0 for the females. While the information on the education of foster parents is reasonably accurate, there is evidence that the education of the natural mother has been overstated by an average of one year (12, 26).

These data again show that while the education of the foster parents is superior to the average for their age and region, the natural parents' education is below the average for their age and region.

Correlations between foster parent education and child *IQ* on successive tests are summarized in Table 4.

Earlier reports on somewhat larger numbers of children showed a slight positive correlation between foster child *IQ* and foster parent education (24, 25, 26). In this array of correlations there is no discernible trend except a consistent lack of statistical relationship. However, it should be pointed out that both the *IQ*'s and the educations represented here are con-

Table 4

	Foster mother education	Foster father education
Child's Test I	−.03 ± .07	.05 ± .07
Child's Test II	+.04 ± .07	.03 ± .07
Child's Test III	.10 ± .07	.03 ± .07
Child's Test IV (1916)	.04 ± .07	.06 ± .07
Child's Test IV (1937)	.02 ± .07	.00 ± .07

fined to the upper segment of the total possible range. As long as the parents are highly selected, and the children as a group also have a limited range of *IQ*'s and are in the upper half of the total population, it is not likely that repetition of similar studies will produce any more significant correlations. Increasing the number of cases may extend the range and sharpen the focus on what little differences exists. These figures are lower than correlations generally reported in the literature for both foster child-foster parent and own-child-parent correlations. However, in other cases the range for both distributions has been wider.

The only conclusions which may be drawn from these data are that the foster parents are above the average of their age and regional group in education and that the children in these homes are above the average in mental development. The differences between these adoptive parents in amount of formal education completed are not reflected in differences in intelligence between the children.

E. Relationships between Mental Development of Adopted Children and Characteristics of Their True Parents

1. *Intelligence*

Intelligence test results were available for 63 of the true mothers. All were based on the 1916 Stanford-Binet except one Terman Group Test, two Otis, and one Wechsler-Bellevue. Since the scores on these tests were consistent with other evidence on the mental adequacy of the mothers, the scores were included. The tests were given by trained examiners, under ordinary testing conditions, usually after the mother had decided to release the baby for adoption. The release was not contingent on the mother's test score and examinations were not made when the mother was ill or obviously upset emotionally.

Table 5 shows the distribution of the true-mother *IQ*'s and child *IQ*'s at a mean age of 13.6 based on the 1916 Stanford-Binet. This test was selected since it offered the maximum available degree of comparability for parent

and child intelligence test scores. The mean *IQ* of these children on the

Table 5
Comparison between Distribution of IQ's (1916 Stanford-Binet)
of True Mothers and Their Children

IQ	Mothers	Children
Number	63	63
Mean	85.7	106
Median	86.3	107
Standard Deviation	15.75	15.10

1937 revision is 10 points higher than on the 1916 revision. If a correction were to be made for the *IQ*'s of the mothers, as some investigators have suggested, the 1937 test scores of the children would be used, with the same relative difference between the two arrays of scores.

A difference of 20 points between the means of mothers and children is not only a statistically reliable difference (CR 9.2) but is also of considerable social consequence.

Previous analysis (26) showed that there was no difference between the mean *IQ*'s of children whose mothers had been examined and those whose mothers' *IQ*'s were unknown. This was confirmed by examination of the present data (see Appendix).

Relationships between mother-child pairs, with regard to *IQ*, expressed in terms of correlation coefficients on 63 cases, are summarized in Table 6.

Table 6

Test I	.00 ± .09
Test II	.28 ± .08*
Test III	.35 ± .07**
Test IV (1916)	.38 ± .07**
Test IV (1937)	.44 ± .07**

*Reliable at the 5 per cent level of confidence (17, p. 212).
**Reliable at the 1 per cent level of confidence (Ibid.).

It is apparent that the above tabulation contains more questions than it answers and can be the source of considerable controversy. Certain conclusions can be drawn, however. Among these are the following: Test scores of children secured during the first two years of life bear no statistical relationship to their own later scores ($r = .35$). By seven years of age a substantial correlation with true mother's *IQ* is reached which remains of the same magnitude in adolescence provided the 1916 Stanford-Binet test is

used with both children and mothers. The correlation is still further increased if the 1937 revision of the Binet is used.

Many reasons can and have been advanced for the low correlation between infant tests and later measures which will not be reviewed here. There is considerable evidence for the position that as a group these children received maximal stimulation in infancy with optimum security and affection following placement at an average of three months of age. The quality and amount of this stimulation during early childhood seemed to have little relation to the foster family's educational and cultural status.

The available data which can be statistically used—occupational classification and formal education—are not sufficiently sensitive to be useful in measuring these less tangible differences in child rearing practises. This point is important for the interpretation of the correlations between the child's *IQ* and his mother's *IQ* because it is possible to throw the weight of interpretation in the direction of either genetic or environmental determinants. If the former point of view is accepted, then the mother's mental level at the time of her examination is considered to reflect her fundamental genetic constitution, and ignores the effects of whatever environmental deprivations or advantages may have influenced her own mental development. Thus it would be assumed that the children of brighter mothers would in turn be brighter than the children of less capable mothers regardless of the type of foster home in which they were placed. The increasing correlation might be interpreted to support this point of view, since the occupational differences between foster parents are not large. It is, however, inconsistent with the evidence that the children's *IQ*'s substantially exceed those of their mothers and that none of them are mentally defective even though a number of the mothers were institution residents. The role of the unknown fathers adds to the complication although the evidence indicates that the fathers resembled their unwed partners in mental level and education (1).

If the so-called environmental point of view is accepted, then the question is raised whether the increasing correlation between child and true mother *IQ* possibly reflects the tendency to place the children of brighter mothers in the more outstanding foster homes, and the influence of these homes becomes increasingly prominent as the child grows older.

The question regarding selective placement can be approached in at least two ways. The first is an inspection of the relationships between such characteristics of the true and foster families as education and occupation. Using these crude measures, correlations of 2.4 between true mother *IQ* and foster parent education and .27 between true mother and foster parent education were found in this sample. Comparisons between true mother characteristics and foster father occupation for the present sampling are summarized in Table 7.

Table 7

| | Foster father occupation | | | | | |
	I	II	III	IV	V	VI
No. of foster fathers	14	17	27	29	2	5
Mean *IQ* of mothers of children in these homes	86	89	87	83	77	90
Number of cases	9	13	20	15	4	2
Mean education of mothers of children in these homes	10	10	10	8	8	8
Number of cases	12	16	28	25	9	2

It is apparent from both types of analyses that while a trend existed, selective placement, as evaluated by these measures was not consistently practiced.

Another approach to this problem of relationship is to examine the data for two contrasting groups of children. Selected for this purpose were: (*a*) Those children whose mothers were known to be mentally defective, with other evidence supporting the known *IQ* of under 70 (*N* = 11). (*b*) Those children whose mothers were above average in intelligence as measured by tests. Since there were only three cases above 110 *IQ*, the next five, in the 105-109 *IQ* range, were also included (N = 8).

Comparisons between the two groups are shown in Table 8. It is evident from the table that there is a marked difference between the intelligence and education of the true mothers of children in Groups (*a*) and (*b*). On the basis of education and occupation the foster parents of both groups are essentially similar, with perhaps a slight advantage for Group (*b*). On the first examination both groups of children were above average. By seven years of age a marked difference in mental level between the two groups is observable which persists into adolescence and is reflected by both the 1916 and 1937 Stanford-Binet tests. While children in Group (*a*) show average mental development as a group, the children in (*b*) show superior mental development. A difference of 25 points in *IQ* has significance socially, educationally, and vocationally.

If reliance were to be placed on these data alone, the inference would be fairly clear. However, comparison of the actual situation in the homes leads to a different conclusion. As a group, the homes of Group (*b*) are superior to the homes of Group (*a*) on every count on which homes can be evaluated. The average income of Group (*b*) is easily double the average income of Group (*a*) families. Five of the eight had sent their children to private schools, nursery schools, or camps for more than one year, reflecting an intelligent interest in superior opportunities, financial stability, and social status. None of the families in Group (*a*) had been either interested or able to afford similar opportunities. All the children in Group (*b*) had had

Table 8
Comparisons between Children of Mothers of
Inferion and of Abive Average Intelligence

	True mother's IQ	True mother's educ.	Foster mid-par. educ.	Foster father occup.	Test I	Test II	Child's IQ Test III	Test IV	Test IV '37
				Group A (N=11)					
Mean	63	7	12	3.2	113	109	105	96	104
Median	64	8	12	III	114	111	96	96	106
				Group B (N=8)					
Mean	111	12	12.5	3.3	116	117	125	118	129
Median	109	12.5	11.5	III	117	112.5	125	117	130

music, dancing, or art lessons, while only 5 of the 11 in Group (*a*) had such training. In the number of books, the extent of participation in church, civic, social, recreational, and cultural organizations, participation in Child Study and *PTA* groups, familiarity with and application of approved child rearing practices and attitudes, the number of toys, school equipment, typewriters, personal radios, the degree of freedom in spending allowances, deciding recreation, hours to be kept and other factors now believed to be essential for optimum social and emotional adjustment, the homes in Group (*b*) were definitely superior to the homes in Group (*a*). The one exception was 72G. This was the home in which the foster mother had been hospitalized for mental illness. The foster father, well educated in a foreign country, is a railroad section supervisor. Finances are limited, intellectual interests are non-existent. For several years this girl has competently managed a household. It is possible to speculate that under more favorable circumstances she too, might have attained higher test scores.

The general conclusions which may be drawn indicate that while in this study an increasing correlation between child *IQ* and true mother *IQ* is observed with increasing age, it cannot be attributed to genetic determinants alone. A more sensitive measure of foster parental competence in child development is necessary before small sample techniques of comparisons and analyses of differences can be fruitful. The present measures of education and occupation do not evaluate the crucial differences between outstanding, average, or less effective homes. The fact remains that the children are considerably superior to their mothers in mental development. There is a socially important difference between a group of people whose average *IQ* is 107-117, depending on the test selected, and another group whose *IQ* is 87. Since the mean for the children is above the average for the population as a whole, it cannot be attributed to the phenomenon of regression alone.

2. Education

In addition to the intelligence test scores there was information on the

education of 92 of the true mothers. Recognizing that it was an unreliable and questionably valid measure of ability, nevertheless, correlations between true mothers' education and child *IQ* were computed. Table 9 summarizes the results.

Table 9

Test I	.04 ± .09
Test II	.31 ± .07*
Test III	.37 ± .06*
Test IV (1916)	.31 ± .06*
Test IV (1937)	.32 ± .06*

*Reliable at the 1 per cent level of confidence (17, p. 212).

Here, too, there was an increase in correlations between the first and second tests, but the relationships then became stationary instead of showing a further increase with subsequent tests. Recalling the still lower correlations between child *IQ* and foster parent education, here again it is advisable to guard against an inclination to over value the significance of correlations of this size.

3. *Occupation*

Since both the true mothers and true fathers of the children originated primarily from the two lowest occupational classifications, attempts to identify a relationship between the mental development of the children and the occupational ranking of the parents were fruitless. The occupational status of the true fathers was occasionally considered in placement plans, but usually the information was not felt to be sufficiently reliable to influence the decision.

Goodenough (8), Terman (29) and others have found that children living with their own parents in the two lower occupational categories have mean *IQ*'s of approximately 95. In contrast, children living with their own parents in the professional and managerial occupations have a mean *IQ* of approximately 115. It is apparent that foster children in adoptive homes of all the occupational levels represented here compare favorably with own children in homes of the upper socio-economic level, rather than following the pattern found in the families from which they originated.

F. Conclusions

Perhaps the most important contribution this study can make to the planning of future research is to point out the inadequacies of easily available data, and the necessity of formulating more clearly the various

criteria used in the selection and assessment of the foster homes and the children. It is clear that the objective data used here, education and occupation, do not represent the real basis for selection and are not closely related to the child's mental development. Judging from the trend of correlations between mother's and child's *IQ*'s, one might conclude that a relationship exists which became increasingly apparent with age. This is complicated by the evidence of selective placement, yet without a parallel relationship between foster parent education and child *IQ*. This one set of figures must not be permitted to overshadow the more significant finding that the children are consistently and unmistakably superior to their natural parents and in fact, follow and improve upon the pattern of mental development found among own children in families like the foster families. What may be the salient features in the foster homes which have produced this development of the children, is only suggested in this study. It is inferred that maximum security, an environment rich in intellectual stimulation, a well balanced emotional relationship, intellectual agility on the part of the foster parents—all these and other factors contributed to the growth of the child. Unfortunately, there is still no scale for the measurement of these dynamic aspects of the foster home situation. The futility of arguments based on correlations involving measures of education and occupation applies to both sides of the discussion.

The conclusions which may be drawn from the material presented here suggest that:

1. The above average mental development of the children adopted in infancy has been maintained into early adolescence. There has been no large scale decline in *IQ* either for the group or for large segments of it, although certain children have shown either wide fluctuation or a steady decline or rise as compared with the first test results.

2. The educational or occupational data available for foster or natural parents in the typical social history record are not sufficient to predict the course of mental development of the children. Other factors, primarily emotional and personal, and probably located in the foster home, appear to have more significant influence in determining the mental growth of the children in this group.

3. The intellectual level of the children has remained consistently higher than would have been predicted from the intellectual, educational, or socio-economic level of the true parents, and is equal to or surpasses the mental level of own children in environments similar to those which have been provided by the foster parents.

The implications for placing agencies justify a policy of early placement in adoptive homes offering emotional warmth and security in an above average educational and social setting.

References

Anderson, C. L., & Skeels, H. M. A follow-up study on a small sampling of the putative fathers in Skodak's study. Unpublished study. Iowa Child Welfare Research Station. State University of Iowa, December, 1941.

Bradway, K. P. *IQ* constancy on the revised Stanford-Binet from the pre-school to the Junior High School Level. *J. Genet. Psychol.*, 1944, **65**, 197-217.

——An experimental study of factors associated with Stanford-Binet *IQ* changes from the preschool to the Junior High School. *J. Genet. Psychol.*, 1945, **66**, 107-128.

Cunningham, B. V. Infant *IQ* ratings evaluated after an interval of seven years. *J. Exper. Educ.*, 1934, **3**, 84-87.

Dexter, E. S. The relation between occupation of parent and intelligence of children. *Sch & Soc.*, 1923, **17**, 612-614.

Driscoll, G. P. The developmental status of the preschool child as a prognosis of future development. Teach. Coll., Columbia Univ., *Child Devel. Monog.*, 1933, No. 13. Pp. 111.

Ebert, E. H. A comparison of the original and revised Stanford-Binet scales. *J. of Psychol.*, 1941, **11**, 47-61.

Goodenough, F. The relation of the intelligence of preschool children to the occupation of their fathers. *Amer J. Psychol.*, 1928, **40**, 284-302.

Goodenough, F. L. & Anderson, J. E. Experimental child Study. New York: Century, 1931. Pp xii+546.

Hallowell, D. K. Stability of mental test ratings for preschool children. *J. Genet. Psychol.*, 1932, **40**, 406-421.

——Validity of mental tests for young children. *J. Genet. Psychol.*, 1941, **58**, 265-288.

Harms, I. E., & Skeels, H. M. Reported education and verified education of mothers of infants committed to the Iowa Soldiers' Orphans' Home during 1940. Unpublished study. Iowa Child Welfare Research Station, State University of Iowa, September, 1941.

Hirt, Z. I. Another study of retests with the 1916 Stanford-Binet Scale. *J. Genet Psychol.*, 1945, **66**, 83-105.

Hoakley, Z. P. A comparison of the results of the Stanford and Terman-Merrill revisions of the Binet. *J. Appl. Psychol.*, 1940, **24**, 75-81.

Layman, J. W. *IQ* changes in older-age children placed for foster-home care. *J. Genet. Psychol.*, 1942-**60**, 61-70.

Leahy, A. M. A study of certain selective factors influencing prediction of the mental status of adopted children in nature-nurture research. *J. Genet. Psychol.*, 1932, **41**, 294-329.

Lindquist, E. F. Statistical Analysis in Educational Research. New York: Houghton Mifflin, 1940. Pp. xii+266.

Merrill, M. A. The significance of *IQ*'s on the Revised Stanford-Binet Scales. *J. Educ. Psychol.,* 1938, 641-651.

National Society for the Study of Education: The Twenty-Seventh Yearbook of the National Society for the Study of Education. Nature and Nurture. Part I. Their Influence Upon Intelligence. Part II. Their Influence Upon Achievement. Bloomington, Ill.: Public School Publishing, 1928. Pp. ix+465, xv+397.

National Society for the Study of Education: The Thirty-Ninth Yearbook of the National Society for the Study of Education. Intelligence: Its Nature and Nurture. Part I. Comparative and Critical Exposition. Part II. Original Studies and Experiments. Bloomington, Ill.: Public School Publishing, 1940. Pp. xviii+471, xviii+409.

Roe, A., Burks, B., & Mittelmann, B. Adult adjustment of foster children of alcoholic and psychotic parentage and the influence of the foster home. *Quart. J. Stud. Alcohol,* 1945, No. 3. Pp. 164.

Satzman, S. The influence of social and economic background on Stanford-Binet performance. *J. Soc. Psychol.,* 1940, **12,** 71-81.

Schmidt, B. G. Changes in personal, social, and intellectual behavior of children originally classified as feebleminded. *Psychol. Monog.,* 1946, **60,** No. 5.

Skeels, H. M. Mental development of children in foster homes. *J. Consult Psychol.,* 1938, **2,** 33-43.

Skodak, M. Children in Foster Homes. *Univ. Iowa Stud. Child Welf.,* 1939, **16,** No. 1. Pp. 165.

Skodak, M., & Skeels, H. A follow-up study of children in adoptive homes. *J. Genet. Psychol.,* 1945, **66,** 21-58.

Snygg, D. The relation between the intelligence of mothers and of their children living in foster homes. *J. Genet. Psychol.,* 1938, **52,** 401-406.

Speer, G. S. The intelligence of foster children. *J. Genet. Psychol.,* 1940, **57,** 49-55.

Terman, L. M., & Merrill, M. A. Measuring Intelligence: A guide to the administration of the new revised Stanford-Binet tests of intelligence. Boston. Mass.: Houghton-Mifflin, 1937. Pp. xiv+461.

Theis, S. Van S. How foster children turn out. New York: New York State Charities Aid Assoc., 1924. Pp. 239.

Woodworth, T. S. Heredity and Environment. New York: Social Science Research Council Bulletin 47, 1941.

2.5   Unknowns in the IQ Equation: A Review of Three Monographs

Sandra Scarr-Salapatek

Institute of Child Development, University of Minnesota, Minneapolis

Environment, Heredity, and Intelligence. Compiled from the *Harvard Educational Review*. Reprint Series No. 2. Harvard Educational Review, Cambridge, Mass., 969. iv, 248 pp., illus. Paper, $4.95.
The IQ Argument. Race, Intelligence and Education. H. J. EYSENCK. Library Press, New York, 1971. iv, 156 pp., illus. $5.95.
LQ. RICHARD HERRNSTEIN, in the *Atlantic,* Vol. 228, No. 3, Sept. 1971, pp. 44-64.

IQ scores have been repeatedly estimated to have a large heritable component in United States and Northern European white populations (*1*). Individual differences in IQ, many authors have concluded, arise far more from genetic than from environmental differences among people in these populations, at the present time, and under present environmental conditions. It has also been known for many years that white lower-class and black groups have lower IQ's, on the average, than white middle-class groups. Most behavioral scientists comfortably "explained" these group differences by appealing to obvious environmental differences between the groups in standards of living, educational opportunities, and the like. But recently an explosive controversy has developed over the heritability of between-group differences in IQ, the question at issue being: If individual differences within the white population as a whole can be attributed largely to heredity, is it not plausible that the average differences between social-class groups and between racial groups also reflect significant genetic differences? Can the former data be used to explain the latter?

To propose genetically based racial and social-class differences is anathema to most behavioral scientists, who fear any scientific confirmation of the pernicious racial and ethnic prejudices that abound in our society. But now that the issue has been openly raised, and has been projected into the public context of social and educational policies, a hard scientific look must be taken at what is known and at what inferences can be drawn from that knowledge.

The public controversy began when A. R. Jensen, in a long paper in the

Reprinted from *Science,* 17 Dec. 1971, *174*, 1223-1228, by permission of the author and the American Association for the Advancement of Science. Copyright 1971 by the American Association for the Advancement of Science.

Harvard Educational Review, persuasively juxtaposed data on the heritability of IQ and the observed differences between groups. Jensen suggested that current large-scale educational attempts to raise the IQ's of lower-class children, white and black, were failing because of the high heritability of IQ. In a series of papers and rebuttals to criticism, in the same journal and elsewhere (2), Jensen put forth the hypothesis that social-class and racial differences in mean IQ were due largely to differences in the gene distributions of these populations. At least, he said, the genetic-differences hypothesis was no less likely, and probably more likely, than a simple environmental hypothesis to explain the mean difference of 15 IQ points between blacks and whites (3) and the even larger average IQ differences between professionals and manual laborers within the white population.

Jensen's articles have been directed primarily at an academic audience. Herrnstein's article in the *Atlantic* and Eysenck's book (first published in England) have brought the argument to the attention of the wider lay audience. Both Herrnstein and Eysenck agree with Jensen's genetic-differences hypothesis as it pertains to individual differences and to social-class groups, but Eysenck centers his attention on the genetic explanation of racial-group differences, which Herrnstein only touches on. Needless to say, many other scientists will take issue with them.

Eysenck's Racial Thesis

Eysenck has written a popular account of the race, social-class, and IQ controversy in a generally inflammatory book. The provocative title and the disturbing cover picture of a forlorn black boy are clearly designed to tempt the lay reader into a pseudo-battle between Truth and Ignorance. In this case Truth is genetic-environmental interactionism (4) and Ignorance is naive environmentalism. For the careful reader, the battle fades out inconclusively as Eysenck admits that scientific evidence to date does not permit a clear choice of the genetic-differences interpretation of black inferiority on intelligence tests. A quick reading of the book, however, is sure to leave the reader believing that scientific evidence today strongly supports the conclusion that U.S. blacks are genetically inferior to whites in IQ.

The basic theses of the book are as follows:

1) IQ is a highly heritable characteristic in the U.S. white population and probably equally heritable in the U.S. black population.

2) On the average, blacks score considerably lower than whites on IQ tests.

3) U.S. blacks are probably a non-random, lower-IQ, sample of native African populations.

4) The average IQ difference between blacks and whites probably represents important genetic differences between the races.

87429

5) Drastic environmental changes will have to be made to improve the poor phenotypes that U.S. blacks now achieve.

The evidence and nonevidence that Eysenck cites to support his genetic hypothesis of racial differences make a curious assortment. Audrey Shuey's review (5) of hundreds of studies showing mean phenotypic differences between black and white IQ's leads Eysenck to conclude:

> All the evidence to date suggests the strong and indeed overwhelming importance of genetic factors in producing the great variety of intellectual differences which we observe in our culture, and much of the difference observed between certain racial groups. This evidence cannot be argued away by niggling and very minor criticisms of details which do not really throw doubts on the major points made in this book [p. 126].

To "explain" the genetic origins of these IQ mean IQ differences he offers these suppositions:

> White slavers wanted dull beasts of burden, ready to work themselves to death in the plantations, and under those conditions intelligence would have been counter-selective. Thus there is every reason to expect that the particular sub-sample of the Negro race which is constituted of American Negroes is not an unselected sample of Negroes, but has been selected throughout history according to criteria which would put the highly intelligent at a disadvantage. The inevitable outcome of such selection would of course be a gene pool lacking some of the genes making for higher intelligence [p. 42].

Other ethnic minorities in the U.S. are also, in his view, genetically inferior, again because of the selective migration of lower IQ genotypes:

> It is known [sic] that many other groups came to the U.S.A. due to pressures which made them very poor samples of the original populations. Italians, Spaniards, and Portuguese, as well as Greeks, are examples where the less able, less intelligent were forced through circumstances to emigrate, and where their American progeny showed signficantly lower IQ's than would have been shown by a random sample of the original population [p. 43].

Although Eysenck is careful to say that these are not established facts (because no IQ tests were given to the immigrants or nonimmigrants in question?). the tone of his writing leaves no doubt about his judgment. There is something in this book to insult almost everyone except WASP's and Jews.

Despite his conviction that U.S. blacks are genetically inferior in IQ to whites, Eysenck is optimistic about the potential effects of radical environ-

mental changes on the present array of Negro IQ phenotypes. He points to the very large IQ gains produced by intensive one-to-one tutoring of black urban children with low-IQ mothers, contrasting large environmental changes and large IQ gains in intensive programs of this sort with insignificant environmental improvements and small IQ changes obtained by Headstart and related programs. He correctly observes that, whatever the heritability of IQ (or, it should be added, of any characteristic), large phenotypic changes may be produced by creating appropriate, radically different environments never before encountered by those genotypes. On this basis, Eysenck calls for further research to determine the requisites of such environments.

Since Eysenck comes to this relatively benign position regarding potential improvement in IQ's, why, one may ask, is he at such pains to "prove" the genetic inferiority of blacks? Surprisingly, he expects that new environments, such as that provided by intensive educational tutoring, will not affect the black-white IQ differential, because black children and white will probably profit equally from such treatment. Since many middle-class white children already have learning environments similar to that provided by tutors for the urban black children, we must suppose that Eysenck expects great IQ gains from relatively small changes in white, middle-class environments.

This book is an uncritical popularization of Jensen's ideas without the nuances and qualifiers that make much of Jensen's writing credible or at least responsible. Both authors rely on Shuey's review (5), but Eysenck's way of doing it is to devote some 25 pages to quotes and paraphrases of her chapter summaries. For readers to whom the original Jensen article is accessible, Eysenck's book is a poor substitute; although he defends Jensen and Shuey, he does neither a service.

It is a maddeningly inconsistent book filled with contradictory caution and incaution; with hypotheses stated both as hypotheses and as conclusions; with both accurate and inaccurate statements on matters of fact. For example, Eysenck thinks evoked potentials offer a better measure of "innate" intelligence than IQ tests. But on what basis? Recently F. B. Davis (6) has failed to find any relationship whatsoever between evoked potentials and either IQ scores or scholastic achievement, to which intelligence is supposed to be related. Another example is Eysenck's curious use of data to support a peculiar line of reasoning about the evolutionary inferiority of blacks: First, he reports that African and U.S. Negro babies have been shown to have precocious sensorimotor development by white norms (the difference, by several accounts, appears only in gross motor skills and even there is slight). Second, he notes that by three years of age U.S. white exceed U.S. black children in mean IQ scores. Finally he cites a (very slight) negative correlation, found in an early study, between sensorimotor

intelligence in the first year of life and later IQ. From exaggerated statements of these various data, he concludes:

> These findings are important because of a very general view in biology according to which the more prolonged the infancy the greater in general are the cognitive or intellectual abilities of the species. This law appears to work even within a given species [p. 79].

Eysenck would apparently have us believe that Africans and their relatives in the U.S. are less highly evolved that Caucasians, whose longer infancy is related to later higher intelligence. I am aware of no evidence whatsoever to support a within-species relationship between longer infancy and higher adult capacities.

Herrnstein's Social Thesis

Thanks to Jensen's provocative article, many academic psychologists who thought IQ tests belonged in the closet with the Rorschach inkblots have now explored the psychometric literature and found it to be a trove of scientific treasure. One of these is Richard Herrnstein, who from a Skinnerian background has become an admirer of intelligence tests—a considerable leap from shaping the behavior of pigeons and rats. In contrast to Eysenck's book, Herrnstein's popular account in the *Atlantic* of IQ testing and its values is generally responsible, if overly enthusiastic in parts.

Herrnstein unabashedly espouses IQ testing as "psychology's most telling accomplishment to date," despite the current controversy over the fairness of testing poor and minority-group children with IQ items devised by middle-class whites. His historical review of IQ test development, including tests of general intelligence and multiple abilities, is interesting and accurate. His account of the validity and usefulness of the tests centers on the fairly accurate prediction that can be made from IQ scores to academic and occupational achievement and income level. He clarifies the pattern of relationship between IQ and these criterion variables: High IQ is a necessary but not sufficient condition for high achievement, while low IQ virtually assures failure at high academic and occupational levels. About the usefulness of the tests, he concludes:

> An IQ test can be given in an hour or two to a child, and from this infinitesimally small sample of his output, deeply important predictions follow—about schoolwork, occupation, income, satisfaction with life, and even life expectancy. The predictions are not perfect, for other factors always enter in, but no other single factor matters as much in as many spheres of life [p. 53].

One must assume that Herrnstein's enthusiasm for intelligence tests rests

on population statistics, not on predictions for a particular child, because many children studied longitudinally have been shown to change IQ scores by 20 points or more from childhood to adulthood. It is likely that extremes of giftedness and retardation can be sorted out relatively early by IQ tests, but what about the 95 percent of the population in between? Their IQ scores may vary from dull to bright normal for many years. Important variations in IQ can occur up to late adolescence (8). On a population basis Herrnstein is correct; the best early predictors of later achievement are ability measures taken from age five on. Predictions are based on correlations, however, which are not sensitive to absolute changes in value, only to rank orders. This is an important point to be discussed later.

After reviewing the evidence for average IQ differences by social class and race, Herrnstein poses the nature-nurture problem of "which is primary" in determining phenotypic difference in IQ. For racial groups, he explains, the origins of mean IQ differences are indeterminate at the present time because we have no information from heritability studies in the black population or from other, unspecified, lines of research which could favor primarily genetic or primarily environmental hypotheses. He is thoroughly convinced, however, that individual differences and social-class differences in IQ are highly heritable at the present time, and are destined, by environmental improvements, to become even more so:

> If we make the relevant environment much more uniform (by making it as good as we can for everyone), then an even larger proportion of the variation in IQ will be attributable to the genes. The average person would be smarter, but intelligence would run in families even more obviously and with less regression toward the mean than we see today [p. 58].

For Herrnstein, society is, and will be even more strongly, a meritocracy based largely on inherited differences in IQ. He presents a "syllogism" [p. 58] to make his message clear.

1. If differences in mental abilities are inherited, and
2. If success requires those abilities, and
3. If earnings and prestige depend on success,
4. Then social standing (which reflects earnings and prestige) will be based to some extent on inherited differences among people.

Five "corollaries" for the future predict that the heritability of IQ will rise; that social mobility wll become more strongly related to inherited IQ differences; that most bright people will be gathered in the top of the social structure, with the IQ dregs at the bottom; that many at the bottom will not have the intelligence needed for new jobs; and that the meritocra-

cy will be built not just on inherited intelligence but on all inherited traits affecting success, which will presumably become correlated characters. Thus from the sucessful realization of our most precious egalitarian, political and social goals there will arise a much more rigidly stratified society, a "virtual caste system" based on inborn ability.

To ameliorate this effect, society may have to move toward the socialist dictum, "From each according to his abilities, to each according to his needs," but Herrnstein sees complete equality of earnings and prestige as impossible because high-grade intelligence is scarce and must be recruited into those critical jobs that require it, by the promise of high earnings and high prestige. Although garbage collecting is critical to the health of the society, almost anyone can do it; to waste high-IQ persons on such jobs is to misallocate scarce resources at society's peril.

Herrnstein points to an ironic contrast between the effects of caste and class systems. Castes, which established artifical hereditary limits on social mobility, guarantee the inequality of opportunity that preserves IQ heterogeneity at all levels of the system. Many bright people are arbitrarily kept down and many unintelligent people are artifically maintained at the top. When arbitrary bounds on mobility are removed, as in our class system, most of the bright rise to the top and most of the dull fall to the bottom of the social system, and IQ differences between top and bottom become increasingly hereditary. The greater the environmental equality, the greater the hereditary differences between levels in the social structure. The thesis of egalitarianism surely leads to its antithesis in a way that Karl Marx never anticipated.

Herrnstein proposes that our best strategy, in the face of increasing biological stratification, is publicly to recognize genetic human differences but to reallocate wealth to a considerable extent. The IQ have-nots need not be poor. Herrnstein does not delve into the psychological consequences of being publicly marked as genetically inferior.

Does the evidence support Herrnstein's view of hereditary social classes, now or in some future Utopia?. Given his assumptions about the high heritability of IQ, the importance of IQ to social mobility, and the increasing environmental equality of rearing and opportunity, hereditary social classes are to some extent inevitable. But one can question the limits of genetic homogeneity in social-class groups and the evidence for his syllogism at present.

Is IQ as highly heritable throughout the social structure as Herrnstein assumes? Probably not. In a recent study of IQ heritability in various racial and social-class groups (9), I found much lower proportions of genetic variance that would account for aptitude differences among lower-class than among middle-class children, in both black and white groups. Social disad-

vantage in prenatal and postnatal development can substantially lower phenotypic IQ and reduce the genotype-phenotype correlation. Thus, average phenotypic IQ differences between the social classes may be considerably larger than the genotypic differences.

Are social classes largely based on hereditary IQ differences now? Probably not as much as Herrnstein believes. Since opportunities for social mobility˜act at the phenotypic level, there still may be considerable genetic diversity for IQ at the bottom of the social structure. In earlier days arbitrary social barriers maintained genetic variability throughout the social structure. At present, individuals with high phenotypic IQ's are often upwardly mobile; but inherited wealth acts to maintain genetic diversity at the top, and nongenetic biological and social barriers to phenotypic development act to maintain a considerable genetic diversity of intelligence in the lower classes.

As P. E. Vernon has pointed out (10), we are inclined to forget that the majority of gifted children in recent generations have come from working-class, not middle-class, families. A larger percentage of middle-class children are gifted, but the working and lower classes produce gifted children in larger numbers. How many more disadvantaged children would have been bright if they had had middle-class gestation and rearing conditions?.

I am inclined to think that intergenerational class mobility will always be weth us, for three reasons. First, since normal IQ is a polygenic characteristic, various recombinations of parental genotypes will always produce more variable genotypes in the offspring than in the parents of all social-class groups, especially the extremes. Even if both parents, instead of primarily the male, achieved social-class status based on their IQ's, recombinations of their genes would always produce a range of offspring, who would be upwardly or downwardly mobile relative to their families of origin.

Second, since, as Herrnstein acknowledges, factors other than IQ—motivational, personality, and undetermined—also contribute to success or the lack of it, high IQ's will always be found among lower-class adults, in combination with schizophrenia, alcoholism, drug addiction, psychopathy, and other limiting factors. When recombined in offspring, high IQ can readily segregate with facilitating motivational and personality characteristics, thereby leading to upward mobility for many offspring. Similarly, middle-class parents will always produce some offspring with debilitating personal characteristics which lead to downward mobility.

Third, for all children to develop phenotypes that represent their best genotypic outcome (in current environments) would require enormous changes in the present social system. To improve and equalize all rearing environments would involve such massive intervention as to make Herrnstein's view of the future more problematic than he seems to believe.

Race as Caste

Races are castes between which there is very little mobility. Unlike the social-class system, where mobility based on IQ is sanctioned, the racial caste system, like the hereditary aristocracy of medieval Europe and the caste system of India, preserves within each group its full range of genetic diversity of intelligence. The Indian caste system was, according to Dobzhansky (*11*), a colossal genetic failure—or success, according to egalitarian values. After the abolition of castes at independence, Brahmins and untouchables were found to be equally educable despite—or because of—their many generations of segregated reproduction.

While we may tentatively conclude that there are some genetic IQ differences between social-class groups, we can make only wild speculations about racial groups. Average phenotypic IQ differences between races are not evidence for genetic differences (any more than they are evidence for environmental differences). Even if the heritabilities of IQ are extremely high in all races, there is still no warrant for equating within-group and between-group heritabilities (*12*). There are eramples in agricultural experiments of within-group differences that are highly heritable but between-group differences that are entirely environmental. Draw two random samples of seeds from the same genetically heterogeneous population. Plant one sample in uniformly good conditions, the other in uniformly poor conditions. The average height difference between the populations of plants will be entirely environmental, although the individual differences in height within each sample will be entirely genetic. With known environments, genetic and environmental variances between groups can be studied. But racial groups are not random samples from the same population, nor are members reared in uniform conditions within each race. Racial groups are of unknown genetic equivalence for polygenic characteristics like IQ, and the differences in environments within and between the races may have as yet unquantified effects.

There is little to be gained from approaching the nature-nurture problem of race differences in IQ directly (*13*). Direct comparisons of estimated within-group heritabilities and the calculation of between-group heritabilities require assumptions that few investigators are willing to make, such as that all environmental differences are quantifiable, that differences in the environments of blacks and whites can be assumed to affect IQ in the same way in the two groups, and that differences in environments between groups can be "statistically controlled." A direct assault on race differences in IQ is vulnerable to many criticisms.

Indirect approaches may be less vulnerable. These include predictions of parent-child regression effects and admixture studies. Regression effects can be predicted to differ for blacks and whites if the two races indeed have

genetically different population means. If the population mean for blacks is 15 IQ points lower than that of whites, then the offspring of high-IQ black parents should show greater regression (toward a lower population mean) than the offspring of whites of equally high IQ. Similarly, the offspring of low-IQ black parents should show less regression than those of white parents of equally low IQ. This hypothesis assumes that assortative mating for IQ is equal in the two races, which could be empirically determined but has not been studied as yet. Interpretable results from a parent-child regression study would also depend upon careful attention to intergenerational environmental changes, which could be greater in one race than the other.

Studies based on correlations between degree of white admixture and IQ scores *within* the black group would avoid many of the pitfalls of between-group comparisons. If serological genotypes can be used to identify persons with more and less white admixture, and if estimates of admixture based on blood groups are relatively independent of visable characteristics like skin color, then any positive correlation between degree of admixture and IQ would suggest genetic racial differences in IQ. Since blood groups have not been used directly as the basis of racial discrimination, positive findings would be relatively immune from environmentalist criticisms. The trick is to estimate individual admixture reliably. Several loci which have fairly different distributions of alleles in contemporary African and white populations have been proposed (*14*). No one has yet attempted a study of this sort.

h² and Phenotype

Suppose that the heritabilities of IQ differences within all racial and social-class groups were .80, as Jensen estimates, and suppose that the children in all groups were reared under an equal range of conditions. Now, suppose that racial and social-class differences in mean IQ still remained. We would probably infer some degree of genetic difference between the groups. So what? The question now turns from a strictly scientific one to one of science and social policy.

As Eysenck, Jensen, and others (*14*) have noted, eugenic and euthenic strategies are both possible interventions to reduce the number of low-IQ individuals in all populations. Eugenic policies could be advanced to encourage or require reproductive abstinence by people who fall below a certain level of intelligence. The Reeds (*15*) have determined that one-fifth of the mental retardation among whites of the next generation could be prevented if no mentally retarded persons of this generation reproduced. There is no question that a eugenic program applied at the phenotypic level of parents' IQ would substantially reduce the number of low-IQ children in the future white population. I am aware of no studies in the black population to

support a similar program, but some proportion of future retardation could surely be eliminated. It would be extremely important, however, to sort out genetic and environmental sources of low IQ both in racial and in social-class groups before advancing a eugenic program. The request or demand that some persons refrain from any reproduction should be a last resort, based on sure knowledge that their retardation is caused primarily by genetic factors and is not easily remedied by environmental intervention. Studies of the IQ levels of adopted children with mentally retarded natural parents would be most instructive, since some of the retardation observed among children of retarded parents may stem from the rearing environments provided by the parents.

In a pioneering study of adopted children and their adoptive and natural parents, Skodak (*16*) reported greater *correlations* of children's IQ's with their natural than with their adoptive parents' IQ's. This statement has been often misunderstood to mean that the children's *levels* of intelligence more closely resembled their natural parents' which is completely false. Although the rank order of the children's IQ's resembled that of their mothers' IQ's, the children's IQ's were higher, being distributed, like those of the adoptive parents, around a mean above 100, whereas their natural mothers' IQ's averaged only 85. The children, in fact, averaged 21 IQ points higher than their natural mothers. If the (unstudied) natural fathers' IQ's averaged around the population mean of 100, the mean of the children's would be expected to be 94, or 12 points lower than the mean obtained. The unexpected boost in IQ was presumably due to the better social environments provided by the adoptive families. Does this mean that phenotypic IQ can be substantially changed?

Even under existing conditions of child rearing, phenotypes of children reared by low IQ parents could be markedly changed by giving them the same rearing environment as the top IQ group provide for their children. According to DeFries (*17*), if children whose parents average 20 IQ points below the population mean were reared in environments such as usually are provided only by parents in the top .01 percent of the population, these same children would average 5 points *above* the population mean instead of 15 points below, as they do when reared by their own families.

Euthenic policies depend upon the demonstration that different rearing conditions can change phenotypic IQ sufficiently to enable most people in a social class or racial group to function in future society. I think there is great promise in this line of research and practice, although its efficacy will depend ultimately on the cost and feasibility of implementing radical intervention programs. Regardless of the present heritability of IQ in any population, phenotypes can be changed by the introduction of new and different environments. (One merit of Eysenck's book is the attention he gives to this point.) Furthermore, it is impossible to predict phenotypic

outcomes under very different conditions. For example, in the Milwaukee Project (*18*), in which the subjects are ghetto children whose mothers' IQ's are less than 70, intervention began soon after the children were born. Over a four-year period Heber has intensively tutored the children for several hours every day and has produced an enormous IQ difference between the experimental group (mean IQ 127) and a control group (mean IQ 90). If the tutored children continue to advance in environments which are radically different from their homes with retarded mothers, we shall have some measure of the present phenotypic range of reaction (*19*) of children whose average IQ's might have been in the 80 to 90 range. These data support Crow's comment on h^2 in his contribution to the *Harvard Educational Review* discussion (p. 158):

> It does not directly tell us how much improvement in IQ to expect from a given change in the environment. In particular, it offers no guidance as to the consequences of a new kind of environmental influence. For example, conventional heritability measures for height show a value of nearly 1. Yet, because of unidentified environmental influences, the mean height in the United States and in Japan has risen by a spectacular amount. Another kind of illustration is provided by the discovery of a cure for a hereditary disease. In such cases, any information on prior heritability may become irrelevant. Furthermore, heritability predictions are less dependable at the tails of the distribution.

To illustrate the phenotypic changes that can be produced by radically different environments for children with clear genetic anomalies, Rynders (*20*) has provided daily intensive tutoring for Down's syndrome infants. At the age of two, these children have average IQ's of 85 while control-group children, who are enrolled in a variety of other programs, average 68. Untreated children have even lower average IQ scores.

The efficacy of intervention programs for children whose expected IQ's are too low to permit full participation in society depends on their long-term effects on intelligence. Early childhood programs may be necessary but insufficient to produce functioning adults. There are critical research questions yet to be answered about euthenic programs, including what kinds, how much, how long, how soon, and toward what goals?

Does h^2 Matter?

There is growing disillusionment with the concept of heritability, as it is understood and misunderstood. Some who understand it very well would like to eliminate h^2 from human studies for at least two reasons. First, the usefulness of h^2 estimates in animal and plant genetics pertains to decisions about the efficacy of selective breeding to produce more desirable pheno-

types. Selective breeding does not apply to the human case, at least so far. Second, if important phenotypic changes can be produced by radically different environments, then, it is asked, who cares about the heritability of IQ? Morton (21) has expressed these sentiments well:

> Considerable popular interest attaches to such questions as "is one class or ethnic group innately superior to another on a particular test?" The reasons are entirely emotional, since such a difference, if established, would serve as no better guide to provision of educational or other facilities than an unpretentious assessment of phenotypic differences.

I disagree. The simple assessment of phenotypic performance does not suggest any particular intervention strategy. Heritability estimates can have merit as indicators of the effects to be expected from various types of intervention programs. If, for example, IQ tests, which predict well to achievements in the larger society, show low heritabilities in a population, then it is probable that simply providing better environments which now exist will improve average performance in that population. If h^2 is high but environments sampled in that population are largely unfavorable, then (again) simple environmental improvement will probably change the mean phenotypic level. If h^2 is high and the environments sampled are largely favorable, then novel environmental manipulations are probably required to change phenotypes, and eugenic programs may be advocated.

The most common misunderstanding of the concept "heritability" relates to the nyth of fixed intelligence: if h^2 is high, this reasoning goes, then intelligence is genetically fixed and unchangeable at the phenotypic level. This misconception ignores the fact that h^2 is a population statistic, bound to a given set of environmental conditions at a given point in time. Neither intelligence nor h^2 estimates are fixed.

It is absurd to deny that the frequencies of genes for behavior may vary between populations. For individual differences within populations, and for social-class differences, a genetic hypothesis is almost a necessity to explain some of the variance in IQ, especially among adults in contemporary white populations living in average or better environments. But what Jensen, Shuey, and Eysenck (and others) propose is that genetic racial differences are necessary to account for the current phenotypic differences in mean IQ between populations. That may be so, but it would be extremely difficult, given current methodological limitations, to gather evidence that would dislodge an environmental hypothesis to account for the same data. And to assert, despite the absence of evidence, and in the present social climate, that a particular race is genetically disfavored in intelligence is to scream "FIRE! . . . I think" in a crowded theater. Given that so little is known, further scientific study seems far more justifiable than public speculations.

Notes

1. For a review of studies, see L. Erlenmeyer-Kimling and L. F. Jarvik, *Science* 142, 1477 (1963. Heritability is the ratio of genetic variance to total phenotypic variance. Heritability is used in its broad sense of total genetic variance/total phenotypic variance.

2. The *Harvard Educational Review* compilation includes Jensen's paper, "How much can we boost IQ and scholastic achievement?," comments on it by J. S. Kagan, J. McV. Hunt, J. F. Crow, C. Bereiter, D. Elkind, L. J. Cronback and W. F. Brazziel, and a rejoiner by Jensen. See also A. R. Jensen, in J. Hellmuth, *Disadvantaged Child.* vol. 3 (Special Child Publ., Seattle, Wash., 1970).

3. P. L. Nichols, thesis, University of Minnesota (1970). Nichols reports that in two large samples of black and white children, seven-year WISC IQ scores showed the same means and distributions for the two racial groups, once social-class variables were equated. These results are unlike those of several other studies, which found that matching socio-economic status did not create equal means in the two racial groups [A. Shuey (5); A. B. Wilson, *Racial Isolation in the Public Schools,* vol. 2 (Government Printing Office, Washington, D.C., 1967)]. In Nichols's samples, prenatal and postnatal medical care was equally available to blacks and whites which may have contributed to the relatively high IQ scores of the blacks in these samples.

4. By interaction, Eysenck means simply $P = G + E$, or "heredity and environment acting together to produce the observed phenotype" (p. 111). He does not mean what most geneticists and behavior geneticists mean by interaction; that is, the *differential* phenotypic effects produced by various combinations of genotypes and environments, as in the interaction term of analysis-of-variance statistics. Few thinking people are not interactionists in Eysenck's sense of the term, because that's the only way to get the organism and the environment into the same equation to account for variance in any phenotypic trait. How much of the phenotypic variance is accounted for by each of the terms in the equation is the real issue.

5. A. Shuey, *The Testing of Negro Intelligence* (Social Science Press, New York, 1966), pp. 499-519.

6. F. B. Davis, *The Measurement of Mental Capacity through Evoked-Potential Recordings* (Educational Records Bureau, Greenwich, Conn., 1972). "As it turned out, no evidence was found that the latency periods obtained . . . displayed serviceable utility for predicting school performance or level of mental ability among pupils in preschool through grade 8" (p.v).

7. *New York Times,* 8 Oct. 1971, p. 41.

8. J. Kagan and H. A. Moss, *Birth to Maturity* (Wiley, New York, 1962).

9. S. Scarr-Salapatek, *Science,* in press.

10. P. E. Vernon, *Intelligence and Cultural Environment* (Methuen, London, 1969).

11. T. Dobzhansky, *Mankind Evolving* (Yale Univ. Press, New Haven, 1962), pp. 234-238.

12. J. Thoday, *J. Biosocial Science* 1, suppl. 3, 4 (1969).

13. L. L. Cavalli-Sforza and W. F. Bodmer, *The Genetics of Human Populations* (Freeman, San Francisco, 1971), pp. 753-804. They propose that the study of racial differences is useless and not scientifically supportable at the present time.

14. T. E. Reed, *Science* 165, 762 (1969); *Am. J. Hum. Genet.* 21, 1 (1969; C. MacLean and P. L. Workman, paper at a meeting of the American Society of Human Genetics (1970, Indianapolis).

15. E. W. Reed and S. C. Reed, *Mental Retardation: A Family Study* (Saunders, Philadelphia, 1965); *Social Biol.* 18, suppl., 42 (1971).

16. M. Skodak and H. WM. Skeels, *J. Genet. Psychol.* 75, 85 (1949).

17. J. C. DeFries, paper for the C.O.B.R.E. Research Workshop on Genetic Endowment and Environment in the Determination of Behavior (3-8 Oct. 1971, Rye, N.Y.).

18. R. Heber, *Rehabilitation of Families at Risk for Mental Retardation* (Regional Rehabilitation Center, Univ. of Wisconsin, 1969). S. P. Strickland, *Am Ed.* 7, 3 (1971).

19. I. I. Gottesman, in *Social Class, Race, and Psychological Development*, M. Deutsch, I. Katz, and A. R. Jensen, Eds. (Holt, Rinehart, and Winston, New York, 1968), pp.11-51

20. J. Rynders, personal communication, November 1971.

21. N. E. Morton, paper for the C.O.B.R.E. Research Workshop on Genetic Endowment and Environment in the Determination of Behavior (3-8 Oct. 1971, Rye, N.Y.).

22. I thank Philip Salapatek, Richard Weinberg, I. I. Gottesman, and Leonard I. Heston for their critical reading of this paper. They are not in any way responsible for its content, however.

2.6 Intellectual Development of Children from Interracial Matings

Lee Willerman*
Alfred F. Naylor
Ntinos C. Myrianthopoulos

If racial differences in intelligence test performance are determined by additive genetic factors which are not sex-linked, then test scores for children of interracial crosses might be independent of maternal race. But if test differences between races are largely environmental in origin, the mothers' race should have an effect on children's performance since she is the primary socializing agent during the preschool years (*1*). In our analysis we assume (in the absence of data) that the mean intelligence of the parents does not differ with either maternal or paternal race combination.

Dichotomous assignment of individuals to either the Negro or white group is inaccurate and suspect on both genetic and social grounds because American Negroes share approximately 21 percent of their genes with

Reprinted from *Science,* 18 Dec. 1970, *170,* 1329-1331, by permission of the author and the American Association for the Advancement of Science. Copyright 1970 by the American Association for the Advancement of Science.

non-Negroes (2) and because 70 percent of a sample of American Negroes has reported a white ancestor (3). Nevertheless, such designations have proven useful in providing insights concerning the occurrence of many biological and social phenomena (4).

The Collaborative Study of Cerebral Palsy, Mental Retardation, and other Neurological and Sensory Disorders of Infancy and Childhood provides data which may be useful in disentangling some of the genetic and environmental interactions. This study is currently following the children born to approximately 42,000 women who registered during pregnancy in 12 institutions throughout the United States (5). These children are routinely given standardized neurological and psychological examinations at various intervals during the first 8 years of life.

Among the information collected before birth of a child is the race and schooling of the father and the race, schooling, and marital status of the mother. The degree of underreporting of fathers of a different race probably depends on the mother's race; white women would tend to report that the father was Negro because it would become obvious at birth; Negro mothers might not report a white mate because light skin is common in Negro infants.

The frequency of interracial mating (disregarding marital status) in the Collaborative Study is approximately 0.38 percent. This should not be taken to be indicative of the rate for the United States since the current sample is approximately 50 percent Negro and is drawn from urban hospital registrants rather than from less-biased census data.

Of the 186 liveborn offspring of interracial matings identified in the Collaborative Study only 88 had reached the age of 4 years and were tested with the Stanford-Binet, abbreviated Form L-M (6), at the time this study was undertaken. The IQ's come from only 10 of the 12 collaborating institutions since the two southernmost ones (Charity Hospital, New Orleans, and University of Tennessee) provided no cases. The IQ's were obtained routinely during the course of regularly scheduled testing for all children in the Collaborative Study.

In another study (7) the mean IQ for control children from uniracial matings matched for hospital of birth and socioeconomic and marital status to the present sample was 104.3 for the children of white matings and 97.4 of the children of Negro matings. The mean IQ for the present sample is 98.7.

The children were also measured and weighed at birth, and their gestational ages were calculated from the mothers' report of her last menstrual period. Interracial matings involved 61 white and 27 Negro mothers; 38 of the children were male and 50 female.

Table 1 shows comparative statistics of available data on maternal education, paternal education, birth weight, birth length, and duration of

gestation by race of the mother of the interracial child. As judged by *t*-tests, none of the differences approach statistical significance, and there is, in

Table 1.
Characteristics of samples of interracial matings by race of mother.

Maternal education (years)	Paternal education (years)	Weight of child at birth (g)	Length of child at birth (cm)	Gestation (weeks)
		White mother		
10.9 ± 2.2 (61)	11.5 ± 2.3 (46)	3207 ± 573 (60)	49.8 ± 2.6 (59)	40.1 ± 2.5 (61)
		Negro mother		
11.0 ± 2.5 (27)	11.0 ± 2.5 (21)	3228 ± 567 (27)	50.1 ± 2.5 (27)	40.2 ± 2.6 (26)

Results are mean ± standard deviation. Numbers in parentheses are the number of subjects.

particular, no suggestion that intrauterine experience or parental education favors the child of a white mother. However, it would be premature to exclude from further consideration differential infection rates or nutritional differences. Because of these close similarities, adjustment for the above variables in the statistical analysis of IQ differences is unnecessary.

Mean education of all white mothers in the Collaborative Study whose 4-year-old children were given the IQ test is 11.1 years, as compared to 10.9 years for the white mothers in Table 1. The 10.4 years for all Negroes in the Collaborative Study whose children were tested at 4 years of age is somewhat lower than the 11.0 years in Table 1 for Negro mothers (*8*). Comparative figures are not available for paternal education.

In the interracial sample 36 percent of the white mothers and 26 percent of the Negro mothers were unmarried at the time of registration. Comparative figures for the entire Collaborative Study are 12 and 23, respectively. Thus, in the present sample, interracial whites have a lower frequency of marriage and Negroes have a higher frequency.

In assessing the postnatal effect of the race of the mother on the IQ of the 4-year-old child it seemed desirable to take into account the marital status of the mother and the sex of the baby since both these factors have been reported as being of importance (*9, 10*). The data showing the three-way combinations of maternal race, sex, and marital status in Table 2 were analyzed from two approaches. The first involved entering the data into a computer program that performed a three-way analysis of variance with least squares adjustments for disproportionality in sample sizes. Statistical interactions were not significant in this analysis and the significant main effects ($F = 4.2$ for 3 and 80 d.f.; $P = .008$) have additive interpretations.

Table 2.
The IQ scores of 4-year-old children categorized by race of mother, sex of child, and marital status. Married implies either legal or common law; unmarried implies single, divorced, separated, or widowed.

Race of mother	Sex of child	Marital status	IQ scores
White	Male	Unmarried	94.7 ± 12.1 (7)
White	Male	Married	100.8 ± 18.3 (20)
White	Female	Unmarried	100.3 ± 15.7 (15)
White	Female	Married	103.8 ± 18.0 (19)
Mean			100.9 ± 16.8 (61)
Negro	Male	Unmarried	67.5 ± 23.3 (2)
Negro	Male	Married	88.4 ± 11.0 (9)
Negro	Female	Unmarried	88.6 ± 13.7 (5)
Negro	Female	Married	105.1 ± 14.1 (11)
Mean			93.7 ± 16.9 (27)
Mean of all			98.7 ± 16.8 (88)

Results are the mean ± standard deviation. The numbers in parentheses are the numbers for each sample.

The first member of each dichotomy, Negro or white mother, male or female child, and married or unmarried marital status, was assigned a score of zero and the second member a score of one. Application of regression procedures yielded the following slopes and standard errors for the main effects: 8.36 ± 3.75 IQ points for race, 8.14 ± 3.52 for sex, and 8.30 ± 3.73 for marital status. If the ratio of each coefficient to its standard error is treated as having a t distribution, all are significant in the 5 to 1 percent range.

However, the interaction between marital status and the mothers' race may be considerable, with marital status resulting in bigger differences among the children of Negro mothers. The maternal race–marital status effect is 13.6 ± 8.4 and, though not statistically significant, is so sizable that it merits further analysis. Similarly, the sex effect seems larger among the children of Negro mothers. In this case the slope is 14.1 ± 7.7, again not statistically significant, but sufficiently large to deserve continued study, especially since the failure to observe statistically significant interactions on these variables is very likely due to small cell sizes.

The data were therefore partitioned in a manner which focused on the two-way interactions, first ignoring sex (Table 3), then ignoring marital status (Table 4). The results indicate that if sex is ignored, maternal race is significant only among males ($P < .05$), and among Negro mothers, it is that among Negro mothers it is the children of the unmarried with the low IQ's ($P < .05$). Alternatively, if marital status is ignored, maternal race is

significant only among males ($P < .05$), and among Negro mothers, it is the male children who have the low IQ's ($P < .05$). Therefore, the male children of unmarried Negro mothers have the lowest IQ's. Among white mothers, the effects of marital status and sex are less, though always consistent with the findings for the children of Negro mothers.

Table 3.
The IQ scores of 4-year-old children categorized by race and marital status of mother (see Table 2).

Race of mother	Marital status	IQ scores
White	Unmarried	98.5 ± 14.7 (22)
White	Married	102.3 ± 18.2 (39)
Negro	Unmarried	82.6 ± 16.1 (7)
Negro	Married	97.6 ± 12.8 (20)

Table 4.
The IQ scores of 4-year-old children categorized by race of mother and sex of child (see Table 2).

Race of mother	Sex of child	IQ scores
White	Male	99.2 ± 17.0 (27)
White	Female	102.3 ± 17.0 (34)
Negro	Male	84.6 ± 12.9 (11)
Negro	Female	99.9 ± 14.0 (16)

Interpretation of the race effect should be tentative since the number of interracial subjects is small. The evidence presented here suggests that environmental factors may play an important role in the lower intellectual performance of Negro preschool children.

Despite no observed differences in mean educational attainment by race of mother, it is possible that child-rearing practices vary between the two groups. Racial differences in dialect usage would tend to militate against the children of Negro mothers on IQ tests, for example. Performance on intelligence and achievement tests might also reveal differences in favor of the white mothers.

The significant sex effect on IQ in favor of females has been reported before the Collaborative Study data (10) and is only one of many cognitive tasks which show females superior to males. Tasks involving relatively simple

perceptual motor skills, such as speed of naming colors, reading, typing, and coding speed, all show female superiority (*11*). However, tasks requiring restructuring of the stimulus field, such as finding a simple pattern embedded in a more complex one, have shown consistent sex differences in favor of males (*11*). It was suggested that sex differences on cognitive tasks may be more adequately explained by physiological differences rather than by child-rearing differences between the sexes. Recent research suggesting a specific perceptual deficit associated with the absence or abnormality of one X chromosome in patients with Turner's syndrome is consistent with that hypothesis (*12*).

The association of single marital status with lower IQ performance has been documented before with interpretation based on increased disorganization in one-parent families (*9*). Since females tend to do most of the child-rearing during the early years even in two-parent families, the relationship remains to be clarified. Lewis (*13*) pointed out that negative effects on children associated with one-parent families tend to diminish when socioeconomic status is controlled. If maternal education can be taken as an index of socioeconomic status, the unmarried group differs only slightly from the mean for the entire sample given in Table 1 [white mothers, 10.5 years (*n* = 22); Negro mothers, 11.3 years (*n* = 7)]. Since the designation of marital status is assigned during pregnancy and there is no information available on whether the postnatal years of the child did in fact agree with this original designation, no firm conclusions can be drawn.

Notes

1. H. Simmons and P. Schoggen, in *The Stream of Behavior,* R. G. Barker, Ed. (Appleton-Century-Crofts, New York, 1963), p. 70.

2. T. E. Reed, *Science* **165**, 762 (1969).

3. M. J. Herskovits, *Pediat. Semin.* **33**, 30 (1926).

4. A. Damon, *Soc. Biol.* **16**, 69 (1969).

5. H. W. Berendes, in *Research Methodology and Needs in Perinatal Studies,* S. S. Chipman, A. M. Lillienfeld, B. G. Greenberg, J. F. Donnelly, Eds. (Thomas, Springfield, Ill., 1966), p. 118. The Collaborative Study, supported by the National Institute of Neurological Diseases and Stroke, has the following participants: Boston Lying-in Hospital; Brown University; Charity Hospital, New Orleans; Children's Hospital of Buffalo; Children's Hospital of Philadelphia; Children's Medical Center, Boston; Columbia University; Johns Hopkins University; Medical College of Virginia; New York Medical College; Pennsylvania Hospital; University of Minnesota; University of Oregon; University of Tennessee; Yale University; and the Perinatal Research Branch, NINDS.

6. L. M. Terman and M. A. Merrill, *Stanford-Binet Intelligence Scale* (Houghton Mifflin, Boston, 1960).

7. L. Willerman, A. F. Naylor, N. C. Myrianthopoulos, J. A. Churchill, unpublished data.

8. S. H. Broman, J. Khanna, J. Weber, in preparation.

9. M. Deutsch and B. Brown, *J. Soc. Issues* XX, 24 (1964).

10. J. E. Singer, M. Westphal, K. R. Niswander, *Child Devel.* **39**, 103 (1968); L. Willerman, S. H. Broman, M. Fiedler, *ibid.* **41**, 69 (1970).

11. B. M. Broverman, E. L. Klaiber, Y. Kabayashi, W. Vogel, *Psychol. Rev.* **75**, 23 (1968).

12. J. Money, *J. Psychiat Res.* **2**, 223 (1964).

13. H. Lewis, in *The Moynihan Report and the Politics of Controversy,* L. E. Rainwater and W. L. Yancey, Eds. (M.I.T. Press, Cambridge, Mass., 1967), p. 314.

* Present address: Department of Muman Genetics, University of Michigan, 1137 E. Catherine Street, Ann Arbor 48104.

2.7 Is 80% of Intelligence Genetically Determined?[1]

Urie Bronfenbrenner
Cornell University

Although Jensen's (1969a, 1969b) argument claiming genetically-based race differences in intelligence has been repeatedly and forcefully attacked (e.g., Scarr-Salapatek 1971a, Gage 1972, Lewontin 1970), his thesis that 80 percent of the variation in intelligence is determined by heredity has been cited as an unassailable fact by his supporters (e g, Eysenck 1971, Herrnstein 1971, Shockley 1972) and, by and large, has been left unchallenged by his critics (e.g., Lewontin 1970, Scarr-Salapatek 1971b). To quote but one representative statement from each quarter, Herrnstein, a leading protagonist of Jensen's views, asserts, "Jensen concluded (as have most other experts in the field) that the genetic factor is worth about 80 percent and that only 20 percent is left to everything else" (1971, p. 56). Lewontin, in his forceful critique and rejection of Jensen's argument for genetically-based race differences, takes no issue with the latter's 80 percent figure for the contribution of heredity: "I shall accept Jensen's rather high estimate without serious argument." (1970, p. 6).

Since Jensen takes his thesis of 80 percent genetic effect as the foundation both for his argument for innate differences in ability between the races, and for his contention that intervention programs with disadvantaged groups have little hope of success, it becomes important, both from the point of view of science and of social policy, to examine the evidence and line of

reasoning that underlie his initial thesis. Jensen's argument rests on inferences drawn primarily from three sets of data:

1. Studies of resemblance between identical twins reared apart.
2. Studies of resemblance between identical vs. fraternal twins reared in the same home.
3. Studies of resemblance within families having own children vs. adopted children.

1. Identical Twins Reared Apart.

Jensen's conclusion from these studies (Burt 1966, Newman, Freeman, and Holzinger (1937), Juel-Nielsen 1964, Shields 1962) that at least 75 percent of variance in intelligence is due to heredity is based on two critical assumptions. First, the environments of separated twins must be uncorrelated; in other words, there must be no tendency to place the twins in similar foster homes. Second, the range of environments into which twins are separated must be as great as that for unrelated children. There is evidence to indicate that neither of these assumptions is met. For example, in the Newman, Freeman, and Holzinger study (1937), rated differences between the social or educational environments of each pair were usually small, and there was a correlation of .55 between separated twins in the number of years of schooling that each received. Such findings illustrate the more general phenomenon of *selective placement,* which has been shown to operate whenever children are separated from their true parents and placed in foster homes or other settings (e.g., Skodak and Skeels 1949). The effects of this process are manifested in correlations between the characteristics of the home into which the child was born and those of the foster home. The selection operates with respect to a variety of variables relevant to psychological development including social status, religion, ethnicity, family structure, and, in particular, values and practices of child rearing. The operation of selective placement with respect to one or more such variables cannot be ruled out in any of the studies, and the resulting correlation between the environments means that estimates of 75 percent for genetic influence are confounded by environmental variance. Further evidence for the presence and effect of correlated environments is presented below.

The evidence also calls into question the assumption that the range of environments into which twins are separated is unrestricted. Findings from adoption studies indicate "a surprising uniformity among adoptive parents" (Pringle 1966) both in their social and psychological characteristics. Thus the possible contribution of environment to differences between separated twins is considerably less than it would be in a population of unrelated children.

The violation of both of these assumptions means that the conclusion of

80 percent as the proportion of variance attributable to heredity is not sustained by the data on identical twins.

2.   Children from Adopted Families.

Jensen concludes that since the correlation between unrelated children brought up in the same home is only .24, the remaining fraction of .76 is due to heredity (1969a, pp. 50-51). This argument requires the rather extraordinary assumption that all differences between children raised in the same home are due only and entirely to genetic differences between them. The possible role of environment (in terms of such factors as differential treatment by parents, or varying experiences in school, peer group, or other settings) is ruled out of consideration. Clearly such an assumption is untenable.

Jensen also relies heavily on studies reporting higher similarity among own vs. adopted children, in particular the finding cited by Honzik (1957) that the correlation between IQ of adopted children was .40 with the IQ of their true mothers but unrelated to the educational level of the foster mothers. In point of fact, in the original study from which these data were taken, Skodak and Skeels (1949) had shown that the correlations for the mothers were significantly confounded by the selective placement of children of more intelligent and better educated mothers in better foster homes. Moreover, the mean IQ of the foster children at age twelve was 106, whereas that of their true mothers was only 86. In an attempt to account for this marked difference, Skodak and Skeels analyzed the characteristics of the home environments among both true and foster families and concluded that the critical factor was the "maternal stimulation . . . and optimum security" provided in the foster homes as a group and especially in those in which the children had shown a marked gain in IQ over a ten-year period. None of these facts bearing on the substantial impact of the environment are reflected in Honzik's conclusions or Jensen's interpretation.

In sum, as in the case of identical twins reared apart, the data from studies of own vs. adopted children likewise fail to support Jensen's claim that 80 percent of the variance in intelligence is genetically determined.

3.   Identical vs. Fraternal Twins Reared Together.

The most widely employed method for estimating the proportion of variance attributable to genetic factors is based on the comparison of within-pair differences for identical vs. same-sex fraternal twins, both groups reared in their own homes. Without getting into technicalities, the basic argument runs as follows. Differences between identical twins can be attributable only to environment since their genetic endowments are the

same. Differences between fraternal twins, however, reflect both environmental and genetic effects, and are larger for that reason. Accordingly, if one subtracts the former variance from the latter, the resulting difference is the amount of variance attributable to heredity. By expressing this variance as a fraction of total variance among individuals, one obtains an estimate of the proportion of total variation attributable to genetic factors in fraternal twins. Since such twins have half their genes in common, the contribution of heredity to variation among unrelated children would be about twice as large. The resulting ratio is referred to as the *heritability coefficient,* and is usually designated as h^2, after Holzinger (1929), who first developed such an index.

Drawing on the results from 25 studies of identical and fraternal twins reared together, as well as other kinship correlations, Jensen obtained a heritability coefficient of .80, which constitutes the primary basis of his claim.

The interpretation of the heritability coefficient as measuring the proportion of variance due to heredity rests on two critical assumptions. First, the environments of identical twins must be no more alike than those for fraternal twins. In the past, investigators have acknowledged that identical twins do grow up in more similar environments but have regarded the difference as a negligible one. An analysis of data published in the last decade reveals that the difference is in fact substantial and contributes significantly to the observed resemblance between identical twins. The analysis draws on three types of evidence. First, systematic studies of the environments of identical vs. fraternal twins indicate that the former are more often placed in similar situations (Husen 1959, Jones 1946, Koch 1966, Shields 1954) and are consistently treated more similarly by their parents (Scarr 1968).

Second, if their more similar environments have significant impact, then identical twins should resemble each other most in those characteristics which are the product of common experience in the family. For example, they should be more similar in verbal than in non-verbal tests of intelligence and in personality traits which relate to interpersonal relations (e.g., extraversion-introversion, dominance-submissiveness) than in intrapsychic qualities (e.g., anxiety, flexibility). Moreover, since parents do not treat boys and girls in the same way, male and female twins should differ in the abilities and traits in which they are most alike, with boys showing greater similarity, and therefore show higher heritability coefficients, in mathematical ability or dominance, and girls in languages or sociability. The results of a series of independent studies (Husen 1959, Gottesman 1966, Nichols 1965a, 1965b, Scarr-Salapatek 1969, 1971b) are in accord with these expectations.

Third, if their more similar environments affect their development, identical twins should be most alike in those social contexts in which parent-child

interaction is most intensive, sustained, and focused on the development of the child. For example, the similarity of identical twins should vary directly with social class and, given present inequities in American society, should be greater among White than Black families. In line with these expectations Scarr-Salapatek (1971b) reports greater similarity, and hence higher heritability coefficients, for twins from advantaged than from disadvantaged socioeconomic groups and in White as against Black families. These findings indicate that for genetic potential to be realized requires an appropriately complex, sustained, and stimulating environment. In accord with this principle, twins from lower class Black groups, who in our society live in suppressive environments, exhibit lower levels of ability and reduced genetic variability as reflected in lower heritability coefficients.

Independent confirmation for this conclusion comes from recent studies of intellectual development in children of mixed Black-White marriages (Willerman *et. al.* 1970). From the point of view of genetic theory, which parent is of which race should make no difference for the child's mental capacity. Yet the data showed a differential effect. Specifically, if the mother was Black, then the child's IQ was closer to the average IQ for Blacks than if the father was Black. Since it is the mother who is the primary agent of child rearing, this result is consistent with the conclusion that the suppressive environments in which Blacks grow up in our society disrupts the process of socialization, with the result that the child of the impoverished environment fails to realize his genetic potential.

The foregoing findings indicate that, contrary to Jensen's assumptions, the greater similarity of environments for identical twins contributes substantially to their greater psychological resemblance. As a result, the heritability coefficient again reflects substantial environmental as well as genetic variance.

Finally, Jensen's argument suffers from an even more serious restrictive condition. To the extent that it is a valid measure, the heritability coefficient reflects the relative contribution of genetic and environmental variance *within* but not *between* families. Yet, it is precisely *between families* that most of the differences in ability occur. It may be true that individual differences among children *within the same family* are more influenced by genetic than by environmental factors, but such a finding implies nothing about variation among children from *different* families. Evidence for the effect of such environmental restriction on the magnitude of heritability coefficients based only on samples of twins can be obtained from data cited by Jensen himself. For example, twins are necessarily of the same age, a circumstance which obviously reduces differences in their environmental experience. Utilizing data provided by Jensen (1969a), one can compute a heritability coefficient from a comparison of siblings with unrelated children

raised in the same family. Siblings, of course, are no more alike than fraternal twins. Just as identical twins have about twice as many genes in common as fraternal twins, so do the latter have about twice as many genes in common as children who are completely unrelated. Accordingly, from this point of view, the genetic contribution to differences in intelligence, as measured by the heritability coefficient, should be approximately the same in both cases. Of course, the critical element is the fact that we are now dealing with children who, though raised in the same family, are of different ages. Although just as similar genetically as fraternal twins, they do not look as alike *at the same point in time.* Hence they are more likely to be treated differently than fraternal twins are, so that the environmental variation is greater. This fact is reflected in the heritability coefficient computed by Jensen's formula from the data cited in his article on siblings vs. unrelated children raised together. The obtained estimate of genetic effect was 68 percent, clearly lower than the 80 percent derived by Jensen from the data on twins. Which value is correct? Obviously, the answer depends on the range of variation present in the environment.

But the contribution of the environment to differences among children raised in the same family is of course less than would obtain for children raised in different households. As Newman, Freeman, and Holzinger pointed out in their pioneering study (1937, p. 347), an unbiased estimate of the relative contribution of heredity and environment to differences between children raised in *different* families could be obtained from a heritability coefficient based on separated identical and separated fraternal twins. They further speculated that, under these circumstances, the percentage of genetic effect, "instead of being about .75 as for twins reared together, might be of the order of .50 or even smaller . . . . The relative role of heredity and environment is thus a function of the type of environment." (p. 347).

It is surprising that no one has followed up on this suggestion. Nor do any published data exist on the degree of similarity between fraternal twins reared apart. Fehr (1969), however, has carried out an alternate analysis comparing separated identical twins with siblings reared apart. As Fehr acknowledges (p. 576), such a comparison is biased toward heredity since identical twins are probably more likely to come from and be placed in correlated environments and, unlike siblings, are always of the same age and sex. As a result, a heritability coefficient based on a comparison of identical twins reared apart with separated siblings would be higher than one in which the contrast group was separated, same-sex fraternal twins. Even so, the estimate of heritability obtained by Fehr was .53, a value substantially below Jensen's figure of .80. Fehr's result also lends support to Newman, Freeman, and Holzinger's prediction of a coefficient of ".50 or even smaller" for separated twins of both types.

But even this estimate can not be generalized to the population at large, in view of the restricted range of environments into which foster children are placed.

We have now concluded our re-examination of evidence and assumptions underlying the thesis of Jensen and others that 80 percent of the variation in human intelligence is genetically determined. The results of our analysis lead to rejection of this thesis both on theoretical and empirical grounds. But what of the fundamental question to which Jensen was so ready to supply an answer? What can be said about the relative contributions of heredity and environment to psychological development? On the basis of the analysis we have undertaken, several conclusions appear to be in order:

1. There can be no question that genetic factors play a substantial role in producing individual differences in mental ability. Many research findings testify to the validity of this statement. Perhaps the most impressive is the fact that the similarity of identical twins reared apart is clearly greater than that of fraternal twins reared together.

2. It is impossible to establish a single fixed figure representing the proportion of variation in intelligence, or any other human trait, independently attributable to heredity vs. environment. Even if one assumes the absolute degree of genetic variation to be a constant, the fact that the relative contribution of each factor depends on the degree of variability present in a given environment and its capacity to evoke innate potential means that the influence of genetic factors will vary from one environmental context to another. *Specifically, whereas the impact of hereditary endowment is considerable in accounting for individual differences among children raised in the same family, the relative importance of the environment becomes much greater in accounting for differences among children raised in different families. This fact is of especial importance since the greatest variation in human abilities occurs across families rather than within them.*

3. Any attempt to identify the independent contribution of heredity and environment to human development confronts the fact of a substantial correlation between these two factors. Moreover, the relation is not uni-directional. It is true, as Jensen points out (1969a, p. 38), that parents of better genetic endowment are likely to create better environments for their children, and that the child, as a function of his genetic characteristics, in fact partially determines the environment that he experiences. The genetically-instigated greater environmental similarity of identical vs. fraternal twins is a case in point. But Scarr-Salapatek's (1971b) research on this same phenomenon provides dramatic evidence that the environment can also determine the extent to which genetic potential is realized. This reverse

relationship calls into question the legitimacy of including covariance between heredity and environment in the proportion of variance due solely to genetic factors, as Jensen does (1969a, p. 39). The impossibility of assigning this covariance unequivocally to one or the other source is further ground for the conclusion that a fixed, single figure representing the proportion of variance attributable to genetic factors cannot be established.

4.   For genetic potential to find expression in terms of level and diversity, requires an appropriately complex and stimulating environment. This fact leads to a new and somewhat ironic interpretation of measures of heritability. Since heritability coefficients are lowest in environments that are most impoverished and suppressive, and highest in those that are most stimulating and enriched, *the heritability coefficient should be viewed not as a measure of the genetic loading underlying a particular ability or trait, but rather as an index of the capacity of a given environment to evoke and nurture the development of that ability or trait.*

5.   Even when the heritability coefficient for a trait in a particular environment is very high, this in no way restricts what might occur in some new environment that might come about or be deliberately constructed. Specifically, contrary to Jensen's contention, *a high heritability coefficient for a particular ability or trait cannot be taken as evidence that the ability or trait in question cannot be substantially enhanced through environmental intervention.* An instructive example is cited by Gage (1972) in a reply to Shockley and Jensen. Gage calls attention to the striking gain in stature exhibited by adults in Western countries over the past 200 years as a function of improved conditions of health and nutrition. He notes further that the heritability of height as determined from twin studies is about .90 higher than that for IO. "If this high heritability index had been derived in the year 1800, would it then have been safe to conclude that height cannot be increased through environmental influences? If that conclusion had been drawn, it would have been wrong." (Gage, 1972, p. 422).

6.   If the heritability coefficient for a given ability or trait in a particular environment is low in comparison with other social contexts, this means that the environment is inadequate for the development of that capacity. Specifically, the low heritability coefficients and depressed levels of measured intelligence, observed in disadvantaged populations especially Blacks, indicate that the environments in which these persons live do not permit the realization of their genetic potential.

7.   In terms of implications for social policy, the foregoing conclusions argue against reliance on methods of selective mating and population control

and in favor of measures aimed at improving existing environments, and even creating new ones better suited to evoke and nurture the expression of genetic potential.

Thus, our analysis has brought us to a paradoxical conclusion. An inquiry into the heritability of inborn capacities has shed new light on the power and potential of the environment to bring about the fuller realization of genetic possibilities.

Notes

[1] A more detailed and technical analysis of evidence and argument bearing on the issues raised in this article is contained in Bronfenbrenner (1972).

References

Bronfenbrenner, U. Nature and nurture: A reinterpretation of the evidence. In press, 1972.

Burt C. The genetic determination of differences in intelligence: A study of monozygotic twins reared together and apart. *British Journal of Psychology,* 1966, *57,* 137–153.

Eysenck, H. J. *The IQ argument.* New York: Library Press, 1971.

Fehr, F. S. Critique of hereditarian accounts. *Harvard Educational Review,* 1969, *39,* 571-580.

Gage, N. L. I.Q. heritability, race differences, and educational research. *Phi Delta Kappan,* January, 1972, 297–307.

Gottesman, I. I. Genetic variance and adaptive personality traits. *Journal of Child Psychology and Psychiatry,* 1966, *7,* 199-208.

Herrnstein, R. IQ. *Atlantic Monthly,* September, 1971, 43-64.

Holzinger, J. The relative effect of nature and nurture influences on twin differences. *Journal of Educational Psychology,* 1929, *20,* 241-248.

Honzik, M. P. Developmental studies of parent-child resemblance in intelligence. *Child Development,* 1957, *28,* 215-228.

Husen, T. *Psychological twin research.* Stockholm: Almqvist & Wiksell, 1959.

Jensen, A. R. Estimation of the limits of heritability of traits by comparison of monozygotic and dizygotic twins. *Proceedings of the National Academy of Sciences,* 1967, *58,* 149-157.

Jensen, A. R. How much can we boost I.Q. and scholastic achievement? *Harvard Educational Review,* Winter, 1969, 1-123. (a)

Jensen, A. R. Reducing the heredity-environment uncertainty: A reply. *Harvard Educational Review,* 1969, *39,* 449-483. (b)

Jones, A. G. Environmental influences on mental development. In Earl Carmichael (ed.), *Manual of child psychology.* New York: Wiley & Sons, 1946, 582-632.

Juel-Nielsen, N. *Individual and environment.* Copenhagen: Munksgaard, 1965.

Koch, H. L. *Twins and twin relations*. Chicago: University of Chicago Press, 1966.

Lewontin, R. C. Race and intelligence. *Bulletin of the Atomic Scientists*, March, 1970, *26*, 2-8.

Newman, H. H., Freeman, F. N., Holzinger, K. J. *Twins: A study of heredity and environment*, Chicago: University of Chicago Press, 1937.

Nichols, R. C. The inheritance of general and specific abilities. *National Merit Scholarship Corporation Research Reports*, 1965, *1*, 1-13. (a)

Nichols, R. C. The National Merit twin study. In G. Vandenberg (ed.), *Methods and goals in human behavior genetics*. New York: Academic Press, 1965, 231-245. (b)

Scarr, S. Environmental bias in twin studies. *Eugenics Quarterly*, 1968, *15*, 34-40.

Scarr, S. Social introversion-extraversion. *Child Development*, 1969, *40*, 823-833.

Scarr-Salapatek, S. Unknowns in the IQ equation. *Science*, 1971, *174*, 1223-1228. (a)

Scarr-Salapatek, S. Race, social class and IQ. *Science*, 1971, *174*, 1285-1295. (b)

Shields, J. Personality differences and neurotic traits in normal twin school children. *Eugenics Review*, 1954 *45*, 213-247.

Shields, J. *Monozygotic twins brought up apart and brought up together*. London: Oxford University Press, 1962. Shockley, W. A debate challenge: Geneticity is 80% for white identical twins' I.Q.'s. *Phi Delta Kappan*, March, 1972, 415-419.

Skodak, M. & Skeels, H. M. A final follow-up study of one hundred adopted children. *Journal of genetic psychology*, 1949, *75*, 85-125.

Willerman, L., Naylor, A. F. & Myrianthopouls, N. C. Intellectual development of children from interracial matings. *Science*, 1970, *170*, 1329-1331.

Part Three
Infancy

In the history of human development, the past decade may well come to be known as the period in which science discovered the human infant, his powers, and his vulnerabilities. From a scientific point of view, infancy was long regarded as a rather dull affair in which a largely passive organism was maturing primarily as a function of inexorable, internally mediated neurological development. The studies included in this section document the demise of this traditional view. The infant emerges not only as vulnerable to external influences even while still in the womb, but also as an active agent, who, given minimum support from his environment, can recoup and even shape his own destiny.

This double theme is seen in the research on the sequellae of prenatal and perinatal damage, as summarized by Birch and as highlighted in Willerman and Broman's demonstration that the psychological consequences of the same degree of prenatal damage are substantially greater among children from families living in suppressive environments than among those growing up in advantaged circumstances. Thus ecological factors are seen to play a crucial role in determining the developmental consequences of abnormalities of pregnancy and birth.

The power of both the infant and his environment to shape the course of development in the early weeks of life is illustrated in a series of studies of mother-infant interaction. Both Korner and Grobstein, working with neonates, and Moss, observing infants at three weeks and three months, call attention to the critical part played by the infant in the formation of a system of mother-infant interaction which then develops its own momentum.

The different trajectories apparently initiated by male and female infants lead to marked sex differences in the first year of life, as documented in the paper by Goldberg and Lewis.

The nature of the mother-infant bond, and the consequences of its disruption, are reflected in the next group of papers. Wahler shows how attachment provides the context for powerful processes of social reinforcement. Spitz's classical study of the effects of maternal separation provides a focal point for Bronfenbrenner's comprehensive review of studies of early deprivation. Especially significant is the finding that, although effects of deprivation appear irreversible in other mammals, the human organism, if again placed in a supportive environment, is able to recover normal function.

The remaining articles in this section document the influence of the broader social environment on the child's development. Rebelsky and Hawks present the first systematic study of father-infant interaction during the earliest months of life. Tulkin and Kagan show how, in this same period, social class already has an impact on the mother's treatment of the child and his corresponding reactions. Finally, in an ingenious resolution of an unanswered question posed by their earlier work, Caudill and Frost show that differences in behavior of American and Japanese mother-infant pairs are a reflection of culture rather than racial origin.

3.1 Health and The Education of Socially Disadvantaged Children

Herbert G. Birch

Introduction

Recent interest in the effect on social and cultural factors upon educational achievement could lead us to neglect certain biosocial factors which through a direct or indirect influence on the developing child affect his primary characteristics as a learner. Such a danger is exaggerated when health and education are administered separately. The educator and the sociologist may concentrate quite properly on features of curriculum, familial environment, motivation, cultural aspects of language organisation, and the patterning of preschool experiences. Such concentration, while entirely fitting, becomes onesided and potentially self-defeating when it takes place independently of, and without detailed consideration of, the child as a biological organism. To be concerned with the child's biology is not to ignore the cultural and environmental opportunities which may affect him. Clearly, to regard organic factors as a substitute for environmental opportunity (Hunt 1966) is to ignore the intimate interrelation between the biology of the child and his environment in defining his functional capacities.

However, it is equally dangerous to treat cultural influences as though they were acting upon an inert organism. Effective environment (Birch 1954) is the product of the interaction of organic characteristics with the objective opportunities for experience. The child who is apathetic because of malnutrition, whose experiences may have been modified by acute or chronic illness, whose or learning abilities may have been affected by some 'insult' to the central nervous system cannot be expected to respond to opportunities for learning in the same way as does a child who has not been exposed to such conditions. Increasing opportunity for learning, though entirely admirable in itself, will not overcome such biologic disadvantages (Birch 1964, Cravioto *et al.* 1966).

There are two considerations with children who have been at risk of a biologic insult. First, such children must be identified and not merely additional but *special* educational opportunities effective for them must be provided. As no socially deprived group can be considered to be homogeneous for any particular disability, groups of children from such backgrounds

Reprinted with abridgment by permission of the author and Spastics International Medical Publications from *Developmental Medecine and Child Neurology*, 1968, *10*, 580-599.

must be differentiated into meaningful subgroups for purposes of remedial, supplemental and habilitative education. Secondly, if conditions of risk to the organism can be identified, principles of public health and of current bio-social knowledge should be utilized by reduce learning handicap in future generations.

Concern for the socially disadvantaged cannot in good conscience restrict itself to the provision either of equal or special educational and preschool opportunities for learning. It must concern itself with all factors contributing to educational failure, among which the health of the child is a variable of primary importance.

Such an argument is not new. The basic relationship between poverty, illness and educational failure has long been known, as has the fact expressed by James (1965) that 'poverty begets poverty, is a cause of poverty and a result of poverty.' What is new is the nature of the society in which such an interaction occurs. As Galbraith (1958) has put it, 'to secure each family a minimum standard, as a normal function of society, would help insure that the misfortunes of parents, discerned or otherwise, were not visited on their children. It would help insure that poverty was not self-perpetuating. Most of the reaction, which no doubt would be almost universally adverse, is based on obsolete attitudes. When poverty was a majority phenomenon, such action could not be afforded . . . An affluent society has no similar excuse for such rigor. It can use the forthright remedy of providing for those in want. Nothing requires it to be compassionate. But it has no high philosophical justification for callousness.'

The pertinence of Galbraith's concern as it applies to the health of children, particularly those in the non-white segments of our population, is underscored by the fact that, according to the Surgeon General Stewart (1967), the United States standing with respect to infant mortality has been steadily declining with respect to other countries. Though we are the richest country our 1964 infant mortality rate of 24.8 per 1,000 live births causes us to rank fifteenth in world standing. Had we had Sweden's rate, the world's lowest, approximately 43,000 fewer infants would have died in that year. Of particular pertinence to the problem of social disadvantage is the fact that the mortality rate for non-white infants is twice as high as that for whites, with the highest rates for the country as a whole in the east south central states, Kentucky, Tennessee, Alabama and Mississippi. Wegman (1966) notes that 'Mississippi again has the dubious distinction of having the highest rate (infant mortality) . . . more than twice that of the lowest state.' Most of this difference could be related to the higher Negro population of Mississippi.

The data on infant mortality have been extended to other features of child health by Baumgartner (1965) and by Densen and Haynes (1967), who have pointed out that although detailed and careful documentation of the

'degree and magnitude of the health problems' of the Negro, Puerto Rican and Indian groups are not readily available, a strikingly dangerous picture may be pieced together as a montage from various public health statistics, research studies and occasional articles. The picture is striking, not merely because it shows these minority groups to be at a significant health disadvantage with respect to the white segment of the population, but because it indicates that the disparity between white and non-white groups is increasing. Thus, while in 1930 twice as many non-white mothers died in childbirth, in 1960 'for every white mother who lost her life in childbirth, four non-white mothers died.' (Baumgartner 1965). In 1940 the number of non-white mothers delivered by poorly trained midwives was 14 times that for white mothers, a discrepancy that rose to 23 times as great by 1960. Gold (1962) pointed out that while the overall death-rate for mothers in childbirth had reached an alltime low of 3.7 per 10,000 live births, this change was largely due to the reduction of the mortality rate among white mothers to 2.6. Non-white mothers had a death-rate four times as great, 10.3, a rate characteristic of white mothers two decades earlier. In generalizing these findings Baumgartner believes 'that the most advantaged non-white family has a poorer chance of having a live and healthy baby than the least advantaged white family.'

In our concern with educational disadvantage we must therefore recognize the excessive risk of ill-health relevant to educational handicap that exists in the children with whose welfare and education we are concerned. To this end I shall discuss some selected features of health and how far they differentiate the population of socially disadvantaged children from other children in the U.S.A.

Prematurity and Obstetric Complications

Few factors in the health history of the child have been as strongly associated with later intellectual and educational deficiencies as prematurity at birth and complications in the pregnancy from which he derives (McMahon and Sowa 1959). Although a variety of specific infections, explicit biochemical disorders, or trauma may result in more clearly identified and dramatic alterations in brain function, prematurity, together with pre- and peri-natal complications, are probably factors which most broadly contribute to disorders of neurologic development (Lilienfeld *et al.* 1955, Pasamanick and Lilienfeld 1955).

A detailed consideration of health factors which may contribute to educational failure must start with an examination of prematurity and the factors associated with it.

Prematurity has been variously defined either by the weight of the child at birth, by the maturity of certain of his physiologic functions, or by gesta-

tional age (Coiner 1960). Independently of the nature of the definition in any society in which it has been studied, prematurity has an excessive representation in the lower social strata and among the most significantly socially disadvantaged. Prematurity in any social group is simultaneously indicative of two separate conditions of risk. In the first place fetuses that are primarily abnormal and characterized by a variety of congenital anomalies are more likely to be born before term than are normal fetuses. Second, infants who are born prematurely, even when no congenital abnormality may be noted, are more likely to develop abnormally than are infants born at term. Thus, Baumgartner (1962) has noted that followup studies have 'indicated that malformation and handicapping disorders (neurological, mental and sensory) are more likely to be found among the prematurely born than those born at term. Thus, the premature infant not only has a poorer chance of surviving than the infant born at term, but if he does survive he has a higher risk of having a handicapping condition.' One consequence of this association between prematurity and neurological, mental, sensory and other handicapping conditions is the excessive representation of the prematures among the mentally subnormal and educationally backward children at school age (Drillien 1964).

Baumgartner (1962) has presented the distribution of live births by birthweight for white and non-white groups in the United States for 1957. For the country as a whole 7.6 per cent of all live births weighed 2,500 g. or less. In the white segment of the population 6.8 per cent of the babies fell in this category, while 12.5 per cent of the non-white infants weighed 2,500 g. or less. The frequency at all levels of low birthweight was twice as great in non-white infants. Baumgartner attributed the high incidence of prematurity among non-whites to the greater poverty of this group. The studies of Donnelly, et al. (1964) in North Carolina, of Thomson (1963) in Aberdeen, Scotland, and of Shapiro et al. (1960 in New York suggest that many factors, including nutritional practices, maternal health, the mother's own growth achievements as a child, as well as deficiencies in prenatal care and birth spacing and grand multiparity, interact to produce group differences between the socially disadvantaged and more advantageously situated segments of the population.

It has sometimes been argued that the excess of low birthweight babies among the socially disadvantaged is largely a consequence of ethnic differences (i.e., Negroes 'naturally' give birth to smaller babies). However, the high association of prematurity with social class in an ethnically homogeneous population such as that in Aberdeen, the finding of Donnelly, et al. that within the Negro group higher social status was associated with reduced frequency of prematurity, the findings of Pakter et al. (1961) that illegitimacy adds to the risk of prematurity within the non-white ethnic group, and the suggestion made by Shapiro et al. that a change for the better in the

pattern of medical care reduces the prevalence of prematurity, all make the ethnically based hypothesis of 'natural difference' difficult to retain.

If gestational age is used instead of birthweight as an indication of prematurity, the non-whites are at an even greater risk than when birthweight is used. In 1958–1959 (Baumgartner 1962) 18.1 per cent of non-white babies born in New York City had a gestational age of 36 weeks or less, in contrast to 8.5 per cent for liveborn white babies.

Both the data on birthweight and the data on gestational age leave little doubt that prematurity and its attendant risks are excessively represented in the non-white segment of the population. Moreover, an examination in detail of regional data such as that provided by Donnelly *et al.* for hospital births in university hospitals in North Carolina indicate clearly that in that community the most advantaged non-white has a significantly greater risk of producing a premature infant than the least advantaged segment of the white population.

For equal degrees of prematurity, non-white infants have a somewhat better chance for survival during the first month of life (Erhardt 1964). However, during the remainder of infancy this likelihood is reversed, particularly for infants weighing between 1,500 and 2,500 g. at birth. Baumgartner, reviewing these data, concludes, 'this observation strongly suggests that inadequate medical care, inadequate maternal supervision, inadequate housing and associated socio-economic deprivations are exerting unfavorable influences on the later survival of those non-white babies who initially appear the more favored. It is apparent that socio-economic factors not only influence the incidence of low birthweight in all ethnic groups, but greatly influence survival after the neonatal period.'

If the low birthweight and survival data are considered distributively rather than categorically, it appears that the non-white infant is subject to an excessive continuum of risk reflected at its extremes by perinatal, neonatal, and infant death, and in the survivors by a reduced functional potential.

The Background of Perinatal Risk

Clearly, the risk of having a premature baby or a complicated pregnancy and delivery begins long before the time of the pregnancy itself. A series of studies carried out in Aberdeen, Scotland on the total population of births of that city (Thomson 1963, Walker 1954, Thomson and Billewicz 1963) indicate that prematurity as well as pregnancy complications are significantly correlated with the mother's nutritional status, height, weight, concurrent illnesses, and the social class of her father and husband. Although the relation among these variables is complex, it is clear that the women born in the lowest socio-economic class and who have remained in this class at marriage were themselves more stunted in growth than other women in the

population, had less adequate dietary and health habits, were in less good general health, and tended to be at excessive risk or producing premature infants. The mother's stature as well as her habits were determined during her childhood, tended to be associated with contraction of the bony pelvis, and appeared systematically related to her risk condition as a reproducer. In analyzing the relation between maternal health and physique to a number of obstetrical abnormalities such as prematurity, caesarean section and perinatal death, Thomson (1959) has shown each of these to be excessively represented in the mothers of least good physical grade. . . .

Dietary Factors—Pre-war and War-time Experience

The physical characteristics of the mother which affect her efficiency as a reproducer are not restricted to height and physical grade. As early as 1933, Mellanby, while recognizing that 'direct and accurate knowledge of this subject in human beings is meagre,' asserted that nutrition was undoubtedly 'the most important of all environmental factors in childbearing, whether the problem be considered from the point of view of the mother or that of the offspring.' It was his conviction that the reduction of a high perinatal mortality rate as well as of the incidence of maternal ill health accompanying pregnancy could effectively be achieved by improving the quality of the diet. Acting upon these views he attempted to supplement the diets of women attending London antenatal clinics and reported a significant reduction in morbidity rates during the puerperium.

Although Mellanby's own study is difficult to interpret for a number of methodologic reasons, indirect evidence rapidly came into being in support of his views. Perhaps the most important of these was the classical inquiry directed by Sir John Boyd-Orr and reported in *Food, Health and Income* (1936). This study demonstrated conclusively that the long recognised social differential in perinatal death rate was correlated with a dietary differential, and that in all respects the average diet of the lower income groups in Britain was inadequate for good health. Two years later McCance *et al.* (1938) confirmed the Boyd-Orr findings in a meticulous study of the individual diets of 120 pregnant women representing a range of economic groups ranging from the wives of unemployed miners in South Wales and Tyneside to the wives of professionals. The diet survey technique which they used and which has, unfortunately, been rarely imitated since, was designed to minimize misreport. The results showed that there was wide individual variation in the intake of all foods which related consistently neither to income nor to intake per kilogram of body weight. But when the women were divided into six groups according to the income available for each person per week, the poorer women proved to be shorter and heavier and to

have lower hemoglobin counts. Moreover, though economic status had little effect on the total intake of calories, fats and carbohydrates, 'intake of protein, animal protein, phosphorus, iron and Vitamin B_1 rose convincingly with income.' The authors of the study offered no conclusions about the possible outcome of the pregnancies involved, but the poorer reproductive performance of the lower class women was clearly at issue. For as they stated, 'optimum nutrition in an adult implies and postulates optimum nutrition of that person as a child, that child as a fetus, and that fetus of its mother.'

A second body of indirect data supporting Mellanby's hypothesis derived from animal studies on the relation of diet to reproduction. Warkany (1944) for example, demonstrated that pregnant animals maintained on diets deficient in certain dietary ingredients produced offspring suffering from malformation. A diet which was adequate to maintain maternal life and reproductive capacity could be inadequate for normal fetal development. The fetus was not a perfect parasite and at least for some features of growth and differentiation could have requirements different from those of the maternal host.

It would divert us from the main line of our inquiry to consider the many subsequent studies in detail. However, Duncan *et al.* (1952), in surveying these studies, as well as the wartime experiences in Britain, have argued convincingly that the fall in stillbirth and neonatal death rate could only be attributed to a reduction in poverty accompanied by a scientific food rationing policy. Certainly there was no real improvement in prenatal care during the war when so many medical personnel were siphoned off to the armed forces. Furthermore, the improvement took place chiefly among those deaths attributed to 'ill defined or unknown' causes—that is among those cases when low fetal vitality seems to be a major factor in influencing survival—and these types of death 'are among the most difficult to influence by routine antenatal practice.' Of all the possible factors then, nutrition was the only one which, improved during the war years (Garry and Wood 1945). Thomson (1959) commented that the result was 'as a nutritional effect' all the more convincing 'because it was achieved in the context of a society where most of the conditions of living other than the nutritional were deteriorating.'

While this National 'feeding experiment' was going on in the British Isles, a more controlled experiment was being carried out on the continent of Europe (Toverud 1950). In 1939 Dr. Toverud set up a health station in the Sagene district of Oslo to serve pregnant and nursing mothers and their babies. Though war broke out shortly after the station was opened, and it became progressively more difficult to get certain protective foods, an attempt was made to insure that every woman being supervised had the recommended amounts of every essential nutrient, through the utilization of

supplementary or synthetic sources when necessary. In spite of food restrictions which became increasingly severe, the prematurity rate among the 728 women who were supervised at the station never went above the 1943 high of 3.4 per cent, averaging 2.2 per cent for the period 1939–1944. Among the unsupervised mothers the 1943 rates was 6.3 per cent and the average for the period 4.6 per cent. In addition, the stillbirth rate of 14.2/1,000 for all women attending the health station was half that of the women in the surrounding districts.

Meanwhile, even as the British and Norwegian feeding experiments were in progress, there were some hopefully never-to-be repeated starvation 'experiments' going on elsewhere. When they were reported after the war, the childbearing experiences of various populations of women under conditions of severe nutritional restriction were to provide evidence of the ways in which deprivation could negatively affect the product of conception, just as dietary improvement appeared able to affect it positively.

Smith (1947), for example, studying infants born in Rotterdam and the Hague during a delimited period of extreme hunger brought on by a transportation strike, found that the infants were shorter and lighter (by about 240 g.) than those born both before and after the period of deprivation. Significantly enough Smith also found that those babies who were five to six month fetuses when the hunger period began appeared to have been reduced in weight as much as those who had spent a full nine months in the uterus on a malnourished mother. He was led to conclude from this that reduced maternal caloric intake had its major effect on fetal weight beginning around the sixth month of gestation. Antonov's study of babies born during the siege of Leningrad (1947) confirmed the fact of weight reduction as well as Smith's observations that very severe deprivation was likely to prevent conception altogether rather than reduce the birthweight. Antonov found that during a six month period which began four months after the start of the siege, there was an enormous increase in prematurity as judged by birth length—41.2 per cent of all the babies born during this period were less than 47 cm. long and fully 49.1 per cent weighed under 2,500 grams. The babies were also of very low vitality—30.8 per cent of the prematures and 9 per cent of the full-term babies died during the period. Abruptly, during the latter half of the year, the birthrate plummeted—along with the prematurity rate. Thus, while 161 prematures and 230 term babies were born between January and June, 1942, five prematures and 72 term babies were born between July and December. Where information was available it suggested that the women who managed to conceive during the latter part of the year, when amenorrhea was widespread, were better fed than the majority, being employed in food industries or working in professional or manual occupations which had food priorities. Antonov concluded that while the fetus might behave for the most part like a parasite, 'the condition of the host, the mother's body, is of great

consequence to the fetus, and that severe quantitative and qualitative hunger of the mother decidedly affects the development of the fetus and the vitality of the newborn child.'

Long after the war, Dean (1951) was able to confirm the Smith and Antonov results with a careful analysis of a series of 22,000 consecutive births at the Landesfrauenklinik, Wuppertal, Germany, during 1937–1948. It was apparent from this series that the small reduction in the average duration of gestation recorded was insufficient to account for the degree of weight reduction observed. The study demonstrated, even more clearly than before, that severe hunger did not merely reduce the mother's ability to maintain the pregnancy to term, but could act directly through the placenta to reduce the growth of the infant. . . .

Obstetrical Care of Lower Class Women

Obstetrical care is markedly different in socially advantaged and disadvantaged segments of the population. A preliminary view of the obstetrical care received by lower-class pregnant women may be obtained from a consideration of Hartman and Sayl's (1965) survey of 1380 births, at the Minneapolis, General Hospital. This hospital which served medically indigent patients living in census tracts having notably high rates of infant mortality delivered 43 per cent of its patients with either no prenatal care of only one third trimester antenatal visit. Of the woman who did attend the hospital's prenatal clinic, 3 per cent made their initial visit during the first trimester, 26 per cent in the second trimester and 71 per cent in the last trimester. Infant mortality appeared to vary according to prenatal care. The mothers having no prenatal care experienced fetal deaths at a rate of 4 per cent, a rate considerably higher than the 0.7 per cent fetal death rate for mothers having one or more visits to the prenatal clinic.

Boek and Boek (1956), in upper New York State, collected their sample through an examination of birth certificates. 1,805 mothers were interviewed and grouped according to social class as determined by the child's father's occupation. The amount and type of obstetric care correlated with social class. Mothers in the lowest social classes tended to seek health care later during pregnancy than higher class women. Lower class mothers tended to use a family doctor for both pre- and post-natal care, rather than the obstetric specialists and pediatricians heavily patronized by upper class women. More than twice as many upper class women attended group meetings for expectant parents than did lower class mothers. Lower class women tended to stay in the hospital fewer days than upper class women, and although the former paid lower doctor's bills since more higher than lower class families had hospital insurance. Three months after the birth of the child fewer lower class women had received postnatal checkups than upper class women and fewer mothers in the lowest social class had

their babies immunized with a triple vaccine or planned to have this done.

The effects of a good, comprehensive health program on pregnancy losses was studied by Shapiro *et al.* (1960), in a comparison of the infant mortality rates for members of the Health Insurance Plan and the general New York City population. Obstetric-gynecology diplomates delivered 72 per cent of the HIP babies. Only 24 per cent of the general New York population received specialist care, and only 5 per cent of non-white babies were delivered by specialists. Because of these radical differences in type of delivery care, the investigators compared the HIP prematurity and perinatal mortality rates only to those New Yorkers who were patients of private physicians. Socio-economic status was judged by the occupation of the father as recorded on birth and death certificates. The white patients who participated in the Health Insurance Plan had their prematurity rate reduced from the 6 per cent rate characteristic for their group in the city as a whole to 5.5 per cent. This reduction just missed statistical significance at the 5 per cent level. In the non-white group the rate was reduced from 10.8 to 8.8 per cent, a difference significant at the .01 level of confidence. Within each specific category of physician used, Shapiro found that white deliveries had a far lower perinatal mortality than non-white for the general New York City group. General service deliveries had a far greater mortality rate than private physician cases in hospitals for both the white and non-white groups. 'Among white deliveries mortality was considerably higher for general service cases than for those under the care of private doctors in each occupation category . . . This raises the interesting question whether the greater mortality in general service is principally due to factors associated with type of care or the setting in which it is received, or whether the poorer risk women within each occupation class tend to turn to general service.'

In view of the potential importance of prenatal care on pregnancy course and outcome and the suggestion that such care is deficient in the lowest socio-economic groups it is important to examine the ethnic distribution of antenatal care. The study of Pakter *et al.* (1961) though restricted to New York City is representative of conditions that exist on a national scale. His findings can be replicated in any urban community having a significantly large non-white population. In rural areas the situation is equally bad. Approximately 30 percent of married Negro mothers and 39 per cent of Puerto Rican mothers received no prenatal care during the first six months of the pregnancy. In contrast, only 13 per cent of white married mothers were subjected to a similar lack of care.

Post-natal Conditions for Development

Densen and Haynes (1967) have indicated that many types of illness are excessively represented in the non-white segments of the population at all

age levels. I have selected one, nutritional status, as the model variable for consideration. A considerable body of evidence from animal experimentation as well as field studies of populations at nutritional risk (Cravioto *et al.* 1966) have suggested a systematic relation between nutritional inadequacy and both neurologic maturation and competence in learning.

At birth the brain of a full-term infant has achieved about one quarter of its adult weight. The bulk of subsequent weight gain will derive from the laying down of lipids, particularly myelin, and cellular growth. Animal experiments on the rat (Davison and Dobbing 1966), the pig (Dickerson *et al.* 1967, McCance 1960) and the dog (Platt *et al.* 1964) have all demonstrated a significant interference in brain growth and differencitation associated with severe dietary restriction, particularly of protein, during the first months of life. In these animals the behavioral effects have been dramatic with abnormalities in some cases persisting after dietary rehabilitation.

The relation of these data to the human situation is made difficult by the extreme severity of the dietary restrictions. More modest restrictions have been imposed by Widdowson (1965) and Barnes *et al.* (1966) and the latter experiments indicated some tendency for poorer learning in the nutritionally deprived animals. Cowley and Griesel's work (1963) suggests a cumulative effect of malnutrition on adaptive behavior across generations.

The animal findings as a whole can be interpreted either as suggesting a direct influence of malnutrition on brain growth and development, or as resulting interference with learning at critical points in development. In either case the competence of the organism as a learner appears to be influenced by his history as an eater. These considerations add cogency to an already strongly held belief that good nutrition is important for children and links our general concerns on the relation of nutrition to health to our concerns with education and the child's functioning as a learner.

Incidents of severe malnutrition appear rarely in the United States today, but there is evidence to suggest that the low income segments of the population suffer from subtle, sub-clinical forms of malnutrition which may be partially responsible for the higher rates of morbidity and mortality of children in this group. Brock (1961) suggests that 'dietary sub-nutrition can be defined as any impairment of functional efficiency or body systems which can be corrected by better feeding.' Since 'constitution is determined in part by habitual diet . . . diet must be considered in discussing the aetiology of a large group of diseases of uncertain and multiple aetiology . . .' The relationship between nutrition and constitution is demonstrated by the fact that the populations of developed nations are taller and heavier than those of technically underdeveloped nations and that 'within a given developed nation children from economically favoured areas are taller and heavier than children from economically under-privileged areas.'

In comparison to the vast body of data available on the diets of peoples

in tropical countries, very little research has been done in recent years on the nutritional status of various economic groups in the United States. The effects of long term subclinical malnutrition on the health of the individual are not yet known, and little research has been directed at this problem since 1939. However, it is instructive to review the studies comparing the diets of low-income people with the rest of the population since these lay the basis for hypothesizing that nutritional differences may have some effect on the overall differences in health and learning ability between groups.

The nutritional differences between lower and higher income individuals begin before birth and continue thereafter. In a study of maternal and child health care in upper New York State, Walter Boek *et al.* (1957) found that babies from low income families were breast fed less often and kept on only milk diets longer than upper income infants. In a study of breast feeding in Boston, Salber and Feinleib (1960) confirmed Boek's results and, 'social class was found to be the most important variable affecting incidence of breast-feeding.'

Social class differences in feeding patterns continue after weaning. Filer and Martinez (1964) studied 4,642 six month old infants from a national representative sample and found that 'infants of mothers with least formal education and in families with lowest incomes are fed more milk formula . . .' and less solid foods at six months old than those from higher educational and economic groups. Class differences in the intake of most nutrients varied primarily according to the amount of milk formula consumed.

The researchers found that for 'almost all nutrients studied, the mean intakes were well above recommended levels. The single exception was iron; more than half of infants do not get the lowest recommended provision—a finding that corroborates the results reported by a number of other investigators.' Iron deficiency was most prevalent among infants of mothers with low educational and income levels. Infants whose mothers attained no more than a grade school education received a mean intake of only 6.7 mg. of iron a day, as compared to the 9.1 mg. mean intake of infants whose mothers had attended high school. Since 'nutritional iron deficiency is widespread and most prevalent in infants in the low socio-economic group,' and iron deficiency is the most common cause of anemia in infants during the first two years of life, malnutrition at least with respect to this nutrient is widely prevalent in lower class infants.

A study of Negro, low-income infants in South Carolina (Jones and Schendel 1966) uncovered more extensive areas of malnutrition in this group; the death-rate for Negro infants in South Carolina was twice the national rate). Thirty-six Negro infants from low income families were tested when they visited a Well-Baby Clinic for routine examinations. The subjects ranged in age from four to ten months. 'The bodyweights of 66 per

cent of the infants were below the 50th percentile in the Harvard growth charts, 34 per cent below the 10th percentile and 9 per cent below the 3rd percentile.' . . .

The researchers concluded that 'it would appear possible that malnutrition may be one of the many underlying causes for the high rate of Negro infant mortality in South Carolina.' Since Greenville County, where the study was conducted, has a relatively small number of infant deaths, 'it is possible that malnutrition may be even more severe and/or prevalent in many other counties of the state.'

Since the sample used in this study is small (36 infants), the results must be viewed as suggestive rather than conclusive. But taken together with the findings on iron intake, a New York study which shows that anemia is common among Negro and Puerto Rican infants (James 1966) and the recent finding of Arneil (1965) that 'some anemia was present in 59 per cent of Glasgow slum children,' the suggestion is strengthened that poor diet may be partly responsible for the poor health of lower socio-economic class children.

The studies so far reviewed have dealt with populations that are in some way representative of the nutritional status of large groups of children. Since these studies are few in number and limited in approach, they cannot give a complete picture of the nutritional status of lower class Americans. Hints about areas of malnutrition which have not thoroughly investigated can be drawn from studies of special groups within the American population. In a survey of the 'Dietary and Nutritional Problems of Crippled Children in Five Rural Counties of North Carolina,' Bryan and Anderson (1965) found that the diets of 73 per cent of the 164 subject sample were less than adequate. The cause for the malnourishment of nine out of ten of the poorly fed children was poor family diet and in only one of ten cases was the malnutrition related to the physical handicap of the child.

Although all the children were from families in the low income group, the researchers found certain significant differentiations between the Negro and white families studied. Seventy-one per cent of the Negro children and 35 per cent of the white children's diets were rated as probably or obviously inadequate. Only a limited number of food items were used and 'in many of the families . . . only one food was cooked for a meal and this would be eaten with biscuits and water, tea or Kool-Aid . . . For the most part, the diet of our low income families contained few foods that are not soft or that require much chewing.' Suggestions of poor nutrition in infancy and childhood can also be drawn from studies of constitutional differences as well as from measurements of food intake.

A study of the nutritional status of junior high school children in Onondaga County, New York (Dibble *et al.* 1965) compared subjects from broadly different economic groups. School 'M' was 94 per cent Negro, while

Schools 'L' and 'J' were overwhelmingly white. The schools were also differentiated on the basis of the occupation of the students' fathers: '. . . of the 58 per cent of the employed fathers from school M, 52 per cent were laborers, whereas only 10 per cent from school L and 38 per cent from school J were in this category.' When the heights and weights of the subjects were compared, a greater percentage of students from the lower-socio-economic class school fell in the short stature and low-weight zones. There was also a tendency for students from the predominantly Negro school to have less subcutaneous fat by ranking of skinfold than students from other schools. . . .

The authors conclude that the differences between nutrition and socio-economic status. These differences are greater than the differences between male and female students, and are related to each other on the various parameters of the study. 'There was a slight indication that the growth of the male subjects in . . . school (M) had not been as great as that of the subjects in the other schools with whom they were compared. This fact was supported by somewhat lower average levels in the other parameters . . .'

Although the students at the predominantly Negro school in Onondaga County did not appear to suffer from gross nutritional deficiences, their diets were significantly less adequate than the subjects from the white, middle-class schools. The investigators did not attempt to link dietary habits with health records, but the results of the study lead to speculations about the relationship between suboptimal diet, rates of infection, school absence and academic performance.

Why Malnutrition?

Why, in a society with an abundant and often enriched food supply, are several groups of the population inadequately nourished. The answer appears to lie in two broad areas: money and information. Cultural differences in food habits and beliefs, though important, appear to lose their significance relatively quickly when adequate funds, higher general education, and sound knowledge of proper nutrition become available. Thus in an article on 'The Nutritional Status of American Negroes,' Jean Mayer (1965) finds that 'the food habits of Negroes belonging to the higher socio-economic classes appear to be essentially those of their white counterparts, (however) it can be fairly stated that in general the state of nutrition of Negroes is inferior to that of whites in the same geographic areas. In some cases, it is vastly inferior.' Just as poverty and lack of education breed poor eating habits among lower economic class Negroes, low income combined with a good education can produce adequate nutrition, as has been shown in a comparison of the dietary habits of students wives with other low income groups (Jeans *et al.* 1952).

In a detailed study of the 'Eating Patterns Among Migrant Families' in Palm Beach County, Florida, Delgado *et al.* (1961), found that a combination of low income, lack of education, lack of kitchen equipment and proper storage facilities contributed to dramatically poor diets in the migrant families.

When the family diets were analyzed in terms of the various nutrients, only 20 per cent of the families met the National Research Council calorie requirements. Thiamine, protein, Vitamin A and iron requirements were not met by over 50 per cent of the families. About 80 per cent did not meet the requirements for calcium and riboflavin and 97 per cent did not have enough Vitamin C. None of the families met stated requirements for milk, green and yellow vegetables; only a few had citrus fruits and tomatoes, potatoes or other fruits and vegetables and eggs; and only 43 per cent of the families met the daily requirements for meat.

Negro migrant agricultural workers have 'the highest proportion of malnourished individuals of any group in the country.' and Mayer (1965) finds the 'shortage of published data in this field striking.' Although lack of money to buy nutritious foods is apparently the major reason for malnourishment, the lack of information about nutrition is also to blame for both the rural and urban Negro diet. A monotonous, limited diet is the rule for Southern rural Negroes and the inadequacy of the diet is exaggerated for Southern urban Negroes for whom the availability of green vegetables is decreased. 'Consumption of fresh vegetables is low and consumption of citrus fruits negligible. Milk consumption is substantially lower than in white families . . . This is for a large part a reflection of lower income; but even at equal income, milk consumption may be lower for Negro families.' Although calorie requirements are usually met in urban families, protein, calcium, thiamine, riboflavin, nicotinic acid, Vitamin A and Vitamin C requirements are often inadequately met.

In the North 'even as approximate a description of the nutritional status of the Negro population is impossible to arrive at.' Mayer observes, however, that familiar Southern foods of minimal nutritional value, such as turnip, mustard greens, kale, okra and plantains, are stocked by stores in northern Negro areas. 'Careful persual of the records available in large cities, as well as the collection of impressions of experienced physicians, dietitians, and health administrators, leaves little doubt that our Negro slums represent the greatest concentration of anemias, growth failures, dermatitis of doubtful origin, accidents of pregnancy and other signs associated with malnutrition.'

Although the studies reviewed here are helpful for their indications and descriptions of areas of suboptimal nutrition in this country, a detailed and comprehensive study of the nutrition of the low income population is still lacking. Since suboptimal nutrition can have social and psychological ramifi-

cations, as well as constitutional and medical results, a more thorough knowledge of the ways in which nutrition can affect the daily life of the individual would be useful for all those who seek to improve the health and social well being of the poor.

Conclusions

In this review I have examined certain selected conditions of health which may have consequences for education. Other factors such as acute and chronic illness, immunizations, dental care, the utilization of health services and a host of other phenomena, perhaps equally pertinent to those selected for consideration, have been dealt with either in passing or not at all but in fact studies of these factors that do exist reflect the same picture that emerges from those variables which have been discussed. In brief, though much of the information is incomplete, and certain aspects of the data are sparse, a serious consideration of available health information leaves little or no doubt that children who are economically and socially disadvantaged and in an ethnic group exposed to discrimination, are exposed to massively excessive risks for maldevelopment.

Such risks have direct and indirect consequences for the functioning of the child as a learner. Conditions of ill health may directly affect the development of the nervous system and eventuate either in patterns of clinically definable malfunctioning in this system or in sub-clinical conditions. In either case the potentialities of the child as a learner cannot but be impaired. Such impairment, though it may in fact have reduced functional consequences under exceptionally optimal conditions for development and education, in any case represents a primary handicap which efforts at remediation may only partially correct.

The indirect effects of ill health or of conditions of suboptimal health care on the learning processes may take many forms. Only two can be nonsidered at this point. Children who are ill nourished are reduced in their responsiveness to the environment, distracted by their visceral state, and reduced in their ability to progress and endure in learning conditions. Consequently, given the same objective conditions for learning, the state of the organism modifies the effective environment and results in a reduction in the profit which a child may derive from exposure to opportunities for experience. Consequently, the provision of equal opportunities for learning in an objective sense is never met when only the school situation is made identical for advantaged and disadvantaged children. Though such a step is indeed necessary, proper and long overdue, a serious concern with the profitability of such improved objective opportunities for socially disadvantaged children demands a concern which goes beyond education and

includes an intensive and directed consideration of the broader environment, the health and functional and physical well-being of the child.

Inadequacies in nutritional status as well as excessive amounts in inter-current illness may interfere in indirect ways with the learning process. As Cravioto, *et al.* (1966) have put it, at least 'three possible indirect effects are readily apparent:

(1) *Loss of learning time.* Since the child was less responsive to his environment when malnourished, at the very least he had less time in which to learn and had lost a certain number of months of experience. On the simplest basis, therefore, he would be expected to show some developmental lags.

(2) *Interference with learning during critical periods of development.* Learning is by no means simply a cumulative process. A considerable body of evidence exists which indicates that interference with the learning process at specific times during its course may result in disturbances in function that are both profound and of long term significance. Such disturbance is not merely a function of the length of time the organism is deprived of the op-portunities for learning. Rather, what appears to be important is the corre-lation of the experimental opportunity with a given state of development— the so-called critical periods of learning. Critical periods in human learning have not been definitively established, but in looking at the consequences associated with malnutrition at different ages one can derive some poten-tially useful hypotheses. The earlier report by Cravioto and Robles (1965) may be relevant to the relationship between the age at which malnutrition develops and learning. They have shown that, as contrasted with older patients, infants under six months recovering from kwashiorkor did not recoup their mental age deficit during the recovery period. In older children, ranging from 15 to 41 months of age, too, the rate of recovery from the initial mental deficit varied in direct relation to chronological age at time of admission. Similarly, the findings of Barrera-Moncada 1963 in children, and those of Keys, *et al.* (1950) in adults, indicated a strong association be-tween the persistence of later effects on mental performance and the age at onset of malnutrition and its duration.

(3) *Motivation and personality changes.* It should be recognized that the mother's response to the infant is to a considerable degree a function of the child's own characteristics of reactivity. One of the first effects of malnutrition is a reduction in the child's responsiveness to stimulation and the emergence of various degrees of apathy. Apathetic behavior in its turn can function to reduce the value of the child as a stimulus and to diminished

the adults' responsiveness to him. Thus, apathy can provoke apathy and so contribute to a cumulative pattern or reduced adult-child interaction. If this occurs it can have consequences for stimulation, for learning, for maturation, and for interpersonal relations, the end result being significant backwardness in performance on later more complex learning tasks.'

However, independently of the path through which bio-social pathology interferes with educational progress, there is little doubt that ill health is a significant variable for defining differentiation in the learning potential of the child. To intervene effectively with the learning problems of disadvantaged children it would be disastrous if we were either to ignore or to relegate the physical condition and health status of the child with whose welfare we are concerned to a place of unimportance. To do so would be to divorce education from health; a divorce which can only have disorganizing consequences for the child. Unless health and education go hand in hand we shall fail to break the twin curse of ignorance and poverty.

References

Antonov, A. N. (1947) 'Children born during the siege of Leningrad in 1942.' *J. Pediat.*, **30**, 250.

Arneil, G. C., McKilligan, H. R., Lobo, E. (1965) 'Malnutrition in Glasgow children.' *Scot. med J.*, **10**, 480.

Barnes, R. H., Cunnold, S. R., Zimmerman, R. R., Simmons, H., MacLeod, R., Krook, L. (1966) 'Influence of nutritional deprivations in early life on learning behaviour of rats as measured by performance in water maze.' *J. Nutr.*, **89**, 399.

Barrera-Moncada, G. (1963) Estudios sobre Alleraciones del Crecimiento y del Desarrollo Psiocológico de Sindrome Pluricarencial Kwashiorkor. Caracas: Editoria Grafos.

Baumgartner, L. (1962) 'The public health significance of low birth weight in the U.S.A., with special reference to varying practices in providing special care to infants of low birth weights.' *Bull. Wld Hlth Org.*, **26**, 175.
———(1965) 'Health and ethnic minorities in the sixties.' *Amer. J. publ. Hlth*, **55**, 495.

Birch, H.G. (1954) 'Comparative psychology.' *In* Marcuse, F. A. (Ed.) Areas of Psychology. New York: Harper.
———(Ed) (1964) Brain Damage in Children: Biological, and Social Aspects. Baltimore: Williams & Wilkins.

Boek, W. E., Boek, J. K. (1956) Society and Health. New York: Putnam.
———and co-worker (1957) Social Class, Maternal Health and Child Care. Albany, N.Y.: New York State Department of Health.

Brock, J. (1961) Recent Advances in Human Nutrition. London: Churchill.

Bryan, H., Anderson, E. L. (1965) 'Dietary and nutritional problems of crippled children in five rural counties of North Carolina.' *Amer. J. publ. Hlth,* **55,** 1,545.

Corner-B. (1960) Prematurity. London: Cassell.

Cowley, J. J., Griesel, R. D. (1963) 'The development of second generation low-protein rats.' *J. genet. Psychol.,* **103,** 233.

Cravioto, J., DeLicardie, E. R., Birch, H. G. (1966) 'Nutrition, growth and neuro-integrative development: an experimental and ecologic study.' *Pediatrics,* **38,** 319.

————Robles, B. (1965) 'Evolution of adaptive and motor behavior during rehabilitation from kwashiorkor.' *Amer. J. Orthopsychiat.,* **35,** 449.

Darby, W. J., Dense, P. M., Cannon, R. O., Bridgeforth, E., Martin, M. P., Kaser, M. M., Peterson, O., Christie, A., Frye, W. W., Justus, K., McClellan, G. W., Williams C., Ogle, P. J., Hahn, P. F., Sheppard, C. W., Crothers, E. L., Newbill, J. A. (1953) 'The Vanderbilt co-operative study of maternal and infant nutrition I. Background. II. Methods, III. Description of the sample data.' *J. Nutr.,* **51,** 539.

————McGanity, W. J., Martin, M. P., Bridegforth, E., Densen, P.M., Kaser, M. M., Ogle, P J., Newbill, J. A., Stockell, A., Ferguson, E., Touster, O., McClellan, G. S., Williams, C., Cannon, R. O. (1953) 'The Vanderbilt co-operative study of maternal and infant nutrition. IV. Dietary, laboratory and physical findings in 2,129 delivered pregnancies.' *J. Nutr.,* **51,** 565.

Davison, A. N., Dobbing, J. (1966) 'Myelination as a vulnerable period in brain development.' *Brit. med. Bull.,* **22,** 40.

Dean, R. F. (1951) 'The size of the baby at birth and the yield of breast milk.' *In* Studies of Undernutrition, Wuppertall, 1946-49. M. C. R. Special Report series, No. 275. Ldon: H.M.S.O. Chap. 28.

Delgado, G., Brumback, C. L., Deaver, M. B. (1961 'Eating patterns among migrant families.' *Publ. Hlth. Rep. (Wash.),* **76,** 349.

Densen, P. M., Haynes, A. (1967) 'Research and the major health problems of Negro Americans. Paper presented at the Howard University Centennial Celebration, Washington. (Unpublished.)

Dibble, M. F., Brin, M., McMullen, E., Peel, A., Chen, N. (1965) 'Some preliminary biochemical findings in junior high school children in Syracuse and Onondaga County, New York.' *Amer. J. clin. Nutr.,* **17,** 218.

Dickerson, J. W., Dobbing, J., McCance, R. A. (1967) 'The effect of under nutrition on the postnatal development of the brain and cord in pigs.' *Proc. roy. Soc. B.,* **166,** 396.

Donnelly, J. F., Flowers, C. E., Creadick, R. N., Wells, H. B., Greenberg, B. G., Surles, K. B. (1964) 'Maternal, fetal and environmental factors in prematurity.' *Amer. J. Obstet, Gynec.* **88,** 918.

Drillien, C. M. (1964) The Growth and Development of Prematurely Born

Children. Edinburgh: Livingstone, Baltimore: Williams & Wilkins.

Duncan, E. H. L., Baird, D., Thomson, A. M. (1952) 'The causes and prevention of stillbirths and first week deaths. I. The evidence of vital statistics.' *J. Obstet. Gyncea. Brit. Emp.*, **59**, 183.

Erhardt, C. L., Joshi, G. B., Nelson, F. G., Kron, B. H., Weiner, L. (1964) 'Influence of weight and gestation on perinatal and neonatal mortality by ethnic group.' *Amer. J. publ. Hlth.* **54**, 1,841.

Filer, L. J., Martinez, G. A. (1964) 'Intake of selected nutrients by infants in the United States: an evaluation of 4,000 representative six-year-olds.' *Clin. Pediat.*, **3**, 633.

Galbraith, J. K. (1958) The Affluent Society. Boston: Houghton Mifflin.

Garry, R. C., Wood, H. O. (1945-46) 'Dietary requirements in human pregnancy and lactation: a review of recent work.' *Nutr. Abstr. Rev.*, **15**, 591.

Gold, E. M. (1962) 'A broad view of maternity care.' *Children*, **9**, 52.

Hartman, E. E., Sayles, E. B. (1965) 'Some reflections on births and infant deaths among the low socio-economic groups.' *Minn. Med.*, **48**, 1,711.

Hunt, E. E. (1966) 'Some new evidence on race and intelligence.' Paper read at the meeting of the New York Academy of Sciences-Anthropology Section, Oct. 24, 1966. (Unpublished).

James, G. (1965) 'Poverty and public health—new outlooks. J. Poverty as an obstacle to health progress in our cities.' *Amer. J. publ. Hlth*, **55**, 1,757.

———(1966) 'New York City's Bureau of Nutrition.' *J. Amer. dietet, Ass.*, **48**, 301.

Jeans, P. C., Smith, M. B., Stearns, G. (1952) 'Dietary habits of pregnant women of low income in a rural state.' *J. Amer. dietet. Ass.*, **28**, 27.

Jones, R. E., Schendel, H. E. (1966) 'Nutritional status of selected Negro infants in Greenville County, South Carolina.' *Amer. J. clin. Nutr.*, **18**, 407.

Kass, E. H. (1960 'Bacteriuria and the prevention of prematurity and perinatal death.' *In* Kowlessar, M. (ed.) Transactions of the 5th Conference on the Physiology of Prematurity. Princeton, 1960.

Keys, A., Brozek, J., Henschel A., Mikelsen, O., Taylor, H. (1950) The Biology of Starvation. Vol. 2. Minneapolis: University of Minnesota Press.

Lilienfeld, A. M., Pasamanik, B., Rogers, M. (1955) 'Relationship between pregnancy experience and the development of certain neuropsychiatric disorders in childhood.' *Amer. J. publ. Hlth*, **45**, 637.

McCance, R. A. (1960 'Severe undernutrition in growing and adult animals. I. Production and general effects.' *Brit. J. Nutr.*, **14**, 59.

———Widdowson, E. M., Verdon-Roe, C. M. (1938) 'A study of English diets by the individual method. III. Pregnant women at different economic levels.' *J. Hyg. (Lond.)*, **38**, 596.

McGanity, W. J., Cannon, R. O., Bridgeforth, E. B., Martin, M. P., Densen, P. M., Newbill, J. A., McClellan, G. S., Christie, A., Peterson, J. O., Darby, W. J. (1954) 'The Vanderbilt co-operative study of maternal and infant nutrition. VI. Relationship of obstetric performance to nutrition.' *Amer J. Obstet. Gynec.,* **67,** 501.

MacMahon, B., Sowa, J. M. (1961) 'Physical damage to the foetus.' *In* Causes of Mental Disorders: A Review of Epidemiological Knowledge, 1959. New York: Milbank Memorial Fund, p. 51.

Mayer, J. (1965) 'The nutritional status of American Negroes.' *Nutr, Rev.,* **23,** 161.

Mellanby, E. (1933; 'Nutrition and child bearing.' *Lancet,* ii, 1,131.

Orr, J. B. (1936) Food, Health and Income. London: Macmillan.

Pakter, J., Rosner, H. J., Jacobziner, H., Greenstein, F. (1961) 'Out-of-wedlock births in New York City. II. Medical aspects.' *Amer. J. publ. Hlth.* **51,** 846.

Pasmanik, B., Lilienfeld, A. M. (1955) 'Association of maternal and fetal factors with development of mental deeficiency. I. Abnormalities in the prenatal and perinatal periods.' *J. Amer. med. Ass.,* **159,** 155.

Platt, B. S., Heard, R. C., Stewart, R. J. (1964) 'Experimental protein-calorie deficiency.' *In* Munro, H. N., Allison, J. B. (Eds.) Mammalian Protein Metabolism. New York: Academic Press. p. 446.

Salber, E. J., Feinleib, M. (1966) 'Breast feeding in Boston.' *Pediatrics,* **37,** 299.

Shapiro, S., Jacobziner, H., Densen, P. M., Weiner, L. (1960) 'Further observations on prematurity and perinatal mortality in a general population and in the population of a prepaid group practice medical care plan.' *Amer. J. publ. Hlth,* **50,** 1,304.

Smith, C. A. (1947) 'Effects of maternal undernutrition upon the new born infant in Holland.' *J. Pediat.,* **30,** 229.

Stewart, W. H. (1957) 'The unmet needs of children.' *Pediatrics,* **39,** 157.

Thomson. A. M. (1959) 'Maternal stature and reproductive efficiency.' *Eugen. Rev.,* **51,** 157.

———(1959) 'Diet in pregnancy. III. Diet in relation to the course and outcome of pregnancy.' *Brit. J. Nutr.,* **13,** 509.

———(1963) 'Prematurity: socio-economic and nutritional factors.' *Bibl. paediat. (Basel),* **81,** 197.

———Billewicz, W. Z. (1963) 'Nutritional status, physique and reproductive efficiency.' *Proc. nutr. Soc.,* **22,** 55.

Toverud, G. (1950) The influence of nutrition on the course of pregnancy.' *Milbank mem Fd. Quart.,* **28,** 7.

U. S. Welfare Administration, Division of Research: (1966) Converging Social Trends—Emerging Social Problems. Welfare Administration Publication No. 6, Washington: U. S. Government.

Walker, J. (1954) 'Obstetrical complications, congenital malformations and

social strata.' *In* Mechanisms of Congenital Malformations. New York: Association for the Aid of Crippled Children. p. 20.

Warkany, J. (1944) 'Congenital malformations induced by maternal nutritional deficiency.' *J. Pediat.,* **25,** 476.

Wegman, M. E. (1966) 'Annual summary of vital statistics, 1965.' *Pediatrics,* **39,** 1,067.

Widdowson, E. M. (1966) 'Nutritional deprivation in psychobiological development: studies in animals.' *In* Proceedings of the Special Session, 4th Meeting of the PAHO Advisory Committee on Medical Research, June, 1965. Washington: World Health Organization.

3.2   Infant Development, Preschool IQ, and Social Class

Lee Willerman
Sarah H. Broman
National Institute of Neurological Diseases and Stroke
Miriam Fiedler
Children's Hospital Medical Center of Boston

Studies relating infant developmental status to later IQ have generally yielded two distinct classes of findings. Those on the negative side have shown essentially no correlation between infant scores and later IQ. (Bayley 1955). Those on the positive side such as Knobloch and Pasamanick (1967), and Erickson (1968) have found moderately high correlations between the earlier and later assessments. Explanations of the negative results have focused upon the lack of overlapping content between infant scales and IQ tests (Anderson 1939), or suggested that poor predictability is evidence for the prepotency of environmental influences in determining IQ (Hunt 1961).

It has been pointed out that the difficulty with some studies yielding negative results is that they were designed in such a way as to minimize the inclusion of abnormal infants or infants from the lower classes. This inter-

Reprinted from *Child Development,* 1970, *41,* No. 1, 69-77, by permission of the author and The Society for Research in Child Development, Inc. Copyright © 1970 by The Society for Research in Child Development, Inc.

pretation has received some support since studies with positive findings have sampled infants likely to have had a much higher incidence of abnormality and have included children from lower socioeconomic strata. Knobloch Rider, Harper and Pasamanick (1956), in obtaining positive findings, utilized a sample of infants, approximately half of which were premature. Erickson's (1968) positive results included infants subsequently found to be mentally defective (mean Cattell IQ = 52). Their findings support the generally held view that infant tests are more useful in predicting low IQs than in predicting average or above average IQs (Illingworth and Birch 1959).

There is some evidence suggesting that the long-term effects of a particular adverse experience during infancy are strongly dependent on socioeconomic status (SES). Werner, Simonian, Bierman, & French (1967) assessed the severity of complications around delivery for a large number of neonates. When these children were given the Cattell Infant Intelligence Scale at 20 months, it was found that social class produced only small differences in IQ if the delivery had been an uncomplicated one, but that social class was strongly related to IQ among deliveries with severe complications. Drillien (1964) found that among full-term infants, social class differences in developmental quotient between the higher and lower classes were approximately of the same magnitude at 4 years of age as they had been at 6 months of age. However, among premature infants, less than 3 pounds 9 ounces, differences in developmental quotient between the higher- and lower-class children were far greater at 4 years than they had been at 6 months. Though based on small numbers of subjects, a reanalysis of Knobloch and Pasamanick's (1967) results also suggests that the risk to the abnormal infant is disproportionately greater when the child comes from a less stimulating cultural milieu. Using the Gesell examination and the Chapin Living-Room Scale (1930) to estimate the degree of cultural stimulation provided in the home, they found that abnormal infants from homes given the highest cultural ratings averaged 5 points increase from the DQ (Developmental Quotient) in infancy to the IQ obtained during the school years. Those abnormal infants from the middle group dropped 28 points from their DQ to IQ, and those from the group given the lowest stimulation rating dropped 16.7 points between DQ and IQ. Among the "normal" cases the respective changes between DQ and IQ were +5, −4, and −11 points. In view of this suggestive differential effect of infant developmental status on IQ as a function of SES, it becomes particularly important to treat SES in a systematic fashion in predicting IQ from infant status. The present report includes a large sample of children widely varying in SES and infant development and relates infant scores to IQs at 4 years of age.

Procedure

Subjects

Subjects were 3037 white children born at Boston Lying-in Hospital (BLI). This hospital is a member of the Collaborative Perinatal Research Project sponsored by the National Institute of Neurological Diseases and Stroke. The project, still in progress, has included gravidae who delivered approximately 50,000 infants at 12 collaborating institutions throughout the country. The children are now being followed until 8 years of age with batteries of neurological, speech, language, hearing, and psychological tests. Only 12 percent of the subjects served by the Medical Center are Negro, and they are not included in the present report. Also excluded were the few children identified as having Down's syndrome. The subjects included in the present analysis are those who received the 8-month as well as the 4-year psychological examinations.

Method

At 8 months of age, the infants were routinely brought to either BLI or to the Children's Hospital Medical Center (CHMC) and administered the Collaborative Research Form of the Bayley Scales of Mental and Motor Development. At 4 years of age these children returned to CHMC and were given the abbreviated version of the Stanford-Binet Intelligence Scale, Form L-M.

The point scores on the infant Mental and Motor Scales were divided as nearly as possible into quartiles and the results are presented as a function of these quartiles. The point scores based on the number of items for which the infant received credit for each of the quartiles are as follows:

Mental Scale, Q4 = $\leq$ 78, Q3, = 79-81, Q2 = 82-84, Q1 = 85-106;
Motor Scale, Q4 = $\leq$ 29, Q3 = 30-33, Q2 = 34-36, Q1 = 37-43.

A socioeconomic index (SEI) devised especially for the project by Myrianthopoulos and French (1968) was employed to assess the SES of the subjects. This multidimensional index is based on the average of a set of rankings of paternal (or other head of household) education and occupation, and family income. The SEI, because it is multidimensional, does not permit a concrete description of the population at various SEI intervals. A graduate student, for example, would rank high on education and occupation, but rank low on income. Another parent with only a high school education, but high income, may have the same SEI, yet there may be substantial differences in their methods of child rearing. Be that as it may, the subjects were arbitrarily divided into three levels of SEI: high, middle, and low. As an oversimplified description of the modal low SEI parent (SEI

0–39), he might be characterized as an unskilled worker having completed no more than 2 years of high school, with a family income of less than $3,500 per year. The middle SEI (40–69) member would be a skilled worker with a high school education and a family income of less than $5,000 per year. The high SEI (70–98) member would have completed at least 1 year of college, be employed as a clerical worker, proprietor or manager, and have a family income of at least $6,000 a year. . . .

Mean Bayley Mental Test scores do not differ significantly between the SEI levels. The mean low SEI Mental Test score = 80.80, middle = 81.23, and high = 81.00.

Shown in figure 1 are the mean Binet IQs by Bayley Mental quartiles for each SEI level. Within each of the SEI levels it can be seen that infants from the lowest quartile (Q) are significantly and consistently lower in IQ at 4 years of age.

As might be expected, the largest main effect is related to SEI, and it is interesting to note that in the low SEI level not even the 4-year olds who were most advanced as infants (Q_1) obtain mean IQs as high as 4-year olds from the high SEI level who were retarded (Q_4) as infants.

Figure 1
Mean 4-Year IQ As a Function of Bayley Mental Quartile at 8 Months and SC

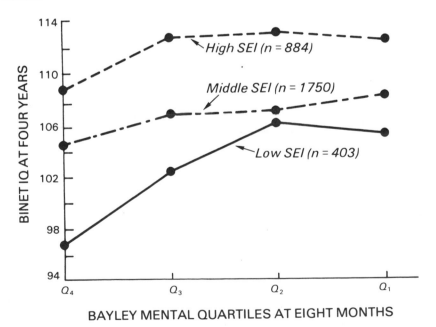

Mean Bayley Motor scores show a slight, but statistically significant relatiinship to SEI. he mean Motor score of the low SEI = 32.46 middle SEI = 32.90, and high SEI = 33.30. The low SEIs differ significantly from both the middle and high SEIs, and the mean difference between the middle and high SEIs is of borderline statistical significance (t low vs. middle = 2.41, $p < .05$, $df = 2151$; t low vs. high = 3.51, $p < .001$, $df = 704$; t middle vs. high = 1.84, $p < .10$, $df = 2632$).

Figure 2 gives mean Binet IQ by Bayley Motor quartiles and SEI. Within each SEI level, infants from the lowest Motor quartile obtain the lowest mean IQs. This figure also shows that the greatest differences in mean IQ between the quartilcs are found among those with the lowest SEI. The maximum difference in IQ within the low SEIs is between those from Q_4 and Q_2, where a mean difference of 10 IQ points exists. Among the middlc SEIs the maximum difference is less, only 4.5 IQ points between Q_4 and Q_1. The maximum IQ difference among the high SEIs is about 6 IQ points, between Q_4 and Q_1. This finding suggests greater vulnerability of poorly developed infants to the adverse effects of environment.

A clearer picture emerges of the increased susceptibility of poorly developed infants to their environment when Mental and Motor scores are

Figure 2

Mean 4-Year IQ As a Function of Bayley Motor Quartile at 8 Months and SC

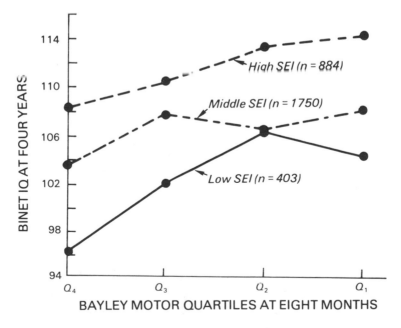

combined and only those infants who performed in the lowest quartiles on both Mental and Motor tests are examined. This small group, only 11.6 percent of the total number of subjects, contains 58 percent of those children with IQ $\leq$ 79 at 4 years. These infants might be said to display no islands of strength. As a contrast group, those infants who are in the highest quartiles on both Mental and Motor tests are presented. These advanced infants might be said to display no weaknesses.

Figure 3 presents the percentages of these retarded and advanced infants who obtained IQs $\leq$ 79 at 4 years as a function of SEI level. Among advanced infants the frequency of occurrence of IQ $\leq$ 79 is unrelated to SEI. However, among infants retarded at 8 months, SEI level is related to subsequent low IQ. Retarded infants were seven times more likely to obtain IQs $\leq$ 79 if they came from the lowest SEI than if they came from the highest SEI χ^2_1 df = 6.34, p < .02 (corrected for continuity).

Figure 3
Percentage of Children IQ $\leq$ 79 at 4 Years as a Function of Quartile Category on Mental and Motor Tests at 8 Months and SC
(N in parentheses)

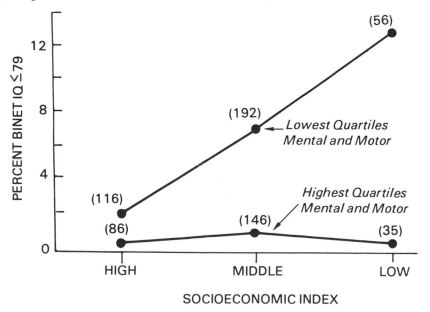

Discussion

The major finding of the present study is that infant developmental status interacts with SES in the incidence of low 4-year IQ. Retarded infant development augurs disproportionately poorer intellectual performance in

the context of low SES than in the context of higher SES, and it appears that retarded low SES infants are more vulnerable to the adverse effects of their environment. Conversely, it seems that advanced infant development can minimize the occurrence of low IQ among low SES individuals. Just how this occurs is a subject for further investigation.

There is no question that the SEI has many weaknesses and that it is not accounting for what influences accelerated infant development. Our data, as well as Bayley and Schaefer's (1964) indicate a very poor relation between social class and test performance in infancy. During the interval between 1 and 2 years, Caldwell and Richmond (1967) have reported moderate correlations between mother's affective and achievement behavior and the child's Cattell IQ. The genic or environmental influences which lead to accelerated early infant maturational status remain a mystery.

Among high SES groups the present results suggest that the infant test is a poorer predictor of later intellectual status. Infant developmental status bore little relation to 4-year IQ. The process by which poorly developed infants from high SES environments overcome their deficits is unclear. However, Drillien (1964) has suggested that even these high SES children will display deficits if they are compared to their siblings. The fact that high SES can mask presumptive constitutional deficits points to the necessity of taking SES into account in gauging the effects of infant experience such as perinatal stress.

These results also suggest that poverty, which produces a higher incidence of perinatal morbidity as well as mortality (Yudkin & Yudkin, 1968) will amplify the IQ deficit in poorly developed infants. The next step in the present research program is to study the fate of neurologically impaired infants as a function of social class.

References

Anderson, J. E. The limitations of infant and preschool tests in the measurement of intelligence. *Journal of Psychology,* 1939, **8,** 351–379.

Bayley, N. On the growth of intelligence. *American Psychologist,* 1955, **10,** 805–818.

Bayley, N. COLR Research form of the Bayley scales of mental and motor development. *Perinatal Research Branch, National Institute of Neurological Diseases and Stroke* (1958).

Bayley, N. Comparisons of mental and motor test scores for ages 1–15 months, by sex, birth order, race, geographical location, and education of parents. *Child Development,* 1965, **36,** 379–411.

Bayley, N., & Schaefer, E. S. Correlations of maternal and child behaviors with the development of mental abilities. Data from the Berkeley Growth Study. *Monographs of the Society for Research in Child Development,* 1964, **29** (6, Serial No. 97).

Caldwell, B., & Richmond, J. B. Social class level and stimulation potential of the home. In J. Hellmuth (Ed.), *Exceptional infant*. Seattle: Special Child Publications, 1967. Pp. 453–466.

Chapin, F. S. *Scale for rating living room equipment*. Minneapolis: Institute of Child Welfare, 1930.

Drillien, C. M. *The growth and development of the prematurely born infant*. Baltimore: Williams & Wilkins, 1964.

Erickson, M. T. The predictive validity of the Cattell Infant Intelligence Scale for young mentally retarded children. *American Journal of Mental Deficiency*, 1968, **72**, 728–733.

Hunt, J. McV. *Intelligence and experience*. New York: Ronald, 1961.

Illingworth, R. S., & Birch, L. B. The diagnosis of mental retardation in infancy: a follow-up study. *Archives of Diseases in Childhood*, 1959, **34**, 269–273.

Knobloch, H., & Pasamanick, B. Prediction from the assessment of neuromotor and intellectual status in infancy. In J. Zubin and G. A. Jervis (Eds.), *Psychopathology of mental development*. New York: Grune & Stratton, 1967. Pp. 387–400.

Knobloch, H.; Rider, R.; Harper, P.; & Pasamanick, B. Neuropsychiatric sequelae of prematurity. *Journal of the American Medical Association*, 1956, **161**, 581–585.

Myrianthopoulos, N. C., & French, K. S. An application of the U. S. Bureau of the Census socioeconomic index to a large diversified population. *Social Science and Medicine*, 1968, **2**, 283–299.

Werner, E.; Simonian, K.; Bierman, J. M.; French, F. E. Cumulative effect of perinatal complications and deprived environment on physical, intellectual, and social development of preschool children. *Pediatrics*, 1967, **39**, 480–505.

Yudkin, S., & Yudkin, G. Poverty and child development. *Developmental Medicine and Child Neurology*, 1968, **10**, 569–579.

3.3 Visual Alertness as Related to Soothing in Neonates: Implications for Maternal Stimulation and Early Deprivation

Anneliese F. Korner
Rose Grobstein
Stanford University School of Medicine

Observations incidental to a study of behavior genetics in neonates (Korner, 1964) suggest that when babies cry and are picked up to the shoulder, they not only stop crying, but they frequently become visually alert, and they scan the environment. We were struck by several implications of this observation: If generally true, this type of soothing would induce a state which is otherwise quite rare in the neonate and which is considered by some to be the optimal state for the infant's earliers learning. According to P. H. Wolff's (1965) observations, this state of alertness occurs spontaneously but from 8 to 16 per cent of the time in the first postnatal week, and it only very gradually increases over subsequent weeks. The infant thus spends only a very minor part of his day in alertness. Yet, in terms of his locomotor helplessness, visual prehension is one of the few avenues at his disposal to make contact and to get acquainted with the environment. If regularly soothing of this type induces a state of alertness, it follows that a baby picked up for crying will have earlier and many more opportunities to scan the environment than an infant left crying in his crib.

In a recent symposium entitled "The Crucial Early Influence: Mother Love or Environmental Stimulation" Frantz (1966), referring to his findings that infants discriminate from birth among visual stimuli, concluded that perceptual experiences play a crucial role in early development. In fact, he could distinguish babies reared at home from institutional infants through their visual responses by the second month of life. While Frantz stressed the importance of perceptual experiences through environmental stimulation, he also stated that the effects of early stimulation would be better understood "if one could pin down the specific kinds of sensory stimulation and perceptual experience often provided optimally by a loving mother." Our observation that babies, when picked up for crying, frequently become visually alert may thus capture one important pathway by which maternal ministrations may inadvertently provide visual experiences.

In this study we set out to investigate how frequently soothing of the type described elicited visual alertness. With the design used to study this

Reprinted from *Child Development,* 1966 *37,* No. 4, 867-876, by permission of author and The Society for Research in Child Development, Inc. Copyright © 1966 by The Society for Research in Child Development, Inc.

problem, it was possible to explore an additional hypothesis. Bell (1963) suggested that infants born to primiparous mothers may, for a number of reasons, respond differently to tactile stimulation than infants of multiparous mothers. We explored the relation between parity and visual alertness in response to soothing by including both types of infants.

Sample

The sample consisted of 12 newborn, breastfed baby girls; six were born to primiparous mothers and six to multiparae. Boys were excluded because it was quite apparent that the comfort derived from being picked up and put to the shoulder was offset by the discomfort of being held close within hours of a circumcision. The babies ranged from 45-79 hours in age; the average was 55 hours old. All were Caucasian. Their birth weights ranged from 6 pounds 8 ounces to 8 pounds 13 ounces. They all had normal vaginal deliveries, received Apgar scores of 8 and above at birth, and they were found to be healthy newborn infants on physical examination.

Method

The infants were tested in a treatment room adjoining the nursery. Temperature and illumination approximated conditions in the nursery. The infants were tested individually after being brought to the treatment room in their own bassinets. They were dressed in shirts and diapers. To facilitate pickups, the infants were placed on the mattress underneath the plastic bassinet usually used for diapering and dressing infants. Since we were interested in soothing crying babies, they were all tested within 1½ hours before a feeding. Occasionally, we had to rouse a sleepy baby by moving her or by flicking her foot. The tests described below were initiated only when the baby was crying. Minimum time between experiments was 1 minute. Since we were interested in comparing each infant with her own tendencies in the various experimental positions, it was of little consequence whether some infants cried harder than others at any given trial. Also, enough trials were given to each infant to randomize the degree of agitation over all the trials.

Diapers were changed before the experiments were started irrespective of need. All infants were tested in four positions:

1. Six trials on the left shoulder.
2. Six trials on the right shoulder.
3. Six trials sitting up.
4. Six control trials in which the baby lay on her back without intervention by the observers.

The "situp" experiments were introduced because it was noted that handling and the upright position alone frequently induced alertness. It was noted, for example, that many babies are alert when they are carried out to their mothers for feeding. In addition to the handling and the upright position, the experience of being put to the shoulder involves warmth, containment, the sense of smell, and the opportunity to establish mouth contract with the shoulder. Differential effects of the two positions could thus be studied.

To insure comparability of handling, the same person did all the interventions. When picked up, the baby's head was supported, and her hands were kept out of reach of her mouth. The same was done in sitting up a baby. Trials in the various positions were done at random.

For 30 seconds following an intervention, alert and scanning behavior was recorded. During the control experiments, the same was done for 30 seconds without an intervention. When the infant opened her eyes during the 30-second experimental period, the trial was scored a "yes." In each instance, the same was done for scanning behavior. Babies varied a great deal in the degree of alertness. Some drowsily opened their eyes; others actively looked around, lifting the head and exploring the experimenter. Some had brief, others had sustained, periods of alertness. Since visual pursuit can be elicited even in drowsy babies (see Wolff, in press), and since it is difficult to equate several brief periods of alertness with one sustained period, the degree and the duration of alertness were not considered in the ratings. "Yes" was scored when the infant opened her eyes and when she scanned the environment at any one time during the 30 seconds of observations. In addition to these observations, the number of spontaneous alert and scanning episodes between experiments was noted for 10 of the 12 subjects.

Observer Reliabilities

Reliabilities between two observers were calculated on the basis of dividing the number of agreements by the combined number of agreements and disagreements. Percentages of agreement were as follows:

1. Opening eyes during "situps" and during controls: 96 per cent.
2. Opening eyes between experiments: 98 per cent.
3. Scanning during "situps" and during controls: 97 per cent.
4. Scanning episodes between experiments: 95 per cent.

Reliability ratings for opening of eyes and scanning during "pickups" would have required a third observer. Since there was very little disagreement between what constituted alerting and scanning behavior during "sit-

ups" and controls and between experiments (the percentages of agreement ranging from 95 to 98), it was felt to be unnecessary to introduce a third observer to rate alert and scanning behavior during "pickups."

Results

Incidence of Alerting in Response to Soothing

Our data confirmed the observation that, when crying infants were put to the shoulder, they not only stopped crying, but each of them also opened her eyes and alerted in the large majority of trials.

An analysis of variance was performed. The difference between "primips"[1] and "multips" was not found to be significant. By contrast, the difference of reactions to the various positions was found to be significant at the 1 per cent level.

The results suggest that handling and the upright position alone did not result in the infant's opening her eyes significantly more often than when no intervention was made.

Incidence of Scanning in Response to Soothing

Since the degree of alertness varied when an infant opened her eyes, active scanning probably was a better measure for testing the effect of soothing on visual alertness. Even with this more stringent criterion for alertness, each baby in this sample alerted and scanned when put to the shoulder, and most did in the majority of the trials.

An analysis of variance was performed. Even though, in absolute terms, the "primips" scanned more, the difference was not statistically significant. By contrast, the difference of reactions to the various positions was again significant at the 1 per cent level.

Spontaneous Alerting and Scanning between Experiments

Spontaneous alerting and scanning between experiments was recorded only in 10 out of 12 cases. The incidence among babies of these episodes varied greatly. The average number of times the "primips" opened their eyes between experiments was 7.8; for "multips," the average was only 3.2. The "primips" scanned on the average of 6.5 times, the "multips" only 3 times. These differences between "primips" and "multips" did not reach significance, probably because of the small number of observations. It is of interest, however, that there is a consistent trend among the three types of observations: In each instance, the "primips" alerted and scanned more frequently than the "multips." This suggests that differences may exist in arousal levels between "primips" and "multips." Our data on crying, not reported here, which shows highly significant differences between "multips" and "primips," would support this hypothesis.

Individual Differences

There were marked differences among babies in their tendency to alert and scan. For example, P4, P5, and M5, tended to alert and scan readily in all positions. By contrast, M3 and P6 had difficulty with both, even when put to the shoulder. There also were marked differences in the capacity to sustain alertness. In some babies these episodes were fleeting; in others they were maintained for long periods of time.

There were particularly marked differences among the infants in their proneness to alert and to scan between experiments. Some babies never did alert and scan, others did very rarely, and a few did quite frequently (range from 0-15 instances, with a mean of 5.5). Infants M3 and P6, who had difficulty alerting when put to the shoulder, also showed very few instances of alerting and scanning between experiments (3 and 0 instances, respectively). By contrast, those infants who alerted and scanned most between experiments were not necessarily the same babies who had the highest frequency of these behaviors when picked up. Very probably, the amount of handling during the entire experimental session affected babies differently, arousing some, not affecting others. One may infer from this that there may be individual differences among babies in the ease with which the state of arousal is changed through manipulation.

Discussion

Visual alertness in the neonate has become the concern of many studies (e.g., Fantz, 1958; 1966; Ling, 1942; White, 1963; Wolff, 1965; 1966; Wolff & White, 1965). This concern on the part of some investigators stems from the observation that visual alertness is not as reflex as most neonatal behavior and, to a large extent, qualitatively resembles the later capacity of attentiveness. In terms of psychoanalytic theory, visual alertness is probably the clearest example of a primary autonomous ego function observable in the newborn. In view of the neonate's locomotor helplessness, visual prehension is one of the infant's few avenues for learning and for getting acquainted with the environment.

Our experiments show that this state of visual alertness, so important for learning, can readily be induced by picking up a crying newborn and putting him to the shoulder. It was possible to do this without difficulty even at a time when, according to Wolff's (1965) findings, the newborn is least likely to be alert, namely, when he is hungry. Wolff's observations demonstrated that during the first week of life his subjects spent, on the average, only 11 per cent of the time in the state of alert inactivity and that 86.4 per cent of this 11 per cent occurred within the first hour after a feeding.

One can only speculate about the causes of the association between this kind of soothing and visual alertness. Neurophysiologically, what may occur is that the soothing action of this intervention lowers the infant's state of

arousal, with the result that the infant goes from crying into the next lower state on the continuum of states and arousal.[2] Waking activity, the next lower state on this continuum, was prevented by the motor restraint imposed by being held to the shoulder. This restraint may have lowered the infant's state of arousal one step further, resulting in the state of alert inactivity. In fact, by preventing the distracting effects of the infant's motor activity, the physical restraint may have enhanced the likelihood of alert behavior. Wolff and White (1965) found this relation to hold: They increased the infants' capacity for attentive behavior by inhibiting motor activity through the use of a pacifier.

In psychologoical terms, the association of soothing and visual alertness may involve the prototype of a reaction which may hold true throughout life: By reducing the intensity of internal needs, the organism can turn outward and attend the external world. Descriptively, this corresponds well with the sequence of events as we observed them.

Our data did not suggest that handling or the upright position alone induced a state of alertness. This was true because, in most cases, handling alone did not lower the infant's state of arousal sufficiently to reduce crying to the point of alertness. The observation that many infants are quietly alert when brought to a feeding suggests that handling and the upright position are more successful in inducing alertness in noncrying or sleepy infants. In those states of arousal, the stimulation of touch, motion, and positional change are rousing rather than soothing. In an intense form, labor and birth which entail extreme stimulation of this type may have arousing effects with similar results. Brazelton (1961) observed that, for a few hours after delivery and before going into a relative state of disorganization, all of his subjects were alert and responsive. They fixed and followed a red ring visually for several minutes at a time. They also attended and often visually followed auditory stimuli. Brazeltons' observations of the altertness of the newly delivered baby are easily confirmed by casual observation. All one has to do is to watch babies as they are admitted to the newborn nursery from the delivery room: Most of them have their eyes wide open and are highly alert.

Of relevance to the alertness-producing effects of both soothing and handling are the numerous studies dealing with the effects of handling and early stimulation on both animals and infants. For the most part, these studies show the importance of early stimulation for the growth and development of the young organism. The specific factors which account for the more favorable development of the "handled" group are usually not spelled out. Levine (1962), noting profound psychophysiological effects of infantile stimulation in the rat, concluded that the sensory routes and mechanisms underlying these effects are not known. He suspects that proprioceptive and kinesthetic stimulation may indicate the sensory routs of effective stimulation. Casler (1961) and Yarrow (1961), in reviews of maternal deprivation studies, concluded that early tactile stimulation appears

necessary for normal human development. Our own observations suggest that tactile stimulation may activate visual behavior. Activation of the visual modality through tactile stimulation may thus be one of the pathways through which early stimulation takes effect. We find support of this hypothesis in White and Castle's (1964) study which demonstrated that institution-reared infants given small amounts of extra handling during their first weeks of life later showed significantly more visual interest in their environment than nonhandled controls.

In the earliest days of life, infant care, for the most part, invites soothing rather than rousing interventions. It is the handling involved in soothing rather than rousing which may make the difference in the neonates' earliest opportunities for visual experiences. Infants in institutions, while usually given adequate physical care, generally are not picked up and soothed when they cry. This may be partly responsible for their earliest deficit.

Mothers of home-reared infants differ, of course, in their readiness to soothe their crying newborn. Our observations suggest that picked-up infants will have many more opportunities to get acquainted with the environment than babies left crying in their cribs. In particular, they will have many more occasions to explore their mothers. Their visual explorations will occur when comforted. This may lower their stimulus barrier under conditions which minimize the danger of being overwhelmed.

Frantz's (1966) findings suggest that visual and perceptual experiences during the neonatal period have lasting developmental effects. With this in mind, our observations raise a host of developmental questions. For example, do babies who are carried around a great deal learn to rely more heavily on the visual modality in their exploration of the environment than babies who do not have this experience as much? How does the development of the infant of another culture who is constantly carried around by his mother differ in this respect? With the added opportunities of exploring the mother, are their differences in time and depth in the infant-mother bond formation and in the development of differentiating self from nonself? Also, are there differences in the onset and strength of stranger and separation anxiety? As Benjamin (1959) has shown, babies who rely heavily on the visual modality will experience stranger and separation anxiety earlier and more severely.

Our observations have not only experiential implications. We also found organismic differences among the infants. Babies differed greatly in their capacity for alert behavior. This finding is confirmed by our larger study (Korner, 1964) involving a bigger sample of neonates and much longer observations. It is reasonable to believe that varying opportunities for visual experiences will affect babies differently depending on their own disposition. Thus an infant with high sensory thresholds may demonstrate the effects of maternal neglect or sensory deprivation more acutely than the infant more capable of providing visual experiences for himself.

Notes

[1] The terms "primips" and "multips" will be used for convenience henceforth to refer to the offspring of primiparous and multiparous mothers, respectively.

[2] For a definition of states of arousal, see Wolff (1959).

References

Bell, R. Q. Some factors to be controlled in studies of the behavior of newborns. *Biol. Neonat.,* 1963, 5, 200-214.

Benjamin, J. D. Prediction and psychopathological theory. In Lucie Jessner & Eleanor Pavenstedt (Eds.), *Dynamic psychopathology in childhood.* New York: Grune & Stratton, 1959, Pp. 6-77.

Brazelton, T. B. Psychophysiologic reactions in the neonate: II. Effect of maternal medication on the neonate and his behavior. *J. Pediat.,* 1961, 58, No. 4, 513-518.

Casler, L. Maternal deprivation: a critical review of the literature. *Monogr. Soc. Res. Child Develpm.,* 1961, 26, No. 2 (Serial No. 80).

Fantz, R. L. Pattern vision in young infants. *Psychol. Rec.,* 1958, 8, 43-47.

Fantz, R. L. The crucial early influence: mother love or environmental stimulation? *Amer. J. Orthopsychiat.,* 1966, 36, No. 2, 330-331. (Abstract)

Korner, Anneliese F. Some hypotheses regarding the significance of individual differences at birth for later development. *The psychoanalytic study of the child.* Vol. 19. New York: International Universities Pr., 1964. Pp. 58-72.

Levine, S. Psychophysiological effects of infantile stimulation. In E. Bliss (Ed.), *Roots of behavior.* New York: Paul Hoeber, 1962, Pp. 246-253.

Ling, Bing-Chung. A genetic study of sustained visual fixation and associated behavior in the human infant from birth to six months: I. *J. genet. Psychol.,* 1942, 61, 227-277.

White, B. L. The development of perception during the first six months of life. Paper read at Amer. Ass. of Advancement of Science, December 30, 1963.

White, B. L., & Castle, P. W. Visual exploratory behavior following postnatal handling of human infants. *Percept. mot. Skills,* 1964, 18, 497-502.

Wolff, P. H. Observations of newborn infants. *Psychosom. Med.,* 1959, 21, 110-118.

Wolff, P. H. The development of attention in young infants. *Ann. N. Y. Acad. Sci.,* 1965, 118, 815-830.

Wolff, P. H. The causes, controls and organization of behavior in the newborn. *Psychological issues.* New York: International Universities Pr., 1966.

Wolff, P. H., C White, B. L. Visual pursuit and attention in young infants. *J. Amer. Acad. Child Psychiat.,* 1965, 4, No. 3, 473-484.

Yarrow, L. J. Maternal deprivation: toward an empirical and conceptual re-evaluation. *Psychol. Bull.,* 1961, 58, 459-590.

3.4 Sex, Age, and State as Determinants of Mother-Infant Interaction

Howard A. Moss
National Institute of Mental Health

A major reason for conducting research on human infants is derived from the popular assumption that adult behavior, to a considerable degree, is influenced by early experience. A corollary of this assumption is that if we can precisely conceptualize and measure significant aspects of infant experience and behavior we will be able to predict more sensitively and better understand adult functioning. The basis for this conviction concerning the enduring effects of early experience varies considerably according to the developmental model that is employed. Yet there remains considerable consensus as to the long term and pervasive influence of the infant's experience.

Bloom (1964) contends that characteristics become increasingly resistant to change as the mature status of the characteristic is achieved and that environmental effects are most influential during periods of most rapid growth. This is essentially a refinement of the critical period hypothesis which argues in favor of the enduring and irreversible effects of many infant experiences. Certainly the studies on imprinting and the effects of controlled sensory input are impressive in this respect (Hess, 1959; White and Held, 1963). Learning theory also lends itself to support the potency of early experience. Since the occurrence of variable interval and variable ratio reinforcement schedules are highly probable in infancy (as they are in many other situations), the learnings associated with these schedules will be highly resistant to extinction. Also, the pre-verbal learning that characterizes infancy should be more difficult to extinguish since these responses are less available to linguistic control which later serves to mediate and regulate many important stimulus-response and reinforcement relationships. Psycho-

Reprinted from the *Merrill-Palmer Quarterly,* 1967, *13,* No. 1, 19-36, by permission of the author and the Merrill-Palmer Institute.

analytic theory and behavioristic psychology probably have been the most influential forces in emphasizing the long-range consequences of infant experience. These theories, as well as others, stress the importance of the mother-infant relationship. In light of the widespread acceptance of the importance of early development, it is paradoxical that there is such a dearth of direct observational data concerning the functioning of infants, in their natural environment, and in relation to their primary caretakers.

Observational studies of the infant are necessary in order to test existing theoretical propositions and to generate new propositions based on empirical evidence. In addition, the infant is an ideally suitable subject for investigating many aspects of behavior because of the relatively simple and inchoate status of the human organism at this early stage in life. Such phenomena is temperament, reactions to stimulation, efficacy of different learning contingencies, perceptual functioning, and social attachment can be investigated while they are still in rudimentary form and not yet entwined in the immensely complex behavioral configurations that progressively emerge.

The research to be reported in this paper involves descriptive-normative data of maternal and infant behaviors in the naturalistic setting of the home. These data are viewed in terms of how the infant's experience structures potential learning patterns. Although the learning process itself is of primary eventual importance, it is necessary initially to identify the organizational factors, in situ, that structure learning opportunities and shape response systems.

A sample of 30 first-born children and their mothers were studied by means of direct observations over the first 3 months of life. Two periods were studied during this 3-month interval. Period one included a cluster of three observations made at weekly intervals during the first month of life in order to evaluate the initial adaptation of mother and infant to one another. Period two consisted of another cluster of three observations, made around 3 months of age when relatively stable patterns of behavior were likely to have been established. Each cluster included two 3-hour observations and one 8-hour observation. The 3-hour observations were made with the use of a keyboard that operates in conjunction with a 20-channel Esterline-Angus Event Recorder. Each of 30 keys represents a maternal or infant behavior, and when a key is depressed it activates one or a combination of pens on the recorder, leaving a trace that shows the total duration of the observed behavior. This technique allows for a continuous record showing the total time and the sequence of behavior. For the 8-hour observation the same behaviors were studied but with the use of a modified time-sampling technique. The time-sampled units were one minute in length and the observer, using a stenciled form, placed a number opposite the appropriate behaviors to indicate their respective order of occurrence. Since each variable can be coded only once for each observational unit, a score of 480

is the maximum that can be received. The data to be presented in this paper are limited to the two 8-hour observations. The data obtained with the use of the keyboard will be dealt with elsewhere in terms of the sequencing of events.

The mothers who participated in these observations were told that this was a normative study of infant functioning under natural living conditions. It was stressed that they proceed with their normal routines and care of the infant as they would if the observer were not present. This structure was presented to the mothers during a brief introductory visit prior to the first observation. In addition, in order to reduce the mother's self-consciousness and facilitate her behaving in relatively typical fashion, the observer emphasized that it was the infant who was being studied and that her actions would be noted only in relation to what was happening to the infant. This approach seemed to be effective, since a number of mothers commented after the observations were completed that they were relieved that they were not the ones being studied. The extensiveness of the observations and the frequent use of informal conversation between the observer and mother seemed to contribute further to the naturalness of her behavior.

The observational variables, mean scores and sample sizes are presented in Table 1. These data are presented separately for the 3-week and the 3-month observations. The inter-rater reliabilities for these variables range from .74 to 1.00 with a median reliability of .97. Much of the data in this paper are presented for males and females separately, since by describing and comparing these two groups we are able to work from an established context that helps to clarify the theoretical meaning of the results. Also, the importance of sex differences is heavily emphasized in contemporary developmental theory and it is felt that infant data concerning these differences would provide a worthwhile addition to the literature that already exists on this matter for older subjects.

The variables selected for study are those which would seem to influence or reflect aspects of maternal contact. An additional, but related consideration in the selection of variables was that they have an apparent bearing on the organization of the infant's experience. Peter Wolff (1959), Janet Brown (1964), and Sibylle Escalona (1962) have described qualitative variations in infant state or activity level and others have shown that the response patterns of the infant are highly influenced by the state he is in (Bridger, 1965). Moreover, Levy (1958) has demonstrated that maternal behavior varies as a function of the state or activity level of the infant. Consequently, we have given particular attention to the variables concerning state (cry, fuss, awake active, awake passive, and sleep) because of the extent to which these behaviors seem to shape the infant's experience. Most of the variables listed in Table 1 are quite descriptive of what was observed. Those which might not be as clear are as follows: *attends infant*—denotes standing close or leaning over infant, usually while in the process of

Table 1
Mean Frequency of Maternal and Infant Behavior
at 3 Weeks and 3 Months

Behavior	3-week observation		3-month observation[a]	
	Males[b] (N = 14)	Females (N = 15)	Males[b] (N = 13)	Females (N = 12)
Maternal variables				
Holds infant close	121.4	99.2	77.4	58.6
Holds infant distant	32.2	18.3	26.7	27.2
Total holds	131.3	105.5	86.9	73.4
Attends infant	61.7	44.2	93.0	81.8
Maternal contact (holds and attends)	171.1	134.5	158.8	133.8
Feeds infant	60.8	60.7	46.6	41.4
Stimulates feeding	10.1	14.0	1.6	3.6
Burps infant	39.0	25.9	20.9	15.3
Affectionate contact	19.9	15.9	32.8	22.7
Rocks infant	35.1	20.7	20.0	23.9
Stresses musculature	11.7	3.3	25.8	16.6
Stimulates/arouses infant	23.1	10.6	38.9	26.1
Imitates infant	1.9	2.9	5.3	7.6
Looks at infant	182.8	148.1	179.5	161.9
Talks to infant	104.1	82.2	117.5	116.1
Smiles at infant	23.2	18.6	45.9	46.4
Infant variables				
Cry	43.6	30.2	28.5	16.9
Fuss	65.7	44.0	59.0	36.0
Irritable (cry and fuss)	78.7	56.8	67.3	42.9
Awake active	79.6	55.1	115.8	85.6
Awake passive	190.0	138.6	257.8	241.1
Drowsy	74.3	74.7	27.8	11.1
Sleep	261.7	322.1	194.3	235.6
Supine	133.7	59.3	152.7	134.8
Eyes on mother	72.3	49.0	91.0	90.6
Vocalizes	152.3	179.3	207.2	207.4
Infant smiles	11.1	11.7	32.1	35.3
Mouths	36.8	30.6	61.2	116.2

[a]Four of the subjects were unable to participate in the 3-month observation. Two moved out of the area, one mother became seriously ill, and another mother chose not to participate in all the observations.

[b]One subject who had had an extremely difficult delivery was omitted from the descriptive data but is included in the findings concerning mother-infant interaction.

caretaking activities; *stimulates feeding*—stroking the infant's cheek and manipulating the nipple so as to induce sucking responses; *affectionate contact*—kissing and caressing infant; *stresses musculature*—holding the infant in either a sitting or standing position so that he is required to support his own weight; *stimulates/arouses infant*—mother provides tactile and visual stimulation for the infant or attempts to arouse him to a higher activity level; and *imitates infant*—mother repeats a behavior, usually a vocalization, immediately after it is observed in the infant.

The sex differences and shifts in behavior from 3 weeks to 3 months are in many instances pronounced. For example, at 3 weeks of age mothers held male infants about 27 minutes more per 8 hours than they held females, and at 3 months males were held 14 minutes longer. By the time they were 3 months of age there was a decrease of over 30% for both sexes in the total time they were held by their mothers. Sleep time also showed marked sex differences and changes over time. For the earlier observations females slept about an hour longer than males, and this difference tended to be maintained by 3 months with the female infants sleeping about 41 minutes longer. Again, there was a substantial reduction with age in this behavior for both sexes; a decrease of 67 and 86 minutes in sleep time for males and females, respectively. What is particularly striking is the variability for these infant and maternal variables. The range for sleep time is 137-391 minutes at 3 weeks and 120-344 minutes at 3 months, and the range for mother holding is 38-218 minutes at 3 weeks and 26-168 minutes for the 3-month observation. The extent of the individual differences reflected by these ranges seem to have important implications. For instance, if an infant spends more time at a higher level of consciousness this should increase his experience and contact with the mother, and through greater learning opportunities, facilitate the perceptual discriminations he makes, and affect the quality of his cognitive organization. The finding that some of the infants in our sample slept a little over 2 hours, or about 25% of the observation time and others around 6 hours or 75% of the time, is a fact that has implications for important developmental processes. The sum crying and fussing, what we term irritability level of the infant, is another potentially important variable. The range of scores for this behavior was from 5-136 minutes at 3 weeks and 7-98 at 3 months. The fact that infants are capable through their behavior of shaping maternal treatment is a point that has gained increasing recognition. The cry is a signal for the mother to respond and variation among infants in this behavior could lead to differential experiences with the mother.

Table 2 presents *t* values showing changes in the maternal and infant behaviors from the 3-week to the 3-month observation. In this case, the data for the males and females are combined since the trends, in most instances, are the same for both sexes. It is not surprising that there are a number of marked shifts in behavior from 3 weeks to 3 months, since the early months

Table 2
Changes in Behavior Between 3 Weeks and 3 Months (N = 26)

Maternal variables	t-values	Infant variables	t-values
Higher at 3 weeks:		*Higher at 3 weeks:*	
Holds infant close	4.43****	Cry	2.84***
Holds infant distant	.56	Fuss	1.33
Total holds	4.00****	Irritable (cry and fuss)	1.73*
Maternal contact		Drowsy	9.02****
(holds and attends)	.74	Sleep	4.51****
Feeds infant	3.49***		
Stimulates feeding	3.42***		
Burps infant	3.28***		
Rocks infant	1.08		
Higher at 3 months:		*Higher at 3 months:*	
Attends infant	5.15****	Awake active	2.47**
Affectionate contact	2.50**	Awake passive	5.22****
Stresses musculature	3.42***	Supine	1.75*
Stimulates/arouses infant	2.63**	Eyes on mother	3.21***
Imitates infant	4.26****	Vocalizes	3.56***
Looks at infant	.38	Infant smiles	6.84****
Talks to infant	2.67**	Mouths	3.69***
Smiles at infant	4.79****		

$8*p < .10$ $**p < .05$ $*** < .01$ $****p < .001$

of life are characterized by enormous growth and change. The maternal variables that show the greatest decrement are those involving feeding behaviors and close physical contact. It is of interest that the decrease in close contact is paralleled by an equally pronounced increase in attending behavior, so that the net amount of maternal contact remains similar for the 3-week and 3-month observations. The main difference was that the mothers, for the later observation, tended to hold their infants less but spent considerably more time near them, in what usually was a vis-à-vis posture, while interacting and ministering to their needs. Along with this shift, the mothers showed a marked increase in affectionate behavior toward the older infant, positioned him more so that he was required to make active use of his muscles, presented him with a greater amount of stimulation and finally, she exhibited more social behavior (imitated, smiled, and talked) toward the older child.

The changes in maternal behavior from 3 weeks to 3 months probably are largely a function of the maturation of various characteristics of the infant. However, the increased confidence of the mother, her greater familiarity with her infant, and her developing attachment toward him will also

account for some of the changes that occurred over this period of time. By 3 months of age the infant is crying less and awake more. Moreover. he is becoming an interesting and responsive person. There are substantial increases in the total time spent by him in smiling, vocalizing, and looking at the mother's face, so that the greater amount of social-type behavior he manifested at three months parallels the increments shown in the mother's social responsiveness toward him over this same period. The increase with age in the time the infant is kept in a supine position also should facilitate his participation in vis-à-vis interactions with the mother as well as provide him with greater opportunity for varied visual experiences.

Table 3 presents the correlations between the 3-week and the 3-month observations for the maternal and infant behaviors we studied. These findings further reflect the relative instability of the mother-infant system over the first few months of life. Moderate correlation coefficients were obtained only for the class of maternal variables concerning affectionate-social responses. It thus may be that these behaviors are more sensitive indicators of enduring maternal attitudes than the absolute amount of time the mother devoted to such activities as feeding and physical contact. The

Table 3
Correlations Between Observations at 3 Weeks and at 3 Months (N = 26)

Maternal variables	*r =*	*Infant variables*	*r =*
Holds infant close	.23	Cry	.28
Holds infant distant	.04	Fuss	.42**
Total holds	.18	Irritable (cry and fuss)	.37*
Attends infant	.36*	Awake active	.25
Maternal contact		Awake passive	.26
(holds and attends)	.25	Drowsy	.44**
Feeds infant	.21	Sleep	.24
Stimulates feeding	.37*	Supine	.29
Burps infant	.20	Eyes on mother	−.12
Affectionate contact	.64****	Vocalizes	.41**
Rocks infant	.29	Infant smiles	.32
Stresses musculature	.06	Mouths	−.17
Stimulates/arouses infant	.23		
Imitates infant	.45**		
Looks at infant	.37*		
Talks to infant	.58***		
Smiles at infant	.66****		

$8 * p < .10$ $* * p < .05$ $* * * < .01$ $* * * * p < .001$

few infant variables that show some stability are, with the exception of vocalizing, those concerning the state of the organism. Even though some of

the behaviors are moderately stable from three weeks to three months, the overall magnitude of the correlations reported in Table 3 seem quite low considering that they represent repeated measures of the same individual over a relatively short period.

Table 4 presents t-values based on comparisons between the sexes for the 3-week and 3-month observations. A number of statistically significant differences were obtained with, in most instances, the boys having higher

Table 4
Sex Differences in Frequency of Maternal and
Infant Behaviors at 3 Weeks and 3 Months

Maternal variables	t-values		Infant variables	t-values	
	3 weeks	3 months		3 weeks	3 months
Male higher:			*Male higher:*		
Holds infant close	1.42	1.52	Cry	1.68	1.11
Holds infant distant	2.64**		Fuss	2.48**	3.47**
Total holds	1.65	1.12	Irritable (cry		
Attends infant	2.66**	1.10	and fuss)	2.23**	2.68***
Maternal contact			Awake active	1.66	.57
(holds and attends)	2.09**	1.57	Awake passive	2.94***	1.77*
Feeds infant	.06	.27	Drowsy		.41
Burps infant	1.67	.69	Supine	2.30**	1.07
Affectionate contact	.90	1.00	Eyes on mother	1.99*	.75
Rocks infant	1.21		Mouths	.64	
Stresses musculature	2.48**	1.67			
Stimulates/arouses					
infant	2.20**	1.53			
Looks at infant	1.97*	1.36			
Talks to infant	1.02	.79			
Smiles at infant	.57				
Female higher:			*Female higher:*		
Holds infant distant		.05	Drowsy	.03	
Stimulates feeding	.62	1.47	Sleep	3.15***	2.87***
Rocks infant		.82	Vocalizes	1.34	.23
Imitates infant	.80	1.76*	Infant smiles	.02	.08
Smiles at infant		.44	Mouths		2.57**

$* \ p < .10 \qquad ** \ p < .05 \qquad *** \ p < .01$

mean scores than the girls. The sex differences are most pronounced at three weeks for both maternal and infant variables. By 3 months the boys and girls are no longer as clearly differentiated on the maternal variables

although the trend persists for the males to tend to have higher mean scores. On the other hand, the findings for the infant variables concerning state remain relatively similar at 3 weeks and 3 months. Thus, the sex differences are relatively stable for the two observations even though the stability coefficients for the total sample are liw (in terms of our variables).

In general these results indicate that much more was happening with the male infants than with the female infants. Males slept less and cried more during both observations and these behaviors probably contributed to the more extensive and stimulating interaction the boys experienced with the mother, particularly for the 3-week observation. In order to determine the effect of state we selected the 15 variables, excluding those dealing with

Table 5
Sex Differences After Controlling for Irritability and
Sleep Time Through Analysis of Covariance

Maternal or infant Behaviors	Sleep time controlled for		Sex with higher mean score	Irritability controlled for		Sex with higher mean score
	3 weeks	3 months		3 weeks	3 months	
Variables	t	t		t	t	
Holds infant close	.30	1.22		.64	1.70	
Holds infant distant	.59	−.20		.92	−.20	
Total holds	.43	.88		.86	1.08	
Attends infant	1.12	1.36		1.91*	.94	Males
Maternal contact (holds and attends)	.62	1.04		1.20	1.12	
Stimulates feeding	.55	1.12		−.09	−1.06	
Affectionate contact	−.46	.91		.56	1.27	
Rocks	.35	−.70		.44	−1.44	
Stresses musculature	1.84*	.71	Males	1.97*	1.40	
Stimulates/arouses infant	2.09**	1.82*	Males	2.43**	2.31**	Males
Imitates infant	−.91	−2.73**	Females	−.63	−2.14**	Females
Looks at infant	.58	1.35		1.17	1.02	
Talks to infant	−.48	.24		.70	.59	
Infant supine	.82	−.03		1.36	.69	
Eyes on mother	.37	.58		1.76*	−.37	Males

* $p < .10$ ** $p < .05$

[a]A positive t-value indicates that males had the higher mean score, a negative t-value indicates a higher mean score for females.

state, where the sex differences were most marked and did an analysis of covariance with these variables, controlling for irritability and another

analysis of covariance controlling for sleep. These results are presented in Table 5. When the state of the infant was controlled for, most of the sex differences were no longer statistically significant. The exceptions were that the *t*-values were greater, after controlling for state, for the variables "mother stimulates/arouses infant" and "mother imitates infant." The higher score for "stimulates/arouse" was obtained for the males and the higher score for "imitates" by the females. The variable "imitates" involves repeating vocalizations made by the child, and it is interesting that mothers exhibited more of this behavior with the girls. This response could be viewed as the reinforcement of verbal behavior, and the evidence presented here suggests that the mothers differentially reinforce this behavior on the basis of the sex of the child.

In order to further clarify the relation between infant state and maternal treatment, product-moment correlations were computed relating the infant irritability score with the degree of maternal contact. The maternal contact variable is based on the sum of the holding and attending scores with the time devoted to feeding behaviors subtracted out. These correlations were computed for the 3-week and 3-month observations for the male and female samples combined and separate. At 3 weeks a correlation of .52 ($p < .01$) was obtained between irritability and maternal contact for the total sample. However, for the female subsample this correlation was .68 ($p < .02$) and for males only .20 (non. sig.). Furthermore, a somewhat similar pattern occurred for the correlations between maternal contact and infant irritability for the 3-month observation. At this age the correlation is .37 ($p < .10$ level) for the combined sample and .54 ($p < .05$ level) for females and $-.47$ ($p < .10$ level) for males. A statistically significant difference was obtained ($t = 2.40$, $p < .05$ level) in a test comparing the difference between the female and male correlations for the 3-month observation. In other words maternal contact and irritability positively covaried for females at both ages; whereas for males, there was no relationship at 3 weeks, and by 3 months the mothers tended to spend less time with the more irritable male babies. It should be emphasized that these correlations reflect within group patterns, and that when we combine the female and male samples positive correlations still emerge for both ages. Since the males had substantially higher scores for irritability and maternal contact than the females, the correlation for the male subjects does not strongly attenuate the correlations derived for the total sample, even when the males within group covariation seems random or negative. That is, in terms of the total sample, the patterning of the males scores is still consistent with a positive relationship between irritability and maternal contact.

From these findings it is difficult to posit a causal relationship. However, it seems most plausible that it is the infant's cry that is determining the maternal behavior. Mothers describe the cry as a signal that the infant needs

attention and they often report their nurturant actions in response to the cry. Furthermore, the cry is a noxious and often painful stimulus that probably has biological utility for the infant, propelling the mother into action for her own comfort as well as out of concern for the infant. Ethological reports confirm the proposition that the cry functions as a "releaser" of maternal behavior (Bowlby, 1958; Hinde, et al., 1964; Hoffman, et al., 1966). Bowlby (1958) states:

> It is my belief that both of them (crying and smiling), act as social releasers of instinctual responses in mothers. As regards crying, there is plentiful evidence from the animal world that this is so: probably in all cases the mother responds promptly and unfailingly to her infant's bleat, call or cry. It seems to me clear that similar impulses are also evoked in the human mother. . . .

Thus, we are adopting the hypothesis that the correlations we have obtained reflect a causal sequence whereby the cry acts to instigate maternal intervention. Certainly there are other important determinants of maternal contact, and it is evident that mothers exhibit considerable variability concerning how responsive they are to the stimulus signal of the cry. Yet it seems that the effect of the cry is sufficient to account at least partially for the structure of the mother-infant relationship. We further maintain the thesis that the infant's cry shapes maternal behavior even for the instance where the negative correlation was noted at 3 months for the males. The effect is still present, but in this case the more irritable infants were responded to *less* by the mothers. Our speculation for explaining this relationship and the fact that, conversely, a positive correlation was obtained for the female infants is that the mothers probably were negatively reinforced for responding to a number of the boys but tended to be positively reinforced for their responses toward the girls. That is, mothers of the more irritable boys may have learned that they could not be successful in quieting boys whereas the girls were more uniformly responsive (quieted by) to maternal handling. There is not much present in our data to bear out this contention, with the exception that the males were significantly more irritable than the girls for both observations. However, evidence that suggests males are more subject to inconsolable states comes from studies (Serr and Ismajovich, 1963; McDonald, Gynther, and Christakos, 1963; Stechler, 1964) which indicate that males have less well organized physiological reactions and are more vulnerable to adverse conditions than females. The relatively more efficient functioning of the female organism should thus contribute to their responding more favorably to maternal intervention.

In summary, we propose that maternal behavior initially tends to be

under the control of the stimulus and reinforcing conditions provided by the young infant. As the infant gets older, the mother, if she behaved contingently toward his signals, gradually acquires reinforcement value which in turn increases her efficacy in regulating infant behaviors. Concurrently, the earlier control asserted by the infant becomes less functional and diminishes. In a sense, the point where the infant's control over the mother declines and the mother's reinforcement value emerges could be regarded as the first manifestation of socialization, or at least represents the initial conditions favoring social learning. Thus, at first the mother is shaped by the infant and this later facilitates her shaping the behavior of the infant. We would therefore say, that the infant, through his own temperament or signal system contributes to establishing the stimulus and reinforcement value eventually associated with the mother. According to this reasoning, the more irritable infants (who can be soothed) whose mothers respond in a contingent manner to their signals should become most amenable to the effects of social reinforcement and manifest a higher degree of attachment behavior. The fact that the mothers responded more contingently toward the female infants should maximize the ease with which females learn social responses.

This statement is consistent with data on older children which indicate that girls learn social responses earlier and with greater facility than boys. (Becker, 1964). Previously we argued that the mothers learned to be more contingent toward the girls because they probably were more responsive to maternal intervention. An alternative explanation is that mothers respond contingently to the girls and not to the boys as a form of differential reinforcement, whereby, in keeping with cultural expectations, the mother is initiating a pattern that contributes to males being more aggressive or assertive, and less responsive to socialization. Indeed, these two explanations are not inconsistent with one another since the mother who is unable to soothe an upset male infant may eventually come to classify this intractable irritability as an expression of "maleness."

There are certain environmental settings where noncontingent caretaking is more likely and these situations should impede social learning and result in weaker attachment responses. Lennenberg (1965) found that deaf parents tended not to respond to the infant's cry. One would have to assume that it was more than the inability to hear the infant that influenced their behavior, since even when they observed their crying infants these parents tended not to make any effort to quiet them. The function of the cry as a noxious stimulus or "releaser" of maternal behavior did not pertain under these unusual circumstances. Infants in institutions also are more likely to be cared for in terms of some arbitrary schedule with little opportunity for them to shape caretakers in accordance with their own behavioral vicissitudes.

Although we have shown that there is a convariation between maternal

contact and infant irritability and have attempted to develop some theoretical implications concerning this relationship, considerable variability remains as to how responsive different mothers are to their infants' crying behavior. This variability probably reflects differences in maternal attitudes. Women who express positive feelings about babies and who consider the well-being of the infant to be of essential importance should tend to be more responsive to signals of distress from the infant than women who exhibit negative maternal attitudes. In order to test this assumption, we first derived a score for measuring maternal responsiveness. This score was obtained through a regression analysis where we determined the amount of maternal contact that would be expected for each mother by controlling for her infant's irritability score. The expected maternal contact score was then subtracted from the mother's actual contact score and this difference was used as the measure of maternal responsivity. The maternal responsivity scores were obtained separately for the 3-week and the 3-month observations. The parents of 23 of the infants in our sample were interviewed for a project investigating marital careers, approximately 2 years prior to the birth of their child, and these interviews provided us with the unusual opportunity of having antecedent data relevant to prospective parental functioning. A number of variables from this material were rated and two of them, "acceptance of nurturant role," and the "degree that the baby is seen in a positive sense" were correlated with the scores on the maternal responsivity measure.[1] Annotated definitions of these interview variables are as follows:

"Acceptance of nurturant role" concerns the degree to which the subject is invested in caring for others and in acquiring domestic and homemaking skills such as cooking, sewing, and cleaning house. Evidence for a high rating would be describing the care of infants and children with much pleasure and satisfaction even when this involves subordinating her own needs.

The interview variable concerning the "degree that the baby is seen in a positive sense" assesses the extent to which the subject views a baby as gratifying, pleasant and non-burdensome. In discussing what she imagines infants to be like she stresses the warmer, more personal, and rewarding aspects of the baby and anticipates these qualities as primary.

Correlations of .40 (p<.10) level) and . 48 (p<.05 level) were obtained between the ratings on "acceptance of nurturant role" and the maternal responsivity scores for the 3-week and 3-month observations, respectively. The "degree that the baby is seen in a positive sense" correlated 38 (p <.10 level) and .44 (p <.05 level) with maternal responsivity for the two ages. However, the two interview variables were so highly intercorrelated ($r = .93$) that they clearly involve the same dimension.

Thus, the psychological status of the mother, assessed substantially before the birth of her infant, as well as the infant's state, are predictive of her maternal behavior. Schaffer and Emerson (1964) found that maternal responsiveness to the cry was associated with the attachment behavior of infants. Extrapolating from our findings, we now have some basis for assuming that the early attitudes of the mother represent antecedent conditions for facilitating the attachment behavior observed by Schaffer and Emerson.

The discussion to this point has focused on some of the conditions that seemingly affect the structure of the mother-infant relationship and influence the reinforcement and stimulus values associated with the mother. Next we would like to consider, in a more speculative vein, one particular class of maternal behaviors that has important reinforcing properties for the infant. This discussion will be more general and depart from a direct consideration of the data. There has been mounting evidence in the psychological literature that the organism has a "need for stimulation" and that variations in the quantity and quality of stimulation received can have a significant effect on many aspects of development (Moss, 1965; Murphy, et al., 1962; White and Held, 1963). Additional reports indicate that, not only does the infant require stimulation, but that excessive or chaotic dosages of stimulation can be highly disruptive of normal functioning (Murphy, et al., 1962). Furthermore, there appear to be substantial individual differences in the stimulation that is needed or in the extremes that can be tolerated. As the infant gets older he becomes somewhat capable of regulating the stimulation that is assimilated. However, the very young infant is completely dependent on the caretaking environment to provide and modulate the stimulation he experiences. It is in this regard that the mother has a vital role.

The main points emphasized in the literature are that stimulation serves to modulate the state or arousal level of the infant, organize and direct attentional processes, and facilitate normal growth and development. Bridger (1965) has shown that stimulation tends to have either an arousing or quieting effect, depending on the existing state of the infant. Infants who are quiet tend to be aroused, whereas aroused infants tend to be quieted by moderate stimulation. Moreover, according to data collected by Birns (1965), these effects occur for several stimulus modalities and with stable individual differences in responsivity. (We found that mothers made greater use of techniques involving stimulation—"stresses musculature" and "stimulates/arouses"—with the males who as a group were more irritable than the females.)

The capacity for stimulus configurations to direct attention, once the infant is in an optimally receptive state also has been demonstrated by a number of studies. Young infants have been observed to orient toward many stimuli (Razran, 1961; Fantz, 1963), and certain stimuli are so compelling

that they tend to "capture" the infant in a fixed orientation (Stechler, 1965). Other studies have demonstrated that infants show clear preferences for gazing at more complex visual patterns (Fantz, 1963). Thus, stimulation can influence the set of the infant to respond by modifying the state of the organism as well as structure learning possibilities through directing the infant's attention. White (1959) has systematically described how stimulation contributes to the learning process in infants. He points out that the infant is provided with the opportunity to activate behavioral potentials in attempting to cope with control stimulation. Motor and perceptual skills eventually become refined and sharpened in the process of responding to stimulus configurations and it is this pattern of learning which White calls "effectance behavior."

Not all levels of stimulation are equally effective in producing a condition whereby the infant is optimally alert and attentive. Excessive stimulation has a disruptive effect and according to drive reduction theorists the organism behaves in ways aimed at reducing stimulation that exceeds certain limits. Leuba (1955), in an attempt to establish rapprochement between the drive reduction view and the research evidence that shows that there is a need for stimulation, states that there is an optimal level of stimulation that is required, and that the organism acts either to reduce or to increase stimulation so as to stay within this optimal range.

The mother is necessarily highly instrumental in mediating much of the stimulation that is experienced by the infant. Her very presence in moving about and caring for the infant provides a constant source of visual, auditory, tactile, kinesthetic and proprioceptive stimulation. In addition to the incidental stimulation she provides, the mother deliberately uses stimulation to regulate the arousal level or state of the infant and to evoke specific responses from him. However, once the infant learns, through conditioning, that the mother is a source of stimulation he can in turn employ existing responses that are instrumental in eliciting stimulation from her. Certain infant behaviors, such as the cry, are so compelling that they readily evoke many forms of stimulation from the mother. It is common knowledge that mothers in attempting to quiet upset infants, often resort to such tactics as using rocking motion, waving bright objects or rattles, or holding the infant close and thus provide warmth and physical contact. The specific function of stimulation in placating the crying infant can be somewhat obscured because of the possibility of confounding conditions. In our discussion so far we have indicated that stimulation inherently has a quieting effect irrespective of learning but that crying also can become a learned instrumental behavior which terminates once the reinforcement of stimulation is presented. However, it is often difficult to distinguish the unlearned from the learned patterns of functioning, since the infant behavior (crying) and the outcome (quieting) are highly similar in both instances. Perhaps the best

means for determining whether learning has occurred would be if we could demonstrate that the infant makes anticipatory responses, such as the reduction in crying behavior to cues, prior to the actual occurrence of stimulation. In addition to the cry, the smile and the vocalization of the infant can become highly effective, and consequently well-learned conditioned responses for evoking stimulation from adult caretakers. Rheingold (1956) has shown that when institutional children are given more caretaking by an adult they show an increase in their smiling rate to that caretaker as well as to other adults. Moreover, for a few weeks after the intensive caretaking stopped there were further substantial increments in the smiling rate, which suggests that the infant after experiencing relative deprivation worked harder in attempting to restitute the stimulation level experienced earlier.

It seems plausible that much of the early social behavior seen in infants and children consists of attempts to elicit responses from others. We mentioned earlier that it has been stressed in recent psychological literature that individuals have a basic need for stimulation. Since the mother, and eventually others, are highly instrumental in providing and monitoring the stimulation that is experienced by the infant, it seems likely that the child acquires expectancies for having this need satisfied through social interactions and that stimulation comes to serve as a basis for relating to others. Indeed, Schaffer and Emerson (1964) have shown that the amount of stimulation provided by adults is one of the major determinants of infants' attachment behavior. Strange as well as familiar adults who have been temporarily separated from an infant often attempt to gain rapport with the infant through acts of stimulation. It is quite common for the father, upon returning home from work, to initiate actions aimed at stimulating the child, and these actions are usually responded to with clear pleasure. Because of the expectancies that are built up some of the provocative behaviors seen in children, particularly when confronted with a nonresponsive adult, could be interpreted as attempts to elicit socially mediated stimulation.

The learning we have discussed is largely social since the infant is dependent on others, particularly the mother, for reinforcements. This dependency on others is what constitues attachment behavior, and the specific makeup of the attachment is determined by the class of reinforcements that are involved. The strength of these learned attachment behaviors is maximized through stimulation, since the mother is often the embodiment of this reinforcement as well as the agent for delivering it. The social aspect of this learning is further enhanced because of the reciprocal dependence of the mother on the infant for reinforcement. That is, the mother learns certain conditioned responses, often involving acts of stimulation, that are aimed at evoking desired states or responses from the infant.

In conclusion, what we did was study and analyze some of the factors which structure the mother-infant relationship. A central point is that the

state of the infant affects the quantity and quality of maternal behavior, and this in turn would seem to influence the course of future social learning. Furthermore, through controlling for the state of the infant, we were able to demonstrate the effects of pre-parental attitudes on one aspect of maternal behavior, namely, the mother's responsiveness toward her infant. Many investigators, in conducting controlled laboratory studies, have stressed that the state of the infant is crucial in determining the nature of his responses to different stimuli. This concern is certainly highly relevant to our data, collected under naturalistic conditions.

Notes

[2] Dr. Kenneth Robson collaborated in developing these variables, and made the ratings.

References

Becker, W. C. Consequences of different kinds of parental discipline. In M. L. Hoffman & Lois W. Hoffman (Eds.), *Review of child development research: I.* New York: Russell Sage Found., 1964, Pp. 169-208.

Birns, B. Individual differences in human neonates' responses to stimulation. *Child Develpm.,* 1965, 36, 249-256.

Bloom, B. S. *Stability and change in human characteristics.* New York: Wiley, 1964.

Bowlby, J. The nature of a child's tie to his mother. *Internat. J. Psychoanal.,* 1958, 39, 350-373.

Bridger, W. H. Psychophysiological measurement of the roles of state in the human neonate. Paper presented at Soc. Res. Child Develpm., Minneapolis, April, 1965.

Brown, Janet L. States in newborn infants. *Merrill-Palmer Quart.,* 1964, 10, 313-327.

Escalona, Sibylle K. The study of individual differences and the problem of state. *J Child Psychiat.,* 1962, 1, 11-37.

Fantz, R. Pattern vision in newborn infants. *Science,* 1963, 140, 296-297.

Hess, E. H. Imprinting. *Science,* 1959, 130, 133-141.

Hinde, R. A., Rowell, T. E., & Spencer-Booth, Y. Behavior of living rhesus monkeys in their first six months. *Proc. Zool. Soc., London,* 1964, 143, 609-649.

Hoffman, H., et al. Enhanced distress vocalization through selective reinforcement. *Science,* 1966, 151, 354-356.

Lennenberg, E. H., Rebelsky, Freda., & Nichols, I. A. The vocalizations of infants born to deaf and to hearing parents. *Vita Humana,* 1965, 8, 23-37.

Leuba, C. Toward some integration of learning theories: The concept of optimal stimulation. *Psychol. Rep.*, 1955, 1, 27-33.

Levy, D. M. *Behavioral analysis.* Springfield, Ill.: Charles C Thomas, 1958.

McDonald, R. L., Gynther, M. D., & Christakos, A. C. Relations between maternal anxiety and obstetric complications. *Psychosom. Med.*, 1963, 25, 357-362.

Moss, H. A. Coping behavior, the need for stimulation, and normal development. *Merrill-Palmer Quart.*, 1965, 11, 171-179.

Murphy, Lois B., et al. *The widening world of childhood.* New York: Basic Books, 1962.

Noirot, Eliane. Changes in responsiveness to young in the adult mouse: the effect of external stimuli. *J. comp. physiol. Psychol.*, 1964, 57, 97-99.

Razran, G. The observable unconscious and the inferable conscious in current Soviet psychophysiology: Interoceptive conditioning, semantic conditioning, and the orienting reflex. *Psychol. Rev.*, 1961, 68, 81-146.

Rheingold, Harriet L. The modification of social responsiveness in institutional babies. *Monogr. Soc. Res. Child Develpm.*, 1956, 21, No. 2 (Serial No. 23).

Schaffer, H. R. & Emerson, Peggy E. The development of social attachments in infancy. *Monogr. Soc. Res. Child Develpm.*, 1964, 29, No. (Serial No. 94).

Serr, D. M. & Ismajovich, B. Determination of the primary sex ratio from human abortions. *Amer J. Obstet. Gyncol.*, 1963, 87, 63-65.

Stechler, G. A longitudinal follow-up of neonatal apnea. *Child Develpm.*, 1964, 35, 333-348.

Stechler, G. Paper presented at Soc. Res. Child Develpm., Minneapolis, April, 1965.

White, B. L. & Held, R. Plasticity in perceptual development during the first six months of life. Paper presented at Amer. Ass. Advncmnt. Sci., Cleveland, Ohio, December, 1963.

White, R. W. Motivation reconsidered: the concept of competence. *Psychol. Rev.*, 1959, 66, 297-323.

Wolff, P. H. Observations on newborn infants. *Psychosom. Med.*, 1959, 21, 110-118.

3.5 Play Behavior in the Year-Old Infant: Early Sex Differences

Susan Goldberg
Michael Lewis

Until recently, the largest proportion of studies in child development gave attention to nursery and early grade school children. The literature on sex differences is no exception. A recent book on development of sex differences which includes an annotated bibliography (Maccoby, 1966) lists fewer than 10 studies using infants, in spite of the fact that theoretical discussions (e.g., Freud, 1938 [originally published in 1905]; Piaget, 1951) emphasize the importance of early experience. Theoretical work predicts and experimental work confirms the existence of sex differences in behavior by age 3. There has been little evidence to demonstrate earlier differentiation of sex-appropriate behavior, although it would not be unreasonable to assume this occurs.

Recently, there has been increased interest in infancy, including some work which has shown early sex differences in attentive behavior (Kagan & Lewis, 1965; Lewis, in press). The bulk of this work has been primarily experimental, studying specific responses to specific stimuli or experimental conditions. Moreover, it has dealt with perceptual-cognitive differences rather than personality variables. There has been little observation of freely emitted behavior. Such observations are of importance in supplying researchers with the classes of naturally occurring behaviors, the conditions under which responses normally occur, and the natural preference ordering of behaviors. Knowledge of this repertoire of behaviors provides a background against which behavior under experimental conditions can be evaluated.

The present study utilized a free play situation to observe sex differences in children's behavior toward mother, toys, and a frustration situation at 13 months of age. Because the Ss were participants in a longitudinal study, information on the mother-child relationship at 6 months was also available. This made it possible to assess possible relations between behavior patterns at 6 months and at 13 months.

Method

Subjects

Two samples of 16 girls and 16 boys each, or a total of 64 infants, were

Reprinted from *Child Development*, 1969, *40*, No. 1, 21-31, by permission of the author and The Society for Research in Child Development, Inc. Copyright © 1968 by The Society for Research in Child Development.

seen at 6 and 13 months of age ($\pm$ 6 days). All Ss were born to families residing in southwestern Ohio at the time of the study. All were Caucasian. The mothers had an average of 13.5 years of schooling (range of 10-18 years) and the fathers had an average of 14.5 years of schooling (range of 8-20 years). The occupations of the fathers ranged from laborer to scientist. Of the 64 infants, 9 girls and 10 boys were first-born and the remaining infants had from 1 to 6 siblings.

The 6-Month Visit

The procedure of the 6-month visit, presented in detail in Kagan and Lewis (1965), included two visual episodes and an auditory episode where a variety of behavioral responses were recorded. The infant's mother was present during these procedures. At the end of the experimental procedure, the mother was interviewed by one of the experimenters, who had been able to observe both mother and infant for the duration of the session. The interviewer also rated both mother and infant on a rating scale. The items rated for the infant included: amount of activity, irritability, response to mother's behavior, and amount of affect. For the mother, the observer rated such factors as nature of handling, amount of playing with the baby, type of comforting behavior, and amount of vocalization to the baby. Each item was rated on a 7-point scale, with 1 indicating the most activity and 7 the least. For the purpose of this study, it was necessary to obtain a measure of the amount of physical contact the mother initiated with the child. Since scores on the individual scales did not result in sufficient variance in the population, a composite score was obtained by taking the mean score for each mother over all three of the touching-the-infant scales. These included: amount of touching, amount of comforting, and amount of play. The composite touch scores (now called the amount of physical contact) resulted in a sufficiently variable distribution to be used for comparison with the 13-month touch data.

The 13-Month Visit

Kagan and Lewis (1965), who employed the same 64 infants for their study, described the procedures used at 6 months, which were similar to those of the present (13-month) study. The only addition was a free play procedure, which will be discussed in detail below.

The playroom, 9 by 12 feet, contained nine simple toys: a set of blocks, a pail, a "lawnmower," a stuffed dog, an inflated plastic cat, a set of quoits (graduated plastic doughnuts stacked on a wooden rod), a wooden mallet, a pegboard, and a wooden bug (a pull toy). Also included as toys were any permanent objects in the room, such as the doorknob, latch on the wall, tape on the electrical outlets, and so forth. The mother's chair was located in one corner of the room.

Procedure

Each *S,* accompanied by his mother, was placed in the observation room. The mother was instructed to watch his play and respond in any way she desired. Most mothers simply watched and responded only when asked for something. The mother was also told that we would be observing from the next room. She held the child on her lap, the door to the playroom was closed, and observation began. At the beginning of the 15 minutes of play, the mother was instructed to place the child on the floor.

Measurement

Two observers recorded the *S*'s behavior. One dictated a continuous behavior account into a tape recorder. The second operated an event recorder, which recorded the location of the child in the room and the duration of each contact with the mother.

Dictated recording. During the initial dictation, a buzzer sounded at regular time intervals, automatically placing a marker on the dictated tape. The dictated behavior account was typed and each minute divided into 15-second units, each including about three typewritten lines. The typed material was further divided into three 5-second units, each unit being one typed line. Independent experimenters analyzed this type material. For each minute, the number of toys played with and amount of time spent with each toy was recorded.

Event recorder. To facilitate recording the activity and location of the child, the floor of the room was divided into 12 squares. For each square, the observer depressed a key on the event recorder for the duration of time the child occupied that square. From this record it was possible to obtain such measures as the amount of time spent in each square and the number of squares traversed. A thirteenth key was depressed each time the child touched the mother. From this record, measure of (*a*) initial latency in leaving the mother, (*b*) total amount of time touching the mother, (*c*) number of times touching the mother, and (*d*) longest period touching the mother were obtained.

The data analysis presented in this report provides information only on sex differences (*a*) in response to the mother and (*b*) in choice and style of play with toys. Other data from this situation are presented elsewhere (Lewis, 1967).

Results

Response to Mother (13 Months)

Open field. Boys and girls showed striking differences in their behavior

toward their mothers (see Table 1). First, upon being removed from their mothers' laps, girls were reluctant to leave their mothers. When Ss were placed on the floor by their mothers, significantly more girls than boys returned immediately—in less than 5 seconds ($p < .05$ for both samples by Fisher Exact Probability test). This reluctance to leave their mothers is further indicated by the time it took the children to first return to their mothers. Girls, in both samples, showed significantly shorter latencies than boys. Out of a possible 900 seconds (15 minutes), girls returned after an average of 273.5 seconds, while boys' average latency was nearly twice as long, 519.5 seconds. This difference was highly significant ($p < .002$, Mann-Whitney U test). All significance tests are two-tailed unless otherwise specified.

Once the children left their mothers, girls made significantly more returns both physical and visual. Girls touched their mothers for an average of 84.6

Table 1
Summary of Infant Behavior to Mother in Free Play Session

Behavior	Girls	Boys	p
Touching mother:			
x latency in seconds to return to mother	273.5	519.5	<.002
x number of returns	8.4	3.9	<.001
x number of seconds touching mother	84.6	58.8	<.03
Vocalization to mother:			
x number of seconds vocalizing to mother	169.8	106.9	<.04
Looking at mother:			
x number of seconds looking at mother	57.3	47.0	<.09
x number of times looking at mother	10.8	9.2	NS
Proximity to mother:			
x time in squares closest to mother	464.1	351.4	<.05
x time in squares farthest from mother	43.8	44.3	NS

seconds, while boys touched their mothers for only 58.8 seconds ($p. < .03$, Mann-Whitney U test). Girls returned to touch their mothers on an average of 8.4 times, and boys 3.9 times ($p < .001$, Mann-Whitney U test). For the visual returns, the number of times the child looked at the mother and the total amount of time spent looking at the mother were obtained from the dictated material. The mean number of times girls looked at the mother was 10.8 (as compared with 9.2 for boys), a difference which was not significant. The total amount of time looking at the mother was 57.3 seconds for girls and 47.0 seconds for boys ($p < .09$, Mann-Whitney U test).

Finally, vocalization data were also available from the dictated material. The man time vocalizing to the mother was 169.8 seconds for girls and 106.9 seconds for boys ($p. < .04$, Mann-Whitney U test).

Another measure of the child's response to his mother was the amount of physical distance the child allowed between himself an his mother. Because

the observers recorded which squares the child played in, it was possible to obtain the amount of time Ss spent in the four squares closest to the mother. The mean time in these squares for girls was 464.1 seconds; for boys, it was 351.4 seconds ($p < .05$, Mann-Whitney U test). Moreover, boys spent more time in the square farthest from the mother, although the differences were not significant.

Barrier frustration. At the end of the 15 minutes of free play, a barrier of mesh on a wood frame was placed in such a way as to divide the room in half. The mother placed the child on one side and remained on the opposite side along with the toys. Thus, the chiild's response to stress was observed.

Table 2
Summary of Infant Behavior During Barrier Frustration

Behavior	Girls	Boys	p
x number of seconds crying	123.5	76.7	<.05
x number of seconds at ends of barrier	106.1	171.0	<.001.
x number of seconds at center	157.7	95.1	<.01

Sex differences were again prominent, with girls crying and motioning for help consistently more than boys (see Table 2). For both samples, amount of time crying was available from the dictated record. Girls' mean time crying was 123.5 seconds, compared with 76.7 seconds for boys ($p < .05$, Mann-Whitney U test). Boys, on the other hand, appeared to make a more active attempt to get around the barrier. That is, they spent significantly more time at the ends of the barrier than girls, while girls spent significantly more time in the center of the barrier—near the position where they were placed ($p < .01$, Mann-Whitney U test).

Toy Preference (13 Months)

A second area of experimental interest was toy preference. When the nine toys were ranked in order of the total amount of time they were played with, girls and boys showed similar patterns of preference.

Table 3 presents each toy and the amount of time it was played with. Play with the dog and cat were combined into one category. The toys which were used most were the lawnmower, blocks, and quoits, and those that were used least were the stuffed dog and cat. On a *post hoc* basis, it seems as if the toys which received the most attention were those that offered the most varied possibilities for manipulation.

Although there were no sex differences in overall toy preference, there were significant sex differences in the amount of time spent with individual toys and in the ways toys were used. Girls played with blocks, pegboard,

Table 3
Mean Time Playing with Toys, by Sex

	Girls	Boys	p
Total time with:			
Mallet	51.7	60.8	...
Bug	50.2	45.3	...
Pail	34.6	22.9	...
Blocks	126.5	77.5	<.03
Lawnmower	220.3	235.6	...
Cat plus dog (combined)	31.0	9.1	<.01
Quoits	122.7	130.3	...
Pegboard	37.2	28.7	<.05
Nontoys	6.9	31.0	<.005
Putting toys in pail	28.2	43.0	...
Banging toys	19.7	34.8	<.05
Lawnmowing on other toys	2.8	9.8	...
Other manipulation of two toys	28.2	10.3	<.05

and with the dog and cat (the only toys with faces) more than boys did ($p < .03$, $p < .03$, $p < .01$, respectively, Mann-Whitney U test).

In terms of style of play, there were also sex differences, Observation of girls' play indicates that girls chose toys which involved more fine than gross muscle coordination, while for boys, the reverse was true—building blocks and playing with dog and cat versus playing with mallet and rolling the lawnmower over other toys. Moreover, boys spent more time playing with the nontoys (doorknob, covered outlets, lights, etc.; $p < .005$, Mann-Whitney U test).

In terms of overall activity level, boys were more active than girls. Girls tended to sit and play with combinations of toys ($p < .05$, Mann-Whitney U test), while boys tended to be more active and bang the toys significantly more than girls ($p < .05$, Mann-Whitney U test). In addition, the children were rated by two observers on the vigor of their play behavior; a rating of 1 was given for high vigor, 2 was given for medium vigor, and 3 for low vigor. These ratings were made from the dictated material for each minute, so that the final score for each S represented a mean of 15 vigor ratings. The interobserver reliability was $p = 0.78$. The boys played significantly more vigorously than girls (mean for boys was 2.45, varying from 1.2 to 3.0; for girls, the mean was 2.65, varying from 1.9 to 3.0 [$p < .05$, Mann-Whitney U test]). This vigor difference was also seen in the style of boys' play; for example, boys banged with the mallet and mowed over other toys. Thus, there were not only significant differences in the choice of toys, but also in the way the toys were manipulated. The data indicate that there are important and significant sex differences in very young children's response to their mothers, to frustration, and in play behavior.

Mother-infant touch (6 months). One possible determinant of the child's behavior toward the mother in the playroom is the mother's behavior toward the child at an earlier age. The 6-month data indicated that mothers of girls touched their infants more than mothers of boys. On the composite score, where 1 indicated most touching and 7 least, there were twice as many girls as boys whose mothers were rated 1-3 and twice as many boys as girls whose mothers were rated 5-7 ($p < .05$, χ^2 test). Moreover, mothers vocalized to girls significantly more than to boys ($p < .001$, Mann-Whitney U test), and significantly more girls than boys were breast-fed rather than bottle-fed ($p < .02$, Mann-Whitney U test). Thus, when the children were 6 months old, mothers touched, talked to, and handled their daughters more than their sons, and when they were 13 months old, girls touched and talked to their mothers more than boys did. To explore this relationship further, mothers were divided into high, medium, and low mother-touch-infant groups (at 6 months), with the extreme groups consisting of the upper and lower 25 per cent of the sample. For the boys at 13 months, the mean number of seconds of physical contact with the mother indicated a linear relation to amount of mother touching (14, 37, and 47 seconds for the low, medium, and high mother-touch groups, respectively; Kruskal-Wallis, $p < .10$). Thus, the more physical contact the mother made with a boy at 6 months, the more he touched the mother at 13 months. For the girls, the relation appeared to be curvilinear. The mean number of seconds of touching the mother for the low, medium, and high mother-touch groups was 101, 55, and 88 seconds, respectively (Kruskal-Wallis, $p < .10$). The comparable distribution for number of seconds close to the mother was 589, 397, and 475 seconds (Kruskal-Wallis, $p < .03$). A girl whose mother initiated very much or very little contact with her at 6 months was more likely to seek a great deal of physical contact with the mother in the play room than one whose mother was in the medium-touch infant group.

Observation of the mothers' behavior when their infants were 6 months old revealed that five of the seven mothers of girls who showed little physical contact were considered by the staff to be severely rejecting mothers. The data suggest that the child of a rejecting mother continues to seek contact despite the mother's behavior. This result is consistent with Harlow's work with rejected monkeys (Seay, Alexander, & Harlow, 1964) and Provence's work with institutionalized children (Provence, 1965; Provence & Lipton, 1962) and suggests that the child's need for contact with his mother is a powerful motive.

Discussion

Observation of the children's behavior indicated that girls were more dependent, showed less exploratory behavior, and their play behavior

reflected a more quiet style. Boys were independent, showed more exploratory behavior, played with toys requiring gross motor activity, were more vigorous, and tended to run and bang in their play. Obviously, these behavior differences approximate those usually found between the sexes at later ages. The data demonstrate that these behavior patterns are already present in the first year of life and that some of them suggest a relation to the mother's response to the infant in the first 6 months. It is possible that at 6 months, differential behavior on the part of the mother is already a response to differential behavior on the part of the infant. Moss (1967) has found behavioral sex differences as early as 3 weeks. In interpreting mother-infant interaction data, Moss suggests that maternal behavior is initially a response to the infant's behavior. As the infant becomes older, if the mother responds contingently to his signals, her behavior acquires reinforcement value which enables her to influence and regulate the infant's behavior. Thus, parents can be active promulgators of sex-role behavior through reinforcement of sex-role-appropriate responses within the first year of life.

The following is offered as a hypothesis concerning sex-role learning. In the first year or two, the parents reinforce those behaviors they consider sex-role appropriate and the child learns these sex-role behaviors independent of any internal motive, that is, in the same way he learns any appropriate response rewarded by his parents. The young child has little idea as to the rules governing this reinforcement. It is suggested, however that as the child becomes older (above age 3), the rules for this class of reinforced behavior becomes clearer and he develops internal guides to follow these earlier reinforced rules. In the past, these internalized rules, motivating without apparent reinforcement, have been called modeling behavior. Thus, modeling behavior might be considered an extension or internalization of the earlier reinforced sex-role behavior. However, it is clear that the young child, before seeking to model his behavior, is already knowledgeable in some appropriate sex-role behavior. In that the hypothesis utilizes both early reinforcement as well as subsequent cognitive elaboration, it would seem to bridge the reinforcement notion of Gewirtz (1967) and Kohlberg's cognitive theory (1966) of identification.

The fact that parents are concerned with early display of sex-role-appropriate behavior is reflected in an interesting clinical observation. On some occasions, staff members have incorrectly identified the sex of an infant. Mothers are often clearly irritated by this error. Since the sex of a fully clothed infant is difficult to determine, the mistake seems understandable and the mother's displeasure uncalled for. If, however, she views the infant and behaves toward him in a sex-appropriated way, our mistake is more serious. That is, the magnitude of her displeasure reveals to us the magnitude of her cognitive commitment to this infant as a child of given sex.

Regardless of the interpretation of the observed sex differences, the free play procedure provides a standardized situation in which young children can be observed without interference from experimental manipulation. While behavior under these conditions may be somewhat different from the young child's typical daily behavior, our data indicate that behavior in the play situation is related to other variables, that behavior can be predicted from earlier events, and that it is indicative of later sex-role behavior. The results of the present investigation as well as the work of Bell and Costello (1964), Kagan and Lewis (1965), and Lewis (in press) indicate sex differences within the first year over a wide variety of infant behaviors. The fact that sex differences do appear in the first year has important methological implications for infant research. These findings emphasize the importance of checking sex differences before pooling data and, most important, of considering sex as a variable in any infant study.

References

Bell, R. Q., & Costello, N. S. Three tests for sex differences in tactile sensitivity in the newborn. *Biologia Neonatorum,* 1964, 1, 335-347.

Freud, S. Three contributions to the theory of sex. Reprinted in *The basic writings of Sigmund Freud.* New York: Random House, 1938.

Gewirtz, J. The learning of generalized imitation and its implications for identification. Paper presented at the Society for Research in Child Development Meeting, New York, March, 1967.

Katan, J., & Lewis, M. Studies of attention in the human infant. *Merrill-Palmer Quarterly,* 1965, 11, 95-127.

Kohlberg, L. A cognitive-developmental analysis of children's sex role concepts and attitudes. In E. Maccoby (Ed.), *The development of sex differences.* Stanford, Calif.: Stanford University Press, 1966.

Lewis, M. Infant attention: response decrement as a measure of cognitive processes, or what's new, Baby Jane? Paper presented at the Society for Research in Child Development Meeting, symposium on "The Role of Attention in Cognitive Development," New York, March, 1967.

Lewis, M. Infants' responses to facial stimuli during the first year of life. *Development Psychology,* in press.

Maccoby, E. (Ed.) *The development of sex differences.* Stanford, Calif.: Stanford University Press, 1966.

Moss, H. Sex, age and state as determinants of mother-infant interaction. *Merrill-Palmer Quarterly,* 1967, 13 (1), 19-36.

Piaget, J. *Play, dreams and imitation in childhood.* New York: Norton, 1951.

Provence, S. Disturbed personality development in infancy: a comparison of two inadequately nurtured infants. *Merrill-Palmer Quarterly,* 1965, 2, 149-170.

Provence, S., & Lipton, R. C. *Infants in institutions.* New York: International University Press, 1962.

Seay, B., Alexander, B. K., & Harlow, H. F. Maternal behavior of socially deprived rhesus monkeys. *Journal of Abnormal and Social Psychology,* 1964, 69 (4), 345-354.

3.6 Infant Social Attachments: A Reinforcement Theory Interpretation and Investigation

Robert G. Wahler

It is generally assumed that an infant's social attachment to a specific individual develops in the third quarter of the first year. To date, the research findings concerning this assumption have been clearly supportive. For example, Schaffer (1958), Schaffer and Callender (1959), and Schaffer and Emerson (1964) have demonstrated that the infant's distress upon being separated from his mother does not emerge until approximately 7 months of age. In addition, evidence from developmental studies of smiling (Ahrens, 1954; Kaila, 1932; Spitz, 1946) suggests that before 6–8 months of age the infant's mother or caretaker is no more effective in eliciting smiles than strangers or moving facial masks. These investigators have concluded that prior to the 6–8 month period the infant is socially indiscriminate; he displays no greater preference for his caretaker than for any other human.

The data generated by the above studies reflect the operational criteria for attachment which the respective investigators have chosen to use. Two criteria have been popular: (*a*) smiling, and (*b*) separation distress. Following the early work of Kaila (1932), Spitz (1946) has argued that the infant's smiling is a social manifestation indicating the experience of pleasure which is stimulated by the presence of a human face. This contention is indirectly supported by studies of Kaila and Spitz and those of Buhler (1937) and Murphy and Murphy (1931), all showing that smiling is selectively elicited by a human or humanoid face from the third month of life on.

Separation distress as a criterion of social attachment is primarily based upon Bowlby's (1958, 1960) conception of the nature and formation of the infant's tie to his mother. According to Bowlby the infant has an inborn

Reprinted from *Child Development,* 1967, *38,* 1079-1088, by permission of the author and The Society for Research in Child Development, Inc. Copyright © 1967 by The Society for Research in Child Development, Inc.

need to seek the proximity of other members of his own species, and this need is reflected in such behavior patterns as clinging, following, sucking, smiling, and crying. He has further argued that the intensity of the need may be gauged by the infant's reactions to a withdrawal of the needed object; the greater his stress or protest following withdrawal the more intense is his need for attachment to the object.

Thus, the currently known developmental picture of social attachment is based upon data generated by the smiling and separation distress criteria of attachment. However, there are excellent grounds for arguing the use of a third and equally meaningful criterion based upon the principles of rein forcement theory (Gewirtz, 1956). Considering the adult as a potential social reinforcer, one could argue that the infant has become socially attached when it can be demonstrated that his behavior is subject to social reinforcement control. That is, the concept of social reinforcement like the concept of social attachment implies that the individual in question is influenced by the social behavior of other individuals; he will frequently engage in behavior which is instrumental in obtaining their approval, affection, reassurance, and nearness.

Using the social reinforcement criterion of attachment, evidence is available to show that the infant may be socially attached to adults at least by the age of 2–3 months. Studies of infants within these age group by Weisberg (1963), Rheingold, Gewirtz, and Ross (1959), and Brackbill (1958) have demonstrated that adult social behavior may serve as an effective set of reinforcers for such infant behaviors as smiling and vocalization. However, none of the studies was designed to assess differences in the reinforcing effectiveness of the infant's mother versus a stranger. Therefore, while these data may be taken to reflect the infant's social attachment to people in general, they do not indicate his attachment to specific individuals.

The reinforcement studies of infant social behavior open the possibility that specific social attachments are formed prior to the third quarter of the first year—perhaps as early as 2–3 months of age. This possibility receives further support from studies which show that the infant can discriminate his mother from strangers by the age of 2–3 months. Ainsworth (1964) has shown that 8–12-week-old African infants will cry differentially, depending upon whether they are held by their mothers or strangers. Likewise, Griffiths (1954) has reported that American infants at this age display mother-stranger discrimination through differential visual attention to the adult's face. Of course, the infant's ability to discriminate familiar from unfamiliar adults cannot by itself be regarded as evidence of attachment—but it is clearly a prerequisite to the formation of specific attachments. Since such discrimination ability is present by the age of 3 months and since the infant is subject to general social reinforcement control at this time, it is also possible that he will be differentially responsive to the social reinforcers

presented by familiar and unfamiliar adults. The present study was designed to produce data relevant to this question.

Method

Subjects, Mothers, Strangers, and Apparatus

Subjects were 13 full-term infants ranging in age from 3 months 7 days to 3 months 26 days (median age, 3 months 18 days). The ratio of males to females was 7:6. The Ss were obtained from a public listing of area births through a procedure which probably produced a some-what biassed sample. This procedure involved sending all parents on the list a letter requesting their participation in the study. Of one hundred parents contacted, fifteen announced their willingness to participate in the study. All infants in this sample were diagnosed by their family pediatricians as physically healthy.

The infants' mothers (Ms) and thirteen female strangers (STs) were involved in the study. The STs were randomly selected from an undergraduate class in child psychology and thus no attempt was made to control the similarity between STs and Ms.

Apparatus consisted of a multichannel event recorder and two operating panels containing pushbutton microswitches. Depression of the microswitches by observers activated selected channels of the event recorder. This apparatus is similar to one described by Lovaas, Freitag, Gold, and Kassorla (1965).

Dependent and Independent Variables

In the few studies which have assessed the presence of reinforcement control in infancy Brackbill, 1958; Reingold et al., 1959; (Weisberg, 1963) vocalization and smiling were selected as dependent variables. Both responses are apparently discrete enough to permit reliable observations and contingent presentation of reinforcing events. In the present study smiling was arbitrarily chosen as the dependent variable.

The above studies also showed that a variety of adult social behaviors may serve as reinforcers. Physical contact with the infant, talking to him, and smiling at him were all effective in increasing the infant rates of smiling and vocalization. In the present study the following combination of adult social behaviors were used as independent variables: (a) the verbal statement, "Hi [infant's name]," (b) a smile, and (c) a light touch on the infant's chest. This combination of events was discretely presented by Ms and STs according to a schedule to be described later.

Procedure

The experiment was conducted in the S's home during the morning or afternoon hours shortly after S's feeding was finished. Each S was seen for

two 15-minute sessions which were spaced 1 or 2 days apart. For the first session either M or a randomly selected ST was involved; in the second session the other member of the pair was used. The member who served in the first session was arbitrarily picked, subject to the restriction that Ms and STs serve first an equal number of times. Since the sample was unequal in number, seven Ms served first and six STs served first.

In both sessions S was placed face up in his crib by his mother and all distracting objects were removed from his range of vision. The two observers then positioned themselves at opposite ends of the crib allowing themselves an unobstructed view of S's face. The observers remained as immobile as possible in these positions while E described the complete procedure to M or ST. When the session began, M or ST was positioned between the observers, leaning over the crib approximately two feet from S's face. The E stood behind M or ST in partial view of S.

Through the use of a stopwatch E kept a record of S's crying during the session. It was decided to drop S from the experiment if his crying exceeded 60 cumulative seconds. Two Ss were dropped from the experiment following this criterion.

Baseline period. For the first 5 minutes of the session M or ST were instructed to remain immobile and quiet, looking at S's face with a fixed, unsmiling expression.

Reinforcement period. For the second 5-minute segment M or ST was instructed to continue her baseline behavior unless signaled by E. Upon E's signal (tap on the shoulder) she presented the reinforcer combination and immediately resumed her baseline behavior. The E, serving as the smiling criterion judge, presented his signals on a continuous schedule immediately following onset of the smiling responses.

Extinction period. For the third 5-minute segment M or ST continued her baseline behavior unless signaled by E. The E's signals continued to serve the same function as in the preceding period. During this period he presented approximately the same number of signals as in the preceding period; however, the signals were now made contingent upon responses other than smiling. For example, vocalization and head turning were frequently reinforced.

Observer recording. During the pilot work the observers were instructed to depress a selected microswitch at the beginning of a smile and to release it when the smile terminated. However, since observer agreement proved unsatisfactory, it was decided to introduce a temporal restriction to the response definition. Observers were now instructed to quickly depress and release a microswitch every 10 seconds if smiling occurred at any time

during the 10-second intervals. The *E* signaled the intervals through a mechanism which produced an audible click every 10 seconds. Thus, one smiling response could be scored per interval, allowing a maximum of 30 smiles for a 5-minute period. Following this response definition, *E* permitted a maximum of one reinforcer combination per interval during the reinforcement periods.

Before a session began, one of the observers was arbitrarily chosen to record the data and the other observer provided a reliability check. To assess the reliability, an agreement or disagreement was tallied for every 10-second interval, and the percentage of agreements between observers was computed for each session. For all sessions reliability checks showed observer agreement of 95 per cent or better.

The observers also recorded behavioral changes in the *M*s and *ST*s. They were instructed to depress a second microswitch every 10 seconds if they observed "appreciable" changes in the behavior of *M*s and *ST*s. Here, reliability checks showed observer agreement of 100 per cent, and behavior changes in *M*s and *ST*s were perfectly correlated with *E*'s signals.

Results

Table 1 shows the total number of mother- and stranger-reinforced smiling responses for the 13 infants during baseline, reinforcement and extinction periods. Reinforcement control was considered to be demonstrated for an infant if his smiling responses were greater in number during the

Table 1
Number of Smiling Responses of 13 Infants Reinforced
by Their Mothers and by Female Strangers

Infants:	Order A: Mothers Presented Before Strangers							Order B: Strangers Presented Before Mothers					
	1	*2*	*3*	*4*	*5*	*6*	*7*	*8*	*9*	*10*	*11*	*12*	*13*
Mothers:													
Baseline	0	7	4	4	4	2	14	3	19	20	5	2	12
Reinforcement	10	21	10	10	2	7	13	8	25	11	9	7	15
Extinction	2	14	3	4	0	1	10	2	15	2	1	0	8
Strangers:													
Baseline	0	1	0	3	0	5	2	6	11	13	14	0	14
Reinforcement	0	9	5	5	2	1	1	7	17	10	9	2	16
Extinction	2	5	0	1	0	3	0	4	10	7	4	0	7
Reinforcement control:													
Mothers	+	+	+	+	−	+	−	+	+	−	+	+	+
Strangers	−	+	+	+	+	−	−	+	+	−	−	+	+

reinforcement period than during either the baseline or extinction periods. As Table 1 indicates, the order effect in the sequence of presenting *M*s and *ST*s to the infants was negligible. A comparison of infants in Orders A and B who did (+) and did not (−) show evidence of reinforcement control reveals only slight differences between the two orders. For the mother-reinforced infants, five were positive and two were negative in Order A; in Order B, five were positive and one was negative. For the stranger-reinforced infants, four were positive and three were negative in Order A; in Order B, four were positive and two were negative. . . .

Discussion

The data reported in this study indicate that the 3-month-old infant is differentially responsive to social reinforcers presented by familiar and unfamiliar adults. In two tests of reinforcer effectiveness, the *M*s used in this study were superior to female *ST*s in their attempts to control the infants' rates of smiling. These findings are not surprising in view of prior research which shows that the infant is subject to adult social reinforcement control by the age of 3 months (Brackbill, 1958; Rheingold, et al., 1959; Weisberg, 1963) and that he is also able to discriminate familiar from unfamiliar adults at this age (Ainsworth, 1964; Griffiths, 1954). By logically extending these findings, one might predict that familiar and unfamiliar adults should also differ in terms of their reinforcement power.

The finding that the *ST*s in this study showed *no* evidence of reinforcement control of the infants is surprising. Three prior studies (Brackbill, 1958; Rheingold et al., 1959; Weisberg, 1963) have shown that unfamiliar adults are effective social reinforcers for the behavior of 3-month-old infants. Thus, the absence of stranger reinforcement control reported in this study should be interpreted with great caution, especially in view of the small number of *S*s on which the findings is based.

The results of this study suggest that the infant's social attachment to a specific individual has undergone significant development by the time that he has reached the age of 3 months. Probably more marked differences in *M-ST* reinforcement control would be evident at later points in the infant's first year of life. This prediction is indirectly supported by research based on the separation distress criterion (Schaffer & Callender, 1959) and smiling criterion (Spitz, 1946 of social attachment. As this research indicates, the infant of 6–8 months makes clear-cut distinctions between familiar and unfamiliar persons through differential smiling and his distress upon being separated from the familiar person. It thus seems likely that prominent differences would also be present at this age between the effectiveness of social reinforcers offered by familiar and unfamiliar persons.

References

Ahrens, R. Beitrag zur Entwicklurg des Physiognomie und Mimikerkennens. *Zeitschrift fur experimentelle und angerwardt Psychologie,* 1954, **2,** 412-454.

Ainsworth, M. D. Patterns of attachment behavior shown by the infant in interaction with his Mother. *Merill-Palmer Quarterly,* 1954, **10,** 51-58.

Bowlby, J. Separation anxiety. *International Journal of Psychoanalysis,* 1960, **41,** 1–25.

Bowlby, J. The nature of the child's tie to his mother. *International Journal of Pschoanalysis,* 1958, **39,** 350–373.

Brackbill, Y. Extinction of the smiling response in infants as a function of reinforcement schedule. *Child Development,* 1958, **29,** 115–124.

Buhler, C. H. *The first year of life.* London: Kegan, Paul, 1937.

Gewirtz, J. L. A program of research on the dimensions and antecedents of emotional dependence. *Child Development,* 1956, **27,** 205–221.

Griffiths, R. *The abilities of babies.* London: Universty of London Press, 1954.

Kaila, E. Die reaktionen des Sauglirgs auf das Menschliche Gesicht. *Annals of Universities Aboensis,* 1932, **17,** 1–114.

Lovaas, O. I., Freitag, G., Gold, V. J., & Kassorla, I. C. Recording apparatus and procedure for observation of behaviors of children in free play settings. *Journal of experimental child Psychology,* 1965, **2,** 108–120.

Murphy, G., & Murphy, L. B. *Experimental social psychology,* New York: Harper & Bros., 1931.

Rheingold, H., Gewirtz, J. S., & Ross, H. W. Social conditioning of vocalization in the infant. *Journal of comparative and physiological Psychology,* 1959, **52,** 68–73.

Schaffer, H. R. Objective observations of personality development in early infancy. *British Journal of medical Psychology,* 1958, **31,** 174–184.

Schaffer, H. R., & Callender, W. M. Psychologic effects of hospitalization in infancy. *Pediatrics,* 1959, **24,** 528–539.

Schaffer, H. R., & Emerson, P. E. The development of social attachments in infancy. *Monographs of the Society for Research in Child Development,* 1964, **29,** 0–77.

Siegel, S. *Nonparametric statistics for the behavioral sciences.* McGraw-Hill Book Co., 1956.

Spitz, R. A. The smiling response: a contribution to the ontogenesis of social relations. *Genetic psychology Monographs,* 1946, **34,** 57–125.

Weisberg, P. Social and non-social conditioning of infant vocalizations. *Child Development,* 1963, **34,** 377–388.

3.7   Hospitalism[2] An Inquiry into the Genesis of Psychiatric Conditions in Early Childhood

Rene A. Spitz, M. D.

The Problem

The term *hospitalism* designates vitiated condition of the body due to long confinement in a hospital, or the morbid condition of the atmosphere of a hospital. The term has been increasingly preempted to specify the evil effect of institutional care on infants, placed in institutions from an early age, particularly from the psychiatric point of view.[2] This study is especially concerned with the effect of continuous institutional care of infants under one year of age, for reasons other than sickness. The model of such institutions is the foundling home.

Medical men and administrators have long been aware of the shortcomings of such charitable institutions. At the beginning of our century one of the great foundling homes in Germany had a mortality rate of 71.5% in infants in the first year of life (1a).[3] In 1915 Chapin (2a) enumerated ten asylums in the larger cities of the United States, mainly on the Eastern seaboard, in which the death rates of infants admitted during their first year of life varied from 31.7% to 75% by the end of their second year. In a discussion in the same year before the American Pediatric Association (3a), Dr. Knox of Baltimore stated that in the institutions of that city 90% of the infants died by the end of their first year. He believed that the remaining 10% probably were saved because they had been taken out of the institution in time. Dr. Shaw of the Albany remarked in the same discussion that the mortality rate of Randalls Island Hospital was probably 100%.

Conditions have since greatly changed At present the best American institutions, such as Bellevue Hospital, New York City, register a mortality rate of less than 10% (4a), which compares favorably with the mortality rate of the rest of the country. While these and similar results were being achieved both here and in Europe, physicians and administrators were soon faced with a new problem: they discovered that institutionalized children practically without exception developed subsequent psychiatric disturbances and became asocial, delinquent, feeble-minded, psychotic, or problem children. Probably the high mortality rate in the preceding period had obscured this consequence. Now that the children survived, the other drawbacks of institutionalization became apparent. They led in this country to the widespread substitution of institutional care by foster home care. . . .

We believe that further study is needed to isolate clearly the various factors operative in the deterioration subsequent to prolonged care in institutions. . . .

Material

With this purpose in mind a long-term study of 164 children was undertaken. In view of the findings of previous investigations this study was largely limited to the first year of life, and confined to two institutions, in order to embrace the total population of both (130) infants. Since the two institutions were situated in different countries of the Western hemisphere, a basis of comparison was established by investigating non-institutionalized children of the same age group in their parents' homes in both countries. A total of 34 of these were observed. We thus have four environments:

Table 1

Environment	Institution No. 1[4]	Corresponding Private Background	Institution No. 2	Corresponding Private Background
Number of Children	69	11	61	23

Procedure

In each case an anamnesis was made which whenever possible included data on the child's mother; and in each case the Hetzer-Wolf baby tests were administered.

Results

For the purpose of orientation we established the average of the Developmental Quotients for the first third of the first year of life for each of the environments investigated. We contrasted these average with those for the last third of the first year. This comparison gives us a first hint of the significance of environmental influences for development.

Table 2

Type of Environment	Cultural and Social Background	Developmental Quotients	
		Average of first four months	Average of last four months
Parental Home	Professional	133	131
	Village Population	107	108
Institution	"Nursery"	101.5	105
	"Foundling home"	124	72

Children of the first category come from professional homes in a large city; their Development Quotient, high from the start, remains high in the course of development.

Children in the second category come from an isolated fishing village of 499 inhabitants, where conditions of nutrition, housing, hygienic and medical care are very poor indeed; their Developmental Quotient in the first four months is much lower and remains at a lower level than that of the previous category.

In the third category, "Nursery", the children were handicapped from birth by the circumstances of their origin, which will be discussed below. At the outset their Developmental Quotient is even somewhat lower than that of the village babies; in the course of their development they gain slightly.

In the fourth category, "Foundling Home", the children are of an unselected urban (Latin) background. Their Development Quotient on admission is below that of our best category but much higher than that of the other two. The picture changes completely by the end of the first year, when their Developmental Quotient sinks to the astonishingly low level of 72.

Thus the children in the first three environments were at the end of their first year on the whole well-developed and normal, whether they were raised in their progressive middle-class family homes (where obviously optimal circumstances prevailed and the children were well in advance of average development), or in an institution or a village home, where the development was not brilliant but still reached a perfectly normal and satisfactory average. The children in the fourth environment, though starting at almost as high a level as the best of the others, had spectacularly deteriorated.

The children in Foundling Home showed all the manifestations of hospitalism, both physical and mental. In spite of the fact that hygiene and precautions against contagion were impeccable, the children showed, from the third month on, extreme susceptibility to infection and illness of any kind. There was hardly a child in whose case history we did not find reference to otitis media, or morbilli, or varicella, or eczema, or intestinal disease of one kind or another. No figures could be elicited on general mortality; but during my stay an epidemic of measles swept the institution, with staggeringly high mortality figures, notwithstanding liberal administration of convalescent serum and globulins, as well as excellent hygienic conditions. Of a total of 88 children up to the age of 2½, 23 died. It is striking to compare the mortality among the 45 children up to 1½ years, to that of the 43 children ranging from 1½ to 2½ years: usually, the *incidence* of measles is low in the younger age group, but among those infected the mortality is higher than that in the older age group; since in the case of Foundling Home every child was infected, the question of incidence does not enter; however, contrary to expectation, the mortality was much higher

in the older age group. In the younger group, 6 died, i.e., approximately 13%. In the older group, 17 died, i.e., close to 40%. The significance of these figures becomes apparent when we realize that the mortality from measles during the first year of life in the community in question, outside the institution, was less than ½%.

In view of the damage sustained in all personality sectors of the children during their stay in this institution we believe it licit to assume that their vitality (whatever that may be), their resistance to disease, was also progressively sapped. In the ward of the children ranging from 18 months to 2½ years only two of the twenty-six surviving children speak a couple of words. The same two are able to walk. A third child is beginning to walk. Hardly any of them can eat alone. Cleanliness habits have not been acquired and all are incontinent.

In sharp contrast to this is the picture offered by the oldest inmates in Nursery, ranging from 8 to 12 months. The problem here is not whether the children walk or talk by the end of the first year; the problem with these 10-month-olds is how to tame the healthy toddlers' curiosity and enterprise. They climb up the bars of the cots after the manner of South Sea Islanders climbing palms. Special measures to guard them from harm have had to be taken after one 10-month-old actually succeeded in diving right over the more than two-foot railing of the cot. They vocalize freely and some of them actually speak a word or two. And all of them understand the significance of simple social gestures. When released from their cots, all walk with support and a number walk without it.

What are the differences between the two institutions that result in the one turning out normally acceptable children and the other showing such appalling effects?

Similarities

Background of the children. Nursery is a penal institution in which delinquent girls are sequestered. When, as is often the case, they are pregnant on admission, they are delivered in a neighboring maternity hospital and after the lying-in period their children are cared for in Nursery from birth to the end of their first year. The background of these children provides for a markedly negative selection since the mothers are mostly delinquent minors as a result of social maladjustment or feeble-mindedness, or because they are psychically defective, psychopathic, or criminal. Psychic normalcy and adequate social adjustment is almost excluded.

The other institution is a foundling home pure and simple. A certain number of the children housed have a background not much better than that of the Nursery children; but a sufficiently relevant number come from socially well-adjusted, normal mothers whose only handicap is inability to support themselves and their children (which is no sign of maladjustment in

women of Latin background). This is expressed in the average of the Developmental Quotients of the two institutions during the first 4 months, as shown in Table II.

The background of the children in the two institutions does therefore not favor Nursery; on the contrary, it shows a very marked advantage for Foundling Home.

Housing Conditions. Both institutions are situated outside the city, in large spacious gardens. In both hygienic conditions are carefully maintained. In both infants at birth and during the first 6 weeks are segregated from the older babies in a special newborns' ward, to which admittance is only permitted in a freshly sterilized smock after hands are washed. In both institutions infants are transferred from the newborns' ward after 2 or 3 months to the older babies' wards, where they are placed in individual cubicles which in Nursery are completely glass enclosed, in Foundling Home glass enclosed on three sides and open at the end. In Foundling Home the children remain in their cubicles up to 15 to 18 months; in Nursery they are transferred after the 6th month to rooms containing four to five cots each.

One-half of the children in Foundling Home are located in a dimly lighted part of the ward; the other half, in the full light of large windows facing southeast, with plenty of sun coming in. In Nursery, all the children have well-lighted cubicles. In both institutions the walls are painted in a light neutral color, giving a white impression in Nursery, a gray-green impression in Foundling Home. In both, the children are placed in white painted cots. Nursery is financially the far better provided one: we usually find here a small metal table with the paraphernalia of child care, as well as a chair, in each cubicle; whereas in Foundling Home it is the exception if a low stool is to be found in the cubicles, which usually contain nothing but the child's cot.

Food. In both institutions adequate food is excellently prepared and varied according to the needs of the individual child at each age; bottles from which children are fed are sterilized. In both institutions a large percentage of the younger children are breast fed. In Nursery this percentage is smaller, so that in most cases a formula is soon added, and in many cases weaning takes place early. In Foundling Home all children are breast-fed as a matter of principle as long as they are under 3 months unless disease makes a deviation from this rule necessary.

Clothing. Clothing is practically the same in both institutions. The children have adequate pastel-colored dresses and blankets. The temperature in the rooms is appropriate. We have not seen any shivering child in either set-up.

Medical Care. Foundling Home is visited by the head physician and the medical staff at least once a day, often twice, and during these rounds the chart of each child is inspected as well as the child itself. For special ailments a laryngologist and other specialists are available; they also make daily rounds. In Nursery no daily rounds are made, as they are not necessary. The physician sees the children when called.

Up to this point it appears that there is very little significant difference between the children of the two institutions. Foundling Home shows, if anything, a slight advantage over Nursery in the matter of selection of admitted children, of breast-feeding and of medical care. It is in the items that now follow that fundamental differences become visible.

Differences

Toys. In Nursery it is the exception when a child is without one or several toys. In Foundling Home my first impression was that not a single child had a toy. This impression was later corrected. In the course of time, possibly in reaction to our presence, more and more toys appeared, some of them quite intelligently fastened by a string above the baby's head so that he could reach it. By the time we left a large percentage of the children in Foundling Home had a toy.

Visual Radius. In Nursery the corridor running between the cubicles, though rigorously white and without particular adornment, gives a friendly impression of warmth. This is probably because trees, landscape and sky are visible from both sides and because a bustling activity of mothers carrying their children, tending them, feeding them, playing with them, chatting with each other with babies in their arms, is usually present. The cubicles of the children are enclosed but the glass panes of the partitions reach low enough for every child to be able at any time to observe everything going on all around. He can see into the corridor as soon as he lifts himself on his elbows. He can look out of the windows, and can see babies in the other cubicles by just turning his head; witness the fact that whenever the experimenter plays with a baby in one of the cubicles the babies in the two adjoining cubicles look on fascinated, try to participate in the game, knock at the panes of the partition, and often begin to cry if no attention is paid to them. Most of the cots are provided with widely-spaced bars that are no obstacle to vision. After the age of 6 months, when the child is transferred to the wards of the older babies, the visual field is enriched as a number of babies are then together in the same room, and accordingly play with each other.

In Foundling Home the corridor into which the cubicles open, though full of light on one side at least, is bleak and deserted, except at feeding time when five to eight nurses file in and look after the children's needs. Most of

the time nothing goes on to attract the babies' attention. A special routine of Foundling Home consists in hanging bed sheets over the foot and the side railing of each cot. The cot itself is approximately 18 inches high. The side railings are about 20 inches high; the foot and head railings are approximately 28 inches high. Thus, when bed sheets are hung over the railings, the child lying in the cot is effectively screened from the world. He is completely separated from the other cubicles, since the glass panes of the wooden partitions begin 6 to 8 inches higher than even the head railing of the cot. The result of this system is that each baby lies in solitary confinement up to the time when he is able to stand up in his bed, and that the only object he can see is the ceiling.

Radius of Locomotion. In Nursery the radius of locomotion is circumscribed by the space available in the cot, which up to about 10 months provides a fairly satisfactory range.

Theoretically the same would apply to Foundling Home. But in practice this is not the case for, probably owing to the lack of stimulation, the babies lie supine in their cots for many months and a hollow is worn into their mattresses. By the time they reach the age when they might turn from back to side (approximately the 7th month) this hollow confines their activity to such a degree that they are effectively prevented from turning in any direction. As a result we find most babies, even at 10 and 12 months, lying on their backs and playing with the only object at their disposal, their own hands and feet.

Personnel. In Foundling Home there is a head nurse and five assistant nurses for a total of forty-five babies. These nurses have the *entire* care of the children on their hands, except for the babies so young that they are breast-fed. The latter are cared for to a certain extent by their own mothers or by wetnurses; but after a few months they are removed to the single cubicles of the general ward, where they share with at least seven other children the ministrations of *one* nurse. It is obvious that the amount of care one nurse can give to an individual child when she has eight children to manage is small indeed. These nurses are unusually motherly, baby-loving women; but of course the babies of Foundling Home nevertheless lack all human contact for most of the day.

Nursery is run by a head nurse and her three assistants, whose duties do not include the care of the children, but consist mainly in teaching the children's mothers in child care, and in supervising them. The children are fed, nursed and cared for by their own mothers or, in those cases where the mother is separated from her child for any reason, by the mother of another child, or by a pregnant girl who in this way acquires the necessary experience for the care of her own future baby. Thus in Nursery each child

has the full-time care of his own mother, or at least that of the substitute which the very able head nurse tries to change about until she finds someone who really likes the child.

Discussion

To say that every child in Nursery has a full-time mother is an understatement, from a psychological point of view. However modern a penal institution may be, and however constructive and permissive its reeducative policies, the deprivation it imposes upon delinquent girls is extensive. Their opportunities for an outlet for their interests, ambitions, activity, are very much impoverished. The former sexual satisfactions as well as the satisfactions of competitive activity in the sexual field, are suddenly stopped: regulations prohibit flashy dresses, vivid nail polish, or extravagant hairdo's. The kind of social life in which the girls could show off has vanished. This is especially traumatic as these girls become delinquent because they have not been able to sublimate their sexual drives, to find substitute gratifications, and therefore do not possess a pattern for relinquishing pleasure when frustrated. In addition, they do not have compensation in relations with family and friends, as formerly they had. These factors, combined with the loss of personal liberty, the deprivation of private property and the regimentation of the penal institution, all add up to a severe narcissistic trauma from the time of admission; and they continue to affect the narcissistic and libidinal sectors during the whole period of confinement.

Luckily there remain a few safety valves for their emotions: 1. the relationship with wardens, matrons and nurses; 2. with fellow prisoners; 3. with the child. In the relationship with the wardens, matrons and nurses, who obviously represent parent figures, much of the prisoner's aggression and resentment is bound. Much of it finds an outlet in the love and hate relationship to fellow prisoners, where all the phenomena of sibling rivalry are revived.

The child, however, becomes for them the representative of their sexuality, a product created by them, an object they own, which they can dress up and adorn, on which they can lavish their tenderness and pride, and of whose accomplishments, performance and appearance they can boast. This is manifested in the constant competition among them as to who has the better dressed, more advanced, more intelligent, better looking, the heavier, bigger, more active—in a word, the better baby. For their own persons they have more or less given up the competition for love, but they are intensely jealous of the attention given to their children by the matrons, wardens, and fellow prisoners.

It would take an exacting experimenter to invent an experiment with

conditions as diametrically opposed in regard to the mother-child relationship as they are in these two institutions. Nursery provides each child with a mother to the nth degree, a mother who gives the child everything a good mother does and, beyond that, everything else she has. Foundling Home does not give the child a mother, nor even a substitute-mother, but only an eighth of a nurse.

We are now in a position to approach more closely and with better understanding the results obtained by each of the two institutions. We have already cited a few: we mentioned that the Developmental Quotient of Nursery achieves a normal average of about 105 at the end of the first year, whereas that of the Foundling Home sinks to 72; and we mentioned the striking difference of the children in the two institutions at first sight. Let us first consider the point at which the developments in the two institutions deviate.

On admission the children of Foundling Home have a much better average than the children of Nursery; their hereditary equipment is better than that of the children of delinquent minors. But while Foundling Home shows a rapid fall of the developmental index, Nursery shows a steady rise. They cross between the 4th and 5th months, and from that point on the curve of the average Developmental Quotient of the Foundling Home drops downward with increasing rapidity, never again to rise (Curve I).

The point where the two curves cross is significant. The time when the children in Foundling Home are weaned is the beginning of the 4th month. The time lag of one month in the sinking of the index below normal is explained by the fact that the Quotient represents a cross-section including all sectors of development, and that attempts at compensation are made in some of the other sectors.

However, when we consider the sector of Body Mastery (Curve II) which is most indicative for the mother-child relationship, we find that the curves of the children in Nursery cross the Body Mastery curve of the Foundling Home children between the 3rd and 4th month. The inference is obvious. As soon as the babies in Foundling Home are weaned the modest human contacts which they have had during nursing at the breast stop, and their development falls below normal.

One might be inclined to speculate as to whether the further deterioration of the children in Foundling Home is not due to other factors also, such as the perceptual and motor deprivations from which they suffer. It might be argued that the better achievement of the Nursery children is due to the fact that they were better provided for in regard to toys and other perceptual stimuli. We shall therefore analyze somewhat more closely the nature of deprivations in perceptual and locomotor stimulation.

First of all it should be kept in mind that the nature of the inanimate perceptual stimulus, whether it is a toy or any other object, has only a very

minor importance for a child under 12 months. At this age the child is not yet capable of distinguishing the real purpose of an object. He is only able to use it in a manner adequate to his own functional needs (23a). Our thesis is that perception is a function of emotion of one kind or another. Emotions are provided for the child through the intervention of a human

Fig. 1
Comparison of Development in "Nursery"
and "Foundlinghome"

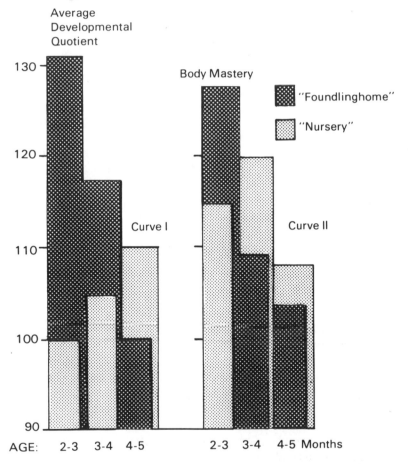

partner, i.e., by the mother or her substitute. A progressive development of emotional interchange with the mother provides the child with perceptive experiences of its environment. The child learns to grasp by nursing at the mother's breast and by combining the emotional satisfaction of that experience with the tactile perceptions. He learns to distinguish animate objects

from inanimate ones by the spectacle provided by his mother's face (28a) in situations fraught with emotional satisfaction. The interchange between mother and child is loaded with emotional factors and it is in this interchange that the child learns to play. He becomes acquainted with his surroundings through the mother's carrying him around; through her help he learns security in locomotion as well as in every other respect. This security is reinforced by her being at his beck and call. In these emotional relations with the mother the child is introduced to learning, and later to imitation. We have previously mentioned that the motherless children in Foundling Home are unable to speak, to feed themselves, or to acquire habits of cleanliness: it is the security provided by the mother in the field of locomotion, the emotional bait offered by the mother calling her child, that "teaches" him to walk. When this is lacking, even children two to three years old cannot walk.

The children in Foundling Home have, theoretically, as much radius of locomotion as the children in Nursery. They did not at first have toys, but they could have exerted their grasping and tactile activity on the blankets, on their clothes, even on the bars of the cots. We have seen children in Nursery without toys; they are the exception—but the lack of material is not enough to hamper them in the acquisition of locomotor and grasping skills. The presence of a mother or her substitute is sufficient to compensate for all the other deprivations.

It is true that the children in Foundling Home are condemned to solitary confinement in their cots. But we do not think that it is the lack of perceptual stimulation *in general* that counts in their deprivation. We believe that they suffer because their perceptual world is emptied of human partners, that their isolation cuts them off from any stimulation by any persons who could signify mother-representatives for the child at this age. The result, as Curve III shows, is a complete restriction of psychic capacity by the end of the first year.

This restriction of psychic capacity is not a temporary phenomenon. It is, as can be seen from the curve, a progressive process. How much this deterioration could have been arrested if the children were taken out of the institution at the end of the first year is an open question. The fact that they remain in Foundling Home probably furthers this progressive process. By the end of the second year the Developmental Quotient sinks to 45, which corresponds to a mental age of approximately 10 months, and would qualify these children as imbeciles.

The curve of the children in Nursery does not deviate significantly from the normal. The curve sinks at two points, between the 6th and 7th, and between the 10th and 12th months. These deviations are within the normal range; their significance will be discussed in a separate article. It has nothing to do with the influence of institutions, for the curve of the village group is nearly identical.

Fig. 2
Comparison of Development in "Nursery"
and "Foundlinghome" During the
First Five Months

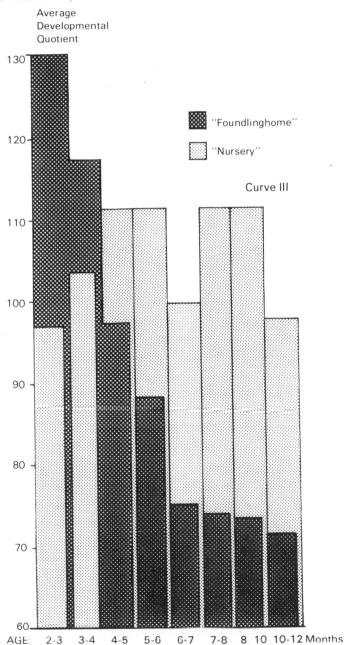

Anaclitic Depression

A circumscribed psychiatric syndrome

In the course of this long term study of infant behavior we encountered a striking syndrome. In the second half of the first year, a few of these infants developed a weepy behavior that was in marked contrast to their previously happy and outgoing behavior. After a time this weepiness gave way to withdrawal. The children in question would lie in their cots with averted faces, refusing to take part in the life of their surroundings. When we approached them we were ignored. Some of these children would watch us with a searching expressions. If we were insistent enough, weeping would ensue and, in some cases, screaming. The sex of the approaching experimenter made no difference in the reaction in the majority of cases. Such behavior would persist for two to three months. During this period some of these children lost weight instead of gaining; the nursing personnel reported that some suffered from insomnia, which in one case led to segregation of the child. All showed a greater susceptibility to intercurrent colds or eczema. A gradual decline in the developmental quotient was observed in these cases.

This behavior syndrome lasted three months. Then the weepiness subsided, and stronger provocation became necessary to provoke it. A sort of frozen rigidity of expression appeared instead. These children would lie or sit with wide-open, expressionless eyes, frozen immobile face, and a faraway expression as if in a daze, apparently not preceiving what went on in their environment. This behavior was in some cases accompanied by autoerotic activities in the oral, anal, and genital zones. Contact with children who arrived at this stage became increasingly difficult and finally impossible. At best, screaming was elicited.

Among the 123 unselected children observed during the whole of the first year of their life we found this clear-cut syndrome in 19 cases. The gross picture of these cases showed many, if not all, of these traits. Individual differences were partly quantitative: i.e., one or the other trait, as for instance weeping, would for a period dominate the picture, and thus would impress the casual observer as the only one present; and partly qualitative: i.e., there was an attitude of complete withdrawal in some cases, as against others in which, when we succeeded in breaking through the rejection of any approach, we found a desperate clinging to the grown-up. But apart from such individual differences the clinical picture was so distinctive that once we had called attention to it, it was easily recognizable by even untrained observers. It led us to assume that we were confronted with a psychiatric syndrome. . . .

Discussion of the Syndrome

The principal symptoms . . . fall into several categories; within each

category we have grouped them on a scale of increasing severity. They are not all necessarily present at the same time, but most of them show up at one point or another in the clinical picture. They are:

Apprehension, sadness, weepiness.
Lack of contact, rejection of environment, withdrawal.
Retardation of development, retardation of reaction to stimuli, slowness of movement, dejection, stupor.
Loss of appetite, refusal to eat, loss of weight.
Insomnia.

To this symptomatology should be added the physiognomic expression in these cases, which is difficult to describe. This expression would in an adult be described as depression. . . .

The factors of color and of sex were explored and do not appear to exert demonstrable influence on the incidence of the syndrome.

The youngest age at which the syndrome was manifested in our series was around the turn of the sixth month; the oldest was the eleventh month. The syndrome therefore seems to be independent of chronological age, within certain limits. . . .

There is one factor which all cases that developed the syndrome had in common. In all of them the mother was removed from the child somewhere between the sixth and eighth month for a practically unbroken period of three months, during which the child either did not see its mother at all, or at best once a week. This removal took place for unavoidable external reasons. Before the separation the mother had the full care of the infant, and as a result of special circumstances spent more time with the child than is usual in a private home. In each case a striking change in the child's behavior could be observed in the course of the four to six weeks following the mother's removal. The syndrome described above would then develop. *No* child developed the syndrome in question whose mother was *not* removed. Our proposition is that the syndrome observed developed only in children who were deprived of their love object for an appreciable period of time during their first year of life.

On the other hand, not all children whose mothers were removed developed the same syndrome. Hence, mother separation is a necessary, but not a sufficient cause for the development of the syndrome. . . .

Prognosis of the Syndrome

Stages of symptoms. The static signs and symptoms are those observable phenomena that we are able to ascertain in the course of one or several observations of the infant in question. We have mentioned them in Part II of our study. One of the outstanding signs is the physiognomic expression of such patients. The observer at once notices an apprehensive or sad or depressed expression on the child's face, which often impels him to ask

whether the child is sick. It is characteristic, at this stage, that the child makes an active attempt to catch the observer's attention and to involve him in a game. However, this outgoing introduction usually is not followed by particularly active play on the part of the child. In the main it is acted out in the form of clinging to the observer and sorrowful disappointment at the observer's withdrawal.

In the next stage the apprehensiveness deepens. The observer's approach provokes crying or screaming, and the observer's departure does not evoke as universal a disappointment as previously. Many of the cases observed by us fall into the period of what has been described as "eight months anxiety" (4b, 9b, 11b, 18b).

The so-called "eight months anxiety" begins somewhere between the sixth and eighth month and is a product of the infant's increasing capacity for diacritic discrimination (19b) between friend and stranger. As a result of this the approaching stranger is received either by what has been described as "coy" or "bashful" behavior, or by the child's turning away, hanging its head, crying, and even screaming in the presence of a stranger, and refusing to play with him or to accept toys. The difference between this behavior and the behavior in anaclitic depression is a quantitative one. While in anaclitic depression, notwithstanding every effort, it takes upwards of an hour to achieve contact with the child and to get it to play, in the eight months anxiety this contact can be achieved with the help of appropriate behavior in a span of time ranging from one to ten minutes. The appropriate behavior is very simple: it consists in sitting down next to the cot of the child with one's back turned to him and without paying any attention to him. After the above mentioned period of one to ten minutes the child will take the initiative, grab the observer's gown or hand—and with this contact is established, and any experienced child psychologist can lead from this into playing with the child's active and happy participation. In the anaclitic depression nothing of the sort occurs. The child does not touch the observer, the approach has to be moderately active on the observer's part, and consists mostly in patient waiting, untiringly repeated attempts at cuddling or petting the child, and incessant offers of constantly varied toys. The latter must be offered with a capacity to understand the nature of the child's refusal. Some toys create anxiety in some children and have an opposite effect on others; for example, some children are attracted by bright colors but are immediately made panicky if a noise such as drumming is provoked in connection with this brightly colored toy. Others may be attracted by the rhythmic noise. Some are delighted by dolls, others go into a panic and can be reassured by no method at the sight of a doll. Some who are delighted by a spinning top will break into tears when it stops spinning and falls over, and every further attempt to spin it will evoke renewed protest.

When finally contact is made the pathognomonic expression does not brighten; after having accepted the observer the child plays without any expression of happiness. He does not play actively and is severely retarded in all his behavior manifestations. The only signs of his having achieved contact is, on the one hand, his acceptance of toys; and on the other, his expression of grief and his crying when left by the observer. That this qualitative distinction is not an arbitrary one can be seen from the fact that in a certain number of the cases in which the anaclitic depression was manifested late, we could observe the eight months anxiety as well as the anaclitic depression at periods distinct from each other. In one case, for instance, the eight months anxiety actually appeared at 0;7 + 14 and had already completely subsided and disappeared when the anaclitic depression was manifested at 0;11 + 2.

In the next stage the outward appearance of the child is that of complete withdrawal, dejection, and turning away from the environment. In the case of these children even the lay person with good empathy for children has no difficulty in making the diagnosis, and will tell the observer that the child is grieving for his mother. . . .

Quantitative signs. Quantitative signs can be detected by consecutive developmental tests which, if compared to each other, will at the beginning of the anaclitic depression show a gradual drop of the developmental quotient; this drop progresses with the progression of the disorder (see fig. 3).

Prognosis: with intervention.

In the beginning of this section we stated that a certain measure could be taken whereupon the syndrome disappeared. The measure taken was in the nature of environmental manipulation. It consisted in returning the mother to the child. The change in the children's observable behavior was dramatic. They suddenly were friendly, gay, approachable. The withdrawal, the disinterest, the rejection of the outside world, the sadness, disappeared as if by magic. But over and beyond these changes most striking was the jump in the developmental quotient, within a period of twelve hours after the mother's return; in some cases, as much as 36.6 per cent higher than the previous measurement.

Thus one would assume that if adequate therapeutic measures are taken, the process is curable with extreme rapidity and the prognosis is good. The last statement requires some qualification. To our regret we have not been and are not in a position to follow the children in question beyond a maximum of eighteen months. It is therefore open to question whether the psychic trauma sustained by them as a consequence of being separated from their mothers will leave traces which will become visible only later in life.

Fig. 3
Variations of Development Quotient

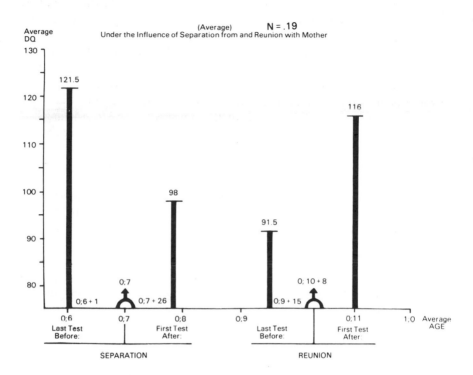

We are inclined to suspect something of the sort. For the sudden astonishing jump in the developmental quotient on the return of the love object is not maintained in all cases. We have observed cases in which, after a period of two weeks, the developmental quotient dropped again. It did not drop to the previous low levels reached during the depression. However, compared to these children's pre-depression performance, the level on which they were functioning after their recovery was not adequate. . . .

Prognosis without intervention.

The main reason why, apart from all physiognomic, behavioral and other traits, we feel justified in speaking of an anaclitic depression going far beyond mourning and even beyond pathological mourning is that we have observed a number of cases in which no intervention occurred and where it

became only too evident that the process was in no way self-limiting. These cases were the ones observed in Foundling Home. In that institution, where medical, hygienic, and nutritional standards were comparable to those obtaining in Nursery, the separation from the mother took place beginning after the third month, but prevalently in the sixth month. However, whereas in Nursery the separation was temporary and the love object was restored after approximately three months of absence, in Foundling Home the love object was not restored. The picture of depression was as clear-cut as in Nursery, with some additional developments: for the picture of children in advanced extreme cases varied from stuporous deteriorated catatonia to agitated idiocy.

If we compare the pictures of the two institutions we are confronted with a syndrome of a progressive nature which after having reached a critical point of development appears to become irreversible. It is this characteristic which causes us to call the picture depression and not mourning. And beyond this, in Foundling Home we encounter a phenomenon more grave than melancholia. Notwithstanding the satisfactory hygiene and asepsis, the rate of mortality of the infants reared there was inordinately high. In the course of two years 34 of the 91 children observed died of diseases varying from respiratory and intestinal infections to measles and otitis media. In some cases the cause of death was in the nature of cachexia. This phenomenon savors of psychosomatic involvement.

No intervention was effective in the case of the longer lasting separation in Foundling Home. This finding is one of the reasons why we spoke of three months as a critical period. The second reason is that in Nursery we observed towards the end of the three months the appearance of that kind of frozen, affect-impoverished expression which had strongly impressed us in Foundling Home. Furthermore, a curious reluctance to touch objects was manifested, combined with certain unusual postures of hands and fingers which seemed to use the precursors of the extremely bizarre hand and finger movements composing the total activity in those infants of Foundling Home whom we described as presenting a picture of stuporous catatonia.

After their recovery in the course of their further development, which to our regret could not be followed beyond one-and-a-half years, the children in Nursery did not show any spectacular changes. As indicated above it, it is therefore impossible at this point to state whether this early depression left any visible traces. One would be inclined to expect it. . . .

Recuperative Trends vs. Institutional Care

An objection might be raised at this point: if anaclitic depression is provoked by inhibiting the locomotion of infants separated from their love object, why is it that a significant number of the infants observed by us in Nursery, the majority in fact, remained unharmed? And what is the reason

for the severe nature of one group of infantile depression, for the milder course of the others?

The answer is that in both cases the outcome depends on the measure of success achieved in this institution in providing the infant with a substitute love object. The separation of the infants from their mothers takes place in Nursery between the sixth and the ninth month. Another of the inmates is then assigned to the care of the motherless child. The substitute mother thus cares for her own child and for a stranger. Though the enlightened management of Nursery exerts the greatest care, their selection is limited by the available number of inmates. Also it is hardly to be expected that a group of delinquent girls, as these were, will furnish very high grade mother substitutes.

We suggest that when the mother substitute is a good one, depression does not develop. Where the mother substitute turns out to be an aggressive, unloving personality. The child is caught between a hostile love object substitute and its own aggressive drive. Bereft of locomotion, it cannot actively seek replacement for the lost love object among the other grown-ups in the institution.

An indirect confirmation of this view is contained in the following table, which refers to the original mother-child relationship. In it we tabulate the number of children and the nature of their depression, on the one hand, the nature of the relations between the child and its mother, on the other. The mother-child relation was established by our observation of the way the mother behaved to her child. For the purpose of corroboration these observations then were compared with the information gathered for this purpose from the unusually able headmatron of Nursery. This somewhat complicated procedure made it impossible to procure reliable data on all the 95 children in question; but we did get them on 64, appearing in the table below.

Table 6
Mother-Child Relation

	Good			Bad		
	Intense	*Moderate*	*Weak*	*Intense*	*Moderate*	*Weak*
Severe Depression	6	11	—	—	—	—
Mild Depression	4	—	3	7	—	4
No Depression	—	—	2	11	2	14

The figures speak for themselves. Evidently it is more difficult to replace a satisfactory love object than an unsatisfactory one. Accordingly depression is much more frequent and much more severe in the cases of good mother-child relationship. In bad mother-child relationship not a single

severe depression occurs. It seems that any substitute is at least as good as the real mother in these cases. . . .

Provisional Conclusions

The contrasing pictures of these two institutions (Nursery and Foundling Home), and the depression syndrome described above show the significance of the mother-child relationship for the development of the child during the first year. Deprivations in other fields, such as perceptual and locomotor radius, can all be compensated by adequate mother-child relations. "Adequate" is not here a vague general term. The examples chosen represent the two extremes of the scale. (These findings should not be construed as a recommendation for overprotection of children. In principle the libidinal situation of Nursery is almost as undesirable as the other extreme in Foundling Home. Neither in the nursery of a penal institution nor in a foundling home for parentless children can the normal libidinal situation that obtains a family home be expected.)

The children in Foundling Home do have a mother—for a time, in the beginning—but they must share her immediately with at least one other child, and from 3 months on, with seven other children. The quantitative factor here is evident. There is a point under which the mother-child relations cannot be restricted during the child's first year without inflicting irreparable damage. On the other hand, the exaggerated mother-child relationship in Nursery introduces a different quantitative factor. To anyone familiar with the field it is surprising that Nursery should achieve such excellent results, for we know that institutional care is destructive for children during their first year; but in Nursery the destructive factors have been compensated by the increased intensity of the mother-child relationship. . . .

Notes

[1]This article is a condensed and edited version of two original articles: 1) Spitz, R. A. Hospitalism: An inquiry into the genesis of psychiatric conditions in early childhood. In A. Freud, *et. al.* (Eds.), The Psychoanalytic Study of the Child. Vol. I. New York: International Universities Press, 1945, 53-74.; and 2) Spitz, R. A., with the assistance of Wolf, K. M. Anaclitic depression: An inquiry into the genesis of psychiatric conditions in early childhood, II. In A. Freud, *et. al.* (Eds.), *The Psychoanalytic Study of the Child.* Vol. II. New York: International Universities Press, 1946, 313-342.

[2]*Hospitalism* tends to be confused with *hospitalization,* the temporary confinement of a seriously ill person to a hospital.

[3]Numbers in parentheses refer to the bibliography at the end of the paper.

[4]Institution No. 1 will from here on be called "Nursery"; and institution No. 2, "Foundling Home".

Bibliography (a)

1a Schlossman, A., "Zur Frage der Säuglingssterblichkeit", *Münchner Med. Wochenschrift*, 67, 1920.

2a Chapin, H. D., "Are Instiutions for Infants Necessary?", *Journal of American Medical Association*, January 1915.

3a Chapin H. D., "A Plea for Accurate Statistics in Infants' Institutions", *Archives of Pediatrics*, October, 1915.

4a Bakwin, H., "Loneliness in Infants", *American Journal of Diseases of Children*, 63, 1942, pp. 30-40.

5a Durfee, H. and Wolf, K., "Anstaltspflege und Entwickling im erstern Lebensjahr", *Zeitschrift fur Kinderforschung*, 42/3, 1933.

6a Lowrey, L. G., "Personality Distortion and Early Institutional Care", *American Journal of Orthopsychiatry*, X, 3, 1940, pp. 576-585.

7a Bender, L. and Yarnell, H., "An Observation Nursery: a Study of 250 Children in the Psychiatric Division of Bellevue Hospital", *American Journal of Psychiatry*, 97 1941, pp. 1158-1174.

8a Goldfarb, W., "Infant Rearing as a Factor in Foster Home Placement", *American Journal of Orthopsychiatry*, XIV, 1944, pp. 162-167.

9a Goldfarb, W., "Effects of Early Institutional Care on Adolescent Personality: Rorschach Data", *American Journal of Orthopsychiatry*, XIV, 1944, pp. 441-447.

10a Goldfarb, W., "Effects of Early Institutional Care on Adolescent Personality", *Journal of Experimental Education*, 12, 1943, pp. 106-129.

11a Goldfarb, W. and Klopfer, B., "Rorschach Characteristics of Institutional Children", *Rorschach Research Exchange*, 8, 1944, pp. 92-100.

12a Ripin, R., "A Study of the Infant's Feeling Reactions During the First Six Months of Life", *Archives of Psychology*, 116, 1930, p. 38.

13a Skeels, H. M., "Mental Development of Children in Foster Homes", *Journal of Consulting Psychology*, 2, 1938, pp. 33-43.

14a Skeels H. M., "Some Iowa Studies of the Mental Growth of Children in Relation to Differentials of the Environment: A Summary", *39th Yearbook, National Society for the Study of Education*, II, 1940, pp. 281 308.

15a Skeels, H. M., Updegraff, R. Wellman, B. L., and Williams H. M., "A Study of Environmental Stimulation; and Orphanage Preschool Project", *University of Iowa Studies in Child Welfare*, 15, 4, 1938.

16a Skodak, M., "Children in Foster Homes", *University of Iowa Studies in Child Welfare*, 16, 1, 1939.

17a Stoddard, G. D., "Intellectual Development of the Child: an Answer to the Critics of the Iowa Studies", *School and Society*, 51, 1940, pp. 529-536.

18a Updegraff, R., "The Determination of a Reliable Intelligence Quotient for the Young-Child", *Journal of Genetic Psychology*, 41, 1932, pp. 152-166.

19a Woodworth, R. S., "Heredity and Environment", *Bulletin* 47 Social Science Research Council, 1941.

20a Jones H. E., "Personal Reactions of the Yearbook Committee", *39th Yearbook, National Society for the Study of Education*, I, 1940, pp. 454-456.,

21a Simpson, M. R., "The Wandering I. Q.", *Journal of Psychology*, 7, 1939 pp. 351-367.

22a Hetzer, H. and Wolf, K., "Baby Tests", *Zeitschrift für Psychologie*, 107, 1928.

23a Bühler, Ch., *Kindheit und Jugend*, Leipzig, 1931, p. 67.

24a Compayré, G., *L'evolution intellectuelle et morale de l'enfant*, Paris, 1893.

25a Stern, Wm., *Psychology of Early Childhood,* London, 1930.
26a Bühler, K., *Die geistige Entwicklung des Kindes,* 4th ed., Jena, 1942, p. 106 and p. 116.
27a Tolman, E. C., *Purposive Behavior,* New York, 1932, p. 27 ff.
28a Gesell, A. and Ilg, F., *Feeding Behavior of Infants* Phila. 1937 p., 21.
29a Gesell, A. and Thompson, H., *Infant Behavior, its Genesis and Growth,* York, 1934, p. 208.

Bibliography (b)

1b Abraham, K. "Notes on the Psychoanalytical Investigation and Treatment of Manic-Depressive Insanity and Allied Conditions", *Selected Papers,* Hogarth, 1927. (Originally 1912.)
2b Abraham, K. "The First Pregenital Stage of the Libido", (Originally, 1916.)
3b Abraham, K. "A Short Study of the Development of the Libido", *ibid.*
4b Bühler, Ch. *Kindheit und Jugend,* Leipzig, 1931.
5b Fenichel, O. *The Psychoanalytic Theory of Neurosis,* Norton, 1945.
6b Frued, S. "Mourning and Melancholia", *Coll. Papers,* IV. (Originally, 1917.)
7b Glover, E. "Examination of The Klein System of Child Psychology", *this Annual,* I, 1945.
8b Harnik J. "Introjection and Projection in the Mechanism of Depression", *Int. J. Psa.* XIII, 1932.
9b Hetzer, H. and Wolf, K. M. "Baby Tests", *Zeit. f. Psychol.,* 107, 1928.
10b Jacobson, E. "Depression; the Oedipus Conflict in the Development of Depressive Mechanisms", *Psa. Quarterly,* XII, 1943.
11b Jersild, A. T. and Holmes, F. B. "Children's Fear", *Child Dev. Mon.,* 20, 1935.
12b Klein, M. "Emotional Life and Ego Development of the Infant, with Special Reference to the Depressive Position", Controversial Series of the London Psychanalytic Society, IV, *Discussion,* March 1944.
13b Klein, M. *The Psycho-Analysis of Children,* London, 1932.
14b Klein, M. "Mourning and Its Relation to Manic-Depression States", *Int. J. Psa.,* XXI, 1940.
15b Klein, M. "The Oedipus Complex in the Light of Early Anxieties", *ibid,* XXVI, 1945.
16b Rank, O. *Das Trauma der Geburt und seine Bedeutung für die Psychoanalyse,* Int. Psa. Verlag, Wien, 1924.
17b Riviere, J. "Original Papers on the Genesis of Physical Conflict in Earliest Infancy", *Int. J. Psa.,* XVII, 1936.
18b Shirley, M. M. *The First Two Years. A Study of Twenty-Five Babies,* Vol. II, Minnesota Press, Minneapolis, 1933.
19b Spitz, R. A. and Wolf, K. M. "The Smiling Response: A Contribution to the Ontogenesis of Social Relations", *Gen. Psychol. Mon.,* XXXIV, I, 1946.
20b Spitz, R. A. "Hospitalism; An Inquiry into the Genesis of Psychiatric Conditions in Early Childhood", *this Annual,* I, 1945.
21b Spitz, R. A. and Wolf, K. M. "Diacritic and Coenesthetic Organizations", *Psa. Rev.,* 32, April, 1945.
22b Watson, J. B. *Psychology from the Standpoint of a Behavorist,* Lippincott, 1919.

3.8 Adult Status of Children with Contrasting Early Life Experiences: A Follow-up Study

Harold M. Skeels
National Institute Of Mental Health

I. Introduction

. . . The present study is a report on the status as adults of two groups of children originally encountered in Iowa institutions. One group experienced what was then regarded as the normal cours of events in a child-caring institution, while the other experienced a specifically designed and implemented intervention program. The findings reported here, are concerned with the question of whether and for how long a time mental development is affected by major changes in early environment and, specifically, with the factors significantly associated with deflections in mental development. It is hoped that these findings will contribute to the growing body of evidence on the effects of deprivation and poverty on the young child's ability to learn.

II. The Original Study

All the children in this study had become wards of the orphanage through established court procedures after no next of kin was found able to provide either support or suitable guardianship. Of the 25 children, 20 were illegitimate and the remainder had been separated from their parents because of evidence of severe neglect and/or abuse. Then as now, the courts were reluctant to sever the ties between child and parents and do so only when clearly presented with no other alternative. All the children were white and of north-European background.

The orphanage in which the children were placed occupied, with a few exceptions, buildings that had first served as a hospital and barracks during the Civil War. The institution was overcrowded and understaffed. By present standards, diet, sanitation, general care, and basic philosophy of operations were censurable. At the time of the study, however, the discrepancies between conditions in the institution and in the general community were not so great and were not always to the disadvantage of the institution. Over the past 30 years, administrative and physical changes have occurred that reflect the economic and social gains of our society. The description of

Excerpted, adapted and reprinted from *Monographs of the Society for Research in Child Development*. Serial No. 105, 1966, *31*, No. 3, by permission. Copyright © 1966 by the Society for Research in Child Development, Inc.

conditions in the institution in the 1930's, therefore, does not apply to the present.

At the time the original study was begun, infants up to the age of 2 years were housed in the hospital, then a relatively new building. Until about 6 months, they were cared for in the infant nursery. The babies were kept in standard hospital cribs that often had protective sheeting on the sides, thus effectively limiting visual stimulation; no toys or other objects were hung in the infants' line of vision. Human interactions were limited to busy nurses who, with the speed born of practice and necessity, changed diapers or bedding, bathed and medicated the infants, and fed them efficiently with propped bottles.

Older infants, from about 6 to 24 months, were moved into small dormitories containing two to five large cribs. This arrangement permitted the infants to move about a little and to interact somewhat with those in neighboring cribs. The children were cared for by two nurses with some assistance from one or two girls, 10 to 15 years old, who regarded the assignment as an unwelcome chore. The children had good physical and medical care, but little can be said beyond this. Interactions with adults were largely limited to feeding, dressing, and toilet details. Few play materials were available, and there was little time for the teaching of play techniques. Most of the children had a brief play period on the floor; a few toys were available at the beginning of such periods, but if any rolled out of reach there was no one to retrieve it. Except for short walks out of doors, the children were seldom out of the nursery room.

At 2 years of age these children were graduated to the cottages, which had been built around 1860. A rather complete description of "cottage life is reported by Skeels et al. (1938) from which the following excerpts are taken:

> Overcrowding of living facilities was characteristic. Too many children had to be accommodated in the available space and there were too few adults to guide them . . . Thirty to thirty-five children of the same sex under six years of age lived in a "cottage" in charge of one matron and three or four entirely untrained and often reluctant girls of thirteen to fifteen years of age. The waking and sleeping hours of these children were spent (except during meal times and a little time on a grass plot) in an average-sized room (approximately fifteen feet square), a sunporch of similar size, a cloakroom, . . . and a single dormitory. The latter was occupied only during sleeping hours. The meals for all children in the orphanage were served in a central building in a single large dining room.
> . . .
> The duties falling to the lot of the matron were not only those involved in the care of the children but those related to clothing and cottage

maintenance, in other words, cleaning, mending, and so forth. . . . With so much responsibility centered in one adult the result was a necessary regimentation. The children sat down, stood up, and did many things in rows and in unison. They spent considerable time sitting on chairs, for in addition to the number of children and the matron's limited time there was the misfortune of inadequate equipment . . . .

No child had any property which belonged exclusively to him except, perhaps, his tooth brush. Even his clothing, including shoes, was selected and put on him according to size. [pp. 10-11].

After a child reached the age of 6 years, he began school. His associates were his cottage mates and the children of the same age and opposite sex who lived on the other side of the institution grounds. Although the curriculum was ostensibly the same as that in the local public school, it was generally agreed that the standards were adjusted to the capabilities of the orphange children. Few of those who had their entire elementary-school experience in the institution's school were able to make the transition to the public junior high school.

The orphanage was designed for mentally normal children. It was perpetually overcrowded, although every opportunity to relieve this pressure was exploited. One such relief occurred periodically when new buildings were opened at other institutions, such as at the schools for the mentally retarded. It was not uncommon for a busload of children to be transferred on such occasions. A valued contribution of the psychologists was the maintenance of lists of children who, on the basis of test scores and observable behavior, were regarded as eligible for transfers.

The environmental conditions in the two state institutions for the mentally retarded were not identical but they had many things in common. Patient-inmates were grouped by sex, age, and general ability. Within any one ward, the patients were highly similar. The youngest children tended to be the most severely disabled and were frequently "hospital" patients. The older, more competent inmates had work assignments throughout the institution and constituted a somewhat self-conscious elite with recognized status.

Personnel at that time included no resident social workers or psychologists. Physicians were resident at the schools for the mentally retarded and were on call at the orphanage. Administrative and matron and caretaking staffs were essentially untrained and nonprofessional. Psychological services were introduced in the orphanage in 1932.

Identification Of Cases

Early in the service aspects of the program, two baby girls, neglected by their feebleminded mothers, ignored by their inadequate relatives, malnour-

ished and frail, were legally committed to the orphanage. The youngsters were pitiful little creatures. They were tearful, had runny noses, and sparse, stringy, and colorless hair; they were emaciated, undersized, and lacked muscle tonus or responsiveness. Sad and inactive, the two spent their days rocking and whining.

The psychological examinations showed developmental levels of 6 and 7 months, respectively, for the two girls, although they were then 13 and 16 months old chronologically. This serious delay in mental growth was confirmed by observations of their behavior in the nursery and by reports of the superintendent of nurses, as well as by the pediatrician's examination. There was no evidence of physiological or organic defect, or of birth injury or glandular dysfunction.

The two children were considered unplaceable, and transfer to a school for the mentally retarded was recommended with a high degree of confidence. Accordingly, they were transferred to an institution for the mentally retarded at the next available vacancy, when they were aged 15 and 18 months, respectively.

In the meantime, the author's professional responsibilities had been increased to include itinerant psychological services to the two state institutions for the mentally retarded. Six months after the transfer of the two children, he was visiting the wards at an institution for the mentally retarded and noticed two outstanding little girls. They were alert, smiling, running about, responding to the playful attention of adults, and generally behaving and looking like any other toddlers. He scarcely recognized them as the two little girls with the hopeless prognosis, and thereupon tested them again. Although the results indicated that the two were approaching normal mental development for age, the author was skeptical of the validity or permanence of the improvement and no change was instituted in the lives of the children. Twelve months later they were re-examined, and then again when they were 40 and 43 months old. Each examination gave unmistakable evidence of mental development well within the normal range for age.

There was no question that the initial evaluations gave a true picture of the children's functioning level at the time they were tested. It appeared equally evident that later appraisals showed normal mental growth accompanied by parallel changes in social growth, emotional maturity, communication skills, and general behavior. In order to find a possible explanation for the changes that had occured, the nature of the children's life space was reviewed.

The two girls had been placed on one of the wards of older, brighter girls and women, ranging in age from 18 to 50 years and in mental age from 5 to 9 years, where they were the only children of preschool age, except for a few hopeless bed patients with gross physical defects. An older girl on the ward had "adopted" each of the two girls, and other older girls served as

adoring aunts. Attendants and nurses also showed affection to the two spending time with them, taking them along on their days off for automobile rides and shopping excursions, and purchasing toys, picture books, and play materials for them in great abundance. The setting seemed to be a homelike one, abundant in affection, rich in wholesome and interesting experiences, and geared to a preschool level of development.

It was recognized that as the children grew older their developmental needs would be less adequately met in the institution for the mentally retarded. Furthermore, they were now normal and the need for care in such an institution no longer existed. Consequently, they were transferred back to the orphanage and shortly thereafter were placed in adoptive homes.

At this point, evidence on the effects of environment on intelligence had been accumulated from a number of studies. The consistent element in normal mental development seemed to be the existence of a one-to-one relationship with an adult who was generous with love and affection, together with an abundance of attention and experiential stimulation from many sources. Children who had little of these did not show progress; those who had a great deal, did.

Since study homes or temporary care homes were not available to the state agency at that time, the choice for children who were not suitable for immediate placement in adoptive homes was between, on the one hand, an unstimulating, large nursery with predictable mental retardation or, on the other hand, a radical, iconoclastic solution, that is, placement in institutions for the mentally retarded in a bold experiment to see whether retardation in infancy was reversible.

By the time these observations were organized into a meaningful whole and their implications were recognized, individual psychological tests were available for all children in the orphanage. As part of a continuing program of observation and evaluation, all infants over 3 months of age were given the then available tests (Kulhmann-Binet and Iowa Tests for Young Children), and were retested as often as changes seemed to occur. Retests at bi-monthly intervals were not uncommon. Older preschoolers were re-examined at 6- to 12-month intervals; school-aged children, annually or biennially. Children who were showing marked delay in development were kept under special observation. .

Children whose development was so delayed that adoptive placement was out of the question remained in the orphanage. The only foreseeable alternative for them was eventual transfer to an institution for the mentally retarded. In the light of the experiences with the two little girls, the possibility was raised that early transfer to such an institution might have therapeutic effects. If not all, then at least some of the children might be able to attain normal mental functioning. In the event they did not, no significant change in life pattern would have occurred, and the child would remain in the situation for which he would have been destined in any case.

This radical proposal was accepted with understandable misgivings by the administrators involved. It was finally agreed that, in order to avoid the stigma of commitment to a state school for the retarded, children would be accepted as "house guests" in such institutions but would remain on the official roster of the orphanage. Periodic re-evaluations were built into the plan; if no improvement was observed in the child, commitment would follow. Insofar as possible, the children were to be placed on wards as "only" children.

In the course of time, in addition to the two little girls who have been described and another transferred to the second of the two institutions at about the same time, 10 more children became "house guests." The transfers were spaced over a year's span in groups of 3, 3, and 4. All went to one institution for the mentally handicapped, the Glenwood State School. Unfortunately, the number of "house guests" exceeded the number of "elite" wards of older girls and necessitated the use of some environments that were less desirable. Consequently, in some wards there were more children, or fewer capable older girls, or less opportunity for extra stimulation, with a resulting variation in developmental patterns.

Experimental Group

The experimental group consisted of the 13 children who were transferred from an orphanage for mentally normal children to an institution for the mentally retarded, as "house guests." All were under 3 years of age at the time of transfer. Their development had been reliably established as seriously retarded by tests and observation before transfer was considered. . . .

Those children who happened to be in the infant to 3-year-old age range, were not ineligible for placement for legal reasons, were not acutely ill, but who were mentally retarded, became members of the experimental group. The entire project covered a span of some three years and was terminated when a change in the administration of the state school reduced the tolerance for such untidy procedures as having "house guests" in an institution. The onset of World War II and the departure of the principal investigator for military service effectively closed the project.

A project such as this could not be replicated in later years because infants were no longer kept exclusively in the orphanage. Temporary boarding homes came to be utilized prior to adoptive placement or for long-term observation and care.

The experimental group consisted of 10 girls and 3 boys, none with gross physical handicaps. Prior to their placement as "house guests" the examinations were routinely administered to them without any indication that they would or would not be involved in the unusual experience.

At the time of transfer, the mean chronological age of the group was 19.4 months (SD 7.4) and the median was 17.1 months, with a range of from

7.1 to 35.9 months. The range of IQ's was from 35 to 89 with a mean of 64.3 (SD 16.4) and a median of 65.0. Additional tests were made of 11 of the 13 children shortly before or in conjunction with the pretransfer tests reported in Table 1, using the Kuhlmann-Binet again or the Iowa Test for Young Children, and the results corroborated the reported scores.

The children were considered unsuitable for adoption because of evident mental retardation. For example, in Case 1, although the IQ was 89, it was felt that actual retardation was much greater, as the child at 7 months could scarcely hold up his head without support and showed little general bodily activity in comparison with other infants of the same age. In Case 3, at 12 months, very little activity was observed, and the child was very unsteady when sitting up without support. She could not pull herself to a standing position and did not creep. Case 11 was not only retarded but showed perseverative patterns of behavior, particularly incessant rocking back and forth. Cases 5, 8, and 13 were classified at the imbecile level. In present-day terms, they would have been labeled "trainable mentally retarded children."

Contrast Group

Since the original purpose of the experiment was to rescue for normalcy, if possible, those children showing delayed or retarded development, no plans had been made for a control or comparison group. It was only after the data had been analyzed that it was found that such a contrast group was available because of the tests that were routinely given to all children in the orphanage. To select such a contrast group, therefore, records were scrutinized for children who met the following criteria:

1. Had been given intelligence tests under 2 years of age.
2. Were still in residence in the orphanage at approximately 4 years of age.
3. Were in the control group of the orphanage preschool study (Skeels et al., 1938).
4. Had not attended preschool.

A total of 12 children were selected on the basis of the criteria and became the contrast group. The mean chronological age of the group at the time of first examination was 16.6 months (SD 2.9), with a median at 16.3 months. The range was from 11.9 to 21.8 months. The mean IQ of the group was 86.7 (SD 14.3) and the median IQ was 90. With the exception of two cases (16 and 24) the children had IQ's ranging from 81 to 103; the IQ's for the two exceptions were 71 and 50 respectively. When the children were examined, it was not known that they were or would become members of any study group. The re-examinations were merely routine retests that were given to all children.

At the ages when adoptive placement usually occurred, nine of the children in the contrast group had been considered normal in mental development. All 12 were not placed, however, because of different circumstances: 5 were withheld from placement simply because of poor family histories, 2 because of improper commitments, 2 because of luetic conditions, 2 because of other health problems, and one because of possible mental retardation.

The subsequent progress of the children in both the experimental and the contrast groups was influenced by individual circumstances. The groups were never identified as such in the resident institution; the members of each group were considered together only in a statistical sense. A child in the experimental group remained in the institution for the mentally retarded until it was felt that he had attained the maximum benefit from residence there. At that point, he was placed directly into an adoptive home or returned to the orphanage in transit to an adoptive home. If he did not attain a level of intelligence that warranted adoptive plans, he remained in the institution for mentally retarded.

The contrast-group members remained in the orphanage until placement. One was returned to relatives, but in most instances the children were eventually transferred to an institution for the mentally retarded as long-term protected residents. A few of the contrast group had been briefly approved for adoptive placement, and two had been placed for short periods. None was successful, however, and the children's decline in mental level removed them from the list of those eligible for adoption.

Description Of Experimental And Contrast Groups

Birth Histories

The birth histories of the two groups were not significantly different. Prematurity was of particular interest in relation to the initial tests of intelligence, as a somewhat slower rate of mental and motor development or possible brain damage or retardation may be associated with it.

The contrast group contained only one instance of prematurity.

There were two cases of Caesarean section, one in the experimental group (Case 11) and one in the contrast group (Case 18), but no effect on mental development was indicated in either case. . . .

Medical Histories

In evaluating the medical histories of both the experimental and contrast groups, little of significance was found in the relation between illnesses and rate of mental growth . . . .

Family Backgrounds

Social histories of the children revealed that all in both the experimental and contrast groups came from homes in which the social, economic, occupational, and intellectual levels were low.

Mothers   Information relating to education was available for 11 of the 13 mothers in the experimental group and for 10 of the 12 mothers in the contrast group. The mean grade completed by mothers of children in the experimental group was 7.8, with a median at grade 8. Only two had any high-school work; one completed grade 11 and one grade 10 (Cases 3 and 6). In one case, it was doubtful if the second grade had been completed (Case 8). Two (Cases 1 and 5) had dropped out of grade 8 at the age of 16.

In the contrast group, the mean grade completed was 7.3, with a median at 7.5. One mother (Case 19) had completed high school and one had an equivalent of ninth-grade education.

Occupational history of mothers, available on seven of the mothers of the experimental group and on nine of the mothers of the contrast group, included mainly housework, either in the homes of their parents or on jobs as domestics. In only one instance was there a higher level (Case 24 of the contrast group); the mother had been a telephone operator and general office worker.

Intelligence tests had been obtained on five of the mothers in the experimental group and on nine of the mothers in the contrast group. The mean IQ for the five mothers of the experimental group was 70.4, with a median at 66. Four mothers had IQ's below 70, and one was classified as normal with an IQ of 100. One additional mother, although not tested, was considered feeble-minded and had gone only as far as the second grade. Of the nine mothers tested in the contrast group, only two had IQ's above 70: one, 79 and the other, 84. The other scores ranged from 36 to 66. The mean IQ was 63, with a median at 62.

Fathers.   Little information was available on the fathers, and in fact, in many cases paternity was doubtful. Ten of the children in each group were illegitimate. In the experimental group, information relating to education was available on only four fathers: Two had completed the eighth grade, one had completed high school, and one had gone to high school, but how far was not known. Occupational status was indicated for only three of the fathers: One was a traveling salesman, one a printer, and one a farmhand.

In the contrast group, educational information was available for four fathers. One had completed high school and was considered talented in music (Case 24), two had completed eighth grade (Case 15 and 18), and one, the sixth grade (Case 21). Occupational data were known for 8 of the

contrast-group fathers: 3 were day laborers, 2 were farmhands, one worked on the railroad section, one was a farm renter, and one was in a C.C.C. camp.

A qualitative analysis of social histories seems to justify the conclusion that within these educational and occupational classifications, the parents represented the lower levels in such groups. Most of the fathers and mothers had dropped out of school because they had reached the limits of achievement and were not, in any sense of the word, average for their grade placements. The same may be said about occupational status.

Description Of The Environments

Experimental Group

Children in the experimental group were transferred from the orphanage nursery to the Glenwood State School, an institution for mentally retarded, and were placed on wards with older, brighter inmate girls. The wards were in a large cottage that contained eight wards with a matron and an assistant matron in charge and with one attendant for each ward. Approximately 30 patients, girls ranging in age from 18 to 50 years, were on each ward. On two wards (2 and 3), the residents had mental ages of from 9 to 12 years. On two other wards (4 and 5), the mental levels were from 7 to 10 years, and on another (ward 7), the mental ages were from 5 to 8 years. With the exception of ward 7, the wards housed few or no younger children other than the experimental "house guests." It was planned to place one, or at the most two, children from the experimental group on a given ward.

As with the first two children, who, by chance, were the first participants in the experiment, the attendants and the older girls became very fond of the children placed on their wards and took great pride in them. In fact, there was considerable competition among wards to see which one would have its "baby walking or talking first. Not only the girls, but the attendants spend a great deal of time with "their children," playing, talking, and training them in every way. The children received constant attention and were the recipients of gifts; they were taken on excursions and were exposed to special opportunities of all kinds. For example, it was the policy of the matron in charge of the girls' school division to single out certain children who she felt were in need of special individualization and to permit them to spend some time each day visiting her office. This furnished new experiences, such as being singled out, receiving special attention and affection, new play materials, additional language stimulation, and meeting other office callers.

The spacious living rooms of the wards furnished ample space for indoor play and activity. Whenever weather permitted, the children spent some time each day on the playground under the supervision of one or more older

girls. Here they were able to interact with other children of similar ages. Outdoors play equipment included tricycles, swings, slides, sand boxes, etc. The children also began to attend the school kindergarten as soon as they could walk. Toddlers remained for only half the morning and 4- or 5-year olds, the entire morning. Activities carried on in the kindergarten resembled preschool rather than the more formal type of kindergarten.

As part of the school program, the children attended daily 15-minute exercises in the chapel, which included group singing and music by the orchestra. The children also attended the dances, school programs, moving pictures, and Sunday chapel services.

In considering this enriched environment from a dynamic point of view it must be pointed out that in the case of almost every child, some one adult (older girl or attendant) became particularly attached to him and figuratively "adopted" him. As a consequence, an intense one-to-one adult-child relationship developed, which was supplemented by the less intense but frequent interactions with the other adults in the environment. Each child had some one person with whom he was identified and who was particularly interested in him and his achievements. This highly stimulating emotional impact was observed to be the unique characteristic and one of the main contributions of the experimental setting.

The meager, even desolate environment in the orphanage has been described. The contrast between the richly stimulating, individually oriented experience of the children in the experimental group and the depersonalizing, mass handling, and affectionless existence in the children's home can hardly be emphasized enough.

Mental Development

The 1922 Kuhlmann Revision of the Binet was used as the standard measure of intelligence, except for two or three tests on children who were 4 years of age or more for whom Stanford-Binet (1916) was used. All examinations were made by trained and experienced psychologists. Test one was the measure of intelligence just prior to transfer. Tests two, three, and the last were given at the end of the experimental period and was the second, third, or fourth, depending on the number of tests available at representative time intervals for a given child.

The comparisons of means, medians, and standard deviations for scores from first to last test for both groups are presented in Table 1 Using the t test, the difference for the experimental group between the means of first and last test was statistically significant at the .001 level. Every child showed a gain of from 7 to 58 points. Three children made gains of 45 points or more, and all but two children gained more than 15 points.

Length of the experimental period was from 5.7 months to 52.1 months.

Table 1
Experimental and Contrast Groups: Mean, Median, and Standard Deviation Comparisons of Mental Growth from First to Last Tests

Measure	Chronological Age, Months	Mental Age, Months	IQ	Chronological Age, Months	Chronological Age, Months	Mental Age, Months	IQ	Length of Experimental Period, Months	Change in IQ, First to Last Test
	Before Transfer			**Transfer**	**After Transfer**				
Experimental Group (N = 13)									
Mean	18.3	11.4	64.3	19.4	38.4	33.9	91.8	18.9	+27.5
Standard deviation	6.6	4.2	16.4	7.4	17.6	13.0	11.5	11.6	15
Median	16.6	10.8	65.0	17.1	36.8	30.0	93.0	14.5	+28
	First Test			**Transfer**	**Last Test**				
Contrast Group (N = 12)									
Mean	16.6	14.2	86.7		47.2	28.7	60.5	30.7	−26.2
Standard deviation	2.9	2.9	14.3		5.9	6.4	9.7	5.8	14.1
Median	16.3	13.6	90.0		49.3	29.3	60.0	28.8	−30.0

Source: Adapted from H. M. Skeels & H. B. Dye (1939, Table 3).

The period was not constant for all children as it depended upon the individual child's rate of development. As soon as a child showed normal mental development, as measured by intelligence tests and substantiated by qualitative observations, the experimental period was considered completed and the child's visit to the school for mentally retarded was terminated. Either he was placed in an adoptive home or returned to the orphanage.

The mental-growth pattern for children in the contrast group was quite opposite that of the experimental group. Using the t test, the difference between the means of first and last tests was statistically significant (p $<.001$) but with the exception of one child who gained 2 points in IQ from first to last test, all children showed losses of from 9 to 45 points. Ten of the 12 children lost 15 or more points in IQ over the period of the study.

In the experimental group, children who were initially at the lower levels tended to make the greater gains. The three children classified at the imbecile level on the first examination made gains of 58, 49, and 45 IQ points. Also, the greatest losses in the contrast group were associated with the highest initial levels. Six children with original IQ's above 90 lost from 29 to 45 points in IQ. While this shift may be partially due to regression, there must have been other factors operating to bring about such a large and consistent change.

Family History and Children's Mental Development

No clear relation between family-history information and the mental-growth pattern of the children could be identified.

That the gains in intelligence evidenced by the children of the experimental group were true gains and not the results of vagaries in testing, seems validated. Improvement was noted independently by members of the medical staff, attendants and matrons, and school teachers. Practice effects could not have been a contributing factor to these gains, as the children in the contrast group, who showed continual losses in IQ, actually had more frequent tests than the children in the experimental group.

Parent Surrogates and Children's Mental Development

A close bond of love and affection between a given child and one or two adults who assume a very personal parental role appears to be a dynamic factor of great importance. Nine of the 13 children in the experimental group were involved in such relationships. The four other children (Cases 2, 9, 10, and 11) tended to be less individualized on the wards, relationships with adults were more general, less intense, and did not involve any individual adult. It is significant that the children who experienced the more intense personal relationships made greater gains than those who were limited to more general interactions. The 9 children in the "personal" group made

gains in IQ ranging from 17 to 58 points, with an average gain of 33.8 points. The 4 children in the more "general" group made gains of from 7 to 20 points, with an average of 14.

Two children (Cases 10 and 11) showed little progress on ward 7 over a period of 1½ years. This ward differed significantly from the others in that it housed 8 to 12 children of younger ages (3 to 8 years), and the older girls were of a lower mental level. The attendant on the ward was especially fine with young children but was unable to give much individual attention because of the large number of young children. At one time it was feared that the two children would continue to be hopelessly retarded. However, they were subsequently placed as singletons on wards with brighter girls and, after a period of six months with the more individualized attention, showed marked gains in intelligence.

First Follow-Up

The experiment ended for each child in the experimental group when the decision was made that he had attained the maximum benefit from his "house-guest" experience. Of the 13, one remained in the institution until adulthood, 5 went directly into adoptive homes from the host institution, 6 had brief periods in the orphanage in transit to adoptive homes, and one was returned to the orphanage for some years and then was committed to the institution for the retarded.

As part of the pre-adoptive procedures and the planned follow-up evaluations, all the children were given individual intelligence tests approximately 2½ years after the close of the experimental period. Thus, the 11 adopted children were tested after approximately 2½ years of living in a family home, and the two children remaining in the institutions, after a similar period of continuing residential care. The mean length of the post-experimental period was 33 months (SD 8.0) and the median 29.8 months, with a range of 21 to 53 months.

The children in the contrast group were still wards of the state institutions and were given routine re-examinations. Those tests that most nearly coincided with the 2-year-interval testing for the experimental group were used for comparison purposes in this study.

For the contrast group, the mean interval between the follow-up tests and the last experimental-period test was 36.0 months (SD 12.2), with a median of 34.2 months. The 1916 Stanford-Binet was used as the standard measure of intelligence since all the children were past 4 years of age. The means, medians and standard deviations for IQ scores recorded after the follow-up tests for children in the experimental and contrast groups are presented in Table 2.

Table 2
Mental Development of Individual Children as Measured by Repeated Intelligence Tests Experimental Group (N = 13)

| | Experimental Period | | | | | | | Follow-up Study | | | | |
| | Before Transfer Initial Test[b] | | Chronological Age, Months, at Transfer | After Transfer Last Test[b] | | Length of Experimental Period, Months | Change in IQ Initial to Last Test | Follow-up Test[a] | | Length of Post-experimental Period, Months | Change in IQ During Post-experimental Period | Total Change in IQ from Initial to Follow-up Test |
	Chronological Age, Months	IQ		Chronological Age, Months	IQ			Chronological Age, Months	IQ			
Mean	18.3	64.3	19.4	38.4	91.8	18.9	+27.5	71.4	95.9	33.0	+ 4.1	+31.6
Standard deviation	6.6	16.4	7.4	17.6	11.5	11.6	15.0	16.7	16.3	8.0	9.1	17.0
Median	16.6	65.0	17.1	36.8	93.0	14.5	+28.0	67.0	94.0	29.8	+ 1.0	+29.0
						Contrast Group (N = 12)						
Mean	16.6	86.7	....	47.2	60.5	30.7	−26.2	83.3	66.1	36.0	+ 5.6	−20.6
Standard deviation	3.2	13.9	....	5.6	9.7	5.8	14.1	12.3	16.5	12.2	13.8	25.6
Median	16.3	90.0	....	49.3	60.0	28.8	−30.0	81.0	66.0	34.2	+ 6.0	−24.0

[b] Kuhlmann-Binet (1922) IQ.
[c] Stanford-Binet (1916) IQ.

Mental Development of the Experimental Group

The mean IQ of the 13 children in the experimental group on the follow-up examination was 95.9 (SD 16.3), and the median was 94.0 For the 11 children who had been placed in adoptive homes after the experimental period, the mean IQ at the time of the follow-up study was 101.4; the range of IQ's was from 90 to 118. Changes in IQ for the 11 children ranged from +16 points to −5 points. The greatest gain (16 points) was made by a child (Case 4) who had been placed in a superior adoptive home; the child (Case 5) showing the only loss was in a home considered to be far below the average of the other adoptive homes.

Losses of 17 and 9 points, respectively, were shown by the two children (Cases 9 and 2) who were not placed in adoptive homes. Case 9 had been returned to the orphanage although it was felt that the move was premature.[2] It was true that she became lost in the orphanage group and received very little, if any, individual attention, but whether her development would have been influenced by a different environment is speculative. Case 2, whose IQ was 77 at the close of the experimental period, had remained in the institution for the mentally retarded and, at the time of the follow-up, was expected to require continuing residential care.

Mental Development of the Contrast Group

To facilitate comparisons between the experimental and contrast groups, the time interval between the examinations during the experimental period and the time of examinations for follow-up purposes were kept as nearly the same as possible. For individual children, the test intervals ranged from 20.1 months to 57.6 months. The mean IQ of the 12 children in the contrast group was 66.1 (SD 16.5), a mean gain of 5.6 points over the last test of the experimental period. Despite this small average gain, 8 of the 12 children showed marked mental deterioration between the initial test and the follow-up test. During the three years following the close of the experimental period, a number of changes were made in the group's living situation. Two children (Cases 15 and 16) were transferred to the Glenwood State School, where they experienced essentially the same type of environment as that of the experimental group, but beginning at an older age. The two were 41 months of age at time of transfer. Thirty-four months following this transfer, Case 16 was examined and obtained an IQ of 80, showing a gain of 24 points. She was returned to the orphanage, therefore, as continued residence in the institution for mentally retarded seemed unwarranted. Case 15, on the other hand, failed to show any gain after 34 months. An examination six months later resulted in an IQ of 52, a 4 point loss.

Six of the contrast children were transferred to the Woodward State Hospital and School following the close of the experimental period. This

transfer was made on a permanent basis, inasmuch as mental retardation and lack of development and adjustment made continued residence in the orphanage seem inadvisable. Four of the children (Cases 14, 17, 18, and 21) were transferred within three months after the close of the experimental period, and the other two (Cases 22 and 24) were transferred 16 months after the close of the experimental period.

The children sent to Woodward experienced a different environment from that of the experimental children who had been "house guests" at Glenwood. The children sent to Woodward were much older at the time of transfer and received, in general, less individual attention and had fewer interactions with adults. They interacted primarily with children of a similar or slightly older chronological age who were mentally more retarded.

Over a period ranging from two to three years, 2 of the 6 transferred children experienced further losses in IQ (Cases 18 and 21), 2 remained relatively constant (Cases 14 and 17), and 2 showed gains (Cases 22 and 24). None attained a level higher than that of borderline intelligence.

The two children who showed marked gains in intelligence had experienced enriched environments. Case 22 was quite the favorite from the time of his transfer. After a year he was placed in the primary group in school. His teacher was especially fond of him and took a great interest in his achievements. The psychologist reported, "Because he was a likable boy with possibilities for improvement under training, he has been given much special attention. His reports show that though he appears quiet and unassuming he has an active imagination and curiosity and often shows initiative." At 6 years of age he surpassed all members of his class in reading skills and in identifying flash cards.

Case 24 was the only one of this transfer group not placed in the nursery ward. He was placed on a ward with older, brighter boys, where his adjustment was consistently satisfactory. Since he was one of the younger boys on the ward, he received additional individual attention from attendants and older boys.

The three contrast children who remained in the orphanage after the close of the original study subsequently also experienced a change of environment. Case 20 did not attend preschool but entered kindergarden at 68 months of age, and he had just completed the year in kindergarten when the follow-up examination was given. Case 23 attended preschool one year, kindergarten one year, first grade one year (with a D average in grades), and, at the time of the follow-up examination, was 9 years of age and in the second grade.

Of the three children who remained in the orphanage, Case 19 had the most enriched and varied experience during the follow-up period and showed by far the greatest gain (22 points) in IQ. Beginning at 5 years of age, he spent one year in preschool and one year in kindergarten. During the year in kindergarten, he was also included in a special mental-growth

· stimulation study, which was carried on by a research assistant from the State University of Iowa (Dawe, 1942), that included an intensified, individualized program of experimental instruction and frequent trips away from the institution. He was the only child from the contrast group included in this special study.

The last of the contrast children to be accounted for (Case 25) was paroled to his grandparents immediately following the close of the experimental period. The home was a very marginal one, and the family had been on relief for years. At the time of the follow-up examination at 8 years of age, the boy was still in the first grade, doing failing work, and was continually "picked on" by other children. A recommendation was made to transfer the boy to an institution for the mentally retarded.

III. The Follow-up Study of Adult Achievement

Statement of the Problem

The purpose of this follow-up study was to obtain answers to a few very simple questions: What happened to the two groups of children when they became adults? How were the differences in mental growth in childhood reflected in adult achievement and adjustment? Were the two divergent pathways maintained or did they converge over the years? Were there significant changes indicating improvement or regression within and between groups? Was there a relation between adult status and such factors as social history, health history, or environmental experiences?

Reality considerations influenced the kind of information that could be secured. Since the study had not been originally planned as a life-time follow-up research, certain details of information, predictions that might have been verified, and base-line data were not available. No provision had been made for subsequent visits and, as far as the subjects and the adopting parents were concerned, relationships with the agencies had long since been terminated. In addition, all the issues relating to privacy and confidentiality arose. In view of the small number of cases, it was essential not only to locate every single subject, but to secure maximum and, if possible, uniform information for each. To jeopardize this goal by making excessive demands for time and details and by probing emotionally charged material did not seem justified. The earlier guidelines of a descriptive natural-history approach were accepted as the most appropriate. No attempt was made to convert the adult follow-up into a more penetrating and detailed assessment of dynamics. Hopefully, this needed aspect of research is being pursued by others.

The adult follow-up study began 20 years after the postexperimental follow-up (Skeels & Skodak, 1965). The initial task was to locate and obtain information on every single case in the two groups. In a study based on such small numbers, the failure to locate even two or three cases could materially limit the conclusions or impressions . . . .

Nature of Interviews

Early in the planning, it had been decided not to give intelligence tests to the subjects, now 25 to 35 years of age, because of the many questions that might arise over their relation to the early childhood tests, and because of the possibility of lack of cooperation. It seemed more appropriate to relate the earlier measures of mental development to the adult educational level, occupation, and general social competence attained by the subjects. Personal interviews were used to secure this information. For the experimental group, the adoptive parents (if living) and the subjects were interviewed, usually separately . . . .

General Overall Findings

Survival Data

All 13 subjects in the experimental group reached adulthood. Among the 11 adoptive homes in which subjects were placed as children, both adoptive parents were deceased in two, and the adoptive parents were divorced in one but the adoptive mother had remarried and maintained a relationship with the subject.

In the contrast group, 11 of the 12 subjects were living; one (Case 16) died at the age of 15 while still a resident of the institution for the mentally retarded. None had been placed in adoptive homes.

Mobility

Among the adoptive parents, 2 of the 11 families had moved out out of the state, one prior to the first follow-up study and the other later. Of the 13 subjects in the experimental group, 6 including the 2 not placed in adoptive homes, still lived in the state. Of the 7 who had moved out of the state, 2 were residing in Minnesota and one each in Arizona, Nebraska, California, Kansas, and Wisconsin.

In the contrast group, 9 of the 11 living subjects still resided within the state of Iowa. One (Case 23) was living in Nebraska, one (Case 22) was located in California (after tracing him from Florida), and he later moved to Montana.

Occupational Levels

The 13 subjects in the experimental group were all self-supporting and neon were words of any institution₁public or private. Two, a boy (Case 1) and a girl (Case 6), however, had spent some time in a state correctional school during adolescence. Nevertheless, no member of the group exhibited evidence of antisocial or delinquent behavior, economic dependency, or need for psychiatric or agency support.

Table 3 summarizes the occupational status of the experimental- and contrast-group subjects and their spouses. The women's vocational achievements cannot be compared directly with those of the men since women do not have equal opportunities for advancement, and early marriage influences their vocational patterns. In the present study, 8 of the 10 girls were married; 2 married shortly after leaving school and had no employment records (Cases 5 and 8). Case 7 took the examination and was accepted as a stewardess for an air line after graduation for high school, but married instead. She worked as a dining-room hostess for a short time after her marriage. The two cases (2 and 9) who had never been placed in adoptive homes worked as domestics.

The occupational status of the 11 living members of the contrast group was significantly different. The contributions to society of the four residents of state institutions were limited to the unskilled tasks assigned to ward patients. One (Case 25) had intermittent paroles to a grandmother; while with her he occasionally mowed lawns or shoveled walks.

One boy (Case 24) was an employee in the institution for the mentally retarded in which he had been a patient for many years. Upon reaching adulthood, it was felt that his retardation was not sufficient to justify his being kept on as a resident. Placement in a community was attempted but failed completely. He was then placed on the employees' payroll in the institution but continued to live on a patient ward; subsequently, he was made a regular employee and transferred to the employees' home. He had no interests other than his work and had no friends among either inmates or employees.

Of the seven who were employed and living in communities, one (Case 21), a male, was still a ward of an institution for the mentally retarded but out on a vocational-training assignment that eventuated in his discharge from the institution. As a dishwasher in a nursing home he earned $60.00 a month and board and room. Two others, one male (Case 17) and one female (Case 15), previously wards of a state institution for the mentally retarded, were discharged from state supervision and worked as dishwashers in small restaurants. One girl (Case 23) remained in the orphanage from infancy to 17 years and was then returned to her mother. She found

Table 3
Experimental and Contrast Groups: Occupations of
Subjects and Spouses

Case No.	Subject's Occupation	Spouse's Occupation	Female Subject's Occupation Previous to Marriage
Experimental Group:			
1 [a]	Staff sergeant	Dental technician	. . .
2	Housewife	Laborer	Nurses' aide
3	Housewife	Mechanic	Elementary school teacher
4	Nursing instructor	Unemployed	Registered nurse
5	Housewife	Semi-skilled laborer	No work history
6	Waitress	Mechanic, semi-skilled	Beauty operator
7	Housewife	Flight engineer	Dining room hostess
8	Housewife	Foreman, construction	No work history
9	Domestic service	Unmarried	. . .
10 [a]	Real estate sales	Housewife	. . .
11 [a]	Vocational counselor	Advertising copy writer [b]	. . .
12	Gift shop sales [c]	Unmarried	. . .
13	Housewife	Pressman-printer	Office-clerical
Contrast Group:			
14	Institutional inmate	Unmarried	. . .
15	Dishwasher	Unmarried	. . .
16	Deceased	. . .	. . .
17 [a]	Dishwasher	Unmarried	. . .
18 [a]	Institutional inmate	Unmarried	. . .
19 [n]	Compositor and typesetter	Housewife	. . .
20 [a]	Institutional inmate	Unmarried	. . .
21 [a]	Dishwasher	Unmarried	. . .
22 [a]	Floater	Divorced	. . .
23	Cafeteria (part time)	Unmarried	. . .
24 [a]	Institutional gardener's assistant	Unmarried	. . .
25 [a]	Institutional inmate	Unmarried	. . .

[a] Male.
[b] B.A. degree.
[c] Previously had worked as a licensed practical nurse.

employment in a cafeteria where her duties were folding napkins around silverware. On paydays, her mother called for her checks and deposited them in the bank for her.

One man (Case 20) had had brief periods of part-time work on a farm during his teens. He spent his childhood in the orphanage and his adolescence in a training school for delinquent boys. He escaped from the training school, got to the West Coast, and within a few months was hospitalized following bizarre behavior and a severe depression. He was returned to his home state and has been hospitalized as mentally ill ever since.

Another boy (Case 22) was a "floater" whose travels had taken him from coast to coast. His vocational activities included plucking chickens in a produce house, washing dishes in a hospital kitchen, and doing the heavy packing for shipment in a stationery company. One trip to Iowa and two to the West Coast were made to locate him.

Still another, the last of the employed subjects in the contrast group to be accounted for was the man (Case 19) who stands out from the group in many ways. He became a compositor and typesetter for a newspaper in a city of 300,000, and his income easily equaled that of all the other employed contrast-group members combined.

Comparisons of Occupational Status . . . .

The percentage distribution of family heads by socio-economic status in the north central region of the United States, 1960, were compared with the distribution of family heads of the experimental and contrast groups. It is apparent that, for the contrast group, again with the consistent exception of Case 19, the subjects are concentrated in the two lowest socio-economic status classifications. The experimental group, however, approximates the distribution of the total population.

Other comparisons of income can be made with census data for employed males in the same general area. Based on principal wage earner, the total experimental group was within the average range of income for employed males in Iowa with earnings of $4,224 as compared to $4,182-$4,782 for men in the labor force; the contrast group, however, had a median annual income of $1,200. If the two unmarried women, with annual incomes of $1,416 and $1,820 are excluded, the median wage for males in the experimental group is $4,800.

There were . . . striking differences in incomes between the experimental and contrast groups. The two unmarried women and one unskilled spouse in the experimental group who earned wages of $2,200 or less, the lowest in the group, still earned more than the lowest seven earners in the contrast group. Only one person in the contrast group, Case 19, earned more than the median of the experimental group.

These achievements are particularly significant in view of the fact that the 11 subjects in the experimental group who were placed in adoptive homes at

young ages were placed in homes of modest level. As would be expected, there had been some reservations about level of achievement subsequent to adoption, and it was deemed advisable to select homes in which the demands for intellectual and educational achievement would not be too great.

Education

Marked differences were found between the two groups in educational attainment. Mean and median school grades completed by experimental-group subjects and their spouses and by the contrast-group subjects are shown in Table 4.

Table 4
Experimental and Contrast Groups: Education of Subjects and Spouses

	Experimental Group	Spouses	Contrast Group	
(*N* = 13)	Grade Completed	Grade Completed	(*N* = 12)	Grade Completed
Mean	11.68	11.60	...	3.95
Median	12.00	12.00	...	2.75

Excluding the two cases not placed in adoptive homes (Cases 2 and 9), the mean grade completed for the experimental group was 12.8 and the median, 12. One subject—a male—(Case 11) had a B. A. degree from a state university and had completed some graduate work; another—a male —(Case 10) graduated from a business college; and three of the girls (Cases 3, 4, and 13) had from one semester to 2½ years of college education.

The education of the spouses was comparable to that of subjects in the experimental group. Excluding the spouse of Case 2, who had never been placed in an adoptive home and had had only a sixth-grade education, the mean grade completed for spouses was 12.2 and the median, 12.0.

The educational levels attained by subjects in the experimental group, and their spouses, compare favorably with the 1960 Census figures for adults of similar ages for Iowa (U. S. Bureau of the Census, 1936b) and for the United States as a whole (U. S. Bureau of the Census, 1963c). In the 1960 Census, the median grade completed by Iowa adults 25 to 34 years of age was 12.4, and of the white population of similar ages in the United States, 12.2.

The educational levels of the subjects in the contrast group were much lower than those of the experimental group. Using the *t* test, the difference

between the means of the experimental and contrast groups was statistically significant at the .001 level.

A direct comparison between the educational attainments of the two groups is difficult. In most instances, children in the contrast group received their education in state institutions for the mentally retarded. Grade levels there are not directly comparable to those in public-school systems. In most instances, grade level reported in this study was based on evidence from standard achievement tests.

Only one subject in the contrast group (Case 19) had an education beyond the eighth grade, and he deserves special mention and explanation. He is not only graduated from high school and had one semester of college but is distinct from the other contrast-group members in that he was the only one with a stable marriage, a family, a home of his own, steady employment in a skilled trade, and earning an income of $6,720 in 1963. He was also the one whose experiences least resembled those of the other contrast children. He had had a moderate hearing loss following bilateral mastoidectomy in infancy, and while it was not regarded as a major disability in preschool years and would not have precluded his attending public school, it was felt that he might receive more individual attention and appropriate instruction at a school for the deaf. Following the close of the first follow-up study he was transferred to a residential school for the deaf and completed high school there. He had the added advantage that the matron of his cottage took a special fancy to him because he was one of the youngest children and had no family. He was a frequent guest in her home and in the home of her daughter and son-in-law.

Marital and Family Status

Experimental Group

Eleven of the 13 subjects in the experimental group had married, and one of the 11 had been divorced. The spouses came from the same type of middle-class working-class families as the adoptive homes of the experimental subjects, which is indicated by the comparable level of education in each pair and was corroborated during the interviews with parents and subjects.

As far as could be observed in the interviews, the marriages gave every indication of stability and permanence. The one divorce was secured by the husband of an experimental subject who alleged that his wife had been unfaithful and neglected the children. Custody of the five children was awarded to him. His wife had spent some time in a facility for delinquent girls during her adolescence.

Nine of the families had children of their own. Making up this second generation at the time of the study were 28 children ranging in age from 1 to 10½ years; 18 were boys and 10, girls.

Arrangements were made for individual intelligence tests to be given these children (Schenke & Skeels, 1965). The Stanford-Binet, form L-M, was given to 22 children, the Stanford-Binet, form L, to one, and the Wechsler Intelligence Scale for Children to 2. The Cattell Infant Intelligence Scale was administered to the three children under 2 years of age.

The 28 children had a mean IQ of 103.9 and a median of 104. The range of IQ's was from 86 to 125, and no child tested below the dull-normal level. Only about half of the children had reached school age, but among those who had, grade achievement was commensurate with age.

Examiners were impressed by the fact that none of the children showed any sign of abnormality or organic pathology, and, as a group, were attractive and physically well developed. Personality development and adjustment were considered well within the normal range. In one or two instances, there was some evidence of feelings of insecurity or lack of self-confidence.

Contrast Group

In the contrast group, only two men of the 11 living subjects, had married, Cases 22 and 19. Case 22 had one child, a boy, and subsequently was divorced. He was living in a modest apartment some distance from his family. The boy was examined in the home of his mother at the age of 6 years, 8 months, on the Stanford-Binet, form L-M. An estimated IQ of 66 was obtained. In the examination, the child evidenced signs of possible brain damage of unknown etiology. The mother indicated that she and the boy's father had maintained no permanent address and had traveled about the country a great deal; as a result the child had been cared for by various persons, including the mother's sister and mother, and other persons. The wife stated that her husband had been quite abusive to the boy frequently striking him during fits of rage. She attributed the child's retarded physical and mental development to the mistreatment he had received in the past. The mother had remarried, and she indicated that her current husband was kind to the child and showed him much consideration.

Case 19 is the subject that consistently was the exception within the contrast group. He was married, had four children, and maintained a comfortable home in a very attractive middle-class residential area. His four children were physically well developed, of average size for age, and were very attractive and nicely adjusted. The oldest child, a boy 5 years, 11 months of age, was doing satisfactory work in the first grade and had an IQ of 107 on the Stanford-Binet, form L. The three younger children were girls; when tested the 4-year-old had an IQ of 117 and the 2-year-old, 119, on form L, and the 9-month-old infant had an IQ of 103 on the Cattell Infant Test.

None of the four girls in the contrast group had married. Two had been sterilized in late adolescence prior to work placement in the community.

In neither experimental nor contrast group was there illegitimacy or indication of serious promiscuity.

Institutional Residence: Time and Costs

One measure of the efficacy of different types of intervention programs is deprived from a comparison of costs. Length of care in institutions and costs of rehabilitation (retraining, casework services, etc.) must be considered in evaluating the advantages and disadvantages of programs. To determine actual costs of institutional care of experimental- and contrast-group children, monthly per capita costs were secured for the years from 1930 to 1963 from the annual and/or biennial reports of the institutions involved. In reviewing these costs over a 30-year period, it is impressive to note that monthly per capita costs for care in the Iowa institutions increased from approximately $20.00 in 1933 to $250.00 in 1963 (exclusive of capital investments). This increase represents not only actual increases in costs and the decreased purchasing power of the dollar, but, also, increased ratios of staff to resident population, marked expansion of professional staff, much less crowding, and more stimulating educational and nursery-life programs, particularly at the Children's Home.

The actual time spent in residence at one or more of the state institutions was computed for each subject from admission and discharge dates. The contrast between the two groups is impressive. Up to the time of this follow-up study, the 13 children in the experimental group had spent a total of 72 years and 5 months in institutional residence, at a total cost to the state of $30,716.01, whereas the 12 children in the contrast group had spent a total of 273 years in residence, at a total cost of $138,571.68.

For children in the experimental group, the mean length of residence was 5 years, 1 month, with a median at 3 years, 3 months. The mean cost was $2,367.75, the median, $890.22. If one excludes the two cases not placed in adoptive homes, the mean and median periods of residence become 2 years, 5 months, and 3 years, 2 months, respectively, with costs materially reduced to a mean of $1,285.12 and a median of $660.96.

For the contrast group, the mean residence period at the time of the follow-up was 22 years, 9 months, with a median at 21 years, 5 months. Since the members of this group were then in their early thirties, many more years of institutional care can be anticipated. The mean cost (1964) of institutionalization was $11,547.64, and the median $9,108.50. Institutional costs for Case 20 were considerably higher than for other institutionalized subjects for a similar period because he spent over 14 years in state mental

hospitals. In thcsc facilities, the per capita cotss increased more rapidly in the 1950's than elsewhere because of the improvement in facilities and treatment.

Per capita costs of care for patient residence do not accurately convey the costs for different types of patients. For example, the placement of infants and young children of normal development was accomplished within weeks or, at most, four to five months after admission. During the placement period, the average cost of care was $72.00 for the typical period of 3 months (Skodak, 1939; Skodak & Skeels 1945; 1949). Then, and even more now, a relatively higher drain on professional and casework services was necessary to facilitate adoptions. However, once the child was placed, there was relatively little demand for further agency service.

The costs cited for the experimental group were markedly increased because of the mental retardation that had already occurred to a diagnosable degree and, consequently, that necessitated the active intervention, based on cooperative staff participation, of two independent facilities.

In institutions for the mentally retarded, long-term custodial cases are allocated relatively little professional time. When rehabilitation of patients is attempted, however, professional staff investment and costs become extremely high. Case 17 was considered by the staff of the institution for the mentally retarded to have been an outstanding example of successful rehabilitation. A period of over six years elapsed from the time the search for work placement was begun until the patient was discharged from state supervision. During that time, the case worker from the institution's Social Service Department made 30 or more visits to the young man and to other individuals. These visits were supplemented by services in the community from other agencies: Vocational Rehabilitation, Family Service, and the Community Center. For a period of more than one year, a social worker from one of the local agencies co-signed all checks drawn by the subject on his bank account before it was decided that he could manage his own affairs. It is not surprising that the costs of restoring a patient to the community in a low-income, occupationally precarious job, have resulted in the scarcity of such programs.

Still another comparison that reflects the differences in achievement between the two groups and that should be considered in evaluating overall costs is that of federal income-tax payments. Tax payments were estimated. . . . . based on 1963 laws . . . .

In the experimental group, these payments were based on family income or on that of the head of the household. Income taxes were paid by all experimental subjects. In the contrast group, on the other hand, four subjects had no income and, therefore, paid no income tax. In the experimental group, the range of tax estimated to have been paid was from $38.00 to $485.00. It should be pointed out that these estimations were based on

deductions for a median of three dependents, whereas, in the contrast group, only Case 19 had any dependents.

Income tax payments were estimated for 1963 only. While it is impossible to predict accurately the future employment stability of a wage earner, the fluctuations in income-tax assessments, or the effects of changing employment patterns, it is reasonable to assume that those subjects employed at the follow-up will continue to have earnings and make tax payments for an additional 20 to 40 years. The continuity of employment for trained or skilled workers is more likely than for the unskilled, who are more vulnerable to fluctuations in jobs. Since the experimental subjects—and Case 19—had better assurance of continued employment, the difference between contributions to society from the experimenal group and costs to society for the contrast group, can be expected to increase with the years.

Analysis of Variable Factors in Relation to Achievement

Medical Histories

An evaluation of the medical histories of the experimental and contrast groups, with few exceptions, revealed no significant relation between illnesses and adult acihevement . . . .

Variables Relating to Natural and Adoptive Parents

It would be useful in many kinds of planning if the developmental course of progeny could be predicted. Information about family histories has been seen as providing the basis for such predictions. By inference, educational attainment, vocational success, and general social conformity have been accepted as indications of genetic differences. The unreliability of these indicators can be judged by inspecting, for example, the differences in average educational level between 1930 and 1960, and the differences in educational attainment between contrasting geographic areas of the United States. Delinquency rates, dependence on community agencies, and "general social adequacy" are influenced by many factors other than individual genetic constitution.

Even if the family history data were predictive, the significant items were frequently missing from the case records. History material on the adopting parents, while not quite as meager, also had omissions, since the adoption agency worker's decision that the petitioners did or did not qualify as adoptive parents was frequently based on a global impression. Such details as school grade completed were likely to be interpreted in the light of the worker's own value system.

With the small numbers of cases involved and the frequency of entries such as "no information" or "unknown," any statistical analysis of . . .

family histories data is not possible. From long experience in evaluating social histories, an inspection of the available information suggests that even if all the missing data were known the total picture for the experimental and contrast groups would not be materially changed.

The sociocultural levels of the biological parents in both the experimental and contrast groups were similar and represented the lower class in American society. Even within this category they represented a lower selection: Many were unemployed, had been known to welfare agencies over the years, or were cited for law infringements.

Adoptive parents of the 11 children in the experimental group could be characterized as coming from the lower middle class. Within this class, in contrast to the biological parents, they represented an upper selection, in that approval for adoptive placement demanded that they be good, solid, substantial citizens in their respective communities and that they be financially capable of supporting a child in the home. The level of these adoptive homes, while representing a marked selection upward in comparison to the natural parents, nevertheless was rated as somewhat below the average level of the adoptive homes in the Skodak-Skeels longitudinal study of 100 adopted children (Skodak, 1939; Skodak & Skeels, 1945; 1949). The selection of relatively modest levels of adoptive homes for the experimental children had been purposeful, and the subsequent development and achievements of the children were similar to or exceeded those that would have been anticipated for natural children in such homes. The question can be raised whether the attainments might have been placed in homes of higher aspirations and stimulation levels. Conceivably, such placement might have resulted in higher achievement. It is equally possible, on the other hand, that excessive demands and pressures might have resulted in lower achievement.

With such small numbers of subjects and with gaps in information, it is impossible to identify relations between achievement of the subjects and specific characteristics of either the adoptive or natural parents.

IV. Implications

At the beginning of the study, the 11 children in the experimental group evidenced marked mental retardation. The developmental trend was reversed through planned intervention during the experimental period. The program of nurturance and cognitive stimulation was followed by placement in adoptive homes that provided love and affection and normal life experiences. The normal, average intellectual level attained by the subjects in early or middle childhood was maintained into adulthood.

It can be postulated that if the children in the contrast group had been placed in suitable adoptive homes or given some other appropriate equivalent in early infancy, most or all of them would have achieved within the normal range of development, as did the experimental subjects.

It seems obvious that under present-day conditions there are still countless infants born with sound biological constitutions and potentialities for development well within the normal range who will become mentally retarded and noncontributing members of society unless appropriate intervention occurs. It is suggested by the findings of this study and others published in the past 20 years that sufficient knowledge is available to design programs of intervention to counteract the devastating effects of poverty, sociocultural deprivation, and maternal deprivation.

Since the study was a pioneering and descriptive one involving only a small number of cases, it would be presumptuous to attempt to identify the specific influences that produced the changes observed. However, the contrasting outcome between children who experienced enriched environmental opportunities and close emotional relationships with affectionate adults, on the other hand, and those children who were in deprived, indifferent, and unresponsive environments, on the other, leaves little doubt that the area is a fruitful one for further study.

It has become increasingly evident that the prediction of later intelligence cannot be based on the child's first observed developmental status. Account must be taken of his experiences between test and retest. Hunt (1964, p. 212) has succinctly stated that,

> . . . In fact, trying to predict what the IQ of an individual child will be at age 18 from a D.Q. obtained during his first or second year is much like trying to predict how fast a feather might fall in a hurricane. The law of falling bodies holds only under the specified and controlled conditions of a vacuum. Similarly, any laws concerning the rate of intellectual growth must take into account the series of environmental encounters which constitute the conditions of that growth.

> The divergence in mental-growth patterns between children in the experimental and contrast groups is a striking illustration of this concept.

> The right of every child to be well born, well nurtured, well brought up, and well educated was enunciated in the Children's Charter of the 1930 White House Conference on Child Health and Protection (White House Conference, 1931). Though society strives to insure this right, for many

years to come there will be children to whom it has been denied and for whom society must provide both intervention and restriction. There is need for further research to determine the optimum modes of such intervention and the most appropriate ages and techniques for initiating them. The present study suggests, but by no means delimits, either the nature of the intervention or the degree of change that can be induced.

The planning of future studies should recognize that the child interacts with his environment and does not merely passively absorb its impact. More precise and significant information of the constitutional, emotional, and responsive-style characteristics of the child is needed so that those environmental experiences that are most pertinent to his needs can be identified and offered in optimum sequence.

The unanswered questions of this study could form the basis for many lifelong research project. If the tragic fate of the 12 contrast-group children provokes even a single crucial study that will help prevent such a fate for others, their lives will not have been in vain.

Notes

Monographs of the Society For Research In Child Development Serial No. 105, 1966 Vol 31, No. 3
2 The return followed a change in administration rather than psychological readiness.

References

Dawe, Helen C. A study of the effect of an educational program upon language development and related mental functions in young children. *Journal of Experimental Education,* 1942, **11,** 200-209.

Hunt, J. McV. The psychological basis for using preschool enrichment as an antidote for cultural deprivation. *Merrill-Palmer Quarterly of Behavior and development,* 1964, **10,** 209-248.

Kirk, S. A. *Early education of the mentally retarded.* Chicago: Univer. of Ill. Pr., 1958.

Kugel, R. B. Familial mental retardation: some possible neurophysiological and psychosocial interrelationships. In A. J. Solnit & Sally Provence (Eds.), *Modern perspectives in child development.* New York: International Universities Press, 1963. Pp. 206-216.

Schenke, L. W., & Skeels, H. M. An adult follow-up of children with inferior social histories placed in adoptive homes in early childhood. Study in Progress, 1965.

Skeels, H. M. The mental development of children in foster homes. *Pedagogical Seminar & Journal of Genetic Psychology.* 1936 **49,** 91-106.

Skeels, H. M. Mental development of children in foster homes. *Journal of Consulting Psychology,* 1938, **2,** 33-43.

Skeels, H. M. Some Iowa studies of the mental growth of children in relation to differentials of the environment: a summary. In *Intelligence: its nature and nurture.* 39th Yearbook, Part II. National Society for the Study of Education, 1940. Pp. 281-308.

Skeels, H. M. A study of the effects of differential stimulation on mentally retarded children: a follow-up report. *American Journal of Mental Deficiency,* 1942, **46,** 340-350.

Skeels, H. M., & Dye, H. B. A study of the effects of differential stimulation on mentally retarded children. *Proceedings & Addresses of the American Association on Mental Deficiency,* 1939, **44,** 114-136.

Skeels, H. M., & Fillmore, Eva A. The mental development of children from underprivileged homes. *Journal of Genetic Psychology,* 1937, **50,** 427-439.

Skeels, H. M., & Skodak, Marie. Techniques for a high-yield follow-up study in the field. *Public Health Reports,* 1965, **80,** 249-257.

Skeels, H. M., Updegraff, Ruth, Wellman, Beth L., & Williams, H. M. A study of environmental stimulation: an orphanage preschool project. *University of Iowa Studies in Child Welfare,* 1938, **15,** No. 4.

Skodak, Marie. Children in foster homes: a study of mental development. *University of Iowa Studies in Child Welfare,* 1939, **16,** No. 1.

Skodak, Marie, & Skeels, H. M. A follow-up study of children in adoptive homes. *Journal of Genetic Psychology* 1945, **66,** 21-58.

Skodak, Marie, & Skeels, H. M. A final follow-up study of one hundred adopted children. *Journal of Genetic Psychology,* 1949, **75,** 85-125.

U. S. Bureau of the Census, 1960. *Methodology and scores of socio-economic status.* Working Paper No. 15. Washington, 1963. P. 13 (a)

U. S. Bureau of the Census. U. S. Census Population, 1960. Vol. I. *Characteristics of the population.* Part 17, Iowa. Washington: U. S. Government Printing Office, 1963. Table 103, pp. 17-333. (b)

U. S. Bureau of the Census. U. S. Census Population, 1960. *Detailed characteristics, United States summary.* Final Report PC (L)-ID Washington: U. S. Government Printing Office, 1963. Table 173, pp. 1-406. (c)

Warner, W. L., Meeker, Marchia, & Eells, H. *Social class in America: the evaluation of status.* New York: Harper's Torchbooks, 1960.

Wellman, Beth L. Our changing concept of intelligence. *Journal of Consulting Psychology,* 1938, **2,** 97-107.

White House Conference on Child Health and Protection. *Addresses and Abstracts of Committee Reports, 1930.* New York: Appleton-Century, 1931.

3.9   Early Deprivation in Monkey and Man

Urie Bronfenbrenner
Cornell University

I. The Problem

This article seeks to examine the effects of early deprivation in primates—monkeys and man; to note continuities and differences across these species in order to gain a better understanding of deprivation in the human infant. But before we begin our investigation of relevant data concerning early deprivation, however, it is necessary to identify the phenomena we shall be considering under the rubric of "early deprivation." In general, we use it to refer to situations in which the organism has been prevented over an extended period in its early life from experiencing conditions and activities normally encountered during this time. Two general types of early deprivation are usefully distinguished:

1. *Drive Deprivation.* At an early period in its life, the organism is prevented from normal gratification of hunger, sucking, or secondary drives acquired through learning.

2. *Stimulus Deprivation.* During infancy the organism is prevented from experiencing stimuli normally encountered in the course of its early life.

Cutting across both of these dimensions is a social parameter, the extent to which either form of deprivation involves reduced contact with other living creatures, most often the mother but also litter mates and, in the case of domestic animals, man.

Having differentiated these broad aspects of early deprivation, we are ready to begin our inquiry. We shall consider first the effects of drive deprivation in monkeys. We shall then repeat the same procedure for the effects of stimulus deprivation. Finally, we shall evaluate the applicability to man of the generalizations derived from the research on monkeys.

II. Maternal Deprivation in Monkeys

Early drive deprivation in monkeys

The importance of sucking in early development has long been speculated upon and theorized about, and the independent contribution of early sucking frustration has been unequivocally demonstrated in monkeys. Benjamin (1961) compared the effects of cup feeding *vs.* bottle feeding in two groups

of eight rhesus monkeys removed from their mother at birth. Counterbalanced with this primary variable was a second factor—the presence of a rocking *vs.* non-rocking mother surrogate (a cylinder or plane covered with terry cloth). The latter variation had to be included because the same animals were simultaneously being used in other researches focused on the effect of rocking in early infancy.

Benjamin's major finding is as follows: the bottle-fed monkeys far exceeded the cup-raised animals in the amount of non-nutritive sucking,[1] thus providing strong evidence for the role of learning in the acquisition of sucking drive in primates. This substantial learned component is apparently superimposed, however, on an innate drive not for sucking *per se* but for generalized oral activity. The evidence for this interpretation comes from a second and equally reliable finding: in comparison with the bottle-fed group, the cup-fed animals engaged in more non-sucking oral activity such as biting or licking the body or objects in the environment. Moreover, there was a negative correlation across individuals between the amount of non-sucking oral activity and the degree of non-nutritive sucking. In Benjamin's view, "this reciprocal relation strongly indicates an underlying persistent oral responsiveness which must assume one form or another. One could apply the label "innate oral drive" to this frequent and persistent oral responsiveness which is not wholly dependent on feeding experience."

Even clearer evidence that "oral responsiveness is not wholly dependent on feeding experience" was a product of serendipity; namely, the essentially fortuitous inclusion in the experiment of rocking *vs.* non-rocking mother surrogates. It turned out that monkeys raised on rocking mother surrogates showed appreciably more non-nutritive sucking than animals raised on stationary surrogates or with no mother surrogates at all. Moreover, the pattern of these differences over time showed an interesting contrast with the results for bottle-*vs.* cup-fed infants. The discrepancy between the latter two groups was evident in the first 10 days of life, reached a maximum before two months, and was beginning to disappear by six months when observations were discontinued. In comparison, the differences associated with rocking and non-rocking mother surrogates did not begin until the monkeys were about 20 days old, reached a maximum at about three months, and were still showing a marked gap at six months when the experiment ended.

This differential pattern leads Benjamin to two conclusions. First, she interprets the near-disappearance of differences between the bottle- and cup-fed group by six months of age as evidence that early sucking frustration "by no means had a permanent or even persistent effect on non-nutritive sucking." It may be premature, however, to generalize this conclusion on at least three counts. First, the experimental animals were not followed up beyond infancy. Second, the monkeys were not in a deprived state when tested. Third, and perhaps most critical, in Benjamin's experiment the

cup-fed animals were subjected to sucking deprivation at birth. But one of her major conclusions was that in monkeys the "need to suck. . . . arises from the association of sucking with the primary reinforcing aspects of feeding." In other words, monkeys who are not so reinforced do not develop a strong sucking drive. Yet these were the only animals subjected to sucking deprivation in Benjamin's experiment.

Benjamin's second conclusion, though far from established, rests on firmer ground. While deprivation of nutritive sucking may have some impact early in life, later in infancy, she asserts, "other variables become dominant." The nature of these "other variables" is suggested not only by Benjamin's own findings on the influence of rocking vs. non-rocking surrogate mothers, but even more strongly by other, earlier results from the same laboratory. To begin with, the original experiment by Harlow and Zimmermann (1958) had likewise shown that contact comfort was far more important for the infant monkey than nutritive sucking. Indeed, in this species the latter variable apparently failed to discriminate even with the infants raised on cloth mothers.[2]

Even more relevant to our concern, however, is the behavior of the experimental animals when placed in an unfamiliar situation such as a playroom. If the cloth mother was absent, the infant's behavior became markedly disturbed. "Vocalization, crouching, rocking and sucking increased sharply." Animals "would rush to the center of the room where the mother was customarily placed, and then run from object to object screaming and crying all the while." In contrast, if the mothers were present, the cloth-reared monkeys would immediately rush to her and clutch her tenaciously, "a response so strong that it can be adequately depicted only by motion pictures." Then gradually the animals would become reassured, and using the mother as a security base, would begin to explore and manipulate the environment. Total emotionality score (based on such behavior as vocalization, crouching, rocking, and sucking) was cut in half when the mother was present. In contrast, monkeys reared by their own mothers showed higher emotionality scores when the cloth mother was present than when she was absent.

In a later publication, Harlow and Zimmermann (1959) report the behavior, in analogous situations, of monkeys raised on wire mothers only. In sharp contrast to children of terry cloth mothers, these animals not only spent much less time on their wire mothers, but the presence of this equally faithful creature rather than reducing emotionality scores, actually raised them somewhat. Instead of clinging, the infants (engaged in convulsive jerking and rocking movements similar to the behavior of deprived and institutionalized human children." They also exhibited "a lack of exploratory and manipulatory behavior . . . similar to that observed in the mother-absent condition for infants raised with the cloth mothers" (p. 6). Harlow

and Zimmermann have also investigated retention effects in animals who had been permanently separated from their "mothers" at about five months of age. Monkeys raised from birth with cloth or wire surrogates or both were examined periodically through tests of visual preference in which the cloth mother was pitted against other stimuli (wire mother, blank box, real infant monkey) as potential reinforcers. The results give clear evidence that the monkeys' orientation toward a cloth surrogate with which they have been raised exhibits all the properties of a learned drive. Animals tested as late as a year after separation still showed preferential and emotional reactions comparable to the results before separation (Harlow and Zimmermann, 1959).

In addition to "contact comfort", Harlow and Zimmermann have identified two other so-called "affectional variables" which evoke drive-like behavior in the infant monkey. The first of these, as already noted, is the presence of rocking motion in the "mother"; the second is the placement of the surrogate at an angle facilitating clinging. While the evidence indicates that both the clinging and rocking properties of the mother enhance the infant's responsiveness, these variables do not appear to match the drive potency of contact comfort *per se*.

Effects of separation from the mother are reported in a study by Seay, Hansen, and Harlow (1962). Four infants ranging from five and a half to seven months of age were separated from their mothers for three weeks by means of Plexiglass panels permitting only auditory-visual contact with the mother. Although the infants were housed in pairs, they showed reactions of emotional disturbance, including "high-pitched screeching and crying, attempts to pass through the Plexiglass barriers and huddling up against the barrier in close proximity to the mother" (p. 126). In addition, the investigators report a "drastic decrease" in the more complex forms of infant-infant interaction such as play, approach, and facial communication. In summarizing their findings, the authors emphasize their relevance to human studies:

> The results of this investigation appear to be in general accord with expectations based upon the human separation syndrome described by Bowlby. The original response of the infants was certainly one of protest —violent and prolonged protest . . . The drastic depression of play following separation is best explained by the trauma of separation (p. 130).

Granted the intensity of the emotional disturbance exhibited by monkeys separated from the mother, the question may nevertheless be raised: What are these infants disturbed about? In the experiment under discussion, they could see the mother, they could hear her; yet these possibilities if anything enhanced rather than reduced their anxieties. Does not this indicate that it is body contact which is the significant variable? And if so, what right do we

have to speak of a secondary drive toward the mother as an object—over and above a need for contact comfort as such?

Two sets of facts give eloquent reply to this challenge. First, the instances described above of separation from the real or cloth mother took place when the monkeys were from five to eight months of age. According to data provided by Harlow, Harlow, and Hanson (1963; Figs. 2-5) "body contacts between mother and infant in monkeys drop sharply after the first month of life and become relatively infrequent by the third month." Second, several of the tests of preference and emotionality administered to monkeys raised with mother surrogates included variations permitting only visual *vs.* direct physical contact with the object; e.g., the animals could choose which "mother" they would look at through a peep hole, or the cloth mother was enclosed in a transparent Plexiglass box (Harlow and Zimmermann, 1959). Although direct physical contact showed the strongest effects, the mere visual presence of the cloth mother had strong attraction for monkeys raised on a cloth surrogate and significantly reduced emotionality scores. Moreover, these effects were still observable in retention tests administered a year after separation from the mother surrogate when the monkeys were 18 months old.

In view of these facts, we cannot attribute the intense emotional disturbance exhibited by monkeys upon separation from real or surrogate mothers solely or even primarily to deprivation of contact comfort. These reactions appear to be specific to removal of an infant from an object which has acquired drive properties in its own right. In short, at least in the case of primates, we can legitimately speak of the development in early infancy of a secondary drive for perceptual contact with the mother. We shall refer to this drive as *maternal dependency*. When frustrated, this acquired need evokes not only the usual effect of heightened drive level, but also a specific syndrome of extreme emotional disturbance. The elements in this pattern can be identified from a real or surrogate mother after a period of contact. There are four major types of reaction: a) a high level of anxiety manifested by squealing, screaming, and fear of the environment; b) inhibition of exploratory and manipulative activities; c) fear, rejection of, and aggressiveness toward other social objects—including substitute mothers and peers; and d) neurotic like, repetitive, self-stimulating movements such as convulsive jerking, self-clutching, or rocking.

How long do separated animals continue to manifest these behaviors? Or, putting the question more generally, what are the long-term effects of maternal separation in monkeys? Unfortunately, no follow-up investigations of this phenomenon have been reported in the literature. In their comprehensive bibliography of research on effects of early experience in monkeys, Mason, Davenport, and Menzel (Newton, 1968) list many studies of animals isolated from the mother at birth, but only one where the infants

were separated after a period of contact with the mother. We do know from Harlow's work that animals removed from their mothers at the age of 8½ months and placed with a cloth surrogate were able to adapt within 48 hours and eventually developed an attachment for the artificial mother, but no information is given on the later behavior of these animals.

At this point, we can only speculate as to the long-term effects of deprivation of dependency drive in monkeys. Taking into consideration such data as we have, we hazard the following generalization. When subjected to maternal separation after a period of dependency, monkeys will in later life exhibit a two-phase pattern of reaction. The initial response to a new situation is one of fear, withdrawal, and defensive aggressiveness. But as the situation becomes familiar, and anxiety becomes allayed, the animal's heightened dependency drive leads to the formation of attachments to inanimate or animate objects in the new environment (e.g. the cloth surrogate) which then serve as sources of security but again give rise to anxiety if removed. In short, the separated animal is likely to be both anxious and dependent.

What if the new environment offers no objects that permit attachment? In that event the effects of frustrated dependency drive became confounded with those of stimulus restriction, a topic we consider in a later section of this chapter.

In summary, the work of Harlow and others on the role of infant experience in the development of the monkey has several implications central to the question of early drive deprivation and its effects. First, tactual stimulation and body contact appear to have drive properties for the infant monkey and probably for other mammal species as well. Second, the drive does not emerge full-blown at birth but develops gradually as a function of the availability of an environment permitting its expression. Thus in Harlow and Zimmermann's data (1958), scores for time spent with the cloth mother rose steadily not reaching a maximum until the infants were over three weeks old. Third, through a process of reinforcement the drive properties of body contact became transferred to the object providing the tactual stimulation—be it a cloth-covered block of wood or a real mother. In this way, an innate biological need is converted through primary reinforcement into a powerful secondary drive. In consequence, separation from the reinforced social object constitutes a form of drive deprivation.

Fourth, the immediate effects of this deprivation attain an extraordinary intensity and scope. In additon to the expected increase in general drive level, there is a strong reaction of pervasive anxiety, stereotyped behavior, and inhibition of normal exploratory and manipulatory activity. We see the second order effects of drive deprivation in cutting the animal off from the reciprocal pattern of motor-sensory stimulation ordinarily provided by the mother-infant relationship. Fifth, since a learned drive takes time to develop

and becomes stronger as a function of length of association with the original sources of primary drive, the effects of maternal separation are likely to be greater if the separation occurs not in the first days of life, but somewhat later. This probability puts a qualification on the general principle that the earlier drive deprivation occurs, the greater its impact.

Finally, the preceding considerations require distinguishing between two types of maternal deprivation which may have rather different consequences for infant behavior. The first is the one we have been discussing, separation of the infant from a "mother-object" toward which the infant has developed a secondary drive through reinforcement by body contact and possibly other associated variables. The second is the complete absence, in the infant's early life, of experience with the object normally serving as the agent of contact comfort, namely an adult female of his species. In this case no drive deprivation is involved since the infant had no opportunity to acquire a secondary drive for association with the real mother. What has occurred is an instance—indeed the classic instance—of stimulus deprivation.

From this point of view it becomes clear that the primary form of early deprivation experienced by Harlow's monkeys raised from birth with mother surrogates was stimulus deprivation rather than deprivation of drive.

Stimulus Deprivation in Monkeys

The behavior of monkeys isolated from birth. The most extensive material bearing on effects of stimulus deprivation in primates comes from investigations of development and behavior in animals removed from the mother at birth. We have already become acquainted with some of the immediate effects of such removal in reviewing Harlow's experiments on contact comfort. We shall now follow the subsequent career of what he later referred to as "motherless monkeys." In addition, we shall draw on material from other studies.

At the time of his original experiments, Harlow had a rather high opinion of the maternal capabilities of his terry-cloth mother.

> . . . a mother, soft, warm and tender, a mother with infinite patience, a mother available twenty-four hours a day, a mother that never scolded her infant and never struck or bit her baby in anger . . . It is our opinion that we engineered a very superior monkey mother, although this position is not held universally by the monkey fathers (Harlow, 1958).

Certainly in the original experiments, the cloth mothers seemed to be living up to expectations. But the product soon began to give grounds for doubt. As early as two or three months of age, children of these "very superior" mothers showed markedly retarded development in their awareness of each other, gestural communication, and mutual play (Harlow, 1962). But the most serious inadequacies of these animals did not become apparent until

they reached maturity. None of them gave any indication of normal sexual behavior. Among a total of 60 monkeys raised on cloth mothers not one male achieved successful mating and only four females have been impregnated, and these with great difficulty.

In all these respects the behavior of the monkeys raised with terry cloth mothers "is indistinguishable from that of monkeys raised in wire cages with no source of contact comfort other than a gauze diaper pad" (Harlow and Harlow, 1962). Clearly with primates contact comfort is not enough.

The preceding quotation focuses our attention on the behavior of monkeys raised in total isolation from birth. Following their comprehensive review of all studies available to date, Mason *et al.* (Newton, 1968) list three principal effects produced by such experience: 1) heightening of excitability to all forms of novel stimulation; 2) self-directed stereotyped activities such as clasping, thumb-sucking, and repetitive movements; 3) impaired social development reflected both in failure to recognize social cues and to respond differentially to animate *vs.* inanimate objects.

But it would be premature to conclude that the data on primates implies that the behavior of mammals isolated from birth will be more similar to that of animals restricted *after* the period of dependency on the mother than that of infants separated from the mother *during* this period. To begin with, the three characteristics listed above represent the long-term rather than the more immediate effects of isolation. This fact is reflected in the qualifying comment by Mason *et al.,* that "the longer period of isolation, the slower the rate of habituation to the new situation." Indeed, there is reason to believe that a prolonged total isolation slows the rate of habituation to a standstill. Witness the following description of the behavior of two monkeys upon their release from a two-year period of "maximum deprivation" involving being housed alone from birth in a cubicle with solid walls:

> They responded to their liberation by the crouching posture with which monkeys typically react to extreme threat. When placed together, each one crouched and made no further response to the other. Paired with younger monkeys from the group raised in partial isolation, they froze or fled when approached and made no effort to defend themselves from aggressive assaults. After another two years, in which they were kept together in a single large cage in the colony room, they showed the same abnormal fear of the sight or sound of other monkeys (Harlow and Harlow, 1962, p. 8).

Similar but less extreme reactions were observed in two monkeys "totally isolated" for the first six months of life. Only after several months of daily experience together in the free environment of a monkey playroom did the animals begin to move and climb about (*Ibid,* p. 8). In contrast monkeys severcly restricted for only 80 days showed deficient behavior initially but

made rapid gains after exposure to the playroom and, after eight months, were rated as almost normal. On the basis of these and other findings, Harlow and Harlow conclude that isolation from birth for a period of six months or more renders the animal "permanently inadequate."

It is apparently these same "permanently inadequate" animals who in later life exhibit marked hyperactivity, for in their review Mason *et al.* state that the "most obvious consequence" of being reared under the "extreme condition" of isolation in small cages is "heightening of excitability." We are led to the conclusion, then, that animals who eventually exhibit highly undifferentiated responses to stimuli, initially upon their very first exposure to unfamiliar objects react by freezing and fright similar to that shown by monkeys separated from real or terry cloth mothers. Interestingly enough, although the present writer could find no reference to the phenomenon in subsequent publications of the McGill group, their very first report describes precisely such a reaction:

> The most striking peculiarity of the restricted animals was the "freezing" behavior which they displayed when they were placed in unfamiliar surroundings, or handled by an experimenter. The animal would hug the floor, forelegs apart, ears back, and eyes staring forward (Clarke, *et al.*, 1951, p. 151).

Similarly, since we now know that monkeys raised only with surrogate mothers were also being subjected to stimulus deprivation, it is significant that the reaction of these animals when first taken out of the cage was also one of fright and withdrawal. The initial response, it will be recalled, was rushing to the "mother" in "abject terror." Only gradually did the infant overcome his fear, this process being facilitated by the presence of a cloth mother.

It seems clear now that stimulus deprivation alone *can* give rise to intense anxiety. But this anxiety is sooner or later dispelled *provided* the deprivation has been partial, short-lived, or has occurred relatively late in the animal's infancy (for example, after 6 months in macaque monkeys).

The evidence also requires us to revise our distinction regarding the differential effects of stimulus restriction *vs.* deprivation of dependency drive. It turns out that at least the immediate effects, and the processes which underlie them, are not so different after all. To begin with, both give rise to anxiety. In the one case, the anxiety is precipitated by separation from the mother; in the other, it is apparently provoked by sudden exposure to an overwhelmingly complex environment. Evidence for the latter point is found in the demonstration by Mason *et al.* (p.) that the intensity of the panic reaction can be markedly reduced through the gradual rather than immediate introduction of a more variegated stimulus situation. Once anxiety is aroused, the initial effect on the separated or restricted infant is the

same; both are overcome by fear and withdraw from the environment. External stimulation is thus shut out. Still subject to stimulus drive, the frustrated animal then resorts to self-stimulation in the form of convulsive stereotyped movements. How long it remains in this encapsulated state depends on the intensity of the anxiety aroused. This, in turn, is a joint function of the developmental state attained by the infant and the severity of the deprivation to which he has been exposed.

It is only when the organism begins to emerge from its immobilized state that differences in the behavior of isolated *vs.* separated animals become apparent. To appreciate the character of these differences, we must examine the effects of stimulus deprivation more concretely. Specifically, we must consider the precise nature of the experience of which an animal is being deprived under conditions of isolation *vs.* separation. Apparently this missing experience can be different in the two situations since the effects of separation—at least the immediate ones—were as readily obtained by removing an infant from his cloth mother as from a real one, whereas no cloth mother, no matter how "soft, and warm, and tender" was able to save her infant from future social maladjustment and childlessness. Having received contact comfort and security, what was it that the motherless monkeys missed in their early childhood that brought about their evolutionary demise?

The nature of deprived experience. The answer, according to Harlow and Harlow, is not something specific to the mother at all. The crucial factor revealed by their data is the opportunity to interact with other animals. In a series of subsequent experiments with three groups of motherless infants, these investigators have demonstrated that "opportunity for optimal infant-infant interaction may compensate for lack of mothering" (Harlow and Harlow, 1962, p. 10). Specifically, infants raised with terry cloth mothers, but given an opportunity to play with each other in a free environment have shown none of the markedly aberrant behavior characteristic of their companions raised individually. It is true that their social development did not proceed as rapidly as that of a control group reared with a real mother, but by the end of the second year of life the early differences had "all but disappeared." A second experiment established the point that "normal mothering" could not by itself produce socially adequate offspring. Each of two infants was kept isolated with his mother from birth until seven months of age and only then introduced to the other's company in a play pen. The animals showed no disposition to play together and exhibited a degree of retardation exceeded only by monkeys raised in total isolation. The importance of the physical environment was further emphasized in a series of experiments in which motherless monkeys were raised in pairs of foursomes in a single cage. These infants spent much of their time clinging together,

"each animal clutching the back of the one just ahead of it in 'choo-choo' fashion" (*Ibid*, p. 10). Placed in a normally stimulating playroom environment, these monkeys nevertheless continued the mutual clinging pattern and "seldom made any attempt to initiate play either with each other or later when they were paired with two normally playful monkeys; for all practical purposes, they never engaged in any play behavior whatsoever" (Harlow, 1963, p. 22). After surveying the evidence on three pairs of what he called "together-together" monkeys, Harlow concludes:

> . . . all have achieved a togetherness which transcends anything which *McCall's Magazine* ever described or imagined. Pairs of animals which obtain this unity are apparently forever denied the full capability of developing the second or any of the subsequent affectional systems [i.e., normal infant-infant and heterosexual interaction]. Although one may idealize a Damon and Pythias relationship, it is not conducive to the survival of the species (Harlow, 1962, p. 223).

> . . . Nothing could attest better to the fundamental differences in the variables underlying infant-mother and infant-infant affectional systems than the fact that the most basic element in the infant-mother systems serves as a destructive force when it appears in the infant-infant affectional relationship (*Ibid*, p. 225).

In actuality this same "basic element" proved equally if not more destructive in the mother-infant relationship as well, so long as the infant was deprived of access to a normal physical environment. We are therefore led to the general conclusion that, in higher mammals, an infant subjected to general stimulus restriction but left in the company of the others becomes bound by the strongly developed drives for body contact and dependency with resultant inhibition of later exploratory, manipulative and social activity. The retardation thus brought about in the animal's psychological development is not so great, however, as that produced by combined physical and social deprivation.

We can see now that the company of other animals, be it the mother or age mates, is not enough to permit normal psychological development. There must also be room and incentive for breaking the ties of contact comfort and dependency to engage in exploratory activity and interactive play.

We are now in a position to answer, at least in part, the question raised earlier regarding the critical element absent in the experience of monkeys reared in isolation or only with a cloth surrogate. This critical element appears to be the opportunity for interaction with "a source of changing stimulation and feed-back requiring progressively more complex adaptation and response." Such a source is normally provided by a living creature of the same species.[3]

In the present instance adequate stimulation and feedback would seem to have been supplied solely by littermates playing in a free environment, rather than by the mother. Does this mean that the mother *qua* mother is dispensable as an agent of rearing and her function can be equally served by age mates? This would seem to be implied by Harlow and Harlow's conclusion that "opportunity for optimal infant-infant interactions may compensate for lack of mothering." Their statement, however, is followed by an important qualification: "This is true at least in so far as infant-infant and sexual relations are concerned. Whether or not maternal behavior or later social adjustment will be affected remains to be seen" (Harlow and Harlow, 1962, p. 10).

Stimulus deprivation assoicated with maternal absence. Such caution seems well-advised if only in recollection of the sobering sequelae to Harlow's original optimism regarding the superior attributes of his cloth mothers. But there are other, more substantive grounds for reservation. To begin with, the critical period of the first six months of life encompasses not only the time of initial interaction with peers but also the interval of most intensive mother-infant interaction. That such interaction facilitates behavior development to a degree not achieved by infant-infant interaction alone is indicated by comparative data on the behavior of monkeys raised with a cloth surrogate *vs.* a real mother but given opportunity for infant-infant play (Harlow, 1963). Differences were observed in three areas. The surrogate group showed considerably more oral behavior which, according to Harlow "is a mark of social inadequacy and infantilism." They were also slower to achieve nomal patterns of mutual play. Finally, there were retarded in developing facial expressions involed in social communication. In this connection Harlow concludes that "early mother-infant association stimulates the formation and differentiation of facial—and probably total bodily —expressions that subsequently facilitate positive social interaction" (p. 16).

Since the latest published observations on these animals were apparently made when they were two years old, we have yet to observe the long-term effects of mother absence on their behavior. Of particular interest in this regard is the behavior of those few adult females who had been raised in complete social isolation and, despite their sexual inadequacy, were successfully impregnated. The Harlows give the following description of one such group of what they call "motherless mothers."

. . . The maternal behavior of all four mothers was completely abnormal, ranging from indifference to outright abuse. Whereas it usually requires more than one person to separate an infant from its mother, these mothers paid no attention when their infants were removed from the cages for the hand-feeding necessitated by the mother's refusal to nurse.

Two of the mothers did eventually permit fairly frequent nursing, but their apparently closer maternal relations were accompanied by more violent abuse (Harlow and Hawlow, 1952, p. 9).

The nature of the abuse typically experienced by the offspring of these "motherless mothers" is graphically depicted in three more recent reports (Harlow, 1963; Seay, Alexander, and Harlow, 1964; Harlow and Harlow, 1965) describing seven mothers in all. The motherless mothers, including some who had been raised on "warm and tender" cloth surrogates, would alternate between complete avoidance of their infants and violent attack including beating their infants, knocking them down, stepping on them and rubbing their faces on the floor. "All seven infants would have died had we not intervened and fed them by hand" (Harlow and Harlow, 1965, p. 309). More generally, then, we can say that an extreme response fatal for the survival of the species results from missing out on a series of transitional experiences. In the case of the motherless monkeys, the transitional experiences are those involved in the gradually changing character of mother-infant interaction over the first six months of life, precisely the period designated by Harlow as crucial for debilitating effects of isolation. It is during this time that the maternal behavior of the monkey undergoes a slow but profound transition. Whereas during the first trimester the female engages primarily in behaviors which are in effect contact-inducing, such as nursing, cradling, and grooming, by the end of this period the mother begins to reject and punish the infant by terminating and prohibiting contact, shaking him, or cuffing him, occasionally hard enough to send him sprawling. Such behavior reaches its maximum at about five months of age after which it abates "not because of a decrease in the mother's readiness to punish" but rather as "a function of the infant's improved ability to avoid punishment" (Harlow, Harlow, and Hansen, 1963, p. 265). In consequence of this maternal rejection "the infant is propelled into closer relation with its peers" (Harlow and Harlow, 1962, p. 9).

In the absence of evidence to the contrary one could argue that an opportunity for infant-infant interaction would be sufficient to equip motherless monkeys with a normal repertoire of maternal motives and behaviors, but this eventuality seems highly unlikely, since infant-infant interaction contains neither the nurturant components nor the aspect of gradual transition which characterize the normal mother-infant relationship. In other words, the pattern of mother-infant interaction contains certain elements important for the development of behavior which are not present in infant-infant play. To the extent that this is so, depriving the infant of an adequate r..other during the first six months of life is likely to reduce his response repertoire and capacity for adaptation. Such deficiencies may be expected not only in .ater social and maternal behavior, as the Harlows

suggest, but to judge from research on other species—also the capacity for problem solving and ability to withstand stress.

Effects of early isolation vs. later maternal separation. Having examined the particular experiences which, when omitted, produce the aberrant behaviors associated with early restriction, we can now return to the issue of similarities and differences between effects of early isolation from the mother *vs.* separation later in infancy. Although the initial reactions of the infant to both are similar, we now see that the long range consequences are likely to differ to the extent that the early-isolated animal has missed certain learning experiences essential for later adaptation. The general effect of such an experimental gap is perhaps best summarized by the term Melzack and Thompson have used to characterize the behavior of their restricted dogs: *ineptitude.* Such animals simply don't know how. They have not learned to perceive and respond differentially to objects in their environment—whether inanimate or animate—and, as a result, are inundated and frightened by the flood of stimuli which they encounter after release from their confinement. The infant separated from the mother later in infancy is in a different situation. His initial problem is not ineptitude but insecurity. Through prior interaction with the mother and exploration using her as a security base, he has acquired some degree of skill in differential response to his environment —again both inanimate an animate. Indeed, it is his capacity for the latter which is the root of his downfall. He recognizes his mother as a distinct entity and when she is gone, he becomes distaught and his capacities for differentiated response are reduced, but not so far reduced that he will fail to discriminate between his own "mother" and a substitute (even though the former be nothing but a cloth-covered piece of wood). More concretely, along with heightened drive level and diffuse anxiety which the separated infant shares with the product of isolation, he also exhibits more differentiated behaviors of selective withdrawal, hostility, protest, and resistance.

In the foregoing analysis we have treated the sequelae of stimulus restriction and frustration of dependency drive as if they were mutually exclusive; and, indeed, in the examples we have cited the two sets of effects were relatively independent of each other. Monkeys isolated from the mother at birth could not be victims of a frustrated maternal dependency drive. This does not mean, however, that the two forms of deprivation cannot have their critical impact simultaneously. The extent to which this is possible depends on the amount of overlap in periods of maximal susceptibility to stimulus restriction on the one hand and frustration of dependency drive on the other. With respect to the latter we have argued that the critical period tends to occur later and last longer as one moves up the phylogenetic scale, with monkeys being maximally susceptible at approximately two

months of age. What is the corresponding chronology for effects of stimulus restriction?

The problem of critical periods. In Harlow's work, animals isolated from birth to six months of age proved beyond redemption whereas others similarly restricted only for the first 80 days of life were able ultimately to attain "almost normal" levels of performance. On this basis Harlow and Harlow conclude that "six months of isolation will render the animals permanently inadequate" whereas "shorter periods of isolation, perhaps 60 to 90 days or even more, are clearly reversible" (1962, pp. 8-9). The same facts, however, allow of another, somewhat different interpretation; namely, the critical period for crippling effects of isolation in monkeys begins at about two months of age. As we have already noted, a major shift in the maternal behavior of the monkey female occurs precisely during the interval under discussion; that is, when the infant is between two and six months of age.

We can conclude now that in monkeys the critical period for effects of stimulus deprivation occurs not earliest but in what might be called middle infancy, centering about the age of weaning. A number of important implications follow from this conclusion. First, subjecting an animal to general restriction only during earliest infancy—i.e., before the critical period begins—should not produce the severe, persistent deficits associated with isolation during the critical period. At this early stage the infant is more a recipient than an active agent, and has not yet developed a strong dependency drive. So long as the organism's basic physiological requirements (e. g., food, warmth) are met, the presence or absence of a wide range of stimuli should therefore be of limited importance, since the infant is capable of responding only minimally to his most immediate physical environment. This does not mean isolation restricted to this early period will be without effect, to begin with, it is not an easy task to provide for the basic physiological needs of a newborn mammal in the absence of a mother. And even if adequate physical care is provided, the absence of tactual stimulation by the mother may cause some initial retardation in acquisition of perceptual-motor skills and in the development of dependency drive, but these losses should be rapidly regained provided the infant is placed in a normal environment before the critical period is reached.

Second, since the "critical period" seems to begin at two months for monkeys, this means, that immediately following birth, there is a kind of "safe" interval in which the infant is comparatively immune from radical effects both of stimulus deprivation and frustration of dependency drive.

Third, the critical period for stimulus restriction is longer than that for deprivation of dependency drive, since the latter presumably passes the danger point at the age of weaning, whereas perceptual restriction after

weaning has been shown to be deleterious in monkeys. But there is nevertheless an interval shortly before weaning when the two critical periods overlap. This means that it is still possible to subject an infant to critical stimulus restriction at a time after he has developed and still retains a strong attachment to the mother and hence is susceptible to frustration of dependency drive as well. Under these circumstances the two forms of deprivation i.e., stimulus and drive) can interact with each other. This in turn means that the effects of stimulus deprivation can differ depending upon whether the restriction is introduced before, during, or after the period of susceptibility to furstration of dependency drive. Specifically, if the animal is isolated from birth for an extended period, as has typically occurred in the research on monkeys, the observed effects are due purely to stimulus restriction and include, as we have seen, an initial reaction of anxiety and withdrawal followed by hyperactivity, diffuseness, and general ineptitude in all spheres of activity—intellectual, emotional, and social. Yet, although these disturbances are attributable solely to stimulus deprivation, dependency drive paradoxically plays a significant role if only by default; that its, the undifferentiated emotional reaction characteristic of early restricted animals and their irresponsiveness to training result in part from the fact that the animal has never developed the normal attachment to a mother which functions both to direct and differentiated response. Lacking this special motivation and training demand, the animal is less susceptible to learning. We see here that stimulus restriction can result not only in drive deprivation; it may actually preclude the development of a drive necessary for the animal's normal psychological growth.

Animals isolated shortly after weaning show a similar but less extreme reaction with some possibility of improvement upon release from restriction. Two considerations argue for the more optimistic prognosis under these circumstances. First, by the time the deprivation is introduced the animals have already developed some capacity for differentiated perception and response in the context of normal mother-child and incipient peer interaction. To the extent that their deficits represent a disorganization of patterns already learned, gradual recovery becomes possible once a normal environment is restored. Second, even though maternal dependency drive no longer has maximal strength after weaning, Harlow's experiments indicate that separation from the mother during later infancy still has considerable impact in terms of drive deprivation. Since animals who have experienced drive frustration are more susceptible to training, it follows that they are more likely to relearn, and learn anew, behavior patterns required for re-establishing and maintaining contact with sources of security and drive reduction that become available upon release from isolation.

But what happens if the animal is isolated from stimuli—including mother—at a time when the critical periods for both types of deprivation

overlap—that is, while the dependency drive is at maximal strength but patterns of reciprocal interaction are still in an inchoate stage of development? Regretably no data are available on this question from the research on monkeys, for in the experiments done to date, other sources of stimulation were always present after the mother was removed. In the absence of such alternative sources of stimulation, one would expect the animal to remain in an encapsulated state closing out and rejecting such minimal external stimulation as was available to him and restoring even more intensively to self-stimulating stereotyped movements. In other words, the isolation would be psychological as well as physical. Under these circumstances one would not expect to see the hyperactivity and diffuse response characteristics of animals restricted prior to or after the period of susceptibility to deprivation of dependency drive. Instead of being welcomed, stimuli from the outside would be actively rejected thus perpetuating and intensifying the effects of stimulus restriction. We therefore arrive at the conclusion that early deprivation will have its most immobilizing and immediately debilitating impact in those instances in which the infant is separated from the mother during the period of maximal dependency drive and placed in a situation in which physical and social stimuli are at a minimum.

But what of the long range impact of this double dose of deprivation? Would it be as incapacitating as the effects of prolonged deprivation from earliest infancy? In the absence of direct evidence, it is impossible to answer this question, for there are arguments on both sides. On the one hand, the psychologically encapsulated state induced by the simultaneous effect of stimulus deprivation and separation from the mother results in even greater alienation from environmental influences than that produced by physical isolation alone and endures longer after the external restrictions have been removed. On the other hand, the animal isolated in middle infancy would have experienced some interaction with the mother and thus developed at least the beginnings of a capacity for differentiated response as well as a dependency drive strong enough to permit the formation of new attachments once the withdrawal reaction is sufficently overcome to permit contact with the environment. About the only conclusion one can draw with any degree of confidence is that the joint effects of stimulus deprivation and frustration of dependency are likely to differ from those of prolonged isolation in early infancy in several respects. First, in the former case there will be an intensification and prolongation into later life of the initial reaction of anxiety, withdrawal, and self-stimulation. Second, the hyperactivity characteristic of the animal isolated from early infancy will not be present, since the strong anxiety reaction has the effect of inhibiting exploratory activity and invasion of the environment. Third, a crude level of social emotional differentiation will be present, taking the form of suspicion, rejection, and aggressiveness toward other animals and humans, including potential mother surrogates. Finally, despite this hostile reaction, the animal

isolated during middle infancy is more likely to show recovery if exposed to a normal or therapeutic environment. These greater recuperative powers derive from the fact that the infant had some opportunity before isolation to develop an incipient capacity for differentiated response and a dependency drive permitting the eventual formation of new attachments which can reinstigate the development of more complex patterns of response.

We have now gone as far as we can in clarifying both the separate and joint effects of stimulus restriction and frustration of dependency drive in monkeys. We turn now to the evidence available for humans.

III. Maternal Deprivation in Humans

It has been possible, in our review of maternal deprivation in monkeys, to identify independent effects of stimulus and drive deprivation. Unfortunately, the data on human maternal deprivation are so confounded as to make such an empirical separation impossible.

The presence of the confounding, however, has not prevented students of human behavior from drawing rather unequivocal conclusions. Typically this has been accomplished by focusing attention on one form of deprivation to the neglect of the other. This selective attention (and inattention) was in no sense deliberate, but rather reflected the theoretical orientation of the investigator. Thus the first extensive studies of maternal deprivation (Goldfarb, 1943a; Ribble, 1943; Bowlby, 1944; Spitz, 1945) were almost without exception stimulated by psychoanalytic hypotheses and carried out by investigators with psychiatric training. Consistent with their orientation, these workers have tended to attribute the observed effects primarily to the absence or interruption of the affectional bond between mother and child. This view is epitomized in Bowlby's militant affirmation at the conclusion of his influential monograph prepared for the World Health Organization; ". . . mother love in infancy and childhood is as important for mental health as are vitamins and proteins for physical health" (1951, p. 158).

The Critique of Spitz and Bowlby.

One of the most important effects of Bowlby's monograph was to stimulate the interest of other researchers, principally psychologists, in the problem of maternal deprivation. We shall not review here the now voluminous scientific literature on the subject, since this has been ably done elsewhere (Casler, 1961; Yarrow, 1961, 1964; Ainsworth, 1962) and most recently both by Casler and O'Connor (Newton, 1968).

The nature of the critique is indicated by the following example from the article by Casler:

It should be clear, then, that (a) no evidence has yet come to light in support of the hypothesis that the emotional, intellectual, and physical

deficiencies or decrements found in maternally deprived children are consequences of the deprivation itself, and that (b) there are many accounts of deprived children who have not suffered ill effects (p. 120).

The underlying thesis of this chapter is that the human organism does not need maternal love in order to function normally. The hypothesis of perceptual deprivation has been offered as an explanatory principle preferable to that of maternal deprivation for the study of the ill effects of institutionalization (p. 125).

The Specific Hypotheses of Spitz and Bowlby.

We mention the critique and rejection of the position of Bowlby and Spitz because we are about to affirm to a contrary conclusion: namely, in this writer's judgement, the original position of these investigators, when carefully examined, turns out to be more specific than its subsequent critics (including Bowlby himself!) have implied, but also, rather than being undermined, is actually supported by results of more recent research, particularly by the animal studies already reviewed in this article.

Since this is a highly unorthodox conclusion, it requires concrete documentation. We begin by calling attention to the fact that neither Bowlby, nor Spitz before him, have claimed that all institutions are necessarily harmful or that all children separated from the mothers "suffer permanent damage."

What are the conditions, then, which Spitz—and Bowlby after him—posit as the antecedents of severe retardation and psychological disturbance in institutionalized infants? For a full answer to this question we must review briefly the reported findings on which the interpretations are based. In his original study, Spitz (1945) described the course of development during the first year of life of children in four environments in two different countries of the Western hemisphere. Two of these environments (one in each country) were institutional and two involved infants from a similar cultural background being raised in their own homes. Whereas, with few exceptions, the infants in one of the institutions (Nursery)—and in both of the control groups—normal development throughout the year (as measured by the Hetzer-Wolf baby test), those in the Foundling Home exhibited a marked drop in developmental quotient from 124 to 72. (During this same period the figures for the corresponding control group of children raised in their own homes were 107 and 108 respectively.) By the end of the second year, the developmental quotient of the Foundling Home infants had fallen to 45. In addition to severe developmental retardation, these children exhibited high susceptibility to infection as well as markedly abnormal behavior ranging from extreme anxiety and bizarre stereotyped movements to profound stupor.

In evaluating the factors accounting for the progressive deterioration among the Foundling Home infants, Spitz gives explicit consideration to the

possibility that it was due to "the perceptual and motor deprivations which they suffer" (p. 11). Nevertheless, he accords primary importance to another factor:

It is true that the children in the Foundling Home are condemned to solitary confinement in their cots. But we do not think that it is the lack of perceptual stimulation *in general* [italics in original] that counts in their deprivation. We believe that they suffer because their perceptual world is emptied of human partners, that their isolation cuts them off from any stimulation by any persons who could signify mother-representatives for the child at this age (p. 68).

In support of this conclusion Spitz offers several lines of evidence and interpretation. First, he calls attention to the fact that the point at which the Foundling Home babies begin to fall below their age-mates in Nursery was between the 4th and 5th months—that is, shortly after they had been separated from the mother through weaning and turned over to the care of a nurse responsible for seven other infants. "The inference," says Spitz, "is obvious. As soon as the babies in Foundling Home are weaned the modest human contacts which they have had during nursing at the breast stop and their development falls below normal" (p. 66). This interruption of human contact, argues Spitz, is critical, since an inanimate perceptual stimulus can only be of minor importance to a child under 12 months of age without "the intervention of a human partner, i. e. by the mother or her substitute." Spitz then develops his thesis as follows:

. . . A progressive development of emotional interchange with the mother provides the child with perceptive experiences of its environment. The child learns to grasp by nursing at the mother's breast and by combining the emotional satisfaction of that experience with tactile perceptions. He learns to distinguish animate objects from inanimate ones by the spectacle provided by his mother's face in situations fraught with emotional satisfaction. The interchange between mother and child is loaded with emotional factors and it is in this interchange that the child learns to play. He becomes acquainted with his surroundings through the mother's carrying him around; through her help he learns security in locomotion as well as in every other respect. This security is reinforced by her being at his beck and call. In these emotional relations with the mother the child is introduced to learning, and later to imitation. We have previously mentioned that the motherless children in Foundling Home are unable to speak, to feed themselves, or to acquire habits of cleanliness: it is the security provided by the mother in the field of locomotion, the emotional bait offered by the mother calling her child, that "teaches" him to walk. When this is lacking, even children two to three years old cannot walk (p. 68).

The reader will note the similarity of the foregoing passage to Harlow's description of mother-infant interaction in monkeys and, in particular, the role of the mother as a security base enabling the infant gradually to explore and manipulate his environment. Moreover, in describing the effect of maternal separation on Founding Home infants, Spitz emphasized the concurrence of two events: first, the separation "cut them off from any stimulation by the mother person"; second, the severing occurred immediately upon weaning at three months of age, a time when dependency relationships are strong. In short, Spitz is emphasizing the specially traumatic effect of simultaneous deprivation of stimulation and dependency drive, a phenomenon we have already noted on the basis of research on early deprivation in mammals.

But the fact that Spitz's analysis is analogous to one that applies in lower mammals does not establish its validity for man. One could still argue, as most modern critics do, that the deterioration observed in the Foundling Home *was* due to "perceptual stimulation in general" and that separation from the mother was not an essential element. To demonstrate that the latter plays a central role, Spitz would have to show that it can bring about extreme reactions even in the absence of general deprivation of the kind encountered in the Foundling Home and, conversely, that in the absence of a severed mother-infant bond, the observed syndrome does not occur.

Although it is not generally acknowledged, this is precisely what Spitz claims to have done in a subsequent report (1946) in which he investigates 19 cases of profound emotional disturbance which did occur among the 123 infants in the Nursery where conditions of general stimulus deprivation did not prevail since the babies were kept in cots permitting free visibility and locomotion and were well provided with toys. The reaction, similar to that observed in the Foundling Home, was one of severe withdrawal and emotional disruption.

While unrelated to sex, race (both Negro and white children were included), or developmental level prior to onset (as measured by the Hetzer-Wolf Test), the syndrome (which Spitz refers to as "anaclitic depression") appeared only in children within a delimited age range, the youngest infant affected being 6 months of age and the oldest 11 months.

With respect to the crucial issue, the source of the disorder, Spitz notes that in all cases, the mother was removed from the child between the sixth and eighth month, and remained absent for a period of three months. Furthermore, no child developed the syndrome whose mother was *not* removed (pp. 319-320).

In calling attention to separation from the mother as a crucial factor in the development of the depressive syndrome, Spitz at the same time emphasizes the exceptions to the rule.

On the other hand, not all children whose mothers were removed developed the same syndrome. Hence, mother separation is a necessary, but not a sufficient cause for the development of the syndrome (p. 320).

In response to the implicit challenge, Spitz then proceeds to develop a hypothesis on the nature of the sufficient conditions and to obtain some data which he views as providing "indirect confirmation" of it (p. 336). This he accomplishes by obtaining ratings by staff members of the quality of the preceding mother-child relationship in those instances in which a separation took place. Among the 26 mothers rated as having a "good" relationship with their infant there were 17 cases of severe and 4 cases of mild depression. Among 38 mothers with a "bad" relationship, there were only 11 cases of depression, all of them mild. The value of X^2 for the 2 × 3 table (not given by Spitz) is significant at better than the .01 level. In other words, depression is both more frequent and more severe in cases of a good mother-child relationship. But even the severance of a warm relationship is not, in Spitz's view, sufficient to produce severe reaction in the child. Two other considerations are relevant. One is the character of the mother substitute. Although he offers no concrete data on this point, Spitz asserts that "when the mother substitute is a good one, depression does not develop" (p. 385). The final critical factor is the opportunity for locomotion. Even in the Nursery, Spitz asserts, such opportunity was severely limited. Under these circumstances, the infant in the second half year of life is prevented from seeking substitute relations with adults through locomotion. In addition,

When motor activity is inhibited in infancy, all normal outlets of the aggressive drive are blocked. In this case only one alternative remains for dealing with the aggressive drive: that is, to direct it against the self.

According to Spitz, this is the explanation for the stereotyped self-stimulation frequently observed among his disturbed cases both in the Foundling Home and Nursery.

In summary, according to Spitz, the factors leading to the development of anaclitic depression in human infants involve separation from a mother with whom the infant has developed a strong dependency and placement in a stimulus restricted environment without adequate mother substitutes. This is not only the position of Spitz but also that of Bowlby in his 1951 monograph which relies heavily on Spitz's work (e. g., pp. 22-23).

Moreover, when one considers the clinical picture presented by Spitz's disturbed infants and the conditions he identifies as giving rise to the disturbance, the similarity with Harlow's experimentally separated monkeys is indeed striking. We have already quoted Harlow's own comments to this

effect, and called attention to the common convergence of determining factors; namely, the simultaneous deprivation of dependency drive and the cutting off of the infant from environmental stimulation, especially the progressively developing reciprocal pattern of interaction with the object of the dependency drive—his mother.

There are of course some differences in pattern for the two species. Perhaps the most prominent of these is the later and longer period of susceptibility in humans. We had concluded that the critical period for the joint impact of stimulus and drive deprivation in monkeys was between 2 and 6 months of age with continued isolation during this four-month interval leading to irreversible damage. In line with Spitz's data cited above, Bowlby identifies the corresponding period of maximal susceptibility in humans as "the second half of the first year of life," (p. 48) with severe deprivation of the type described (i. e., no adequate mother substitute and restricted opportunity for locomotion) having permanent effects if continued "at least three months and probably more than six" (p. 47).

The question of the validity of these conclusions remains, however, and cannot be accepted without corroborative data from other studies which have been better designed and more satisfactorily reported.

As already indicated, it is this writer's contention that such studies do exist in appreciable number and quality. Indeed, some of the very investigators who have interpreted their work as clearly contradicting Spitz's position have produced the data most consistent with his formulation.

The Dennis Studies.

A case in point is the research of Dennis and his colleagues (Dennis and Najarian, 1957; Dennis, 1960; Dennis and Sayegh, 1965) on children raised in orphanages in Lebanon and Iran.[4] These papers describe institutions which certainly equal and perhaps exceed Spitz's Foundling Home in the barrenness and restrictiveness of the physical environment in which the infants were raised. For example, in the Lebanese orphanage, infants were kept swaddled from birth to four months of age or later, the sides of cribs were covered so that normally only the ceiling could be seen, the ratio of caretakers to children was 1 to 10, with the result that adults seldom approached the child during feeding times, toys and play equipment were limited, and the environment continued to be minimally stimulating until the child entered kindergarten at about four years of age. When tested with the Cattell infant scale during the first year of life, the babies appeared to be normal at two months of age but "greatly retarded" between the ages of three and twelve months. Yet, children between 4½ and 6 years old, who had spent all their lives in the institution, scored "almost normal" on a series of performance tests of mental ability. With respect to the emotional behavior of their subjects, Dennis and Najarian report as follows:

In the absence of objective techniques, we can only report a few impressions. The Creche infants were readily approachable and were interested in the tests. Very few testing sessions were postponed because of crying, from whatever cause. There was very little shyness or fear of strangers, perhaps because each infant saw several different adults. In the cribs there was very little if any crying that did not seem attributable to hunger or discomfort. However, some of the older babies developed automatisms such as arching the back strongly, or hitting some part of the body with the hand, which may have represented a type of "stimulation hunger." It was almost always possible to get the infants over two months of age to smile by stroking their chins or cheeks or by shaking them slightly. The older children, like the infants, were friendly and approachable. However, such observations are not meant to imply that other personality consequences could not be found if adequate techniques existed (p. 12).

Although some signs of emotional disturbance are evident in the above description, it clearly does not approach the picture of profound disorder presented by Spitz and Bowlby.

After detailed examination of the experiences available to the children at various ages, Dennis concludes that "the retardation prevailing between three and twelve months of age seems to be due to the lack of learning situations comparable to the test situations" (p. 12). While acknowledging that "Spitz's data and ours agree in finding that environmental conditions can depress infant test scores after the second month of life," Dennis and Najarian reject Spitz's interpretation of the cause of the decline and argue that the latter's findings can be adequately explained without reference of maternal deprivation:

. . . We suggest that an analysis of the relationship between test items and the conditions prevailing in the Foundling Home would reveal that retardation could readily be explained in terms of learning opportunities (p. 10).

As for the role of emotional factors in their own research, the authors assert:

. . . There is nothing to suggest that emotional shock, or lack of mothering or other emotion-arousing conditions, were responsible for behavioral retardation (p. 12).

Finally, pointing to the fact that their subjects achieved normal levels when tested at 4½ to 6 years of age despite early retardation and continued sojourn in a restricted environment, Dennis and Najarian emphasize that their study "does not support the doctrine of the permanency of early environmental effects" (p. 12).

As a further test of the hypothesis that the retardation of infants in the orphanage is due largely to poverty of experiences relevant to the testing situation, Dennis and Sayegh (1965) have recently published an experimental study in which one group of infants was provided supplementary experiences relevant to test performance. Following a month of such training for one hour a day, the experimental group showed a gain in developmental quotient four times that achieved by matched controls. The results are interpreted as demonstrating that appropriate experience "can result in rapid increases in behavioral development in the part of environmentally retarded infants" (p. 81).

Dennis's studies in Iranian institutions (Dennis, 1960) describe similar conditions and effects and arrive at similar conclusions; for example:

> The retardation of subjects . . . is believed due to the restriction of specific kinds of learning opportunities. . . . In the light of these findings, the explanation of retardation as being due primarily to emotional factors is believed to be untenable" (p. 59).

In view of such statements, how can we assert, as we do, that Dennis's findings are not in conflict with Spitz's and Bowlby's formulations? Let us recall that these formulations stipulate as the necessary conditions for evoking severe disturbance not simply physical deprivation and lack of maternal care but placement in such an environment immediately upon separation from a mother toward whom the child had developed a strong dependency relationship. Such a relationship is hardly likely to have developed for infants in the Lebanese orphanage since "all children in the creche are received shortly after birth" either from a maternity hospital or simply by having been "left on the doorstep of the institution" (p. 1). Ironically, Dennis acknowledges this very point in arguing that Spitz's hypothesis of "a break of the emotional attachment to the mother" could not explain the early retardation exhibited by the orphanage infants since in the creche, "the conditions for the formation of an emotional tie to a specific individual were never present" and, hence, "no breach of attachment would have occurred" (p. 10).[5] According to Spitz's own data, however, in the absence of such an emotional tie one should expect neither a marked depressive reaction nor enduring damage to the child. Any effects would be attributable to stimulus deprivation alone, unexcerbated by the critical additional impact of simultaneous deprivation of dependency drive.

The Effects of Early Dependency Frustration in Humans.

A substantial body of literature points in the same direction as our conclusions about Spitz's work (Bayley 1932, Bridges 1932, Ahrens 1954, Ambrose 1961, Gewirtz 1965, Yarrow 1956, 1962, 1964).

A particularly instructive research, because of its seemingly paradoxical

character, is Rheingold's (1961) comparative analysis of the effects of marked differences in environmental stimulation upon the social and exploratory behavior of three-month old infants. The comparison involved infants being raised in an institution *vs.* those brought up in their own home. The technique of time-sampling was used for observing care-taking behavior. The results showed marked differences favoring the home environment. "Home infants were cared for in 44 per cent of the observations, the institution infant on 15 per cent" (p. 151). Specific behaviors occurring significantly more frequently in the home environment included talking to the infant, looking at him, smiling, holding, feeding, showing affection, playing, patting, etc.

The primary measures of infant development involved a series of tests administered by the examiner. These included a series of manipulative tasks (i. e., how the infant holds and manipulates a rattle) and social reactions to a greeting ("Hello, baby, how are you?") with note being taken of both *positive facil and vocal responses* (e. g., smiling and *negative* ones (e.g., frowning, fussing, crying).

Contrary to Rheingold's expectation, responses of the two groups in the standarized situation, while showing no difference in reaction to toys, showed significant differences in social behavior. In the investigator's words:

> . . . not only were the institution infants as interested and as competent, but also they were more positively responsive to the examiner than the home infants. They smiled more quickly and more often; they more often vocalized and reached out a hand. On almost every measure of a positive, self-extending nature they were more reactive and more responsive, although not always to a degree sufficient for statistical significance. They appeared more eager and more delighted (p. 164).

Rheingold therefore concludes:

> The results indicate that the lesser amount of environmental stimulation provided by the institution did not blunt the interest of the institution infants in people and objects, or reduce their competence in responding to them. It did appear, however, to be associated with a quicker, fuller and more positive response to a social object (p. 166).

But the infants' responses to the standardized situations do not tell the whole story. At the time that caretaking activities were observed in both settings, records of the babies' behavior were taken as well. Here the results were in the opposite direction. In comparison with the institution children, the infants in their own homes vocalized over twice as much in general and seven times as much to the caretaker. They spent over ten times as much time in looking, touching an object, or playing with toys (which were in much richer supply in the home). The only time in which institution babies

significantly surpassed their family-reared age mates was in the frequency with which an infant was observed with a bottle in his mouth.

In seeking an explanation for this paradoxical pattern of results, Rheingold gives first consideration to the hypothesis that the infants in the institution were showing the effects of short-term deprivation. "It was as though they were happier to see a person, because they saw persons less often, they were more ready to be stimulated" (p. 164).

Rheingold then suggests, rather timorously, a second possibility, which is much more in keeping with the research results we have just been reviewing.

An alternative hypothesis, however, may be entertained, one based upon the assumption that the home infant is already capable of discriminating between his mother and another person, between the familiar person and the strange. Accordingly, it would follow that to the institution infant with his greater experience of many caretakers, any person would appear less different. The home infant, to be sure, *did* regard the person, but we may surmise that, with many of the accustomed cues missing, his positive responses were accordingly diminished. The negative responses, although few in number, may have been distress reactions to the sight, sound an touch of a strange person.

Rheingold feels, however, that "before this hypothesis can be accepted," corroborative evidence is necessary.

Such corroborative evidence has recently become available in another comparative study of infant devvelopment in home *vs.* institution which presents results opposite to those obtained by Rheingold and also different from previous studies of the particular behavior in question; namely, the smiling response Gewirtz (1965), using standarized experimental procedures, has compared the development of smiling to four different settings in Israel: 1) an institution for infants, 2) a day nursery, 3) a kibbutz and 4) children raised in their own families. In the institution 5 or 6 infants housed in the same room were in the care of a nurse usually professionally trained. Caretakers were rotated every few months and sometimes oftener. In the kibbutz, "much thought and effort" were devoted to the care and upbringing of children. Infants were reared primarily by a professionally trained caretaker responsible for four or five children, but also spent considerable time with their parents. They not only visited the children's house frequently, but the youngster also spent considerable time at home with his parents, here he routinely had a "corner" of his own. As a result the kibbutz child had "two focal environments." The day nursery served children of working mothers for 8 or 9 hours a day, 6 days a week. The ratio of caretakers per child was typically lower than that for the institution, but only children 8 months of age or over were admitted.

The smiling response was tested in a manner similar to that employed by previous investigators (Sptiz and Wolf, 1946; Ambrose, 1961). Specifically, "Upon approaching S, and for 2 minutes thereafter . . . Exhibited to S an unresponding 'blank face,' aligned with S's face at a distance of 2 feet." (p. 10) The statistically reliable results may be summarized as follows:

1.   Infants in the family and Kibbutz setting smiled earlier (2 months of age) and reached a maximum level sooner (at 4 months) than babies in institutions (one month later in each instance).

2.   After reaching a maximum, the frequency of smiling responses dropped off sharply with age for institution and day nursery children and moderately for kibbutz youngsters, but maintained the same high level for children raised in their own families through 18 months of age.

Gewirtz attributes the differences in level and rate of development of the smiling response in the several environments to the frequency with which caretakers (including parents) reinforce smiling by a change in their own behavior. This interpretations is, of course, consistent with the previously discussed experimental studies by Brackbill (1958) and Rheingold, Gewirtz and Ross (1959) demonstrating the efficacy of social reinforcement in increasing infant smiling and vocalization.

But though logically consistent with the above experiments, Gewirtz's curves for the development of the smiling response differed in two major respects from those previously reported by Spitz and Wolf (1946) and Ambrose (1961); the Israeli infants began smiling a month earlier, and, even in the insitution and day nursery groups, showed a much more gradual decline after reaching a maximum around 6 months of age. Both Spitz and Wolf, and Ambrose interpret the sharp drop of this age as a function of the infant's developing ability to distinguish familiar persons from strangers. On this basis children raised in their own families should be the ones exhibiting the sharpest decline, whereas in Gekirtz's sample they differed from the other three groups in showing no drop at all.

In seeking an explanation for these departures from results of previous studies, Gewirtz calls attention to a difference in procedure. In his own research, before the child was tested there was a warm-up period during which the examiner observed the child while talking with the caretaker or mother. If the observer caught the eye of a potential subject "she might smile or talk to him at a distance and even approach particular S's or groups of children, concentrating on particular S's" (pp. 8-9). Then, after a ten minute withdrawal, the examiner would return to begin the experiment proper. Moreover, the extent of the preliminary interaction depended in part on the observer's judgment, and a review of examiners' reports indicated that the interaction tended to be more intense with children living in their own families than in the other three settings.

In other words, in Gewirtz's experiment the babies had an opportunity to get used to the stranger and even to receive some reinforcement from him through social interaction. In the author's words:

> To the extent that the familiarization procedure was successful . . . the data could provide a valid picture of the strength of the smile response to the stimulus of a not totally unfamiliar woman's face, involving, we would imagine, rather little "fear" of the stranger (p. 36).

Needless to say, no such familiarization procedure was employed in previous studies of the smiling response nor, we would now add, in Rheingold's experiment prior to administering the tests of social development. It is this fact, we believe, that explains why her insitutional babies scored higher in social responsiveness than home-reared infants, whereas Gewirtz got just the opposite result.

Effects in Adolescence and Adulthood. How late? We have observed in Pringle and Bossio's study that by 14 years of age intellectual and language defects attributable to early deprivation development is not broken down by age. In a follow-up study of some of his original cases, Goldfarb (1947) reported evidence of maladjustment)based on ratings by caseworkers) in his subjects at 14 years of age. In addition, in line with the inference we have already drawn from comparing his earlier data with those of Pringle and Bossio, he found greater maladjustment among cases admitted before *vs.* after six months of age.

What of effects beyond adolescence? This writer has been able to find only two studies bearing on this question. Beres and Obers (1950) examined a sample of 38 young adults who had been institutionalized in early infancy (typically in the first year of life) for periods ranging up to four years. Although the authors report some continuity between the early deprivation experience and later personality characteristics, they are primarily impressed by the absence of serious psychological disorder in their subjects and the gradual recovery to normal levels of functioning.

> Our chief interest in this group focuses on the fact that considerable improvement to the level of satisfactory social adjustment was possible following the experience of extreme deprivation in infancy. We may again emphasize that the satisfactory adjustment in five of the seven cases did not become evident until latency or early adolescence. In their earlier years they showed varying degrees of unsatisfactory adjustment, and if our observations had been limited only to those years, we would have had to put them in one of the categories of ego maldevelopment. The implication is that the arrest of ego and superego development which characterizes the cases suffering from emotional deprivation in infancy is

not an irreversible process, and that further development of ego and superego is possible. . . .

Other authors have stressed the permanancy of the psychological effects of extreme deprivation in infancy. Our findings are at variance with their conclusions (pp. 231-232).

The Question of Long-Term Effects. The question of the permanence of effects of early stimulus deprivation in humans remains an important one. The work of Dennis suggests that substantial recovery is possible even after prolonged restriction in early infancy once the child finds himself in a more stimulated environment. Generalizability from Dennis's finding is limited, however, by the fact that the only aspects of child behavior evaluated were perceptual-motor development and (at the 4½ and 5 year old level) intelligence as measured by performance tests. But, according to Bowlby (1951) when chidren are exposed to early deprivation, "not all aspects of development are equally affected. Least affected is neuro-muscular development, including walking, other locomotor activities, and manual dexterity" (p. 20). The most affected are speech, "the ability to express being more affected than the ability to understand" (p. 20) and emotional adjustment, in particular the capacity to establish and maintain genuine emotional attachments, these affective disorders not becoming fully apparent until later childhood and adolescence (Ibid, pp. 39-36). It will be recalled that, in like manner, Harlow's "motherless monkeys" exhibited greatest disturbance in the spheres of communication and relation to others, with the full impact of early deprivation on behavior in these areas not becoming evident until the animals reached maturity.

Confirmation of Bowlby's conclusion involving the relative vulnerability of different aspects of psychological development comes from a subsequent investigation by Pringle and Bossio (1960). In a study of intellectual, emotional, and social development of 188 institutionalized children 8, 11, and 14 years of age, these researchers examined the relation of degree of impairment to three factors: (1) age of first separation from the mother (before or after 5*th* birthday); (2) length of institutional residence; and (3) extent of contact with family after institutionalization (through visits, letters, gifts, etc.). Intellectual function was measured by the Wechsler Intelligence Scale for Children, which provides for separate scores on verbal and performance sections. Whereas none of the three factors was associated with differences on the performance scale, the verbal scale showed significantly lower scores (a difference of 8 points in IQ) for children separated early and for those having no contact with their families after admission. Length of stay in the institution, however, proved to be unrelated to the degree of deficit in verbal intelligence.

The investigators also administered tests of reading ability and language skill. The results showed that "extent of backwardness in language development was considerably larger than that in intelligence or reading achievement" (p. 157). Again scores were lowest for chidren separated early and bereft of contac with their families after institutionalization, with length of stay showing no reliable effect.

In addition, examination of the tables in Pringle and Bossio's report reveals a feature not emphasized in their analysis. Since the data are tabulated separately for three age groups (8-, 11-, and 14-year olds), one may ask how each of the above relationships varies with age. It turns out that significant relationships are found only for the two younger age groups and never for the 14-year olds. Correspondingly the differences between means for the early and later separated children decreases in size with age. In other words, no deficit in verbal intelligence and language development associated with early separation from the mother could be reliably detected by the time the children were 14 years old.

The failure of time spent in the institution to predict the extent of verbal impairment suggests that it is the initial impact of removal from mother to institution which is critical for intellectual impairment. Support for this interpretation comes from data on the emotional adjustment of subjects in the sample. The results of two standardized assessment procedures, as well as clinical interviews, revealed a "high incidence" of emotional maladjustment. Furthermore, an analysis of symptoms exhibited by the children indicated that "maladjustment is to a large extent due to separation . . . rather than to the effects of institutional life" (p. 86). For example, among all problem behaviors appearing on the Bristol Social Adjustment Guides, the one which was observed in the greatest number of children (65%) was "anxiety or uncertainty about adult interest or affection."

In view of such findings, Pringle and Bossio then examined the relation between the degree of emotional disorder an reading achievement. Results showed that backward readers were four times as frequent among children classified as "maladjusted" as among the "stable group."

When examined more fully, Pringle and Bossio's description of the emotional reaction of their subjects shows even greater similarity to that of early deprived animals. For example, consider the five behaviors observed most frequently among the children in their sample; in addition to those we have already commented on—dependency anxiety (65%) and educational backwardness (60%)—those included "restlessness or inability to concentrate" (50%), "unforthcomingness" (34%), "depression" (25%) and "hostility to adults or children" (20%).

Scaled down to their simian equivalents, these characteristics parallel Harlow's descriptions of early deprived monkeys. Moreover, in its commingling of dependency anxiety, hyperactivity, and withdrawal, the picture

resembles more closely not the behavior of monkeys isolated from birth but of those separated from the mother in middle infancy. Nor is this surprising when we take into account the fact that Pringle and Bossio's early deprived group included infants separated from the mother at any time between birth and five years of age (no further breakdown was made). It seems likely, therefore, that we are dealing with a group of children most of whom were subjected to the joint impact of stimulus deprivation and frustration of dependency drive.

Separate vs. joint effects.   We are thus left with the questions of the nature of long-term effects specific to stimulus restriction alone. For this purpose we would need to compare later behavior in children subjected to deprivation beginning before *vs.* after six months of age. Regrettably none of the studies in the literature carries out such a comparison. Some light is shed on the question, however, by data presented in one of Goldfarb's pioneering reports (1943 b) This is a study of "the effects of early institutional care on adolescent personality. At the time of testing, the sample of 15 had an average age of 12 years with a range from 10 to 14: thus they are close in age—though a year older and more homogeneous— than the children in Pringle and Bossio's study (median of 11 years, range 8-14). The significance of the earlier study for our concern lies in the fact that the children had entered the institution at an average age of 4½ months (with a standard deviation of 2 months), the latest admission being at 9 months of age. In other words, most of the 15 cases experienced separation before the critical 6 month level. Accordingly, if we are willing to make the admittedly risky assumption that children were institutionalized for roughly the same reasons in England in the middle 1950's (the locale and date of fieldwork in Pringle and Bossio's study) as they had been in America in the early 40's (Goldfarb's research), any differences in degree and type of impairment exhibited by the two groups at adolescence might reflect in part the differential long range effects of stimulus deprivation during earliest infancy on the one hand, and, on the other, of the combined influence in middle infancy of stimulus restriction and frustration of dependency drive.

Roughly comparable data from the two studies are available in two areas: 1) verbal and performance IQ's (based on the Wechsler Bellevue in the American study, WISC in England); 2) observed frequency of problem behaviors.

The data suggest the following differences between the two groups in degree and type of psychological impairment.

1.   The adolescents in Institution A, most of whom were deprived before six months of age, show greater intellectual deficit generally and are retarded in non-verbal as well as verbal capacity. The later-separated children in

Institution B manifest deficiencies only in verbal intelligence. The differences favoring Institution B obtain despite the fact that these children were about a year younger at the time of testing.

2. A similar general result is evident in the area of emotional development with only 7% of children classified as "normal" in Institution A *vs.* 39% as "stable" in Institution B. In terms of specific behaviors, both samples of early deprived adolescents exceed foster home controls in frequency of problems in school achievement, inability to concentrate, hyperactivity, and craving for affection. At the same time, there is a difference in the general pattern of behavior exhibited by the two groups. The most salient characteristics of adolescents deprived mainly before six months of age are an impaired capacity in forming relationships, inability to concentrate, restlessness, and craving for affection. In contrast, among those deprived after six months of age, adult affection is their most frequent symptom. nly then do restlessness and inability to concentrate come into the picture. This pattern of similarities and contrasts, it will be observed, parallels that we have previously encountered in comparing the behavior of infant macaques isolated from birth *vs.* those separated from a mother or mother surrogate in middle infance (see pp. above). Specifically, in the latter case, both humans and monkeys show signs of dependency anxiety.

Problems of interpretation. Again the consistency of the human data with results of animal research does not establish its validity. Not only does the evidence rest on shaky foundations (e. g., buttressed at one end by only 15 cases), but questions arise about interpretation as well. For example, since the American sample is one year older, this might account for the lower salience of dependency anxiety in the pattern of behavior for the group. Fortunately, a check on this interpretation is possible from an earlier report by Goldfarb (1943 b) on a sample of 20 eight-year olds from the same institution, all admitted before 6 months of age, who were rated on some of the same behavior items later employed with 12-year olds. In comparing the results with those already cited for the older group, three trends become apparent.

First, there is a general increase in reported problem behavior with age among early-deprived children. It is impossible to say, however, whether this represents a genuine increase or simply a shift in the raters' standards of judgment. Second, the relatively constant rank order of items in the two age groups suggests little change in pattern of problem behavior over time. In particular, there is no evidence that among children separated in the first half year of life dependency behavior is more frequent than at younger age levels. On the contrary, such behavior appears to take time to develop.

A second problem in interpretation cannot be so easily resolved. This is the question of comparability in conditions within the two institutions.

Although Goldfarb provides no description of the institutional environment in his original publications, he indicates in a later report (1955) that babies were kept in individual cubicles up till nine months of age and in general suggests conditions similar to those observed in Spitz's Foundling Home. Since no information whatever is available about conditions in the institution in Pringle and Bossio's study, we cannot exclude the possibility that the difference between the two groups is mainly a product of a more restrictive or otherwise distinctive environment in Goldfarb's orphanage.

If the two institutions were in fact comparable, with the English setting being similar to that described by Goldfarb and Spitz, then another question arises. According to Spitz's hypothesis, infants separated from the mother after six months of age and placed in an environment in which locomotion is restricted show retardation and emotional trauma more severe than that exhibited by infants deprived earlier in life. Moreover, in the former circumstance, deprivation continuing much beyond five months is presumed to have irreversible effects. In other words, the most affected children should be found in the English rather than the American sample. Yet, the data in Table 1 show greater damage in the latter. This remains the case even when we focus attention on the sub-group from Institution B which brackets most closely the critical period of the second six months of life. These are the adolescents classified in the category "early entrance/long stay"; that is, children who had been admitted before five years of age and had spent at least one-third of their lives in the institution. The mean verbal IQ for this sub-group, 82.0, is still appreciably higher than the corresponding mean for Goldfarb's deprived cases, 74.3.

Of course, one could argue that the failure of this sub-sample to show the expected inferiority could be due to the fact that it also included cases separated after the first year of life. Nevertheless, our comparison calls into question an important corollary of the Spitz-Bowlby hypothesis. As we have seen, these early students of the problem had asserted that continued maternal deprivation beginning in the second half year of life would not only have more damaging effects than separation before six months, but also that deprivation during the critical period—if continued for five months or beyond—would have lasting effects. It is the second part of this proposition which is challenged by our comparative analysis. Instead, it points to an opposite conclusion; namely, even though the *immediate* effects are more debilitating when maternal deprivation takes place during the second half year of life, the reverse is true for *long term* consequences; the chilrren more severely affected nevertheless recuperate more quickly. In other worlds, rather than supporting Spitz and Bowlby's view on this issue, the data are more in line with the proposition that although the joint effects of stimulus restriction and frustration of dependency drive are more debilitating than those of stimulus restriction alone, they are more susceptible to

recovery through subsequent interaction with the environment, whereas the sequel of stimulus restriction in earliest infancy are more likely to persist into later life.

Despite the regrettable lack of control groups and objective measures, the two preceding reports are sufficiently unequivocal in their results to indicate that many children subjected to the debilitating effects of early deprivation of the type encountered in impersonal institutions can show substantial recovery in later life. This is not to imply, however, that they are unaffected. To be free of debilitating psychopathology is not synonymous with optimal psychological functioning. The possibility cannot be ruled out that a comparison against a control group with non-deprived background might reveal superiority for the latter in such spheres as abstract thinking, capacity to delay gratification, and ability to establish and maintain enduring relationships with others.

Nor do these results signify that more extreme or long lasting forms of early deprivation would not have correspondingly severe and persistent effects. Specifically, the evidence from work with monkeys strongly suggests that permanent debility might result if human infants were deprived early in life from any contact with other people—peers as well as adults. We can probably consider ourselves fortunate that we have no body of data bearing on this issue.

"Together-together" humans. The foregoing consideration calls to mind another question, however, on which some evidence is available. The question is that posed by Harlow's contention—to which we took exception —that in monkeys "infant-infant interactions can compensate for lack of mothering." Does such a statement apply to humans? In a sense, our conclusion in the preceding paragraph implies an affirmative reply, for if children in institutions with low staff-child ratios ultimately regain initial losses, presumably interaction with peers has played a substantial part in the process.

But the issue is more complex. Although a Rhesus monkey can feed himself at birth, a human infant cannot. The intercession of another member of the species is required. Normally—even in institutions—these other members are almost invariably adults, at least until the child is three or four years old. But what if at the earliest possible age children are left to themselves? Do they—like Harlow's infant monkeys—provide the necessary stimulation for each other? And if they do, does it make any difference in the final outcome?

At least one study suggests a positive answer to both of these questions. Freud and Dann (1951) have examined the results of an unusual "experiment in upbringing . . . not the outcome of an artificial and deliberate laboratory setup but of a combination of fateful outside circumstances" (p.

127). The subjects were six young children—between 3 and 4 years old at the time the study began—whose parents had been deported or killed by the Nazis during the infants' first year of life (typically in the first six months), and who had grown up in the Tereszin concentration camp. There they "had led the existence of inmates of a Ward within a restricted space, with few or no toys, with no opportunities for moving about freely . . ." (p. 153). "The Ward was staffed by nurses and helpers, themselves undernourished and overworked. Since Tereszin was a transit camp, deportations were frequent . . ." (p. 127). After liberation from the camp,

. . . the children wandered from one place to another with several [five or six] complete changes of adult environment. . . .

. . . none of the children had known other circumstances of life than those of a group setting. They were ignorant of the meaning of "a family" (p. 129).

When studied at Bulldog's Bank nursery at four years of age, these children showed many of the characteristics we have come to expect as sequelae of early deprivation. They were described as "hypersensitive, restless, aggressive, difficult to handle" (p. 186). But at the same time they differed dramatically from children brought up in institutions, where care, though limited, is regularly provided by adults and only by adults. The nature of the difference is indicated by the following excerpts:

The children's positive feelings were centered exclusively in their own group. It was evident that they cared greatly for each other and not at all for anybody or anything else. They had no other wish than to be together and became upset when they were separated from each other, even for short moments. No child would consent to remain upstairs while the others were downstairs, or vice versa, and no child would be taken for a walk or on an errand without the others. If anything of the kind happened, the single child would constantly ask for the other children while the group would fret for the missing child.

This insistence on being inseparable made it impossible in the beginning to treat the children as individuals or to vary their lives according to their special needs . . . (p. 131).

When together, the children were a closely knit group of members with equal status, no child assuming leadership length of time, but each one exerting a strong influence on the others by virtue of individual qualities, peculiarities, or by the mere fact of belonging . . . (p. 132).

The children's unusual emotional dependence on each other was borne out further by the almost complete absence of jealousy, rivalry and

competition, such as normally develop between brothers and sisters or in a group of contemporaries who come from normal families . . . (p. 133).

The authors interpret the atypical behavior of their charges as follows:

> . . . The children were without parents in the fullest sense of the word, i. e., not merely orphaned at the time of observation, but most of them without an early mother or father image in their unconcious minds to which their earliest libidinal strivings might have been attached. Consequently, their companions of the same age were their real love objects and their libidinal relations with them of a direct nature, not merely the products of laborious reaction formation and defenses against hostility. This explains why the feelings of the six children toward each other show a warmth and spontanety which is unheard of in ordinary relations between young contemporaries (pp. 166-167).

In the light of the other research—both on animals and humans—reviewed in this monograph, this writer would offer a somewhat different interpretation. Freud and Dann appear to assume an innate drive for emotional attachment to another human being. Such an assumption seems neither necessary nor warranted to explain the strong dependency needs of the Bulldogs Bank children. Rather, the drive can be presumed to have developed gradually in the same way and for the same reasons that it develops in the course of normal mother-infant relations—namely through reinforcement by drive reduction of contact comfort, stimulation and related primary needs. In this case the only consistent agents of such drive reduction turned out to be age mates rather than the mother. In this connection, it is noteworthy that the children are described as having been "conscientiously cared for" during infancy by adult inmates in the concentration camp but that "deportations were frequent." In other words, during the first year of life the infants were subjected to intermittent reinforcement and hence strengthening of drives for contact comfort and dependency.

Although at first strongly resistent and aggressive toward adults, in response to the consistent attention of staff members at the nursery the children gradually began to exhibit positive attitudes, in several instances developing attachments of unusual intensity. Marked progress was also shown in the other areas in which the children had exhibited disturbance and deficit, e. g., excessive fears and anxieties, compulsive movements, retarded modes of thinking, and language problems. In this connection, Freud and Dann take issue with "the belief held by many that every disturbance of the mother relationship during this vital phase [in their terms, the "oral" period] is invariably a pathogenic factor of specific value" (pp. 162-163). Pointing to the severe deprivation of "mother love" experienced by their subjects,

they emphasize that, despite certain "anomalies" in emotional life and Ego attitudes", the children

. . . were neither deficient, delinquent nor psychotic. They had found an alternative placement for their libido and, on the strength of this had mastered some of their anxieties, and developed social attitudes. That they were able to acquire a new language in the midst of their upheavals, bears witness to a basically unharmed contact with their environment (p. 168).

The persistence of these children in seeking satisfaction for their dependency drive and their ability to maintain substantial functional integrity in the face of repeated rejection call to mind Harlow's eloquent description of infant monkeys born to "motherless mothers":

. . . One of the things that would unnerve experimenters was to watch the desperate efforts of these babies to make contact with the abnormal mother. She would beat them and knock them down; they would come back and make contact; the mothers would rub their face into the floor; they would wriggle free and again attempt contact. The power, insistence and demandingness of the infant to make contact and the punishment the infant would accept would make strong men reach the point that they could hardly bear to observe this unmaternal behavior (Harlow, 1963, p. 25).

Significantly, a recent study (Seay, Alexander, and Harlow, 1964), which compares the behavior of these same infants during the first six months of life with a control group reared by normal mothers, finds no important differences between the two groups.

The important finding concerning infant-infant interactions is that the infants of the MM [motherless mothers] group developed very effective play patterns. On the basis of subsequent data we know, moreover, that the infants developed strong and specific affectional bonds for each other. It is perfectly obvious that inadequate or abusive mothering was a variable of little importance in the long-term development of the infant-infant social interactions (p. 151).

This testimony to the capacity of the infant monkey to exploit even a minimal mother-infant relationship has its human counterpart in a statement by one who is generally thought of as the chief protagonist of the contrary view, asserting the vulnerability of babies to permanent damage from maternal deprivation. The quotation below from Rene Spitz (Spitz and Wolf, 1946) constitutes a fitting summary for our discussion of the long range effects of early deprivation in humans.

. . . if we may be permitted to speak somewhat metaphysically of the urge to live, then we may say that at birth very little of this urge appears to be present in any organized fashion, but, that it develops powerfully in the course of the first few months; once developed, it pursues those alleys which seem to promise its gratification with incredible tenacity. The lines along which the urge to live appears to develop are those of security and assurance of gratification of various needs such as hunger, thirst, comfort, and warmth. All these are insured by the presence of the human partner. Once the road to contact with the human partner has opened for the infant it will pursue it regardless of disappointments and obstacles with that incredible tenacity which characterizes the urge to live. To discourage this tenacity in the pursuit of social contact, once it has come into being, would again require deep and fundamental modifications of the general environment (p. 105).

Notes

[1] Food deprivation as a possible confounding variable can apparently be ruled out, since Benjamin reports no reliable differences in weight between the bottle-fed and cup-fed groups.

[2] It is difficult to judge the reliability of Harlow and Zimmermann's findings since no significance tests are cited. Igel and Calvin assert, however, that in their study with dogs the reliable difference favoring lactating vs. non-lactating mothers was "contrary to the Wisconsin findings" (Op. cit., p. 304).

[3] The question may be raised as to whether normal development could not be achieved simply by placing the infant alone in an enriched physical environment including moving objects providing sensori-motor feedback of various kinds. Since this experimental variation has as yet not been carried out by Harlow or other investigators, this alternative hypothesis cannot be ruled out of consideration. Given the complexities of the interaction patterns described above, however, it seems highly unlikely that a totally inanimate environment could provide adequate substitute experience.

[4] We shall not discuss here an earlier study (Dennis, 1938), anteceding Spitz's publications by seven years, which purported to show that "practically all responses of the first year of life may be developed autogenously . . . those which are learned through the intercession of other persons are few and relatively unimportant" (p. 187). As Stone (1954) has nicely demonstrated, the conditions and findings of the experiment, far from supporting Dennis's claim, actually point to the contrary conclusion.

[5] This is not the only time that Spitz's own hypothesis has been used against him. For example, Orlansky (1949) in what appears to be the first published attack on the "mothering" hypothesis, writes: "It should be noted that in the cases of anaclitic depression reported by Spitz the children affected had been accustomed since brith to the care and attention of their mothers. One wonders if the same reaction would have occurred had they . . . not been accustomed to such personal attention during their first half year of life" (p. 16).

References

Ahrens, R. Beitrag zur Entwicklung des Physionomie und Mimikerkennens. *Zeit. F. Exp. U. Angew. Psychol.*, 1954, *2*, 99-633.

Ainsworth, M. D. The effects of maternal deprivation: a review of findings and controversy in the context of research strategy. In *Deprivation of maternal care: A re-assessment of its effects.* Geneva: W. H. O. Public Health Papers, No. 14, 1962.

Akrawi, S. *The strength of the oral drive as related to the age and method of weaning.* A thesis submitted for the degree of Master of Arts. Cornell University Graduate School, 1960.

Ambrose, J. A. The development of the smiling response in early infancy. In B. Foss (Ed.), *Determinants of infant behavior.* London: Matheun; New York: Wiley, 1961, pp. 179-201.

Bayley, N. A study of the crying of infants during mental and physical tests. *J. of Genetic Psych.*, 1932, Vol. XL, No. 2, 306-329.

Beach, F. A. and Jaynes, J. Effects of early experience upon the behavior of animals. *Psychol. Bull.*, 1954, *51*, 239-263.

Benjamin, L. S. The effect of bottle and cup feeding on the nonnutritive sucking of the infant Rhesus monkey. *J. Comp. Physiol. Psychol.*, 1961, *54*, 230-237.

Beres, D. and Obers, S. The effects of extreme deprivation in infancy on psychic structure in adolescence. *Psychoanal. Stud. of the Child.*, 1950, *5*, 121-140.

Bernstein, A. Some relations between techniques of feeding and training during infancy and certain behavior in childhood. *Genet. Psychol. Monogr.*, 1955, *51*, 3-44.

Bernstein, L. A note on Christie's "Experimental naivete and experimental naivete". *Psychol. Bull.*, 952, *49*, 38-40.

Bernstein, L. A reply to Scott *J. Abnorm. Soc. Psychol.*, 1956, *53*, 141-142.

Bernstein, L. The effects of variations in handling upon learning and retention. *J. Comp. Physiol. Psychol.*, 1957, *50*, 162-167.

Birch, H. G. Sources of order in the maternal behavior of animals. *Amer. J. Orthopsychist.*, 1956, *26*, 279-284.

Bowlby, J. Forty-four juvenile thieves: Their characters and home life. *Int. J. Psycho-Anal.*, 1944, *25*, 107-128.

Bowlby, J. *Maternal care and mental health.* World Health Organization, 1951.

Brackbill, Y. Extinction of the smiling response in infants as a function of reinforcement schedule. *Child Develpm.*, 1958, *29*, 115-124.

Bridges, K. M. B. Emotional development in early infancy. *Child Develpm.*, 1932, *3*, 324-341.

Burdina, V. N., Krasuskiy, V. K. and Chebikin, D. A. K voprosu o

zavisimosti formirovaniya vishei nervnoi deyatel'nosti sobak ot uslovii ikh vospitania v ontogeneze. *Zhurnal Visshei Nervnoi Deyatel'nosti.*, 1960, Vol. X, pp. 427-434.

Butler, R. A. Discrimination learning by rhesus monkeys to visual-exploration motivation. *J. Comp. Physiol. Psychol.*, 1953, *46*, 95.

Butler, R. A. Incentive conditions which influence visual exploration. *J. Exp. Psychol.*, 1954, *48*, 19.

Caldwell, B. M. The effects of infant care. In Hoffman, M. L. and Hoffman, L. W. (Eds.), *Review of child development research.* New York: Russell Sage Foundation, 1964, pp. 9-87.

Casler, L. Maternal deprivation: A critical review of the literature. *Monogr. Soc. Res. Child Develpm.*, 1961, *26*, No. 2.

Casler, L. The effects of extra tactile stimulation on a group of institutionalized infants. *Genet. Psychol. Monogr.*, 1965, *71*, (1), 137-175.

Chow, K. L. and Nissen, H. W. Intervocular transfer of learning in visually naive and experienced infant chimpanzees. *J. Comp. Physiol. Psychol.*, 1955, *48*, 224-237.

Davis, H. V., Sears, R. R., Miller, H. C., and Brodbeck, A. J. Effects of cup, bottle, and breast feeding on oral activities of newborn infants. *Pediatrics,* 1948, *2*, 549-558.

Da, C. *This simian world.* New York and London: Alfred A. Knopf, 1936.

Denenberg, V. H. The effects of early experience. In Hafez, E. S. E. (Ed.), *The behavior of domestic animals.* Baltimore: Williams and Wilkins, 1962.

Denenberg, V. H. and Naylor, J. C. The effects of early food deprivation upon adult learning. *Psychol. Rec.*, 1957, *7*, 75-77.

Dennis, W. Infant development under conditions of restricted practice and of minimum social stimulation. *J. Genet. Psychol.*, 1938, *53*, 149-158.

Dennis, W. Causes of retardation among institutional children: Iran. *J. Genet. Psychol.*, 1960, *96*, 47-59.

Dennis, W. and Najarian, P. Infand development under environmental handicap. *Psychol. Monogr.*, 1957, *71*, No. 7.

Dennis W. and Sayegh, Y. The effect of supplementary experiences upon the behavioral development of infants in institutions. *Child Develpm.*, 1965, *36*, No. 1, 81-90.

Fredeen, R. C. Cup feeding of new born infants. *Pediatrics*, 1948, *2*, 544-548.

Frederickson, E. Composition: The effects of infantile experience upon adult behavior. *J. Abn. Soc. Psychol.*, 1951, *46*, 406-409.

Freud, A. and Dann, S. An experiment in group upbringing. *Psychoanal. Stud. Child.*, 1951, *6*, 127-168.

Ganz, L. and Riesen, A. H. Stimulus generalization to hue in the dark-reared macaque. *J. Comp. Physiol. Psychol.*, 1962, *55*, 92-99.

Gauron, E. F. and Becker, W. C. The effects of early sensory deprivation on adult rat behavior under competition stress: An attempt at replication of a study of Alexander Wolf. *J. Comp. Physiol. Psychol.*, 159, *52*, 689-693. 689-693.

Gewirtz, J. L. The course of infant smiling in four child-rearing environments in Israel. In Foss, B. M. (Ed.), *Determinants of infant behavior*, III. New York: Wiley, 1965.

Gewirtz, J. L. and Baer, D. M. The effects of brief social deprivation on behaviors for a social reinforcer. *J. Abnorm. Soc. Psychol.*, 1958, *56*, 49-56.

Gibson, E. J. and Walk, R. D. The effect of prolonged exposure to visually presented patterns on learning. *J. Comp. Physiol. Psychol.*, 1956, *49*, 239-242.

Goldfarb, W. Infant rearing and problem behavior. *Amer. J. Orthopsychiat.*, 1943, *13*, 249-265. (a)

Goldfarb, W. The effects of early institutional care on adolescent personality. *J. Exp. Educ.*, 1943, *12*, 106-129. (b)

Goldfarb, W. Variations in adolescent adjustment of institutionally reared children. *Amer. J. Orthopsychiat.*, 1947, *17*, 449-457.

Goldfarb, W. Emotional and intellectual consequences of psychological deprivation in infancy: A revaluation. In Hoch, P. H. and Zubin, J. (Eds.), *Psychopathology of childhood*. Grune & Stratton, 1955, pp. 105-119.

Harlow, H. F. The nature of love. *Amer. Psychol.*, 1958, *13*, 673-685.

Harlow, H. F. The maternal affectional system. In Foss, B. M. (Ed.), *The determinants of infant behavior*. New York: John Wiley & Sons, 1963, pp. 3-33.

Harlow, H. F. Development of the second and third affectional systems in macaque monkeys. In Tourlenees, T. T., Pollack, S. L. and Himwich, H. E., (Eds.), *Research approaches to psychiatric problems*, 1962, pp. 209-229.

Harlow, H. F., and Harlow, M. K. Social deprivation in monkeys. *Scientific Amer.*, 1962, *207*, 136-144.

Harlow. H F., and Harlow, M. K. The affectional systems. In Schrier, S. M., Harlow, H. F. and Stollnitz, F. (Eds.), *Behavior of nonhuman primates*, Vol. II. New York: Academic Press, 1965, pp. 287-334.

Harlow, H. F., Harlow, M. K. and Hansen, E. W. The maternal affectional system of rhesus monkeys. In Rheingold, H. F. (Ed.), *Maternal behavior in animals*. New York: Wiley, 1963, pp. 254-281.

Harlow, H. F. and Zimmerman, R. R. *Proceedings of the American Philosophical Society*, 1958, *102*, 501-509.

Harlow, H. F. and Zimmerman, R. R. Affectional responses in the infant monkey. *Science*, 1959, *1*, 421-432.

Hartup, W. W. Dependence and independence. In Stevenson, H. W., Kagan, J. and Spiker, C. (Eds.), *Child psychology: The sixty-second yearbook*

of the National Society for the Study of Education, Part 1. Chicago, Ill.: Univ. of Chicago Press, 1963, pp. 333-363.

Hebb, D. O. The effects of early experience on problem-solving at maturity. *Amer. Psychol.*, 1947, *2*, 306-307.

Heinstein. M. I. Behavioral correlates of breast-bottle regimes under varying parent-infant relationships. *Monogr. Soc. Res. Child Develpm.*, 1963, *4*, No. 4, 1-61.

Held, R. and Hein, A. Movement-produced stimulation in the development of visually guided behavior. *J. Comp. Physiol. Psychol.*, 1963, *56*, 872-876.

Holmberg, A. R. *Nomads of the long bow: The Siriono of Eastern Bolivia.* Smithsonian Institute of Social Anthropology Publication No. 10, Washington, D. C.: United States Government Printing Office, 1950.

Hopper, H. E. and Pinneau, S. R. Frequency of regurgitation in infancy as related to the amount of stimulation received from the mother. *Child Develpm.*, 1957, *28*, 229-235.

Klackenberg, G. Studies in maternal deprivation in infants' homes. *Acta Paediat*, 1956, *45*, 1-12.

Landreth, C. *The psychology of early childhood.* Knopf, 1958.

Lashley, K. S. and Russell, J. T. The mechanism of vision. XI. A preliminary test of innate organization. *J. Genet. Psychol.*, 1934, *45*, 136-144.

Levy, D. M. Finger-sucking and accessory movements in early infancy. (An etiological study). *Amer. J. Psychiat.*, 1928, *7*, 881-918.

Levy, D. *Maternal overprotection.* New York: Columbia University Press, 1943.

Luchins, A. S. and Forgus, R. H. The effect of differential post-weaning environments on the rigidity of an animal's behavior. *J. Genet. Psychol.*, 1955, *86*, 51-58

Maas, H. Long-term effects of early childhood separation and group care. *Vita Humana*, 1963, *6*, 34-56.

Meier, G. W. and McGee, R. K. A re-evaluation of the effect of early perceptual experience on discrimination performance during adulthood. *J. Comp. Physiol. Psychol.*, 1959, *52*, 390-395.

Melzack, R. and Thompson, W. R. Effects of early experience on social behavior. *Canad. J. Psychol.*, 1956, *10*, 82-90.

Morgan, G. A. and Ricciuti, H. N. Infants' responses to strangers during the first year. Unpublished mimeographed manuscript, Cornell University, 1965.

Newton, Grant (Ed.), *Early Experience and Behavior.* Springfield, Ill.: C. C. Thomas, 1968.

Nissen, H. W., Chow, K. L. and Sennes, J. Effects of restricted opportunity for tactual, kinesthetic, and manipulative experience on the behavior of a chimpanzee. *Amer. J. Psychol.*, 1951, *64*, 485-507.

O'Connor, N. The evidence for the permanently disturbing effects of

mother-child separation. *Acta Psychol.*, 1965, *12*, 174-191.

Orlansky, H. Infant care and personality. *Psychol. Bull.*, 1949, *46*, 1-48.

Ottinger, D. R., Denenberg, V. H. and Stephens, M. W. Maternal emotionality multiple mothering, and emotionality in maturity. *J. Comp. Physiol. Psychol.*, 1963, *56*, 313-317.

Ourth, L. and Brown, K. B. Inadequate mothering and disturbance in the neonatal period. *Child Develpm.*, 1961, *32*, 287-295.

Pinneau, S. A critique on the articles by Margaret Ribble. *Child Develpm.*, 1950, *21*, 203-228.

Pinneau, S. The infantile disorders of hospitalism and anaclitic depression. *Psychol. Bull.*, 1955, *52*, 429-452.

Pringle, M. L., Kellmer and Bossio, V. A study of deprived children. *Vita Humana*, 1958, *1*, 65-91, 142-169.

Rheingold, H. L. The effect of environmental stimulation upon social and exploratory behavior in the human infant. In B. M. Goss (Ed.), *Determinants of infant behavior*. New York: Wiley, 1961, pp. 143-171.

Rheingold, H. L., Gewirtz, J. L., and Ross, H. W. Social conditioning of vocalizations in the infant. *J. Comp. Physiol. Psychol.*, 1959, *52*, 68-73.

Ribble, M. *The rights of infants: Early psychological needs and their satisfactions*. Columbia Univ. Press, 1943.

Riesen, A. H. The development of visual perception in man and chimpanzee. *Science*, 1949, *106*, 107-108.

Riesen, A. H. Arrested vision. *Sci. Amer.*, 1950, *183*, 16-19.

Riesen, A. H. Post-partum development of behavior. *Chicago Med. School Quart.*, 1951, *13*, 17-24.

Riesen, A. H. Plasticity of behavior: Psychological aspects. In Harlow, H. F. and Woolsey, C. N. (Eds.), *Symposium of biological and chemical bases of behavior*. Madison, Wis.: Univ. of Wis. Press, 1958, pp. 425-450.

Riesen, A. H. Studying perceptual development using the technique of sensory deprivation. *J. Nerv. Ment. Dis.*, 1961, *132*, 21-25.

Roberts, E. Thumb and finger sucking in relation to feeding in early infancy. *Amer. J. Dis. Child.*, 1944, *68*, 7-8.

Ross, S., Fisher, A. and King, D. Sucking behavior: A review of the literature. *J. Genet. Psychol.*, 1957, *91*, 63-81.

Roudinesco, J. and Appell, G. Les repercussions de la stabulation hospitaliere sur le developpement psycho-moteur des jeunes enfants. *La semaine des hopitaux de Paris*, 1959, *26*, No. 47, 2271-2273.

Schaffer, H. R. Objective observations of personality development in early infancy. *Brit. Mod. Psychol.*, 1958, *31*, 174-184.

Schaffer, H. R. Some issues for research in the study of attachment behaviour. In B. M. Foss (Ed.), *Determinants of infant behavior II*. London: Methuen, 1963.

Schaffer, H. R. Changes in developmental quotient under two conditions of

maternal separation. *Brit. J. Soc. Clin. Psychol.*, 1965, *4*, 39-46.

Schaffer, H. R. and Callender, W. M. Psychological effects of hospitalization in infancy. *Pediatrics*, 1959, *24*, 528-539.

Schaffer, J. R. Emerson, P. E. The development of social attachments in infancy. *Monogr. Soc. Res. Child Devel.*, 1964, *29*, No. 2 (Serial No. 93).

Sears, R. and Wise, G. W. Relation of cup-feeding in infancy to thumbsucking and the oral drive. *Amer. J. Orthopsychiat.*, 1950, *20*, 123-138.

Seay, B., Alexander, B. K. and Harlow, H. F. Maternal behavior of socially deprived rhesus monkeys. *J. Abnorm. Soc. Psychol.*, 1964, *69*, No. 4, 345-354.

Seay, B., Hansen, E. and Harlow, H. F. Mother-infant separation in monkeys. *J. Child Psychol. and Psychiat.*, 1962, *3*, 123-132.

Seitz, P. F. D. The maternal instinct in animal subjects. *Psychosom. Med.*, 1958, *20*, 215-226.

Spitz, R. A. Hospitalism: An inquiry into the genesis of psychiatric conditions in early childhood, Part I. *Psychoanal. Stud. Child*, 1945, *1*, 53-74.

Spitz, R. A. The smiling response: A contribution to the ontogenesis of social relations. *Genet. Psychol. Monogr.*, 1946, *34*, 57-125.

Spitz, R. A. Reply to Dr. Pinneau. *Psychol. Bull.*, 1955, *52*, 453-458.

Spitz, R. A. and Wolf, K. M. Anaclitic depression: An inquiry into the genesis of psychiatric conditions in early childhood (II). *Psychoanal. Stud. Child*, 1946, *2*, 313-342.

Stone, L. J. A critique of studies of infant isolation. *Child Developm.*, 1954, *25*, 9-20.

Theis, S. V. *How foster children turn out.* New York: State Charities Aid Ass., 1924.

Thompson, W. R. and Molzack, R. Early environment. *Scientific American*, 1956, *194*, 38-42.

vonSenden, M. *Faum-und Gestaltauffassung bei operieten Blindge-borenen vor und nach der Operation.* Leipzig: Barth, 1932.

Wolf, A. The dynamics of the selective inhibition of specific functions in neurosis: A preliminary report. *Psychosom. Med.*, 1943, *5*, 27-38.

Yarrow, L. J. The relationship between nutritive sucking experiences in infancy and non-nutritive sucking in childhood. *J. Genet. Psychol*, 1954, *84*, 149-162.

Yarrow, L. J. The development of object relationships during infancy and the effects of a disruption of early mother-child relationships. *Amer. Psychologist*, 1956, *11*, 423. (abstract)

Yarrow, L. J. Maternal deprivation: Toward an empirical and conceptual reevaluation. *Psychol. Bull.*, 1961, *58*, 459-490.

Yarrow, L. J. Research in dimensions of early maternal care. *Merrill-Palmer Quarterly of Behavior and Development*, 1963, *9*, No. 2, 101-114.

Yarrow, L. J. Separation from parents during early childhood. In M. L. Hoffman and L. W. Hoffman (Eds.), *Review of child development research*, Vol. I. New York: Russell Sage Foundation, 1964, pp. 89-136.

Yarrow, L. J. and Goodwin, M. S. *Effects of change in mother figure during infancy on personality development.* Progress Report, 1963, Family and Child Services, Washington, D. C.

3.10 Fathers' Verbal Interaction With Infants in the First Three Months of Life

Freda Rebelsky
Cheryl Hanks
Boston University

In his review of the psychological literature on the father, John Nash (1965) suggests that most American psychologists regard the United States as a matriocentric child-rearing society. In support of this statement, Nash cites numerous publications dealing with child-rearing practices and parent-child relations which make no mention of the father, thereby equating parent with mother, and child-rearing practices with mothers' child-rearing practices.

The dearth of studies that deal with fathers may be partially explained by the fact that fathers are not as available for study as mothers. It may also be due to the fact that psychologists consider fathers unimportant to child rearing and, therefore, make less of an effort to study them. In the light of recent studies of the effects of father absence, this assumption does not seem tenable: the absence (or presence) of a father does seem to have important effects, especially on the male child (Carlsmith 1964; Lynn & Sawrey 1959). Carlsmith's (1964) study of the relationship between father absence and the aptitude patterns of male college students showed that the effects were greatest if a father left when his son was 0-6 months old. Thus it appears that, especially in infancy, the presence or absence of a father is

Reprinted from *Child Development*, 1972, *42*, 63-68, by permission of the author and The Society for Research in Child Development, Inc. Copyright © 1971 by The Society for Research in Child Development, Inc.

important to the subsequent development of male children. It is difficult to explain many of the data that we do have because there have been no studies on fathers' interactions with infants. The present study, part of a larger study of infant vocalization (Lenneberg, Rebelsky, & Nichols 1965), was designed to supply some basic descriptive data on fathers' verbal interactions with their infants.

Method

Subjects

The sample consisted of 10 normal, full-term white, winter-born babies, seven males and three females. They were born into lower-middle-to upper-middle-class families who lived in Boston suburbs. Only two of the babies were firstborn. The sample was obtained through professional contacts with pediatricians. The research was presented to the parents as a general study of how infants live, what they do, etc., with the explanation that such basic data are not as yet known. The experimenter explained that she did not want to interfere in any way with the household schedule and that no changes in the babies' normal environment or routine should be made for E's convenience.

Procedure

Beginning in the second week of life, 24-hour tape recording were made approximately every 2 weeks for a 3-month period. Thus, there were six 24-hour observation periods for each infant. A microphone approximately the shape of a half-dollar, with a cord of about 27 feet, was attached to the infant's shirt such that the infant could be moved around without removing him from the sound field. The microphone picked up both the noises emitted by the infant and the noises to which he was exposed. In order to eliminate silent periods on the tapes, a recording instrument (described more fully in Chan, Lenneberg, & Rebelsky 1964) was operated by a voice key which turned the recorder off if there was a silence of more than 20 seconds, and turned it on if there was noise in the sound field.

Coding the tape recordings. Two coders listed to the tapes for the 10 infants and recorded the duration, time of day, and activity occurring each time a father vocalized to his infant. Ten percent of the tapes were coded by both coders, with an interjudge reliability of over .90 for each of the items scored. An interaction began with a father vocalizing to his infant and ended if there was an interval of silence longer than 30 seconds. The silent period was not included in the interaction time.

Results

The data indicate that fathers spend relatively little time interacting with their infants. The mean number of interactions per day was 2.7, and the average number of seconds per day was 37.7. While there were large individual differences, even the father with the most interactions spent an average of only 10 minutes, 26 seconds interacting with his infant each day. This is low when compared with the Moss data on mothers' verbal interactions with their infants (Moss 1967). Table 1 summarizes the group data on fathers' daily interactions with their infants. In addition, there was a Spearman rank correlation of $+.72$ between the number of interactions per father and the mean length of each father's interaction. This is significant at the 0.5 level ($p < .05$).

As might be expected, fathers talked to their babies most often in the morning hours before going to work (41 percent of all interactions) and in the evening hours after work (33 percent of all interactions).

The amount of father's interactions varied by the age and sex of their infants. Unlike mothers, who increase their vocalization time during the first 3 months of life (Moss 1967; Rebelsky 1967), seven out of 10 fathers spent less time vocalizing to their infants during the last half of the study (8-12 weeks) than in the first half (2-6 weeks). This decrease of vocalization over time is more marked among the fathers of female infants. While all three of the fathers of female infants decreased their number of vocalizations during the last 6 weeks, only four out of seven fathers of male infants decreased their numbers of vocalizations in the same time period. None of these interactions reached significance.

Table 1
**Means and Ranges of Fathers' Daily Interactions
with Their Infants**

	Number of Seconds per Day	Number of Interactions per Day	Length of Interactions in Seconds
Mean	37.7	2.7	13.9
Range	0–1,370	0–17	4–220

Of the 164 verbal interactions of these fathers with their infants, about half (54 percent) were during caretaking activities (e.g., diapering, feeding) and 46 percent were not during caretaking (see table 2).

When the data are analyzed in terms of the kinds of activities that were occurring while the father was vocalizing to his infant, the decrease of vocalization during caretaking activities is largely responsible for the overall

decrease in vocalization over time. With only one exception, all fathers decreased their number of vocalizations during caretaking activities during the second three observations. On the other hand, the number of vocalizations during noncaretaking activities remained about the same for the fathers of male infants, but decreased somewhat for the fathers of female infants.

Discussion

Fathers talk infrequently and for short periods of time to their infants in the first 3 months of life. When compared with similar data on mothers' verbalizations to infants (Moss 1967; Rebelsky 1967), the data suggest that fathers do some things differently from mothers. For example, whereas mothers increase their vocalization time during their infants' first 3 months, seven of the 10 fathers in this study spent less time verbalizing to their infants during the last month and a half compared with the first month and a half of life.

Like mothers, fathers seem to behave differently toward male and female infants; however, the differential behavior of fathers toward their infants is opposite from the differential behavior of mothers. While the fathers of female infants verbalized more than did the fathers of male infants at 2 weeks and 4 weeks of age, Moss's data show that mothers of male infants vocalized more than mothers of female infants at 3 weeks of age (Moss

Table 2

Sex Differences in Development Trends in the Number of Fathers' Verbal Interactions during Caretaking and Noncaretaking Activities

	Weeks 2, 4, 6			Weeks 8, 10, 12		
	Male	*Female*	*Total*	*Male*	*Female*	*Total*
Vocalization during caretaking	24(52%)	34(64%)	58(59%)	13(34%)	17(62%)	30(46%)
Vocalization not during caretaking	22(48%)	19(36%)	41(41%)	25(66%)	10(38%)	35(54%)
Total	46(100%)	53(100%)	99(100%)	38(100%)	27(100%)	65(100%)

1967, p. 23). By the time infants reach 3 months of age, these patterns are reversed. Fathers of male infants vocalize somewhat more than do fathers of female infants at 12 weeks; by 12 weeks, mothers of female infants vocalize more than mothers of male infants (Moss 1967). To account for this data, Moss suggests that mothers initially respond more to male infants because the infants are awake more and are generally more irritable than female

infants. He suggests that the shift in behavior at 3 months is due to the more reinforcing nature of the mother's interactions with her less-irritable female infant (Moss 1967).

While this explanation is reasonable, it cannot be extended to apply to the data which show a shift in the opposite direction on the part of fathers. However, it may easily be that mothers and fathers are responding to different things in their infants. For example, the mother may be responding to the sex-related behavior of her infant, whereas the father may be initially responding more to his role of father-of-daughter as a more nurturant, verbal role than the role of father-of-son. This suggestion receives some support from our finding that fathers of female infants verbalize more during caretaking activities than do fathers of male infants. If this is true, it may be that father absence has greater effects on males than on females because fathers of female infants define their role as more similar to the maternal role (i.e., nurturant) than do fathers of male infants. This is at best a tentative hypothesis; moreover, it does not clarify the father's definition of his role as father-of-son.

This study has raised some interesting questions. We now know that the patterns of mothers' and fathers' vocalizations to infants differ, but we do not know about other than vocal interactions of the fathers. It may be that fathers are more physical than verbal with their infants; it may be that fathers interact more physically with sons and more verbally with daughters. We do know that the presence or absence of a father has effects on the subsequent development of his children. What we now need are more comprehensive observations of fathers' interactions with their children to determine how they do interact so that we can hypothesize more clearly about how the effects we have seen might occur.

References

Carlsmith, L. Effect of early father absence on scholastic aptitude. *Harvard Educational Review*, 1964, 34, 3-21.

Chan, C. H.; Lenneberg, E. H.; & Rebelsky, F. G. Apparatus for reducing play-back time of tape recorded, intermittent vocalization. In U. Bellugi & R. Brown (Eds.), The acquisition of language. *Monographs of the Society for Research in Child Development,* 1964, 29 (1, Serial No. 92), 127-130.

Lenneberg, E. H.; Rebelsky, F. G.; & Nichols, I. A. The vocalizations of infants born to deaf and to hearing parents. *Human Development*, 1965, 8, 23-37.

Lynn, D. B., & Sawrey, W. L. The effects of father absence on Norwegian boys and girls. *Journal of Abnormal and Social Psychology,* 1959, 59, 258-262.

Moss, H. A. Sex, age and state as determinants of mother-infant interaction. *Merrill-Palmer Quarterly,* 1967, 13, 19-36.

Nash, J. The father in contemporary culture and current psychological literature. *Child Development,* 1965, 36, 261-297.

Rebelsky, F. G. Infancy in two cultures. *Nederlands Tijdschrift voor de Psychologie,* 1967, 22, 379-385.

3.11 The Mother-Child Relationship and the Father-Absent Boy's Personality Development

Henry B. Biller

In a recent article this author reviewed data pertaining to the personality development of the father-absent boy (Biller, 1970). A tentative conclusion was that variations in the mother-child relationship are associated with individual differences among father-absent boys. The present paper contains a fuller description and discussion of data relating to the mother's influence on the father-absent boy's personality development. Some indirect evidence from studies of children's personality development in father-present homes is cited and many untested hypotheses and speculations are presented. It is hoped that this paper will stimulate further thinking and research in this sparsely explored area.

Matriarchal Homes

There is considerable evidence that the boy's masculine development is impeded in the maternally dominated, father-present home (e.g., Biller, 1969a; Hetherington, 1965; Moulton et al., 1966). A number of investigators, studying families from diverse sociocultural backgrounds, have reported a strong relationship between maternal dominance and sex-role related difficulties among father-absent or paternally deprived males (Biller, 1970). A striking example of maternal domination occurs in matriarchal families which are very common in lower-socioeconomic neighborhoods (Miller, 1958). . . .

Reprinted with slight abridgment from the *Merrill-Palmer Quarterly of Behavior and Development,* 1971, *17,* 3, 227-241, by permission of the author and the Merrill-Palmer Institute.

Mother's Views of the Absent Father

Maternal attitudes relating to the father seem to be important in the personality development of children in intact homes (Grunebaum et al., 1962; Helper, 1955; Sears, 1953). Grunebaum et al. (1962), in a clinical study of academically underachieving boys, contended that a contributing factor to the boys' difficulties was the mothers' perceptions that their husbands were inadequate and incompetent . . .

The mother's attitude regarding masculinity and men, including her reactions to her son's masculine behavior, forms a significant part of the mother-son relationship. Her perception of the boy's father seems to frequently generalize to her son. However, it could be predicted that the degree to which a mother perceives her son as similar to his father is related to the boy's behavioral and physical characteristics as well as to particular maternal attitudes. For example, if her son very much resembles his father, facially and physically, it seems more likely that the mother would expect the boy's behavior to approximate his father's than if there was little father-son resemblance. As Bell (1968) points out, the stimulus value of the child and his impact on parental behavior has not received enough research attention.

Maternal Overprotection

In families where maternal overprotection exists, the father generally seems to play a very submissive and ineffectual role (Levy, 1943). Where the father is absent the probability of a pattern of maternal overprotection seems to be increased. Most fathers are very critical of having their children overprotected and most fathers also serve as models for independent behavior. The child's developmental stage at the onset of father-absence is no doubt an important variable. The infant or pre-school age father-absent boy seems likely to be overprotected by his mother, whereas if father-absence began when the boy was older, he might be expected to take over many of the responsibilities his father had previously assumed.

Stendler (1952) suggested that there are two critical periods in develop-ment of overdependency: (a) at around nine months, when the child first begins to test out and see if his mother will meet his dependency needs; and (b) from two to three years of age, when the child must give up his perceived control of his mother and learn to act independently in culturally approved ways. Father-absence, especially during this later period, could make the child prone to over-dependency. Comparing the family histories of 20 first-grade children rated as overdependent by their teachers, with 20 matched children, Stendler (1954) found that overdependency was common in families where the father was absent or ineffectual. Of the 20

overdependent children, 13 lacked the consistent presence of the father in the home during the first three years of life as compared to only 6 in the control group. In addition, the 6 relatively father-absent children in the control group had generally been without their fathers for a much shorter time than the overdependent children. Stendler pictured the role of the father as one which discouraged the mother's overprotecting tendencies and actively encouraged independent activity, especially in the boy. Unfortunately, Stendler (1954) did not do separate data analyses for boys and girls.

Stolz et al.'s (1954) analysis of retrospective maternal reports suggested that mothers whose husbands were away in military service tended to restrict their infants' locomotor activities to a greater extent than did mothers whose husbands were present; but, again, the results of this study might be more meaningful if the researchers had done separate analyses in terms of sex of child. Tiller (1958) reported similar results with mothers of eight- and nine-year-old Norwegian children whose fathers were seldom-home sailors. With respect to both sons and daughters, these mothers were more overprotective, as judged by maternal interview data and by the children's responses to a structured doll play test, than were the mothers of matched father-present children. Biller (1969b) also found that mothers of father-absent boys were less encouraging of masculine behavior than were mothers of father-present boys. In the father-absent families, many of the mothers' informal responses suggested that they were very fearful of their children being physically injured.

It is interesting to note that in intact homes fathers seem to vary their own behavior more as a function of sex of child than do mothers. In intact homes, fathers are reported to be more concerned with sex-typing and to more often base their expectations and reinforcements on the basis of sex of child (Goodenough, 1957; Johnson, 1963; Tasch, 1955). Romney's (1965) reanalysis of Barry, Bacon, and Child's (1957) cross-cultural findings suggests that, in societies where there is relatively little father availability, emphasis on children being compliant prevails; whereas in societies with high father availability, children are expected to be assertive. In the father-absent home, the degree to which the mother can take over the sex-role differentiation function seems of critical importance in the child's personality development (Colley, 1959).

Sociocultural Factors

Some studies suggest that maternal overprotection is not common in lower-class families (Heckscher, 1967; Kardiner & Ovesey, 1591; McCord, McCord, & Thurber, 1962; Rohrer & Edmonson, 1960). Socioeconomic status seems related to the frequency of maternal overprotection. The opportunity for a lower-class mother to overprotect a father-absent son may be less because she is more often engaged in a full-time job than is a middle-class mother (Heckscher, 1967). Second, there seems less of a

social stigma attached to father-absence among lower-class families as compared to middle-class families (King, 1945). A mother without a husband who has young children is a more common phenomenon in the lower class. The middle-class mother may be more predisposed to feel guilty because her child, particularly her son, is being deprived of a father. She may be more likely to try to make this up to the boy and overprotect and overindulge him.

On the other hand, there is evidence to suggest that maternal rejection and neglect are quite common among husbandless lower-class mothers (Heckscher, 1967; Kardiner & Ovesey, 1951; McCord, McCord & Thurber, 1962; Rohrer & Edmonson, 1960). Lower-class mothers without husbands seem particularly concerned with their own needs and their day-to-day existence and often withdraw from their children. There is some evidence that boys are more often rejected than girls (Beller, 1967; Bronfenbrenner, 1967; Dai, 1953; Pettigrew, 1964).

In any case, either overprotection or rejection would seem to reduce the probability of the boy's feeling a sense of worth in terms of his maleness. However, it does seem that maternal indifference or rejection would make a boy more prone to be indiscriminately influenced by the gang milieu. The maternally overprotected father-absent boy may be quite timid and retiring in peer interactions, whereas it seems more probable that the maternally rejected father-absent boy will act out aggressively and choose masculine activities and attitudes in order to gain the respect of his peers. Nevertheless, both overprotected and rejected father-absent boys seem likely to be low in underlying masculinity of sex-role orientation.

The frequent negative attitude of lower-class mothers towards their sons, and males in general, seems to contribute to the meaningfulness of the gang milieu for boys. The boy who feels neglected or rejected can have his needs for attention, recognition, and affection satisfied by becoming a member of a gang. Masculinity of an aggressive acting-out nature (in relation to typically middle-class standards) is valued by the gang, and behaviors perceived as feminine are fearfully avoided. Such an atmosphere may help bolster the boy's self-image, if he has the ability to perform in an aggressive-competitive manner, but it often leads to rigid and narrow interpersonal and cognitive functioning. For example, because women are usually authority figures in the school situation, many boys resent participation in the intellectual pursuits, perceiving such activities as feminine.

The general economic and social difficulties of the husbandless mother cannot be overlooked (Glasser & Navarre, 1965; Hartley, 1960; Kriesberg, 1967). Kriesberg (1067) clearly summarized the frequent plight of the mother whose husband is absent:

His absence is likely to mean that his former wife is poor, lives in generally poor neighborhoods, and lacks social, emotional, and physical

assistance in child rearing. Furthermore, how husbandless mothers accommodate themselves to these circumstances can have important consequences for their children (1967, p. 288).

The degree to which the fatherless family has available social and economic resources influences the child's interpersonal and educational opportunities. The lower-class child seems even more disadvantaged by fatherlessness than does the middle-class child.

Maternal values related to social and economic factors can be readily transmitted to the child. Because of differing maternal reinforcement patterns, middle-class father-absent children seem to be less handicapped in intellectual pursuits than are lower-class father-absent children. One could predict that a father-absent boy strongly identified with an intellectually oriented mother is at an advantage in certain facets of school adjustment since he might find the transition from home to the typically feminine oriented classroom quite comfortable. There is some rather impressionistic data (Hilgard, Neuman, & Fisk, 1960; Levy, 1943) which suggest that among middle-class father-absent boys, those who have overprotective and/or academically striving mothers do well in school, particularly in tasks where verbal skills and conformity are rewarded.

Intensity of Mother-Child Relationship

Father-absence would often seem to lead to an increase in the intensity of the emotional relationship between mother and child, especially during infancy and early childhood. Incidents of sexual play between mother and infant son during post-partum taboos for husband-wife sexual intercourse are frequently cited in anthropological reports; post-partum taboos lasting two to three years are common and during this time the family is relatively father-absent. Stephens (1962) presented cross-cultural evidence indicating that long post-partum taboos tend to make mothers closer to their children and less husband-centered. In such societies, mothers apparently are more attentive and succorant, as well as more indulgent of dependency in their young children than mothers in societies in which post-partum taboos are of short duration. There are also some interesting anthropological data which suggest that males often experience sex-role conflicts in societies in which children, during their first few years of life, have a relatively exclusive relationship with their mothers (Bacon, Child, & Barry, 1963; Burton & Whiting, 1961; Stephens, 1962). Variations in sociocultural background, particularly those reflected in terms of prevalent patterns of mothering, may account for marked differences between father-absent and father-present children in some societies but not in others (Ancona, et al., 1964; Lynn & Sawrey, 1959).

Levy (1943) reported that excessive physical contact is a frequent concomitant of maternal overprotection (and paternal underinvolvement).

of 19 cases of maternal overprotection involving boys, he found that 6 of the boys slept with their mothers long past infancy, 3 of them during adolescence. In almost one-half of the clinical cases involving father-absent pre-adolescent and adolescent boys in Wylie and Delgado's (1959) study, mother and son slept together in the same bed or bedroom. In reviewing relevant psychoanalytic case studies, Neubauer (1960) described how difficult sex-role development is for the young father-absent boy who has a highly sexualized relationship with his mother. Such an intense relationship affords the boy little opportunity to interact with masculine role models. In addition, the boy's inability to cope with his sexual feelings toward his mother may lead to a defensive feminine identification (Freud, 1947).

A close, binding mother-son relationship in the context of father-absence or low father-availability appears to be an important factor contributing to difficulties in heterosexual relationships (Hilgard, Neuman, & Fisk, 1960; Neubauer, 1960; Winch, 1949) and in the etiology of male homosexuality (Bieber, et al., 1962; West, 1967). Both an intense relationship with the mother and little opportunity to observe appropriate interpersonal relations between adult males and females seem more likely for the father-absent as compared to the father-present boy.

Stoller (1968) described several boys who felt that they were really females. These transsexual boys had extremely close physical relationships with their mothers. Mutual body contact during infancy was especially intense and there was much evidence that the mothers reinforced many forms of feminine behavior in their sons. It is of particular interest that in none of these cases was the father masculine or involved in the family. Stoller's book is replete with references to his and other therapists' case studies suggesting that disturbed sex-role and sexual development in males is associated with an overly-intense, relatively exclusive mother-son relationship.

In addition to lacking a male role model during the pre-school years, the father-absent boy seems more likely to be confronted by a mother who does not reinforce such behavior if it occurs. (The boy's sex-role development would seem additionally handicapped if the mother was not secure in her own sex-role identification.) As father-absent boys enter into situations with boys from intact homes, especially as they begin school, they may be ignored for their lack of masculine behavior and/or negatively reinforced for their feminine behavior. Many father-absent boys who are strongly motivated to adopt masculine behavior will do so. Yet at home their mothers may react negatively to such behavior, thus creating conflict.

Boys who are extremely emotionally and instrumentally dependent upon their mothers may not become involved in the masculine subculture. Some boys with strong but less intense mother-son relationships might learn to act feminine in the presence of their mothers and masculine with their peers.

Where the mother is not so overprotective, such boys may learn to act masculine even to the point of overcompensation. However, situations where conflicting response tendencies are called forth cannot be completely avoided and there is likely to be much sex role conflict. Keeping behavior consistent with an internal standard of masculinity-femininity, which Kagan (1964) stressed as a central motivational process, would seem much more difficult and anxiety-producing for the father-absent individual.

Father-absent boys seem particularly likely to develop certain interpersonal difficulties associated with sex-role development. Ruth Hartley (1959) through interviews with eight- to eleven-year-old boys from father-present homes described the following types of sex-role development: (a) overly-intense masculine striving combined with rigidity concerning male and female activities and hostility toward women, (b) overly-intense masculine striving combined with rigidity concerning male and female activities but no hostility towards women; (c) inclinations and attempts to withdraw from the masculine role and related activities; and (d) a positively integrated and balanced sex role. It could be predicted that behaviors related to (a), (b), and (c) would be more frequently displayed by father-absent boys than by father-present boys. But in order to make meaningful predictions, peer group interactions, the quality of the mother-child relationship, and various family structure variables have to be carefully considered.

Such family structure variables as birth order and age and sex of siblings can interact with maternal behavior to influence the father-absent child's personality development. Studying father-present children, a number of researchers have found that boys with brothers are more masculine than boys with sisters, especially in two child families where the children are close in age (Biller, 1968a; Brim, 1958; Sutton-Smith, Roberts, & Rosenberg, 1964). There is some evidence that among father-absent boys, those with brothers suffer less of a deficit in academic aptitude than do those with sisters (Sutton-Smith, Rosenberg, & Landy, 1968). If a father-absent boy is an only child or the only boy in an all female family, the probability of maternal overprotection seems increased. On the other hand, if the boy, during his early years, has frequent opportunity to interact with older male siblings, peers, or adults who encourage the development of his autonomy and assertiveness, the chances of a close-binding mother-son relationship seem lessened.

Positive Mothering

Some researchers have suggested that the mother-son relationship can have either a positive or a negative effect on the father-absent boy's personality development. Such a conclusion was reached by McCord, McCord, and Thurber (1962) when they analyzed social workers' observations of 10- to 15-year-old lower-class boys. They found that the presence

of a rejecting and/or disturbed mother was related to various behavior problems (sexual anxiety, regressive behavior, and criminal acts) in father-absent boys, but father-absent boys who had seemingly well-adjusted mothers were much less likely to have such problems.

Pedersen (1966), studying military families, reported evidence suggesting that psychologically healthy mothers may be able to counteract the effects of father-absence. Mothers of a group of emotionally disturbed 11- to 15-year-old boys were themselves found to be significantly more disturbed (in terms of the MMPI) than mothers of a comparable group of nondisturbed children. Both the emotionally disturbed and nondisturbed children had experienced relatively long periods of father-absence, but it was only in the disturbed group that degree of father-absence was related to level of emotional disturbance (measured by the Rogers Scale of Adjustment).

Hilgard, Neuman, and Fisk (1960), in an investigation of adults who as children had fathers who died, stressed the importance of the mother's ego strength. The mother's ability to utilize her own and outside resources and assume some of the dual functions of mother and father with little conflict appeared strongly related to her child's adjustment as an adult. Hilgard, Neuman, and Fisk emphasized that such women were relatively feminine while their husbands were alive but that they were secure enough in their basic sex-role identifications to perform some of the traditional functions of the father after he had died. These researchers also felt that the mother's ego strength rather than her warmth or tenderness was the essential variable in her child's adjustment. Excessive maternal warmth and affection may be related to maternal overprotection, particularly among father-absent children.

A mother who is generally dominant and competent in interpersonal and environmental interaction can provide her child with an effective model. However, parental dominance seems to facilitate a child's personality development only if the dominant parent allows the child sufficient freedom and responsibility to initiate effective parental behaviors that he has observed (Biller, 1969a). A serious problem that the young boy from a typical matriarchal family faces is that his mother often does not allow and/or encourage him to display competent behaviors. The mother frequently seems to interfere with the boy's attempts at mastery and to reward his dependency upon her.

Cooley (1959) postulated that: "Even in a father's absence, an appropriately identified mother will respond to the boy 'as if' he were a male and will expect him to treat her as a male would treat a female [1959, p. 173]." It seems reasonable to suppose that a mother could facilitate her father-absent boy's sex-role development by having a positive attitude toward the absent father and males in general, and by consistently encouraging masculine behavior in her son. Biller (1969b) found that for father-absent

kindergarten age boys, degree of maternal encouragement of masculine behavior, as measured by a multiple-choice questionnaire, was significantly related to masculinity as assessed by a game preference measure and a multidimensional rating scale filed out by teachers. In father-absent families, mothers who accepted and reinforced aggressive and assertive behavior appeared to have much more masculine sons than mothers who discouraged such behavior.

Since the father-son relationship appears more critical than the mother-son relationship when the father is present (Biller & Borstelmann, 1967), it could be predicted that maternal encouragement and expectations concerning sex-appropriate and sex-inappropriate behavior are less important when the father is present than when he is absent. For instance, a masculine and salient father would seem able to outweigh the effects of a mildly overprotecting mother. However, it is hypothesized that the mother's behavior is the most critical variable in facilitating or inhibiting masculine development in the young father-absent boy. It is assumed that the mother can, by reinforcing specific responses and expecting masculine behavior, increase the boy's perception of the incentive value of the masculine role. This, in turn, would seem to promote a positive view of males as salient and powerful, thus motivating the boy to imitate their behavior.

An overview of previous research (Biller, 1970) suggests that father-absence generally has more of an effect on the boy's sex-role orientation (his underlying perception and evaluation of his maleness and/or femaleness) than it does on his sex-role preference (his choice of particular sex-typed activities and attitudes) or his sex-role adoption (how masculine and/or feminine he behaves in social or environmental interaction). Sex-role preference and sex-role adoption seem easier to influence, at least after a child reaches school age, than does sex-role orientation; and it may be that the mother's behavior during the pre-school years has more impact on the boy's sex-role preference and sex-role adoption than it does on his sex-role orientation. However, it could be speculated that if a father-absent boy learns a masculine preference and adoption on the basis of both consistent maternal and peer group reinforcement, he is likely to view himself and his masculinity positively, and to develop a masculine sex-role orientation at least by his middle school years.

There is some evidence that father-absence before the age of five has more effect on the boy's sex-role development than does father-absence after the age of five (Biller, 1970), and it may be that the mother-child relationship is particularly important when the boy becomes father-absent early in life. In a recent study, Biller and Bahm (1971) discovered that degree of perceived maternal encouragement for aggressive and assertive behavior was highly related to the masculinity of junior high school boys who had become father-absent before the age of five. Among the early

father-absent boys, perception of clearcut maternal encouragement for appropriate sex-typed behaviors (as assessed by a Q-sort technique) was associated with high masculinity of self-concept, as measured by an adjective check list.

It is hoped that future research will lead to the delineation of the kinds of maternal behaviors, and the dimensions of the mother-child relationship, that are relevant to the father-absent boy's personality development. This author has described elsewhere Biller, 1970) some of the specific conceptual issues and methodological considerations that must be taken into account if research comparing father-absent and father-present boys is going to yield more clearly interpretable results. Longitudinal investigations including both observational and experimental methods may be especially important in gaining a detailed understanding of the effects of variations in the mother-son relationship on the father-absent boy's personality development. Biller and Weiss (1970) reviewed some research concerning the effects of father-absence on the girl's personality development and it would seem that investigators studying the impact of father-absence should systematically examine possible differential effects of the mother-child relationship as a function of sex of child. Findings from such research may be useful for programs designed to maximize the interpersonal and intellectual potential of father-absent children and to help mothers in father-absent families to become more effective parents.

Summary

A review of available data suggests that the mother-son relationship can have either a positive or a negative effect on the father-absent boy's sex-role and personality development. Research relating to matriarchal families, maternal overprotection, and maternal rejection indicates that mothers in father-absent homes and mothers in homes where the father is relatively ineffectual often undermine their sons' feelings of masculine adequacy and ability to function interpersonally. The importance of the mother having a positive attitude towards males and her son participating in masculine activities, and generally expecting and encouraging masculine behavior in her son was emphasized. It was pointed out that an attempt to understand the impact of the mother-child relationship on the father-absent boy must consider such factors as socio-cultural background, peer group interaction, and length and timing of father-absence.

References

Ancona, L., Cesa-Bianchi, M., & Bocquet, C. Identification with the father in the absence of the paternal model: Research applied to children of

navy officers. *Archivo di Psicologia Neurologia e Psichaitria,* 1964, **24,** 339-361.

Bach, G. R. Father-fantasies and father typing in father-separated children. *Child development.,* 1946, **17,** 63-80.

Bacon, M. K., Child, I. L., & Barry, H., III. A cross-cultural study of correlates of crime. *J. Abnorm. Soc. Psychol.,* 1963, **66,** 291-300.

Barclay, A. G. & Cusumano, D. Father-absence, cross-sex identify, and field-dependent behavior in male adolescents. *Child Developm.,* 1967, **38,** 243-250.

Barry, H., III., Bacon, M. K., & Child, I. L. A cross-cultural survey of some sex differences in socialization. *J. Abnorm. Soc. Psychol.,* 1957, **55,** 327-332.

Bell, R. Q. A reinterpretation of the direction of effects in studies of socialization. *Psychol. Rev.,* 1968, **75,** 81-95.

Beller, E. K. Maternal behaviors in lower-class Negro mothers. Paper persented at the meeting of the Eastern Psychological Association, Boston, April, 1967.

Bieber, I, *et al. Homosexuality: A psychoanalytic study.* New York: Basic Books, 1962.

Biller, H. B. A multiaspect investigation of masculine development in kindergarden are boys. *Genet. Psychol. Monogr.,* 1968a, **76,** 89-139.

Biller, H. B. A note on father-absence and masculine development in young lower-class Negro and white boys. *Child Developm.,* 1968b, **39,** 1003-1006.

Biler, H. B. Father dominance and sex-role development in kindergarten age boys. Developm. Psychol., 1969a, **1,** 87-94.

Biller, H. B. Father absence, maternal encouragement and sex-role development in kindergarten age boys. *Child Developm.,* 1969b, **10,** 539 546.

Biller, H. B. Father absence and the personality development of the male child. *Developm. Psychol.,* 1970, **2,** 181-201.

Biller, H. B. & Bahm. R. M. Father absence, perceived maternal behavior, and masculinity of self-concept among junior high school boys. *Developm.* 1971, **4.**

Biller, H. B. & Borstelmann, L. J. Masculine development: An integrative review. *Merrill-Palmer Quart.,* 1967, **13,** 253-294.

Biller, H. B. & Weiss, S. D. The father-daughter relationship and the personality development of the female. *J. Genet. Psychol.,* 1970, **114,** 79-93.

Brim, O. G. Family structure and sex role learning by children: A further analysis of Helen Koch's data. *Sociomet.,* 1958, **21,** 1-16.

Bronfenbrenner, U. The psychological costs of quality and equality in education. *Child Developm.,* 1967, **38,** 909-925.

Burton, R. V. & Whiting, J. W. M. The absent father and cross-sex identity

Merrill-Palmer Quart., 1961, **1,** 85-95.

Colley, T. The nature and origin of psychological sexual identity. *Psychol. Rev.,* 1959, **66,** 165-177.

Dai, B. Some problems of personality development among Negro children. In C. Kluckhohn, H. A. Murray, & D. M. Schneider (Eds.), *Personality in nature, society, and culture.* New York: Knopf, 1953. Pp. 545-566.

Dinitz, S., Dynes, R. R. and Clarke, A. C. Preferences for male or female children: Traditional or affectional? *Marr. Fam. Liv.,* 1954, **16,** 128-130.

Frazier, E. F. *The Negro family in the United States.* Chicago: Univer. of Chicago Press, 1939.

Freud S. *Leonardo Da Vinci: A study in psychosexuality.* New York: Random House, 1947.

Glasser, P. & Navarre, E. Structural problems of the one-parent family. *J. Soc. Iss.,* 1965, **21,** 98-109.

Goodenough, E. W. Interest in persons as an aspect of sex differences in the early years. *Genet. Psychol. Monogr.,* 1957, **55,** 287-323.

Gronseth, E. The impact of father absence in sailor families upon the personality structure and social adjustment of adult sailor sons, Part I. In N. Anderson (Ed.), *Studies of the family; Vol. 2.* Gottingen: Vandenhoeck and Ruprecht, 1957. Pp. 97-114.

Grunebaum, M. G., Hurwitz, I., Prentice, N. M., & Sperry, B. M. Fathers of sons with primary neurotic learning inhibition. *Amer. J. Orthopsychiat.,* 1962, **32,** 462-473.

Hartley, R. E. Sex-role pressures and the socialization of the male child. *Psychol. Rep.,* 1959, **5,** 457-468.

Hartley, R. E. The one-parent family. In *Reference papers on children and youth.* White House Conference on Children and Youth, 1960.

Heckscher, B. T. Household structure and achievement orientation in lower class Barbadian families, *J. Marr. Fam.,* 1967, **29,** 521-526.

Helper, M. M. Learning theory and the self concept. *J. Abnorm. Soc. Psychol.,* 1955, **51,** 184-194.

Hetherington, E. M. A developmental study of the effects of sex of the dominant parent on sex-role preference, identification, and imitation in children. *J. Personal. Soc. Psychol.,* 1965, **2,** 188-194.

Hilgard, J. R., Neuman, M. F., & Fisk, F. Strength of adult ego following bereavement. *Amer. J. Orthopsychiat.,* 1960, **30,** 788-798.

Johnson, M. M. Sex-role learning in the nuclear family. *Child Developm.,* 1963, **34,** 319-333.

Kagan, J. Acquisition and significance of sex-typing and sex-role identity. In M. L. Hoffman & L. W. Hoffman (Eds.), *Review of child development research, Vol. 1.* New York Russell Sage, 1964, Pp. 137-167.

Kardiner, A. & Ovesey, L. *The mark of oppression.* New York: Norton,

1951.

King, C. E. The Negro maternal family: A product of an economic and cultural system. *Soc. Forces,* 1945, **24,** 100-104.

Kriesberg, L. Rearing children for educational achievement in fatherless families. *J. Marr. Fam.,* 1967, **29,** 288-301.

Levy, D. M. *Maternal overprotection.* New York: Columbia Univer. Press, 1943.

Leob, J. & Price, J. R. Mother and child personality characteristics related to parental marital status in child guidance cases. *J. Consult. Psychol.,* 1966, **30,** 112-117.

Lynn, D. B. A note on sex differences in the development of masculine and feminine identification. *Psychol. Rev.,* 1959, **66,** 126-135.

Lynn, D. B. & Sawrey, W. L. The effects of father absence on Norwegian boys and girls. *J. Abnorm. Soc. Psychol.,* 1959, **59,** 258-262.

McCord, J., McCord, W., & Thurber, E. Some effects of paternal absence on male children. *J. Abnorm. Soc. Psychol.,* 1962, **64,** 361-369.

Miller, W. B. Lower-class culture as a generating milieu of gang delinquency. *J. Soc. Iss.,* 1958, **14,** 5-19.

Moulton, P. W., Burnstein, E., Liberty, D., & Altucher, N. The patterning of parental affection and dominance as a determinant of guilt and sex-typing. *J. Personal. Soc. Psychol.,* 1966, **4,** 356-363.

Neubauer, P. B. The one-parent child and his oedipal development. *Psychoanal. Studies Child,* 1960, **15,** 286-309.

Pedersen, F. A. Relationships between father-absence and emotional disturbance in male military dependents. *Merrill-Palmer Quart.,* 1966, **12,** 321-331.

Pettigrew, T. F. *A profile of the Negro American.* Princeton: Van Nostrand, 1964.

Rainwaiter, L. Crucible of identity. *Daedalus,* 1966, **95,** 172-216.

Rohrer, J. H. & Edmonson, M. S. *The eighth generation.* New York: Harper, 1960.

Romney, A. K. Variations in household structure as determinants of sex-typed behavior. In F. Beach (Ed.), *Sex and behavior.* New York: Wiley, 1965. Pp. 208-220.

Sears, P. S. Child-rearing factors related to playing of sex-typed roles. *Amer. Psychol.,* 1953, **8,** 431 (abstract).

Stendler, C. B. Critical periods in socialization and overdependency. *Child Developm.,* 1952, **23,** 3-12.

Stendler, C. B. Possible causes of overdependency in young children. *Child Developm.,* 1954, **25,** 125-146.

Stephens, W. N. *The oedipus complex: Cross-cultured evidence.* Glencoe, Ill.: Free Press, 1962.

Stoller, R. J. *Sex and gender.* New York: Science House, 1968.

Stolz, L. M. et al. *Father relations of war born children.* Stanford: Stanford Univer. Press, 1954.

Sutton-Smith, B., Roberts, J. M., & Rosenberg, B. G. Sibling associations and role involvement. *Merrill-Palmer Quart., 1964,* **10,** 25-38.

Sutton-Smith, B., Rosenberg, B. G., & Landy, F. Father-absence effects in families of different sibling compositions. *Child Developm.,* 1968, **39,** 1213-1221.

Tasch, R. J. Interpersonal perceptions of fathers and mothers. *J. Genet. Psychol.,* 1955, **87,** 59-65.

Tiller, P. O. Father-absence and personality development of children in sailor families. *Nordisk Psychologi's Monography Series,* 1958, 9, 1-48.

West, D. J. *Homsexuality.* Chicago: Aldine, 1967.

Winch R. F. The relation between loss of a parent and progress in courtship. *J. Soc. Psychol.,* 1949, **29,** 51-56.

Wylie, H. L. & Delgado, R. A. A pattern of mother-son relationship involving the absence of the father. *Amer. J. Orthopsychiat.,* 1959, **29,** 644-649.

3.12 Mother-Child Interaction in the First Year of Life

Steven R. Tulkin
State University of New York at Buffalo

Jerome Kagan
Harvard University

Psychologists have begun to take more seriously the idea that experiences during infancy may influence development, although the specific functional relations between early experiences and later cognitive skills or personality traits remain unclear. The failure to understand these functional relations has prompted many social scientists and public officials to use categorical labels like "culturally deprived" to designate types of children. These labels are demeaning to the particular groups so labeled and are misleading because they suggest that one group can judge another by noting how similar others are to themselves. Most discussions of cultural deprivation contribute little to our understanding of human development because

Reprinted from *Child Development,* 1972, *43,* 31-41, by permission of the author and The Society for Research in Child Development, Inc. Copyright © 1972 by The Society for Research in Child Development, Inc.

they do not examine the effects to *specific experiences* on developmental processes.[1]

The purpose of the present report is to examine the experiences of infants from different social class backgrounds. Hess and Shipman (1965) observed preschool children and reported that middle-class mothers engaged in more "meaningful" verbal interchanges with their children than working-class mothers. It is less clear, however, whether mothers' behaviors with infants also reflect this difference. Descriptive reports of the experiences of young children in poor families (Pavenstedt 1965, 1967) suggest that social class differences in mother-infant interaction exist, but there has been little systematic observation.

Method

The present study reports data collected from 30 middle-class and 26 working-class Caucasian mothers. Middle class was defined as (*a*) one or both parents having graduated from college and (*b*) the father working in a professional job. Working class was defined as (*a*) either one or both parents having dropped out of high school (but neither having any college) or (*b*) the father working in a semiskilled or unskilled job. Each mother was observed at home for 2 hr on two separate days with her firstborn baby girl, who was approximately 10 months of age. Premature infants and infants with abnormal medical histories were excluded from the study.

Observation periods were 20 min long, separated by 5-min rest periods. Thus there were six observation periods scheduled for each visit. Mothers were told that the observer (the first author) was investigating infants' behaviors in natural settings, and that it was important for her to act naturally and to engage in her normal activities so that the day would appear "typical" to the infant. The observer carried a small battery-operated timer which, every 5 sec, emitted a soft tone which the observer heard through an earphone. Code sheets each contained 30 1 x 2-inch squares, and at the sound of the tone, the observer moved his pencil into the next square. Presence of a particular behavior during a 5-sec interval was noted on the code sheet by a number or letter representing that behavior. A particular variable could only be tallied once per 5-sec interval.

The variables to be examined in the present report were defined as follows:

1. Location: distance of mother from infant, coded each time it changed.
    a) Face to face.
    b) Within 2 feet (within arm's distance).
    c) More than 2 feet away.
2. Physical contact

a) Kiss: mother's lips touch child.

b) Hold: mother supports child's weight (mother carries child, child sits on mother's lap, etc.).

c) Active physical contact: mother tickles child, bounces child on lap, throws child in air, etc.

3. Prohibitions: mother interferes with or stops an act that had already begun.

   a) Verbal prohibition: negative command (e.g., "stop that" or "don't do that").

   b) Physical prohibition: mother stops child's motor activity or takes object from child.

   c) Prohibition ratios: To control for possible differences in fants' activity levels which could result in some infants receiving more prohibitions than others, a ratio was computed in which the total number of maternal prohibitions was divided by the number of 6-sec intervals in which the infant was either walking or crawling. Another possible bias was that infants moving around on the floor would have more opportunities to engage in behaviors that might be prohibited; thus a second ratio was computed in which the total number of maternal prohibitions was divided by the amount of time that the infant was free to crawl or walk on the floor.

4. Maternal vocalization: mother says words to child. Analyzed separately for each location in category 1.

5. Keeping infant busy: mother provides activity for child.

   a) Entertain: mother holds attention of child by nonverbal sounds, body movements such as peek-a-boo, or holding the attention of the child through a toy—such as shaking a rattle. If words were used in conjunction with an entertainment behavior, category 4 was also coded.

   b) Give object: mother gives child an object and makes no effort to hold child's attention.

Infant behaviors were also recorded, but will not be discussed in the present paper.

In addition to the discrete behaviors described above, several other variables were obtained by examining sequences of mother and infant behaviors. These variables were not directly coded in the homes but were drived at a later time from the discrete behaviors of mothers and infants:

1. Positive responses to noverbal behaviors: coded when infant touched mother or gave an object to mother if this behavior was followed,

within the same or the following 5-sec interval, by any maternal behavior in categories 2, 4, or 5 above.

2. Percentage of reciprocal vocalization: defined as the percentage of the child's vocalizations which were followed, within the same or the following 5-sec interval, by a maternal vocalization.
3. Response to child's frets: positive maternal responses (categories 2, 4, 5 and/or moving to within 2 feet of child) were analyzed following "spontaneous" frets, that is, frets for which there was no apparent cause.
4. Interaction: defined by both mother and infant acting in response to each other. Although either could initiate the interaction, infant had to respond to mother's behaviors and mother had to respond to infant's. The interaction went on as long as each responded to the other's behaviors within the same of the following 5-sec interval. Examples of interaction sequences are: infant touches mother, mother picks up infant, infant vocalizes; mother tickles infant, infant smiles, mother tickles, etc. Interaction could not be initiated by a fret or prohibition, and if it occurred with 1 min of a fret or prohibition, it was analyzed separately. Two variables describing the interaction are (a) the number of times interaction was initiated (labeled "interaction episodes") and (b) the total amount if interaction (labeled "total interaction").

Table 1
Percentages of Agreement on Home-Observation Variables for Pretest Infants (N = 10)

Variable	Median Percentage	Range of Percentages
Location	92.0	90–97
Physical contact	90.0	74–95
Prohibitions	84.5	75–100
Maternal vocalizations	81.5	70–88
Entertain	81.5	71–93
Give object	86.5	75–100

When the observers found that their level of agreement was satisfactory, the computation of reliabilities began. Ten "reliability" infants were each observed for 2 hr and percentages of agreement were computed. Percentages were based on tallies from each page of the coding booklet representing a 2½-min segment). These were computed by dividing the number of agreements per page by the total number of agreements and disagreements per page, for each infant. Resulting percentages appear in table 1. The overall range was 70%-100% agreement, and the median percentages were all above 80. For some variables, the frequencies were too low to permit analysis on a page-by-page basis; therefore Pearson product-moment correlations were also computed between the records of

the two observers, on the basis of the total number of tallies for each subject over the 2-hr period. These correlations are presented in table 2. All correlations were above .90. Reliabilities were not computed for variables derived from the coding sheets, as specific rules were followed (e.g., if maternal vocalization follows child vocalization in either the same or the following 5-sec interval, code as reciprocal vocalization).

Table 2
Between-Subject Correlations of Home-Observation Variables
for Pretest Infants (N = 10)

Variable	Correlation
Location	.99
Kiss	.96
Hold	.99
Active physical contact	.97
Verbal prohibitions	.99
Physical prohibitions	.97
Maternal vocalization	.99
Entertain	.94
Give object	.98

Note.—All correlations are significant beyond the .01 level of confidence.

It should be noted that although there was no class difference in the amount of infant fretting or crying, or in the frequency of maternal prohibition, all maternal behaviors with 1 min of an infant fret or a maternal prohibition were analyzed separately to reduce the variance which might be attributable to differences among the infants.

If other people interacted with the child, their behavior was recorded in categories identical with those listed for maternal behaviors. An additional variable was the total amount of time another adult interacted with the infant.

Variables describing particular aspects of the infant's environment were also recorded during the home visits. The number of toys available and the number of other environmental objects played with (pots, pans, magazines, etc.) were recorded at the end of each 20-min observation period. The location of the infant was coded by recording the number of minutes which the child spent in a playpen, in a high chair, in a crib, etc. Infants who were placed in walkers or who were free to walk or crawl on the floor were further described by recording the number of minutes during which they were free to roam around any part of the home, rather than being restricted to a particular area. The free-movement condition was labeled "no barriers." Location variables were summed over the entire 4 hr of observation, yielding a range of 0–240 min. The number of minutes that the television or radio were played during each home visit was similarly recorded. Finally,

a "crowdedness ratio" was computed for each home by dividing the number of people living in the dwelling unit by the number of rooms.

After the final observation period, the observer spoke informally with mothers about what they felt was important for mothers to do during their infant's first year of life.

Reliability.—The first author "taught" the above coding system to another observer by their jointly observing 10 pretest infants at home, coding maternal and infant behaviors aloud, and discussing any disagreements.

Results

Environmental variables Table 3 presents data on the infants' homes. The environments of the infants in the two class groups differed along two particular dimensions. First, there was more "extraneous noise" in the working-class children's environments. The infants lived in more crowded homes, had more interaction with adults other than their mothers, and spent more time in front of television sets than their middle-class counterparts. Second, working-class infants had less opportunity to explore and manipulate their environments. They had somewhat fewer toys and fewer environmental objects (pots, pans, magazines, etc.) with which to play, and spent less time with "no barriers."

Maternal behavior Table 4 presents the behavioral observations. Total interaction was greater in the middle-class group, but analysis of specific behaviors revealed that class differences were larger in some areas than in

Table 3
Class Differences in Home Environments

Variable	Working Class Mean	Working Class SD	Middle Class Mean	Middle Class SD	p [a]
Crowdedness ratio (people per room)	0.761	0.172	0.597	0.143	.001
No. of 5-sec intervals with interaction with other adults	114.500	165.676	40.433	68.783	.029
Minutes of TV	109.621	92.025	30.033	60.791	.001
Minutes of radio	39.276	55.776	66.467	68.692	.101
No. of toys within reach in 20-min period	6.016	2.491	7.011	2.181	.117
No. of environmental objects played with in 20-min period	3.215	1.557	4.531	1.696	.004
Minutes with no barriers	114.500	77.480	168.600	65.296	.006

[a] Independent t tests; two-tailed.

others. Class differences in maternal *behaviors*, in fact, paralleled the findings noted above for "nonbehavioral" variables. The majority of differences centered around the mother's verbal behavior and her attempts to "keep her infant busy." Other aspects of maternal behavior did not reveal social class differences. There was no class difference in the amount of time mothers spent in close proximity to their infants (within 2 ft), although the middle-class mothers more often placed their infants in a face-to-face position. There were also no significant differences for frequencies of kissing, holding, or active physical contact. Contrary to expectations, no class differences were found in the frequency of maternal prohibitions, even when controls were introduced for the amount of time infants were free to crawl around and explore. Finally, when infants touched their mothers or handed objects to their mothers, working-class mothers responded positively as often as middle-class mothers.

The paucity of social class differences for nonverbal variables was in sharp contrast with the dramatic differences found for the mothers' verbal behaviors. Every verbal behavior coded was more frequent among middle-class mothers. There was no social class difference in the infants' tendencies to vocalize spontaneously, a result which suggests that the differences in maternal vocalization were not attributable to initial differences among the infants.[2]

Middle-class mothers more often entertained their infants and more often gave their infants things with which to play. They also responded to a higher percentage of the infants' spontaneous frets and responded more quickly.

It was noted above that working-class infants were involved in interaction with adults other than their mothers more often than middle-class infants; thus the present analysis—by limiting itself to *maternal* behaviors—might not reflect the overall amount of social interaction experienced by the infant. Additional anaylses were made noting every occurrence of specific behaviors directed toward the infants, whether or not the mother was involved. These analyses yielded social class differences similar to those reported in table 4. Thus, regardless of the degree to which the mothers shared their child-rearing responsibilities with others, infants from middle- and working-class families had different experiences.

It should be noted that the present report deals specifically with differences *between* the two social class groups. Large within-class differences were also observed in the present study, however, and it would be erroneous to conclude that middle-class children were "enriched" while working-class children were "deprived." The class differences appear to be attributable to a subgroup of middle-class mothers who were highly verbal with their infants—rather than to a "deprivation" which is uniquely characteristic of working-class families.

Table 4
Maternal Behaviors Observed at Home

Variable	Working Class		Middle Class		p^a
	Mean	SD	Mean	SD	
Interaction:					
Interaction episodes	36.08	19.69	65.97	36.31	.001
Total interaction	132.50	83.44	251.83	144.46	.001
Location:					
Over 2 ft from child	1,402.73	536.38	1,243.27	488.03	.249
Within 2 ft	1,424.50	515.29	1,525.60	459.54	.441
Face to face	53.19	53.66	110.77	113.69	.022
Physical contact:					
Kiss	4.00	6.13	5.73	5.32	.262
Total holding	210.73	179.71	265.17	154.54	.228
Active physical contact	21.42	23.99	31.37	24.01	.128
Prohibitions:					
Verbal only	15.50	9.85	18.33	14.75	.409
Physical only	12.19	10.89	11.00	9.87	.669
Prohibitions ÷ time on floor	36.19	24.72	33.93	51.85	1.000
Prohibitions ÷ walk and crawl	19.04	13.69	16.50	15.20	.522
Responses to nonverbal behaviors:					
Positive response (%), child					
touches mother	56.36	22.50	63.89	21.03	.206
Positive response (%), child					
offers object to mother	90.65	15.44	86.40	16.22	.410
Maternal vocalization:					
Over 2 ft away	17.65	15.36	40.57	33.84	.002
Within 2 ft	148.77	73.92	329.37	183.81	.001
Face to face	19.00	15.97	38.20	28.48	.004
Total maternal vocalization	192.00	88.30	422.40	206.41	.001
Reciprocal vocalization (%)	11.27	6.12	20.70	10.19	.001
Keeping infant busy:					
Entertainment	54.65	40.46	99.13	62.08	.003
Give objects	26.23	19.72	38.53	14.76	.010
Response to spontaneous frets:					
Frets (%) to which					
mother responded	38.36	15.15	58.41	25.46	.001
Latency to respond					
(no. of 5-sec intervals)	1.98	0.70	1.62	0.54	.032

NOTE.—All numbers (except percentages) refer to the number of 5-sec intervals in which the behavior occurred. The possible range is 0-2,880.

[a] Independent t tests; two-tailed.

Discussion

The results indicate that more middle-class than working-class mothers were extensively involved in verbal interactions with their infants and were more likely to provide their infants with a greater variety of stimulation.

These findings parallel previous reports of (*a*) minimal social class differences in the affective elements of mother-child interaction (Bayley & Schaefer 1960; Kagan & Freeman 1963) and (*b*) larger differences in verbal interaction and cognitive stimulation (Levine, Fishman, & Kagan 1967; Shipman & Hess 1966). In fact, Moss, Robson, and Pedersen (1969) found that "less well-educated mothers" provided more physical stimulation for their infants than better-educated mothers. Working-class mothers, then, care for their infants as extensively as middle-class mothers; differences occur mainly in areas involving maternal stimulation of cognitive development.

It is important to understand why the mothers in the present sample interacted with their infants in this manner, and to examine the implications of the present findings for infant intervention programs. Informal discussions with mothers suggested that one source of variance in maternal behavior was the mother's concept of her infant. Some working-class mothers did not believe that their infants possessed the ability to express "adult-like" emotions or to communicate with other people. Hence, these mothers felt that it was futile to attempt to interact with their infants. One working-class mother who constantly spoke to her daughter lamented that her friends chastized her for "talking to the kid like she was three years old." Some working class mothers felt that it was only important for a mother to speak to her infant after the infant began to speak. Weikart and Lambie (1969) also noted that lower-income mothers were hesitant "to involve themselves in anything as silly as talking to a baby." Thus, one objective of infant intervention projects might be to emphasize the importance of early verbal stimulation.

Second, working-class mothers seemed to feel that they could not have much influence on the development of their children. Many believed that infants are born with a particular set of characteristics, and that environmental influence on the development of their children. Many believed that Schumer (1967) also observed that lower-income mothers "seemed to see themselves as powerless, helpless, and . . . not able to do anything" to effect the development of their children. This philosophy may be indicative of a general sense of fatalism which develops when working-class people find that they have little power to effect changes in their environment. Thus, a mother's attitudes toward her children are not independent of social and economic conditions, and interventionists must realize that attempts to change maternal *behaviors* without regard to the source of the behaviors— or the relation between these behaviors and other aspects of the social system—may not succeed.

Various other maternal beliefs also appeared to influence behaviors. Some mothers in both class groups, for example, believed that children should be able to explore and discover things for themselves in an atmosphere of

minimal adult-imposed structure; other mothers believed in early teaching of "right and wrong" and worried about their children being spoiled. Infants in the former group spent less time in playpens, were prohibited less, and were allowed to play with more environmental objects. Similarly, some mothers stressed the importance of independence training for their infants. One middle-class mother said that she had to teach her daughter "to go out, . . . to become more independent when she's not near me." She went on to say that she didn't believe that a child should be picked up "for no reason at all, just because maybe she's fussing to be picked up." This mother had the lowest amount of interaction in the middle-class group. Other mothers stressed the importance of extensive mother-infant contact and felt that the child had to learn to be dependent before she could learn to be independent. These mothers had more interaction with their daughters. In each case, mothers had fairly specific ideas about the type of child behaviors they were attempting to develop and acted in accord with this model.

It is important for interventionists to respect the values of the families with whom they are working and not attempt to convert other people to their own value systems. One of the goals of intervention programs should be to encourage parents to recognize the influence they have over their children's development and to understand the consequences of various types of experiences. We must retain a relativistic posture, however, and not insist that one pattern of intellectual skills and personality traits is optimal for all children.

Notes

[1] A complete discussion of how the "cultural deprivation" concept has hindered our understanding of developmental processes can be found in Tulkin (in press).

[2] Infants' spontaneous vocalization rates were difficult to assess because mothers often elicited vocalization from their infants by entertainment, tickling, maternal vocalizations, etc. It wes decided to construct a "solitary-vocalization ratio," which was defined as follows: frequency of infant vocalizations when the mother was over 2 ft away, divided by the number of 5-sec intervals during which the mother was over 2 ft away. For middle-class infants, the ratio was 24.81 with a standard deviation of 5.46; for working-class infants, the ratio was 22.97 with a standard deviation of 7-13. The class difference was not significant.

References

Bayley, N., & Schaefer, E. Relationships between socio-economic variables and the behavior of mothers toward young children. *Journal of Genetic Psychology,* 1960, 96, 61-77.

Hess, R. D., & Shipman, V. C. Early experience and the socialization of cognitive modes in children. *Child Development,* 1965, 36, 869-886.

Kagan, J., & Freeman, M. The relation of childhood intelligence, maternal be-

haviors, and social class to behavior during adolescence. *Child Development,* 1963, 34, 899-911.

Levine, J.; Fishman, C.; & Kagan, J. Sex of child and social class as determinants of maternal behavior. Paper presented at the meeting of the Society for Research in Child Development, New York, March 1967.

Minuchin, S.; Montalvo, B.; Guerney, B. G.; Rosman, B. L.; & Schumer, F. L. *Families of the slums: an exploration of their structure and treatment.* New York: Basic, 1967.

Moss, H. A.; Robson, K. S.; & Pederson, F. Determinants of maternal stimulation of infants and consequences of treatment for later reactions to strangers. *Developmental Psychology,* 1969, I, 239-246.

Pavenstedt, E. A comparison of the child rearing environment of upper-lower and very low-lower class families. *American Journal of Orthopsychiatry,* 1965, 35, 89-98.

Pavenstedt, E. (Ed.) *The drifters.* Boston: Little, Brown, 1967.

Shipman, V. C., & Hess, R. D. Early experience in the socialization of cognitive modes in children: a study of urban Negro families. Paper presented at the Conference on Family and Society, Merrill-Palmer Institute, April 1966.

Tulkin, S. R. An analysis of the concept of cultural deprivation. *Developmental Psychology,* in press.

Weikart, D. P., & Lambie, D. Z. Early enrichment infants. Paper presented at the meeting of the American Association for the Advancement of Science, Boston, December 1969.

3.13 A Comparison of Maternal Care and Infant Behavior in Japanese-American, American, and Japanese Families

William Caudill, Ph.D.
National Institute of Mental Health
Bethesda, Maryland

Lois Frost, M.A.
Corvallis, Oregon

Earlier reports from this on-going research project have dealt with a comparison of the everyday behavior of mothers and three-to-four-month old infants in middle-class homes in Japan and America (Caudill and Weinstein 1969, Caudill 1971). These earlier analyses show that the

American mothers do more lively chatting to their babies, and that as a result the American babies have a generally higher level of vocalization and particularly they respond with greater amounts of happy vocalization and gross motor activity. The Japanese mothers, on the other hand, do more vocal lulling, carrying and rocking of their babies, and as a result the Japanese babies are more physically passive; in addition, the Japanese babies have a greater amount of unhappy vocalization as their mothers take longer to respond to such signals for attention. Thus, because of the different styles of caretaking in the two cultures it appears that by three-to-four months of age the infants have already learned (or have been conditioned) to behave in culturally distinctive ways and that this has happened out of awareness and well before the development of language. If true, these findings have major thoretical implications for the understanding of personality development in relation to the transmission and persistence of cultural patterns of emotion, cognition, and behavior in human groups.

Two somewhat opposed arguments might be directed against the interpretation just given to the earlier findings. The first argument is that the behavioral differences between the Japanese and American infants might be due more to group genetic factors than to cultural learning or conditioning (see, for example, Freedman and Freedman 1969). The second argument is that as social change takes place in a human group, succeeding generations of mothers will care for their babies in a different fashion and that this will result in significant shifts in the behavior of the babies (see, for example, Bronfenbrenner 1958).

Comparable data obtained from Japanese-American mothers and infants can provide information to help settle both of these arguments, and this is the task set for this paper. Japanese Americans tend to marry within their own group, and hence the children of these intra-group marriages are genetically Japanese. If the first argument is the more true, then group genetic factors should remain as an important influence on the behavior of Japanese-American infants and they should be closer to Japanese than to American infants in their degree of physical passivity, lesser total vocalization, and greater unhappy vocalization.[1] In support of the second argument, the vast majority of Japanese immigrants came to the mainland of the United States between 1890-1924, and Japanese-American mothers are now having the third generation of babies to be born in this country. Since, as indicated more fully below, Japanese Americans have so successfully adapted to American middle-class life, the present generation of mothers ought to be rearing their babies in American style and the babies should be responding accordingly; that is, the Japanese-American infants should be closer to American than to Japanese infants in their degree of high physical activity, greater total vocalization, and particularly greater happy vocalization.

Background of the Japanese Americans

The Japanese Americans are an extraordinarily interesting group of people to study (see Caudill 1952, Caudill and DeVos 1956, Kitano 1969). At the end of the nineteenth, and during the beginning of the twentieth, century fairly large groups of Japanese immigrated either directly to the mainland of the United States, or to Hawaii. These people called themselves Issei—meaning first generation. They came largely from farming families in the southern part of the Japanese islands, and for a short while they worked as laborers in the United States, but on the mainland they soon shifted to being independent truck and garden farmers and small business-men in and around the major cities of California, Washington, and Oregon. At first the immigrant Issei were largely men, but as they found that they were not going to return to Japan, they arranged for marriages in their home prefectures and the brides came to join them in the United States.

At the beginning of World War II the Japanese Americans on the Pacific Coast numbered about 130,000 persons (with an additional 160,000 persons in Hawaii). By this time the citizen children of the Issei, known as Nisei—meaning second generation—had achieved a very high educational level and were in their early to mid-twenties when war broke out. During the war, the Japanese Americans were first placed in relocation camps, and later allowed to migrate to Middle Western and Eastern cities, but could not return to the Pacific Coast until after the war. The Nisei made an outstanding record in the armed services of the United States.

Both during and after World War II, the Nisei moved quickly into predominantly white collar and professional occupations and established themselves as solidly middle class. They were able to do this, despite highly visible racial differences, because of the high degree of compatibility between Japanese and American middle-class values—both cultures emphasizing at that time educational attainment, hard work, and long-range goals (see Caudill and DeVos 1956). The phrase "compatibility of values" is important because although the values of the Nisei and those of middle-class Americans were similar, they were far from being the same. Americans looking at the Nisei thought that they were just like themselves when, in considerable part, the Nisei were operating on a Japanese set of values that worked very well in the middle-class American world.

By 1970 the Nisei were well into middle age, and their children, known as Sansei—meaning third generation—also had achieved a very high educational level, and were beginning to establish their own families. The children in these families are known as Yonsei—meaning fourth generation—and this article is concerned with the behavior of Sansei mothers and their Yonsei babies.

At the present time many of the Sansei are critical of their Nisei parents for being so establishment-minded and so successful in the white American middle-class world; and some of the Sansei, at least on university campuses, are beginning to try to form themselves into a radical group. As a group, however, the Sansei have come rather late to radicalism and are rather mild in their demonstration of it compared with their Black, Spanish-American, and White counterparts. Most of those Sansei who have graduated from high school and college, established families, and are working in white collar and professional jobs, give every evidence of being law-abiding middle-class American citizens.

Given the foregoing historical background, the Sansei should in the area of family life and child rearing look very much like middle-class Americans. At the same time, and in light of the compatibility rather than identity of values discussed earlier, it could be expected that a good many Japanese ideas on how to care for and rear children will have been passed down, largely out of awareness, from Issei to Nisei to Sansei mothers. In research terms, then, the expectation is that the behavior both of Sansei mothers and their Yonsei babies will, for the most part, be closer to that of the American sample, but in some regards there will still be evidence of a Japanese cultural heritage.[2]

Sample Populations and Method

The Japanese and American samples have been fully described in Caudill and Weinstein (1969). In general, naturalistic observations were made on two consecutive days during 1961-1964 in the homes of 30 Japanese and 30 white American first-born, three-to-four month old infants equally divided by sex, and living in intact middle-class urban families. Data on the ordinary daily life of the infant were obtained by time-sampling, one observation being made every fifteenth second over a ten-minute period in terms of a pre-determined set of categories concerning the behavior of the mother (or other caretaker) and the behavior of the infant, resulting in a sheet containing 40 equally spaced observations. There was a five-minute break between observation periods, and ten observation sheets were completed on each of the two days, giving a total of 800 observations for each case. In the analysis already published, these data were analyzed by multivariate analysis of variance using three independent variables: culture (Japanese, American), father's occupation (salaried, independent), and sex of infant (male, female). The effects of each of these independent variables were examined while controlling on the other two variables, and culture proved overwhelmingly to be the most important variable. Interactions between the independent variables revealed nothing of importance. Essentially the same methods of data analysis are used in arriving at the results reported in this article,

except that, for reasons given below, only culture and sex of infant are used as independent variables.

The Japanese-American sample was gathered by the junior author, Lois Frost, after she had read the article by Caudill and Weinstein (1969). Using the same methods, she carried out observations during 1969-70 in Sacramento, California, in the homes of 21 Sansei mothers having a three-to-four month old Yonsei baby (in general, see Frost 1970). All of the Sansei families are middle class as measured by the occupation and education of the father, and the education of the mother. By occupation, 11 of the fathers have professional and managerial positions, 7 are white collar and clerical workers, and 3 are in skilled trades; by education, 10 of the fathers are college graduates, 4 have some college training, and 7 are high school graduates. By education, 8 of the mothers are college graduates, 11 have so.ne college training, and 2 are high school graduates. All of the fathers work as salaried employees in large businesses, and for this reason the classification by father's occupation into salaried and independent families is omitted as a variable in the analyses in this article.[3]

Among the 21 Yonsei infants, 7 are male and 14 are female, and 11 are first-born and 10 are later-born. Because the sex distribution is more equal and all infants are first-born in the Japanese and American samples, we did a complete internal analysis of the Japanese-American data using sex and birth order as independent variables. The results are almost entirely negative.[4] We feel it is possible, therefore, to make a direct comparison of the data from the three cultural groups.

After the junior author had collected her data, she wrote to the senior author informing him of her study. He then arranged to visit her for consultation and for the purpose of doing a reliability check. In January, 1971, the two authors carried out observations together in the homes of four infants in order to obtain data for testing inter-observer reliability and for the standardization of scores on the dependent variables used in describing infant and caretaker behaviors. The terms "caretaker" and "mother" are used as interchangeable in this paper because the caretaker was the mother in over 90 per cent of the observations in each of the three cultures. Table 1 gives the names of the dependent variables used in the analyses along with an estimate of their reliability and the weights used for standardization scores.

The names of the dependent variables are fairly self-explanatory, and have been defined in detail in previous publication (Caudill and Weinstein 1969). The junior author used these detailed definitions in collecting her data (see Frost 1970). A brief explanation of the variables is, however, useful for the reader. Starting with the infant behaviors, "awake" is reciprocal with "asleep" and therefore only the scores for "awake" are used here. "Breast or bottle" must be in the infant's mouth at the time of observation

Table 1

Observer Reliability and Weights Used For Standardization of Frequencies of Observations Across Cultures

Dependent Variables	Average Percent Agreement per Case*			Weight Used for Standardization†		
	Japanese (7 cases)	American (3 cases)	Japanese American (4 cases)	Japanese (7 cases)	American (3 cases)	Japanese American (4 cases)
Infant Behavior						
Awake	98	100	100	...	...	...
Breast or Bottle	99	100	97	...	...	...
All Food	99	99	98	...	.98	...
Finger or Pacifier	92	84	85	...	.94	1.02
Total Vocal	91	80	73	1.04	.86	...
Unhappy	89	88	73	1.05	1.07	.97
Happy	70	70	72	1.10	.64	1.04
Active	69	74	77	.91	.75	.90
Baby Plays	85	93	75	.96	1.07	1.28
Caretaker Behavior						
Presence of	99	100	100	...	...	...
Feeds	99	100	99	...	...	...
Diapers	95	96	94	.98	.93	1.09
Dresses	84	99	85	1.06	1.03	1.17
Positions	49	77	56	1.75	.71	.62
Pats or Touches	78	87	59	.82	.84	.69
Other Care	85	85	72	.97	.86	.80
Plays with	67	86	85	1.34	1.16	.93
Looks at	94	90	99	...	1.06	...
Talks to	90	83	88	...	.83	.94
Chats	90	83	89		.83	.96
Lulls	94	100	78	...	...	...
In Arms	100	99	97	...	...	...
Rocks	90	88	91	.95	...	1.02

*Agreement between two observers as to the presence (Yes) or absence (No) of a behavior is classified within four cells: (a) Yes/Yes, (b) Yes/No, (c) No/Yes, (d) No/No. Percent agreement is computed as the ratio of (2a) to (2a + b + c), thus avoiding the use of the somewhat spurious agreement on absence of behavior.

Weight used to standarize frequencies across cultures is computed as the ratio of (Sum of Caudill's Presence Scores) to (Sum of Other Observer's Presence Scores).

in order to be scored. "All food" is a composite variable combining the additive variables of "breast or bottle" and "semi-solid food" such as commercially prepared baby foods, crackers, biscuits, and so forth which must be in the infant's mouth at time of observation. Since there is very little use of semi-solid food at three-to-four months of age in Japan, we do not include this variable here, but rather use the composite variable of "all food." "Finger or pacifier" denotes all such actions as sucking on a finger or

hand, or sucking on other objects such as a pacifier or the edge of a blanket. "Total vocal" is a composite variable combining the additive variables of "unhappy" and "happy" vocalizations which must be distinctive voiced sounds; other sounds such as hiccups and coughs are not scored as vocalization. "Active" means gross bodily movements, usually of the arms and legs, and does not include minor twitches or startles. "Baby plays" is a composite variable meaning that the baby was playing with an object at the time of observation which was either a "toy," his "hand" or other part of his body, or an "other object" such as a blanket or the edge of a crib. The three additive detailed variables are combined here into the composite variable of "baby plays."

Turning to the caretaker behaviors, "presence of" means that the caretaker must be able both to see and hear the baby at the time of observation. "Feeds" means that the caretaker is offering the infant the breast, bottle, or food. "Diapers" is restricted to the checking for wetness and the taking off and putting on of the diaper and its cover, plus assisting the baby to urinate or defecate, and the cleaning, powdering, and oiling of the baby's body. All other removal, putting on, or rearranging of clothing is scored as "dresses." "Positions" is the manipulation of the baby's body to make him more comfortable. "Pats or touches" is a combined variable meaning rhythmic stroking or patting as in burping, or that the caretaker's hand is resting on the baby's body with the apparent intent of soothing. "Other care" is a general category including other caretaking acts such as adjusting the covers under which the baby is lying, wiping his face, or taking his temperature. "Plays with" means that the caretaker is attempting to amuse or entertain the baby by such acts as playing peek-a-boo, showing the baby a toy, and so forth. "Looks at" means that the caretaker is specifically directing her visual attention to the baby. "Talks to" is a composite variable combining the additive variable of "chats" and "lulls." "Chats" means that the caretaker is talking or singing to the baby in a lively fashion, "lulls" is a very delimited behavior, and means that the caretaker is softly humming or singing a lullaby, or making repetitive comforting noises, with the apparent intent of soothing and quieting the baby or getting him to go to sleep. "In arms" means that the baby is being held in the caretaker's arms or lap, or is being carried by the caretaker. "Rocks" includes all conscious acts of the caretaker to cause the baby to sway rhythmically back and forth; it is not scored when the infant is being carried and is merely being moved up and down by the normal walking motion of the caretaker.

In assessing the reliabilities shown in Table 1 we used the severe criterion of requiring agreement as to the presence of a particular behavior at the level of the individual observation. Because of the visual difficulty, however, under conditions of actual observation of picking the correct column for time on the form in which to check the presence of a behavior, we counted agreement if the two observers had checked the same column or contiguous

columns for the presence of a particular behavior. In some places in the raw data for the reliability check, the observers have obviously recorded the same behavior for the infant and caretaker over a ten-minute sheet of 40 columns but are consistently off one column across the entire sheet.

In general the reliability of the dependent variables is satisfactory in each of the three cultures. Altogether there are only three instances in which reliability is poor: a level of 49 per cent in the Japanese data and of 56 per cent in the Japanese-American data on "positions," and a level of 59 per cent in the Japanese-American data on "pats or touches." In part, satisfactory reliability is related to the frequency of occurrence of a dependent variable, and the relative frequency of occurrence of the behaviors of infant and caretaker can be seen in the tables given later in the discussion of the findings.

As pointed out in earlier publication (Caudill and Weinstein 1969), a variable can be satisfactorily reliable and still be "biased." That is, compared to the scores of a constant observer (Caudill in all three cultures), separate observers in each culture (Notsuki for the Japanese, Weinstein for the American, and Frost for the Japanese American) may differ proportionately from the constant observer in the same or in opposite directions. For example, on "total vocal" Caudill had 104 per cent as many scores as Notsuki, 86 per cent as many as Weinstein, and had the same proportion, 100 per cent, as Frost. In order to eliminate these differences where present, the scores of the separate observers are standardized to those of the constant observer. Thus, in the example given for "total vocal" Notsuki's scores are increased by a weight of 1.04, Weinstein's are decreased by a weight of .86, and there is no change in Frost's scores. The weights used to standardize the scores for the dependent variables across the three cultures can be seen in Table 1. Without standardization, it is quite possible to have satisfactory reliability among observers within several cultures, but not to know whether the general perception of the observers is the same or different across cultures.

In this article we are primarily interested in the relative position of the Japanese Americans in comparison with the other two cultural groups on *each* of the behaviors of infant and caretaker considered singly. Thus, our main technique of analysis was an analysis of variance in which the dependent variables were the behaviors of infant and caretaker, and the independent variables were sex of infant and cultural group. In examining the effects of one independent variable we always controlled for the effects of the other. For each dependent variable we made a series of all possible paired-group comparisons (Japanese and American, Japanese and Japanese American, and American and Japanese American).[5] We also did a Pearsonian correlational analysis of the dependent variables for each culture in order to look at patterns of intercorrelation, and we will make a limited use of these patterns in reporting our findings.

Findings

In all three sets of paired comparisons for the dependent variables none of the interactions between the independent variables are significant, and there are no findings by sex of infant. Cultural differences, however, are highly significant as can be seen in Tables 2 and 3. The mean frequencies given for the dependent variables in the tables represent their average occurrence over 800 observations for each case, and all significant differences between cultural groups are reported on the basis of a two-tailed test.

The findings for the dependent variables by cultural group are reported on two separate tables because earlier published comparisons of Japanese and Americans (Caudill and Weinstein 1969) showed that the dependent variables divided into two groupings which we called a) the expression and caretaking of the infant's "basic biological needs," and b) "styles of behavior" by the infant and caretaker. In general, the Japanese and Americans showed no difference in the first grouping, but were distinctively different in the second grouping. We expected that the Japanese Americans would also show no difference in the expression and care of the infant's basic needs, and would be closer to the Americans in styles of behaving. On the whole, the results are as expected, but with some surprises, particularly in the case of basic needs.

Table 2
Paired Cultural Comparisons of Variables Related
to Care of The Infant's Basic Needs

	Mean Frequencies			Cultural Comparisons		
Dependent Variables	Japanese (30 cases)	American (30 cases)	Japanese American (21 cases)	Japanese and American p<	Japanese and Japanese American p<	Americ'an and Japanese American p<
Infant Behavior						
Awake	499	489	511	...	...	...
Breast or Bottle	66	55	77	...	...	...
All Food	68	74	112	...	0.001	0.05
Caretaker Behavior						
Presence of	549	414	489	0.01	...	...
Feeds	74	70	113	...	0.01	0.01
Diapers	23	17	38	...	0.001	0.001
Dresses	13	13	4	...	0.001	0.001
Pats or Touches	34	46	53	...	0.05	...
Other Care	17	23	11	...	...	0.05
Looks at	247	293	288	...	...	...

On Table 2 it can be seen that there are no differences in any of the paired comparisons for the amount of time the baby is "awake," and this argues for the biological similarity of the infants with regard to the needs for sleep and awakeness. There also are no statistical differences for the amount of time spent in the intake of milk from "breast or bottle," although the Japanese-American mean is the highest on this variable. On the intake of "all food," however, the Japanese-American babies are significantly greater than the babies in either of the other groups. The reason for this is obviously due to the greater intake of "semi-solid food" (which is the difference between the means for "breast or bottle" and "all food") by the Japanese-American babies when coupled with their higher mean on "breast or bottle."

From the above results it is clear that the Japanese-American mother is making a greater use *both* of milk and semi-solid food in the feeding of her baby, and this shows up in the finding that the Sansei mother is greater than either the Japanese or the American mother on the variable of "feeds." The Sansei mother appears to have taken on the American pattern of a greater use of semi-solid food without having given up the Japanese pattern of a somewhat greater use of milk, and thus she appears as a sort of super-care-taker in the matter of feeding. Given this finding, it is not surprising that the Sansei mother is also doing more diapering than the mothers in the other two groups, and also has a higher mean on patting and touching as a large part of the behavior included under this latter variable consists of burping the baby.

On the remaining variables in Table 2, there are no differences in the paired comparisons on the variable of "looks at," and the Sansei mother is intermediate between the Japanese and American mothers in the amount of time she is in the "presence of" her baby. The significantly lesser amount of time spent by the Sansei mother in dressing her baby compared with the mothers in the other two groups is probably related to differences in climate; observations were evenly spaced throughout the year in all three cultures, and on the average it is colder in Tokyo and Washington, D. C., than it is in Sacramento. Thus, the Yonsei baby was probably more lightly clothed during the winter months. The same reasoning is applicable for the Sansei mother's lower mean on "other care" as this variable includes such behavior as adjusting bedclothes, wiping runny noses, and so forth.

Turning to Table 3, the main variables of interest in terms of the questions with which we began this paper are the vocalization and activity of the infant, and the verbalization to the infant by the caretaker. As can be seen, the Yonsei baby is more like the American than the Japanese baby in his greater amount of happy vocalization and physical activity, and in his lesser amount of unhappy vocalization. Equally, the Sansei mother is more like the American than the Japanese mother in the greater amount of

Table 3
Paired Cultural Comparisons of Variables Related
to Styles of Behaving

Dependent Variables	Mean Frequencies			Cultural Comparisons		
	Japanese (30 cases)	American (30 cases)	Japanese American (21 cases)	Japanese and American $p<$	Japanese and Japanese American $p<$	American and Japanese American $p<$
Infant Behavior						
Finger or Pacifier	70	170	45	0.001	...	0.001
Total Vocal	95	115	135	...	0.05	...
Unhappy	67	44	27	0.01	0.001	0.05
Happy	30	59	111	0.001	0.001	0.001
Active	51	95	111	0.001	0.01	...
Baby Plays	83	170	102	0.001	...	0.05
Caretaker Behavior						
Positions	9	19	25	0.001	0.001	...
Plays with	40	23	71	0.05	0.05	0.001
Talks to	104	121	214	...	0.001	0.001
Chats	80	119	205	0.01	0.001	0.001
Lulls	23	2	14	0.001	...	0.01
In Arms	204	132	193	0.05	...	0.05
Rocks	49	17	17	0.01	0.05	...

chatting she does to her baby. Moreover, the infant's happy vocalization and the caretaker's chatting to infant are significantly correlated in the American (.39, $p < 0.05$) and Japanese-American (.57, $p < 0.01$) data, but are not so in the Japanese data (-.09, *n.s.*). These results indicate that American and Sansei mothers are making a greater, and more discriminating (see Caudill 1971), use of their voices as a means of communicating with their babies and the babies respond accordingly—the more the mother chats to the baby, the more he is happily vocal. The Sansei mothers are also more like the American mothers in several other regards—they do more positioning and less rocking of their babies than do the Japanese mothers. Thus, the major finding from Table 3 is that the Japanese-American mothers and infants are closer in their style of behavior to their American than to their Japanese counterparts.

In some respects, however, the data in Table 3 also show that the Japanese-American mothers and infants have retained certain patterns of behavior from their Japanese cultural heritage. The Sansei mother is more like the Japanese mother in the greater amount of time she spends in playing with her baby, and this finding is probably related to the finding that the

Yonsei baby is more like the Japanese baby in playing less by himself. In addition, the Yonsei and Japanese babies are alike in that they do less non-nutritive sucking on "finger or pacifier" than do the American babies. Finally, the Sansei mother is more like the Japanese mother in doing more carrying of the baby in her arms and lulling.[6]

Conclusion

In general, the main conclusion to be drawn from these data is that the behavior of the Japanese-American mothers and infants is closer to that of the Americans than to that of the Japanese. This is particularly true for the great amount of lively chatting the Sansei mother does to her baby who, in turn, responds with increased happy vocalization and physical activity.

In answer to the arguments with which we began this paper, it would seem, first of all, that the greater activity and happy vocalization of the American baby in contrast to the Japanese baby do not seem to be genetic in origin because the Yonsei baby is like the American baby in these regards even though he is genetically Japanese. Secondly, it would seem that both cultural change and cultural persistence are operating to influence the behavior of the Sansei mothers and their Yonsei babies. On the whole, Sansei mothers have come to behave like other American mothers, but it is also true that in come respects they act like Japanese mothers. And, as would be expected, the Yonsei babies respond appropriately and learn to behave in ways that reflect the cultural style of their parents.

Notes

1. Beyond the possible influence of group genetic factors, the question of the effects of nutritional differences might be asked concerning the feeding of babies among Japanese, Americans, and Japanese Americans. Roughly speaking, there is greater use of breast feeding for a longer period after birth among Japanese mothers and they also delay the introduction of semi-solid food longer (usually until about the beginning of the third month) than do American or Japanese-American mothers (who start semi-solid food at about the end of the first month). In terms of the nutritional adequacy of the infant's diet, however, there is probably little difference among the three groups since all of the families in each group are urban, middle-class, and without serious economic problems.

2. For a more general discussion, supported by research data, of this question of ethnic identity across three generations of Japanese Americans see Masuda, Matsumoto, and Meredith (1970).

3. The distinction between working as a salaried employee in a large business and working as an owner or employee in a small business is an important one in Japan and has a meaningful influence on the nature of interpersonal relations in the family. For this reason we designed the study of American and Japanese infants to include this distinction as an independent variable. In the analysis of the American and Japanese data (see Caudill and Weinstein 1969) this variable proved to be of no

importance in the American families, and to be of only minor, but still meaningful, importance in the Japanese families where the caretakers in the Japanese independent business families were more present and doing more talking to, carrying, and locking of their babies who, probably as a consequence, were more awake.

4. In the internal analysis of the Japanese-American data no interactions are significant, and there are no findings by sex of infant. There is a hint when the dependent variables are considered singly, that first-born Yonsei infants may be more active, happily vocalizing, and playing by themselves than are later-born infants; but, none of the canonical correlations are significant when the entire group of infant dependent variables are considered collectively.

5. Before doing our paired comparisons of the three cultural groups, we also ran an analysis using all three cultures (Japanese, American) and sex of infant (male, female) as independent variables in one analysis in order to assure ourselves that we were not capitalizing on extremes in making our paired comparisons. In this overall analysis no interactions are significant, and there are no findings by sex. The comparisons by culture are highly significant, but the similarities and differences between cultural groups appear more clearly in the paired-group analyses.

6. The Japanese pattern of soothing the baby and getting him to go to sleep is usually a combination of carrying in arms while also lulling and rocking. The Sansei mother seems to have given up rocking, but she still carries and lulls the baby more than the American mother. Frost's more qualitative notes which were made in addition to her quantitative observations provide a number of illustrations of such behavior. For example: "Mrs. H. does not rock her child to sleep, but she plays soft music, holds him in her arms, and dances with him until he falls asleep. She does this before both his morning and afternoon nap. She says that sometimes she spends as much as an hour dancing with him."

References

Bronfenbrenner, Urie. 1958. Socialization and social class through time and space. *In* Eleanor E. Maccoby, Theodore M. Newcomb, and Eugene L. Hartley, eds. Readings in social psychology, third edition. New York, Henry Holt.

Caudill, William. 1952. Japanese American personality and acculturation. Genetic Psychology Monographs 45: 3–102.

1971. Tiny dramas: vocal communication between mother and infant in Japanese and American families. *In* William Lebra, ed. Mental health research in Asia and the Pacific, Volume Two. Honolulu, East-West Center Press.

Caudill, William, and George DeVos. 1956. Achievement, culture and personality: the case of the Japanese Americans. American Anthropologist 58: 1102–1126.

Caudill, William, and Helen Weinstein. 1969. Maternal care and infant behavior in Japan and America. Psychiatry 32: 12–43.

Clyde, Dean J., Elliot M. Cramer, and Richard J. Sherin. 1966. Multivariate statistical programs. Coral Gables, Florida, Biometrics Laboratory, University of Miami.

Frost, Lois. 1970. Child raising techniques as related to acculturation among Japanese Americans. Unpublished Master's thesis in anthropology, Sacramento State College.

Freedman, D. G., and N. C. Freedman. 1969. Behavioral differences between Chinese-American and European-American newborns. Nature, Vol. 224, No. 5225, p. 1227 only, December 20.

Kitano, Harry H. L. 1969. Japanese Americans: the evolution of a subculture. Englewood Cliffs, New Jersey, Prentice-Hall.

Masuda, Minoru, Gary H. Matsumoto, and Gerald M. Meredith. 1970. Ethnic identity in three generations of Japanese Americans. Journal of Social Psychology 81: 199–207.

Part Four
Early Childhood

It is in this period that the effect of ecological factors on human development becomes most clearly apparent. Social structure shapes patterns of family interaction and, thereby, the course of the child's behavior and growth. In making the case for the small family, Lieberman summarizes research on the effects of family size. Rothbart documents differences in mother-child interaction as a function of the child's ordinal position. Bee and her colleagues provide a view, at a later stage of development, of the trajectory of progressive class differences in mother-child interaction. And the studies by Parke and Baumrind document the impact of differing patterns of discipline on the development of the child.

Next, the importance of parents in preschool intervention programs is reflected in the reports of specific studies by Gray, and Klaus and Karnes *et. al.*, and in Schaefer's comprehensive survey of research on compensatory programs. The evidence indicates that the often marked gains in measured intelligence and other variables achieved in such programs tend to "wash out" if the program does not involve persons who constitute part of the child's enduring environment in the home, the peer group, the school, or the community.

The role of these extrafamilial contexts is examined in the next set of studies: Freud and Dann's dramatic follow-up of children rescued from Nazi concentration camps demonstrates the power of the children's group in sustaining emotional security and psychological growth. The way in which "social labeling" of the child can affect others' treatment

of him, and thereby his own capacity to function, is demonstrated by Brophy and Goods' study of teacher behavior.

The influence of that new and now ubiquitous member of virtually every American family—the television set—is examined in the next three articles. The first, by Liebert, provides a concrete example of the experimental studies which served as a basis for the Surgeon General's report. The second, by Holden, summarizes these studies. In the third, written especially for this volume, Garbarino calls attention to a major omission in the research carried out to date on the effects of television on children.

Finally, the last two articles in the section remind us of the crippling realities of life for thousands of children in America today. While presenting sharp contrasts in method, Gil's systematic survey of child abuse and Coles' graphic description of life in the alley converge in testifying to the pervasive role of violence in the daily lives of thousands of children growing up in our society.

4.1 Reserving a Womb: Case for the Small Family

E. James Lieberman, M.D., M.P.H., F.A.P.H.A.

"If people only made prudent marriages, what a stop to population there would be!"—Thackeray.

If conceiving babies were nearly as hard as rearing them well, small families would be more common. Some parents feel that child rearing is not more hazardous with a large family, and many good results are in evidence. But for most of us, child rearing is so complicated and challenging that there is not much to be taken for granted. New knowledge about child development, emphasis on the importance of the early years, and the discovery of subtle but significant differences between newborn infants all lend weight to the idea that "maternal instinct" while essential is not enough.[1] Sound information is needed, too. The profusion of articles and books on child rearing is not an indictment of the American family but public testimony of myriad private concerns that are entirely appropriate for parents of this and any age.

Trends in the United States

In the United States average family size has fluctuated from as many as eight per woman in colonial days to 2.3 during the depression and over three since then. The birth rate has been falling steadily in recent years, but the national growth rate is still ahead of most other industrialized countries. This growth is due not to uncontrolled reproduction among the poor, but to the deliberate attainment of three and four children by the more prosperous majority of our population. In fact, the poor prefer smaller families than the average but attainment of their goals has been more difficult. It takes only two children to replace two parents in the next generation, if the children survive to reproductive maturity. Since there is a slight amount of attrition, the actual size of family required for a stable population is 2.2, given our present standards of health and longevity.

Most Americans determine their family size on personal, not demographic considerations. Of course, population growth cannot go on indefinitely in a finite space, with finite resources. Anyone who has lately tried to get out of a large city on Friday afternoon or into a national park for a weekend will probably conclude that there are enough people here already! Hopefully, we have sufficient time and individual and community wisdom to bring family size and community size into harmonious relationship on

Reprinted from the *American Journal of Public Health* 1970, 60, 87–92, by permission of the author and the American Public Health Association.

a voluntary basis.

Surveys indicate that the two-child family was preferred by more people in 1940 than in the last decade. The three- and four-child family seems to be gaining as an ideal. There is an astonishing number of unplanned pregnancies even in recent years and, what is worse, a good many unwanted children. Family building is a process in which the ideals of inexperience are transformed by realities of parenthood with the result that preferred family size may change. Experts in both child development and demography attest to the great significance of the difference between family size of four, three, and two.[2,3]

There is a good deal of research on family size and birth order,[4] but little that can make precise distinctions between two, three, and four children— the range which is the most common preference today. Furthermore, the studies do not take into account whether the children in these families were wanted or unwanted—often a difficult thing to ascertain. Presumably, wanted children in large families will do as well or better than unwanted children in small families, but as would be expected, there are more unwanted children in large families than in small families.

Family Size Effects on Children

The 1964 Presidential Task Force on Manpower Conservation found that about 70 per cent of Selective Service mental rejectees come from families of four children or more, though only 33 per cent of the nation's children come from such families. A further breakdown shows that 47 per cent of rejectees come from the 11 per cent of children who are members of families with six or more offspring! Interpretation is difficult because large family size and poverty are associated and cannot be separated for analysis.[6]

The Scottish Mental Survey of 1947 gets around this difficulty by separating the effects of social class and family size in its measure of intelligence. All 11-year-olds were subjects of the study, which showed progressive decline in intelligence score with increasing family size regardless of social class. Scores did correlate with social class too: the richer, the better. But family size took its toll within each grouping, so that children of small lower class families excelled those from the large middle class homes, and so on.[7] In the United States several studies have shown that the development of intellect is favored by the small family environment. One interpretation is that parents have less time for verbal interaction with a larger number of children; verbal proficiency is the crux of success in intelligence tests and in education generally.

Concerning personality development, important work on family density —number and spacing of children—has been done at the National Institute of Mental Health. Second and later-born boys were studied for vigor and lethargy at birth, and for dependence or independence at age two and a half.

The findings contest the stereotype that children from large (high density) families are more self-reliant and mature. In the nursery school setting they demand more frequent contact with teacher than their peers from small families, which the scientists theorize is due to relative maternal deprivation at home. Even at birth, there are significant differences, the infants from smaller families being more vigorous and responsive. But when the differences at birth are controlled for, those at two and a half remain significant, i.e., there is an environmental as well as a congenital factor. Social class did not influence the results. As might be expected, in the more congested families, observers found significantly less contact with the child initiated by the mother. There was no correlation between family density and friendliness with peers, so the teacher-seeking behavior cannot be written off as extroversion.[9]

Other studies show that (1) successive children do not receive the parental warmth granted their predecessors,[10] and (2) relative maternal unconcern toward younger siblings characterizes some large families.[11] Child development specialists stress the importance of maternal deprivation due to illness, death, or separation. It is likely that another form of maternal and paternal deprivation occurs regularly in crowded families and, furthermore, that this is related to prolonged dependency behavior.

Physical development also seems to be retarded by increased family size. A British study found that average height and weight for age decreased as family size increased, despite the fact that birth weights increase with parity. This may be due to poorer nutrition or factors affecting it; e.g., emotion or infection. Birth spacing may be important in that the older child receives less attention at mealtime when a new baby is born.[12]

Eighth- and eleventh-grade students from small families in Michigan reported better relations with their parents than those from larger families.[13] In a study of Ohio fifth-graders from families of at least two children, researchers found that offspring in smaller families had more favorable relations with both parents and siblings.[14]

Not all studies favor small families. Some researchers have been unable to show any significant difference between large and small families on criteria of adjustment.[15,16] Bossard and Boll[17] sum up their survey as follows: Small families have the advantage of more parental attention, but possible disadvantage of too much intensive parenthood, pressure to achieve, and exaggerated feeling of importance in a group; large families tend to be less planned, with less intensive parenting, early acceptance of realities, more crises, more group emphasis with organization, discipline, conformity and specialization of function among children. The small family theme is planning, rationalism and prudence oriented toward achievement in a complex, changing society. The desire for a large family, significantly, is not prominent among offspring of prolific parents: only 30 per cent of children from large families endorsed the idea wholeheartedly.

Effects Upon Parents

A recent British study found more ill health—both physical and mental —in parents of larger families, especially mothers, which is attributed to the increased strain imposed upon them by caring for a larger number of children. There was no association between family size and income and none between social class and health in the population sampled.[18]

Other studies have found (1) in discordant marriages, the chance for successful outcome decreases as the number of children increases[19]; (2) happiness was associated with the desire for children, whether couples had any or not at the time, and poorest adjustment was found among those with unwanted children[20]; (3) an inverse relationship existed between marital adjustment and family size, i.e., more children, less adjustment; also, there was a correlation between marital adjustment and success in controlling fertility according to the desires of the couple[21]; (4) having more than one child early in marriage correlated with poorer marital adjustment.[22]

Family planning is clearly related to marital adjustment, and good communication between spouses is known to correlate with effective family planning.[23] Good marriages get better with parenthood and the poor ones get more children. This phenomenon deserves closer attention because it is a very vicious cycle of maladaptation.

Discussion

The two-child family does not seem so oppressively small when we note that, at various times and places, it has become the mode and without grievous consequences; for example, in contemporary Scandinavia, Japan, and Hungary, and in segments of populations, such as women college graduates and Jewish couples in this country.

Most of the accidental pregnancies that occur nowadays turn out to be the first and second children. Many couples whose use of contraceptives, if any, has been casual, will start family planning conscientiously only after reaching their desired family size. This laxity can jeopardize marital stability and compromise the development of infants born too close together. Besides those marriages that occur because the girl is pregnant, there are many more "young marrieds" who become parents before they smooth out their nuptial ruffles. Although divorce rates have remained relatively constant, the number of children affected (1.18 per divorce) has increased significantly, reflecting the rising proportion of couples with children.

Prudence in the matter of starting a family requires some interval for marital adjustment. Young couples need and can well afford an interval of marriage without children. Child spacing is also an important matter, all of which comes down to a strong recommendation that couples learn and

adopt effective famliy planning measures from the start of their sexual relationship. By practicing birth control at the outset, couples are more likely to gain the experience and skill necessary to achieve the desired number and spacing of offspring. This is important for parents who want the best in life for their children.

It is more rational and responsible to have few or none than to have unwanted children. The decision to have a child will rarely be clear-cut; ambivalence, conscious or unconscious, will often be present: a wanted child is sometimes or somehow not wanted, and vice versa. Our society is unequivocal about the desirability of marriage and child rearing, and for most of human history that social imperative expressed the statistical necessity for birth rates to keep ahead of high death rates. The necessity is now gone—in terms of human history not long gone—and while social pressure for large families has lessened, the very small family or childless couple is apparently still in some disfavor.

"You should have as many children as you can afford" is a precept that has a surprising following, even today, despite the fact that "affording" economically may have little to do with competence in child rearing. A community with finite resources cannot "afford" a rich child any better than a poor one. Each child takes up a seat in school, a bed in the hospital, and eventually a parking place. Given the burgeoning knowledge of child development and the demographic picture, it is timely to begin educating school children about family size and structure,[24] so as to remove any stigma associated with small family size and to provide people with the knowledge and the means necessary to realize their parental wishes.

It is high time for more of the attitude: "We want to raise two children well, with time left over for adult pursuits for both husband and wife." Indeed, there is some research evidence to support the idea that the woman who wants to work will be a better mother for half a day with a part-time job and good help than for a full day with no relief and no chance to exercise and replenish her adult capacities. The part-time working mother of one or two children can have time enough for both activities and have wifely charm to spare.[25,26]

Two children would be sufficient for more of us if (1) we could have the choice of sex; (2) we were not afraid of losing a child, and (3) we did not need to make good our mistakes with the firstborn by having extra chances later. In a few more dceades, we will probably be able to choose the sex of our offspring. It is true that the smaller the family, the greater the emotional investment in each child and the more overwhelming is the prospect of losing one, but odds are extremely good that a one-year-old will survive to adulthood and the main hindrance thereto—accidental death—is preventable. As for recouping our errors, this is a dubious practice on several counts; prevention is worth more than a pound of cure. Greater readiness for

parenthood should reduce the number of false starts, and where trouble has already occurred, investment of resources—family and professional—for that child is likely to be a better prescription than trying once again.

Actions speak louder than words and sanctions for small families would be enhanced by the behavior of social pacesetters as well. The more affluent members of society cannot merely sanction small families for the poor, as if those with less money should have fewer children. The most important psychological advantages for having few children apply to the rich as well as to the poor. Of course, one cannot completely separate economic from psychological advantages. The Institute of Life Insurance recently estimated that the cost of rearing a child to age 18 for a family with an annual income of $6,600 amounted to $23,800, not including college!

There is a way to have more children without increasing the population. Nowadays, adoption agencies are more willing to consider requests from fertile couples. There are still many unadopted children—a tragedy which is overwhelming, if we dare to contemplate it. Some people who have the means and the desire for many children may find an optimum answer in the combination of natural and adopted children. At present, adoption is the one sure way to balance the sexes in a family.

The small family question is more than a matter of quality—good or bad—versus quantity, but quality of diverse kinds. Most parents will recognize some minute differences between their children at birth, perhaps despite what they have been told about environment and heredity. But how many know enough, have time enough, or have sanctions from wherever it counts to exploit the individualities of their different children?

I would hate to see a standardized family emerge as the price of population stability. There will be some who will want one child or none and a few who will want many. Since more individualization of children and parents can occur in small families, we can expect healthy variety not only to endure but thrive under conditions where all children are wanted children, and overpopulation is no longer a threat.

Acknowledgement

The author wishes to acknowledge the valuable assistance of Mrs. Susan Roth in the preparation of this paper.

References

Bell, Richard Q. A. Reinterpretation of the Direction of Effects in Studies of Socialization. Psychology. Rev. 75:81-95, 1968.

Westoff, C. F. "The Fertility of the American Population." In: Population: The Vital Revolution. Freedman, R. (ed.). New York: Anchor, 1964, pp. 110-122.

Day, L. H., and Day, A. T. Too Many Americans. Boston: Houghton, 1964; New York: Delta, 1965.

Clausen, J. A. Family Size and Birth Order As Influences Upon Socialization and Personality: Bibliography and Abstracts. New York: Soc. Science Research Council, 1965 (mimeo.), p. 182.

Westoff, C. F.; Potter, R. G.; and Sagi, P. C. The Third Child. Princeton, N. J.: Princeton University Press, 1963.

President's Task Force on Manpower Conservation. One Third of a Nation. Washington, D. C.: Gov. Ptg. Office, 1964.

Scottish Council for Research in Education. Social Implications of the 1947 Scottish Mental Survey. London, 1953, p. 48.

Clausen, J. A. Family Structure, Socialization and Personality. Rev. Child Development Res. Hoffman and Hoffman (eds.). New York: Russell Sage Foundation, 1966, pp. 1-54.

Waldrop, Mary F., and Bell, R. Q. Relation of Preschool Dependency Behavior to Family Size and Density. Child Development 35:1187-1195, 1964.

Lasko, J. Parent Behavior Toward First and Second Children. Genetic Psychol. Monogr. 49:97-137, 1954.

Kent, N., and Davis, R. Discipline in the Home and Intellectual Development. Brit J. Med Psychol., 1957, pp 27-33.

Grant, M. W. Family Size. Brit. J. Social Med. 18:35-42, 1964.

Nye, F. I. Sibling Number, Broken Homes, and Adjustment. Marriage & Family Living 14:327-30, 1952.

Hawkes, G. R.; Burchinal, L.; and Gardner, B. Size of Family and Adjustment of Children. Ibid. 20:65-58, 1958.

Hamilton, G. V. In: Christensen. H. T.. and Philbrick, R. E. Family Size a a Factor in the Marital Adjustments of College Couples. Am. Soc. Rev. 17:306-312, 1952.

Leslie, G. R. The Family in Social Context. New York: Oxford, 1967, pp. 514-516.

Bossard, J. H. S., and Boll, E. The Large Family System. Philadelphia: University of Pennsylvania Press, 1956.

Hare, E. H., and Shaw, J. K. A Study in Family Health: Health in Relation to Family Size. Brit. J. Psychiat. 3:475, 461-466 (June), 1965.

Mowrer, E. R., et al. Domestic Discord. Chicago: Chicago University Press, 1928 (cited by Lewis Terman, et al. Psychological Factors in Marital Happiness. New York: McGraw, 1938, p. 173.

Burgess, E. W., and Cottrell, L. S. Predicting Success or Failure in Marriage. New York: Prentice-Hall, 1939, p. 260.

Reed, R. B. Social and Psychological Factors Affecting Fertility: The Interrelationship of Marital Adjustment, Fertility Control, and Size of Family. Milbank Mem. Fun Quart. 25:383-425, 1947.

Hurley, J. R., and Palonen, D. Marital Satisfaction and Child Density Among University Student Parents. J. Marr. Fam. 29:483-484, 1967.

Rainwater, L. Family Design. Chicago: Aldine, 1965.

Wayland, S. R. "Family Planning and the School Curriculum." In: Family Planning and Population Programs. Berelson, B. (ed.). Chicago: University of Chicago Press, 1966, pp. 353-362.

Yarrow, M. R.; Scott, P.; and deLeeuw, C. Childrearing in Families of Working and Nonworking Mothers. Sociometry 25:122-140, 1962.

Morrow, W. R., and Wilson, R. C. "Family Relations of Bright High-Achieving and Under-Achieving High School Boys." In: Underachievement. Kornich, M. (ed.). Springfield: Thomas, 1965, pp. 188-199.

Etzioni, A. Sex Control, Science and Society. Science 161:1107-1112 (Sept.), 1968.

Addenda

Christensen, H. T. Children in the Family: Relationship of Number and Spacing to Marital Success. J. Marr. Fam. 30:2, 283-289 (May), 1968.

Datta, L.-E. Birth Order and Potential Scientific Creativity. Sociometry 31:1, 76-88 (Mar.), 1968.

Groat. H. T., and Neal, A. G. Social Psychological Correlates of Urban Fertility. Am. Sociolog. Rev. 32:6, 945-959 (Dec.), 1967.

Pohlman, E. Psychology of Birth Planning. Cambridge: Schenkman, 1969.

Population Council. American Attitudes on Population Policy: Recent Trends. Studies in Family Planning No. 30 (May), 1968.

Tuckman, J., and Regan, R. A. Size of Family and Behavioral Problems in Children. J. Genet. Psychol. 111:151-160, 1967.

4.2   Birth Order and Mother-Child Interaction in an Achievement Situation

Mary K. Rothbart
Stanford University

Most research on the effects of birth order has concentrated on identifying personality characteristics that vary as a function of ordinal position. Although such research often concludes with hypotheses about differing socialization experiences for children of different ordinal posi-

Reprinted from Rothbart, Mary K. Birth order and mother-child interaction in an achievement situation. *Journal of Personality and Social Psychology,* 1971, *17,* No. 2, 113-120. Copyright © 1971 by the American Psychological Association, and reproduced by permission.

tions, only a few studies have attempted to observe the actual behavior of parents toward children of differing birth order. The present study presents a test of hypotheses about differential socialization of first- and later-born children in an achievement situation. It is part of a larger study in which mothers' interactions with firstborn and second-born children were observed in a structured interaction setting.

The general finding that the firstborn tends to gain greater eminence in school and later life (Altus, 1966; Sampson, 1965; Schachter, 1963), though recently disputed (Bayer, 1966), has led to questions about the kinds of parental expectations and pressures for success exerted upon the firstborn as compared with the second born. In addition, numerous studies have considered possible IQ differences between firstborn and later-born children (Sampson, 1965). These studies often have had conflicting results; in infant tests (Bayley, 1965; Cushna, 1966), slight differences in favor of firstborns have been found. Bayley, however, reports that these differences are small, and seem to have no cumulative effect or relation to later intelligence test scores.

What, then, are other variables that might prompt the firstborn to higher academic levels in later life? It has been suggested that greater parental pressures are directed toward the firstborn's achievement and acceptance of responsibility (Davis, 1941; McArthur, 1956; Rosen, 1961). that the firstborn is often given the role of parent surrogate (Sutton-Smith, Roberts, & Rosenberg, 1964), that the parents talk and interact more with the firstborn (Bossard, 1945), and pay more attention to the firstborn (Koch, 1954). Rosen (1961) and Phillips (1956) have proposed that since parents have no frame of reference in their expectations for the firstborn, they tend to overestimate his ability more than the second born's, setting higher standards for his performance.

Work done on the relation of birth order and eminence thus suggests numerous questions for this study: Do parents exert greater pressure on their firstborn to excel in his work? Do parents have higher or more unrealistic expectations for their first child's performance? Do parents interact more with the first child? Are parents more likely to praise and criticize the performance of the first child than the second? When a parent instructs his child, are his explanations more complex and at a higher level for the firstborn than the second? In the present study these questions were investigated through an observation of mothers supervising their firstborn or second-born children in the performance of a variety of tasks.

Method

The experimenter compared mother-child interactions for 5-year-old firstborn and second-born boys and girls from two-child, same-sex fami-

lies. In a 2×2 design, sex of child and birth order were the independent variables. Mothers were asked to supervise their children in the performance of five different tasks, two of which involved explanations by the mother.

Subjects

Subjects were kindergarten children from the Palo Alto Unified School District and their mothers. Subjects were chosen from two-child families only, where both children were of the same sex and there was an approximate age difference of 2 years between the subject and his sibling. Half of the subjects had a 3-year-old younger sibling; half had a 7-year-old older sibling. Of a total of 56 subjects, 30 were girls and 26 were boys. Distributions were matched with respect to age of the subject and age difference with the sibling. Approximately the same proportion of children in each group (67 %) came from professional homes. One important variable on which groups were not matched was age of mother, with mothers whose second-born children were 5 years old, as would be expected, significantly older than mothers whose firstborn children were 5 years old.

Mothers were introduced to the study by a letter from the school district director or research, who described the purpose of the study as investigating differences between children of different birth orders. After the mothers had received the letter, sessions were scheduled by telephone. Of over 60 mothers asked to take part in the study and pretest, only 2 were unable to participate.

Procedure

All interaction sessions were held in a specially equipped trailer provided by Stanford University's Laboratory of Human Development. Since subjects came from all parts of the city, the trailer was located at four different schools, providing the same situation for all subjects. The trailer was divided into three rooms, with two large rooms at either end and a small central observation room containing one-way mirrors and recording equipment. Tasks were performed in one large room; children played with toys in the other large room while the mother was given instructions. In the case of six firstborn boys and seven firstborn girls, the younger sibling was also present in the toy room, since the experimenters offered baby-sitting to participating mothers. Two experimenters, the author and another woman experienced in working with children, were present for all sessions. When the mother and child arrived, introductions were made, and subjects were shown the experimental room. One experimenter then invited the child to come into the playroom for a short time.

The mother was then seated at a card table, and instructions were given to her by the experimenter. The instructions, developed with the help of nine pretest subjects, began:

What we'd like to try to do as soon as [name of child] comes back in is to set up and record several simple situations that you probably go through with him fairly often. Most of the situations will involve you describing or explaining something to him, or supervising his work on a problem. Of course, it's best if you can be as natural as possible, and act toward him as you usually do.

The mother was then introduced to the five tasks she was to engage in with her child. The situations were as follows:

Conversation. The mother was asked first of all to ask her child what he had seen in the other room, to "get an idea of his usual conversation." The playroom contained a special toy (a set of dump trucks), along with a workbench, coloring book, paper, crayons, and two children's books. The mother did not know what the playroom contained. The conversation was designed to put subjects at ease at the beginning of the session, to provide an indication of the number of questions asked the child by his mother, and the specificity and correctness of the child's recall.

Cartoons. The mother was asked to show her child two four-frame "Peanuts" cartoons by the artist Charles Schulz, and to explain to him what was happening in the cartoons. The cartoons offered a set of somewhat ambiguous stimulus materials that the mother could structure a great deal or not at all. The mother could simply read the cartoon, she could point out emotions displayed by the cartoon characters, and for one cartoon, she could draw a moral lesson. It was thus possible to get a measure of the complexity of the mother's explanation, along with the amount of time she spent explaining the cartoons.

Picture. Mothers were given a picture of 20 zoo animals and were asked, initially, to show the child the picture for a 3-minute period. During this time, the mother, or child, or both could name the animals aloud. The mother was then to turn the picture over for 3 minutes and ask the child to remember as many of the animals as he could. She was allowed to prompt him as much as she wished. The mother was also asked to estimate the number of animals her child would be likely to remember, after being told that the average child of his age would remember 10 animals. This situation proved to be a powerful measure of the mother's pressure on the child to perform well. Most children attempted to stop

the task at some point during the recall period, and a measure was made of pressure exerted on the child to continue.

Explanation. Mothers were given a simple diagram of the workings of a water tap, along with an extremely complicated written description of how a water tap works. The language was technical, and included some information about water pressure that was tangential to the explanation. The mother was asked to show the diagram to the child, and explain to him in her own words how the water tap worked. This situation allowed a measure of complexity and length of the mother's explanation, along with her use of praise and criticism.

Puzzle. The last situation was a difficult geometric puzzle, on which the mother was asked to supervise her child. She was given a model of how the puzzle should look when it was completed, and told that she could help the child as much as she wanted without actually showing him the solution to the puzzle. The time allowed for working on the puzzle was 6 minutes, after which the experimenter made sure that the child successfully completed the puzzle if he had not yet done so. The mother was also asked to estimate how quickly her child would be likely to solve the puzzle on a 6-point scale ranging from "very slowly and with difficulty" to "very rapidly."

After the mother was given the initial instructions, she was provided with a shorter written version of the oral instructions, and the child was returned to the room to begin the tasks. The experimenter remained in the room with the mother and child to answer the mother's questions about procedure and to make sure the correct order of tasks was followed. The entire session was tape-recorded.

After the tasks were completed, the child was given paper construction materials, and the mother, a questionnaire to complete during a 15-minute period while the experimenter was out of the room. (These data have not yet been analyzed.) The mother was also asked if she and the child would straighten the room before the experimenter returned. Two brooms, one large and one child-size, were conspicuously located in the corner of the room, and the experimenter noted the extent of the child's involvement in the cleanup. When the 15 minutes had elapsed, the experimenter returned to ask the mothers a few questions about rules she had for her children, and the session was then terminated. (Interview data have also not yet been analyzed.)

Coding procedures and reliabilities

Coding for data analysis was based for the most part on tape recordings of the five tasks completed by the mother and child. This coding

was blind, with all tape recordings coded by the author and 21 recordings coded independently by a second rater for reliability. In addition, length of interactions was timed, and the child's level of performance on the conversation, picture, and puzzle was rated. The average reliability coefficient was .92; the only achievement scale with a reliability of .80 or below was the mother's structuring of the puzzle task, where $r = .79$.

The basic statistical analysis for all variables was a two-way analysis of variance (Sex × Birth Order). In addition, items on the same general variable, for example, mother's pressure for achievement, were intercorrelated. When correlations were significant at the .01 level, standard scores of these measures were added to form larger scales, and analyses of variance, applied to scale scores. When individual variables failed to correlate or Ns were unequal, separate analyses were carried out.

Results

Results are summarized in Tables 1, 2, and 3. For all measures, the meaning of a score corresponds to the name of the scale. For example, a high score on the pressure for achievement variable indicates strong pressure for achievement. In data analysis, it was first necessary to determine whether performance of firstborns and second borns differed significantly on the tasks assigned them. If there were actual differences in the success or failure of first- and second borns, these differences might have, in turn, differentially affected their mothers' behavior, greatly complicating an interpretations of differences on maternal variables.

Measures of the child's performance, including the number of playroom objects described in the conversation, number of zoo animals recalled, and time to complete the puzzle, failed to correlate with each other. The direction of recall differences was the same, with higher means for first children, but no significant differences were found (see Table 1). The time required to solve the puzzle showed a significant interaction ($F = 5.34$, $df = 1/51$, $p < .05$), with firstborn girls and second-born boys taking longer to solve the puzzle. The puzzle was fortunately the last task assigned, so differential child performance on the puzzle could not have affected the mother's behavior toward her child on any subsequent tasks.

The first general maternal variable examined was the mother's estimate of her child's performance. It was thought that this variable would be reflected in (a) the mother's response to a direct question about her child's likely performance on a concrete task; (b) a measure of complexity of the mother's explanation, with mothers who have higher estimates of their child's performance using more complex and detailed concepts in their explanations; and (c) the mother's structuring of tasks for her

child. If the mother of the second born is more aware of her child's level of understanding, she might be expected to give him a more structured introduction to a task.

Table I
Means and Standard Deviations for Variables
Describing Child's Behavior

Area and Variable	Girls				Boys			
	Firstborn		Second born		Firstborn		Second born	
	M	SD	M	SD	M	SD	M	SD
Performance								
Conversation	4.91	4.08	3.92	3.01	5.80	3.39	4.33	2.87
Picture	9.60	4.63	8.53	3.02	8.38	4.73	7.46	4.14
Puzzle time	3.38	1.33	2.87	1.42	2.42	.90	3.35	1.45
Adoption of responsibility								
Cleanup involvement	3.43	1.28	3.21	1.25	3.30	1.95	2.38	1.43

Mothers estimated their child's performance for both the picture and puzzle tasks. For the picture estimate, there was a barely significant birth-order effect ($F = 3.31$, $df = 1/48$, $p < .10$), with mothers tending to have a higher estimate of the first child's performance; however, a stronger interaction ($F = 5.55$, $df = 1/48$, $p < .05$) indicated that the birth-order difference was contributed by the mother's higher estimate for the first girl than for the second girl (see Table 2). The direction of estimates was reversed for the puzzle, with higher estimates for firstborn boys and second-born girls, and no indication of a birth-order effect. The puzzle differences were not significant.

Two measures were made of the mother's complexity of explanation. For the water tap explanation, a count was made of the number of technical terms used by the mother, for example, "water pressure," "valve," and "cylindrical stopper." For the cartoons, a count was made of the number of different features of the picture described, for example, sizes of cars, number of pieces of the snowman, and of interpretations made by the mother (e.g., "The little dog is copying the big dog."). The two measures of complexity failed to correlate significantly with each other, but the direction of differences for both measures was the same: mothers tended to give a more complex description to the first child. This difference was only significant for the water tap explanation ($F = 4.35$, $df = 1/52$, $p < .05$).

Measures were also made of the mother's structuring of tasks, that is, the amount of information she gave the child about what would happen in a task and what he would be expected to do. Structuring for the pic-

ture and the puzzle surprisingly failed to correlate. There were no significant differences found in structuring the picture task, or agreement in direction of findings for the picture and puzzle. For structuring the puzzle, a strong interaction was found ($F = 9.61$, $df = 1/51$, $p < .01$). Mothers structured the puzzle task more for firstborn girls and second-born boys, those groups that in fact performed less well on the puzzle than the other two groups.

A second general variable thought to correlate with later achievement of the child was the sheer amount of interaction of the mother with the child. This was measured by the amount of time spent in the conversation and explanation and the number of questions asked by the mother in the conversation, cartoons, and explanation tasks. Since time spent in conversation and explanation correlated .47, these variables were combined, and analysis showed no differences for either the grouped or separate data. Standard scores of number of questions were also combined, yielding only a barely significant sex difference ($F = 3.35$, $df = 1/52$, $p < .10$), with mothers tending to ask more questions of their daughters than of their sons (see Table 2).

Table 2
Means and Standard Deviations for Variables
Describing Mother's Behavior

Area and Variable	Girls				Boys			
	Firstborn		Second born		Firstborn		Second born	
	M	SD	M	SD	M	SD	M	SD
Expectations								
Picture estimate	12.13	3.93	9.07	1.83	10.25	2.83	11.00	2.31
Puzzle estimate	3.27	.96	3.60	1.05	3.50	.80	3.00	1.22
Explanation complexity	8.47	5.98	5.40	2.77	7.00	4.30	5.85	2.61
Cartoon complexity	5.27	1.75	5.20	2.48	5.92	3.04	5.00	2.61
Picture structuring	1.93	1.10	2.07	1.10	2.00	1.21	1.92	1.11
Puzzle structuring	2.47	.74	1.80	.86	1.92	.79	2.54	.66
Length of interaction								
Conversation and								
explanation time	4.06	2.16	4.23	1.92	3.38	1.47	4.17	1.17
Number of questions	6.98	3.11	5.98	1.67	5.27	2.22	5.49	1.64
Pressure for success								
Pressure for naming	3.07	.70	2.13	1.13	2.75	.87	2.15	1.14
Pressure for remembering	2.90	.32	1.50	.71	2.17	.71	2.20	.79
Anxious intrusiveness	3.33	1.50	2.47	1.13	2.50	1.00	1.85	.90
Praise and criticism								
Praise	1.27	1.66	1.40	1.82	1.82	1.82	.84	1.02
Tells child he is correct	19.87	8.04	19.20	9.10	17.17	10.47	19.31	9.59
Tells child he is incorrect	3.87	4.85	2.07	2.15	1.33	.98	2.77	3.06

The difference probably proposed most often about achievement socialization of firstborn and later-born children involves the prediction of greater pressures for success and greater parental involvement in the firstborn's performance. The first direct measure of pressure for achievement was pressure for naming, a rating of the speed at which zoo animals were named by the mother and child, that is, whether there was leisurely discussion or whether animals were named rapidly and repeated several times before the end of the period. Pressure for remembering rated the mother's reaction to the child's desire to stop trying to recall the names of animals—whether she allowed him to stop or insisted that he continue until the time was up. The two scales were positively correlated with each other ($r = .30$, $p < .05$), and both showed highly significant birth-order effects (pressure for naming, $F = 8.87$, $df = 1/51$, $p < .01$; pressure for remembering, $F = 8.05$, $df = 1/38$, $p < .01$), with mothers exerting more pressure on firstborns than on second borns. Ns for the pressure for remembering variable were smaller, since not all subjects attempted to stop working on the task. The pressure for remembering variable also showed a significant interaction ($F = 9.76$, $df = 1/38$, $p < .01$), with greater differential pressure for girls than for boys (see Table 2).

More indirect measures of achievement variables were amount of time spent in conversation and explanation, and the number of questions asked by the mother. As described above, no differences were found in interaction time, while mothers showed a tendency to ask more questions of their daughters than their sons, with no birth-order effects.

After doing all coding, raters made an overall judgment of the extent to which the mother seemed to intrude herself into the child's performance in a worried or anxious way. Raters achieved good agreement ($r = .88$) on this variable, and it yielded a significant birth-order effect ($F = 5.92$, $df = 1/51$, $p < .05$), with mothers showing higher anxious intrusiveness for firstborns than for second borns. A significant sex difference was also found ($F = 5.45$, $df = 1/51$, $p < .05$), with mothers exerting more anxious intrusiveness on girls than on boys (see Table 2). The intrusiveness variable was included in intercorrelations for both pressure and help-giving variables. It correlated with conversation time ($r = .34$, $p < .01$); the number of questions asked in the conversation, cartoons, and explanation (rs $= .38$, $.26$, and $.41$, ps $< .01$, $.05$, and $.01$, respectively; the mother's help giving on the picture ($r = .48$, $p < .01$); and on the puzzle ($r = .41$, $p < .01$), even though these last two measures failed to correlate with each other.

A related variable was the extent to which the mother evaluated and reinforced her child's ongoing performance through the use of praise and criticism. If the mothers were more involved in their firstborn's performance, they might be expected to give him more praise and criticism.

Since the number of occurrences of praise and criticism were relatively small, they were initially combined over all tasks except the conversation. The direction of differences for use of criticism was opposite to that of use of praise. The data, however, were confounded by the fact that the second-born girl and firstborn boy had actually performed better on the puzzle task than the firstborn girl and second-born boy. When praise and criticism data from the puzzle task were discarded, the differences for praise were in the same direction, that is, for more praise to the second-born girl and firstborn boy, but not significant. The frequencies of use of criticism were so low that a chi-square test was performed to see whether the four groups differed according to the mothers' use of criticism (see Table 3). There was a slight tendency for mothers of firstborn girls to use criticism more than the other groups. ($\chi^2 = 6.67$, $p < .10$, two-tailed).

A closely related measure, this one taken over all situations except the puzzle, was the number of times the mother told her child that he was correct or incorrect. There were no significant differences in telling the child he was correct, but a significant interaction was found for telling the child he was incorrect ($F = 4.31$, $df = 1/51$, $p < .05$), with the mother more likely to tell the firstborn girl or the second-born boy that he had done something wrong.

Table 3
Chi-Square for Mother's Criticism of Child

	Girls		Boys	
Reaction	First-born	Second-born	First-born	Second-born
Mother criticizes	8	2	2	4
Mother does not criticize	7	13	9	9

Note.— $x^2 = 6.67$, $p < .10$.

Finally, in an attempt to measure the mother's encouragement of her child's responsible behavior, a rating was made of the child's involvement in cleaning up the room. Ratings of cleanup were made from the experimenter's descriptions, with a scale ranging from the mother doing all of the cleanup (low score) to the child doing all of the cleanup (high score). The cleanup scale yielded a significant interaction ($F = 8.39$, $df = 1/47$, $p < .01$), with a larger difference between firstborn and second-born boys in the direction of firstborn boys participating more in the cleanup.

Discussion

The present study showed no tendency for mothers to interact more with firstborns, or to have a general overestimation of the firstborn's ability. Indeed, there was a notable lack of correlation among measures intended to assess the mother's estimate of her child's ability. The mother's behavior appears to be affected more by the nature of the particular task than by some general notion of her child's ability. This finding may not be surprising in view of the fact that subjects were 5 years old at the time of the study; the mothers would have had sufficient time to observe that their children were more successful at some tasks than at others. It seems likely that any generalized overestimate of the firstborn child's ability would be more evident in the mother's behavior toward the infant or very young child than toward the 5 year old.

The strongest birth-order difference among the estimate measures was the mother's tendency to give a more complex technical explanation to the firstborn; on the less technical cartoons, differences were in the same direction, but not significant. Apparently, even if the mother does not show a generalized overestimate of the first child's ability, she nevertheless uses more complex language with the firstborn than the second-born child. Whether she is overrating the firstborn child's ability to understand or simply providing him with better intellectual stimulation than the second-born child is a question for further research.

In considering measures of maternal pressure for success, a comparison of this study's findings with those of Hilton (1967) is of value. She gave mothers differential information about their child's success or failure in order to compare mothers' interactions with firstborn and second-born children on a puzzle task. Hilton reported greater maternal interference with firstborn and only children (grouped together) on several variables: mothers of firstborn and only children were rated as "more involved," were more likely to initiate work on the puzzle task, and gave more task-oriented suggestions and direct help to the firstborn child. While a detailed analysis of maternal help-giving data from the present study is not completed, the measure of overall anxious intrusiveness is highly relevant to the question of maternal interference with the firstborn. Mothers of firstborns were rated as more intrusive than mothers of second borns, with mothers also more intrusive toward girls than boys. Another finding which may be related to interference is that mothers exerted more pressure for achievement on the firstborn in the picture task, just as mothers of firstborns were more likely to initiate the puzzle task in Hilton's study. Results of both studies suggest that mothers are more intrusive into the performance of firstborn than second-born children, although the present study found this accentuated for the firstborn girl. It is possible that the mother's greater interference with the first-

born provides such a readily accessible source of support that the first-born may depend more on others for support in achievement situations. The firstborn's later success in school may be mediated to some extent by his dependency on others for setting standards for his performance.

A major difference in the findings of the two studies, however, is that while Hilton failed to find consistent differences in the mother's behavior as a function of the sex of the child, results of the present study favor the view that maternal behavior toward the first- or second-born child is also influenced by his sex. For example, the firstborn girl seems to have evoked the most extreme responses from the mother. The pressure for remembering variable showed greater differential pressure on the first-born girl as compared to the second-born girl, in addition to a birth-order difference; the mother gave a higher estimate of her firstborn girl's per-formance on the picture; the mother was more likely to tell the first girl she was incorrect, and showed a tendency to be more likely to criticize her; and the mother showed most anxious intrusiveness toward the first-born girl. There is a striking similarity between these findings and those of Cushna (1966), reported by Sutton-Smith and Rosenberg (1970). Cushna's subjects were 16–19-month-old children from middle-class families. When mothers were asked to determine their children's perfor-mance on a number of tasks, mothers were found to be more involved in influencing the performance of firstborn children, but in different ways for boys and girls. Mothers were more supportive and cautious in direct-ing their boys, but more demanding, exacting, and intrusive toward their firstborn girls.

The second-born girl seems to be shown both less criticism and less pressure to achieve than the firstborn girl. Her mother expected less from her on the picture task, and less often told her that she was incor-rect. The firstborn boy shared with the firstborn girl greater maternal pressure for achievement, but only on the first part of the picture task; the birth-order difference on the pressure for remembering variable was contributed chiefly by the mother's pressure on the firstborn girl. The mother gave her firstborn boy a more complex explanation and showed greater anxious intrusiveness toward the firstborn than the second-born boy, but showed no greater intrusiveness toward the firstborn boy than toward the second-born girl. The direction of differences was also for the firstborn boy to be told he was incorrect less often than was the second-born boy. The mother's pressure for the firstborn boy's achieve-ment and intrusiveness into his performance thus seems somewhat tempered in comparison with her pressures on the firstborn girl. Finally, the second-born boy seems to have received less pressure and inter-ference from the mother than the firstborn boy, but was also more likely to be told that he was incorrect than the firstborn boy.

It is interesting to speculate about the more extreme pressure and intrusiveness exhibited toward the firstborn girl in this study. One possibility is that of all ordinal positions, the mother most closely identifies with the firstborn girl, since the firstborn girl most resembles the mother at any given time. This could lead to both greater pressure for achievement and to less satisfaction with the child's performance, since it is difficult to fulfill high expectations. The mother may also feel something of an attraction toward the firstborn boy that would temper her behavior toward him, and a sense of rivalry toward the firstborn girl, in a role reversal of the Oedipal triangle. Her feelings, both positive and negative, may be less extreme toward the second-born girl or boy. It was found in a previous study (Rothbart & Maccoby, 1966) that parents tended to respond more permissively toward a child's voice of the opposite sex; this differential reaction may be stronger for the firstborn in the family, and less accentuated in the parent's reaction to the later born.

An additional finding of interest is that while firstborn boys were involved in the cleanup to as great an extent as either first- or second-born girls, the second-born boy was less likely to be involved in the cleanup. Cleaning up, while a measure of adoption of responsibility, is an activity that is also highly sex typed in the feminine direction. The differences found may reflect a ceiling effect in the behavior of girls which could mask a higher adoption of responsibility for the firstborn to be found in a more neutral (or masculine) activity. In addition, the findings may reflect the greater masculine identification of the second-born boy in an all-male family that has been reported elsewhere (Rosenberg & Sutton-Smith, 1964).

It should be noted that the findings of the present study are very limited. Only two-child, same-sex families were involved, with only *mother*-child interaction observed. The value of observing fathers interacting with their children seems apparent from the Sex × Birth Order interactions found in this study. We might expect that in such research, the firstborn boy would occupy the extreme position occupied by the firstborn girl in the present study. It would also be of value to include cross-sex sibling pairs and families of a larger size than two children, although with needed controls for size of family, sex, and spacing of siblings, such research becomes very difficult.

References

Altus, W. D. Birth order and its sequelae. *Science*, 1966, 151, 44–49.
Bayer, A. E. Birth order and college attendance. *Journal of Marriage and Family Living*, 1966, 28, 480–484.

Bayley, N. Comparisons of mental and motor test scores for ages 1 – 15 months by sex, birth order, race, geographical location, and education of parents. *Child Development*, 1965, 36, 379 – 411.

Bossard, J. H. S. Family modes of expression. *American Sociological Review*, 1945, 10, 226 – 237.

Cushna, B. Agency and birth order differences in very early childhood. Paper presented at the meeting of the American Psychological Association, New York, September 1966.

Davis, A. American status systems and the socialization of the child. *American Sociological Review*, 1941, 6, 345 – 354.

Hilton, I. Differences in the behavior of mothers toward first- and later-born children. *Journal of Personality and Social Psychology*, 1967, 7, 282 – 290.

Koch, H. L. The relation of "Primary Mental Abilities" in five- and six-year olds to sex of child and characteristics of his sibling. *Child Development*, 1954, 25, 209 – 223.

McArthur, C. Personalities of first and second children. *Psychiatry*, 1956, 19, 47 – 54.

Phillips, E. L. Cultural vs. intropsychic factors in childhood behavior problem referrals. *Journal of Clinical Psychology*, 1956, 12, 400 – 401.

Rosen, B. C. Family structure and achievement motivation. *American Sociological Review*, 1961, 26, 574 – 585.

Rosenberg, B. G., & Sutton-Smith, B. Ordinal position and sex-role identification. *Genetic Psychology Monographs*, 1964, 70, 297 – 328.

Rothbart, M. K. *Birth order and mother-child interaction.* (Doctoral dissertation, Stanford University) Ann Arbor, Mich.: University Microfilms, 1967. No. 67-7961.

Rothbart, M. K., & Maccoby, E. E. Parents' differential reactions to sons and daughters. *Journal of Personality and Social Psychology*, 1966, 4, 237 – 243.

Sampson, E. E. The study of ordinal position: Antecedents and outcomes. In B. Maher (Ed.), *Progress in experimental personality research.* Vol. 2. New York: Academic Press, 1965.

Schachter, S. Birth order, eminence, and higher education. *American Sociological Review*, 1963, 28, 757 – 767.

Sutton-Smith, B., Roberts, J. M., & Rosenberg, B. G. Sibling associations and role involvement. *Merrill-Palmer Quarterly of Behavior and Development*, 1964, 10, 25 – 38.

Sutton-Smith, B., & Rosenberg, B. G. *The sibling.* New York: Holt, Rinehart & Winston, 1970.

4.3   Social Class Differences in Maternal Teaching Strategies and Speech Patterns

Helen L. Bee,
Lawrence F. Van Egeren,
Ann Pytkowicz Streissguth
Barry A. Nyman,
Maxine S. Leckie
University of Washington

Many studies of children and parents are based on the assumption that parents, particularly mothers, mediate between the child and the outer world, and in so doing transfer to the child the benefits and limitations of their own personalities, conflicts, and cognitive and emotional resources. While most research within this framework has dealt with personality development, there is recent evidence that the quality of mother-child interactions influences the child's cognitive development as well (cf. Bee, 1967; Bing, 1963; Witkin, Dyk, Faterson, Goodenough, & Karp, 1962). Bing (1963) found differential patterns of children's cognitive ability related to maternal behavior in a structured interaction situation and to mothers' reports of child-rearing practices, while Bee (1967) demonstrated a relationship between a child's susceptibility to distraction and certain features of the parents' interactions with him.

Distinctive mother-child relationships have also been used recently to account for social class differences in children's cognitive abilities. Hess (1968), for example, contended that children from disadvantaged homes are not *unsocialized* when they reach school, but are socialized in a way that fosters substandard learning. Hess and Shipman (1965, 1967, 1968) proposed that two of the major dimensions of social class differences related to children's learning are the maternal speech and the maternal teaching strategies.

In comparing teaching strategies of middle- and lower-class black mothers with their 4-year-old children, Hess and Shipman (1965) found that middle-class mothers used more direct and efficient teaching strategies than lower-class mothers. The quality of the mother's teaching strategy was in turn related to the level of the child's cognitive functioning. In fact, the maternal teaching behavior was as good a predictor of the child's cognitive behavior as IQ measures.

The importance of maternal speech was first emphasized by Bernstein (1961). He postulated the presence of two "linguistic modes" used for

Reprinted from *Developmental Psychology,* 1969, *1*, No. 6, 726-734. Copyright © 1969 by the American Psychological Association and reproduced by permission.

communication and organization of experience. Lower-class parents, he suggested, typically use a "public" language mode, characterized by a very rigid and restricted grammatical usage. Middle-class parents typically use a "formal mode," in which language is used more flexibly, exploiting its structural possibilities for richer and more varied communication. The existence of such social class differences in language modes was later demonstrated by Bernstein (1962a, 1962b), and by Hess and Shipman (1965, 1967, 1968), who found that middle-class parents used more complex syntax, longer sentences, more qualifying (discriminating) modifiers, and fewer personal pronouns. Hess and Shipman also found a connection between the linguistic mode used by the mother and the child's level of cognitive functioning.

The present study was designed to provide a general replication of earlier findings on social class differences in maternal language behavior and teaching strategies, and to explore further the dimensions of mother-child interactions that may be associated with the child's cognitive development. To do so, mother-child interactions were observed in both structured and unstructured settings and the mother's behavior language was studied in an interview.

The research reported is part of a larger project in which social class differences in both mother-child interaction and children's cognitive functioning were studied as a starting point for an evaluation of a Head Start program. The present report deals only with the social class differences in mother-child interactions and maternal language. Subsequent publications will report on social class differences in children's cognitive functioning, patterns of mother-child interaction, and the impact of Head Start experience.

Method

Subjects

The subjects were 114 children (aged 4-0 to 5-5) and their mothers, 76 lower social class families (37 boys and 39 girls), and 38 middle-class families (22 boys and 14 girls).

Half of the lower-class sample eventually entered a Head Start program, and were selected from the list of applicants at six Head Start centers. The remaining 38 lower-class families were obtained through a variety of sources: (a) families who had applied to Head Start but were ineligible either because they lived outside the areas serviced by the local program, or because their income was somewhat over the Office of Economic Opportunity poverty guidelines, and (b) families living in public housing projects who had 4-year-olds eligible for Head Start but who had not applied.

The middle-class group consisted of University of Washington Staff and student families. Thirty-eight volunteer families with children of the appropriate age were located by means of a letter sent to all graduate students at the University.

A comparison of the two social class groups on a number of demographic variables appears in Table 1. The two groups differed in the ways that are typically used to define social class. Middle-class families had significantly higher income, the mothers were better educated, and there were fewer children. In addition, fathers were present in all but two of the middle-class homes, but in only 34 of 76 lower-class homes.

Two features of the middle-class sample require some special comment. First, middle-class families were intentionally selected whose educational level and academic achievement motivation was higher than for the typical middle-class family. This particular comparison group was chosen because we were interested in familial variables related to (and predictive of) school success in children, and wished to maximize the difference in expected school success. Second, the middle-class sample was entirely white, while the lower-class sample was two-thirds black. This was a direct and unavoidable result of the other selection criteria, since approximately two thirds of the local Head Start children are black, and almost 100% of the University graduate students are white. The reader should bear in mind that when we refer to the "middle-class" sample, we refer to "highly-educated white middle-class" families—the families whose children typically excel in school.

Table 1
Comparison of Lower-class and Middle-class Groups on Demographic Variables

Variable	Lower class[a] $\overline{X}$	Middle class[b] $\overline{X}$	t
Family income	$4,594	$6,852	4.97**
Mother's education in yr.	11.46	14.89	8.01**
No. siblings or other children in home	3.44	2.55	2.75*
No. adults in home	1.63	2.00	3.33*
Child's age in mo.	53.238	53.895	<1.00

[a] $N = 76$.
[b] $N = 38$.
*$p < .01$.
**$p < .001$.

Procedures and scores derived

Each mother and child was seen in a four-part session lasting approximately 1½ hours. The pair was first brought into the "waiting room" where their interaction was observed and recorded (by one of two observers) for 10 minutes. The mother was then interviewed while the child was given a series of 13 brief tests of cognitive and motivational behavior. The mother and child were then reunited for a series of problem-solving interactions, administered by one of two experimenters, in which the mother's teaching strategies were observed and recorded. Only the interactional and interview behavior are presented in this article; the details of the individual tests given to the children are described elsewhere (Bee, Nyman, Pytkowitz, Sarason, & Van Egeren, 1968).

Waiting room. The 12 × 13 foot waiting room was furnished with a couch, armchair, and magazine table in one corner, with toys (paper and crayons, mailbox, jack-in-the-box, trucks and cars, toy piano, knock-out bench, and small rubber animals and people) scattered throughout the room on small tables and on the floor. The floor of the room was marked into equal quadrants so that the child's movement could be recorded. An observer watching through a one-way mirror recorded mother and child verbalizations in coded categories. Every 15 seconds, the observer also scored the mother's level of attention to her child in one of four categories and recorded the child's movement about the room and from one toy to another. The observation was terminated after 10 minutes and the observer, using notes and a tape recording of the interaction, made final scorings in each category.

A total of 20 scores were derived from the waiting room situation. Verbal responses by the mother were scored in one of seven categories, as below. The percentage of agreement for each category, based on 12 families scored by two independent observers, is given in parentheses.

1. Control: An attempt by the mother to stop or modify the child's activity in preemptory fashion. (85%)
2. Suggestion: A helpful statement soliciting a change or modification of the child's activity. (85%)
3. Information: A statement directed at informing or giving facts. (83%)
4. Question: A statement directed at asking, interrogating, or inquiring. (88%)
5. Approval: A statement giving a favorable opinion of the child's activity or product. (85%)
6. Ignoring: Lack of response when the child made a specific bid for help or attention. (91%)

7. Disapproval: A statement giving an unfavorable opinion of the child's activity or product. (85%)

The child's verbalizations and movements were scored in one of nine categories, as below.

8. General seeking: A general bid for help, assistance, or attention. (89%)
9. Question: A request for specific information. (84%)
10. Demand: A statement from the child demanding an action from the mother. (88%)
11. Information: A statement giving information gratuitously. (85%)
12. Rejection: A rejection of the mother's control, suggestion, or question statement. (100%)
13. Acceptance: Acceptance of a control, suggestion, or question statement from the mother. (78%)
14. Ignoring: No response to a control, suggestion, or question from the mother. (85%)
15. Toy shifts: Movement from one toy to another.
16. Space shifts: Movement from one quadrant of the room to another.

The mother was also scored, every 15 seconds, in one of the following four categories, according to her level of attention to the child.

17. Level 0, no attention: Mother did not look up or speak to the child. (80%)
18. Level 1, occasional but brief attention: Mother glanced at, but did not speak to the child. (65%)
19. Level 2, moderate attention: Mother looked at the child for a substantial portion of the period, or spoke occasionally. (80%)
20. Full attention: Mother looked at the child continuously, and may have spoken in addition. (77%)

Raw scores (category frequencies) were converted to rate-per-minute scores for each category.

The interrater agreement for the verbalization and attention categories, as shown above, ranged from 65 to 100% with only three categories falling below 80%. No reliability estimates were obtained for space or toy shifts.

Problem solving.   Mother and child were brought together in a separate room for the problem-solving interaction. Two problems, a "toy-rearrangement" task and a "house-building" task, were administered, but because the toy-rearrangement task proved to be too easy for many

of the children, only the house-building task was scored and analyzed. For the house-building task the mother and child were seated on one side of a table with the experimenter on the other side. The experimenter showed the child a toy house constructed out of 17 blocks, with seven different shapes and four colors. The child was given an identical 17-block set and instructed to build a house that was just the same as the model. The mother was then told: "You can give as much or as little help as you like, whatever you think will help—to do his best." Mother and child were then allowed to work on the house until the task was completed. If no progress was being made and the mother was not making any effort to encourage the child to continue, the session was terminated at 10 minutes.

Verbal interactions were recorded on tape and transcribed, with all scoring of verbalizations by mother and child done from the typed transcripts. Nonverbal intrusive behavior by the mother was recorded by the experimenter at the time of the interaction.

Each of the mother's verbalizations was scored in 1 of 11 content categories, but because many categories of verbalization did not occur frequently enough for comparison, or because they were not task relevant, the analysis presented here relates to only 4 major verbal categories, and 1 nonverbal category. As before, the percentage of agreement, based on 92 families scored by two independent raters, is given in parentheses.

1. Nonquestion suggestion: A statement indicating what the mother wants the child to do next (e.g., "Find a yellow one like this."). (89%)
2. Question suggestion: Suggestion, as above, but stated in interrogative form (e.g., "Where does this yellow one go?"). (91%)
3. Positive feedback: An expression of approval about what the child had already done, or general approval of the child (e.g., "Good."). (90%)
4. Negative feedback: An expression of disapproval about what the child had already done, or general disapproval of the child (e.g., "That's not too good."). (81%)
5. Nonverbal intrusion: Placement of a block or other physical problem solving such as moving the model, or handing the child a block to use.

All suggestions from the mother, whether they were stated in interrogative form or not, were also scored on a 3-point scale of specificity:

6. Level 1: Orienting suggestions, focusing strategies, suggestions that restrict the attention to some major segment of the task (e.g.,

"Look at the lady's house." "Let's start on the front."). (85%)

7. Level 2: Suggestions about specific pieces, or specific locations on the house, but not both (e.g., "Find a yellow one like this."). (73%)
8. Level 3: Solutions. Suggestions indicating both which piece was to be used and where it was to be placed (e.g., "Put that one over here."). (75%)

Of the seven child-verbalization categories, those that occurred with sufficient frequency to be analyzed were:

9. Acceptance: A verbal acceptance of a suggestion from the mother. (71%)
10. Rejection: A verbal rejection of a suggestion from the mother. (52%)
11. Dependency bids: A verbal bid for help, attention, or approval. (84%)

The responses in each category were summed for each mother and child. Since the amount of time spent on the task was variable, raw scores were converted to rate-per-minute scores.

All protocols were scored from the transcripts by both experimenters, disagreements were discussed, and a common score obtained. Percentage of agreement, as reported above, ranged from 73 to 91% for the maternal behavior categories, and from 52 to 84% for the child-behavior categories. No reliability estimate is available for nonverbal intrusions since they were scored only by the experimenter who administered the tests.

Interview.   The 45-minute interview with the mother included a biographical data sheet, 26 standard open-ended questions, and 4 role-playing questions. The analysis of syntactical features of the mothers' speech was based on the first 5 open-ended questions, and only they will be of concern here. These questions asked the mother to describe her child, to indicate the "best" thing about him, the things about him that were of most concern to her; what was the most important thing she thought she could give to or do for her child; and what she tried to teach him.

The analysis of the mother's speech, based on transcriptions of the interview, yielded five scores:

1. Quantity of speech: total number of words spoken.
2. Mean sentence length: total number of words divided by the total number of complete sentences.
3. Adjective/verb quotient: total number of adjectives divided by the total number of verbs.

4. Syntactic complexity: number of subordinate clauses divided by the number of sentences.
5. Percentage of personal pronouns: number of personal pronouns divided by the total number of words.

Since scoring of the speech sample involved simple counting procedures, no reliability estimates were calculated.

Results

Waiting room

In comparison to lower-class mothers, middle-class mothers were less controlling, less disapproving, and gave more information to their children in the waiting room. Middle-class mothers also gave their children more attention; they were scored more frequently at Attention Level 2, and less frequently at Attention Level 1. Middle-class children, in comparison to lower-class children, were lower in acceptance of controls and questions, higher in spontaneous information statements, and lower on both toy and space shifts.

Problem solving

Comparisons of the two groups indicated first that the middle-class mothers and children spent significantly more time on the house-building task than did the lower-class mothers and children. Second, the middle-class mothers' suggestions to their children were less specific than the suggestions given by lower-class mothers, and in comparison to lower-class mothers, middle-class mothers gave more suggestions in the form of questions. Finally, the middle-class mothers more often told their children what they were doing correctly rather than what they were doing wrong. Middle-class children did not differ from their lower-class peers in their reactions to or requests for help.

Interview

Significant social class differences were obtained on all five measures of maternal speech. Middle-class mothers used more words, longer sentences, greater syntactic complexity, a higher adjective-verb quotient, and a lower percentage of personal pronouns.

Differences in maternal behavior associated with race of mother and sex of child

Since the lower-class group included both blacks and whites, while the middle-class group was entirely white, the possibility exists that race rather than social class accounts for the differences in behavior described above. In addition, there were differing numbers of boys and

girls in the various racial and social class groups. To assess both effects, two-way analyses of variance were performed on each variable described above, with sex of child and a combination of racial and social class groups as the two between-subjects variables. Lower-class blacks were compared with lower-class whites and middle-class whites.

Main effects on the race-social class comparison were obtained for 12 variables, but follow-up analyses showed that the differences were clearly racial in only four instances. That is, in only four cases were the two white groups equivalent, and both significantly different from the lower-class black group. Black mothers were significantly lower than both white groups on rate of positive feedback, question suggestions, and total interaction in the problem-solving session. Black children were significantly lower on information statements in the waiting-room situation. In the case of total interaction in the problem-solving session, the differences are somewhat misleading, since there were also differences between the groups in the total time spent on the problem. When the mean *rate* of interaction was determined for each group, the white lower-class group showed the highest rate (16.1 statements per minute), with the lower-class black group the lowest (12.1 statements per minute).

In addition to those variables on which clear racial differences were obtained, there were four on which all groups differed from each other. On three of these (mother's suggestions at Specificity Level 1, mother's physical intrusiveness, and child's bids for help during problem solving) the differences were such that the lower-class black group was lowest, followed in order by the lower-class white and the middle-class white groups. On one variable (mother's rate of negative feedback), all groups differed, but in this instance it was the lower-class white group that showed the highest rate of negative feedback, followed in turn by the lower-class black and middle-class white groups. On one additional variable (mother's suggestions at Specificity Level 2) lower-class white mothers differed from both remaining groups.

In no instance was a main effect of sex of child obtained. However, sex of child interacted with the racial-social class breakdown on 14 variables. The pattern of interaction varied greatly from one variable to another, and there was no systematic effect to be noted. In some instances the social class or racial differences were more marked for boys, in some instances for girls, with neither the mother-child interaction situation nor the type of variable differentiating the two types of pattern.

Discussion

The data presented here provide a clear and consistent portrait of social class differences in maternal behavior. Middle-class mothers, regard-

less of the situation, used more instruction, less physical intrusion, less negative feedback, and were generally more in tune with the child's individual needs and qualities. Their speech patterns were also notably more complex than those of the lower-class mothers. Several specific features of the results deserve separate comment.

First, it is clear from the analysis of maternal speech that there were social class differences in linguistic codes of the type described by Bernstein (1961, 1962a, 1962b) for a British sample and by Hess and Shipman (1965, 1967, 1968) for a Midwest black sample. The speech of middle-class mothers, in the present study, was similar on all five language measures to what Bernstein has referred to as the "formal" or "elaborated" mode. The fact that these differences were related to social class rather than race, taken together with previous findings by Hess and Shipman and by Bernstein, suggests that social class differences in linguistic style are stable and pervasive.

The second major portion of the results concerns the maternal teaching strategies in the problem-solving setting. The strategy used by many middle-class mothers on the house-building task seems to be optimal in a number of respects. The middle-class mother tended to allow her child to work at his own pace, offered many general structuring suggestions on how to search for a solution to the problem, and told the child what he was doing that was correct. She allowed the child to take his time and seldom worked on the house herself. Such a procedure seemed to encourage the child to explore the problem on his own and did not focus attention on his failures. The general structure offered by the mother may help the child to acquire learning sets (strategies) that will generalize to future problem-solving situations. In contrast, the lower-class mother as a rule did not behave in ways that would encourage the child to attend to the basic features of the problem. Her suggestions were highly specific, did not emphasize basic problem-solving strategies, and seldom required reply from the child. Indeed, she often deprived the child of the opportunity to solve the problem on his own by her nonverbal intrusions into the problem-solving activity. In the use of such a strategy, there is very little demand made on the child's capacities to respond, and it is difficult to imagine that the child learns much from such an interaction that would generalize to other problem-solving settings.

This analysis of the problem-solving interaction also suggests the importance of certain new types of dependent variables. In particular, the division of the form of suggestions into questions and nonquestions appears to be a potentially fruitful approach. Certainly the implications for the child of a predominantly interrogative style, as opposed to an imperative style, are substantial, since questions provoke thought and

verbal replies, while imperative statements generally demand only a specific action.

The third major source of data in the present study was the unstructured waiting-room situation. During the 10-minute wait, the interactions of lower-class mothers and their children were more negative and restrictive than the interactions of middle-class mothers and children. Lower-class mothers were less attentive and made more controlling and disapproving statements to the child. This greater control and disapproval of lower-class mothers is consistent with findings from previous studies of social class differences in child-rearing practices, summarized by Bronfenbrenner (1958). In addition, the negative-restrictive pattern in the waiting room also bears some similarity to behavior in the problem-solving setting, where lower-class mothers were more critical and controlling and appeared to be less sensitive to the child's rhythm of activity.

Thus far we have discussed the differences in maternal behavior as though they represent relatively enduring aspects of the different environments surrounding the middle- and lower-class child. This general interpretation rests on two important assumptions. The first is that the behavior of the mothers in the laboratory is not atypical of their interaction with their children at home. The second is that the children, by their own behavior, did not place radically different response demands on the two groups of mothers.

Concerning the first assumption, it was obvious to the interviewers and observers that to some extent the mothers and children were on their "good" behavior in the laboratory. And yet we were also impressed with the spontaneity, cooperativeness, and relaxed and frank attitude of most mothers in both groups. We could detect no obvious systematic differences between the two groups of mothers in situational anxiety or genuine involvement in the tasks set for them.

Concerning the second assumption, the two groups of children differed little in the problem-solving situation. The lower-class child's greater hyperactivity (space shifts and toy shifts) in the waiting room may have made some contribution to the lower-class mother's high rate of controlling and disapproving statements there, but the lower-class mother's tendency toward control in the problem-solving setting, where the children differed little, suggests that the greater tendency toward control of the lower-class mother is not simply a response to a more-difficult-to-manage child.

Finally, although a discussion of the social class differences in the test performance of the children in our sample will be presented in a later paper, a further word should be said about the implications of the social

class differences in maternal behavior obtained here. Our findings, as those of Hess and Shipman, provide evidence of an impoverished language environment and ineffectual teaching strategies experienced by the lower-class child. Such a child may learn a good deal about what *not* to do, or at least about global rules of conduct, but he may not be well equipped with the language tools or learning sets required for a systematic approach to the analysis of problems. He has not, judging from our results, been encouraged to learn general techniques of problem solving, and he has not been exposed to the highly differentiated language structure that is most suitable for verbally mediated analysis of the environment. If the mother's role as a teacher is as important for the child's cognitive functioning as it would appear to be, then it is not surprising that there are large social class differences in the measured cognitive functioning of children, and in their ultimate school performance.

References

Bee, H. L. Parent-child interaction and distractibility in 9-year-old children. *Merrill-Palmer Quarterly*, 1967, **13**, 175 – 190.

Bee, H. L., Nyman, B. A., Pytkowicz, A. R., Sarason, I. G., & Van Egeren, L. A study of cognitive and motivational variables in lower and middle class preschool children: An approach to the evaluation of the impact of Head Start, Volume I. University of Washington Social Change Evaluation Project, Contract 1375, Office of Economic Opportunity, 1968.

Bernstein, B. Social class and linguistic development: A theory of social learning. In A. H. Halsey, J. Floud, & C. A. Anderson (Eds.), *Education, economy, and society*. New York: Free Press, 1961.

Bernstein, B. Linguistic codes, hesitation phenomena, and intelligence. *Language and Speech*, 1962, **5**, 31 – 46. (a)

Bernstein, B. Social class, linguistic codes, and grammatical elements. *Language and Speech*, 1962, **5**, 221 – 240. (b)

Bing, E. Effect of child rearing practices on development of differential cognitive abilities. *Child Development*, 1963, **34**, 631 – 648.

Bronfenbrenner, U. Socialization and social class through time and space. In E. E. Maccoby, T. M. Newcomb, & E. L. Hartley (Eds.), *Readings in social psychology*. (3rd ed.) New York: Holt, 1958.

Hess, R. D. Early education as socialization. In R. D. Hess & R. M. Bear (Eds.). *Early education*. Chicago: Aldine, 1968.

Hess, R. D., & Shipman, V. Early experience and the socialization of cognitive modes in children. *Child Development*, 1965, **34**, 869 – 886.

Hess, R. D., & Shipman, V. Cognitive elements in maternal behavior. In

J. P. Hill (Ed.), *Minnesota symposium on child psychology*. Vol. 1. Minneapolis: University of Minnesota Press, 1967.

Hess, R. D., & Shipman, V. Maternal influences upon early learning: The cognitive environments of urban pre-school children. In R. D. Hess & R. M. Bear (Eds.), *Early education*. Chicago: Aldine, 1968.

Witkin, H. A., Dyk, R. B., Faterson, H. F., Goodenough, D. R., & Karp, S. A. *Psychological differentiation*. New York: Wiley, 1962.

4.4 Some Effects of Punishment on Children's Behavior

Ross D. Parke

A casual review of magazines, advice to parent columns, or (until recently) the psychological journals quickly reveals that there is considerable controversy concerning the usefulness of punishment as a technique for controlling the behavior of young children. For many years, the study of the impact of punishment on human behavior was restricted to armchair speculation and theorizing. In part, this paucity of information was due to the belief that punishment produced only a temporary suppression of behavior and that many undesirable side-effects were associated with its use. Moreover, ethical and practical considerations prohibited the employment of intense punishment in research with human subjects—especially children—thus contributing to this information gap.

Through both studies of child rearing and laboratory investigations, however, some of the effects of punishment on children's social behavior are being determined. It is the main aim of this paper to review these findings and assess the current status of our knowledge concerning the effects of punishment.

Timing of Punishment

A number of years ago at Harvard's Laboratory of Human Development, Black, Solomon and Whiting (1960) undertook a study of the ef-

Reprinted with permission from *The Young Child: Reviews of Research*, Vol. II, pp. 264–283. Copyright © 1972 by The National Association for the Education of Young Children, 1834 Connecticut Ave. N.W., Washington D.C. 20009.

fectiveness of punishment for producing "resistance to temptation" in a group of young puppies. Two training conditions were used. In one case, the dogs were swatted with a rolled-up newspaper just *before* they touched a bowl of forbidden horsemeat. The remaining pups were punished only *after* eating a small amount of the taboo food. On subsequent tests—even though deprived of food—the animals punished as they approached the food showed greater avoidance of the prohibited meat than did animals punished after committing the taboo act. This study is the prototype of a number of studies recently carried out with children, and it illustrates the importance of the *timing* of the punishment for producing effective control over children's behavior.

In recent studies of the effects of timing of punishment on children's behavior, the rolled-up newspaper has been replaced by a verbal rebuke or a loud noise, and an attractive toy stands in place of the horsemeat. For example, Walters, Parke and Cane (1965) presented subjects with pairs of toys—one attractive and one unattractive—on a series of nine trials. The six- to eight-year-old boys were punished by a verbal rebuke, "No, that's for the other boy," when they chose the attractive toy. As in the dog study, one group of children was punished as they approached the attractive toy, but before they actually touched it. For the remaining boys, punishment was delivered only after they had picked up the critical toy and held it for two seconds. Following the punishment training session, the subjects were seated before a display of three rows of toys similar to those used in the training period and were reminded not to touch the toys. The resistance-to-deviation test consisted of a 15-minute period during which the boy was left alone with an unattractive German-English dictionary and, of course, the prohibited toys. The extent to which the subject touched the toys in the absence of the external agent was recorded by an observer located behind a one-way screen. The children's data paralleled the puppy results: the early punished children touched the taboo toys less than did the boys punished late in the response sequence. This timing of punishment effect has been replicated by a number of investigators (Aronfreed & Reber, 1965; Parke & Walters, 1967; Cheyne & Walters, 1969).

Extensions of this experimental model indicate that this finding is merely one aspect of a general relation: *the longer the delay between the initiation of the act and the onset of punishment, the less effective the punishment for producing response inhibition.* This proposition is based on a study in which the effects of four delay of punishment positions were examined (Aronfreed, 1965). Using a design similar to Walters, Parke and Cane (1965), Aronfreed punished one group of children as they reached for the attractive toy. Under a second condition, the subject was permitted to pick up the attractive toy and was punished at the

apex of the lifting movement. Under a third condition, six seconds elapsed after the child picked up the toy before punishment was delivered. In the final group, six seconds after the child picked up the toy he was asked to describe the toy and only then was punishment administered. The time elapsing between the experimenter's departure until the child made the first deviation steadily decreased as the time between the initiation of the act and the delivery of punishment increased.

Punishment may be less effective in facilitating learning as well as less effective in facilitating resistance to temptation if the punishment is delayed. Using a learning task in which errors were punished by the presentation of a loud noise combined with the loss of a token, Walters (1964) found that punishment delivered immediately after the error speeded learning more than did punishment which was delayed 10 seconds or 30 seconds.

In addition, the importance of timing of punishment may be contingent on a variety of other features of punishment administration, such as the intensity of the punishment, the nature of the agent-child relationship, and the kind of verbal rationale accompanying the punishment. The effects of these variables will be examined in the following sections.

Intensity of Punishment

It is generally assumed that as the intensity of punishment increases the amount of inhibition will similarly increase. It is difficult to study severity of punishment in the laboratory due to the obvious ethical limitations upon using potentially harmful stimuli in experimentation with children. Until recently most of the evidence concerning the relative effectiveness of different intensities of punishment derived either from animal studies or from childrearing interview studies.

The animal studies (e.g., Church, 1963), in which electric shock is most often used as the punishing stimulus, have supported the conclusion that more complete suppression of the punished response results as the intensity of the punishment increases. On the other hand, the childrearing data relating to the effects of intensity on children's behavior have not yielded clear cut conclusions. It is difficult, however, to assess the operation of specific punishment variables using rating scales of parent behavior because most of these scales confound several aspects of punishment, such as frequency, intensity, and consistency (Walters & Parke, 1967). Differences between scale points may, therefore, be due to the impact of any of these variables, either alone or in combination.

Recent laboratory studies have avoided some of these short-comings and have yielded less equivocal conclusions concerning the effects of

punishment intensity on children's behavior. Using the resistance-to-deviation approach already described, Parke and Walters (1967) punished one group of boys with a soft tone (65 decibels) when they chose an attractive but prohibited toy. A second group heard a loud tone (96 decibels) when they chose the attractive toy. In the subsequent temptation test, children who were exposed to the loud punisher were less likely to touch the prohibited toys in the experimenter's absence than were boys exposed to a less intense version of the tone. This finding has been confirmed using a noxious buzzer as the punishing stimulus (Cheyne & Walters, 1969; Parke, 1969).

This research has also yielded some suggestive evidence concerning the impact of intensity variations on other aspects of punishment such as timing (Parke, 1969). Under conditions of high intensity punishment, the degree of inhibition produced by early and late punishment was similar. Under low intensity conditions, however, the early punished subjects showed significantly greater inhibition than did subjects punished late in the response sequence. Thus, timing of punishment may be less important under conditions of high intensity punishment. However, the generality of this conclusion is limited by the narrow range of delay of punishment intervals that have been investigated. Perhaps when punishment is delayed over a number of hours, for example, this relationship would not hold. Further research is clearly required.

Other research has indicated, however, that high intensity punishment may not always lead to better inhibition or be more effective in controlling children's behavior than low intensity punishment. A study by Aronfreed and Leff (1963), who investigated the effects of intensity of punishment on response inhibition in a temptation situation, illustrates this possibility. Six- and seven-year old boys were given a series of choice trials involving two toys roughly comparable in attractiveness, but which differed along certain stimulus dimensions that the child could use to distinguish between punished and nonpunished choices. For two groups, a simple discrimination between red and yellow toys was required; the other groups of subjects were exposed to a complex discrimination between toys which represented passive containers and toys with active internal mechanisms. The punishment consisted of verbal disapproval (no), deprivation of candy, and a noise. The intensity and quality of the noise were varied in order to control the noxiousness of the punishment. Following training, each child was left alone with a pair of toys of which the more attractive one was similar in some respects to the toys that had been associated with punishment during the training procedure. Provided that the discrimination task was relatively simple, response inhibition was more frequently observed among children who received high intensity punishment. When the discrimination task was difficult,

however, "transgression" was more frequent among children under the high intensity punishment than among children who received the milder punishment. Thus, the complex discrimination task combined with high intensity punishment probably created a level of anxiety too high for adaptive learning to occur. When subtle discriminations are involved, or when the child is uncertain as to the appropriate response, high intensity punishment may create emotional levels that clearly interfere with learning and therefore retard inhibition of undesirable behaviors.

Nature of the Relationship Between the Agent and Recipient of Punishment

The nature of the relationship between the socializing agent and the child is a significant determinant of the effectiveness of punishment. It is generally assumed that punishment will be a more effective means of controlling behavior when this relationship is close and affectional than when it is relatively impersonal. This argument assumes that any disciplinary act may involve in varying degrees at least two operations—the presentation of a negative reinforcer and the withdrawal or withholding of a positive one (Bandura & Walters, 1963). Physical punishment may, in fact, achieve its effect partly because it symbolizes the withdrawal of approval or affection. Hence, punishment should be a more potent controlling technique when used by a nurturant parent or teacher.

Sears, Maccoby and Levin (1957) provided some evidence in favor of this proposition. Mothers who were rated as warm and affectionate and who made relatively frequent use of physical punishment were more likely to report that they found spanking to be an effective means of discipline. In contrast, cold, hostile mothers who made frequent use of physical punishment were more likely to report that spanking was ineffective. Moreover, according to the mothers' reports, spanking was more effective when it was administered by the warmer of the two parents.

A study by Parke and Walters (1967) confirmed these child-rearing findings in a controlled laboratory situation. In this investigation, the nature of the experimenter-child relationship was varied in two interaction sessions prior to the administration of punishment. One group of boys experienced a 10-minute period of positive interaction with a female experimenter on two successive days. Attractive constructional materials were provided for the children and, as they played with them, the female experimenter provided encouragement and help and warmly expressed approval of their efforts. A second group of boys played with relatively unattractive materials in two 10-minute sessions while the experimenter sat in the room without interacting with the children. Fol-

lowing these interaction sessions, the children underwent punishment training involving verbal rebuke and a noxious noise for choosing incorrect toys. In the subsequent test for response inhibition, children who had experienced positive interaction with the agent of punishment showed significantly greater resistance to deviation than boys who had only impersonal contact.

It is difficult to determine whether this effect is due to an increase in the perceived noxiousness of the noise when delivered by a previously friendly agent or whether the result derives from the withdrawal of affection implied in the punitive operation. Probably it was a combination of these two sources of anxiety which contributes to our findings. A study by Parke (1967), while not directly concerned with the relative importance of these two components, shows that nurturance-withdrawal alone, unaccompanied by noxious stimulation, can effectively increase resistance to deviation in young children. Two experimental treatments were employed. In one condition—the continuous nurturance group— the subjects, six- to eight-year-old boys and girls, experienced 10 minutes of friendly and nurturant interaction with either a male or female experimenter. Subjects in the nurturance-withdrawal group experienced five minutes of nurturant interaction, followed by five minutes of nurturance-withdrawal during which the experimenter turned away from the child, appeared busy, and refused to respond to any bid for attention. Following these manipulations, all subjects were placed in a resistance-to-deviation situation, involving a display of attractive, but forbidden, toys. In the instructions to the subject, it was made clear that if the subject conformed to the prohibition, the experimenter would play with him upon returning. In this way the link between resistance-to-deviation and nurturance was established. As in previous experiments, a hidden observer recorded the child's deviant activity during the 15-minute period that the adult was absent from the room. The results provided support for the hypothesis, with subjects in the nurturance-withdrawal group deviating significantly less often than subjects in the continuous-nurturance condition. However, it was also found that nurturance-withdrawal influenced girls to a greater degree than boys, and that the effect was most marked with girls experiencing withdrawal of a female agent's nurturance.

These data are consistent with previous studies of nurturance-withdrawal, which have indicated that withdrawal of affection may motivate the previously nurtured child to engage in behavior that is likely to reinstate the affectional relationship (e.g., Hartup, 1958; Rosenblith, 1959, 1961). In the present study, the greater resistance to deviation of the subjects in the inconsistent nurturance condition may thus reflect an at-

tempt to win back the experimenter's approval through conformity to his prohibition.

Reasoning and Punishment

In all of the studies discussed, punishment was presented in a relatively barren cognitive context. Very often, however, parents and teachers provide the child with a rationale for the punishment they administer. Is punishment more effective when accompanied by a set of reasons for nondeviation? Field studies of child rearing suggest that the answer is positive. For example, Sears, Maccoby and Levin (1957), in their interview investigation of child-rearing practices, found that mothers who combine physical punishment with extensive use of reasoning reported that punishment was more effective than mothers who tended to use punishment alone. Field investigations, however, have yielded little information concerning the relative effectiveness of different aspects of reasoning. In the child-training literature, reasoning may include not only descriptions of untoward consequences that the child's behavior may have for others, but also the provision of examples of incompatible socially acceptable behaviors, explicit instructions on how to behave in specific situations, and explanations of motives for placing restraints on the child's behavior. Moreover, these child-training studies do not indicate the manner in which the provision of reasons in combination with punishment can alter the operation of specific punishment parameters such as those already discussed — timing, intensity, and the nature of the agent-child relationship.

It is necessary to turn again to experimental studies for answers to these questions. First, laboratory investigations have confirmed the field results in that punishment is more effective when accompanied by a rationale. Parke (1969), for example, found that when children, in addition to being punished, were told that a toy was "fragile and may break," greater inhibition occurred than when children were punished without an accompanying rationale. In a later experiment, Parke and Murray (1971) found that a rationale alone is more effective than punishment alone. However, comparison of the results of the two studies indicates that the combination of punishment and a rationale is the most thoroughly effective procedure.

To understand the impact of reasoning on the timing of punishment effect, let us examine a pioneering set of studies by Aronfreed (1965). In the earlier timing experiments, cognitive structure was minimized and no verbal rationale was given for the constraints placed on the child's behavior. In constrast, children in a second group of experiments were

provided, in the initial instructions, with a brief explanation for not handling some of the toys. In one variation, for example, the cognitive structuring focused on the child's intentions. When punished, the child was told: "No, you should not have *wanted* to pick up that thing." The important finding here was that the addition of reasoning to a *late*-timed punishment markedly increased its effectiveness. In fact, when a verbal rationale accompanied the punishment the usual timing of punishment effect was absent; early- and late-timed punishments were equally effective inhibitors of the child's behavior. Other investigators have reported a similar relation between reasoning operations and timing of punishment (Cheyne & Walters, 1969; Parke, 1969). In these latter studies, the reasoning procedures presented in conjunction with punishment did not stress intentions, but focused on the consequences of violation of the experimenter's prohibition.

The delay periods used in all of these studies were relatively short. In everyday life, detection of a deviant act is often delayed many hours or the punishment may be postponed, for example, until the father returns home. An experiment reported by Walters and Andres (1967) addressed itself directly to this issue. Their aim was to determine the conditions under which a punishment delivered four hours after the commission of a deviant act could be made an effective inhibitor. By verbally describing the earlier deviation at the time that the punishment was administered, the effectiveness of the punishment was considerably increased in comparison to a punishment that was delivered without an accompanying restatement. An equally effective procedure involved exposing the children to a videotape recording of themselves committing the deviant act just prior to the long-delayed punishment. A partially analogous situation, not studied by these investigators, involves parental demonstration of the deviant behavior just before delivering the punishing blow. In any case, symbolic reinstatement of the deviant act, according to these data, seems to be a potent way of increasing the effectiveness of delayed punishment.

A question remains. Do reasoning manipulations alter the operation of any other parameters besides the timing of the punishment? Parke (1969) examined the modifying impact of reasoning on the intensity and nurturance variables. When no rationale was provided, the expected intensity of punishment effect was present: high intensity punishment produced significantly greater inhibition than low intensity punishment. However, when a rationale accompanied the punishment, the difference between high and low intensity of punishment was not present.

As noted earlier, children who experience nurturant interaction with the punishing agent prior to punishment training deviate less often than

subjects in the low nurturance condition. However, this effect was present in the Parke (1969) study only when no rationale accompanied the noxious buzzer. When the children were provided with a rationale for not touching certain toys, the children who had experienced the friendly interaction and the children who had only impersonal contact with the agent were equally inhibited during the resistance-to-deviation test period. Taken together, these experiments constitute impressive evidence of the important role played by cognitive variables in modifying the operation of punishment.

A common yardstick employed to gauge the success of a disciplinary procedure is the permanence of the inhibition produced. It is somewhat surprising, therefore, that little attention has been paid to the stability of inhibition over time as a consequence of various punishment training operations. One approach to this issue involves calculating changes in deviant activity occurring during the resistance-to-deviation test session in experimental studies. Does the amount of deviant behavior increase at different rates, for example, in response to different training procedures? As a first step in answering this question, Parke (1969) divided

Figure 1:
Stability of Duration of Deviation over Three Five-minute Periods for High-cognitive and Low-cognitive Structure Conditions.

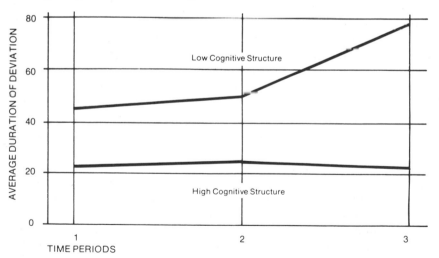

the 15-minute resistance-to-deviation test session into three five-minute periods. As Figure 1 indicates, the low cognitive structure subjects (no rationale) increased their degree of illicit toy touching over the three

time periods while the degree of deviation over the three intervals did not significantly change for the high cognitive structure (rationale provided) subjects. Cheyne and Walters (1969) have reported a similar finding. These data clearly indicate that the stability of inhibition over time was affected by the reasoning or cognitive structuring procedures. The most interesting implication of this finding is that inhibition — or internalization — may *require* the use of cognitively-oriented training procedures. Punishment techniques that rely solely on anxiety induction, such as the noxious noises employed in many of the experiments discussed or the more extreme forms of physical punishment sometimes used by parents, may be effective mainly in securing only short-term inhibition.

Figure 2:
Stability of Inhibition over One Week
with and Without Reinstatement.

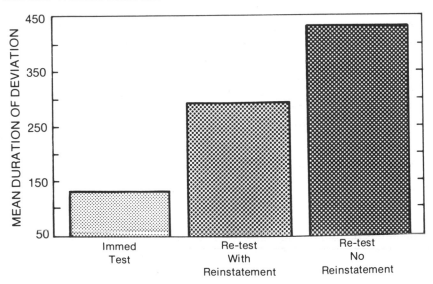

However, children often forget a rationale or may not remember that a prohibition is still in force after a lengthy time lapse. A brief reminder or re-instatement of the original punisher or rationale may be necessary to insure continued inhibition. To investigate the impact of such re-instatement on the stability of inhibition was the aim of an experiment by Parke and Murray (1971). In this study, following the typical punishment training procedure, the seven- to nine-year-old boys were tested immediately for resistance-to-deviation and then re-tested in the same situation one week later. Half of the children were "reminded" of the earlier training

by the experimenter. For example, in the case of the boys who were punished by a buzzer during the training session, the experimenter sounded the buzzer a single time and reminded the children that it signalled that they should not touch the toys ("You shouldn't touch the toys"). For children who received rationales unaccompanied by any punishment, the experimenter merely re-stated the rationale ("Remember, those toys belong to another boy" or "They are fragile and may break") before leaving the children alone with the toys. For the remaining children, no reminder or re-instatement of the earlier training was provided. As Figure 2 indicates, re-instatement of the original training clearly increased the permanence of the response inhibition.

The type of research reviewed here does not provide us with any information concerning the relative effectiveness of reasoning procedures for producing behavioral control at different ages. It is likely that developmental trends will be discovered in light of recent Russian work (e.g., Luria, 1961) which indicates that the child's ability to use verbal behavior to control motor responses increases with age. Possibly with younger children response inhibition will be most successfully achieved by a reliance on physical punishment techniques which stress the production of anxiety. With older children, punishment techniques which diminish the role of anxiety and which stress the role of verbal control of motor behavior through the appeal to general rules will be more effective in producing response inhibition (Parke, 1970).

Consistency of Punishment

In naturalistic contexts, punishment is often intermittently and erratically employed. Consequently, achieving an understanding of the effects of inconsistent punishment is a potentially important task. Data from field studies of delinquency have yielded a few clues concerning the consequences of inconsistency of discipline. Glueck and Glueck (1950) found that parents of delinquent boys were more "erratic" in their disciplinary practices than were parents of nondelinquent boys. Similarly, the McCords (e.g., McCord, McCord & Howard, 1961) have found that erratic disciplinary procedures were correlated with high degrees of criminality. Inconsistent patterns involving a combination of love, laxity, and punitiveness, or a mixture of punitiveness and laxity alone were particularly likely to be found in the background of their delinquent sample. However, the definition of inconsistency has shifted from study to study in delinquency research, making evaluation and meaningful conclusions difficult (Walters & Parke, 1967).

To clarify the effects of inconsistent punishment on children's aggressive behavior, Parke and Deur (Parke & Deur, 1970; Deur & Parke,

1970) conducted a series of laboratory studies. Aggression was selected as the response measure in order to relate the findings to previous studies of inconsistent discipline and aggressive delinquency. An automated Bobo doll was used to measure aggression. The child punched the large, padded stomach of the clown-shaped doll and the frequency of hitting was automatically recorded. In principle, the apparatus is similar to the inflated punch toys commonly found in children's homes. To familiarize themselves with the doll, the boys participating in the first study (Parke & Deur, 1970) punched freely for two minutes. Then the children were rewarded with marbles each time they punched the Bobo doll for a total of 10 trials. Following this baseline session, the subjects experienced one of three different outcomes for punching: termination of reward (no outcome), receipt of marbles on half the trials and a noxious buzzer following the other half, of consistent punishment by the buzzer. Half the children were also told that the buzzer indicated that they were playing the game "badly," while the remaining boys were informed that the buzzer was a "bad noise." All the boys had been informed that they could terminate the punching game whenever they wished. The main index of persistence was the number of hitting responses that the child delivered before voluntarily ending the game. The results were clear: subjects in the no outcome group made the greatest number of punches, while the continuously punished children delivered the fewest punches; the inconsistently punished children were in the intermediate position. The results were not affected by the labeling of the buzzer; whether the buzzer meant "playing the game badly" or "a bad noise" made no difference. This laboratory demonstration confirms the common child-rearing dictum that intermittent punishment is less effective than continuous punishment.

Parents and other disciplinary agents often use consistent punishment only after inconsistent punishment has failed to change the child's behavior. To investigate the effectiveness of consistent punishment *after* the child has been treated in an inconsistent fashion was the aim of the next study (Deur & Parke, 1970). Following the baseline period, subjects underwent one of three different training conditions. One group of boys were rewarded for 18 trials, while a second group of children received marbles on nine trials and no outcome on the remaining trials. A final group of boys was rewarded on half of the trials but heard a noxious buzzer on the other nine trials. The children were informed that the buzzer indicated that they were playing the game "badly."

To determine the effects of these training schedules on resistance to extinction (where both rewards and punishers were discontinued) and on resistance to continuous punishment (where every punch was punished) was the purpose of the next phase of the study. Therefore, half of the

children in each of the three groups were neither rewarded nor punished for hitting the Bobo doll and the remaining subjects heard the noxious buzzer each time they punched. The number of hitting responses that the child made before voluntarily quitting was, again, the principal measure.

The results are shown in Figure 3. The punished subjects made fewer hitting responses than did subjects in the extinction condition, which suggests that the punishment was effective in inhibiting the aggressive behavior. The training schedules produced particularly interesting results. The inconsistently punished subjects showed the greatest resistance to extinction. Moreover, these previously punished children tended to persist longer in the face of consistent punishment than the boys in the other training groups. The effects were most marked in comparison to the consistently rewarded subjects. The implication is clear: the socializing agent using inconsistent punishment builds up resistance to future attempts to either extinguish deviant behavior or suppress it by consistently administered punishment.

The particular form of inconsistency employed in this study represents only one of the variety of forms of inconsistency which occurs in naturalistic socialization. Consistency, as used in the present research, refers to the extent to which a single agent treats violations in the same

Figure 3:
Mean Number of Punches in Post-training Period as a Function of Consistency of Reward and Punishment.

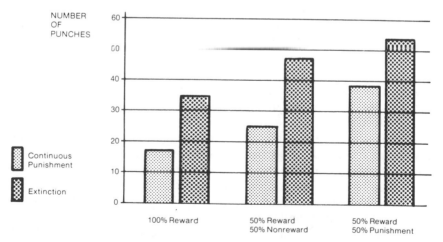

manner each time such violations occur. Of equal importance would be studies of inter-agent inconsistency. For example, what effect will one parent rewarding aggressive behavior and the other parent punishing the

same class of behaviors have on the persistence of aggressive response patterns? Similar inconsistencies between teacher and parental treatment of deviant behavior and the discrepancies between peer and teacher reactions require examination.

Undesirable Consequences of Punishment

The foregoing paragraphs indicate that punishment is effective in producing response suppression. Nevertheless, punishment may have undesirable side-effects which limit its usefulness as a socializing technique. In the first place, the teacher or parent who employs physical punishment to inhibit undesirable behaviors may also serve as an aggressive model. Bandura (1967) has summarized this viewpoint as follows: "When a parent punishes his child physically for having aggressed toward peers, for example, the intended outcome of this training is that the child should refrain from hitting others. The child, however, is also learning from parental demonstration how to aggress physically. And the imitative learning may provide the direction for the child's behavior when he is similarly frustrated in subsequent social interactions" (1967, p. 43).

Evidence supporting this position is, at best, indirect. There is a sizable body of data indicating a relation between the frequent use of physical punishment by parents and aggressive behavior in their children (Becker, 1964). However, the increases in aggression could possibly be due to the *direct* encouragement that punitive parents often provide for behaving aggressively outside the home situation. Alternatively, highly aggressive children may require strong, physically punitive techniques to control them. Thus, even if it is assumed that the punitive parent acts as an aggressive model there is no evidence demonstrating that children imitate the aggressive behaviors the disciplinarian displays while punishing the child. It is recognized that exposure to aggressive models increases aggressive behavior in young children (Bandura, 1967). It is of questionable legitimacy, however, to generalize from Bobo doll studies to children imitating a physically punitive adult who is often carrying out a justified spanking in line with his role as parent or teacher.

The results of a study by Slaby and Parke (1968) are relevant. Children were exposed to a film-mediated model who was disciplined for touching prohibited toys. In one case, the film agent "spanked" the child for touching the toys. In the second case, the adult on the film "reasoned" with the deviant model after detecting the violation of the prohibition. In addition to testing the child's resistance to deviation, the amount of aggression that a child would direct to a peer was assessed. Under the guise of helping the experimenter teach the other child arithmetic problems, the subject was given the opportunity to punish the

other child by "punching" him each time he made a mistake. A punch was administered by depressing a button on the subject's panel which activated a punching machine in the adjacent room. Both the number and intensity of punches were recorded for each subject. The subjects who saw the physically punitive disciplinarian were more aggressive than the children exposed to the verbal reasoning sequence.

The effect was most marked, however, in the case of subject-observers who were the same age as the film model (seven-year-olds). Older children tended not to show the effect. Clearly, model-subject similarity is an important factor in this type of imitation study and replication of the study with film models of different ages is necessary. The results for the seven-year-olds are shown in Figure 4.

Figure 4:
Aggression and Type of Disciplinary Model.

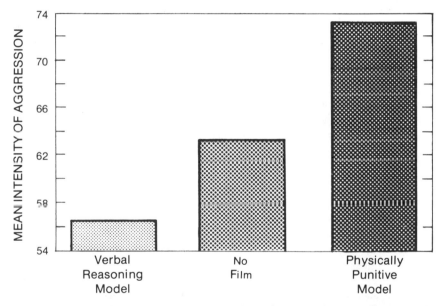

Another undesirable consequence of punishment is the effect on the agent-child relationship. As a result of punishment, the child may be motivated to avoid the punishing parent or teacher. Consequently, the socialization agent may no longer be able to direct or influence the child's behavior. Conditions such as the classroom often prevent the child from physically escaping the presence of the agent. Continued use of punishment in an inescapable context, however, may lead to passivity and withdrawal (Seligman, Maier & Solomon, 1969) or adaptation to the punishing stimuli themselves. In any case, whether escape is possible or

not, the quality of the agent-child relationship may deteriorate if punishment is used with high frequency; punishment administered by such an agent will, therefore, be less effective in inhibiting the child.

The undesirable effects of punishment mentioned here probably occur mainly in situations where the disciplinary agents are indiscriminately punitive. In child-training contexts where the agent rewards and encourages a large proportion of the child's behavior, even though selectively and occasionally punishing certain kinds of behavior, these side effects are less likely to be found (Walters & Parke, 1967).

Reinforcement of Incompatible Responses: An alternative to punishment

In light of these undesirable consequences, it may be worthwhile to consider other ways in which deviant behavior can be controlled. Reinforcement of incompatible responses is one such technique. Brown and Elliot (1965) asked several nursery school teachers to ignore aggressive acts and only encourage behaviors that were inconsistent with aggression, such as cooperation and helpfulness. Encouraging these alternative behaviors resulted in a marked decrease in classroom aggression. More recently, Parke, Ewall and Slaby (1972) have found that encouraging college subjects for speaking helpful words also led to a decrease in subsequent aggression. In an extension of this work, Slaby (1970) found a similar effect for eight- to 12-year-old children. The lesson is clear: speaking in a manner that is incompatible with aggression may actually inhibit hostile actions. Words, as well as deeds, can alter our physical behaviors. The advantage of the incompatible response technique for controlling behavior is that the unwanted side-effects associated with punishment can be avoided.

Conclusion

This review leaves little doubt that punishment can be an effective means of controlling children's behavior. The operation of punishment, however, is a complex process and its effects are quite varied and highly dependent on such parameters as timing, intensity, consistency, the affectional and/or status relationship between the agent and recipient of punishment, and the kind of cognitive structuring accompanying the punishing stimulus.

It is unlikely that a socialization program based solely on punishment would be very effective; the child needs to be taught new appropriate responses in addition to learning to suppress unacceptable forms of behavior. "In fact, in real-life situations the suppressive effect of punishment is usually only of value if alternative pro-social responses are elicit-

ed and strengthened while the undesirable behavior is held in check. The primary practical value of studies of parameters that influence the efficacy of punishment is . . . to determine the conditions under which suppression will most likely occur" (Walters & Parke, 1967, p. 217). From this viewpoint, punishment is only one technique which can be used in concert with other training tools such as positive reinforcement to shape, direct, and control the behavior of the developing child.

References

Aronfreed, J. Punishment learning and internalization: Some parameters of reinforcement and cognition. Paper read at biennial meeting of Society for Research in Child Development, Minneapolis, 1965.

_____. *Conduct and Conscience.* New York: Academic Press, 1968.

Aronfreed, J. & Leff, R. The effects of intensity of punishment and complexity of discrimination upon the learning of an internalized inhibition. Unpubl. mss., Univ. of Pennsylvania, 1963.

Aronfreed, J. & Reber, A. Internalized behavioral suppression and the timing of social punishment. *J. pers. soc. Psychol.*, 1965, 1, 3–16.

Bandura, A. The role of modeling processes in personality development. In W. W. Hartup & Nancy L. Smothergill (Eds.), *The Young Child: Reviews of Research.* Washington: National Association for the Education of Young Children, 1967. Pp. 42–58.

Bandura, A. & Walters, R. H. *Social Learning and Personality Development.* New York: Holt, Rinehart & Winston, 1963.

Becker, W. C. Consequences of different kinds of parental discipline. In M. L. Hoffman & L. W. Hoffman (Eds.), *Review of Child Development Research,* Vol. 1. New York: Russell Sage Foundation, 1964. Pp. 169–209.

Black, A. H., Solomon, R. L. & Whiting, J. W. M. Resistance to temptation in dogs. Cited by Mowrer, O. H. *Learning Theory and the Symbolic Processes.* New York: John Wiley, 1960.

Brown, P. & Elliot, R. Control of aggression in a nursery school class. *J. exp. child Psychol.*, 1965, 2, 103–107.

Cheyne, J. A. & Walters, R. H. Intensity of punishment, timing of punishment, and cognitive structure as determinants of response inhibition. *J. exp. child Psychol.*, 1969, 7, 231–244.

Church, R. M. The varied effects of punishment on behavior. *Psychol. Rev.*, 1963, 70, 369–402.

Cowan, P. A. & Walters, R. H. Studies of reinforcement of aggression: I. Effects of scheduling. *Child Develpm.*, 1963, 34, 543–551.

Deur, J. L. & Parke, R. D. The effects of inconsistent punishment on aggression in children. *Develpm. Psychol.*, 1970, 2, 403–411.

Glueck, S. & Glueck, E. *Unraveling Juvenile Delinquency.* Cambridge: Harvard Univ. Press, 1950.

Hartup, W. W. Nurturance and nurturance-withdrawal in relation to the dependency behavior of preschool children. *Child Develpm.,* 1958, 29, 191–201.

Luria, A. R. *The Role of Speech in the Regulation of Normal and Abnormal Behavior.* New York: Liveright, 1961.

McCord, W., McCord, J. & Howard, A. Familial correlates of aggression in non-delinquent male children. *J. abnorm. soc Psychol.,* 1961, 62, 79–93.

Parke, R. D. Nurturance, nurturance-withdrawal and resistance to deviation. *Child Develpm.,* 1967, 38, 1101–1110.

———. The role of punishment in the socialization process. In R. A. Hoppe, G. A. Milton, & E. C. Simmel (Eds.), *Early Experiences and the Processes of Socialization.* New York: Academic Press, 1970. Pp. 81–108.

———. Effectiveness of punishment as an interaction of intensity, timing, agent nurturance and cognitive structuring. *Child Develpm.,* 1969, 40, 213–236.

Parke, R. D. & Deur, J. The inhibitory effects of inconsistent and consistent punishment on children's aggression. Unpubl. mss., Univ. of Wisconsin, 1970.

Parke, R. D., Ewall, W. & Slaby, R. G. Hostile and helpful verbalizations as regulators of nonverbal aggression. *J. pers. soc. Psychol.,* 1972, in press.

Parke, R. D. & Murray, S. Re-instatement: A technique for increasing stability of inhibition in children. Unpubl. mss., Univ. of Wisconsin, 1971.

Parke, R. D. & Walters, R. H. Some factors determining the efficacy of punishment for inducing response inhibition. *Monogr. Soc. Res. Child Develpm.,* 1967, 32 (Serial No. 109).

Rosenblith, J. F. Learning by imitation in kindergarten children. *Child Develpm.,* 1959, 30, 69–80.

———. Imitative color choices in kindergarten children. *Child Develpm.,* 1961, 32, 211–223.

Sears, R. R., Maccoby, E. E. & Levin, H. *Patterns of Child Rearing.* Evanston, Ill.: Row, Peterson, 1957.

Seligman, M. E. P., Maier, S. F. & Solomon, R. L. Unpredictable and uncontrollable aversive events. In F. R. Brush (Ed.), *Aversive Conditioning and Learning.* New York: Academic Press, 1969.

Slaby, R. G. Aggressive and helpful verbalizations as regulators of behavioral aggression and altruism in children. Unpubl. doctoral dissertation, Univ. of Wisconsin, 1970.

Slaby, R. G. & Parke, R. D. The influence of a punitive or reasoning model on resistance to deviation and aggression in children. Unpubl. mss., Univ. of Wisconsin, 1968.

Walters, R. H. Delay-of-reinforcement effects in children's learning. *Psychonom. Sci.,* 1964, 1, 307 – 308.

Walters, R. H. & Andres, D. Punishment procedures and self-control. Paper read at Annual Meeting of the American Psychological Association, Washington, D. C., Sept., 1967.

Walters, R. H. & Parke, R. D. The influence of punishment and related disciplinary techniques on the social behavior of children: Theory and empirical findings. In B. A. Maher (Ed.), *Progress in Experimental Personality Research,* Vol. 4. New York: Academic Press, 1967. Pp. 179 – 228.

Walters, R. H., Parke, R. D. & Cane, V. A. Timing of punishment and the observation of consequences to others as determinants of response inhibition. *J. exp. child Psychol.,* 1965, 2, 10 – 30.

4.5 Some Thoughts About Childrearing

Diana Baumrind, Ph.D.

Introduction

I want to speak with you today about my research findings relating patterns of parental authority to dimensions of competence in young children, and to share with you the conclusions I draw from those findings.

There are a few points I want to make before I discuss the findings themselves. . . .

1. First, there is no such thing as a *best* way to raise children. Each individual family's total life situation is unique. A generalization which makes sense on a probability basis must be tailored to fit an individual family's situation, if indeed it fits at all. It is each parent's responsibility

This selection was originally presented as a talk to the Children's Community Center in Berkeley, California, May 14, 1969, by Diana Baumrind, Research Psychologist and Principle Investigator for the Parental Authority Research Project, University of California at Berkeley. The program of research discussed in this paper was supported by research grant HD-02228 from the National Institute of Child Health and Human Development, U.S. Public Health Service.

to become an expert on his own children, using information in books or parent effectiveness encounter groups or, best of all, by careful observation and intimate communication with the child.

2.   Secondly, the generalizations which I make have a reasonable probability of being true for a particular sample, but the extent to which that sample is representative of a population, say eight years later, remains in question. Moreover, the extent to which any individual family is similar to the families in the sample affects how relevant the findings are for that family. In addition, the relationships found are not strong enough to predict for the individual family.

3.   Third, to have any social meaning at all, research findings must be *interpreted* and integrated. Yet the interpretations I make of my findings may well be disputed by other equally expert investigators. I will speak *strongly* for my interpretations because I am that sort of person. But each of you must evaluate the relevance to your own family of what I say, and you must do so in the light of your personal value system and experience.

I should tell you that my *subjective* assurance about what I say rests as much upon my personal experience as a parent, as on my research findings. I have three daughters whose ages are 11, 13 and 15. My theories and my practice coincide rather well (I think), and I am subjectively satisfied with the effectiveness of what I call "authoritative parental control" in achieving my *personal* aim. I will generalize to say it is possible, if parents wish to—IF parents wish to—to control the behavior of children, even of adolescents, and to do so without suppressing the individuality and willfulness of the child or adolescent. What gets in the way of most parents who *do* wish to control the behavior of their children more effectively is lack of *expertness* as parents, *indecisiveness* about the application of power, *anxiety* about possible harm resulting from demands and restrictions, and *fear* that if they act in a certain way they will lose their children's love. Nowadays I think more parents are concerned about maintaining the approval of their children than vice versa, and, indeed, many parents become paralyzed with indecision when their authority is disputed, or their children are angered by discipline.

Now I will tell you something about my research.

Research Variables

For the past eight years my staff and myself have been gathering data on the behavior of preschool children in nursery schools and in structured laboratory situations. Each child studied has been observed for at least three months. These data were related to information obtained about the parent-child interaction, and about the parents' beliefs and

values. We made two home visits to each family between the difficult hours of five to eight in the evening, then subsequently interviewed the mother and father separately. So far more than 300 families have participated in the study, most of them middle-class, well educated families.

A. Child Variables

I think it is important to tell you what kinds of behavior we were looking for so that you will know what I mean by such general terms as "competence" when speaking of the child, or "authoritative parental control" when speaking of the parent.

In all correlational studies of children's social behavior, at least two dimensions are revealed. One dimension may be called *Responsible versus Socially Disruptive Behavior*. The other dimension may be called *Active versus Passive Behavior.* These two dimensions are independent of each other—that is, a socially responsible child can run the gamut from very active and self-assertive to very quiet and socially passive. Or, a socially disruptive child may be an active terrorist or he may be sullen, passive and detached from other children.

When we call a child *socially responsible*, we mean that relative to other children his age the child takes into account the ongoing activities of other children enough not to disrupt them—he will facilitate the routine of the group; he does not actively disobey or undermine the rules of the school; he can share possessions with other children; he is sympathetic when another child needs hlep; he does not try to get another child into trouble, and so on.

When we speak of a child as *active*, we are referring to the independent, self-motivated, goal-oriented, outgoing behavior of the child. When we call a child highly active, he is relative to other children his age likely to go after what he wants forcefully, to show physical courage, to be a leader, to feel free to question the teacher, to persevere when he encounters frustration, to show originality in his thinking, and so on.

72 very explicitly defined items were used by the raters to describe each child in relation to these two dimensions.

When I report my findings to you later on and I speak of the most *competent* group of children, I am speaking about children who were rated by the observers as being very active and very responsible. I am comparing these children to other children who are less competent in the sense that raters judged them to be lacking in self-assertiveness and self-control, or to be socially disruptive.

Clearly, any definition of competence makes certain tacit assumptions about the proper relationship of the individual to society. The child is *competent* to fulfill himself and succeed in a given society. The same qualities might not be as effective in a differently organized society. To

the extent that an investigator believes that successful accommodation to the ongoing institutions of a society defines competence, he will stress the *social responsibility* dimension of competence. If an investigator believes in revolutionary change, he may reject social responsibility as a criterion of competence. To the extent that an investigator values thrust, potency, dominance, and creative push, he will stress *activity* as a dimension of competence. If, by contrast, he believes in an Eastern ideal—such as Zen Buddhism—an investigator may reject dominance and push as criteria of competence, emphasizing instead receptivity, openness, egolessness, and unwilled activity. My definition of *competence* assumes the importance both of accommodation to social institutions, and of self-assertive and individualistic action in relation to these institutions. In the preschool years, I regard the development of *social responsibility* and of *individuality* as equally important for both sexes, although I suppose that our society, at least in the past, has placed the emphasis in adulthood on activity and individuality for boys, and on responsibility and conformity for girls.

B. Parent Variables

Now I would like to tell you about what we were looking for when we observed parents with their children. Our focus has been upon facets of parental authority which might conceivably predict dimensions related to competence in young children. More specifically, we measured dimensions such as the following:

1. *Directive versus nondirective behavior*—that is, the extent to which the child's life is governed by clear regulations and the parent in charge sets forth clearly the daily regimen for the child.
2. *Firm versus lax enforcement policy*—the extent to which the parent enforces directives, resists coercive demands of the child, requires the child to pay attention to her when she speaks, and is willing to use punishment if necessary to enforce her demands.
3. *Expects versus does not expect participation in household chores*—we measured the extent to which parents require the child to help with household tasks, to dress himself, to put his toys away, and to behave cooperatively with other family members.
4. *Promotes respect for established authority versus seeks to develop an equalitarian, harmonious relationship with child*—here we sought to measure what is generally thought of as authoritarian control and its opposite, i.e. the extent to which the parent assumes a stance of personal infallibility on the basis of her role as parent rather than on the basis of her specific competencies and responsibilities, and requires of the child that he defer to her without question.

We also measured such variables as:

1. The extent to which the parent encourages self-assertion and independent experimentation.

2. The extent to which the parent uses reason and explanation when directing the child.

3. The extent to which the parent values individuality in behavior and appearance by contrast or in addition to social acceptability.

Methods Used to Study Parent Attitudes and Behavior

In studying parental attitudes and practices we used a variety of methods. As I have already indicated, we visited the home on two occasions between the hours of five and eight, and took complete notes on the interactions which transpired. We then interviewed the mother and the father separately, discussing with each the possible ways in which the presence of the observer might have affected the behavior witnessed during the home visit. We talked with parents about their general position on child-rearing, their attitudes towards permissiveness, directiveness, and the use of reason, what their ideals were for their child, and so on.

Some parents have asked how we thought the presence of the observer in the home affected the interactions we witnessed. Our general conclusion is that while most families censored some behavior (such as intense emotional shows of love or anger), the interactions we observed and rated with regard to the variables we were measuring predict pretty well how parents interact with their children. We may think about the information we obtain from home visits somewhat as we do about on-the-job tests for a prospective employee. An employer can predict the typing efficiency of a prospective employee from a five-minute typing test on standardized material. While the typist will not handle all kinds of typing tasks in the same way that she does the typing test copy, her handling of the test copy will predict pretty accurately her general speed, her knowledge of format, and her ability to spell. Under the kind of pressure that preschoolers produce during the hours of five and eight, parents generally become sufficiently involved with their customary tasks so that they fall back upon their most practiced responses, modifying these perhaps in accord with their ideals. Very few parents sought consciously to disguise this customary behavior. Since our focus is upon conscious childrearing practices and values, the observational situation is reasonably successful in providing relevant information about parental practices and values. If we were concerned primarily with incidents of highly charged emotional events, direct observation in the home would probably not have provided us with the needed information. Most studies of the effects of childrearing practices in the past have used less

valid data than home visits. They have relied upon psychological tests, or self-report, or experimental observation in the laboratory setting. With all its drawbacks, then, we found that the combination of direct observation in the home setting, with interview and self-report, gave us relatively valid information of the kind we were seeking.

Conclusions from the Study

These are the general conclusions which we drew from our data about the childrearing antecedents of *responsible versus irresponsible behavior* and *active versus passive behavior.*

In the middle-class group we studied, parental practices which were intellectually stimulating and to some extent tension-producing (e.g., socialization and maturity demands and firmness in disciplinary matters) were associated in the young child both with self-assertion and social responsibility. Techniques which fostered self-reliance whether by placing demands upon the child for self-control and high-level performance, or by encouraging independent action and decision-making, were associated in the child with responsible and independent behavior. Firm discipline in the hope did not produce conforming or dependent behavior in the nursery school. For boys, especially, the opposite was true. Firm, demanding behavior on the part of the parent was not correlated with punitiveness or lack of warmth. The most demanding parents were, in fact, the warmest.

These conclusions concerning the effects of diciplinary practices are consistent with the findings of a second study we conducted (Baumrind, 1967). In that study, a group of nursery school children who were both responsible and independent were identified. These children were self-controlled and friendly on the one hand, and self-reliant, explorative, and self-assertive on the other hand. They were realistic, competent, and content by comparison with the other two groups of children studied. In the home setting, parents of these children were consistent, loving and demanding. They respected the child's independent decisions, but were very firm about sustaining a position once they took a stand. They accompanied a directive with a reason. Despite vigorous and at times conflictual interactions, their homes were not marked by discord or dissensions. *These parents balanced much warmth with high control, and high demands with clear communication about what was required of the child.* By comparison with parents of children who were relatively immature, parents of these highly mature children had firmer control over the actions of their children, engaged in more independence training, and did not reward dependency. Their households were better coordinated and the policy of regulations clearer and more effectively enforced. The child was more satisfied by his interactions with his parents. By comparison

with parents of children who were relatively unhappy and unfriendly, parents of the mature children were less authoritarian, although quite as firm and even more loving.

A Position on Childrearing

I would like now to move from a report of research findings into a presentation of some of my conclusions about childrearing. I want to make clear that experts in the field disagree just as parents do. The meaning I derive from my research findings is affected by my personal values and life experience, and is not necessarily the meaning another investigator would derive.

I have been quoted as opposing permissiveness, and to a certain extent that is true. I would like to describe my position on permissiveness in more detail. I think of the permissive parent as one who attempts to behave in a nonevaluative, acceptant and affirmative manner toward the child's impulses, desires and actions. She consults with him about policy decisions and gives explanations for family rules. She makes few demands for household responsibility and orderly behavior. She presents herself to the child as a resource for him to use as he wishes, not as an ideal for him to emulate, nor as an active agent responsible for shaping or altering his ongoing or future behavior. She allows the child to regulate his own activities as much as possible, avoids the exercise of control, and does not insist that he obey externally defined standards. She attempts to use reason and manipulation, but not overt power, to accomplish her ends.

The alternative to adult control, according to Neill, the best known advocate of permissiveness, is to permit the child to be self regulated, free of restraint, and unconcerned about expression of impulse, or the effects of his carelessness. I am quoting from *Summerhill* now:

> *Self-regulation means the right of a baby to live freely, without outside authority in things psychic and somatic.* It means that the baby feeds when it is hungry; that it becomes clean in habits only when it wants to; that it is never stormed at nor spanked; that it is always loved and protected (1964, p. 105, italics Neill's).

> *I believe that to impose anything by authority is wrong. The child should not do anything until he comes to the opinion—his own opinion—that it should be done* (1964, p. 114, italics Neill's).

> Every child has the right to wear clothes of such a kind that it does not matter a brass farthing if they get messy or not (1964, p. 115).

Furniture to a child is practically nonexistent. So at Summerhill we buy old car seats and old bus seats. And in a month or two they look like wrecks. Every now and again at mealtime, some youngster waiting for his second helping will while away the time by twisting his fork almost into knots (1964, p. 138).

Really, any man or woman who tries to give children freedom should be a millionnaire, for it is not fair that the natural carelessness of children should always be in conflict with the economic factor (1964, p. 139).

Permissiveness as a doctrine arose as a reaction against the authoritarian methods of a previous era in which the parent felt that her purpose in training her child was to forward not her own desire, but the Divine Will. The parent felt that since the obstacle to worldly and eternal happiness was self-will, that the subduing of the will of the child led to his salvation. The authoritarian parent of a previous era was preparing his child for a hard life in which success depended upon achievment, and in which strength of purpose and ability to conform were necessary for success. With the advent of Freudian psychology and the loosening of the hold of organized religion, educated middle-class parents were taught by psychologists and educators to question the assumptions of their own authoritarian parents. Spock's 1946 edition of *Baby and Child Care* advocated the psychoanalytic view that full gratification of infantile sucking and excretory and sexual impulses were essential for secure and healthful adult personalities. The ideal educated, well-to-do family in the late 40's and 50's was organized around unlimited acceptance of the child's impulses, and around maximum freedom of choice and self-expression for the child.

However by 1957 Spock himself changed his emphasis. He said, in the 1957 edition of his famous book, "A great change in attitude has occurred and nowadays there seems to be more chance of conscientious parent's getting into trouble with permissiveness than with strictness."

I would like now to examine certain of the assumptions which have been made in support of permissiveness, most of which, when examined in a research setting, have not been supported.

1. One assumption previously made was that scheduled feeding and firm toilet training procedures have as their inevitable consequences adult neuroses. This apparently is not so. Unless the demands put upon the infant are unrealistic — as might be the demand for bowel training at five months — or the parent punishes the infant cruelly for failure to live up to her demands — scheduled feeding and firm toilet training do not appear to be harmful to the child.

2. A second assumption, that punishment, especially spanking, is harmful to the child, or not effective in controlling behavior, is also not supported by recent research findings. On the contrary, properly administered punishment has been shown by the behavior therapists to be an effective means of controlling the behavior of children. This hardly comes as a surprise to most parents. Brutal punishment *is* harmful to the child. Threats of punishment not carried out are harmful to the child. A parent who threatens to punish must be prepared to deal with escalation from the child by prompt administration of punishment. She cannot appease. Otherwise the threat of punishment will actually *increase* the incidence of undesirable behavior, since it is just that undesirable behavior which will cause the parent to cancel the punishment, in an attempt to appease the child.

While *prompt* punishment is usually most effective, it is important for the parent to be certain that the child knows exactly why he is being punished, and what kind of behavior the parent would prefer and why. While extremely rapid punishment following a transgression works best in training a rat or a dog, a human child is a conscious being and should be approached as one. It should not be enough for a parent, except perhaps in critical matters of safety, to *condition* a child to avoid certain kinds of behavior by prompt punishment. The parent's aim is to help the child control his own behavior, and that end requires the use of reason and the bringing to bear of moral principles to define what is right and what is wrong conduct.

Properly administered punishment, then, provides the child with important information. The child learns what it is his parent wants, and he learns about the consequences of not conforming to an authority's wishes.

3. A third assumption that advocates of permissiveness have made is that unconditional love is beneficial to the child, and that love which is conditional upon the behavior of the child is harmful to the child. I think that the notion of unconditional love has deterred many parents from fulfilling certain important parental functions. They fail to train their children for future life and make them afraid to move towards independence. Indulgent love is passive in respect to the child — not requiring of the child that he become good, or competent, or disciplined. It is content with providing nourishment and understanding. It caters to the child and overlooks petulance and obnoxious behavior — at least it tries to. The effect on the child of such love is often not good. Once the child enters the larger community, the parents are forced to restrict or deprive. Accustomed as the child is to immediate gratification, he suffers greater deprivation at such times than he would if he were accustomed to associating discipline with love. He does not accept nor can he tolerate unpleasant consequences when he acts against authority figures. Such a

child, even when he is older, expects to receive, and is not prepared to give or to compromise. The rule of reciprocity, of payment for value received, is a law of life that applies to us all. The child must be prepared in the home by his parents to give according to his ability so that he can get according to his needs.

The parent who expresses love unconditionally is encouraging the child to be selfish and demanding while she herself is not. Thus she reinforces exactly the behavior which she does not approve of—greedy, demanding, inconsiderate behavior. For his part, the child is likely to feel morally inferior for what he is, and to experience conflict about what he should become. I believe that a parent expresses her love most fully when she demands of the child that he become his best, and in the early years helps him to act in accordance with *her* image of the noble, the beautiful and the best, as an initial model upon which he can create (in the adolescent years) his own ideal.

On the other hand, I do believe that to the extent that it is possible, a parent's *commitment* to the child should be unconditional. That is, the parent should stay contained *in* the experience with the child, no matter what the child does. Parental love properly expressed comes closest in my mind to the Christian notion of *Agape*. The parent continues to care for the child because it is her child and not because of the child's merits. Since she is human, the quality of her feeling for him depends upon the child's actions, but her interest in his welfare does not depend upon his actions and is abiding. This abiding interest is expressed not in gratifying the child's whims, nor in being gentle and kind with him when he is being obnoxious, nor in making few demands upon him, nor in approval of his actions, nor even in approving of what he is as a person. Unconditional *commitment* means that the child's interests are perceived as among the parent's most important interests, and that (no matter what the child does) the parent does not desert the child. But the love of a parent for a child must be demanding—not demanding of the unconditional commitment it offers—but rather demanding of the reciprocal of what it offers. The parent has the right—indeed, the duty—to expect obedience and growth towards mature behavior, in order that she can discharge her responsibilities to the child, and continue to feel unconditional commitment to his welfare. (Only parents are required, as an expression of love, to give up the object of that love, to prepare the object of love to become totally free of the lover.)

Authoritative versus Authoritarian Parental Control

Now that I have discussed the concept of permissiveness in childrearing, I would like to explain the distinction which I make between *authoritarian* and *authoritative* parental control.

I think of an *authority* as a person whose expertness befits him to tell another what to do, when the behavioral alternatives are known to both. An authority does not have to *exercise* his control, but it is recognized by both that by virtue of his expertness and his responsibility for the actions of the other, he is fit to exercise authority in a given area.

By *authoritative parental control* I mean that, in relation to her child, the parent should be an authority in the sense just defined.

1. *In order to be an authority, the parent must be expert.* It seems to me that many parents and teachers have come to the conclusion that they are not expert on matters which pertain to the young people placed in their charge. Therefore, since they are not expert, they abandon their role as authorities. I think instead that they should become more expert. Parents often do need more information about children of all ages than they have, in order to be expert. But much of what a parent needs to know she can learn from observing her child and listening to him. A parent must permit her child to be a socialization agent for her, as well as the other way, if the parent is to acquire the information about the child and his peer group that she needs in order to make authoritative decisions about matters which affect the child's life. Unlike the authoritarian parent, the authoritative parent modifies her role in response to the child's coaching. She responds to suggestions and complaints from the child and then transmits her own more flexible norms to her child. In this way, by becoming more expert, the parent legitimates her authority and increases her effectiveness as a socializing agent.

2. *In order to be authoritative, the parent must be willing and able to behave rationally, and to explain the rationale for her values and norms to the child.* The parent does not have to explain her actions all the time to the child, especially if she knows that the child knows the reason but is engaging in harrassment. But a parent does need to be sure that she herself knows the basis for her demands, and that the child also knows, within the limits of his understanding, the reasons behind her demands.

In authoritarian families the parent interacts with the child on the basis of formal role and status. Since the parent has superior power, she tells the child what to do and does not permit herself to be affected by what he says or does. Where parents do not consult with children on decisions affecting the children, authority can only rest on power. As the child gets older and the relative powers of parent and child shift, the basis for parental authority is undermined. Even the young child has the perfect answer to a parent who says, "you must do what I say because I am your mother," and that answer is, "I never asked to be born." The adolescent can add, "Make me," and many say just that when parents

are unwise enough to clash directly with an adolescent on an issue on which the adolescent has staked his integrity or autonomy.

3. *In order to be authoritative, the parent must value self-assertion and willfulness in the child.* Her aim should be to prepare the child to become independent of her control and to leave her domain. Her methods of discipline, while firm, must therefore be respectful of the child's actual abilities and capacities. As these increase, she must share her responsibilities and perogatives with the child, and increase her expectations for competence, achievment, and independent action.

I believe that the imposition of authority even against the child's will is useful to the child during the first six years. Indeed, power serves to legitimate authority in the mind of the child, to assure the child that his parent has the power to protect him and provide for him.

The major way in which parents exercise power in the early years is by manipulating the reinforcing and punishing stimuli which affect the child. What makes a parent a successful reinforcing agent or an attractive model for a child to imitate is his effective power to give the child what he needs — i.e., the parent's control over resources which the child desires, and his willingness and ability to provide the child with these resources in such a manner and at such a time that the child will be gratified and the family group benefitted. Thus, practically as well as morally, gratification of the child's needs within the realistic economy of the family, is a precondition for the effective imposition of parental authority. An exploited child cannot be controlled effectively over a long period of time. The parent's ability to gratify the child and to withhold gratification legitimates his authority. The child, unlike the adolescent, has not yet reached the level of cognitive development where he can legitimate authority, or object to its imposition, on a principled basis.

By early adolescence, however, power based on physical strength and control of resources cannot and should not be used to legitimate authority. The young person is now capable of formal operational thought. He can formulate principles of choice by which to judge his own actions and the actions of others. He has the conceptual ability to be critical even though he may lack the wisdom to moderate his criticism. He can see clearly many alternatives to parental directives; and the parent must be prepared to defend rationally, as she would to an adult, a directive with which the adolescent disagrees. Moreover, the asymmetry of power which characterizes childhood no longer exists at adolescence. The adolescent cannot be forced physically to obey over any period of time.

When an adolescent refuses to do as his parent wishes, it is more congruent with his construction of reality for the parent simply to ask him, "why not?". Through the dialogue which ensues, the parent may learn

that his directive was unjust; or the adolescent may learn that his parent's directive could be legitimated. In any case, a head-on confrontation is avoided. While head-on confrontation won by the parent serves to strengthen parental authority in the first six years, it produces conflict about adult authority during adolescence.

Although a young person need feel no commitment to the social ethic of his parents' generation, he does have, while he is dependent upon his parents, a moral responsibility to obey rational authority, i.e. authority based on explicit, mutually-agreed-upon principles. The just restrictions on his freedom provide the adolescent with the major impetus to become self-supporting and responsible to himself rather than to his parents.

The Relationship of Individual Freedom to Control

To an articulate exponent of permissiveness in childrearing, such as Neill, freedom for the child means that he has the liberty to do as he pleases without interference from adult guardians and, indeed, with their protection. Hegel, by contrast, defines freedom as the appreciation of necessity. By this he means that man frees himself of the objective world by understanding its nature and controlling his reactions to its attributes. His definition equates the concept of freedom with power to act, rather than with absence of external control. To Hegel, the infant is enslaved by virtue of his ignorance, his dependence upon others for sustenance, and his lack of self-control. The experience of infantile omnipotence, if such he has, is based on ignorance and illusion. His is the freedom to be irresponsible, a very limited freedom, and one appropriate only for the incompetent.

For a person to behave autonomously, he must accept responsibility for his own behavior, which in turn requires that he believe the world is orderly and susceptible to rational mastery and that he has or can develop the requisite skills to manage his own affairs.

When compliance with parental standards is achieved by use of reason, power, and external reinforcement, it may be possible to obtain obedience and self-correction without stimulating guilt reactions. To some extent the parent's aggressiveness with the child stimulates counteraggressiveness and anger from the child, thus reducing the experience of guilt and of early internalizations of standards whose moral bases cannot yet be grasped. When the child accepts physical punishment or deprivation of privileges as the price paid for acts of disobedience, he may derive from the interaction greater power to withstand suffering and deprivation in the service of another need or an ideal and, thus, increased freedom to choose among expanded alternatives in the future.

Authoritarian control and permissive noncontrol both shield the child

from the opportunity to engage in vigorous interaction with people. Demands which cannot be met or no demands, suppression of conflict or sidestepping of conflict, refusal to help or too much help, unrealistically high or low standards, all may curb or understimulate the child so that he fails to achieve the knowledge and experience which could realistically reduce his dependence upon the outside world. The authoritarian and the permissive parent may both create, in different ways, a climate in which the child is not desensitized to the anxiety associated with nonconformity, nor willing to accept punishment for transgressions. Both models minimize dissent, the former by suppression and the latter by diversion or indulgence. To learn how to dissent, the child may need a strongly held position from which to diverge and then be allowed under some circumstances to pay the price for nonconformity by being punished. Spirited give and take within the home, if accompanied by respect and warmth, may teach the child how to express aggression in self-serving and prosocial causes and to accept the partially unpleasant consequences of such actions.

The body of findings on effects of disciplinary practices give provisional support to the position that authoritative control can achieve responsible conformity with group standards without loss of individual autonomy or self-assertiveness.

4.6 The Early Training Project: A Seventh-Year Report

Susan W. Gray
Rupert A. Klaus
George Peabody College for Teachers, Nashville, Tennessee

The Early Training Project as been a field research study concerned with the development and testing over time of procedures for improving the educability of young children from low-income homes. The rationale, the general design and methodology, and findings through the second year of schooling have been reported in some detail by Klaus and Gray (1968). A briefer report, up to school entrance, is given in Gray and Klaus (1965). The purpose of this report is to present the findings at the end of the fourth grade, 3 years after all experimental intervention had ceased.

Reprinted from *Child Development*, 1970, *41*, 909-924, by permission of the senior author and The Society for Research in Child Development, Inc. Copyright © 1970 by The Society for Research in Child Development, Inc.

The major concern of the Early Training Project was to study whether it was possible to offset the progressive retardation observed in the public school careers of children living in deprived circumstances. In addition, the writers undertook to study the spillover effect upon other children in the community and upon other family members.

The general research strategy was one of attempting to design a research "package" consisting of variables which—on the basis of research upon social class, cognitive development, and motivation—might be assumed to be relevant to the school retardation which is observed in deprived groups and which at the same time might be subject to the effects of manipulation. Because this was a problem with major social implications, we also tried to design a general treatment approach which would be feasbile to repeat on a large scale in the event that the procedure proved successful.

Subjects were 88 children born in 1958. Sixty-one of these lived in a city of 25,000 in the upper South. The remaining 27, who served as a distal control group, resided in a similar city 65 miles away. The children were all Negro. When we initiated the study the schools of the city were still segregated; we chose to work with Negro children because in this particular setting we had reason to believe that our chances of success were greater with this group.

The children were selected on the basis of parent's occupation, education, income, and housing conditions. At the beginning of the study, incomes were considerably below the approximate $3,000 used as the poverty line for a family of four. Occupations were either unskilled or semiskilled; the educational level was eighth grade or below; housing conditions were poor. The median number of children per family at the beginning of the study was five; in about one-third of the homes there was no father present.

From the 61 children in the first city three groups were constituted by random assignment. The first group (T1) attended, over a period of three summers, a 10-week preschool designed to offset the deficits usually observed in the performance of children from disadvantaged homes. In addition, this group had 3 years of weekly meetings with a specially trained home visitor during those months in which the preschool was not in session. The second group (T2) had a similar treatment, except that it began a year later; the children received two summers of the special preschool and 2 years of home visits. The third group (T3) became the local control group, which received all tests but no intervention treatment. The fourth group (T4), the distal control group, was added to the design because of the somewhat ghetto-type concentration of Negroes in the first city. The local and distal control groups also made possible the study of spillover effects upon children and parents living in proximity to the experimental children. The general layout of the experimental design is given in table 1. By reading down the columns, one may see the particular treatment and testing

Table 1
Layout of General Research Design

Treatment Time	Three Summer Schools (T1)	Two Summer Schools (T2)	Local Controls (T3)	Distal Controls (T4)
First winter (1961–1962)	Criterion development, curriculum planning, general tooling up			
First summer (1962)	Pretest, summer school, posttest	Pretest, posttest	Pretest, posttest	Pretest, posttest
Second winter (1962–1963)	Home visitor contacts	. . .	. . .	. . .
Second summer (1963)	Pretest, summer school, posttest	Pretest, summer school, posttest	Pretest, posttest	Pretest, posttest
Third winter (1963–1964)	Home visitor contacts	Home visitor contacts	. . .	. . .
Third summer (1964)	Pretest, summer school, posttest	Pretest, summer school, posttest	Pretest, posttest	Pretest, posttest
Fourth winter (1964–1965)	Home visitor contacts	Home visitor contacts	. . .	. . .
Fourth summer (1965)	Follow-up tests	Follow-up tests	Follow-up tests	Follow-up tests
Fifth summer (1966)	Follow-up tests	Follow-up tests	Follow-up tests	Follow-up tests
Seventh summer (1968)	Follow-up tests	Follow-up tests	Follow-up tests	Follow-up tests

sequence followed for each of the four groups. Periodic testing is continuing for the children through elementary school.

The Intervention Program

The overall rationale for the intervention program grew out of the literature on child-rearing patterns in different social classes, plus the writers' own observations in low-income homes. On the basis of this study, the intervention program for children was organized around two broad classes of variables: attitudes relating the achievement, and aptitudes relating to achievement. Under attitudes we were particularly interested in achievement motivation, especially as it concerns schooltype activities, in persistence, in ability to delay gratification; generally interested in typical

school materials, such as books, crayons, puzzles, and the like. We were also concerned with the parents' attitude toward achievement, particularly in their aspirations for their children, especially as they related to schooling.

In the broad class of aptitude variables relating to achievement, we were particularly interested in perceptual and cognitive development and in language. Children from low-income homes have been shown to have deficits in these areas, all of which appear closely related to school success in the primary grades.

In the summer months, for 10 weeks the children met in assembled groups. Each of the two experimental groups had a head teacher, who was an experienced Negro first-grade teacher. There were, in addition, three or four teaching assistants. These assistants were divided about equally as to race and sex.

The work with the parents in the project was carried on largely through a home-visitor program in which a specially trained preschool teacher made weekly visits to each mother and child. Both the home program and the school program are described in considerable detail in Gray, Klaus, Miller, and Forrester (1966) and in Klaus and Gray (1968).

Prior to and after each summer session, children in all four groups were tested on several instruments. From the first summer certain standardized tests of intelligence and language were used, along with a number of less formal instruments. At the end of first grade, achievement tests were added. This testing schedule is shown in table 1. In general the .05 level of significance was used.

Results

The detailed results of the testing program through May 1966, the end of the second grade for the children, are given in Klaus and Gray (1968). This paper gives the results as they relate to the spring and summer testings of 1968 with some additional information on performance of younger siblings. The same kinds of analyses were used for the 1968 data as were used in the earlier paper.

In 1968 the following tests were administered to all children still residing in middle Tennessee: the Stanford-Binet, the Peabody Picture Vocabulary Test, and the Metropolitan Achievement Test. The analyses here reported are based only upon those children available for testing with the exception of one child in the distal control group.

The Stanford-Binet scores are given in table 2, and are portrayed graphically in figure 1. A Lindquist (1953) type 1 analysis of the results of 1962-68, in terms of IQ, gave a significant F of 4.45 for the four groups, F of 16.81 for repeated measures, and F for interaction of groups over time of 3.51. All of these were significant at the .01 level or beyond. Next an

analysis was made by the use of orthogonal comparisons. The two experimental groups remained significantly superior to the two control groups. The comparison of the first and the second experimental groups for 1968

Table 2
Mean Stanford-Binet MA and IQ Scores for the Four Treatment Groups at Each Administration

Date of Administration	T1(N = 19) MA (Mo)	IQ	T2(N = 19) MA (Mo)	IQ	T3(N = 18) MA (Mo)	IQ	T4(N = 23) MA (Mo)	IQ
May 1962	40.7	87.6	43.8	92.5	40.3	85.4	40.3	86.7
August 1962	50.7	102.0	46.9	92.3	44.3	88.2	43.4	87.4
May 1963	55.6	96.4	56.0	94.8	53.2	89.6	50.4	86.7
August 1963	59.3	97.1	60.6	97.5	55.0	87.6	52.3	84.7
August 1964	68.0	95.8	71.6	96.6	62.3	82.9	59.4	80.2
August 1965	83.8	98.1	86.3	99.7	79.4	91.4	77.0	89.0
June 1966	88.7	91.2	93.4	96.0	86.8	87.9	82.9	84.6
July 1968	106.0	86.7	111.4	90.2	104.7	84.9	96.2	77.7

showed an F of less than 1.00. The comparison of the two control groups, however, yielded an F that, although not conventionally significant, was still large enough (3.52 where $F_{.95} = 3.96$) to be suggestive of a sharper decline

Fig. 1.—Mental ages for the four groups on the Stanford-Binet Test

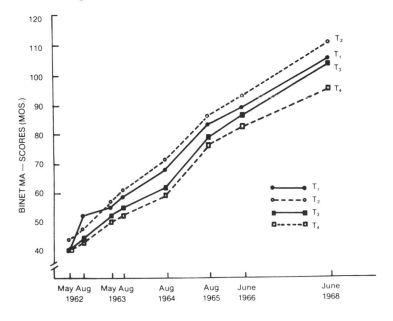

in the distal than in the local control group. As was true of earlier analyses, the larger part of the variance appeared to be carried by the second experimental group and the distal control group.

The scores across the 10 administrations of the Peabody Picture Vocabulary Test are given in table 3 in MA and IQ form. A Lindquist (1953) Type 1 analysis of variance was performed for the MA scores. For groups F was 5.16, indicating a significant effect of the experimental treatment upon the children's performance. For repeated testings F was 376.73, an effect that would be clearly expected when MA scores were used. These were selected in preference to IQ scores on this particular test since the IQ scores appear to lack discrimination at certain levels. The interaction between groups and time was nonsignificant. Orthogonals were next used. Here was found that T1 + T2 was significantly greater than T3 + T4 up until 1968, in which year differences were not significant. As may be seen from table 3, differences in mean scores were still apparent. Heterogeneity had increased over time, however, so that differences were no longer significant. In no analysis at any point of time was either experimental group significantly superior to the other. Nor did either control group show itself to be significantly superior to the other one.

Table 3
Mean PPVT Mental Age Scores and IQ Equivalents for the Four Treatment Groups for the 10 Administrations

Date of Administration	Test Form	$T1(N=19)$ MA (Mo)	IQ	$T2(N=19)$ MA (Mo)	IQ	$T3(N=18)$ MA (Mo)	IQ	$T4(N=23)$ MA (Mo)	IQ
May 1962	A	30.0	69.5	30.6	70.1	29.4	66.4	32.2	74.0
August 1962	B	36.8	75.3	33.1	63.9	32.7	65.8	30.7	62.8
May 1963	A	44.8	79.0	40.7	69.6	39.1	69.3	39.5	69.8
August 1963	B	45.0	78.4	50.7	83.6	38.4	64.0	37.6	63.8
May 1964	B	55.6	81.2	60.1	85.5	45.8	65.4	48.7	70.9
August 1964	A	59.1	83.0	62.0	87.0	50.6	72.4	48.7	69.6
June 1965	B	74.2	89.0	76.2	90.3	67.6	83.0	67.3	84.0
August 1965	A	70.6	86.2	76.5	91.8	65.4	80.2	66.3	83.4
June 1966	A	78.1	86.7	81.9	89.3	75.4	83.9	71.2	80.7
July 1968	A	96.4	84.5	100.3	86.7	91.7	81.8	89.3	78.7

The results for the Metropolitan Achievement Test are given in table 4. A Lindquist (1953) Type 1 analysis was performed on each subtest, and orthogonal comparisons made. In the interest of brevity a table of orthogonal comparisons is not given. In 1965, at the end of first grade, the experimental children were significantly superior on three of the four tests used at that time: world knowledge, word discrimination, and reading. For arithmetic computation scores, F was less than 1.00. The local controls were

Table 4
Metropolitan Achievement Test Grade Equivalent Mean Scores
for the Various Subtests for the Three Administrations

Subtest and Year	T1	T2	T3	T4
Word knowledge:				
1965	1.69	1.73	1.79	1.37
1966	2.32	2.47	2.29	1.98
1968	3.58	3.90	3.54	3.27
Word discrimination:				
1965	1.68	1.81	1.82	1.37
1966	2.64	2.73	2.65	2.20
1968	3.73	3.95	3.76	3.47
Reading:				
1965	1.72	1.82	1.84	1.46
1966	2.52	2.75	2.56	2.11
1968	3.52	3.89	3.72	3.10
Arithmetic computation:				
1965	1.52	1.62	1.54	1.43
1966	2.41	2.55	2.49	2.05
1968	3.92	4.07	4.06	3.79
Spelling:				
1966	2.42	2.85	2.60	1.99
1968	4.26	4.69	4.24	3.67
Language:				
1968	3.52	4.00	3.63	3.17
Arithmetic problem solving and concepts:				
1968	3.31	3.54	3.75	3.26

also somewhat superior to the distal controls on these tests, an indication possibly of horizontal diffusion or, either in interaction or independently, a somewhat better instructional program. In 1966 five subtests were given. This time only two were significant, word knowledge and reading. On the other three tests, however, the F's ranged from 2.69 to 2.84, suggesting probabilities at about the .10 level. In neither year was T1 significantly superior to T2. The highest F was 1.16, where $F_{.95}$ is 3.97. In the comparisons of T3 and T4, T3 was superior to T4 on reading and arithmetic computation. On word knowledge, word discrimination, and spelling the F's ranged from 3.19 to 3.85, suggesting probabilities beyond the .10 level ($F_{90} = 2.77$). At the end of the fourth year no significant effects were found with the single exception of reading, on which T3 was superior to T4. There is some suggestion of residual effect since, in six of superior to T4. There is some suggestion of residual effect since, in six of the seven possible comparisons of experimentals and controls, the experimentals were superior. Also, on all seven possible comparisons the local control group was superior to the distal control group.

The Stanford-Binet was administered in all four groups to those younger

siblings who were of testable age. This was first done in 1964 and again in 1966. In 1964, 57 children were tested. Fifty of these same children were tested again in 1966, along with 43 additional siblings who were too young to test in 1964.

An analysis of covariance was performed on these scores, with the IQs at first testing of the target-age children used as the covariable. Also, where there were two younger siblings in the same family, one was dropped, so that the analysis was based on 87 children. Separate analyses were also performed for the 1964 and the 1966 results of all children who were retested. In addition, an analysis was performed on the 1966 results for those children who were being tested for the first time.

On all younger siblings tested in 1966 F between groups was not significant at the .05 level (F = 3.97). It was significant beyond the .10 level, and therefore we made further analyses. Orthogonal comparisons were used. All orthogonal comparisons showed significant differences for the testing of all younger siblings in 1966: the combined experimental group siblings were superior to the combined control group siblings; the T1 siblings were superior to the T2 siblings; and the T3 siblings were superior to the T4 siblings. When the children who were tested for the first time are separated out, it is clear, both in the 1966 and the 1964 data, that most of the variance was being carried by younger siblings closer in age to the target-age children. There are some interesting implications of these general results on younger siblings which will be examined in more detail in the Discussion.

Discussion

The results on the one test of intelligence which was used consistently, from the initiation of the program in 1962 until the testing at the end of the fourth grade in 1968, are very much in line with what might be expected. For this was an intervention program that used a broad-gauge approach and which was relatively successful in terms of improving the educability of young children from low-income homes. Intervention caused a rise in intelligence which was fairly sharp at first, then leveled off, and finally began to show decline once intervention ceased. The control groups on the other hand tended to show a slight but consistent decline with the single exception of a jump between entrance into public school and the end of first grade. Differences between experimentals and controls on Stanford-Binet IQ were still significant at the end of the third year after intervention ceased. All four groups have shown a decline in IQ after the first grade, but the decline, as shown in figure 1, tended to be relatively parallel. Perhaps the remarkable thing is that with the relatively small amount of impact over time differences should still be significant. After all, the child experienced only five mornings

of school a week for 10 weeks for two or three summers, plus weekly home visits during the other 9 months for 2 or 3 years. This suggests that the impact was not lost. It was not sufficient, however, to offset the massive effects of a low-income home in which the child had lived since birth onward.

The results on the PPVT showed a pattern that is not dissimilar. There was a rise during intervention, including the first grade, then a leveling off and a slight decline. Here, however, difference between groups, although consistent, was no longer significant.

The importance of the school situation for the maintenance or loss of a gain should be weighed. The children for the most part remained in schools in which the entire population was Negro. Eight of the local children at the end of first grade did enroll in schools that had previously been all white. Four more changed during the next 2 years. None of the distal children attended schools with white children. Since in this area, as in many places, race tends to be confounded with social class, the children in the study did not in general have the advantage of classmates with relatively high expectancies. There is some evidence that in both of the all-Negro schools the general teaching-learning situation, although fair, was less adequate than in the schools that have formerly been all white. This, plus the continuing effect of the home situation and the immediate community, took its toll. There are some data on achievement-test scores to be presented later which suggest the impact of the two all-Negro schools which most of the children attended.

On the one achievement battery administered from first to fourth grade, the Metropolitan Achievement Test (table 4), significant differences did not appear in 1968 on any of the subtests with sole exception of the reading score, in which the local control group was superior to the distal control group. The experimentals had been superior to the controls on three tests in 1965 and on two tests in 1966. One might interpret this as showing that the intervention program did have measurable effects upon test performance at the end of first grade, but that by the end of fourth grade, the school program had failed to sustain at any substantial level the initial superiority. Although disappointing, this is perhaps not surprising in a test battery so dependent upon specific school instruction.

An interesting sidelight is thrown on the matter by looking at the performance on the Metropolitan Achievement Test of the eight children from the local school who enrolled in previously all-white schools at the end of first grade. An attempt was made, on the basis of first-grade achievement tests and home ratings of educational aspirations, to match these eight children with eight who remained in the Negro school. Admittedly, this is a chancy business, and one which should not be taken too seriously. Table 5 presents the gains in grade equivalents on the Metropolitan Achievement

Table 5

Mean Gains on the MAT over a 3-Year Period for Eight ETP Children in Integrated Schools and Matches in Negro Schools

| | Mean Gains 1965–1968 | | | |
	Word Knowledge	Word Discrimination	Reading	Arithmetic
ETP *S*s in integrated schools beginning Fall 1965	3.1	2.8	2.7	2.9
ETP *S*s in Negro schools matched to the first group on Spring 1965 MAT and on verbal rating by home visitor	1.7	2.0	1.6	1.7
Difference	1.4	0.8	1.1	1.2

Tests from the end of first grade to the end of fourth grade. On the four subtests common to both grade levels, the picture is a clear one of more gain in the children who changed schools, varying from .8 to 1.4 years greater gain. These data did not seem appropriate for subjection to statistical analysis. They do suggest, however, the fairly obvious: that performance on achievement tests is directly related to school experience. The children who changed schools have made approximately "normal" gain for their 3 years; the children who did not change have gained 2 years or less during the 3 years from first through fourth grade.

The results on the younger siblings are to the writers among the most interesting findings of the study. We have termed the process by which such results are achieved and the product of that process "vertical diffusion," to suggest that this is a spread of effect down the family from the mother and possibly the target-age child to a younger child. In this study the effects of the older sibling and the mother upon the younger child were confounded. Some research currently being carried on under the direction of one of the writers has made possible the separation of the influence of mother and older siblings. Results so far indicate that most of the effect is coming from the mother. It is plausible to assume that the role of the mother was the more influential since considerable effort was expended by the home visitor over a period of 3 years with the first experimental group and over 2 years with the second experimental group. The emphasis of the home intervention was on making the mother a more effective teacher, or more generally, an effective educational change agent for her target-age child. Also worthy of note is the finding that vertical diffusion appeared more clearly in the younger siblings born in 1959 and 1960, who were within 1-2½ years in age to the older siblings. The siblings born in 1961 and 1962, when pulled out for separate analysis, did not show an effect which approached statistical signifiance. Vertical diffussion also appeared more operative in the first than in the second experimental group. A plausible explanation is that interven-

tion lasted a year longer with the first group and began a year earlier. There is also in the data some suggestion of a process we have examined in more detail elsewhere (Klaus & Gray 1968), one that may be termed horizontal diffusion, the spread of effect from one family to another. This we have in general analyzed by comparing the local and distal control groups. Here we find that the younger siblings in the local control group showed themselves to be superior to the distal control group.

To the extent that the findings on vertical diffusion have generality, they seem to point to the efficacy of a powerful process in the homes, presumably mediated by the parent, which may serve to improve the educability of young children. Before a second conclusion is reached by the reader, however, to the effect that "parent education" is the answer, we would like to point out that our procedure was clearly parent education with a difference. It was conducted in the homes; it was done by skilled preschool teachers with some experience in working in the homes; it was highly concrete and specific to a given mother's life situation; it was continuous over a long period of time. Indeed, parent education probably is the answer, but in low-income homes a very different kind of parent education from that usually provided may be needed.

Seven years after the Early Training Project began, in 1969, intervention programs for young children from low-income homes were nationwide. These programs differ tremendously in the length and timing of the intervention, in the objectives and consistency with which they are followed, in the degree of specificity of the program, and in the length and extent of follow-up study of the sample.

It is hardly surprising, with the wild heterogeneity of such programs, that nationwide assessment of programs, such as the Westinghouse Survey of Project Head Start (1969), would find relatively small evidence of positive effects upon the child's achievement and personal adequacy. Leaving aside all the problems of measuring personal adequacy and even achievement in young children, such lack of results is only to be expected in situations where the bad or inappropriate so cancels out the good that little positive effect can be found, especially if the evaluation is somewhat premature.

At this point in time it seems appropriate to look more closely at those programs which have clearly followed an adequate research design, specified and carefully monitored their treatments, and conducted adequate follow-up study of the sample. Such programs are relatively few in number, for their history is short.

In the Early Training Project we have been more fortunate than most. The study was initiated nearly 4 years before the tidal wave of interests in such early intervention that came about through such nationwide programs as Project Head Start and Titles 1 and 111 of the Elementary and Secondary Education Act. We have worked in a setting in which we have been free from administrative pressures either to change our procedures or to make

premature conclusions from our data. The two communities in which families live have had little outward mobility; even at the end of 7 years attrition is only a minor problem. For these reasons we believe the data collected over 7 years with our four groups of children do shed some light upon the problem of progressive retardation and the possibility that it can be offset.

Our answer as to whether such retardation can be offset is one of cautious optimism. The effects of our intervention program are clearly evidenced through the second year of public schooling, 1 year after intervention ceased. There is still an effect, most apparent in the Stanford-Binet, after 2 more years of nonintervention. Our data on horizontal and vertical diffusion, especially the latter, give us some hope that intervention programs can have a lasting effect that goes beyond the children that were the target of that intervention program.

Still, it is clear from our data, with a parallel decline across the four groups in the second through fourth grades, that an intervention program before school entrance, such as ours, cannot carry the entire burden of offsetting progressive retardation. By some standards the Early Training Project might be seen as one of relatively massive intervention. And yet a colleague of ours (Miller 1970) has estimated that in the years prior to school entrance the maximum amount of time that the children in the project could have spent with the Early Training Project staff was approximately 600 hours, less than 2 percent of their waking hours from birth to 6 years. Perhaps the remarkable thing is that the effect lasted as well and as long as it did. In a similar vein, we have estimated the amount of these contacts in the home as a maximum of 110 hours, or about 0.3 percent of the waking hours of the child from birth to 6 years. Surely it would be foolish not to realize that, without massive changes in the life situation of the child, home circumstances will continue to have their adverse effect upon the child's performance.

In 1968 we wrote: "The most effective intervention programs for preschool children that could possibly be conceived cannot be considered a form of innoculation whereby the child forever after is immune to the effects of a low-income home and of a school inappropriate to his needs. Certainly, the evidence on human performance is overwhelming in indicating that such performance results from the continual interaction of the organism with its environment. Intervention programs, well conceived and executed, may be expected to make some relatively lasting changes. Such programs, however, cannot be expected to carry the whole burden of providing adequate schooling for children from deprived circumstances; they can provide only a basis for future progress in schools and homes that can build upon that early intervention."

In 1969 we saw no reason to alter this statement. Our seventh-year results only serve to underscore its truth.

References

Gray, S. W., & Klaus, R. A. An experimental preschool program for culturally deprived children. *Child Development,* 1965, 36, 887-898.

Gray, S. W.; Klaus, R. A. Miller, J. O.; & Forrester, B. J. *Before first grade.* New York: Teachers College Press, Columbia University, 1966.

Klaus, R. A., & Gray, S. W. The early training project for disadvantaged children: a report after five years. *Monographs of the Society for Research in Child Development,* 1968, 33 (4, Serial No. 120).

Lindquist, E. F. *The design and analysis of experiments in psychology and education.* Boston: Houghton Mifflin, 1953.

Miller, J. O. Cultural deprivation and its modification; effects of intervention. In C. H. Haywood (Ed.), *Social-cultural aspects of mental retardation.* Boston: Appleton-Century-Croft, 1970.

Westinghouse Learning Corporation. *The impact of Head Start: an evaluation of the Head Start experience on children's cognitive and affective development.* Westinghouse Learning Corporation, Ohio University, 1969.

4.7 Educational Intervention at Home by Mothers of Disadvantaged Infants

Merle B. Karnes,
James A. Teska,
Audrey S. Hodgins,
Earladeen D. Badger
University of Illinois, Urbana

Operation Head Start has, of course, generated widespread concern with compensatory education for disadvantaged preschool children, but it has also created an interest of a somewhat different sort: an interest in preventive programs of very early intervention which might forestall the developmental deficiencies characteristic of disadvantaged children by the age of 3 or 4 (Karnes, Hodgins, & Teska 1969; Karnes, Studley, Wright, & Hodgins 1968; Kirk 1969; Radin & Weikart 1967; Schaefer 1969; Weikart 1969). This investigation is based on similar assumptions of preventive programming through early intervention together with the notion that the mother might well serve as the primary agent of that intervention. During

Reprinted from *Child Development,* 1970, *41,* 925-935, by permission of the senior author and The Society for Research in Child Development, Inc. Copyright © 1970 by The Society for Research in Child Development, Inc.

weekly meetings, mothers in disadvantaged families were provided a sequential educational program to use at home in stimulating the cognitive and verbal development of their children and were instructed in principles of teaching which emphasized positive reinforcement. In addition to these child-centered activities, a portion of each meeting was devoted to mother-centered goals related to fostering a sense of dignity and worth as the mother demonstrated self-help capabilities within the family setting and the community at large.

Method

Recruitment

Twenty mothers (including two grandmothers responsible for the care of the child) with infants between the ages of 12 and 24 months were recruited from the economically depressed neighborhoods of Champaign-Urbana, a community of 100,000 in central Illinois. Staff workers at the offices of Aid to Dependent Children (ADC) and the Public Health Department were primary referral sources. In addition, an interviewer canvassed acutely disadvantaged sections of the city to locate families new to the community or otherwise unknown to the referring agencies. Sixteen of the 20 mothers who comprised the original training group were ADC recipients. The families of the remaining four children met the OEO poverty definition acceptable for Head Start admission.

During these initial contacts, the mother was asked if she was willing to attend a 2 hour meeting each week where she would be instructed in teaching techniques to use with her infant at home. In order to make appropriate baby-sitting arrangements for her children, she would be paid $1.50 an hour to attend these meetings. Transportation would also be provided. She was asked, further, to agree to apply these teaching techniques with her infant each day. She would not be paid for this work at home, but the toys used to implement the instructional program would be given to her baby. Finally, it was explained that the infant would be tested to determine how successful the mother had been as a teacher. Although the mothers readily acknowledged the importance of education to their children, they did not recognize their contribution to that enterprise. The suggestion that they could learn ways to stimulate the cognitive and language development of their babies at home was received with skepticism, and many mothers agreed to participate with only a limited commitment.

Characteristics of the Mothers

Fourteen Negro and one Caucasian mother completed the 15-month training program. Five of these mothers had been born in the North (Illinois), and the others had migrated from the South, principally from

Mississippi but also from Arkansas. The ages of these mothers ranged from 22 to 55 years, with a median of 26 years. Their educational levels ranged from 5 to 13 years, with a mean of 9.5 years. These mothers had from one to 12 children, with a mean of 4.9 children. Only two mothers were employed on a full-time basis outside the home. With one exception (a family in which the mother worked a 16-hour day at a factory assemblyline job and an evening food-service job), the annual income of these families did not exceed $4,000.

The average attendance of the 15 mothers who continued in the program was more than 80 percent. The five mothers who left the program had an average attendance of less than 60 percent during the first 7 months.

Initial Characteristics of the Children

The initial mean chronological age of the 15 infants who completed the intervention was 20 months, with a range of 13 to 27 months. Five of these subjects were female and 10 were male. No child attended a day-care center or was enrolled in a preschool prior to or during this 2-year study.

A control (no intervention) group could not be maintained over the 2-year period, and the effectiveness of the mother training program is evaluated through comparisons between the scores on standardized instruments of the 15 children in the experimental group and 15 children of similar age with similar background characteristics chosen from a group of over 50 disadvantaged children who had been tested prior to intervention in the larger research project. The age range (31 to 44 months) within the experimental group at the conclusion of the program was divided into approximate thirds, and each third was comparably represented in the control group so that the ages of the control subjects would closely match those of the experimental children in range as well as mean. Within these age groupings, each experimental child was matched by a control child of the same race and sex. Further, the control child closely approximated his experimental match in the following family background characteristics: number of children in the family, working mother, birthplace of mother, educational level of mother, presence of father or father surrogate, and welfare aid (ADC) to the family. Since the effect of the interactions of these factors on the development of the child is unknown, background characteristics were matched on an individual rather than a group basis. A summary of these characteristics for both groups appears in table 1.

In spite of the careful effort to establish a comparable control group, a conspicuous variable remains uncontrolled. The mothers of the experimental children demonstrated a concern for the educational development of their children by participating in the training program over a 2-year period. A parallel level of motivation cannot be established for the mothers of the control children. This variable is, however, controlled in a second compari-

Table 1
Background Characteristics

Variable	Experimental Group	Control Group
Mean Binet CA (months)	37.9	38.3
Race:		
Negro	14	14
Caucasian	1	1
Sex:		
Male	10	10
Female	5	5
Mean number of children	4.9	4.7
Working mother	2	2
Mother's birthplace:		
Illinois	5	4
Mississippi	7	6
Other South	3	5
Mean educational level of mother (years)	9.5	9.1
Father (or surrogate) present	11	7
ADC	10	9

son. Six children in the experimental group had older siblings for whom test scores were available at similar chronological ages (within 12 months) and prior to the mothers' enrollment in the training program. The experimental child and his sibling control were not necessarily the same sex, but there were four males and two females in each group. Further, *all* data—the scores for the six experimental children and their sibling controls as well as the scores for the 15 experimental children and their matched controls—were obtained within a 3-year period; thus, family dynamics and community milieu remained relatively constant.

Evaluation Procedure

At the conclusion of the program, the 15 children in the experimental group received the Stanford-Binet Intelligence Scale, form L-M, and the experimental edition of the Illinois Test of Psycholinguistic Abilities (ITPA). The matched control and the sibling control children had been tested with these instruments in connection with recruitment for the larger research project. All tests were administered by qualified psychological examiners at a school site.

The Intervention

First Year

To encourage discussion, the 20 mothers met in two groups of 10 throughout the 7-month intervention of the first year. The weekly meetings were divided between child- and mother-centered activities. The first catego-

ry, the presentation of educational toys and materials with an appropriate teaching model, required strong staff leadership. The mother-centered activities involved group discussion with the intention that the group would provide its own vehicle for attitude change through interactions among the members. Two staff members conducted these weekly 2-hour meetings; one functioned as a group leader while the other served as a recorder. After the meeting, both staff members made a written evaluation of the content presented and the interactions within the group. Staff members made monthly (more often when necessary) home visits to reinforce the teaching principles introduced at the meetings and to help each mother establish a positive working relationship with her baby. They observed the appropriateness of the infant curriculum as well as the mother's effectiveness in communicating teaching strategies. Certain principles of teaching were repeated often at the weekly meetings and were encouraged during home visits:

1. If you have a good working relationship with your child, you can become an effective teacher. A good relationship is based on mutual respect.

2. Be positive in your approach. Acknowledge the child's success in each new task, even when the child simply tries to do as he is instructed. Minimize mistakes, show the right way immediately, have the child attempt the task again, and praise him.

3. Break a task into separate steps. Teach one step at a time, starting with the simplest. Do not proceed to the next step until the child is successful with the first.

4. If the child does not attend or try to do as instructed (and you are absolutely sure he can do what is asked), put the toys away until later. Do not scold, beg, or bribe. This time together should be fun for both of you.

Toys were the instructional media for the intellectual and language stimulation of the infant but were, of course, equally important as the media in which a positive interaction between mother and child occurred; they included nested cans and boxes, snap and string beads, graduated rings, a form box, and masonite shapes in various colors and sizes. The materials used in the Kirk tutorial study served as an initial guide and are described in Painter (1968). In addition, art materials (crayons, scissors, play dough, and chalk and slate), inexpensive books, a lending library of wooden inlay puzzles (three to 12 pieces), simple lotto games, toys for unstructured play (pounding bench, busy box, and musical ball), and toys to demonstrate transfer of learning (a stack tower and interlocking cubes) were provided. A home project which proved very successful in stimulating verbal responses was a picture scrapbook. The mother or older children in the family cut pictures from magazines which the infant was able to identify by naming or pointing and pasted these pictures in the scrapbook. "Reading" this book

together fostered a sense of accomplishment shared by mother and child. A child's table and chair and a laundry basket for toy storage were supplied to encourage organization and good work habits. While the books were intended to foster language interactions between mother and child, all program toys created opportunities for verbal development. As the leader demonstrated teaching techniques with each new toy, she used key words which the mothers were to use and which they were to encourage their children to say. Initial work periods for mother and child were 10 minutes but lengthened as the child's attention span grew and the selection of toys increased.

The choice of discussion topics for the mother-centered portion of the meetings was guided by response to previous material. Child discipline, birth control, and the generation gap were among the topics which stimulated discussion. On occasion, pamphlets or magazine excerpts were distributed for reading prior to discussion sessions. Several films (*Guess Who's Coming to Dinner?* and *Palmour Street*) and speakers (a black-power advocate and a family-planning counselor) were included as were a trip to the public library to obtain library cards and to explore the resources of the children's library and a visit to a demonstration nursery school.

A more detailed description of the instructional program implemented by the mothers during the first year and a discussion of certain critical variables in mother participation and child performance can be found in Karnes and Badger (1969).

Second Year

The structure of the program the second year was patterned after that of the first year, and 15 of the original 20 mothers continued to attend weekly 2-hour meetings over an 8-month period. They were again paid to attend these sessions and transportation was provided. The group met as a single unit with only one staff member, with the exception of a group-leader trainee who participated during the last 2 months. Program responsibilities (note-taking during meetings, group leadership, program planning, and home visits) were shared by the mothers to develop their leadership capabilities.

Many of the child-centered activities of the second year extended those initiated the first year. Form perception, introduced the first year with the form box and the masonite shapes, was reinforced the second year with masonite templates. Most children were able to recognize and name three shapes and to distinguish big, little, and middle-sized. Matching skills acquired in the first year in object lotto games were incorporated into classification activities the second year. All children regularly used the art materials and pasted their own projects (snowmen, geometric shapes, collages) into a scrapbook. The lending library of wooden inlay puzzles was enlarged to include puzzles of 20 pieces.

New concepts and activities expanded the instructional goals of the first year. Each mother and child received a set of three books from which regular assignments were given, and mothers were encouraged to model the presentations offered by the teacher. A sequence of visual-motor activities from the Frostig Program for the Development of Visual Perception (Frostig and Horne 1964) was used to emphasize left-to-right progression and visual-motor coordination. Children learned to sort objects or pictures into two categories, and older children were able to sort by six categories at the same time. The ability to distinguish among the alphabet letters *A* through *F* was also developed in this manner. Rubber counting units and felt cutouts of familiar figures were used in patterning experiences. All children learned to sequence colored rods of five lengths and were exposed to seriational and dimensional vocabulary. Mothers encouraged the children to match concrete objects with pictured objects in inexpensive word books. Color and number concepts were emphasized with all program materials. In addition, a lending library of toys and materials which included picture files, puppets, beaded numeral cards, pegboards, blocks, and children's books was available for shared use.

The mother-centered aspect of the meetings during the second year emphasized topics related to programs of community involvement. Interactions during meetings were consistently lively. Mothers volunteered suggestions during the instructional demonstrations and offered comment on the teaching principles presented by the staff leader. Such spontaneous contributions had not been evident the first year and indicate improved self-confidence. Compared with their first-year reactions to guest speakers, the mothers seemed more receptive. Leadership capabilities emerged within the group during the year. Five mothers presented talks and moderated the discussion that followed. One mother served as notetaker at meetings for the year. Four mothers were trained to carry out home visits and performed ably. The group planned and presented a demonstration meeting for visitors from an out-of-state teachers college. Four mothers presented a taped panel discussion on family planning, and one mother arranged for a speaker on black history.

The confidence and capabilities demonstrated by the mothers within the program were reflected in increased community involvement. Four mothers assumed responsibility in the summer recruitment of Head Start children, and one was hired as an assistant teacher and promoted later to the position of head teacher. Two mothers spoke of their experiences in the mother training program at a Head Start parent meeting. Finally, total group involvement was demonstrated at a local Economic Opportunity Council meeting called to discuss the possibility of establishing a parent-child center in the community. Twelve of the 15 mothers attended this meeting and were, in fact, the only persons indigenous to the neighborhood in attendance.

Results

The Matched Control Comparison

On both standardized measures, the performances of the experimental group were significantly superior to those of the control group (table 2). The mean Binet IQ of the children whose mothers had worked with them at home was 16 points above that of the children who had received no intervention. The ITPA performance of the experimental group closely approximated its mean chronological age, and that of the control group was nearly 6 months below its chronological age. Since seven of the 15 control subjects scored below the normative range of the ITPA total and were arbitrarily assigned the lowest normative age score, the mean of this group is artificially inflated.

The Sibling Control Comparison

Greater differences in intellectual functioning and language development were found between the experimental subjects and their siblings than between the matched groups. The 28-point difference in Binet IQ between

Table 2
Experimental (N = 15) and Matched Control (N = 15)
Groups, Stanford-Binet and ITPA

Variable	Binet CA (Months)		Binet MA (Months)		Binet IQ		ITPA Total Language-Age Difference Score (Months)[a]	
	Exp.	Control	Exp.	Control	Exp.	Control	Exp.	Control
Mean	37.9	38.3	41.8	35.5	106.3	90.6	−0.8	−5.9
Standard deviation	3.92	3.45	6.84	5.43	12.46	9.87	6.59	5.42
Difference	0.4		6.3		15.7		5.1	
t[b]	0.24		2.72		3.70		2.25	
Level of significance	N.S.		.01[b]		.0005[b]		.025[b]	

[a]To relate ITPA language age and chronological age and to compensate for slight differences in mean chronological ages between groups, a language-age *difference score* was computed by subtracting each child's chronological age at the time of testing from his language-age score. For example, a child who was 36 months old with a total language-age score of 32 months received a difference score of −4 months. All ITPA data are presented in this form. Children who scored below the norms provided for convention was required in three instances in the experimental group and in seven instances in the matched control.

[b]One-tailed test.

the six experimental children and their sibling controls was, in spite of the small sample, significant (table 3). Virtually no overlap in the range of IQ

scores was found between the two groups. In the experimental group, scores ranged from 99 to 134, and in the sibling control group, from 71 to 102. Three of the six experimental subjects obtained scores of 124 or above. The experimental group achieved a mean acceleration in language development (ITPA) of 3 months, while the sibling control group scored nearly 4 months below its mean chronological age. The t for this difference approaches significance at the .05 level.

Discussion

The comparability of a control group established after the intervention interval may be open to serious question. In this study, family background and mother motivation variables were of particular concern. Mother motivation, demonstrated to be high in the experimental group, may well have been lower in the matched control group, and differences in performance between these groups might, therefore, have been magnified. On the basis of this assumption, smaller differences would have been found between sibling groups than between matched groups. Such was not the case. In the sibling comparison, where mother motivation and family background characteristics were controlled, differences between experimental and control subjects were larger than those between matched groups, and suggest that the comparison with the matched control group was legitimate.

The results of this study endorse the effectiveness of the mother training

Table 3
Experimental (N = 6) and Sibling Control (N = 6) Groups,
Groups, Stanford-Binet and ITPA

Variable	Binet CA (Months)		Binet MA (Months)		Binet IQ		ITPA Total Language-Age Difference Score (Months)[a]	
	Exp.	Control	Exp.	Control	Exp.	Control	Exp.	Control
Mean	38.2	40.3	46.5	36.7	116.7	89.0	3.0	−3.8
Standard deviation	3.33	3.20	6.95	5.76	12.43	10.28	7.68	7.73
Difference	2.1		9.8		27.7		6.8	
t[b]	0.86		3.00		5.90		2.54	
Level of significance	N.S.		.05		.01		.10	

[a]Children who scored below the norms provided for the ITPA total were arbitrarily assigned the lowest total language-age score (30 months). This scoring convention was not employed for any of the six experimental children used in the sibling comparison but was applied to one of the six sibling controls.

[b]For correlated pairs of means.

program in altering in positive ways the development of disadvantaged children before the age of 3. The 16-point Binet IQ difference between the infants whose mothers worked with them at home and the control infants nearly equals the 17-point Binet IQ difference between the experimental and control subjects in the Schaefer study, where the educational intervention was carried out by college graduates who served as tutors, visiting the child at home for 1 hour a day, 5 days a week, over a 21-month period. In the Kirk study, where professional tutors were used in a similar way over a 1-year period, the mean Binet IQ of the experimental group was seven points higher than that of the control. Since at home intervention by mothers can be budgeted at a fraction of the cost of tutorial intervention, the direction for further research in preventive programs of very early intervention seems clear. Further, programs which train the mother to serve as the agent for intervention hold potential for developing her self-help capabilities and sense of personal worth, pivotal factors in effecting broader changes within the disadvantaged family. Not only may the mother represent the ideal agent for fostering an improved school prognosis for the young disadvantaged child, but through group interaction she may extend this sense of responsibility for infant, self, and family to the wider community in which they live.

The encouraging implications of this study must be interpreted with caution. Three-year-old disadvantaged children have been found to make gains in a structured preschool setting (Karnes, Hodgins, Stoneburner, Studley, and Teska 1968) comparable to the difference between the experimental and control subjects in this study. The superiority of intervention before the age of 3 is not demonstrated unless earlier gains are more stable than the disappointingly transitory gains attained in preschools for the disadvantaged. It may be that gains obtained by intervention through the mother that affects the child's total environment on a sustained basis will prove more stable and will be reflected in later school competency. Conclusions based on the performance of 3-year-old children are obviously premature, but the results of this study suggest that a program of mother training can do much to prevent the inadequate cognitive and linguistic development characteristic of the disadvantaged child.

References

Frostig, M., & Horne, D. *The Frostig program for the development of visual perception.* Chicago: Follett, 1964.

Karnes, M. B., & Badger, E. Training mothers to instruct their infants at home. In M. B. Karnes, Research and development program and pre-school disadvantaged children, Vol. 1. Final Report, May 1969, Project No. 5-1181, Contract No. OE6-10-235, Bureau of Research, Office of

Education, U.S. Department of Health, Education, and Welfare. Pp. 245-263.

Karnes M. B.; Hodgins, A. S.; Stoneburner, R. L.; Studley, W. M.; & Teska, J. A. Effects of a highly structured program of language development on intellectual functioning and psycholinguistic development of culturally disadvantaged three-year-olds. *Journal of Special Education,* 1968, 2, 405-412.

Karnes, M. B.; Hodgins, A. S.; & Teska, J. A. The impact of at-home instruction by mothers on performance in the ameliorative preschool. In M. B. Karnes, Research and development program on preschool disadvantaged children. Vol. 1. Final Report, May 1969, Project No. 5-1181, Contract No. OE6-10-235, Bureau of Research, Office of Education, U.S. Department of Health, Education, and Welfare. Pp. 205-212.

Karnes, M. B.; Studley, W. M.; Wright, W. R.; & Hodgins, A. S. An approach for working with mothers of disadvantaged preschool children. *Merrill-Palmer Quarterly,* 1968, 14, 184-183.

Kirk, S. A. The effects of early education with disadvantaged infants. In M. B. Karnes, Research and development program on preschool disadvantaged children. Vol. 1. Final Report, May 1969, Project No. 5-1181, Contract No. OE6-10-235, Bureau of Research, Office of Education, U. S. Department of Health, Education, and Welfare. Pp. 233-248.

Painter, G. *Infant education.* San Rafael, Calif.: Dimensions, 1968.

Radin, N., & Weikart, D. P. A home teaching program for disadvantaged preschool children. In D. P. Weikart (ed.). *Preschool intervention: a preliminary report of the Perry Preschool Project.* Ann Arbor, Mich.: Campus, 1967. Pp. 105-116.

Schaefer, E. S. A home tutoring program. *Children,* 1691, 16, 59-61.

Weikart, D. P. Ypsilanti Carnegie Infant Education Project. Progress Report, Ypsilanti, Michigan, Ypsilanti Public Schools, Department of Research and Development, 1969.

4.8   Parents as Educators: Evidence from Cross-Sectional, Longitudinal and Intervention Research

Earl S. Schaefer

An awareness of the major role of the parent as educator is emerging from child development research. Research findings now suggest the need to return to a traditional comprehensive definition of education as opposed to a restricted, professional and institutional one. Definitions of education such as "the act or process of rearing or bringing up . . ." and "the process of providing with knowledge, skill, competence or usually desirable qualities of behavior and character . . ." (*Webster's Third New International Dictionary of the English Language*, Unabridged. Springfield, Mass.: G. & C. Merriam Co., 1965) apply to the activities of parents as well as professional teachers. However, the classroom model of education has focused on the school-age child in the classroom, in company with a professional educator, learning academic subjects through formal instruction in order to earn academic credentials. Webster's definitions of educator, "one skilled in teaching" and "a student of the theory and practice of teaching" are currently applied primarily, if not exclusively, to the professional educator. Accumulating research on parent behavior and child development now suggests the need to develop a life time and life space perspective on education which recognizes the major educational role of parents.

A review of recent trends in early childhood and early education research may explain the increasing interest in the educational role of parents. From research findings, a rationale for early education can be developed emphasizing provision of experience that contributes to intellectual development. One response, from a classroom perspective, is to speed the development of preschool education. Other responses are to develop enriched day care programs and child-centered home tutoring programs. Although these programs have led to immediate gains in mental test scores, evaluations after termination of the intensive child-centered enrichment show significant declines in IQ. Such findings have led to recognition of the need for continued education in order to foster continued development (Klaus & Gray, 1968; Schaefer, 1970).

The development of programs to train parents to foster the intellectual development of their children has been yet another major response to the need for early and continuing education of the child. Whether brief parent training programs will be sufficient to have long-term effects upon

Reprinted with permission from *The Young Child: Reviews of Research*, Vol. II. Copyright © 1972 by The National Association for the Education of Young Children, 1834 Connecticut Ave. N.W., Washington D.C. 20009.

parents' education of their children is as yet undetermined. Perhaps a comprehensive system of education that integrates the collaborative efforts of the family, the community, the mass media, and the schools must be developed to provide a continuing educational impact upon the child.

The history of education also suggests a need to develop a comprehensive view that recognizes the role of parents in the educational process. The initial *thesis* of education through life experience in the family and community was followed by the *antithesis* of academic education in the schools. As a result, the educational professions and institutions often assume a restricted classroom perspective rather than the more comprehensive life time and life space perspective on education. Child development research now suggests that academic education in the schools will not solve the problems of low academic achievement of disadvantaged groups, again suggesting the need to support the child's education in the family and community. Increasing recognition of the impact of the mass media, particularly television, and of their potential effectiveness in education, also suggests the need for the development of a *synthesis* that will strengthen and integrate the educational contributions of various social units.

Increasing awareness of the role of the parent in the child's education is shown by an analysis of parental involvement in early education (Hess et al., 1970). Parental roles in the classroom education of children—parents as supporters, service givers, and facilitators; parents as teacher aides and volunteers in the classroom; and parents as policy makers and partners in the operation of the school—were differentiated from more independent roles of parents as learners and parents as teachers of their own children. The research reviewed here strongly supports the need to view parents as students of educational methods and as teachers in their own right. An analysis of major characteristics of children's interaction with parents also supports the view that parents are teachers and increases the credibility of findings concerning parental influences on child development. The combination of these different characteristics of parent-child interaction suggests that their cumulative impact upon the child's development would be substantial. Contrasting these characteristics of parent-child interaction with characteristics of children's interaction with the child care and education professions and institutions suggests that strengthening and supporting family care and education of the child should be a major focus in child development programs.

Conceptualization of Parent Behavior

Reviews of the extensive literature on maternal deprivation by Bowlby (1951), Yarrow (1961), and Ainsworth (1962) have contributed sub-

stantially to understanding deprivation and its effects. Ainsworth's review suggests distinction of: "(a) insufficiency of interaction implicit in deprivation; (b) distortion of the character of the interaction, without respect to its quantity; and (c) the discontinuity of relations brought about through separation." Ainsworth recognized that various combinations of these types of deprivation occur. Converging conceptual models for parent behavior derived from ratings support Ainsworth's categories for they clearly distinguish hostile detachment (including neglect and ignoring) from hostile involvement (including nagging and irritability) (Schaefer, 1971). Recent studies suggest a further distinction between the amount of emotional support and the amount of educational stimula-

Table 1
Major Characteristics of the Parent's Interaction with the Child.

	Major Characteristics of the Parent's Interaction with the Child
Priority	Parents influence the early development of relationships, language, interests, task-oriented behaviors, etc.
Duration	The parent's interactions with the child usually extend from birth to maturity.
Continuity	The parent-child interaction is usually not interrupted, particularly in early childhood, apart from brief separations. Concern about such interruptions has led to research on maternal separation and deprivation.
Amount	The total amount of time spent in parent-child interaction, particularly one-to-one interaction, is usually greater than with other adults.
Extensity	The parent shares more different situations and experiences with the child than do other adults.
Intensity	The degree of involvement between parent and child, whether that involvement is hostile or loving, is usually greater than between the child and other adults.
Pervasiveness	Parents potentially influence the child's use of the mass media, his social relationships, his exposure to social institutions and professions, and much of the child's total experience, both inside and outside the home.
Consistency	Parents develop consistent patterns of behavior with their children.
Responsibility	Both society and parents recognize the parent's primary responsibility for the child.
Variability	Great variability exists in parental care of children, varying from extremes of parental neglect and abuse to extremes of parental acceptance, involvement, and stimulation.

tion provided by parents. Lack of educational stimulation seems to be related to school achievement problems while lack of emotional support is more closely related to emotional problems (Werner, Bierman & French, 1971).

Hess (1969), based on an extensive review, has developed a list of parent behaviors that have been found to be related to intellectual development and academic achievement. Similar lists of parental variables can be found in studies by Rupp (1969) and Wolf (1964) and in others summarized elsewhere in this review. The Hess list is as follows:

A. *Intellectual Relationship*
   1. Demand for high achievement
   2. Maximization of verbal interaction
   3. Engagement with and attentiveness to the child
   4. Maternal teaching behavior
   5. Diffuse intellectual stimulation
B. *Affective Relationship*
   1. Warm affective relationship with child
   2. Feelings of high regard for child and self
C. *Interaction Patterns*
   1. Pressure for independence and self-reliance
   2. Clarity and severity of disciplinary rules[1]
   3. Use of conceptual rather than arbitrary regulatory strategies

Intra-Family Resemblance

Roff's (1950) review of intra-family resemblances in personality characteristics has provided a great deal of evidence that parents influence the development of attitudes, opinions, and interests in their children. Hartshorne et al. (1930) found relatively high correlations between parents and children in a test of moral knowledge and opinion and Newcomb and Svehla (1937) found substantial correlations between parents and children in attitudes toward the church, war, and communism. Somewhat lower correlations have been found between fathers and sons in vocational interests and even lower, but usually positive correlations, in personality inventory scores. Reports by high school children about their own use and their parent's use of psychoactive drugs suggest that patterns of heavy drug use are heavily influenced by parental example (Smart & Fejer, 1970). Children who reported that their mothers used tranquilizers nearly every day were eight times as likely to report their own use of tranquilizers as were children who reported that their mothers never used tranquilizers. Use of one psychoactive drug by parents, both mothers and fathers, was found to influence use of many other psy-

choactive drugs by their children. Thus, Smart and Fejer (1970) suggested that "A likely hypothesis is that students are modeling their drug use after parents' use. . . ."

Early Emergence of Levels of Intelligence

In the area of intellectual and language development, relatively stable differences in mean mental test scores between socioeconomic groups emerge in the second and third year of life (Terman & Merrill, 1937; Hindley, 1965). This may be interpreted as evidence of the early and continuing influence of parental stimulation. Studies show that the mean IQs of different groups tend to remain stable during the school years (Terman & Merrill, 1937; Kennedy, 1969), or the mean IQs of disadvantaged groups may even decline in regions of relative deprivation (Coleman, 1966). Apparently, the typical school does not improve the level of intellectual functioning that is established and maintained by the family and community under these circumstances. Schaefer (1970), from a summary of findings on early language development and intellectual development concluded, "The evidence of the coincidence of the emergence of early language skills with the emergence of mental test differences between social groups, of the relationship of verbal skills with socioeconomic status, ethnic groups, IQ scores, reading achievement and academic and occupational success, supports a conclusion that the education of the child should begin prior to or at the beginning of early language development." Relations between maternal behavior and child language behavior at five months (Rubenstein, 1967) and 10 months of age (Tulkin, 1971) can be interpreted as evidence of influence of parent behavior upon early language development and, perhaps, later cognitive development.

Studies of Children in Institutions and Adoptive Homes

Another source of evidence showing the educational influence of parents is the study of language development of children reared in institutions (Skeels et al. 1938; Pringle & Bossio, 1958). Skeels et al. reported: "At most ages the orphanage children had a vocabulary only one-fourth to one-half that of Iowa City children of average intelligence and the same age. Explanations of this extreme retardation were advanced; namely, that the orphanage situation was characteristically deficient in the factors known to be associated with good language development — such factors as adult-child ratio, parent goals for child achievement, standard of acceptability of verbal expression, number of hours being read to and being told stories, breadth of experiences, and extensions of environment." Skeels et al. pointed out that study of the orphanage

group "demonstrates to some extent what average homes operating in an average social milieu accomplish in the way of mental stimulation, by showing what may happen when children are bereft of such influences."

Other studies by Skeels (1940) and his coworkers at the University of Iowa provided additional data on the role of the environment in intellectual development. A study of infants in an institution for higher level retarded girls (Skeels & Dye, 1939) who received a relatively high stimulation from patients and staff, as contrasted to infants who received relatively little stimulation in an orphanage, showed substantial IQ increases in the stimulated group and substantial decreases in the unstimulated group. Subsequently, most of the stimulated group were adopted while the unstimulated group remained in the orphanage. A follow-up showed very large differences in the social competence of the two groups at maturity (Skeels, 1966). Not only the early stimulation in the institution, but also the continued stimulation in the adoptive homes, contributed to the intellectual functioning and social competence of the experimental group.

A study by Skeels and Harms (1948) of children in good adoptive homes whose natural parents were either mentally retarded or of very low socio-economic status yielded surprising results. The adopted children of mentally retarded natural mothers achieved a mean IQ of 105.5, children whose natural fathers were laborers had a mean IQ of 110.3, and children with both laborer fathers and mentally retarded mothers had a mean IQ of 104.1. Mental retardation in the children "with known inferior histories" who were placed in adoptive homes in infancy was no greater than that of a random sample of the population and the frequency of superior intelligence was somewhat greater than would be expected. Skodak and Skeels (1949) also reported a 20-point IQ difference between adopted children and their natural mothers, with a maternal mean of 86 and a child mean of 106. These data suggest that a radical change in environment can produce a major change in intellectual functioning between generations.

Despite the substantial differences between mean IQs of the adopted children and their natural mothers, Skodak and Skeels reported higher correlations between the IQs of the adopted children and those of their natural mothers than with characteristics of the adoptive parents. Thus, the data indicate that genetics may determine the potential for intellectual development but the quality of the environment may determine the level of intellectual functioning that is achieved.

Cross-Sectional Studies

A number of cross-sectional studies have provided detailed analysis of parent variables that are related to children's mental test scores. Milner

(1951) interviewed both mothers and children to determine family variables that were related to high and low language scores on the *California Test of Mental Maturity*. High scoring children had more books, were read to more often, had more meal time conversation with parents, and received less harsh physical punishment. Interpretation of the findings is obscured by the great differences in socioeconomic status between low and high scoring groups. Milner recognized the problem in her statement, "The findings listed above may be restated, substituting for the words *mothers of low scorers and high scorers*, the words *lower-class mothers and middle-class mothers* respectively." Milner's study suggests that different socio-economic groups have different patterns of parent behavior that are partially determined by their adaptation to their life situation but also are related to their children's intellectual development.

Kent and Davis (1957) interviewed parents of samples of school children, juvenile offenders, and psychiatric outpatient clinic referrals and classified the type of discipline used as normal, demanding, over-anxious, and unconcerned. The parents of the school children showed the highest percentage of normal discipline, the parents of the juvenile offenders showed the highest percentage of unconcerned discipline, and the parents of the psychiatric outpatient clinic referrals showed the highest percentages of demanding and overanxious discipline. Among the school sample, children of demanding parents had the highest IQ scores and had higher verbal than performance scores; children of unconcerned parents had the lowest IQ scores and reading scores. This study suggests that insufficiency of emotional support and intellectual stimulation results in lower intelligence and academic achievement than moderate degrees of distortion – demanding and overanxious discipline – but both insufficiency and distortion may be related to different types of maladjustment.

Interviews and mailed questionnaires focusing upon parental rejection and punitiveness have been correlated with *California Test of Mental Maturity* scores (Hurley, 1965; 1967). An association between parent rejection and low mental test scores was found for different measures and for different samples, with higher correlations between the mothers' education and the daughters' IQ and low correlations for the higher educational groups of parents. Although a number of studies support the conclusion that rejection tends to be negatively related to intellectual development (Baldwin, Kalhorn & Breese, 1945; Bayley & Schaefer, 1964; Kagan & Freeman, 1963; Kagan, 1964; Honzig, 1967), different findings for different socioeconomic groups and for boys and girls in different studies suggest a possible interaction between socioeconomic group, sex of child, and parent behavior as these influence the intellectual development and academic achievement of children. Perhaps different socio-

economic groups have different expectations for boys and girls that are related to parent behavior and child development.

Interviews with parents of fifth grade children about family educational processes (Dave, 1963; Wolf, 1964) have isolated a number of parental variables that are related to academic achievement and intellectual development. Family process was found to be more highly related to intelligence and achievement than was socioeconomic status. Rupp (1969) tested hypotheses about the relation of parent practices to reading success through a questionnaire study of a range of socioeconomic groups. Cultural-pedagogical patterns of child rearing were related to socioeconomic status within the lower socioeconomic groups, but not within the higher socioeconomic groups in which the fathers had at least high school educations. A second study of children from very low socioeconomic groups from the first grade of the primary school also showed significant relations between parent behavior and attitudes and the children's reading achievement.

Although the cross-sectional studies of parent behavior and child development yield consistent findings, their interpretation is unclear. The results may reflect the parent's response to the child's behavior rather than parental influence upon the child's development. Further, methods that have been used in these studies—interviews, questionnaires, and inventories—may not yield valid information on the parents' behavior. The longitudinal studies that have used repeated observations of a parent's actual behavior as observed in familiar situations, provide more valid data upon which to interpret parent influences on child development.

Longitudinal Studies

Analyses of data collected in several early longitudinal studies show significant correlations between observations of maternal behavior in early childhood and the child's subsequent mental test scores (Baldwin, Kalhorn & Breese, 1945; Bayley & Schaefer, 1964; Honzig, 1967; Kagan & Freeman, 1963; Kagan, 1964). Since the maternal behavior was often observed prior to the appearance of the correlations with the children's intelligence, it is less likely that the parent behavior is a response to the child's intelligence. Small sample sizes, inconsistent results for boys and girls, difficulties in controlling for social class in these small samples, and the utilization of the data for purposes not foreseen at the time they were collected, have limited the usefulness of these early studies. However, the major trends in the significant relations found between parent behavior and the child's intellectual growth have been replicated in several major studies.

A longitudinal study of ability and educational attainment of approximately 5,000 children born in 1946 in England, Scotland, and Wales documents the influence of the home and of the school (Douglas, 1964). Significant differences between social classes were found in standards of infant care and management, use of medical services, interest in the child's school progress, age at which the parents wished the child to leave school, and the desire for the child to enter grammar school — higher standard, academic education. Children of manual working-class parents showed a relative decline in tests of mental ability and school achievement between eight and 11 years of age. They also had a lower chance of going to grammar school even when measured ability was controlled. The parents' interest in their children's school progress was measured by frequency of mothers' visits to the school, requests to speak to the principal as well as the teacher, and by fathers' visits. These showed striking differences between social classes. The author concluded that "The influence of level of parents' interest on test performance is greater than that of any of the three other factors — size of family, standard of home (housing), and academic record of the school — which are included in this analysis, and it becomes increasingly important as the children grow older." After controlling for socioeconomic level of the family, variations in the children's test scores were much more related to variations in degree of parent interest than to variations in the quality of the schools.

Another English longitudinal study, reported by Moore (1968), concerned material gathered from home visits. Toys, books, and experiences available to the child were rated, as were example and encouragement in the home for the development of language, emotional atmosphere of the home, and general adjustment of the child at two and a half years of age. Although these qualities of home influences were only slightly related to the child's early intelligence test scores, the relations with reading quotient at seven years and IQ at eight years were substantial. The family variables gave better predictions of IQ and reading, even after controlling for social class, than did maternal vocabulary or education. The control for social class and the early data on family variables increase the credibility of the interpretation that parent practices influence the child's development.

Werner, Bierman and French (1971) presented a longitudinal study of the effects of perinatal complications and of socioeconomic status, educational stimulation, and emotional support upon achievement problems, learning problems, and emotional difficulties of children. Socioeconomic status, educational stimulation, and emotional support showed moderate inter-correlations ranging from .37 to .57. These were all significantly

related to school achievement and learning problems (IQ, perceptual, and language problems) at 10 years of age with the highest relations for educational stimulation. Emotional problems were most highly related to lack of emotional support. The findings that the child's learning, achievement, and emotional problems were more related to indices of family environment than with socioeconomic status is similar to Douglas' (1964) and Moore's (1968) findings. The authors also concluded that "Ten times more children had problems attributed to the effects of a poor environment than to the effects of serious perinatal stress." Relations between perinatal stress and the child's competence decreased with age but relations of environmental factors and competence increased with age. At 20 months of age only a four-point difference in IQ was found between children from the least and most favored environments but at 10 years of age a 20-point difference was found between children who received the least and most educational stimulation in the home.

Hess (1969) has summarized some of the significant findings from a short-term longitudinal study that correlated measures on 160 middle-class and lower-class mothers collected at the child's age of four years with the child's school performance two to four years later. Among the variables that were related significantly to reading readiness, reading achievement and grades given by teachers were availability and use of home educational resources, the mother's personal optimism and number of out-of-home activities. Maternal behaviors in teaching the child use of an *Etch-A-Sketch* that were related to later achievement included number of models shown the child, number of specific turning directions, orientation to the task, praise and encouragement, and specificity of maternal feedback. Maternal language scores and indices of affection — support toward the child, warmth in block-sorting task, and affectionateness in teaching tasks — also predicted later school achievement. Apparently the mother's teaching behavior, the experiences she provides, and the model she sets for the child are important influences.

Evidence that low intelligence test scores are not only developed but maintained by adverse environments of neglect and cruelty has been reported by Clarke and Clarke (1959). Their studies of mentally retarded adolescents and young adults show an average IQ increase of 16 points during the six-year period after they left their adverse home environments with 33 percent showing IQ increments of 20 points or more. The Clarkes interpret their results as showing recovery from deprivation and state that "the amount of measured recovery can be taken as a minimal estimate of original damage" with the probability that the data are an underestimate of damage. The Clarkes' data are valuable not only for

showing the extent to which adverse environments can influence intellectual development but also for showing the possibility of at least partial recovery, even in early maturity.

Intervention Research

An increasing number of researchers are turning from descriptive and correlational studies of parent behavior and child development to research on programs that, through varied methods, teach parents methods for fostering the intellectual development and academic achievement of their children. Klaus and Gray (1968) utilized visitors actively to engage parents in the education of their own children as a supplement for a preschool program. Significant differences were found in mental test scores between the control children and those who had been involved in both the preschool and home visitor programs. Although the amount of difference between experimental and control groups decreased after termination of the special program, differences between groups persisted during the first years of elementary education. Evidence of vertical diffusion, i.e., that the younger children in the experimental group families also showed more rapid development, was found. The authors expressed guarded optimism about the long-range effects of two or three years work with the mothers, stating that the disadvantaged mother may be unable to provide a home situation that would maintain the development of the child and that the schools are, in general, unable to provide alone for the education of the child. Their concluding statement is an excellent summary of the evidence from intervention research,

> . . . the evidence is overwhelming in indicating that . . . performance results from the continual interaction of the organism with its environment. Intervention programs, well conceived and executed, may be expected to make some relatively lasting changes. Such programs, however, cannot be expected to carry the whole burden of providing adequate schooling for children from deprived circumstances; they can provide only a basis for future progress in schools and homes that can build upon that early intervention.

More recently, Gray (1970) has contrasted a preschool program with a program that taught mothers to foster the development of their children. The home program showed equal effectiveness at far lower cost as well as allowing vertical diffusion to younger children in the family and horizontal diffusion through the neighborhood. Gray's results suggest that a home program that teaches a mother to teach her child might either be an alternative or a supplement for a preschool program.

Weikart and Lambie (1969) have utilized trained educators to teach parents how to support their child's education in conjunction with half-day preschool programs. The combined programs, after successive refinement over a period of years, have resulted in mean IQ gains of up to 30 points in low IQ disadvantaged children. Weikart and his colleagues are currently working with parents of infants in the first year of life to determine the effectiveness of very early parent-centered intervention but have not yet reported the results.

Gordon (1968) has used paraprofessional parent educators to teach parents specific infant education exercises during the first year of life. The *Griffith Mental Development Scales* at 12 months of age showed significant differences between the experimental group and a control group, with significant differences in eye-hand, personal-social, and hearing-speech skills and little difference in locomotor and performance skills. The design of this project will evaluate the effects of intervention during the first, second, and third years of life and will evaluate the effects of brief early intervention as contrasted to continued intervention.

Levenstein (1970) conceptualized books and toys as "Verbal Interaction Stimulus Materials," had toy demonstrators use the carefully selected materials in home visits with mothers, had mothers use them under the supervision of the demonstrator, and encouraged mothers to use the materials that were left in the home. With approximately 32 visits over a seven-month period her two- and three-year-old subjects showed a mean IQ gain of approximately 17 points—from an IQ of 85 to 102. Levenstein also found that the child's IQ level can be maintained or increased by a reduced number of visits the following year. In Levenstein's initial studies, professional social workers were used as toy demonstrators but in more recent studies paraprofessionals have been trained for that role. Karnes, Teska, Hodgins and Badger (1970) worked with small groups of mothers of infants in the first and second year of life on child-centered educational activities and materials. Co-operation and attendance was lower for working mothers and only 15 of the initial group of 20 mothers completed the second year of the program. Highly significant differences in IQ were found between the experimental group of children and matched controls and the experimental group and their sibling controls. The authors expressed caution about long-term effects as contrasted to the long-term effects of preschool programs at later ages but concluded ". . . the results of the study suggest that a program of mother training can do much to prevent the inadequate cognitive and linguistic development characteristic of the disadvantaged child."

The promising results of these parent-centered intervention programs show that working with mothers is an effective method for producing

gains in intellectual functioning. Parent-centered, as contrasted to child-centered, early intervention programs have equal immediate effectiveness, greater long-term effectiveness, are less expensive, and produce vertical and horizontal diffusion through the family and community. However, the longer the time interval between the intervention and the evaluation, the less significant the effects of the program. These results suggest not only the need for early and continuing education of the child but also early and continuing support for parents in their roles as educators of their own children and as students of the theory and practice of education in the home.

A major question about the future of intervention programs designed to increase parental effectiveness in the education of their children is whether these programs would have significant effects in upper socioeconomic groups as well as in disadvantaged groups and whether intensive parental stimulation contributes substantially to superior levels of functioning as well as fostering average levels of functioning. Evidence by Moore (1968) that early parent behaviors are related to intelligence and reading achievement even after controlling for socioeconomic status and by Douglas (1964) that degree of parental involvement in the child's education is related to mental test scores at 10 years in all socioeconomic groups suggests that intervention to improve parent education would have significant effects in all socioeconomic groups. Fowler (1962) reviewed records of "25 superior IQ children, all of whom learned to read by the age of three. . . . Of these, 72 percent had definitely enjoyed a great deal of unusually early and intensive cognitive stimulation. For the other 28 percent evidence regarding the quality and quantity of stimulation was lacking in the records." Current intervention research on disadvantaged groups should be extended to other socioeconomic groups to obtain evidence of the degree to which intellectual functioning can be changed in more varied populations. The result of that study would suggest whether programs to improve parental education should be offered to all or only to disadvantaged groups.

Summary

The accumulating evidence suggests that parents have great influence upon the behavior of their children, particularly their intellectual and academic achievement, and that programs which teach parents skills in educating their children are effective supplements or alternatives for preschool education. These data should influence future education policies and programs. A critical decision will be whether to devote manpower and money to child-centered extensions of academic education or to develop a comprehensive system of education that strengthens and

supports parental education in the home, effective use of the mass media, and collaboration between the school, the home, and the mass media. This review suggests that an exclusive focus upon academic education will not solve the major educational problems. A major task for our child care and educational institutions and professions will be the development of a support system for family care and education. Major changes in professional roles and responsibilities, in training, and in educational policies and programs will be required to achieve a goal of equal education in the home as well as in the school.

Notes

1. The literature that was interpreted as "clarity and severity of disciplinary rules" could be interpreted instead as setting of high standards and enforcement of rules, rather than severity, which may imply hostility or rejection.

References

Ainsworth, M. D. The effects of maternal deprivation: A review of findings and controversy in the context of research strategy. In Deprivation of Maternal Care: A Reassessment of its Effects. *Public Health Papers*, 14, Geneva: World Health Organization, 1962.

Baldwin, A. L., Kalhorn, J. & Breese, F. H. Patterns of parent behavior. *Psychol. Monogr.*, 1945, 58, 3.

Bayley, N. & Schaefer, E. S. Correlations of maternal and child behaviors with the development of mental abilities: Data from the Berkeley Growth Study. *Monogr. Soc. Res. Child Develpm.*, 1964, 29, 6.

Bowlby, J. Maternal care and mental health. 2nd ed. Geneva: World Health Organization: Monograph Series, No. 2, 1951.

Clarke, A. D. B. & Clarke, A. M. Recovery from the effects of deprivation. *Acta Psychologica*, 1959, 16, 137–144.

Coleman, J. S. *Equality of Educational Opportunity*. Washington: U.S. Government Printing Office, 1966.

Dave, R. T. The identification and measurement of environmental process variables that are related to educational achievement. Unpubl. doctoral dissertation, Univ. of Chicago, 1963.

Douglas, J. W. *The Home and the School: A Study of Ability and Attainment in the Primary School*. London: MacGibbon & Kee, 1964.

Fowler, W. Cognitive learning in infancy and early childhood. *Psychol. Bull.*, 1962, 59, 116–152.

Gordon, I. J. Early child stimulation through parent educators. A progress report to the Children's Bureau. U.S. Dept. of H. E. W., Gainesville, Fla., 1968.

Gray, S. Home visiting programs for parents of young children. Paper presented at the meeting of the National Association for the Education of Young Children. Boston, 1970.

Gray, S. W. & Klaus, R. The early training project: A seventh year report. John F. Kennedy Center for Research on Education and Human Development. George Peabody College, 1969.

Hartshorne, H., May, M. & and Shuttleworth, F. K. *Studies in the Organization of Character.* New York: MacMillan, 1930.

Hess, R. D. Parental behavior and children's school achievement; implications for Head Start. In E. Grotberg (Ed.), *Critical Issues in Research Related to Disadvantaged Children.* Princeton: Educational Testing Service, 1969.

Hess, R. D., Block, M., Costello, D., Knowles, R. T. & Largan, D. Parent involvement in early education. In Edith H. Grotberg (Ed.) *Day Care: Resource for Decisions.* Washington: Office of Economic Opportunity, 1971.

Hess, R. D., Shipman, V. C., Brophy, J. & Bear, R. B. (In collaboration with A. Adelberger). The cognitive environment of urban pre-school children: follow-up phase. Report to Children's Bureau. Social Security Administration, U.S. Dept. of H.E.W., 1969.

Hindley, C. B. Stability and change in abilities up to five years: Group trends. *J. Child Psychol. Psychiat.*, 1965, 6, 85-99.

Honzig, M. P. Environmental correlates of mental growth: Prediction from the family setting at 21 months. *Child Develpm.*, 1967, 38, 337-364, 1967.

Hurley, J. R. Parental acceptance-rejection and children's intelligence *Merrill-Palmer Qtrly.*, 1965, 11, 19-31.

————. Parental malevolence and children's intelligence. *J. Consult. Psychol.*, 1967, 31, 199-204.

Irwin, O. Infant speech: Effect of systematic reading of stories. *J. Speech Hearing Res.*, 1960, 3, 187-190.

Kagan, J. Erratum. *Child Develpm.*, 1964, 35, 1397.

Kagan, J. & Freeman, M. Relation of childhood intelligence and social class to behavior during adolescence. *Child Develpm.*, 1963, 34, 899-901.

Karnes, M. B. & Badger, E. Training mothers to instruct their infants at home. In M. B. Karnes (Ed.), *Research and Development Program on Preschool Disadvantaged Children.* Project Report to the U.S. Dept. of H.E.W., 1969.

Karnes, M. B., Teska, I. A., Hodgins, A. S. & Badger, E. D. Educational intervention at home by mothers of disadvantaged infants. *Child Develpm.*, 1970, 41, 925-935.

Kennedy, W. A. A follow-up normative study of Negro intelligence and achievement. *Monogr. Soc. Res. Child Develpm.*, 1969, 34, 2.

Kent, N. & Davis, D. R. Discipline in the home and intellectual development. *Brit. J. Med. Psychol.*, 1957, 30, 27–34.

Klaus, R. A. & Gray, S. W. The educational training program for disadvantaged children: A report after five years. *Monogr. Soc. Res. Child Develpm.*, 1968. 33, 4.

Levenstein, P. Cognitive growth in preschoolers through verbal interaction with mothers. *Am. J. Orthopsychiat.*, 1970, 40, 426–32.

Milner, E. A. A study of the relationship between reading readiness in grade one school children and patterns of parent-child interaction. *Child Develpm.*, 1951, 22, 95–112.

Moore, T. Language and intelligence: A longitudinal study of the first eight years. Part II: Environmental correlates of mental growth. *Human Develpm.*, 1968, 11, 1–24.

Newcomb, T. & Svehla, G. Intra-family relationships in attitude. *Sociometry*, 1937, 1, 271–283.

Pringle, M. L. & Bossio, V. A study of deprived children. *Vita Humana*, 1958, 1, 65–92.

Roff, M. Intra-family resemblence in personality characteristics. *J. Psychol.* 1950, 30, 199–227.

Rubenstein, J. Maternal attentiveness and subsequent exploratory behavior of the infant. *Child Develpm.*, 1967, 38, 1089–1100.

Rupp., J. C. C. *Helping the Child to Cope with the School: A Study of the Importance of Parent-Child Relationships with Regard to Elementary School Success.* Groningen: Walters-Noordhoff, 1969.

Schaefer, E. S. Need for early and continuing education. In V. M. Denenberg, (Ed). *Education of the Infant and Young Child.* New York: Academic Press, 1970.

Schaefer, E. S. Development of hierarchial configurational models for parent behavior and child behavior. J. P. Hill (Ed.), *Minnesota Symposia on Child Psychology*, Vol. V., Minneapolis: Univ. of Minnesota Press, 1971.

Shramm, W., Lyle, J. & Parker, E. W. *Television in the Lives of Our Children.* Stanford: Stanford Univ. Press, 1961.

Skeels, H. M. Some Iowa studies of the mental growth of children in relation to differentials of the environment: A summary. In G. M. Whipple (Ed.), *Intelligence: Its Nature and Nurture.* 39th Yearbook, Part II, National Society for the Study of Education. 1940. 281–308.

———. Adult status of children with contrasting early life experiences. *Monogr. Soc. Res. Child Development.* 1966, 31, 3.

Skeels, H. M. & Dye, H. B. A study of the effects of differential stimula-

tion on mentally retarded children. *Proceedings of the American Association on Mental Deficiency.* 1939, 44, 114–136.

Skeels, H. M. & Harms, I. Children with inferior social histories; their mental development in adoptive homes. *J. Genetic Psychol.*, 1948, 72, 283–294.

Skeels, H. M., Updegraff, R., Wellman, B. L. & Williams, H. M. A study of environmental stimulation: An orphanage preschool project. *Univ. of Iowa Studies in Child Welfare.* 1938, 15, No. 4.

Skodak, M. & Skeels, H. M. A final follow-up of one hundred adopted children. *J. Genetic Psychol.*, 1949, 75, 85–125.

Smart, R. G. & Fejer, D., Drug use among adolescents and their parents: Closing the generation gap in mood modification. Paper presented at the meeting of the Eastern Psychiatric Research Association. Nov., 1970.

Terman, L. M. & Merrill, M. A. *Measuring Intelligence: A Guide to the Administration of the New Revised Stanford-Binet Tests of Intelligence.* New York: Houghton Mifflin, 1937.

Tulkin, S. R. Infant's reaction to mother's voice and stranger's voice. Social class differences in the first year of life. Paper presented at the meeting of the Society for Research in Child Development. Minneapolis. April 1971.

Weikart, D. P. & Lambie, D. Z. Ypsilanti-Carnegie Infant Education Project Progress Report. Dept. of Research & Development. Ypsilanti Public Schools, Ypsilanti, Mich., 1969.

Werner, E. E., Bierman, J. M. & French, F. E. *The Children of Kauai. A Longitudinal Study from the Prenatal Period to Age Ten.* Honolulu: Univ. of Hawaii Press. 1971.

Wolf, R. M. The identification and measurement of environmental process variables related to intelligence. Unpubl. doctoral dissertation, Univ. of Chicago, 1964.

Yarrow, L. I. Maternal deprivation: Toward an empirical and conceptual reevaluation. *Psych. Bull.*, 1961, 58, 459.

4.9   An Experiment in Group Upbringing

Anna Freud
Sophie Dann

Introduction

The experiment to which the following notes refer is not the outcome of an artificial and deliberate laboratory setup but of a combination of fateful outside circumstances. The six young children who are involved in it are German-Jewish orphans, victims of the Hitler regime, whose parents, soon after their birth, were deported to Poland and killed in the gas chambers. During their first year of life, the children's experiences differed; they were handed on from one refuge to another, until they arrived individually, at ages varying from approximately six to twelve months, in the concentration camp of Tereszin.[1] There they became inmates of the Ward for Motherless Children, were conscientiously cared for and medically supervised, within the limits of the current restrictions of food and living space. They had no toys and their only facility for outdoor life was a bare yard. The Ward was staffed by nurses and helpers, themselves inmates of the concentration camp and, as such, undernourished and overworked. Since Tereszin was a transit camp, deportations were frequent. Approximately two to three years after arrival, in the spring of 1945, when liberated by the Russians, the six children, with others, were taken to a Czech castle where they were given special care and were lavishly fed. After one month's stay, the 6 were included in a transport of 300 older children and adolescents, all of them survivors from concentration camps, the first of 1000 children for whom the British Home Office had granted permits of entry. They were flown to England in bombers and arrived in August 1945 in a carefully set-up reception camp in Windermere, Westmoreland where they remained for two months. When this reception camp was cleared and the older children distributed to various hostels and training places, it was thought wise to leave the six youngest together, to remove them from the commotion which is inseparable from the life of a large children's community and to provide them with peaceful, quiet surroundings where, for a year at least, they could adapt themselves gradually to a new country, a new language, and the altered circumstances of their lives.

This ambitious plan was realized through the combined efforts of a

Reprinted with slight abridgment from *The Psychoanalytic Study of the Child*, Vol. VI, pp. 127–168, by permission of the author and the International Universities Press, Inc. Copyright 1951 by International Universities Press, Inc.

number of people. A friend of the former Hampstead Nurseries, Mrs. Ralph Clarke, wife of the Member of Parliament for East Grinstead, Sussex, gave the children a year's tenancy of a country house with field and adjoining woodland, "Bulldogs Bank" in West Hoathly, Sussex, containing two bedrooms for the children, with adjoining bathrooms, a large day nursery, the necessary staff rooms, a veranda running the whole length of the house and a sun terrace.

The Foster Parents' Plan for War Children, Inc., New York, who had sponsored the Hampstead Nurseries during the war years 1940–1945, took the six children into their plan and adopted Bulldogs Bank as one of their colonies. They provided the necessary equipment as well as the financial upkeep.

The new Nursery was staffed by Sisters Sophie and Gertrud Dann, formerly the head nurses of the Baby Department and Junior Nursery Department of the Hampstead Nurseries respectively. A young assistant, Miss Maureen Wolfison, who had accompanied the children from Windermere was replaced after several weeks by Miss Judith Gaulton, a relief worker. Cooking and housework was shared between the staff, with occasional outside help.

The children arrived in Bulldogs Bank on October 15, 1945. The personal data of the six, so far as they could be ascertained, were the following:

Name	Date and Place of Birth	Family History	Age at Arrival in Tereszin	Age at Arrival in Bulldogs Bank
John	18.12.1941 Vienna	Orthodox Jewish working-class parents. Deported to Poland and killed.	Presumably under 12 months	3 years 10 months
Ruth	21.4.1942 Vienna	Parents, a brother of 7 and a sister of 4 years were deported and killed when Ruth was a few months old. She was cared for in a Jewish Nursery in Vienna, sent to Tereszin with the Nursery.	Several months	3 years 6 months
Leah	23.4.1942 Berlin	Leah and a brother were illegitimate, hidden from birth. Fate of mother and brother unknown. Brother presumed killed.	Several months	3 years 5 months Arrived 6 weeks after the others. owing to a ringworm infection.

Name	Date and Place of Birth	Family History	Age at Arrival in Tereszin	Age at Arrival in Bulldogs Bank
Paul	21.5.1942 Berlin	Unknown	12 months	3 years 5 months
Miriam	18.8.1942 Berlin	Upper middle-class family. Father died in concentration camp, mother went insane, was cared for first in a mental hospital in Vienna, later in a mental ward in Tereszin where she died.	6 months.	3 years 2 months
Peter	22.10.1942	Parents deported and killed when Peter was a few days old. Child was found abandoned in public park, cared for first in a convent, later, when found to be Jewish, was taken to the Jewish hospital in Berlin, then brought to Tereszin.	Under 12 months	3 years

Meager as these scraps of information are, they establish certain relevant facts concerning the early history of this group of children:

(i)   that four of them (Ruth, Leah, Miriam, Peter) lost their mothers at birth or immediately afterward; one (Paul) before the age of twelve months, one (John) at an unspecified date;

(ii) that after the loss of their mothers all the children wandered for some time from one place to another, with several complete changes of adult environment. (Bulldogs Bank was the sixth station in life for Peter, the fifth for Miriam, etc. John's and Leah's and Paul's wanderings before arrival in Tereszin are not recorded.);

(iii) that none of the children had known any other circumstances of life than those of a group setting. They were ignorant of the meaning of a "family";

(iv) that none of the children had experience of normal life outside a camp or big institution.[4]

Behavior Toward Adults on Arrival

On leaving the reception camp in Windermere, the children reacted badly to the renewed change in their surroundings. They showed no

pleasure in the arrangements which had been made for them and behaved in a wild, restless, and uncontrollably noisy manner. During the first days after arrival they destroyed all the toys and damaged much of the furniture. Toward the staff they behaved either with cold indifference or with active hostility, making no exception for the young assistant Maureen who had accompanied them from Windermere and was their only link with the immediate past. At times they ignored the adults so completely that they would not look up when one of them entered the room. They would turn to an adult when in some immediate need, but treat the same person as nonexistent once more when the need was fulfilled. In anger, they would hit the adults, bite or spit. Above all, they would shout, scream, and use bad language. Their speech, at the time, was German with an admixture of Czech words, and a gradual increase of English words. In a good mood, they called the staff members indiscriminately *Tante* (auntie), as they had done in Terezin; in bad moods this changed to *blöde Tante* (silly, stupid auntie). Their favorite swearword was *blöder Ochs* (the equivalent of "stupid fool"), a German term which they retained longer than any other.

Group Reactions

Clinging to the Group

The children's positive feelings were centered exclusively in their own group. It was evident that they cared greatly for each other and not at all for anybody or anything else. They had no other wish than to be together and became upset when they were separated from each other, even for short moments. No child would consent to remain upstairs while the others were downstairs, or vice versa, and no child would be taken for a walk or on an errand without the others. If anything of the kind happened, the single child would constantly ask for the other children while the group would fret for the missing child.

This insistence on being inseparable made it impossible in the beginning to treat the children as individuals or to vary their lives according to their special needs. Ruth, for instance, did not like going for walks, while the others greatly preferred walks to indoor play. But it was very difficult to induce the others to go out and let Ruth stay at home. One day, they actually left without her, but kept asking for her until, after approximately twenty minutes, John could bear it no longer and turned back to fetch her. The others joined him, they all returned home, greeted Ruth as if they had been separated for a long time and then took her for a walk, paying a great deal of special attention to her. . . .

Inability to be separated from the group showed up most glaringly in

those instances where individual children were singled out for a special treat, a situation for which children crave under normal circumstances. Paul, for example, cried for the other children when he was taken as the only one for a ride in the pony cart, although at other times such rides were a special thrill to him as well as to the others. On another, later, occasion the whole group of children was invited to visit another nursery in the neighborhood. Since the car was not large enough to take everybody, Paul and Miriam were taken earlier by bus. The other four, in the car, inquired constantly about them and could not enjoy the trip nor the pleasures prepared for them, until they were reunited.

Type of Group Formation

When together, the children were a closely knit group of members with equal status, no child assuming leadership for any length of time, but each one exerting a strong influence on the others by virtue of individual qualities, peculiarities, or by the mere fact of belonging. At the beginning, John, as the oldest, seemed to be the undisputed leader at mealtimes. He only needed to push away his plate, for everybody else to cease eating. Peter, though the youngest, was the most imaginative of all and assumed leadership in games, which he would invent and organize. Miriam too played a major role, in a peculiar way. She was a pretty, plump child, with ginger hair, freckles and a ready smile. She behaved toward the other children as if she were a superior being, and let herself be served and spoiled by them as a matter of course. She would sometimes smile at the boys in return for their services, while accepting Leah's helpfulness toward herself without acknowledgment. But she, too, did not guide or govern the group. The position was rather that she needed a special kind of attention to be paid to her and that the other children sensed this need and did their best to fulfill it. The following are some recorded examples of this interplay between Miriam and the group:

November 1945.—Miriam, on a walk, has found a tiny pink flower, carries it in her hand but loses it soon. She calls out "flower!" and John and Paul hurry to pick it up for her, a difficult task since they wear thick gloves. Miriam drops the flower again and again, never makes an attempt to pick it up herself, merely calls "flower!" and the boys hurry to find it.

March 1946.—From the beginning Miriam liked to sit in comfortable chairs. In the winter she would drag such a chair to the fireplace, put her feet on the fire guard and play in that position. When outdoor life began again, Miriam had a chair in the sandbox. She even helped

weed the garden while sitting in a chair. But it did not happen often that she had to fetch a chair herself usually the other children carried it into the garden for her. One day, Miriam and Paul played in the sandbox after supper. Suddenly Paul appears in the house to fetch Miriam's chair. When told that the evening was too cold already for outdoor play and that they had better both come in, he merely looks bewildered and says: "But Miriam wants chair, open door quickly."

May 1946. — Miriam drops her towel, turns around and says: "Pick it up, somebody." Leah picks it up for her.

July 1946. — Miriam enters the kitchen, calls out: "Chair for Miriam, quickly." She looks indignant when she sees no child in the kitchen and nobody to obey her orders. She does not fetch the chair herself but goes out again.

August 1946. Ruth is found in Miriam's bed in the morning and is asked to get up. Miriam replies instead of Ruth: "Oh no, she much better stays here. She has to wait to fasten Miriam's buttons."

August 1946. — Miriam bangs her hand on the table and says to John: "Can't you be quiet when I want to talk?" John stops talking.

The children's sensitiveness to each other's attitudes and feelings was equally striking where Leah was concerned. Leah was the only backward child among the six, of slow, lower average intelligence, with no outstanding qualities to give her a special status in the group. As mentioned before, Leah's arrival in Bulldogs Bank was delayed for six weeks owing to a ringworm infection. During this period the five other children had made their first adaptation to the new place, had learned some English, had established some contact with the staff and dropped some of their former restlessness. With Leah's coming, the whole group, in identification with her, behaved once more as if they were all newcomers. They used the impersonal *Tante* again instead of first names for the members of staff. They reverted to talking German only, shouted and screamed and were again out of control. This regression lasted approximately a week, evidently for the length of time which Leah herself needed to feel more comfortable in her new surroundings.

Positive relations within the group. Absence of envy, jealousy, rivalry, competition

The children's unusual emotional dependence on each other was borne out further by the almost complete absence of jealousy, rivalry and competition, such as normally develop between brothers and sisters or in a group of contemporaries who come from normal families. There

was no occasion to urge the children to "take turns"; they did it spontaneously since they were eager that everybody should have his share.
Since the adults played no part in their emotional lives at the time, they
did not compete with each other for favors or for recognition. They did
not tell on each other and they stood up for each other automatically
whenever they felt that a member of the group was unjustly treated or
otherwise threatened by an outsider. They were extremely considerate
of each other's feelings. They did not grudge each other their possessions (with one exception to be mentioned later), on the contrary lending
them to each other with pleasure. When one of them received a present
from a shopkeeper, they demanded the same for each of the other children, even in their absence. On walks they were concerned for each
other's safety in traffic, looked after children who lagged behind, helped
each other over ditches, turned aside branches for each other to clear
the passage in the woods, and carried each other's coats. In the nursery
they picked up each other's toys. After they had learned to play, they
assisted each other silently in building and admired each other's productions. At mealtimes handing food to the neighbor was of greater importance than eating oneself.

Behavior of this kind was the rule, not the exception. The following
examples merely serve the purpose of illustration and are in no way outstanding. They are chosen at random from the first seven months of the
children's stay in Bulldogs Bank:

October 1945.—John, daydreaming while walking, nearly bumps
into a passing child. Paul immediately sides with him and shouts at the
passer-by: "Blöder Ochs, meine John, blöder Ochs Du!" ["Stupid
fool, my John, you stupid fool!"]

November 1945.—John refuses to get up in the morning, lies in his
bed, screams and kicks. Ruth brings his clothes and asks: "Willst Du
anziehen?" ["Don't you want to put them on?"] Miriam offers him her
doll with a very sweet smile. John calms down at once and gets up.

November 1945.—John cries when there is no cake left for a second
helping for him. Ruth and Miriam offer him what is left of their por-
tions. While John eats their pieces of cake, they pet him and comment
contentedly on what they have given him. . . .

December 1945.—Paul has a plate full of cake crumbs. When he
begins to eat them, the other children want them too. Paul gives the
biggest crumbs to Miriam, the three middle-sized ones to the other
children, and eats the smallest one himself. . . .

December 1945.—Paul loses his gloves during a walk. John gives

him his own gloves, and never complains that his hands are cold. . . .

January 1946. — A visitor gives sweets to the children in the kitchen. Peter and Leah immediately demand a sweet for Miriam who is alone in the nursery. . . .

March 1946. — John has a temper tantrum when a ladybird, which he has caught, flies away. Leah hurries to him, strokes his hair, picks up his basket and all the carrots which he dropped out. She carried both John's and her own full baskets on the way home. . . .

March 1946. — Paul receives a parcel with clothes, toys and sweets from his American foster parents, a new experience in the children's lives. The excitement is great but there is no sign of envy. The children help to unpack, hold whatever Paul gives them to hold, welcome what he gives them as presents but accept the fact that he is, and remains, the owner of most of the contents of the parcel. . . .

April 1946. — On the beach in Brighton, Ruth throws pebbles into the water. Peter is afraid of waves and does not dare to approach them. In spite of his fear, he suddenly rushes to Ruth, calls out: "Water coming, water coming," and drags her back to safety. . . .

Discrimination between group members. Antipathies and friendships

Although the positive reactions of the children extended to all members of the group, individual preferences or their opposite were not lacking. There was a certain discrimination against Leah on the part of the other girls, as the following recordings indicate:

February 1946. — When Miriam cries, Leah runs immediately to comfort her, although Miriam each time screams: "Not Leah," and then accepts comfort from the other children.

April 1946. — Ruth is very helpful toward Leah, looks after her on walks and helps her to dress and undress. But her behavior indicates that these actions are duties, imposed by Leah's comparative clumsiness, rather than acts of friendship.

There were, further, close and intimate friendships between individual children, as for example between Paul and Miriam.

October 1945. — On his first evening in Bulldogs Bank, Paul goes to bed, saying with a deep sigh: "My Miriam."

October 1945. — Paul is very fond of Miriam. He gives her toys and serves her at mealtimes. Sometimes he takes her doll, walks with it round the room and returns it to her.

November 1945. — On her third day in Bulldogs Bank, Miriam had

been given a doll from which she became inseparable in day- and nighttime. No other child was allowed to touch it except Paul who sometimes took it for a walk round the room.

On November 11, Miriam gives the doll to Paul when saying good night and goes to sleep without it.

On November 12, she gives him the doll again in the evening but later cries in her bed. Paul, who has the doll in bed with him, gets up and calls through the closed door: "Miriam, dolly!" Miriam gets her doll and Paul goes to sleep without it. . . .

Aggressive Reactions within the Group

With the exception of one child the children did not hurt or attack each other in the first months. The only aggressiveness to which they gave vent within the group was verbal. They quarreled endlessly at mealtimes and on walks, mostly without any visible provocation. . . .

The disputes ended sometimes in a general uproar, sometimes in a concerted attack on any adult who had tried to interfere and appease the quarrel; mostly the quarrel merely petered out when some new event distracted the children's attention.

After the children had entered into more normal emotional relationships with the adults and had become more independent of each other, word battles diminished and were replaced to some degree by the fights normal for this age. This second phase lasted approximately from January to July, when the relations between the children became peaceful again on a new basis.

The only child whose reactions did not fit in with the general behavior of the group was Ruth. She behaved like the others so far as being inseparable from the group was concerned, did not want to be left alone and worried about absent children. She also did her share of comforting others or of helping Leah, the latter especially after Leah begun to call her "my Ruth." But apart from these reactions, she was moved by feelings of envy, jealousy and competition, which were lacking in the other children and which made her actions stand out as isolated instances of maliciousness or spitefulness. In this connection it is interesting to remember that Ruth is the only child among the group who has a recorded history of passionate attachment to a mother substitute. The evidence is not sufficient to establish with certainty that it is this past mother relationship which prevented her from merging completely with the group, and which aroused normal sibling rivalry in her. On the other hand, the difference between her and the other children's behavior together with the difference in their emotional histories seems too striking to be a mere coincidence.

The following are instances of Ruth's negative behavior in the group. Between October and January these instances were daily events. They lessened considerably after she had formed a new attachment to Sister Gertrud and they disappeared almost altogether after June. . . .

October 1945.—Ruth takes other children's toys, shows a very pleased, triumphant expression.

October 1945.—Peter has to wear a bonnet to protect a bandage where he has cut his head. Ruth takes off his bonnet repeatedly.

November 1945.—Peter gets soap in his eyes at bathtime and cries. Ruth watches him. When he has almost ceased crying, her watchful expression changes suddenly to a malicious one. She snatches the piece of soap and tries to put it into Peter's eye.

November 1945.—Each child receives a sweet. Ruth keeps hers until the others have finished eating theirs. Then she offers her sweet to one child after the other, withdrawing it as soon as the child touches it. Repeats this for twenty minutes and again later until the children stop paying attention to her. . . .

January 1946.—John, Miriam and Peter are isolated with stomatitis. Ruth cannot stand the extra care given to them and takes out her jealousy on Paul and Leah by hitting and biting them. Her aggressiveness ceases again when the patients recover. . . .

May 1946.—The children pick flowers which grow behind high nettles. They are warned to avoid being stung. John continues but moves and picks carefully. After a while he cries out as he gets stung: "Die Ruth, die Ruth push " Ruth stands behind him, pushing him into the nettles with a malicious expression on her face. . . .

Aggressiveness Toward the Adults

As reported above, the children behaved with strong and uncontrolled aggression toward the adults from their arrival. This aggression was impersonal in its character, not directed against any individual and not to be taken as a sign of interest in the adult world. The children merely reacted defensively against an environment which they experienced as strange, hostile and interfering.

On arrival it was striking that the form of aggressive expression used by the children was far below that normal for their age. They used biting as a weapon, in the manner in which toddlers use it between eighteen and twenty-four months. Biting reached its peak with Peter, who would bite anybody and on all occasions when angry; it was least pronounced

with Leah who showed very little aggression altogether. For several weeks John and Ruth would spit at the adults, Ruth also spitting on the table, on plates, on toys, looking at the adults in defiance. Similarly, Peter, when defying the staff, urinated into the brick box, on the slide, into the toy scullery, or wetted his knickers.

After a few weeks, the children hit and smacked the adults when angry. This happened especially on walks where they resented the restrictions imposed on them in traffic.

Shouting and noisy behavior was used deliberately as an outlet for aggression against the adults, even though the children themselves disliked the noise.

Toward spring these very infantile modes of aggressiveness gave way to the usual verbal aggressions used by children between three and four years. Instead of hitting out, the child would threaten to do so, or would say: "Naughty boy, I make noise at you," and then shout at the top of their voices. Other threats used by the children were: "Doggy bite you." Paul once used: "Froggy bite you." After a visit to Brighton in April, where Peter had been frightened of the waves, a new threat was used by them: "You go in a water." They sometimes tried to find a water so as to carry out the threat.

From the summer 1946 onward, the children used phrases copied from the adults to express disapproval: "I am not pleased with you."

The following samples of aggressive behavior are chosen from a multitude of examples of similar or identical nature during the first three months.

October 1945.—Mrs. X from the village returns the clean laundry. Both John and Peter spit at her when she enters the nursery.

October 1945.—A painter works in the nursery with a high ladder. Peter, who climbs on the ladder, is lifted down by Sister Gertrud. He spits at her and shouts: "Blöde Tante, blöder Ochs!" ["Stupid auntie, stupid fool."] . . .

October 1945.—John hits Mrs. Clarke repeatedly.

November 1945.—Sister Gertrud polishes shoes and tells Ruth not to play with the shoe polish. Ruth spits at her, throws the box with polish down the stairs and runs through the house, shouting: "Blöder Ochs, Gertrud."

First Positive Relations With the Adults

The children's first positive approaches to the adults were made on

the basis of their group feelings and differed in quality from the usual demanding, possessive behavior which young children show toward their mothers or mother substitutes. The children began to insist that the members of the staff should have their turn or share; they became sensitive to their feelings, identified with their needs, and considerate of their comfort. They wanted to help the adults with their occupations and, in return, expected to be helped by them. They disliked it when any member of staff was absent and wanted to know where the adults had been and what they had done during their absence. In short, they ceased to regard the adults as outsiders, included them in their group and, as the examples show, began to treat them in some ways as they treated each other.

Sharing with the Adults

Christmas 1945. — The children are invited to a Christmas party in Mrs. Clarke's house. They receive their presents with great excitement. They are equally thrilled when they are handed presents for the staff, they call out: "For Gertrud," "For Sophie" with great pleasure, and run back to Mrs. Clarke to fetch more presents for them.

December 1945. — When Mrs. Clarke, who has been visiting, leaves, Ruth demands to be kissed. Then all the children have to be kissed. Then John and Ruth call out: "Kiss for Sophie."

December 1945. — The children are given sweets in the shop and demand a "sweet for Sophie." After leaving the shop, they want to make sure that she has received the sweet. Sister Sophie opens her mouth for inspection and, in so doing, loses her sweet. The children are as upset as if they had lost one of their own sweets. John offers his but Sister Sophie suggests that she can wait to get another on returning home. When they reach home after an hour's walk with many distracting events, Peter runs immediately to the box of sweets to fetch one for Sophie.

Considerateness for the adults

November 1945. — When the children are told that one of the staff has a day off and can sleep longer in the morning, they try to be quiet. If one or the other forgets, the others shout: "You quiet. Gertrud fast asleep."

November 1945. — Sister Sophie has told the children that the doctor has forbidden her to lift heavy weights. Paul asks: "Not too heavy?," whenever he sees her with a tray or bucket.

May 1946. — Leah, though a noisy child, tries hard to keep quiet when her Judith is tired.

Equality with the adults. Helpfulness

December 1945. — The children become keen on fetching from the kitchen what is needed. They carry logs, set chairs and tables. They help to dress and undress themselves and to tidy up.

January 1946. — Ruth sees a woman with a shopping bag in the street. She approaches her and takes one handle silently to help carrying it.

April 1946. — The children are alone in the nursery after breakfast. Ruth and Peter each take a broom and sweep up the rubbish. When Sister Sophie enters, they call to her: "We tidy up nicely."

May 1946. — Miriam begins to help Sister Sophie in the kitchen when the latter is called away. When she returns Miriam has dried four big dishes, twelve bowls, sixteen spoons and has placed them tidily on a tray.

On a similar occasion Miriam is found on a chair in front of the sink, her arms up to the elbows in soapy water, with most of the washing-up done. . .

Sensitiveness to adults. Identification

March 1946. — Ruth and John lag far behind on a walk. When they reach the others eventually, Peter calls to them: "You naughty boys, you dragging behind; Sophie calling and calling and calling. You not coming, Sophie cross and sad!" Then he turns to Sister Sophie and says in a low voice: "You still cross and sad?" When she nods, he repeats his speech.

May 1946. — While the children are picking bluebells, Sister Sophie listens intently to the calling of birds. Paul suddenly puts his hand into hers and says: "You cross with everybody?" Though she assures him that she is not cross, merely absent-minded, he leaves his hand in hers to comfort her.

Second Phase of Positive Relations to Adults.
Personal Relationships

Several weeks after arrival in Bulldogs Bank the first signs of individual personal attachments to adults appeared, alongside with and superimposed on the relationships based on community feelings. These new attachments had many of the qualities which are well known from the relationship of young children to their mothers or mother substitutes. Attitudes such as possessiveness, the wish to be owned, exclusive clinging, appeared, but they lacked the intensity and inexorability which is

one of the main characteristics of the emotional life at that age. During the year's stay at Bulldogs Bank these ties of the children to the adults in no way reached the strength of their ties to each other. The children went, as it were, through the motions and attitudes of mother relationships, but without the full libidinal cathexis of the objects whom they had chosen for the purpose.

Examples of owning and being owned

Miriam was the first to say "Meine Sophie, my Sophie" at the end of October.

Peter, the youngest, was the next to show a personal attachment. At the end of November he cried on several occasions when Sister Gertrud left the room. He began to say: "Meine Gertrud" and shortly afterward called himself "Gertrud's Peter." He picked flowers for her and liked her to bathe him. But his attachment was in no way exclusive and he did not mind being with somebody else. He was fond of Sister Sophie too and disliked her going away.

Ruth very soon afterward showed a first preference for Mrs. Clarke. She began showing pleasure in seeing her, kissed her once spontaneously and said on another occasion: "Is bin [I am] Mrs. Clarke's Ruth."

Leah was a clinging child who made advances to every visitor and even to people passing in the street. She became attached to the assistant Judith, would hold her hand on walks, picked flowers for her and sang sometimes all day long: "My Judith bathes me all the time!" But the apparent warmth of this relationship was belied by the fact that she continued to attach herself to every stranger.

John called the young assistant "his" Maureen. His attachment showed more warmth than those of the others but was broken again, unluckily, by Maureen's leaving.

Examples of conflicting relationships

Several children had considerable difficulties in choosing their mother substitutes, their positive feelings wavering uncertainly between the adult figures. John, after being left by Maureen, attached himself to Sister Gertrud, and shortly afterward became fond of Sister Sophie. Neither relationship was exclusive or very passionate and consequently he seemed to have no difficulties in maintaining both simultaneously. In contrast to this, Miriam, who was attached equally to Sisters Sophie and Gertrud, suffered badly from the consequent conflict of feeling. She lived in a constant state of tension without finding relief and satisfaction

in her relationships. During Sister Sophie's absence, she "wrote" and dictated long letters to her and she was full of happiness on Sister Sophie's return. But the preference for Sister Sophie, which seemed established at the time, gave way once more to a preference for Sister Gertrud in the course of a few weeks.

Examples of resentment of separations

Even though the children's attachments to their mother substitutes took second place in their emotional lives, they deeply resented the absences or the leaving of the adults.

January 1946. — Sister Sophie has left the house together with Mrs. Clarke. When she returns a few hours later, Peter refuses to say good night to her. He turns to the other side and says: "You go, you go to a Mrs. Clarke."

March 1946. — When Sister Sophie returned to Bulldogs Bank after an absence of two months, Peter refused to let her do anything for him for a week, would not even take bread or sweets from her. Whenever she left the house, he asked: "You go in a London?"

He regained his affection for her through a process of identification with her interests. Five weeks after her return the children played that they took a bus ride to London. When asked what they wanted to do there, Peter said: "Go in a Miss X's house." Peter saying: "Miss X all better?" From then onward, he called the patient "Peter's Miss X," cuddled and kissed Sister Sophie and held her hand on walks although the children usually preferred to walk on their own. . . .

Example of attachment to a mother substitute

The only child to choose a real mother substitute was Ruth, an exception which is easily explainable on the basis of her former attachment to the superintendent of the Children's Ward in Tereszin. She chose as her object Sister Gertrud, and developed toward her the same demandingness, aggressive possessiveness and wish for exclusive attention which had characterized her earlier relationship, a mixture of emotions which is well known from children in the toddler stage and at later ages from those who have gone through the experience of loss, separation, rejection and disappointments in their earliest object relationships. Ruth's lack of satisfaction and insecurity expressed itself with regard to Sister Gertrud in the constantly repeated phrase: "And Ruth? And Ruth?"

Example of a passionate father relationship

The only child to form a passionate relationship to a father figure was Miriam. Since Miriam arrived in Tereszin at the age of six months, her

father having been killed some time previously, it cannot be presumed that what she went through was a past father relationship transferred to a new object, rather that it was the need for a father which found a first outlet in this manner:

> *January 1946.* — Mr. E., a neighbor, visits the Nursery for a whole afternoon and teaches the children songs. At the time, Miriam seems more interested in his picture book than in his person. But in the evening she begins to cry for him. She wakes up in the night twice and cries for him and keeps asking for him during the next two days.

> *March 1946.* — Miriam has seen Mr. E. more often lately. He has brushed her hair once in the evening and she insists on his doing it again. On evenings when he does not come, her hair is not brushed at all since she will not allow anybody else to touch it.

> She blushes whenever she sees him. About twenty times a day she says: "Meine Mr. E. — meine Sophie."

> *March 1946.* — Mr. E. says about Miriam: "I have never seen anything like her. That girl is puffing and panting with passion." . . .

Oral Erotism. Masturbation

There was a further factor which accounted for the children's diminished capability to form new object relationships. As children for whom the object world had proved disappointing, and who had experienced the severest deprivations from the oral phase onward they had had to fall back to a large degree on their own bodies to find comfort and reassurance. Therefore oral-erotic gratifications persisted with each child in one form or another. Ruth, besides, had a habit of scratching herself rhythmically until she bled, and of smearing with the blood. One child, Paul, suffered from compulsive masturbation.

Peter, Ruth, John and Leah were all inveterate thumb-suckers, Peter and Ruth noisily and incessantly during the whole day, John and Leah more moderately, gradually reducing it to bedtime only. Miriam sucked the tip of her tongue, manipulating it with her teeth until she fell asleep. With Peter, sucking changed in spring to "smoking" carried out with match sticks, twigs, grass blades, then again to sucking his thumb when cross, angry, or at bedtime only. With Ruth sucking persisted even while she was carrying out interesting activities such as threading beads or playing with plasticene.

Since the children's sucking was noisy and obvious they often heard remarks from passers-by or in shops that they should stop or that "their thumbs would be cut off." Contrary to their usual oversensitiveness they

remained completely indifferent on such occasions, not even needing reassurance. Sucking was such an integral and indispensable part of their libidinal life that they had not developed any guilt feelings or conflicting attitudes concerning it.

That the excess of sucking was in direct proportion to the instability of their object relationships was confirmed at the end of the year, when the children knew that they were due to leave Bulldogs Bank and when sucking in daytime once more became very prevalent with all of them.

This persistence of oral gratifications, more or less normal under the circumstances, which fluctuated according to the children's relations with the environment, contrasted strongly with Paul's behavior, where compulsive sucking and masturbation manifested themselves as a complicated and, at the time, inaccessible symptom.

Paul, in his good periods was an excellent member of the group, friendly, attentive and helpful toward children and adults, and capable of friendship as the examples on pages 135 f. show. Though not aggressive himself, he was always ready to come to another child's rescue and take up arms against an aggressor. But when he went through one of his phases of compulsive sucking or masturbating, the whole environment, including the other children, lost their significance for him. He ceased to care about them, just as he ceased to eat or play himself. He did not bother to take part in his favorite communual activities such as sorting the laundry or lighting fires. He did not defend himself, or anybody else, merely cried passively when something or somebody made him unhappy. These spells attacked him at any time of the day, while playing, when eating at the table, and during work. He was only free of masturbation on walks, when he sometimes sucked his thumb but otherwise showed a completely changed, cheerful and interested attitude.

In masturbating Paul used his hands, soft toys, picture books, a spoon; or rubbed himself against furniture or against other people. When sucking, his whole passion was concentrated on face flannels or towels which he sucked while they were hanging on their hooks. He also used a corner of his dungarees, of his coat and the arms of a doll, which he sucked while it was hanging from his mouth. For a period of several weeks he treated the children's used bibs or feeders as so many fetishes, rubbing them rhythmically up and down his nose while sucking, treasuring all six feeders in his arms, or pressing one or more between his legs. When on a walk, he sometimes looked forward to these ecstasies with passionate excitement, rushing into the nursery on coming home with the joyous exclamation "Feeder—feeder!" Since he was indifferent to the same feeders when they were freshly laundered, it may be concluded that his erotic excitation was connected with the smell belonging to a feeding situation.

Relations to the Outside World

In Tereszin, i.e., up to the ages of three to three and one half, the children had led the existence of inmates of a Ward, within a restricted space, with few or no toys, with no opportunities for moving about freely, for contact with animals, for observing nature. They had not shared or observed the lives of ordinary people and, in the absence of strong emotional ties to the people who looked after them, they had lacked the normal incentives for imitating the adults and for identifying with them. Consequently, their knowledge of the external world, their ability to understand and to deal with it, were far below the level of their ages and of their intelligence.

Indoor and Outdoor Activities

During their first weeks in Bulldogs Bank, the children were unable to use play material. The only toys which attracted their attention from the start were the soft toys, dolls and teddy bears which were adopted as personal possessions and not so much played with as used for auto-erotic gratification (sucking, masturbation), or in replacement of it. All the children without exception, took their dolls or teddy bears to bed with them. When a child failed to do so in the evening, it would invariably wake up in the middle of the night, crying for the missing object.

The first play activity, which the children carried out with passionate eagerness, was the pushing of furniture, the usual favorite occupation of toddlers who have just learned to walk. They began their day in the morning with pushing chairs in the nursery and returned to this activity at intervals during the day, whenever they were free to do so. After they had learned to play in the sandpit, they used sand for the same purpose, pushing a supply of it along the whole front of the veranda by means of an inverted chair. They would revert to pushing furniture even on coming home from long walks, or when tired.

Gradual progress in their physical ability to handle objects and to manage their own possessions coincided with the growth of the children's emotional interest in the adult world. This led to the wish to "help," to share the work of the adults and, as described above, to fetch and carry, to set chairs and tables, etc., activities which were carried out surprisingly well. For a short while, the wish to be equal to the adults in these matters led to a frenzy of independence, as the following example shows:

In November, the children are taken for their first bus ride. The situation has been explained to them beforehand, also that the ride will be short and that they will have to get out quickly at the bus stop. They have promised to co-operate, and they leave their seats without protest at the appointed time. But when the conductor and a passenger

try very kindly to help them down the steps, they push them away, and shout and scream that they want to do it alone. Finally Miriam lies on the road, her face almost blue with fury, Paul sits next to her, kicking and screaming, the others cry and sob.

While such a phase of independence brought marked increases in the skill and range of the children's activities, in periods of an opposite emotional nature the advances seemed to be lost once more. In January all the children went through a phase of complete passivity, and dependence on the adults, corresponding to the change of their relationships with them from the more impersonal community feelings to warmer personal attachments. During this time they refused to do anything for themselves, wanted to be fed, dressed, etc., and did not co-operate in work. Their ambivalent attitude toward the adults, the outgoing and withdrawal of emotion toward them, was reflected in the sphere of activities by violent demands to be helped and looked after like a helpless infant, coupled with an equally violent refusal to accept the care. In such moods the children would run away from being dressed, push the tables and chairs away when they had been set for a meal, refuse to carry even their own belongings, etc.

After approximately six months stay in Bulldogs Bank, these violent upheavals gave way to more ordinary and stable modes of progress.

In March 1946 the children began to lose interest in their soft toys and took picture books to bed with them for "reading." For some time each child was content to have any book. From April onward the children demanded books in which they were particularly interested.

When Miriam received her postcard from Mr. E. and "wrote" her answer on it before going to sleep in the evening, "reading" came to an end and "writing" took its place. Several children had received letters and parcels from their American foster parents and "wrote" to them in bed. At first they used pencils indiscriminately, after a while they chose their colors. The imaginary letters written at that time dealt with matters such as Sister Sophie's absence, news about animals, flowers, etc., i.e., interests in the external world which had taken the place of the exclusive autoerotic activities of the bedtime hour.

In the second half of their year in Bulldogs Bank, the children became increasingly interested in the usual nursery school occupations. At the end of the year they had become able to concentrate on an occupation for as much as an hour. They had become able to handle scissors, pencils, paint brushes, blunt needles, and enjoyed painting, cutting out, doing puzzles and threading beads. Even then they preferred "grownup work" to nursery occupations and carried it out very efficiently.

After the beginnings, which had showed the children to be backward in their play by as much as eighteen months or two years, it was all the more impressive to watch the speed with which they passed through

consecutive stages of play activity making up for development which had been missed.[2]

Absence of adequate experience with consequent backwardness in understanding and behavior was even more striking outdoors than indoors. The children lacked both the city child's knowledge of traffic, shops, busy streets, etc., and the country child's familiarity with animals, trees, flowers and all types of work. They knew no animals except dogs, which were objects of terror. They did not know the name of a single plant and had never picked or handled flowers. They seemed to know no vehicles and were completely oblivious of the dangers of the road. Consequently their walks on the country road, through the village or the lanes and paths were exciting events during which innumerable new impressions crowded in on them.

Parallel to the speed of their development in the sphere of play, the children passed rapidly through the various stages of experience and behavior with regard to outdoor events, which are usually gone through between the ages of two and four. Their interest in animals, once awakened, was accompanied by the usual animal play, identification with animals and observation of animals. Interest in cars went from an initial terror of being "made too-too by a car" to a pride in being able to manage crossings, to admonish others to do so, and to distinguish between the types of car. Before they left Bulldogs Bank the children had acquired the experience normal for country children of their age. They knew most trees and practically all the common flowers by name and asked for information when meeting new specimens. They distinguished weeds from plants; they picked flowers with long stems instead of tearing their heads off as at first. They were greatly helped in making up for lost time by the interest of the village people who showed them their animals, permitted them to come into their gardens, gave them flowers, explained their tools, allowed them to look inside their vans or behind counters, all of it new experiences of unique importance for the children.

Retardation in modes of thinking

In dealing with the mass of experience which crowded in on them, the children revealed, during the first weeks, some characteristic peculiarities which are worth noting in individuals of their ages.

A first perception of an object, or the experiencing of an event, together with the naming of it, left an impression on their minds far overriding all later ones in strength and forcefulness. This was clearly demonstrated on several occasions.

A pony in the field had been introduced to the children as a donkey by mistake, and the first ducks which they met had been misnamed geese. In both cases it took several weeks to undo the wrong connection between object and word. In spite of repeated efforts at correction, the

children clung to the names connected with their first image of the animal.

The first leaf shown to the children was an ivy leaf. For a whole month every green leaf was called ivy leaf.

When the children noticed a plane overhead for the first time and asked where it was going, they were told that it was going to France. "Going to France" remained a fixed attribute of every plane from then onward. During the whole year they called out: "Aeroplane going to France," whenever they heard a plane overhead.

The first time that letter writing had come into the children's lives was on the occasion of Sister Sophie's absence. All later letters, imagined or dictated by them retained the opening phrases which they had used then: "Dear Sophie in a London in a Miss X's house. Miss X all better," regardless of the fact that Sister Sophie had returned long ago and that the letters were addressed to other people.

The first English song which the children learned in Bulldogs Bank was "Bah bah black sheep." Though they learned and sang many other nursery rhymes during their stay, "Bah bah black sheep" remained in a class of its own. They would sing it when cheerful or as a treat for somebody on special occasions.

When talking of people the children would name them according to their most interesting attribute or possession, or would name these objects after them. Mrs. Clarke, for example, had two small dogs which were the first friendly dogs known to the children and played an important role in helping them to overcome their terror of dogs. In December all children called Mrs. Clarke: "Miss Clarke's doggies." Objects given by her to the children were called by the same name. A big electric stove which came from her house was called by Peter: "Miss Clarke's doggies." Green porridge bowls given by her as a Christmas present were called Mrs. Clarke by everybody.

December 1945.—When washing up, John says: "You wash Mrs. Clarke. I dry Mrs. Clarke. Look at that, Mrs. Clarke all dry."

January 1946.—Ruth throws Peter's green bowl on the floor. Three children shout: "Mrs. Clarke kaputt, poor Mrs. Clarke all kaputt."

The examples quoted in this chapter reveal primitive modes of thinking which are shown by children in their second year of life. The overwhelming strength of a first link between an object or event and its name is characteristic for the time when children first learn to speak, or—to express it in metapsychological terms—when word representations are first added to the images (object representations) in the child's mind. The inability to distinguish between essential and nonessential attributes of an object belongs to the same age (see example of aeroplanes). Instances of naming where this is directed not to a single limited object but to a

whole idea related to it (see example of "Miss Clarke's doggies") are forms of "condensation," well known from the primary processes which reveal themselves normally in dream activity, and continue in the second year of life as a mode of waking thought.

That these infantilisms in the sphere of thinking were not based on a general mental retardation with the children under observation was borne out by their adequate, adapted reasoning and behavior in situations with which they felt familiar (such as household tasks, community affairs, etc.); that they were not merely a function of the reversal in their emotional development is suggested by the fact that they overcame them before their libidinal attachments had changed decisively. That the rapid growth of life experience brought about an equally rapid advance in the modes of dealing with it mentally, suggests rather that it was the extreme dearth of new perceptions and varied impressions in their most impressionable years which deprived the children of the opportunity to exercise their mental functions to a normal degree and consequently brought about a stunting of thought development. . . .

Language Problems

While passing through the phases of development as described above, the children had the added task of learning a new language, a necessity which made adaptation more difficult since it rendered them inarticulate in the transition period. They talked German on arrival, mixed with Czech which they had picked up after leaving Tereszin. Ruth's mixture of German and Czech was especially difficult to understand. The members of the staff began to talk English in front of the children and with them after a week and ceased talking German altogether after approximately seven weeks.

Surprisingly enough, there was no violent refusal on the part of the children to adopt the new language. The only outbursts of this kind came from Paul. In October, while repeating English words, which he liked to do, he became furious suddenly: "Is nicht motor car, is Auto, blöde Tante!" "Nicht good morning Paul, guten Morgen Paul!" On the other hand, Paul was the first to realize that the new language was essential to make contact with the village people. At the time when the other children still looked unhappy and withdrawn, he attracted everybody's attention by a very pleasant smile. People smiled and waved at him, though he could only say "hallo" in answer. His first English sentence was spoken in a deliberate effort to make contact:

In December, the children passed one of the cottages whose owner came to the gate and gave flowers to them. Paul said: "Flowers," after some thinking "Lovely flowers," and then "Many lovely flowers, thank you!" The woman was so pleased that she kissed him.

John and Peter followed Paul in using their English words to draw attention to themselves, and soon used more English than German nouns. In a transitional phase they used composite nouns, made up of both languages, such as "auto-car," "doggy-Hund," "dolly-Puppe," "Löffel-spoon," etc. The girls, who were worse speakers altogether, followed much more slowly. The first adjectives and adverbs were used from the fifth week after beginning.

It was of evident concern to the children that the difference in their speed of learning English caused differences between them where there had been unity before. Many of their word battles centered around these points, as the following examples show:

December (at mealtime). —
Leah: "Brot."
Ruth: "Is bread."
Leah: "Brot."
Ruth (half crying): "Nis Brot, is bread."
Leah (shouting): "Brot."
Ruth (crying): "Is bread."
Paul: "Is bread, blöder Ochs Leah."
John: "Is nis blöder Ochs."
Paul (shouting): "Is blöder Ochs John."
John (screaming): "Is nis blöder Ochs."
Sister Sophie: "Don't cry, nobody is a blöder Ochs."
Paul (as loud as possible): "Blöder Ochs du, blöder Ochs Sophie."
John: "Sophie is nis blöder Ochs."
Peter (all smiles): "Nis blöder Ochs Sophie."
Paul: "Is hau dich" (turns against Peter).
Peter: "Please bread."
Paul gets bread for Peter and passes it to him.

January (At mealtime). —
Paul: "Look, ich big Teller, siehst du?"
John: "Nis Teller, is plate."
Paul: "Oh nein."
John: "Is nis Teller, is in endlich [English?] plate."
Paul (shouts): "Oh nein."
Sister Sophie: "John is quite right, Teller is plate in English."
Paul: "Look, ich big plate."
John: "Clever boy John."
Peter: "No, clever boy Sophie," etc.

These differences disappeared again after January, when the whole group spoke English, among themselves as well as to the adults. They tried to express everything in English, using a picturesque language where the absence of verbs made expression difficult. . . .

For a long time the children clung to the German negation *nicht* (which must have played an overwhelmingly great part in their restricted lives). For some weeks in spring it was used together with its English counterpart as "not-nicht," before it was finally dropped.

The only German word which the children retained throughout the year was *meine* (my). Although the children knew and used the English equivalent, they would revert to the German *meine* when very affectionate: "Meine Gertrud," "Meine dolly."

By August the last German words, with this single exception, had disappeared, though the understanding of the German lanugage as such had ceased much earlier. When a visitor talked German to the children in April, they laughed as if at a joke. In May, a German prisoner of war talked German to Ruth who looked completely blank. In June another visitor who knew the children from Windermere talked German to them; there was absolutely no reaction.

With the adaptation to the new language the children had made a further decisive step toward the break with their past, which now disappeared completely from their consciousness.

Conclusion

"Experiments" of this kind, which are provided by fate, lack the satisfying neatness and circumscription of an artificial setup. It is difficult, or impossible, to distinguish the action of the variables from each other, as is demonstrated in our case by the intermingled effects of three main factors: the absence of a mother or parent relationship; the abundance of community influence; and the reduced amount of gratification of all needs. It is, of course, impossible to vary the experiment. In our case, further, it proved impossible to obtain knowledge of all the factors which have influenced development. There remained dark periods in the life of each child, and guesswork, conclusions and inferences had to be used to fill the gaps.

Under such circumstances, no claim to exactitude can be made for the material which is presented here and it offers no basis for statistical considerations. This experiment staged by fate accentuates the action of certain factors in the child's life (demonstrated through their absence or their exaggerated presence). . . .

The six Bulldogs Bank children are, without doubt, "rejected" infants in this sense of the term. They were deprived of mother love, oral satisfactions, stability in their relationships and their surroundings. They were passed from one hand to another during their first year, lived in age group instead of a family during their second and third year, and were uprooted again three times during their fourth year. A description of the

anomalies which this fate produced in their emotional life and of the retardations in certain ego attitudes is contained in the material. The children were hypersensitive, restless, aggressive, difficult to handle. But they were neither deficient, delinquent nor psychotic. They had found an alternative placement for their libido and, on the strength of this, had mastered some of their anxieties, and developed social attitudes. That they were able to acquire a new language in the midst of their upheavals, bears witness to a basically unharmed contact with their environment. . . .

Notes

1. Theresienstadt in Moravia.

2. See in this respect the paper by Lotte Danzinger and Lieselotte Frankl (2) on the test results with Albanian infants who, according to custom, spend their first year tied down in their cradle. The authors watched some of these infants being taken out of the cradle and allowed to play with toys. While they at first appeared extremely backward in comparison with other children, they nearly caught up with them (thought not completely), when they had played with the toys for some hours only. As explanation, the authors suggest that inner processes of maturation had taken place and progressed in spite of the deprivations.

See also Phyllis Greenacre's comprehensive article on "Infant Reactions to Restraint" (4).

References

Burlingham, D. T. *Twins*, Imago Publ. Co., London, 1951.

Danziger, L. and Frankl, L. "Zum Problem der Funktionsreifung," *Ztsch. f. Kinderforschung*, XLIII, 1934.

Freud, A. and Burlingham, D. *Infants Without Families*, Int. Univ. Press, New York, 1944.

Greenacre, P. "Infant Reactions to Restraint," in *Personality*, edited by Clyde Kluckhohn and Henry A. Murray. A. Knopf, New York, 1948.

Werner, H. *Comparative Psychology of Mental Development*, Follet, Chicago, 1948.

4.10 Teacher's Communication of Differential Expectations for Children's Classroom Performance: Some Behavioral Data

Jere E. Brophy
Thomas L. Good

Rosenthal and Jacobson (1968) assert on the basis of controversial research presented in *Pygmalion in the Classroom* that teachers' expectations for student performance function as self-fulfilling prophecies. The "expectancy effects" in the Oak School experiment described in *Pygmalion* are not as consistent as the authors' interpretations of them would suggest, however, and even the support that they do provide is questionable on methodological grounds (Barber and Silver, 1968; Snow, 1969; Thorndike, 1968). Even if the data and their interpretation are accepted, the Rosenthal and Jacobson work remains only a demonstration of the *existence* of expectancy effects; their study did not address itself to any of the events intervening between the inducement of teacher expectations and the administration of the criterion achievement test. The present study focuses on these intervening processes, applying the method of classroom interaction analysis to identify and document differential teacher behavior communicating different teacher expectations to individual children.

The lack of data concerning the causal mechanisms at work in the Rosenthal and Jacobson study, combined with the tendency in most secondary sources to oversimplify or exaggerate their findings has cast an aura of magic or mystery around expectation effects. Consequently, it is important to conceptualize such phenomena as outcomes of observable sequences of behavior. The explicit model assumed in the present research may be described as follows:

(a)   The teacher forms differential expectations for student performance;
(b)   He then begins to treat children differently in accordance with his differential expectations;
(c)   The children respond differentially to the teacher because they are being treated differently by him;
(d)   In responding to the teacher, each child tends to exhibit behavior which complements and reinforces the teacher's particular expectations for him;

Excerpted and reprinted from Jere E. Brophy and Thomas L. Good, *Teachers' Communication of Differential Expectations for Children's Performance: Some Behavioral Data*, Report Series No. 25, The Research and Development Center for Teacher Education, The University of Texas at Austin, 1969, by permission.

(e) As a result, the general academic performance of some children will be enhanced while that of others will be depressed, with changes being in the direction of teacher expectations;

(f) These effects will show up in the achievement tests given at the end of the year, providing support for the "self-fulfilling prophecy" notion.

A series of interrelated studies will be required to systematically investigate the full model from beginning (how do teachers form differential expectations in the first place?) to end (how do children change so as to begin to conform more closely to teacher expectations?). The present study deals with the second step: given differential teacher expectations, how are they communicated to the children in ways that would tend to cause the children to produce reciprocal behavior? To begin to answer this question, the present study approached the problem through classroom interaction analysis. In contrast to the usual classroom interaction study, however, the present research focused on dyadic interaction between the teacher and individual children.[1]

METHOD

Subjects

The research was carried out in four first-grade classrooms in a small Texas school district which serves a generally rural and lower-class population. However, a large military base located within the district contributes about 45 per cent of the students in the school in which observations were taken. Children from the base tend to be from more urban backgrounds and of a somewhat higher socio-economic status than the local children. The ethnic composition of the school is about 75 per cent Anglo-American, 15 per cent Mexican-American and ten per cent Afro-American, which is representative of the general population of the area.

Research was carried out in four of the nine first-grade classrooms in the school, chosen because there were no assistant teachers present to complicate the picture (the other five classrooms had pre-service teacher interns assisting the head teacher). The four teachers involved were asked to rank the children in their class in the order of their achievement. These instructions were deliberately kept vague to encourage the teachers to use complex, subjective criteria in making their judgments. The rankings were then used as the measure of the teachers' expectations for classroom performance for the children in their classes. In each class, three boys and three girls high on the teacher's list (highs) and three boys and three girls low on the teacher's list (lows) were selected

for observational study. The highs were simply the first six elegible children on the list. This was generally true also for the lows, although a few children low on the lists were excluded from the study because they could not speak English fluently or because of suspected emotional or biological disturbance. Substitutes for each type of child (high boys, high girls, low boys, low girls) were also identified and these were individually observed on days when children in the designated sample were absent.

The teachers had been told that the study was concerned with the classroom behavior of children of various levels of achievement. They were not informed that their own behavior as well as that of the children was being specifically observed. Furthermore, the teachers thought that observations were being taken on everyone in the class and did not know that specific subgroups had been selected for study. By selecting subjects from the extremes of the distributions of teacher's rankings, the chances of discovering differential teacher treatment of the students were maximized. However, the school practiced tracking, achieving homogeneity within the nine classrooms by grouping the children according to readiness and achievement scores. Thus, at least in terms of test scores, objective differences among the children (and, therefore, objective support for the validity of teacher expectations) was minimized.

Observation System

Since the object of the research was to focus on differential treatment of different children, the observation system developed was addressed only to dyadic contacts between the teacher and an individual child, with lecture-demonstration and other teacher behavior directed to the class as a group being ignored. Although the types of interactions coded were partly dictated by the range of situations seen in pilot studies, certain features of the coding system were built in for their specific relevance to the study of communication of differential teacher expectations. One major and consistent feature was that the source of the interaction was always coded, so that it would be determined later whether the interaction was initiated by the teacher or by the child. . . .

Other than the large class differences, the data are most notable for the consistency of expectancy group differences on variables measuring the tendency to seek out the teacher and initiate contact with her. Children for whom the teacher held high expectations (highs) raised their hands more frequently and initiated more procedural and especially more work-related interactions than did children for whom the teachers held low expectations (lows). The class x expectancy group interactions with regard to child-initiated contacts reflect degree rather than

direction of effect. The highs exceeded the lows in each class for hand raising, initiating work-related interactions, and total child-initiated response opportunities (the hand-raising effect excludes Class 1, where it could not be assessed because the teacher never asked open questions while her class was being observed). The highs also exceeded the lows in three of the four classes in initiating procedural interactions. There was a negligible reversal in Class 2, where this type of interaction was very infrequent (highs averaged 1.50, lows averaged 1.67). The only exception to the pattern of significant differences between highs and lows in child-initiated interactions occurred in the measure of calling out answers in the reading groups. The mean difference is in favor of the highs, but it is not a significant difference and the effect occurred in only one of the four classes. The data for child-initiated contacts may be summarized, then, in the statement that, outside the reading group at least, the highs seek out the teacher and initiate interactions with her more frequently than the lows. The difference is especially notable in work-related interactions: the highs much more frequently show their work to the teacher or ask her questions about it, and they initiate many more response opportunities.

The data for contacts initiated or controlled by the teacher are less clear than for those initiated by the children. The highs were called on more frequently to answer open questions, but the teacher initiated more procedural and work-related interactions with the lows and afforded them slightly more response opportunities. None of these differences reach significance, however. The only significant difference occurred with teacher-afforded behavioral criticisms, which more frequently went to the lows than the highs. This effect showed an important interaction with sex, due to the high frequency of teacher criticisms directed at boys in the low group. Males in the low group averaged 8.25 teacher behavior criticisms, as compared with 2.25 for boys in the high group (the corresponding figures for girls are 1.58 and 1.83). Sex also interacted with expectancy in the measure of hand raising, and again the boys in the low group were notably different from the other three groups. These boys averaged 6.25 on the hand-raising measure as compared to 17.75 for the boys of the high group (corresponding figures for the girls are 11.50 and 15.58).

The data regarding interactions initiated or controlled by the teacher may be summarized as follows: there is a tendency for the teachers to initiate more contacts with the lows than with the highs, but the teachers cannot be said to have been compensating for the superiority of the highs in child-initiated contacts because the trend is not completely consistent and because the only significant differences occur with teacher criticism rather than with work-related contacts or provision of response

opportunities. While the data for child-initiated contacts showed strong expectancy group differences, the measures of teacher-initiated interactions were much more closely related to sex than to expectancy. Boys were higher than girls on all measures of teacher-initiated contacts; significantly so for work-related interactions, behavioral criticisms, and total teacher-afforded response opportunities. When teacher-child dyadic contacts of all types are totaled, a clear difference favoring boys is evident; there is no difference between expectancy groups. Differences between the highs and the lows are in quality rather than quantity of interaction with the teacher. . . .

The highs produced more correct answers and fewer incorrect answers than the lows, had fewer problems in the reading groups, and achieved higher average scores on the Stanford Achievement Test given at the end of the year. They also were given more praise and less criticism than the lows by the teachers. The direction of difference follows this pattern in all four classes for every variable except for the total correct answers, where the group means were equal in one class. Thus the class by expectancy interactions affected the degreee but not the direction of expectation effects.

Sex effects also appeared, with boys producing more correct answers and receiving more criticism than girls. The other, nonsignificant, differences in favor of boys are consistent with the finding noted above that boys tend to have more interactions with the teacher than girls. A sex by expectancy group interaction occurs for the measure of total criticism which is similar and related to the one reported for behavioral criticism. For the boys in the low group, teacher criticism was present in 32.50 per cent of their dyadic contacts with the teacher. The corresponding figure for the high boys is 13.25 per cent, for the low girls 16.17 per cent and for the high girls 8.25 per cent.

In summary, the data show that teacher expectancy consistently predicts objective measures of classroom performance, objective achievement test scores, and rates of teacher praise and criticism. . . .

Significant group differences on these measures suggest that the teachers were systematically, although not necessarily deliberately or consciously, treating one group more favorably than the other. The first two measures concern provision of response opportunities to the children, and may be considered in combination with the data previously discussed. Since the highs create more response opportunities for themselves than the lows, do the teachers compensate for this by calling on the lows more frequently? The data suggest only a slight tendency in this direction at best. The teachers definitely do not compensate by asking the lows more direct questions, since the mean on this variable for the lows is less than that for the highs, although not significantly. The mean for direct questions in the low group would have been increased if "dis-

cipline" questions had been included in their figures. These were very special questions which appeared only in the low group, but not with sufficient frequency to be analyzed as a separate variable. "Discipline" questions were direct questions which ostensibly asked for academic content ("what's the next word, John?"), but which were directed at children not paying attention. In these instances the teacher's questions appeared to function as control techniques rather than as response opportunities, and so they were not included in the totals for the direct questions. If they had been included the results would have been an increase in the mean for direct questions in the low group, but this mean value would still be below that for the highs.

The one teacher measure which does suggest some compensation concerns the teacher's behavior in calling on children to answer open questions. When the number of times the child is called on is weighted by the number of times he raised his hand to seek a response opportunity, the resulting recognition rates showed a significant difference in favor of the lows. However, this difference seemed more due to the large difference in hand raising rate between the two groups of children rather than to any systematic compensation efforts by the teachers. The recognition rates are not adjusted for the fact that more highs than lows were likely to be raising their hands seeking an opportunity to answer a given question, so that a single response opportunity had less effect on the recognition rates of the highs than on those of the lows. The rates may be adjusted by treating the highs and the lows as groups and discounting hand raising by other members of the group when one member of the group is called on. When the hand raising totals are reduced in this manner, the resultant recognition rates still favor the lows, although the difference no longer approaches statistical significance.

In summary, the data on quantity of contacts are neutral with regard to expectation effects. The highs initiate more work-related contacts and create more response opportunities for themselves than do the lows, but there is no unequivocal evidence to suggest that the teachers are systematically either exaggerating or compensating for these differences among the children.

The data for the last five variables comprise the major findings of the study, since they provide direct evidence that the teachers' differential expectations for performance were being communicated in their classroom behavior. The measures involved are all concerned with the teachers' reactions to the children's attempts to answer questions and read in the reading group. All are percentage or ratio measures which take into account absolute differences in the frequencies of the various behaviors involved so as to enable a direct comparison to be made between the teachers' behavior toward the two groups when faced with equivalent situations. The data show that the teachers consistently favored the

highs over the lows in demanding and reinforcing quality performance. Despite the fact that the highs gave more correct answers and fewer incorrect answers than did the lows, they were more frequently praised when correct and less frequently criticized when incorrect or unable to respond. Furthermore, the teachers were more persistent in eliciting responses from the highs than they were with the lows. When the highs responded incorrectly or were unable to respond, the teachers were more likely to provide a second response opportunity by repeating or rephrasing the question or giving a clue than they were in similar situations with the lows. Conversely, they were more likely to supply the answer or call on another child when reacting to the lows than the highs. This group difference was observed both for difficulties in answering questions and for problems in reading during reading group. Finally, the teachers failed to give any feedback whatever only 3.33 per cent of the time when reacting to highs, while the corresponding figure for lows is 14.75 per cent, a highly significant difference.

Group differences in the direction of expectancy effects occur for all four classes on three variables; small reversals occur in the measure of criticism following wrong responses in one class and in the measure regarding teachers' reactions to reading problems in another class. These are the only measures for which the class by expectancy interaction is significant.

Significant sex effects also appear as they have previously. These show that boys receive more direct questions from the teacher than girls and that they are praised more frequently when giving correct answers. The difference on direct questions fits in with the general finding that boys tend to have more interactions of all kinds with the teachers than girls. The data concerning praise are more surprising, in view of the preponderance of criticism toward boys noted earlier. Taken together, the data on teacher praise and criticism suggest that the teachers are generally more evaluative in responding to boys and more objective in responding to girls. Boys are praised more often after correct responses and criticized more often after incorrect responses or failures to respond, although the latter difference is not statistically significant. The general preponderance of critical comments toward boys noted earlier is apparently due to behavioral criticisms rather than to critical comments made during work-related interactions.

Discussion

The data which show objective differences among the children related to their sex and achievement levels, are quite consistent with previous findings. The finding that high-achieving students receive more teacher praise and support (Hoehn, 1954; de Groat and Thompson, 1949;

Good, 1970) was confirmed in the present study. Hoehn's suggestion that the differences between high and low achieving students in the inter-action with their teachers were in quality rather than quantity of interaction is also compatible with present findings. The finding that teachers have more disapproval contacts with boys than girls has also been frequently reported (Meyer and Thompson, 1956; Lippitt and Gold, 1959; Jackson and Lahaderne, 1967). Meyer and Thompson, (1956) also reported greater praise toward boys, as was found in the present study in work-related interactions. Taken together, the findings on sex differences in the present study may be summarized as follows: boys have more interactions with the teacher than girls and appear to be generally more salient in the teacher's perceptual field. Teachers direct more evaluative comments toward boys, both absolutely and relatively. The largest and most obvious absolute difference in evaluative comments occur with teacher criticism and disapproval, which are directed far more frequently at boys. However, much of this difference appears to come in the form of behavioral criticisms and disciplinary contacts rather than criticisms of academic performance in work-related contacts. The difference appears attributable to more frequent disruptive behavior among boys which brings criticism upon themselves rather than to a consistent teacher set or bias toward being more critical toward boys than girls in equivalent situations. The latter statement agrees closely with the conclusion of Davis and Slobodian (1967), who studied teacher provision of response opportunities and evaluation of children's performance in reading groups.

While sex differences are attributable to objective differences in the classroom behavior of the children, the data show that differences related to teacher expectancy are only partly attributable to the children themselves. When the latter differences are statistically controlled through the use of percentage measures, it is seen that the teachers systematically discriminate in favor of the highs over the lows in demanding and reinforcing quality performance. Teachers do, in fact, communicate differential performance expectations to different children through their classroom behavior, and the nature of this differential treatment is such as to encourage the children to begin to respond in ways which would confirm teacher expectancies. In short, the data confirm the hypothesis that teachers' expectations function as self-fulfilling prophecies, and they indicate some of the intervening behavioral mechanisms involved in the process. Despite large differences in the frequencies of the various behaviors observed in the four classrooms, expectancy effects were consistent across the four teachers (two of the teachers favored the highs on four of the last five measures, while the other two favored the highs on all five measures).

Although the direction of difference in treatment of highs and lows

was constant across teachers, there were observable differences in degree. In particular, one teacher stood out as extreme in this regard, while another showed relatively small differences, even though the direction of difference was constant. It is of interest that the latter teacher, who showed the least discrimination between highs and lows, was the teacher who did not group the children by achievement in her classroom seating pattern. It is also worthy of note that although the teachers' expectations were highly related to the children's achievement test scores within classes, the achievement scores are not so closely related to the previous readiness and achievement data which were used as the basis of tracking into classrooms. That is, the class achievement of some classes was higher than expected, while that of others was lower. While not enough classes were included to allow a statistical test, the data suggest that the achievement levels of the classes were related to the teachers' performance demands and expectations. . . .

Notes

1. In the study of dyadic interaction the individual child (or teacher-child dyad) becomes the unit of analysis, rather than the class as a group. For a discussion of the advantages of this method for studying traditional teacher effectiveness variables and of applications of the method to problems that cannot be approached through ordinary interaction analysis methods, see Good and Brophy (1969).

References

Barber, T. X. and Silver, M. J. Fact, fiction and the experimenter bias effect. *Psychological Bulletin Monographs*, 1968, **70**, 6, Part 2.

Davis, O. L. Jr. and Slobodian, J. J. Teacher behavior toward boys and girls during first grade reading instruction. *American Educational Research Journal*, 1967, **4**, 261–269.

de Groat, A. F. and Thompson, G. G. A study of the distribution of teacher approval and disapproval among sixth grade pupils. *Journal of Experimental Education*, 1949, **18**, 57–75.

Good, T. L. Which pupils do teachers call on? *Elementary School Journal*, 1970, **70**, 190–198.

Good, T. L. and Brophy, J. Analyzing classroom interaction: a more powerful alternative. Report Series No. 26, Research and Development Center for Teacher Education, The University of Texas at Austin, 1969.

Hoehn, A. J. A study of social status differentiation in the classroom behavior of nineteen third-grade teachers. *Journal of Social Psychology*, 1954, **39**, 269–292.

Jackson, P. W. and Lahaderne, H. M. Inequalities of teacher-pupil contacts. Expanded version of a paper delivered at the American Psychological Association Meeting, New York City, September, 1966.

Lippitt, R. and Gold, M. Classroom social structure as a mental health problem. *Journal of Social Issues*, 1959, **15**, 40–49.

Meyer, W. J. and Thompson, G. G. Sex differences in the distribution of teacher approval and disapproval among sixth-grade children. *Journal of Educational Psychology*, 1956, **47**, 385–396.

Rosenthal, R. and Jacobson, L. *Pygmalion in the Classroom: Teacher Expectation and Pupils' Intellectual Development*. New York: Holt, Rinehart and Winston, Inc., 1968.

Snow, R. E. Unfinished pygmalion. *Contemporary Psychology*, 1969, **14**, 197–199.

Thorndike, R. L. Review of Rosenthal, R. and Jacobson, L. Pygmalion in the Classroom. *American Educational Research Journal*, 1968, **5**, 708–711.

4.11 Some Immediate Effects of Televised Violence On Children's Behavior

Robert M. Liebert
State University of New York at Stony Brook

Robert A. Baron
Purdue University

In his review of the social and scientific issues surrounding the portrayal of violence in the mass media, Larsen (1968) noted that we may begin with two facts: "(1) Mass media content is heavily saturated with violence, and (2) people are spending more and more time in exposure to such content [p. 115]." This state of affairs has been used by both laymen and professionals as the basis for appeals to modify the entertainment fare to which viewers, particularly children and adolescents, are exposed (Merriam, 1964; Walters, 1966; Walters & Thomas, 1963; Wertham, 1966). Other writers, however, have argued that the kind of violence found on television or in movies does not necessarily influence

Reprinted from Liebert, Robert M. and Robert A. Baron. Some immediate effects of televised violence on children's behavior. *Developmental Psychology*, 1972, *6*, No. 3, 469–475. Copyright © 1972 by the American Psychological Association. By permission.

observers' "real-life" social behavior (Halloran, 1964; Klapper, 1968). A few have even characterized the portrayal of violence as potentially preventing the overt expression of agression, at least under some circumstances (Feshbach, 1961; Feshbach & Singer, 1971).

In view of the controversy, it is hardly surprising that recent years have seen a substantial increase in the number of experimental studies directed to this issue. An effort has been made to determine whether children will learn and/or be disinhibited in their performance of agressive acts as a function of exposure to symbolic aggressive models (e.g., in cartoons, movies, stories, and simulated television programs). This research has indicated consistently that children may indeed *acquire*, from even a very brief period of observation, certain motoric and verbal behaviors which are associated with aggression in life situations. More specifically, it has been repeatedly shown that after viewing a film which depicts novel forms of hitting, kicking, and verbal abuse, children can, when asked to do so, demonstrate this learning by reproducing these previously unfamiliar behaviors with a remarkable degree of fidelity (Bandura, 1965; Hicks, 1965). Taken together with the large body of research on the observational learning of other behaviors (Flanders, 1968), the available evidence appears to leave little doubt that the learning of at least some aggressive responses can and does result from television or movie viewing.

Equally important, however, is the question of whether the observation of violence will influence children's performance of aggressive acts when they have *not* been specifically asked to show what they have seen or learned. Several experiments appear to provide evidence relating to this issue (Bandura, Ross, & Ross, 1961, 1963a, 1963b; Rosekrans & Hartup, 1967). In these studies, subjects have typically been exposed to live or filmed aggressive scenes, then placed in a free play situation with a variety of toys or other play materials. Results obtained with these procedures have shown repeatedly that the exposure of young children to aggression produces increments in such play activities as punching inflated plastic clowns, popping balloons, striking stuffed animals, and operating mechanized "hitting dolls."

It has been argued by critics (Klapper, 1968) that findings such as those reviewed above are not directly relevant to the question of whether exposure to televised aggression will increase children's willingness to engage in behavior which might actually harm another person. Since this criticism was advanced, a human victim has replaced the inanimate target in at least four more recent investigations (Hanratty, 1969; Hanratty, Liebert, Morris, & Fernandez, 1969; Hanratty, O'Neal, & Sulzer, 1972; Savitsky, Rogers, Izard, & Liebert, 1971). These later studies have

demonstrated clearly that exposure to the behavior of filmed aggressive models may lead young children to directly imitate aggression against a human, as well as a "toy," victim.

Despite the newer evidence, critics may still question whether exposure to the type of violence generally depicted on regularly broadcast television shows will produce similar effects. Likewise, it is important to consider the possible *disinhibitory* effects (cf. Lovaas, 1961; Siegel, 1956) rather than only the direct *imitative* effects of observing aggressive models. Although such effects have previously been observed with adult subjects and violent scenes taken from motion pictures (e.g., Berkowitz, 1965; Berkowitz & Rawlings, 1963; Walters & Thomas, 1963), in no previous investigation known to the authors has the influence of televised violence on interpersonal aggression been examined for young children. It was with these latter questions that the present research was primarily concerned. We sought to determine whether exposure to violent scenes taken directly from nationally telecast programs increases the willingness of young children to engage in aggressive acts directed toward another child.

Method

Participants

Population sampled. The sample was drawn both from Yellow Springs, Ohio, a small college town, and from a larger and more conservative neighboring community, Xenia. The participants were brought to Fels Research Institute in Yellow Springs by one of their parents, in response to a newspaper advertisement and/or a letter distributed in local public elementary schools asking for volunteers to participate in a study of the effects of television on children. To assure that no potential participants were turned away because of scheduling inconveniences, parents were invited to select their own appointment times (including evenings or weekends), and transportation was offered to those who could not provide it for themselves.

Subjects. The subjects were 136 children, 68 boys and 68 girls. Sixty-five of the participants were 5 or 6 years of age at the time of the study; the remaining 71 subjects were 8 or 9 years of age. Within each age group and sex the children were assigned randomly to the treatment conditions. Approximately 20% of the children in this study were black; virtually all of the remainder were white. The economic backgrounds from which these participants came was widely varied. Although eco-

nomic characteristics were not used as a basis for assignment to treatments, inspection suggested that the procedure of random assignment had adequately distributed them among the experimental groups.

Experimental personnel. One of the investigators greeted the parent and child at the outset, served as the interviewer, and obtained informed parental consent for the child's participation. A 28-year-old white female served as experimenter for all the children, and two other adult females served as unseen observers throughout the experiment.

Design

A $2 \times 2 \times 2$ factorial design was employed. The three factors were sex, age (5 – 6 or 8 – 9 years old), and treatment (observation of aggressive or nonaggressive television sequences).

Procedure

Introduction to the situation. Upon the arrival of parent and child at the institute, the child was escorted to a waiting room containing nonaggressive magazines and other play materials while the parent was interviewed in a separate room. During the interview, the nature of the experiment was disclosed to the parent, questions were invited and answered, and a written consent to the child's participation was obtained.[1]

Experimental and control treatment. After the interview, but without permitting the parent and the child to interact, the experimenter escorted each subject individually to a second waiting room containing children's furniture and a television video-tape monitor. The television was then turned on by the experimenter, who suggested that the child watch for a few minutes until she was ready for him. The experimenter left the child to watch television alone for approximately $6\frac{1}{2}$ minutes; the subjects were in fact continuously observed through a concealed camera and video monitor. For all groups, the first 120 seconds of viewing consisted of two 1-minute commercials video-taped during early 1970. The first of these depicted the effectiveness of a certain paper towel, and the second advertised a humorous movie (rated G). The commercials were selected for their humor and attention-getting characteristics.

Thereafter, children in the experimental group observed the first $3\frac{1}{2}$ minutes of a program from a popular television series, "The Untouchables." The sequence, which preserved a simple story line, contained a chase, two fist-fighting scenes, two shootings, and a knifing. In contrast, children in the control group viewed a highly active $3\frac{1}{2}$-minute video-taped sports sequence in which athletes competed in hurdle races, high

jumps, and the like. For all subjects, the final 60 seconds of the program contained a commercial for automobile tires. Before the end of this last commercial, the experimenter reentered the room and announced that she was ready to begin.

Assessment of willingness to hurt another child. The subject was next escorted by the experimenter from the television room to a second room and seated at a response box apparatus modeled after the one employed by Mallick and McCandless (1966). The gray metal response box, which measured approximately 17 × 6 inches, displayed a red button on the left, a green button on the right, and a white light centered above these two manipulanda. The word "hurt" appeared beneath the red button, while the word "help" appeared beneath the green button. Several plastic wires led from the response box to a vent in the wall. The experimenter explained to the subject that these wires were connected to a game in an adjacent room and that "one of the other children is in the next room right now and will start to play the game in just a minute." She further explained that the game required the player in the other room to turn a handle and that the white light would come on each time the other child in the next room started to turn the handle, thus activating the red and green buttons.

The experimenter continued:

When this white light comes on, you have to push one of these two buttons. If you push this green button, that will make the handle next door easier to turn and will help the child to win the game. If you push this red button, that will make the handle next door feel hot. That will hurt the child, and he will have to let go of the handle. Remember, this is the *help* button, and this is the *hurt* button [indicating]. See, it says *help* and *hurt*. . . . You have to push one of these two buttons each time the light goes on, but you can push whichever one you want to. You can always push the same button or you can change from one button to the other whenever you want to, but just remember, each time the light goes on, you can push only one. So if you push this green button then you help the other child and if you push this red button then you hurt the other child. Now if you push this green button for *just a second*, then you *help the other child just a little*, and if you push this red button down for *just a second*, then you *hurt the other child just a little*. But if you push this green button down a little longer, then you help the other child a little more, and if you push this red button down a little longer, then you hurt the other child a little more. *The longer you push the green button, the more you help the*

other child and *the longer you push the red button, the more you hurt the other child.*

This explanation, with slightly varied wording, was repeated a second time if the child did not indicate comprehension of the instructions. After being assured that the subject understood the task, the experimenter left the room.[2]

Although all the subjects were led to believe that other children were participating, there was, in fact, no other child; the entire procedure was controlled in the next room so as to produce 20 trials, with an intertrial interval of approximately 15 seconds. Each child's response to each trial (appearance of the white light) and the duration of the response, recorded to the hundredth of a second, was automatically registered. When the subject had completed 20 trials, the experimenter reentered the room and announced that the game was over.

Assessment of aggressive play.   The influence of televised violence on the children's subsequent play activities was also explored, although this issue was of secondary interest in the present research (the study being primarily concerned with interpersonal aggression rather than aggression aimed at inanimate objects). After completing the button-pushing task, the child was escorted to a third room (designated the "play room") across the hallway. The room contained two large tables, on each of which appeared three attractive nonaggressive toys (e.g., a slinky, a cookset, a space-station) and one aggressive toy (a gun or a knife). Two inflated plastic dolls, 36 inches and 42 inches in height, also stood in the room. The child was told that he would be left alone for a few minutes and that he could play freely with any of the toys.

All the children were observed through a one-way vision mirror, and their aggressive behavior was recorded using a time-sampling procedure. One point was scored for the occurrence of each of three predetermined categories of aggressive play (playing with the knife, playing with the gun, assaulting either of the dolls) during the first 10 seconds of each of ten $\frac{1}{2}$-minute periods. In order to assess interobserver reliability for this measure, 10 subjects were observed independently by the two observers. Their agreement using the scoring procedures was virtually perfect ($r = .99$).

At the end of the play period, the experimenter reentered the room and asked the child to recall both the television program which he had seen and the nature of the game he had played. (All children included in the analyses were able to recall correctly the operation of the red and green buttons and the essential content of the television programs to which they had been exposed.) The child was then escorted to the lounge where the parent was waiting, thanked for his or her participation, re-

warded with a small prize, and asked not to discuss the experiment with his or her friends.

Results

Willingness to Hurt Another Child

The single overall measure which appears to capture the greatest amount of information in this situation is the total duration in seconds of each subject's aggressive responses during the 20 trials. Since marked heterogeneity of variance was apparent among the groups on this measure, the overall $2 \times 2 \times 2$ analysis of variance was performed on square-root transformed scores (i.e., $x' = \sqrt{x} + \sqrt{x+1}$, Winer, 1962). The means for all groups on this measure are presented in Table 1. The analysis itself reveals only one significant effect: that for treatment conditions ($F = 4.16$, $p < .05$). Children who had observed the aggressive program later showed reliably more willingness to engage in interpersonal aggression than those who had observed the neutral program.

Several supplementary analyses, which may serve to clarify the nature of this overall effect, were also computed. For example, a subject's total duration score may be viewed as the product of the number of times he aggresses and the average duration of each of these aggressive responses. Moreover, these two measures are only moderately, although reliably, related in the overall sample ($r = +.30$, $p < .05$). Analysis of variance for the average duration of the hurt responses reveals only a significant program effect that directly parallels the effects for total duration ($F = 3.95$, $p < .05$). The means for all groups on this measure are

Table 1
Mean Total Duration (Transformed) of Aggressive Responses in All Groups

Program shown	5–6-year-olds		8–9-year-olds	
	Boys	*Girls*	*Boys*	*Girls*
Aggressive	9.65	8.98	12.50	8.53
N	15	18	20	17
Nonaggressive	6.86	6.50	8.50	6.27
N	15	17	18	16

presented in Table 2. In contrast, analysis of the frequency measures fails to show any significant effects, although the tendency for the younger children is in the same direction.

Table 2

Mean Average Durations (Total Duration/Number of Hurt Responses) of Aggressive Responses in all Groups

Program shown	5–6-year-olds		9–8-year-olds	
	Boys	Girls	Boys	Girls
Aggressive	3.42	2.64	5.18	3.07
Nonaggressive	2.55	2.09	2.07	1.57

Note.—The number of subjects for each cell in this analysis is the same as that shown in Table 1.

Helping Responses

One possible explanation of the higher total aggression scores shown by the aggressive program group is that these children were simply more aroused than their nonaggressive treatment counterparts. To check on this interpretation, an overall analysis of variance was performed on the total duration of the help responses, employing the same square-root transformation described above. Presumably, if general arousal accounted for the effects of the hurt measure, the aggressive program groups should also show larger help scores than the nonaggressive program groups. However, contrary to the general arousal hypothesis, the effect of the treatments on this measure was not significant; the overall F comparing the aggressive program subjects' prosocial responses with those of the nonaggressive program observers was only 1.17. The one effect of borderline significance which did appear in this analysis was a Program $\times$ Sex $\times$ Age interaction ($F = 3.91$, $p \cong .05$). As can be seen in Table 3, in which these data are presented, the interaction results from the very large helping responses shown by older girls who saw the aggressive program and the relatively large helping responses shown by younger girls who saw the nonaggressive one.

Table 3

Mean Total Duration (Transformed) of Helping Responses in All Groups

Program shown	5–6-year-olds		8–9-year-olds	
	Boys	Girls	Boys	Girls
Aggressive	10.81	11.66	11.32	19.97
Nonaggressive	10.76	14.12	11.59	10.69

Note.—The number of subjects for each cell in this analysis is the same as that shown in Table 1.

Discussion

The overall results of the present experiment provide relatively consistent evidence for the view that certain aspects of a child's willingness to aggress may be at least temporarily increased by merely witnessing aggressive television episodes. These findings confirm and extend many earlier reports regarding the effects of symbolically modeled aggression on the subsequent imitative aggressive behavior of young observers toward inanimate objects (e.g., Bandura, Ross, & Ross, 1963a; Hicks, 1965; Rosekrans & Hartup, 1967). Likewise, the present data are in accord with other studies which have shown disinhibition of both young children's aggressive play and older viewers' willingness to shock another person after observing filmed aggressive modeling. As in many earlier studies, subjects exposed to symbolic aggressive models regularly tended to behave more aggressively than control group subjects tested under identical circumstances. Further, the present results emerged despite the brevity of the aggressive sequences (less than 4 minutes), the absence of a strong prior instigation to aggression, the clear availability of an alternative helping response, and the use of nationally broadcast materials rather than specially prepared laboratory films.

The various measures employed, considered together, provide some clarification of the nature of the effects obtained in the overall analysis. The significant effect for the total duration measure appears to stem predominantly from the average duration of the subjects' aggressive responses. In fact, as seen in Table 2, the group means on this measure did not overlap; the *lowest* individual cell mean among those who observed the aggressive program was higher than the *highest* mean among those groups who observed the nonaggressive program.

It should also be recalled that the instructions given to all children emphasized that a brief depression of the hurt button would cause only minimal distress to the other child, while longer depressions would cause increasingly greater discomfort. This fact, coupled with the finding that the overall average duration of such responses was more than 75 % longer in the aggressive program group than in the control group, suggests clearly that the primary effect of exposure to the aggressive program was that of reducing subjects' restraints against inflicting severe discomfort on the ostensible peer victim, that is, of increasing the *magnitude* of the hurting response. With the exception of the older girls, this effect was not paralleled by an increment in the corresponding measures of helping; thus it cannot be attributed to simple arousal effects.

It should be noted that the measure of aggressive play responses was obtained after all the subjects had been given an opportunity to help or hurt another child. Thus the observed effects might reflect an interaction between the programs and some aspect of the hurting/helping opportu-

nity rather than the simple influence of the programs themselves. While the present data do not permit us to address the possibility of such interactions directly, it is clear that the obtained results are consistent with earlier studies in which other types of aggressive scenes were used and where there were no such intervening measures.

The present experiment was designed primarily to determine whether children's willingness to engage in interpersonal aggression would be affected by the viewing of violent televised material. Within the context of the experimental situation and dependent measures employed, it appeared that this was indeed the case. However, it is clear that the occurrence and magnitude of such effects will be influenced by a number of situational and personality variables. It is thus important to examine the antecedents and correlates of such reactions to violence in greater detail. In view of the fact that a child born today will, by the age of 18, have spent more of his life watching television than in any other single activity except sleep (Lesser, 1970), few problems seem more deserving of attention.

Notes

1. Since no specific information could be provided in public announcements or over the telephone, it appeared necessary to have parents accompany their children to the institute in order to assure that no child participated without the informed consent of his parents. In order to defray the costs of transportation, baby sitters for siblings who remained at home, and the like, and to eliminate economic biases which might otherwise have appeared in the sample, a $10 stipend was given the parent of each participant. No parent who appeared for the interview declined to allow his or her child to participate.

2. Nine children, all in the 5–6-/year-old age group, were terminated prior to the collection of data because they refused to remain alone, cried, or left the experimental situation. Twenty-three other children participated in the entire experiment but were not included in the sample. Of these, 14 (5 in the younger age group and 9 in the older group) did not understand or follow instructions for the response box 7 (3 younger and 4 older children) played or explored the room instead of watching television. The data for the remaining 2 children were not recorded properly due to the technical difficulties. All potential participants brought to the institute by their parents who were not eliminated for the reasons listed above were included in the experimental sample.

References

Bandura, A. Influence of models' reinforcement contingencies on the acquisition of imitative responses. *Journal of Personality and Social Psychology*, 1965, **1**, 589–595.

Bandura, A., Ross, D., & Ross, S. A. Transmission of aggression through imitation of aggressive models *Journal of Abnormal and Social Psychology*, 1961, **63**, 575–582.

Bandura, A., Ross, D., & Ross, S. A. Imitation of film-mediated aggres-

sive models. *Journal of Abnormal and Social Psychology*, 1963, **66**, 3 – 11. (a)

Bandura, A., Ross, D., & Ross, S. A. Vicarious reinforcement and imitative learning. *Journal of Abnormal and Social Psychology*, 1963, **67**, 601 – 607. (b)

Berkowitz, L. Some aspects of observed aggression. *Journal of Personality and Social Psychology*, 1965, **2**, 359 – 369.

Berkowitz, L., & Rawlings, E. Effects of film violence on inhibitions against subsequent aggression. *Journal of Abnormal and Social Psychology*, 1963, **66**, 405 – 412.

Feshbach, S. The stimulating versus cathartic effects of a vicarious aggressive activity. *Journal of Abnormal and Social Psychology*, 1961, **63**, 381 – 385.

Feshbach, S., & Singer, R. D. *Television and aggression*. San Francisco: Jossey-Bass, 1971.

Flanders, J. P. A review of research on imitative behavior. *Psychological Bulletin*, 1968, **69**, 316 – 337.

Halloran, J. D. Television and violence. *The Twentieth Century*, 1964, **174**, 61 – 72.

Hanratty, M. A. Imitation of film-mediated aggression against live and inanimate victims. Unpublished master's thesis, Vanderbilt University, 1969.

Hanratty, M. A., Liebert, R. M., Morris, L. W., & Fernandez, L. E. Imitation of film-mediated aggression against live and inanimate victims. *Proceedings of the 77th Annual Convention of the American Psychological Association*, 1969, **4**, 457 – 458. (Summary)

Hanratty, M. A., O'Neal, E., & Sulzer, J. L. The effect of frustration upon imitation of aggression. *Journal of Personality and Social Psychology*, 1972, **21**, 30 – 34.

Hicks, D. J. Imitation and retention of film-mediated aggressive peer and adult models. *Journal of Personality and Social Psychology*, 1965, **2**, 97 – 100.

Klapper, J. T. The impact of viewing "aggression": Studies and problems of extrapolation. In O. N. Larsen (Ed.), *Violence and the mass media*. New York: Harper & Row, 1968.

Larsen, O. N. *Violence and the mass media*. New York: Harper & Row, 1968.

Lesser, G. S. Designing a program for broadcast television. In F. F. Korten, S. W. Cook, & J. I. Lacey (Eds.), *Psychology and the problems of society*. Washington, D.C.: American Psychological Association, 1970.

Lovaas, O. I. Effect of exposure to symbolic aggression on aggressive behavior. *Child Development*, 1961, **32**, 37 – 44.

Mallick, S. K., & McCandless, B. R. A study of catharsis of aggression.

Journal of Personality and Social Psychology, 1966, **4**, 591–596.

Merriam, E. We're teaching our children that violence is fun. *The Ladies' Home Journal*, 1964, **52**, 44, 49, 52.

Rosekrans, M. A., & Hartup, W. W. Imitative influences of consistent and inconsistent responses consequences to a model on aggressive behavior in children. *Journal of Personality and Social Psychology*, 1967, **7**, 429–434.

Savitsky, J. C., Rogers, R. W., Izard, C. E., & Liebert, R. M. The role of frustration and anger in the imitation of filmed aggression against a human victim. *Psychological Reports*, 1971, **29**, 807–810.

Siegel, A. E. Film-mediated fantasy aggression and strength of aggressive drive. *Child Development*, 1956, **27**, 365–378.

Walters, R. H. Implications of laboratory studies for the control and regulation of violence. *The Annals of the American Academy of Political and Social Science*, 1966, **364**, 60–72.

Walters, R. H., & Thomas, E. L. Enhancement of punitiveness by visual and audiovisual displays. *Canadian Journal of Psychology*, 1963, **16**, 244–255.

Wertham, F. Is T.V. Hardening us to the war in Vietnam? *New York Times*, December 4, 1966.

Winer, B. J. *Statistical principles in experimental design*. New York: McGraw-Hill, 1962.

4.12 TV Violence: Government Study Yields More Evidence, No Verdict

Constance Holden

The Surgeon General's report on what watching violence on television does to youth was released last month and promptly sank out of the public eye.

Nonetheless, framers of the report, which was 2½ years in the making and is based in large part on research funded by the National Institute of Mental Health (NIMH), regard it as a significant step toward establishing that a causal relation, however modest, exists between violence viewing and aggressive behavior in young people.

Reprinted from *Science*, 11 Feb. 1972, *175*, 608–611, by permission of the author and the American Association for the Advancement of Science. Copyright 1972 by the American Association for the Advancement of Science.

One million dollars were spent on research for the study, which was modeled on the landmark Surgeon General study that in 1964 announced that cigarette smoking was bad for the health. Requested in 1969 by Senator John Pastore (D-R.I.), chairman of the Senate communications subcommittee, the study was conducted by a special staff set up within NIMH and was headed by Eli Rubinstein, then assistant director for extramural programs and behavioral sciences.

The study was directed by a committee of 12 psychologists, social scientists, and communications experts—including two broadcasting industry executives—appointed by former Secretary of Health, Education, and Welfare Robert Finch.

The committee was not charged with making policy recommendations (regulating communications is outside the purview of HEW), and there are none. The final product is five volumes of research, topped by the committee's 279-page summary report, which attempts, not very successfully, to weave together various research results into some coherent generalizations. The summary winds up with the following: "We can tentatively conclude that there is a modest relationship between exposure to television violence and aggressive tendencies." Indications are that "the causal relation operates only on some children (who are predisposed to be aggressive)," and the report postulates that a "third variable" exists (the first two being violence viewing and violence doing), which sets the cause-and-effect phenomenon into action.

Some observers regard the committee report as over-cautious, in view of the inordinately large role television plays in the life of the average American. Some statistics from the report: 96 percent of American homes have at least one set; the average home set is on for at least 6 hours a day; most children start regular watching—at least 2 hours a day—by the time they are 2 or 3 years old. The typical 16-year-old has spent as much time in front of the tube as in school. *TV Guide* has the largest circulation of any magazine in the country.

The violence committee has been susceptible to criticism from the beginning (*Science*, 22 May 1970) because, unlike the smoking committee, which contained no tobacco people, five of its members have ties with the television industry.

Furthermore, the three major networks were given the option of vetoing nominations to the committee, a privilege not accorded any scholarly organizations (seven men were vetoed, all of whom had done research on television violence or had spoken sharply about the industry). George Comstock, a Rand communications research specialist who served as senior research coordinator, says the unfair selection process was a source of some ill feeling between committee and staff and within the committee. He also believes the heavy industry representation resulted in a watered-down report in which some strong individual opinions were

sacrificed for the sake of unanimity. (According to Comstock, the staff dubbed the committee "the network five, the naive four, and the scientific three.")

Others associated with the project, including Rubinstein, political scientist Ithiel de Sola Pool, and psychologist Alberta Siegel, say that the committee was not polarized along industry and nonindustry lines and insist that the report's strength lies in its unanimity.

The methods, at any rate, have not been called into question. The staff had a free hand in determining procedures within the broad areas of research determined by the committee, and all contracts were reviewed by normal NIMH ad hoc committees. The research projects covered a wide range, including surveys of television producers; analysis of audience reaction to commercials; attempts to uncover "third variables" such as sex, age, IQ, socioeconomic status, and family relationships; comparison of blacks and whites under the same viewing circumstances; polls of mothers and children on children's viewing habits; analyses of various kinds of violence (implied, threatened, senseless, justified, feigned, self-directed, and so forth); and reviews of Swedish, Israeli, and British broadcasting policies.

Studies had three focuses: the testing of long-term effects of violence (defined as "the overt expression of physical force against others or self, or the compelling of action against one's will on pain of being hurt or killed"), its immediate effects, and effects of TV on general behavior.

Some 7500 young people were involved in the studies—most of them were teen-agers, but some were as young as 4 and 5.

Comstock says some field studies were added to the literature that back up evidence hitherto gained only from controlled experiments. One was a project in which families were filmed watching television in their native habitats and their behavior and reactions monitored minute-by-minute. In another study, the facial expressions of children were watched to gauge their emotional reactions. One of the most useful studies, says Comstock, was a longitudinal one, in which a population of 19-year old boys, whose viewing habits had been studied a decade before, was subjected to a "cross-lag" analysis. This analysis allegedly confirms that there is a significant correlation between viewing violence on television and subsequent aggressive behavior.

Pool says that despite these positive findings the national press botched its coverage by following the lead of the *New York Times*, which was the first to break the story under the head "TV Violence Held Unharmful to Youth."

But such a generalization is not incomprehensible in view of the stream of ambiguities and qualified statements contained in the report.

For example, the nature of violence itself is by no means clear. In

three different studies of programming, football was ignored by one research time, classified as "highly violent" by another, and "nonviolent" by still another.

Dead ends abound: the report says, "in two studies, for example, the relationship between violence viewing and aggression was found to be as strong or stronger for girls than it was for boys, while in another study virtualy no relationship was found for girls."

Again, in another study, three groups of children were subjected, respectively, to a "prosocial" program (Misterogers Neighborhood), a violent program, and a "neutral" program. It was found that children of low socioeconomic status (SES) became more cooperative and sharing with each other after watching the prosocial program, but high SES children didn't. "Rather, the high-status children showed an increase in prosocial interpersonal behavior after viewing aggressive programming." Findings such as these have convinced researchers that there is no point in testing further the hypothesis that most children react to violence in a uniform way.

Conclusiveness having proved elusive, the question arises as to what should be done next. "The real question," says Percy Tannenbaum of Berkeley, who contributed to the studies (but was blackballed from the committee), "is when do we as a society take action on a subject, even when all the evidence is not in." Or, "When do we take action if even a small percentage of the population is affected in an undesirable way." Leon Eisenberg, a Johns Hopkins Medical School psychiatrist and another blackballee, also expressed concern over how much evidence is needed to prove the desirability of change. He compared the present network attitude toward violence on television to the official nonresponse when researchers during the 1930's suggested that cigarettes were damaging to health. In both instances, says Eisenberg, the dominant opinion was that positive proof of harm should precede corrective action, rather than that the alleged offender must furnish positive proof of harmlessness. "The committee took a very narrow view which lets the industry entirely off the hook." says Eisenberg.

Several researchers involved in the study have been highly critical of the committee's conclusions. Robert Liebert of the State University of New York at Stony Brook says the report is at best "misleading," because the results of the study were in fact "impressively strong and remarkably consistent" in establishing a correlation between viewing violence on television and viewer aggression. Monroe Lefkowitz of the New York State Department of Hygiene has written the Pastore committee, accusing the violence committee of making a weak interpretation of research findings and criticizing the procedure whereby members were selected.

Indeed, it is unlikely that the report will galvanize the television industry into an orgy of self-scrutiny. A survey of producers that was included in the project indicated that these professionals believe people like violence, so that's what they give them. "The TV industry is almost totally divorced from any social science research," says Siegel, although Klapper says CBS has been engaged in social research since 1963.

Jack McLeod of the University of Wisconsin, who with Steven Chaffee conducted one of the project's major studies, says he believes the report will help erase two misconceptions on the part of broadcasters. Now that there are field studies that back up experimental data, he says, industry can no longer label experiments as "artificial." Also, doubt has been cast on the "bad-boy" hypothesis, which says that only naturally naughty kids will be affected by video violence.

The most immediate impact of the study will be, presumably, to stimulate more research. The prime areas of need, according to the report, are identifying characteristics that predispose a child to aggressive behavior; ascertaining what reactions occur at different ages; discovering how the context of violence on television affects reactions; and identifying what fare other than violence induces aggression. The committee also sees a great need for investigating the reactions of very young children to television. Infants are the most difficult to study because lengthy, tedious observations must be relied upon in lieu of interrogation.

(According to a group of Boston mothers called Action for Children's Television, commercialism is a greater source of dismay than violence. They say that during toddler-aimed shows—particularly the Saturday morning fare, which is known among nonfans as "kidvid ghetto"—up to three times as many commercials are showered on innocent viewers as during adults shows. They have petitioned the Federal Communications Commission to outlaw commercials at prime tot time.)

The surgeon general's study may be a way to gain a foothold on the larger impact of television on society—the tastes and values it imparts, and the subtle force it has in molding children's concepts of the roles of various races, sexes, and minority groups.

These larger questions may get an airing during the week of hearings on the report to be held by Pastore's sub-committee, starting 21 March. A staff member says the object of the hearings will be to elicit the kinds of policy recommendations that the committee was barred from making. Testimony has been solicited from various government agencies, as well as from the seven individuals who were vetoed from the committee— including two prominent researchers in the field, Leonard Berkowitz of the University of Wisconsin and Albert Bandura of Stanford University.

Changing the ways of the television industry is slow going, particularly since the protections afforded by the First Amendment mean that real

efforts to improve the quality of video fare will have to be voluntary. But researchers feel that the Surgeon General's report has accumulated new evidence that, if pursued, will add up to significant social pressure on broadcasters to make better use of their rich and powerful medium.

4.13 A Note on the Effects of Television Viewing

James Garbarino
Cornell University

Concern with the effects of television viewing began with the earliest introduction of broadcast and reception facilities in the late 1930's and early 1940's. As early as 1936, the question was raised by the British social psychologist T. H. Pear, "What differences will television make to our habits and mental attitudes?" (Pear, 1936). —.Some thirty-six years and numerous investigations later, Pear's question remains largely unanswered.

The most recent compendium of research findings, the report to the Surgeon General, entitled *Television and Growing Up: The Impact of Televised Violence*, (1972) is addressed almost exclusively to the problem of assessing the relation of television to aggressive behavior in children and adolescents. In addition, some attention is given to matters such as the number of hours viewed, development of program choice, program content, and "changing patterns of television use." What is disturbing about the report to the Surgeon General is that like much of the research which has gone before, it fails to address the question of the effect of television on the socialization process within the family. More specifically: How does the television viewing both by the child and his parents affect parent-child interaction? How does the use of television as a "babysitter" by parents affect the parent-child relationship? How does the child's free and largely autonomous access to such powerful entertainment affect his other activities?

While little has been done to answer these questions directly there is indirect evidence which is germane and illuminating. Relevant data are cited in the report to the Surgeon General, as well as in two previous large scale investigations (Schramm, Lyle, and Parker, 1961; Himmelweit, Oppenheim, and Vince, 1958). But the facts seem to have gone

unnoticed because of the inadequacy of the perspective which looks only for direct effects upon the child, rather than viewing the impact on the family interactional system.

Much of the relevant research was done in the transitional period—i.e. the 1950's—when alternatives to the "television culture" were still viable. A major reason reported for initial purchase of a television set was to bring the family together in the home (Riley, Cantwell, and Ruttiger, 1949; Hamilton and Lawless, 1956). Yet television viewing was shown to be a largely non-interactive activity. One study reported that 78 percent of the respondents indicated no conversation occurring during viewing except at specified times such as commercials (and 60 percent indicated that no other activity was engaged while viewing) (Maccoby, 1951). The same investigator described the television viewing setting in the following terms:

> The television atmosphere in most households is one of quiet absorption on the part of the family members who are present. The nature of the family social life during a program could be described as "parallel" rather than interactive, and the set does seem quite clearly to dominate family life when it is on. (Maccoby, 1951, p. 428)

Such is the role of television in family interaction—or lack of it—as described in the early 1950's. Distressingly, 36 percent of respondents in one survey reported that television viewing was the only family activity participated in during the week (Hamilton and Lawless, 1956). This same study concluded that television viewing became a substitute for social activity both within and outside the family circle.

If this evidence suggests anything, it is that—at least during the 1950's—television contributed to "parallel" rather than "interactive" social activity within the family. That this had an effect upon the "habits and mental attitudes" of the viewers—adults and children—seems at the very least plausible. That television had a direct effect upon child rearing patterns seems clearer.

It has been repeatedly found that parents generally do not know how many hours their children view television (e.g., Albert and Melaine, 1958). This result has generally been intepreted as strictly a methodological problem—which to be sure it is. But it is also a substantive finding—or at least can be, given the proper conceptual framework. The fact that children watch television to an extent which is not precisely known to their parents supports the notion that television provides a dimension of experience which is often independent of adult supervision, discussion, guidance, etc.. For example, the choice of viewing time and programs is largely a decision of the child (Hess and Goldman, 1962; Lyle and Hoffman, 1971; McLeod et. al., 1971). The rising number of households

in which there are two or more sets—over thirty-five percent in 1969 (Statistical Abstract 1969)—can only contribute to the autonomy of children's viewing. That this independence from parental association and influence may generalize to other areas seems not implausible.

Earlier surveys did probe the relation of television to the process of child rearing. In one study mothers were asked: "Has TV made it easier or harder to take care of the children at home?" Fifty-four percent replied "easier," thirty-three percent replied "no difference," and three percent replied "harder" (Maccoby, 1951). One investigator reported the following comment from a mother in this regard: "It's much easier—it's just like putting him to sleep" (Maccoby, 1951, p. 429). The same investigator concluded that, "Mothers comment that TV keeps the children much quieter—there is less roughhousing and less bothering the parents with questions." (Maccoby, 1951, p. 440). In response to the statement, "TV keeps the children quiet," in one study 62 percent replied "strongly agree," 26 percent replied "somewhat agree," and 12 percent replied, "disagree." (Hess and Goldman, 1961).—.What were those children doing while they were so quiet? Was their "silence" enhancing their attachment to people, to activities, or simply to television sets? The question is a rhetorical one. The answer is, of course, a matter of speculation.

To assess the impact of television viewing upon socialization—for present and future generations as the children of the "television culture" become the parents of that culture—is a problem of a magnitude at least as great as that to which the report to the Surgeon General is addressed. The early findings suggest that television had a disruptive effect upon interaction and thus presumably human development, which by the year 1972 may have become not an anomaly but a pervasive element of the culture; by 1972, 96 percent of all American households had one or more television sets and an average viewing time in excess of two hours per day (Report to the Surgeon General, 1972). It is not unreasonable to ask: "Is the fact that the average American family during the 1950's came to include two parents, two children and a television set somehow related to the psycho-social characteristics of the young adults of the 1970's?"

Except for the sketchy data presented above we do not know the answer. And, because television has become an inextricable part of the culture, we may now not be able to find out.

References

Albert, R. and Meline, H., The influence of social status on the uses of television, *Public Opinion Quarterly*, 1958, **22**, 145–151.

Belson, W., Measuring the effects of television: A description of method, *Public Opinion Quarterly*, 1958, **22**, 11 – 18.

Hamilton, R. and Lawless, R., Television within the social matrix, *Public Opinion Quarterly*, 1956, **20**, 393 – 403.

Hess, R. and Goldman, H., Parents' views of the effect of television on their children, *Child Development*, 1962, **33**, 411 – 426.

Himmelweit, H. T., Oppenheim, A. N., and Vince, P., *Television and the child: An empirical study of the effects of television on the young*, London: Oxford University Press, 1958.

Maccoby, E., Television: Its impact on school children, *Public Opinion Quarterly*, 1951, **15**, 423 – 444.

Merrill, I., Broadcast viewing and listening by children, *Public Opinion Quarterly*, 1961, **15**, 263 – 276.

Pear, T. H., What television might do, *Listener*, November 18, 1936.

Rees, M., Achievement motivation and content preferences, *Journalism Quarterly*, 1967, **44**, 688 – 692.

Riley, J., Cantwell, F. and Ruttiger, K., Some observations on the social effects of television, *Public Opinion Quarterly*, 1949, **13**, 223 – 234.

Robinson, J., Television and leisure time: Yesterday, today and (maybe) tomorrow, *Public Opinion Quarterly*, 1969, **33**, 210 – 222.

Schramm, W., Lyle, J., and Parker, E. B., *Television in the lives of our children*, Stanford: Stanford University Press, 1961.

Surgeon General's Scientific Advisory Committee, *Television and growing up: The impact of televised violence*, Washington, D.C.: U. S. Government Printing Office, 1972.

Sweetser, F., Home television and behavior: Some tentative conclusions, *Public Opinion Quarterly*, 1955, **19**, 79 – 84.

United States Department of Commerce, *Statistical Abstract of the United States*, Washington D.C.: U. S. Government Printing Office, 1969.

4.14   Violence Against Children: Physical Child Abuse in the United States

David G. Gil

. . . The impetus for professional and public interest in physical abuse of children was provided in the forties by observations of roentgenologists of cases of unexplained multiple fractures of the long bones of young children found in conjunction with subdural hematomas (swelling or bleeding under the skull between the brain and its protective membrane). Subsequent intensive clinical studies of these strange cases by social workers, pediatricians, and psychiatrists in children's hospitals, clinics and child protective agencies in many communities throughout the country led to the suspicion and eventual confirmation that these unexplained injuries of children were often inflicted by their own parents and caretakers. As a result of these and many other studies, physical abuse of children came to be viewed as a widespread and important medical and social problem, which often resulted in serious, irreversible damage to the physical well-being and emotional development of children and which sometimes even caused their death. The types of injuries inflicted upon children were found to range from minor, superficial bruises and cuts· through burns, scaldings, fractures and internal injuries, to intentional starvation, dismemberment and severe injuries to the brain and central nervous system. The circumstances under which the injuries were inflicted were equally varied and ranged from simple disciplinary measures through uncontrollable angry outbursts, often under the influence of alcohol to premeditated murderous attacks.

Opinions varied widely with respect to the etiology and dynamics of the phenomenon and the characteristics of individuals and families involved. Many investigators concluded that physical abuse of children was an expression of severe personality disorders on the part of the perpetrators who attacked the children in their care. Many students of the phenomenon also noted that severe disturbances of family relationships as well as environmental strains and stresses such as those related to life in poverty were significantly associated with incidents of child abuse. Finally, investigators also noted that some children, because of unusual congenital or acquired characteristics, may occasionally be more prone to provoking abusive attacks against themselves than other, more "normal" children. Definite knowledge as to the nature and scope of physical

Excerpted by permission of the author and publishers from pp. 2–3, 58–60, 122, 133–148 of David G. Gil, *Violence Against Children: Physical Child Abuse in the United States*, Cambridge, Mass.: Harvard University Press (for the Commonwealth Fund), Copyright, 1970, by the President and Fellows of Harvard College.

child abuse was lacking at the time the present series of studies was initiated, however, and widely differing views were held concerning the social, psychological, legal, and administrative treatment and handling of incidents of child abuse. Some professionals expressed optimistic views concerning the potential of therapeutic intervention with abusive parents, while others questioned seriously the value of such intervention, and suggested that emphasis be given to assuring the safety of the abused child by removing him from his family. . . .

One item in the survey was designed to provide an indirect, rough estimate of the upper limit of the annual incidence of child abuse in the United States population. Respondents were asked whether they personally knew families involved in incidents of child abuse resulting in physical injury during the twelve months preceding the interview. Forty-five, or 3 percent of the 1520 respondents, reported such personal knowledge of 48 different incidents in the course of one year. The comprehension of respondents of the definition of child abuse as used in the survey was tested in the interview by means of a supplementary questionnaire that required detailed description and actual identification of each child-abuse incident of which they claimed personal knowledge during the preceding year. In this way the attempt was made to ascertain that all incidents reported in response to this question did indeed occur, and fit the definition used in the survey.

At the time of the survey there were about 110 million adults, 21 years of age and over in the United States, who constituted the universe sampled by the survey. Sample proportions obtained in the survey may be extrapolated to this universe within a known margin of error, which in the case of 3 percent, at the 95 percent level of confidence, is less than 0.7 percent. Accordingly, it is possible to state that 2.3 percent to 3.7 percent of 110 million adults, or 2.53 to 4.07 million adults throughout the United States, knew personally families involved in incidents of child abuse during the year preceding the October 1965 survey.

If each of these adults knew a different family involved in abusing and injuring a child, the number of families abusing children during the year preceding the survey would equal the number of adults having personal knowledge of such families. In that unlikely case the figures 2.53 and 4.07 millions, respectively, would represent, with 95 percent certainty, the lower and upper limits of the annual, nationwide incidence of child abuse resulting in some injury known outside the home of abused children. It must be remembered in this context that some incidents of child abuse are completely unknown beyond the confines of the abused child's home. Information concerning such completely invisible incidents was not expected to be revealed by means of a survey of the type discussed here.

The actual incidence rate of child abuse known outside the abused child's home is, however, likely to be lower than suggested by the foregoing discussion, since some of the 2.53 to 4.07 million adults who according to this estimate personally knew families involved in child-abuse incidents are likely to have known the same family. Data from the survey do not permit an estimate of the proportion of incidents known to more than one person. As far as could be ascertained, there were no multiple known cases at all among those known to the respondents of the survey. Common sense suggests, however, that some of the families involved in abusing children are likely to be known personally to more than one person, and therefore the total number of families known to have abused children is likely to be considerably smaller than the total number of individuals having personal knowledge of such families. Accordingly, the survey provided only an estimate of the *upper limit* in the total United States population of the incidence of child abuse resulting in injury from minimal to fatal, and known beyond the confines of the abused child's home. This upper limit for the year ending October 1965 was between 2.53 and 4.07 million for a population of about 190 million, or about 13.3 to 21.4 incidents per 1000 persons. The actual incidence rate, however, was not determined by the survey and is likely to be considerably lower.

It should be noted once more that this estimate of the upper limit of the annual incidence of child abuse is very rough, having been obtained by means of an indirect method, the reliability and validity of which are unknown. . . .

Ed. Note: Rates of abuse were found to be highest among families of low socioeconomic background, in families headed by females, and in which the birth rate was above average. . . .

While, as already mentioned, nearly all incidents of abuse in the sample cohort took place in the child's own home, they usually occurred in the presence of several persons besides the victim and the perpetrator. Other children from the same household were on the scene in 62.2 percent of the cases, the mother or substitute in 25.9 percent, the father or substitute in 4.6 percent, other adult members of the household in 5.9 percent, children from outside the household in 3.4 percent, and adults from outside the household in 8.2 percent.

The injured child's health and welfare may depend to a considerable extent on actions taken subsequent to an abusive incident. Delay in obtaining help may have serious consequences. A set of items in the comprehensive study focused on this issue. It was learned that the perpetrators themselves initiated help for the victims in 21.2 percent of the incidents. In 35.7 percent of the incidents, members of the victim's household other than the perpetrator initiated help. Thus in 56.9 percent of the cases the child's own family acted to obtain help once they noticed the

results of the abusive treatment. School or child-care personnel initiated help in 16.4 percent of the cases, and in 31.7 percent others, such as neighbors or visiting relatives, initiated help for the child. Occasionally help was initiated simultaneously by more than one source. . . .

To gain understanding of physical abuse of children as a phenomenon in American society it seems necessary to overcome the emotional impact of specific incidents, to go beyond the level of clinical diagnosis of individual cases, and to examine trends revealed by data on large cohorts of cases against the background of broader social and cultural forces. To conduct such an examination was the objective of the nationwide studies. The following observations suggest a conceptual framework derived from substantive findings of these studies. Based on this framework, several measures to reduce the incidence of physical child abuse in the United States are recommended.

A key element to understanding physical abuse of children in the United States seems to be that the context of child-rearing does not exclude the use of physical force toward children by parents and others responsible for their socialization. Rather, American culture encourages in subtle, and at times not so subtle, ways the use of "a certain measure" of physical force in rearing children in order to modify their inherently nonsocial inclinations. This cultural tendency can be noted in child-rearing practices of most segments of American society. It is supported in various ways by communications disseminated by the press, radio, and television, and by popular and professional publications.

Approval of a certain measure of physical force as a legitimate and appropriate educational and socializing agent seems thus endemic to American culture. Yet differences do exist between various segments of American society concerning the quantity and quality of physical force in child-rearing of which they approve, and which they actually practice. Thus, for instance, families of low socioeconomic and educational status tend to use corporal punishment to a far greater extent than do middle-class families. Also, different ethnic groups, because of differences in their history, experiences, and specific cultural traditions, seem to hold different views and seem to have evolved different practices concerning the use of physical force in child-rearing.

Although excessive use of physical force against children is considered abusive and is usually rejected in American tradition, practice, and law, no clear-cut criteria exist, nor would they be feasible, concerning the specific point beyond which the quantity and quality of physical force used against a child is to be considered excessive. The determination of this elusive point is left to the discretion of parents, other caretakers, professional personnel, health, education and welfare agencies, the police, and the courts. Implied in this ambiguous situation is the fol-

lowing question: What kind of forces singly, or in various combinations, result at certain times in culturally unacceptable "excessive" or "extreme" use of physical force against children on the part of caretakers? In other words, why and under what conditions do some persons go beyond a culturally sanctioned level of physical violence against children? Findings from the nationwide surveys suggest the following set of forces:

1. environmental chance factors;
2. environmental stress factors;
3. deviance or pathology in areas of physical, social, intellectual, and emotional functioning on the part of caretakers and/or the abused children themselves;
4. disturbed intrafamily relationships involving conflicts between spouses and/or rejection of individual children;
5. combinations between these sets of forces.

Judging by these forces. one concludes that the phenomenon of physical abuse of children should be viewed as multidimensional rather than uniform with one set of causal factors. Its basic dimension upon which all other factors are superimposed is the general, culturally determined permissive attitude toward the use of a measure of physical force in caretaker-child interaction, and the related absence of clear-cut legal prohibitions and sanctions against this particular form of interpersonal violence. A second dimension is determined by specific child-rearing traditions and practices of different social classes and ethnic and nationality groups, and the different attitudes of these groups toward physical force as an acceptable measure for the achievement of child-rearing objectives. A third dimension is determined by environmental chance circumstances, which may transform an otherwise acceptable disciplinary measure into an unacceptable outcome. A fourth dimension is the broad range of environmental stress factors which may weaken a person's psychological mechanisms of self-control, and may contribute thus to the uninhibited discharge of aggressive and destructive impulses toward physically powerless children, perceived to be causes of stress for real or imaginary reasons. The final dimension is the various forms of deviance in physical, social, intellectual, and emotional functioning of caretakers and/or children in their care, as well as of entire family units to which they belong.

The following substantive findings from the nationwide studies support the conceptual framework presented here. Culturally determined, permissive attitudes toward the use of physical force against children, and tolerant attitudes toward the perpetrators of such acts, were brought out most convincingly in the opinions expressed by a majority of respondents to the public opinion survey. Next, a majority of nearly 13,000

abusive incidents reported through legal channels during 1967 and 1968 resulted from more or less acceptable disciplinary measures taken by caretakers in angry response to actual or perceived misconduct of children in their care. Furthermore, a large majority of families involved in these reported incidents of abuse belonged to socioeconomically deprived segments of the population whose income and educational and occupational status were very low. Moreover, families from ethnic minority groups were overrepresented in the sample and study cohorts. Environmental chance factors were often found to have been decisive in transforming acceptable disciplinary measures into incidents of physical abuse resulting in injury, and a vast array of environmental stress situations were precipitating elements in a large proportion of the incidents. Finally, a higher than normal proportion of abused children, their abusers, and their families revealed a wide range of deviance and pathology in areas of physical, social, intellectual, and emotional functioning.

Before presenting a set of recommendations based on this conceptual framework, several more specific comments concerning selected substantive findings seem indicated.

Physical abuse of children does not seem to be a "major killer and maimer" of children as it was claimed to be in sensational publicity in the mass media of communication. Such exaggerated claims reflect an emotional response to this destructive phenomenon which, understandably, touches sensitive spots with nearly every adult, since many adults may themselves, at times, be subject to aggressive impulses toward children in their care. In spite of its strong emotional impact, and the tragic aspects of every single incident, the phenomenon of child abuse needs to be put into a more balanced perspective. Its true incidence rate has not been uncovered by the nationwide surveys. It seems, nevertheless, that the scope of physical abuse of children resulting in serious injury does not constitute a major social problem, at least in comparison with several more widespread and more serious social problems that undermine the developmental opportunities of many millions of children in American society, such as poverty, racial discrimination, malnutrition, and inadequate provisions for medical care and education.

Reporting levels and rates of physical child abuse did increase in several states from 1967 to 1968, while they decreased in several others. A net increase of about 10 percent occurred during this period throughout the United States. Increases in reporting rates have been interpreted by communications media and other sources as evidence of an increase in real incidence rates. Analysis of reporting patterns, however, does not support such an interpretation. Intrastate changes over time and interstate differences in levels and rates of reporting were found to be associated with differences in legal and administrative provisions and differences in professional concern and actions. They are therefore unlikely to

reflect differences and changes in real incidence rates, and claims concerning increases or decreases of real incidence rates are based on insufficient and unreliable evidence.

Although the real incidence rate of all physical child abuse remains unknown in spite of reporting legislation, cohorts of officially reported incidents are likely to be a more adequate representation of the severe-injury segment of the physical child-abuse spectrum than of lesser or no-injury segments, since severity of injury is an important criterion in reporting. If, then, the 6,000 to 7,000 incidents that are reported annually through official channels are, as a group, an approximate representation of the severe segment of the nationwide abuse spectrum, then the physical consequences of child abuse do not seem to be very serious in the aggregate. This conclusion is based on data concerning the types and severity of injuries sustained by children of the 1967 and 1968 study cohorts. Over half these children suffered only minor injuries, and the classical "battered child syndrome" was found to be a relatively infrequent occurrence. Even if allowance is made for underreporting, especially of fatalities, physical abuse cannot be considered a major cause of mortality and morbidity of children in the United States.

Turning now to an epidemiologic perspective, it should be noted that physical abuse of children, and especially more serious incidents, were found to be overconcentrated among the poor and among nonwhite minorities, and thus seem to be one aspect of the style of life associated with poverty and the ghetto. While it may be valid to argue, on the basis of much evidence, that the poor and nonwhites are more likely to be reported for anything they do or fail to do, and that their overrepresentation in cohorts of reported child abuse may be in part a function of this kind of reporting bias, it must not be overlooked, nevertheless, that life in poverty and in the ghettos generates stressful experiences, which are likely to become precipitating factors of child abuse. The poor and members of ethnic minorities are subject to the same conditions that may cause abusive behavior toward children in all other groups of the population. In addition, however, these people must experience the special environmental stresses and strains associated with socioeconomic deprivation and discrimination. Moreover, they have fewer alternatives and escapes than the nonpoor for dealing with aggressive impulses toward their children. Finally, there is an additional factor, the tendency toward more direct, less inhibited, expression and discharge of aggressive impulses, a tendency learned apparently through lower-class and ghetto socialization, which differ in this respect from middle-class mores and socialization.

Of considerable interest in terms of the forces contributing to child abuse are findings concerning the troubled past history of many abused children, their parents and perpetrators, and the relatively high rates of

deviance in areas of bio-psycho-social functioning of children and adults involved in abuse incidents. In many instances manifestations of such deviance were observed during the year preceding the reported incident. Deviance in functioning of individuals was matched by high rates of deviance in family structure reflected in a high proportion of female-headed households and households from which the biological fathers of abused children were absent. In terms of family structure it is also worth noting that, as a group, families of physically abused children tend to have more children than other American families with children under age 18.

The age distribution of abused children and their parents was found to be less skewed toward younger age groups than had been thought on the basis of earlier, mainly hospital-based, studies. This difference in findings seems due to the fact that younger children tend to be more severely injured when abused and are, therefore overrepresented among hospitalized abused children. More boys than girls seem to be subjected to physical abuse, yet girls seem to outnumber boys among adolescent abused children. Although more mothers than fathers are reported as perpetrators of abuse, the involvement rate in incidents of child abuse is higher for fathers and stepfathers than for mothers. This important relationship is unraveled when account is taken of the fact that nearly 30 percent of reported abuse incidents occur in female-headed households. Altogether, nearly 87 percent of perpetrators are parents or parent substitutes.

Mention should be made of observations which support the hypotheses that some children play a contributive role in their own abuse, since their behavior seems to be more provocative and irritating to caretakers than the behavior of other children. Such atypical behavior may derive from constitutional or congenital factors, from environmental experiences, or from both.

Many children in the study had been abused on previous occasions, and siblings of many abused children were abused on the same or on previous occasions. Many perpetrators were involved in incidents of abuse on previous occasions, and many had been victims of abuse during their childhood. The high rate of recidivism reflected in these findings indicates that the use of physical force tends to be patterned into child-rearing practices and is usually not an isolated incident.

Circumstances precipitating incidents of abuse are quite diverse, yet underlying this diversity there seems to be a rather simple structure. A factor analysis of the circumstances of 1,380 abusive incidents of the sample cohort resulted in the following refined typology of circumstances of child abuse:

    a.   Psychological rejection leading to repeated abuse and battering;
    b.   Disciplinary measures taken in uncontrolled anger;

c. Male babysitter acting out sadistic and sexual impulses in the mother's temporary absence, at times under the influence of alcohol;

d. Mentally or emotionally disturbed caretaker acting under mounting environmental stress;

e. Misconduct and persistent behavioral atypicality of a child leading to his own abuse;

f. Female babysitter abusing child during mother's temporary absence;

g. Quarrel between caretakers, at times under the influence of alcohol.

Recommendations

Measures aimed at the prevention or the gradual reduction of the incidence and prevalence of specified social phenomena cannot be expected to achieve their purpose unless they are designed and executed in a manner that assures intervention on the causal level. Applying a public health model of preventive intervention to the phenomenon of physical abuse of children and proceeding on the conceptualization of its etiology, which has been presented above, I suggest the following measures:

I. Since culturally determined permissive attitudes toward the use of physical force in child-rearing seem to constitute the common core of all physical abuse of children in American society, systematic educational efforts aimed at gradually changing this particular aspect of the prevailing child-rearing philosophy, and developing clear-cut cultural prohibitions and legal sanctions against the use of physical force as a means for rearing children, are likely to produce over time the strongest possible reduction of the incidence and prevalence of physical abuse of children.

What is suggested here is, perhaps, a revolutionary change not only in the child-rearing philosophy and practices of American society but also in its underlying value system. Such a thorough change cannot be expected to occur overnight on the basis of a formal decision by governmental authority. What would be required is an extended, consistent effort in that direction which must eventually lead to a series of changes in our system of values and in the entire societal fabric.

It is important to keep in mind in this context that educational philosophies tend to reflect a social order and are not its primary shapers. Education tends to recreate a society in its existing image, or to maintain its relative status quo, but it rarely if ever creates new social structures. Violence against children in rearing them may thus be a functional aspect of socialization into a highly competitive and often violent society, one that puts a premium on the uninhibited pursuit of self-interest and

that does not put into practice the philosophy of human cooperativeness which it preaches on ceremonial occasions and which is upheld in its ideological expressions and symbols. The elimination of violence from American child-rearing philosophy and practice seems therefore to depend on changes in social philosophy and social reality toward less competition and more human cooperativeness, mutual caring, and responsibility.[1]

The foregoing considerations suggest that a close connection may indeed exist between culturally acceptable violence against children and culturally unacceptable violence among adults and among various groups in American society. These considerations also suggest that to the extent that American society may succeed in reducing the amount of violence and abuse which it inflicts collectively on children in the course of their socialization, it may reduce the amount of violence in interpersonal and intergroup relations among adults in this country, and perhaps even in international relations on a global scale.

If physical force could gradually be eliminated as a mode of legitimate interaction between caretakers and children, some other more constructive modes of interaction would have to replace it. Children who were exposed to more constructive relationship patterns would be likely to learn from this experience and to carry it over into their adult relationships. They would no longer be exposed, as they are now, to conflicting signals from their parents and caretakers according to which violence is valued both positively and negatively, but would integrate into their personalities and into their consciousness a value that would reject violence as a mode of human interaction.

Eschewing the use of physical force in rearing children does not mean that inherently nonsocial traits of children would not need to be modified in the course of socialization. It merely means that alternative educational measures would have to replace physical force, since physical force, while perhaps an effective agent of change in human behavior, seems to result in too many undersirable, long-term side effects. Child-rearing literature and practice no doubt offer such alternative means of achieving the socially desirable modifications of nonsocial inclinations of children.

It should be recognized that giving up the use of physical force against children may not be easy for adults who were subjected to physical force and violence in their own childhood and who have adopted the existing value system of American society. Moreover, children can sometimes be very irritating and provocative in their behavior and may strain the tolerance of adults to the limit. Yet in spite of these realities, which must be acknowledged and faced openly, society needs to work toward the gradual reduction and, eventually, complete elimination of physical violence

toward its young generation if it is serious about its expressed desire to prevent the physical abuse of children.

As a first, concrete step toward developing eventually comprehensive legal sanctions against the use of physical force in rearing children, the Congress of the United States and legislatures of the states could outlaw corporal punishment in schools, juvenile courts, correctional institutions, and other child-care facilities. Such legislation would assure that children would receive the same protection against physical attack outside their homes as the law provides for adult members of society. Moreover, such legislation is also likely to affect child-rearing attitudes and practices in American homes, for it would symbolize society's growing rejection of violence against children.[2]

To avoid misinterpretations it should be ntoed here that rejecting corporal punishment does not imply favoring unlimited permissiveness in rearing children. To grow up successfully, children require a sense of security that is inherent in nonarbitrary structures and limits. Understanding adults can establish such structures and limits through love, patience, firmness, consistency, and rational authority. Corporal punishment seems devoid of constructive educational value, since it cannot provide that sense of security and nonarbitrary authority. Rarely, if ever, is corporal punishment administered for the benefit of the attacked child, for usually it serves the immediate needs of the attacking adult who is seeking relief from his uncontrollable anger and stress. And finally, physical attack by an adult on a weak child is not a sign of strength, for it reflects lack of real authority, and surrender to the attacker's own uncontrollable impulses.

2. Poverty, as has been shown, appears to be related to the phenomenon of physical abuse of children in at least four ways. First, the cultural approval of the use of physical force in child-rearing tends to be stronger among the socioeconomically deprived strata of society than among the middle class. Secondly, there seems to be less inhibition to express and discharge aggressive and violent feelings and impulses toward other persons among members of socioeconomically deprived strata than among the middle class. Thirdly, environmental stress and strain are considerably more serious for persons living in poverty than for those enjoying affluence. Finally, the poor have fewer opportunities than the nonpoor for escaping occasionally from child-rearing responsibilities.

These multiple links between poverty and physical abuse of children suggest that one important route toward reducing the incidence and prevalence of child abuse is the elimination of poverty from America's affluent society. No doubt this is only a partial answer to the complex issue of preventing violence against children, but perhaps a very impor-

tant part of the total answer, and certainly that part without which other preventive efforts may be utterly futile. Eliminating poverty also happens to be that part of the answer for which this nation possesses the necessary resources, assuming willingness to redistribute national wealth more equitably, and for which it possesses the knowledge of how to effect a change—provided that an unambiguous, high priority, national commitment is made to the unconditional elimination of poverty by assuring to all members of society, without discrimination, equal opportunity to the enjoyment of life through:

    a. adequate income derived from employment whenever feasible, or assured by means of a system of nonstigmatizing guaranteed-income maintenance based on legal entitlement rather than on charity and bureaucratic discretion;

    b. comprehensive health care and social services;

    c. decent and adequate housing and neighborhoods, free from the stigmatizing milieu and conditions of many existing public-housing programs;

    d. comprehensive education fitting inherent capacities and assuring the realization of each person's potential;

    e. cultural and recreational facilities.

3. Deviance and pathology in areas of physical, social, intellectual, and emotional functioning of individuals and of family units were found to be another set of forces that may contribute to the incidence and prevalence of physical abuse of children. Adequate preventive or ameliorative intervention once an individual or a family is affected by such conditions is known to be very complicated. However, it is also known that these conditions tend to be strongly associated with poverty; the elimination of poverty is therefore likely to reduce, though by no means to eliminate, the incidence and prevalence of these various dysfunctional phenomena. The following measures, aimed at the prevention and amelioration of these conditions and at the strengthening of individual and family functioning should be available in every community as components of a comprehensive program to reduce the incidence of physical abuse of children and also to help individuals and families once abuse has occurred:

a. Comprehensive family-planning programs including the repeal of all legislation concerning medical abortions. The availability of family-planning resources and medical abortions are likely to reduce the number of unwanted and rejected children, who are known to be frequently victims of severe physical abuse and even infanticide. Such provisions would assure that no family would have to increase beyond a size desired by parents and beyond their capacity to care for the children. Women, in-

cluding single women, would not have to become mothers unless they felt ready for this role. It is important to recall in this context that families with many children, and households headed by females, are overrepresented among families involved in physical abuse of children.

b. Family-life education and counseling programs for adolescents and adults in preparation for marriage and after it. Such programs should be developed in accordance with the assumption that there is much to learn about married life and parenthood which one does not know merely on the basis of sexual and chronological maturity, and that marital and parental relationships can be enriched like all human relationships if one is willing to work toward such enrichment. While such programs should be geared primarily to the strengthening of "normal" families, they could also serve as a screening device for the identification of incipient deviance in any area of individual and family functioning. Such programs should be offered within the public school systems of communities in order to avoid their becoming identified in the mind of the public with deviance-focused agencies.

c. A comprehensive, high quality, neighborhood-based, national health service, financed through general tax revenue and geared not only to the treatment of acute and chronic illness, but also to the promotion and assurance of maximum feasible physical and mental health for everyone.

d. A range of high quality, neighborhood-based social, child-welfare, and child-protective services geared to the reduction of environmental and internal stresses on family life, and especially on mothers who carry major responsibility for the child-rearing function. Such stresses are known to precipitate incidents of physical abuse of children, and any measure that would reduce these stresses would also indirectly reduce the incidence of child abuse. Family counseling, homemaker and housekeeping services, mothers' helpers and babysitting services, family and group day-care facilities for preschool and school-age children are all examples of such services. They would all have to be licensed publicly to assure quality. They should be available on a full coverage basis in every community to all groups in the community and not only to the rich or the very poor. Nor should such services be structured as emergency services; they should be for normal situations, in order to prevent emergencies. No mother should be expected to care for her children around the clock, 365 days a year. Substitute care mechanisms should be routinely available to offer mothers opportunities for carefree rest and recreation.

Every community needs also a system of social services geared to the assistance of families and children who cannot live together because of severe relationship and/or reality problems. Physically abused children

belong frequently to this category, and in such situations the welfare of the child and of the family may require temporary or permanent separation. The first requirement for dealing adequately with such situations is diagnostic service capable of arriving at sound decisions which take into consideration the circumstances, needs, and rights of all concerned. Next, a community requires access to a variety of facilities for the care of children away from their homes.

The administration of services and provisions suggested here should be based on a constructive and therapeutic rather than a punitive philosophy, if they are to serve the ultimate objective—the reduction of the general level of violence and the raising of the general level of human well being throughout the entire society.

The three sets of measures proposed are aimed at different levels and aspects of physical abuse of children. The first set would attack the culturally determined core of the phenomenon; the second set would attack and eliminate a major condition to which child abuse is linked in many ways; the third set approaches the causes of child abuse indirectly. It would be futile to argue the relative merits of these approaches; all three are important and should be utilized simultaneously. The basic questions seems to be not which measure to select for combating child abuse but whether American society is indeed committed to the well being of all its children and to the eradication of all violence toward them, be it violence perpetrated by individual caretakers, or violence perpetrated collectively by society. If the answer to this question is an unambiguous yes, then the means and the knowledge are surely at hand to progress toward this objective.

Notes

1. See Urie Bronfenbrenner, *Two Worlds of Childhood* (New York, Russell Sage Foundation, 1970).

2. A unique step in the direction recommended here was taken on June 2, 1970, by the United States District Court in Boston when Chief Judge Charles Wyzanski issued a permanent injunction against corporal punishment in any form under any circumstances in all Boston public schools.

4.15 Like It Is In The Alley

Robert Coles

In the alley it's mostly dark, even if the sun is out. But if you look around, you can find things. I know how to get into every building, except that it's like night once you're inside them, because they don't have lights. So, I stay here. You're better off. It's no good on the street. You can get hurt all the time, one way or the other. And in buildings, like I told you, it's bad in them, too. But here it's o.k. You can find your own corner, and if someone tries to move in you fight him off. We meet here all the time, and figure out what we'll do next. It might be a game, or over for some pool, or a coke or something. You need to have a place to start out from, and that's like it is in the alley; you can always know your buddy will be there, provided it's the right time. So you go there, and you're on your way, man."

Like all children of nine, Peter is always on his way—to a person, a place, a "thing" he wants to do. *"There's this here thing we thought we'd try tomorrow"*, he'll say; and eventually I'll find out that he means there's to be a race. He and his friends will compete with another gang to see who can wash a car faster and better. The cars belong to four youths who make their money taking bets, and selling liquor that I don't believe was ever purchased, and pushing a few of those pills that *"go classy with beer."* I am not completely sure, but I think they also have something to do with other drugs; and again, I can't quite be sure what their connection is with a "residence" I've seen not too far from the alley Peter describes so possessively. The women come and go—from that residence and along the street Peter's alley leaves.

Peter lives in the heart of what we in contemporary America have chosen (ironically, so far as history goes) to call an "urban ghetto." The area was a slum before it became a ghetto, and there still are some very poor white people on its edges and increasing numbers of Puerto Ricans in several of its blocks. Peter was not born in the ghetto, nor was his family told to go there. They are Americans and have been here *"since way back before anyone can remember."* That is the way Peter's mother talks about Alabama, about the length of time she and her ancestors have lived there. She and Peter's father came north *"for freedom."* They did not seek out a ghetto, an old quarter of Boston where they were expected to live and where they would be confined, yet at least some of the time solidly at rest, with kin, and reasonably safe.

Reprinted by permission of *Daedalus*, Journal of the American Academy of Arts and Sciences, Boston, Mass. Fall 1968, *The Conscious of the City*.

No, they sought freedom. Americans, they moved on when the going got "*real bad*," and Americans, they expected something better someplace, some other place. They left Alabama on impulse. They found Peter's alley by accident. And they do not fear pogroms. They are Americans, and in Peter's words: "*There's likely to be another riot here soon. That's what I heard today. You hear it a lot, but one day you know it'll happen.*"

Peter's mother fears riots too—among other things. The Jews of Eastern Europe huddled together in their ghettos, afraid of the barbarians, afraid of the *Goyim*, but always sure of one thing, their God-given destiny. Peter's mother has no such faith. She believes that "*something will work out one of these days.*" She believes that "*you have to keep on going, and things can get better, but don't ask me how.*" She believes that "*God wants us to have a bad spell here, and so maybe it'll get better the next time—you know in Heaven, and I hope that's where we'll be going.*" Peter's mother, in other words, is a pragmatist, an optimist, and a Christian. Above all she is American: "*Yes, I hear them talk about Africa, but it don't mean anything to us. All I know is Alabama and now it's in Massachusetts that we are. It was a long trip coming up here, and sometimes I wish we were back there, and sometimes I'd just as soon be here, for all that's no good about it. But I'm not going to take any more trips, no sir. And like Peter said, this is the only country we've got. If you come from a country, you come from it, and we're from it, I'd say, and there isn't much we can do but try to live as best we can. I mean, live here.*"

What is "life" like for her over there, where she lives, in the neighborhood she refers to as "here"? A question like that cannot be answered by the likes of me, and even her answer provides only the beginning of a reply: "*Well, we does o.k., I guess. Peter here, he has it better than I did, or his daddy. I can say that. I tell myself that a lot. He can turn on the faucet over there, and a lot of the time, he just gets the water, right away. And when I tell him what it was like for us, to go fetch that water—we'd walk three miles, yes sir, and we'd be lucky it wasn't ten—well, Peter, it doesn't register on him. He thinks I'm trying to fool him, and the more serious I get, the more he laughs, so I've stopped.*

"*Of course it's not all so good, I have to admit. We're still where we were, so far as knowing where your next meal is coming from. When I go to bed at night I tell myself I've done good, to stay alive and keep the kids alive, and if they'll just wake up in the morning, and me too, well then, we can worry about that, all the rest, come tomorrow. So there you go. We do our best, and that's all you can do.*"

She may sound fatalistic, but she appears to be a nervous, hard-working, even hard-driven woman—thin, short, constantly on the move. I

may not know what she "really" thinks and believes, because like the rest of us she has her contradictions and her mixed feelings. I think it is fair to say that there are some things that she can't say to me — or to herself. She is a Negro, and I am white. She is poor, and I am fairly well off. She is very near to illiterate, and I put in a lot of time worrying about how to say things. But she and I are both human beings, and we both have trouble — to use that word — "communicating," not only with each other, but with ourselves. Sometimes she doesn't tell me something she really wants me to know. She has forgotten, pure and simple. More is on her mind than information I might want. And sometimes I forget too: *"Remember you asked the other day about Peter, if he was ever real sick. And I told you he was a weak child, and I feared for his life, and I've lost five children, three that was born and two that wasn't. Well, I forgot to tell you that he got real sick up here, just after we came. He was three, and I didn't know what to do. You see, I didn't have my mother to help out. She always knew what to do. She could hold a child and get him to stop crying, no matter how sick he was, and no matter how much he wanted food, and we didn't have it. But she was gone — and that's when we left to come up here, and I never would have left her, not for anything in the world. But suddenly she took a seizure of something and went in a half hour, I'd say. And Peter, he was so hot and sick, I thought he had the same thing his grandmother did and he was going to die. I thought maybe she's calling him. She always liked Peter. She helped him be born, she and my cousin, they did."*

Actually, Peter's mother remembers quite a lot of things. She remembers the "old days" back South, sometimes with a shudder, but sometimes with the same nostalgia that the region is famous for generating in its white exiles. She also notices a lot of things. She notices, and from time to time will remark upon, the various changes in her life. She has moved from the country to the city. Her father was a sharecropper and her son wants to be a pilot (sometimes), a policeman (sometimes), a racing-car driver (sometimes), and a baseball player (most of the time). Her husband is not alive. He died one year after they all came to Boston. He woke up vomiting in the middle of the night — vomiting blood. He bled and bled and vomited and vomited and then he died. The doctor does not have to press very hard for "the facts." Whatever is known gets spoken vividly and (still) emotionally: *"I didn't know what to do. I was beside myself. I prayed and I prayed, and in between I held his head and wiped his forehead. It was the middle of the night. I woke up my oldest girl and I told her to go knocking on the doors. But no one would answer. They must have been scared, or have suspected something bad. I thought if only he'd be able to last into the morning, then we could get some help. I was caught between things. I couldn't leave him to go get a*

policeman. And my girl, she was afraid to go out. And besides, there was no one outside, and I thought we'd just stay at his side, and somehow he'd be o.k., because he was a strong man, you know. His muscles, they were big all his life. Even with the blood coming up, he looked too big and strong to die, I thought. But I knew he was sick. He was real bad sick. There wasn't anything else, no sir, to do. We didn't have no phone and even if there was a car, I never could have used it. Nor my daughter. And then he took a big breath and that was his last one."

When I first met Peter and his mother, I wanted to know how they lived, what they did with their time, what they liked to do or disliked doing, what they believed. In the back of my mind were large subjects like "the connection between a person's moods and the environment in which he lives." Once I was told I was studying "the psychology of the ghetto," and another time the subject of "urban poverty and mental health." It is hoped that at some point large issues like those submit themselves to lives; and when that is done, when particular but not unrepresentative or unusual human beings are called in witness, their concrete medical history becomes extremely revealing. I cannot think of a better way to begin knowing what life is like for Peter and his mother than to hear the following and hear it again and think about its implications: *"No sir, Peter has never been to a doctor, not unless you count the one at school, and she's a nurse I believe. He was his sickest back home before we came here, and you know there was no doctor for us in the county. In Alabama you have to pay a white doctor first, before he'll go near you. And we don't have but a few colored ones. (I've never seen a one.) There was this woman we'd go to, and she had gotten some nursing education in Mobile. (No, I don't know if she was a nurse or not, or a helper to the nurses, maybe.) Well, she would come to help us. With the convulsions, she'd show you how to hold the child, and make sure he doesn't hurt himself. They can bite their tongues real, real bad.*

"Here, I don't know what to do. There's the city hospital, but it's no good for us. I went there with my husband, no sooner than a month or so after we came up here. We waited and waited, and finally the day was almost over. We left the kids with a neighbor, and we barely knew her. I said it would take the morning, but I never thought we'd get home near suppertime. And they wanted us to come back and come back, because it was something they couldn't do all at once—though for most of the time we just sat there and did nothing. And my husband, he said his stomach was the worse for going there, and he'd take care of himself from now on, rather than go there.

"Maybe they could have saved him. But they're far away, and I didn't have money to get a cab, even if there was one around here, and I thought to myself it'll make him worse, to take him there.

*"My kids, they get sick. The welfare worker, she sends a nurse here,
and she tells me we should be on vitamins and the kids need all kinds of
check-ups. Once she took my daughter and told her she had to have her
teeth looked at, and the same with Peter. So, I went with my daughter,
and they didn't see me that day, but said they could in a couple of
weeks. And I had to pay the woman next door to mind the little ones,
and there was the carfare, and we sat and sat, like before. So, I figured,
it would take more than we've got to see that dentist. And when the
nurse told us we'd have to come back a few times—that's how many, a
few—I thought that no one ever looked at my teeth, and they're not
good, I'll admit, but you can't have everything, that's what I say, and
that's what my kids have to know, I guess."*

What *does* she have? And what belongs to Peter? For one thing, there
is the apartment, three rooms for six people, a mother and five children.
Peter is a middle child with two older girls on one side and a younger
sister and still younger brother on the other side. The smallest child was
born in Boston: *"It's the only time I ever spent time in a hospital. He's
the only one to be born there. My neighbor got the police. I was in the
hall, crying I guess. We almost didn't make it. They told me I had bad
blood pressure, and I should have been on pills, and I should come
back, but I didn't. It was the worst time I've ever had, because I was
alone. My husband had to stay with the kids, and no one was there to
visit me."*

Peter sleeps with his brother in one bedroom. The three girls sleep in
the living room, which is a bedroom. And, of course, there is a small
kitchen. There is not very much furniture about. The kitchen has a table
with four chairs, only two of which are sturdy. The girls sleep in one big
bed. Peter shares his bed with his brother. The mother sleeps on a
couch. There is one more chair and a table in the living room. Jesus
looks down from the living room wall, and an undertaker's calendar
hangs on the kitchen wall. The apartment has no books, no records.
There is a television set in the living room, and I have never seen it off.

Peter in many respects is his father's successor. His mother talks
things over with him. She even defers to him at times. She will say
something; he will disagree; she will nod and let him have the last word.
He knows the city. She still feels a stranger to the city. *"If you want to
know about anything around here, just ask Peter,"* she once said to me.
That was three years ago, when Peter was six. Peter continues to do
very poorly at school, but I find him a very good teacher. He notices a
lot, makes a lot of sense when he talks, and has a shrewd eye for the
ironic detail. He is very intelligent, for all the trouble he gives his teachers. He recently summed up a lot of American history for me: *"I wasn't
made for that school, and that school wasn't made for me."* It is an old

school, filled with memories. The name of the school evokes Boston's Puritan past. Pictures and statues adorn the corridors — reminders of the soldiers and statesmen and writers who made New England so influential in the nineteenth century. And naturally one finds slogans on the walls, about freedom and democracy and the rights of the people. Peter can be surly and cynical when he points all that out to the visitor. If he is asked what kind of school he would *like*, he laughs incredulously. *"Are you kidding? No school would be my first choice. They should leave us alone, and let us help out at home, and maybe let some of our own people teach us. The other day the teacher admitted she was no good. She said maybe a Negro should come in and give us the discipline, because she was scared. She said all she wanted from us was that we keep quiet and stop wearing her nerves down, and she'd be grateful, because she would retire soon. She said we were becoming too much for her, and she didn't understand why. But when one kid wanted to say something, tell her why, she told us to keep still, and write something. You know what? She whipped out a book and told us to copy a whole page from it, so we'd learn it. A stupid waste of time. I didn't even try; and she didn't care. She just wanted an excuse not to talk with us. They're all alike."*

Actually, they're all *not* alike, and Peter knows it. He has met up with two fine teachers, and in mellow moments he can say so: *"They're trying hard, but me and my friends, I don't think we're cut out for school. To tell the truth, that's what I think. My mother says we should try, anyway, but it doesn't seem to help, trying. The teacher can't understand a lot of us, but he does all these new things, and you can see he's excited. Some kids are really with him, and I am, too. But I can't take all his stuff very serious. He's a nice man, and he says he wants to come and visit every one of our homes; but my mother says no, she wouldn't know what to do with him, when he came here. We'd just stand and have nothing to talk about. So she said tell him not to come; and I don't think he will, anyway. I think he's getting to know."*

What is that teacher getting to know? What *is* there to know about Peter and all the others like him in our American cities? Of course Peter and his friends who play in the alley need better schools, schools they can feel to be theirs, and better teachers, like the ones they *have* in fact met on occasion. But I do not feel that a reasonably good teacher in the finest school building in America would reach and affect Peter in quite the way, I suppose, people like me would expect and desire. At nine Peter is both young and quite old. At nine he is much wiser about many things than my sons will be at nine, and maybe nineteen. Peter has in fact taught me a lot about his neighborhood, about life on the streets, about survival: *"I get up when I get up, no special time. My mother has Alabama in her. She gets up with the sun, and she wants to go to bed*

when it gets dark. I try to tell her that up here things just get started in the night. But she gets mad. She wakes me up. If it weren't for her shaking me, I might sleep until noon. Sometimes we have a good breakfast, when the check comes. Later on, though, before *it comes, it might just be some coffee and a slice of bread. She worries about food. She says we should eat what she gives us, but sometimes I'd rather go hungry. I was sick a long time ago, my stomach or something — maybe like my father, she says. So I don't like all the potatoes she pushes on us and cereal, all the time cereal. We're supposed to be lucky, because we get some food every day. Down South they can't be sure. That's what she says, and I guess she's right.*

"Then I go to school. I eat what I can, and leave. I have two changes of clothes, one for everyday and one for Sunday. I wait on my friend Billy, and we're off by 8:15. He's from around here, and he's a year older. He knows everything. He can tell you if a woman is high on some stuff, or if she's been drinking, or she's off her mind about something. He knows. His brother has a convertible, a Buick. He pays off the police, but Billy won't say no more than that.

"In school we waste time until it's over. I do what I have to. I don't like the place. I feel like falling off all day, just putting my head down and saying good-bye to everyone until three. We're out then, and we sure wake up. I don't have to stop home first, not now. I go with Billy. We'll be in the alley, or we'll go to see them play pool. Then you know when it's time to go home. You hear someone say six o'clock, and you go in. I eat and I watch television. It must be around ten or eleven I'm in bed."

Peter sees rats all the time. He has been bitten by them. He has a big stick by his bed to use against them. They also claim the alley, even in the daytime. They are not large enough to be compared with cats, as some observers have insisted; they are simply large, confident, well-fed, unafraid rats. The garbage is theirs; the land is theirs; the tenement is theirs; human flesh is theirs. When I first started visiting Peter's family, I wondered why they didn't do something to rid themselves of those rats, and the cockroaches, and the mosquitoes, and the flies, and the maggots, and the ants, and especially the garbage in the alley which attracts so much of all that "lower life." Eventually I began to see some of the reasons why. A large apartment building with many families has exactly two barrels in its basement. The halls of the building go unlighted. Many windows have no screens, and some windows are broken and boarded up. The stairs are dangerous; some of them have missing timber. (*"We just jump over them,"* says Peter cheerfully.) And the landowner is no one in particular. Rent is collected by an agent, in the name of a "realty trust." Somewhere in City Hall there is a bureaucrat who unquestiona-

bly might be persuaded to prod someone in the "trust"; and one day I went with three of the tenants, including Peter's mother, to try that "approach." We waited and waited at City Hall. (I drove us there, clear across town, naturally.) Finally we met up with a man, a not very encouraging or inspiring or generous or friendly man. He told us we would have to try yet another department and swear out a complaint; and that the "case" would have to be "studied," and that we would then be "notified of a decision." We went to the department down the hall, and waited some more, another hour and ten minutes. By then it was three o'clock, and the mothers wanted to go home. They weren't thinking of rats anymore, or poorly heated apartments, or garbage that had nowhere to go and often went uncollected for two weeks, not one. They were thinking of their children, who would be home from school and, in the case of two women, their husbands who would also soon be home. "*Maybe we should come back some other day*," Peter's mother said. I noted she didn't say *tomorrow* and I realized that I had read someplace that people like her aren't precisely "future-oriented."

Actually, both Peter and his mother have a very clear idea of what is ahead. For the mother it is "*more of the same.*" One evening she was tired but unusually talkative, perhaps because a daughter of hers was sick: "*I'm glad to be speaking about all these things tonight. My little girl has a bad fever. I've been trying to cool her off all day. Maybe if there was a place near here, that we could go to, maybe I would have gone. But like it is, I have to do the best I can and pray she'll be o.k.*"

I asked whether she thought her children would find things different, and that's when she said it would be "*more of the same*" for them. Then she added a long afterthought: "*Maybe it'll be a little better for them. A mother has to have hope for her children, I guess. But I'm not too sure, I'll admit. Up here you know there's a lot more jobs around than in Alabama. We don't get them, but you know they're someplace near, and they tell you that if you go train for them, then you'll be eligible. So maybe Peter might someday have some real good steady work, and that would be something, yes sir it would. I keep telling him he should pay more attention to school, and put more of himself into the lessons they give there. But he says no, it's no good; it's a waste of time; they don't care what happens there, only if the kids don't keep quiet and mind themselves. Well, Peter has got to learn to mind himself, and not be fresh. He speaks back to me, these days. There'll be a time he won't even speak to me at all, I suppose. I used to blame it all on the city up here, city living. Back home we were always together, and there wasn't no place you could go, unless to Birmingham, and you couldn't do much for yourself there, we all knew. Of course, my momma, she knew how to make us behave. But I was thinking the other night, it wasn't so good back there either.*

Colored people, they'd beat on one another, and we had lot of people that liquor was eating away at them; they'd use wine by the gallon. All they'd do was work on the land, and then go back and kill themselves with wine. And then there'd be the next day—until they'd one evening go to sleep and never wake up. And we'd get the Bossman and he'd see to it they got buried.

"Up here I think it's better, but don't ask me to tell you why. There's the welfare, that's for sure. And we get our water and if there isn't good heat, at least there's some. Yes, it's cold up here, but we had cold down there, too, only then we didn't have any *heat, and we'd just die, some of us would, every winter with one of those freezing spells.*

"And I do believe things are changing. On the television they talk to you, the colored man and all the others who aren't doing so good. My boy Peter, he says they're putting you on. That's all he sees, people 'putting on' other people. But I think they all mean it, the white people. I never see them, except on television, when they say the white man wants good for the colored people. I think Peter could go and do better for himself later on, when he gets older, except for the fact that he just doesn't believe. *He don't believe what they say, the teacher, or the man who says it's getting better for us—on television. I guess it's my fault. I never taught my children, any of them, to believe that kind of thing; because I never thought we'd ever have it any different, not in this life. So maybe I've failed Peter. I told him the other day, he should work hard, because of all the 'opportunity' they say is coming for us, and he said I was talking good, but where was my proof. So I went next door with him, to my neighbor's, and we asked her husband, and you know he sided with Peter. He said they were taking in a few here and a few there, and putting them in the front windows of all the big companies, but that all you have to do is look around at our block and you'd see all the young men, and they just haven't got a thing to do. Nothing."*

Her son also looks to the future. Sometimes he talks—in his own words—"big." He'll one day be a bombadier or "*something like that.*" At other times he is less sure of things: "*I don't know what I'll be. Maybe nothing. I see the men sitting around, hiding from the welfare lady. They fool her. Maybe I'll fool her, too. I don't know what you can do. The teacher the other day said that if just one of us turned out o.k. she'd congratulate herself and call herself lucky.*"

A while back a riot excited Peter and his mother, excited them and frightened them. The spectable of the police being fought, of white-owned property being assaulted, stirred the boy a great deal: "*I figured the whole world might get changed around. I figured people would treat us better from now on. Only I don't think they will.*" As for his mother, she was less hopeful, but even more apocalyptic: "*I told Peter we were*

going to pay for this good. I told him they wouldn't let us get away with it, not later on." And in the midst of the trouble she was frightened as she had never before been: *"I saw them running around on the streets, the men and women, and they were talking about burning things down, and how there'd be nothing left when they got through. I sat there with my children and I thought we might die the way things are going, die right here. I didn't know what to do: if I should leave, in case they burn down the building, or if I should stay, so that the police don't arrest us, or we get mixed up with the crowd of people. I've never seen so many people, going in so many different directions. They were running and shouting and they didn't know what to do. They were so excited. My neighbor, she said they'd burn us all up, and then the white man would have himself one less of a headache. The colored man is a worse enemy to himself than the white. I mean, it's hard to know which is the worst."*

I find it as hard as she does to sort things out. When I think of her and the mothers like her I have worked with for years, when I think of Peter and his friends, I find myself caught between the contradictory observations I have made. Peter already seems a grim and unhappy child. He trusts no one white, not his white teacher, not the white police-man he sees, not the white welfare worker, not the white storekeeper, and not, I might add, me. There we are, the five of us from the 180,-000,000 Americans who surround him and of course 20,000,000 others. Yet, Peter doesn't really trust his friends and neighbors, either. At nine he has learned to be careful, wary, guarded, doubtful, and calculating. His teacher may not know it, but Peter is a good sociologist, and a good political scientist, a good student of urban affairs. With devastating accuracy he can reveal how much of the "score" he knows; yes, and how fearful and sad and angry he is: *"This here city isn't for us. It's for the people downtown. We're here because, like my mother said, we had to come. If they could lock us up or sweep us away, they would. That's why I figure the only way you can stay ahead is get some kind of deal for yourself. If I had a choice I'd live someplace else, but I don't know where. It would be a place where they treated you right, and they didn't think you were some nuisance. But the only thing you can do is be care-ful of yourself; if not, you'll get killed somehow, like it happened to my father."*

His father died prematurely, and most probably, unnecessarily. Among the poor of our cities the grim medical statistics we all know about become terrible daily experiences. Among the black and white families I work with — in nearby but separate slums — disease and the pain that goes with it are taken for granted. When my children complain of an earache or demonstrate a skin rash I rush them to the doctor. When I have a headache, I take an aspirin; and if the headache is per-

sistent, I can always get a medical check-up. Not so with Peter's mother and Peter; they have learned to live with sores and infections and poorly mended fractures and bad teeth and eyes that need but don't have the help of glasses. Yes, they can go to a city hospital and get free care; but again and again they don't. They come to the city without any previous experience as patients. They have never had the money to purchase a doctor's time. They have never had free medical care available. (I am speaking now of Appalachian whites as well as southern blacks.) It may comfort me to know that every American city provides some free medical services for its "indigent," but Peter's mother and thousands like her have quite a different view of things: "*I said to you the other time, I've tried there. It's like at City Hall, you wait and wait, and they pushes you and shove you and call your name, only to tell you to wait some more, and if you tell them you can't stay there all day, they'll say 'lady, go home, then.' You get sick just trying to get there. You have to give your children over to people or take them all with you; and the carfare is expensive. Why if we had a doctor around here, I could almost pay him with the carfare it takes to get there and back for all of us. And you know, they keep on having you come back and back, and they don't know what each other says. Each time they starts from scratch.*"

It so happens that recently I took Peter to a children's hospital and arranged for a series of evaluations which led to the following: a pair of glasses; a prolonged bout of dental work; antibiotic treatment for skin lesions; a thorough cardiac work-up, with the subsequent diagnosis of rheumatic heart disease; a conference between Peter's mother and a nutritionist, because the boy has been on a high-starch, low-protein, and low-vitamin diet all his life. He suffers from one attack of sinus trouble after another, from a succession of sore throats and earaches, from cold upon cold, even in the summer. A running nose is unsurprising to him — and so is chest pain and shortness of breath, due to a heart ailment, we now know.

At the same time Peter is tough. I have to emphasize again *how* tough and, yes, how "politic, cautious and meticulous," not in Prufrock's way, but in another way and for other reasons. Peter has learned to be wary as well as angry; tentative as well as extravagant; at times controlled and only under certain circumstances defiant: "*Most of the time, I think you have to watch your step. That's what I think. That's the difference between up here and down in the South. That's what my mother says, and she's right. I don't remember it down there, but I know she must be right. Here, you measure the next guy first and then make your move when you think it's a good time to.*"

He was talking about "*how you get along*" when you leave school and go "*mix with the guys*" and start "*getting your deal.*" He was telling me

what an outrageous and unsafe world he has inherited and how very carefully he has made his appraisal of the future. Were I afflicted with some of his physical complaints, I would be fretful, annoyed, petulant, angry — and moved to do something, see someone, get a remedy, a pill, a promise of help. He has made his "adjustment" to the body's pain, and he has also learned to contend with the alley and the neighborhood and *us*, the world beyond: *"The cops come by here all the time. They drive up and down the street. They want to make sure everything is o.k. to look at. They don't bother you, so long as you don't get in their way."*

So, it is live and let live — except that families like Peter's have a tough time living, and of late have been troubling those cops, among others. Our cities have become not only battlegrounds, but places where all sorts of American problems and historical ironies have converged. Ailing, poorly fed, and proud Appalachian families have reluctantly left the hollows of eastern Kentucky and West Virginia for Chicago and Dayton and Cincinnati and Cleveland and Detroit, and even, I have found, Boston. They stick close together in all-white neighborhoods — or enclaves or sections or slums or ghettos or whatever. They wish to go home but can't, unless they are willing to be idle and hungry all the time. They confuse social workers and public officials of all kinds because they both want and reject the city. Black families also have sought out cities and learned to feel frightened and disappointed.

I am a physician, and over the past ten years I have been asking myself how people like Peter and his mother survive in mind and body and spirit. And I have wanted to know what a twentieth-century American city "means" to them or "does" to them. People cannot be handed questionnaires and asked to answer such questions. They cannot be "interviewed" a few times and told to come across with a statement, a reply. But inside Peter and his brother and his sisters and his mother, and inside a number of Appalachian mothers and fathers and children I know, are feelings and thoughts and ideas — which, in my experience, come out casually or suddenly, by accident almost. After a year or two of talking, after experiences such as I have briefly described in a city hall, in a children's hospital, a lifetime of pent-up tensions and observation comes to blunt expression: *"Down in Alabama we had to be careful about ourselves with the white man, but we had plenty of things we could do by ourselves. There was our side of town, and you could walk and run all over, and we had a garden you know. Up here they have you in a cage. There's no place to go, and all I do is stay in the building all day long and the night, too. I don't use my legs no more, hardly at all. I never see those trees, and my oldest girl, she misses planting time. It was bad down there. We had to leave. But it's no good here, too, I'll tell you. Once I woke up and I thought all the buildings on the block were falling*

down on me. And I was trying to climb out, but I couldn't. And then the next thing I knew, we were all back South, and I was standing near some sunflowers — you know, the tall ones that can shade you if you sit down.

"No, I don't dream much. I fall into a heavy sleep as soon as I touch the bed. The next thing I know I'm stirring myself to start in all over in the morning. It used to be the sun would wake me up, but now it's up in my head, I guess. I know I've got to get the house going and off to school."

Her wistful, conscientious, law-abiding, devoutly Christian spirit hasn't completely escaped the notice of Peter, for all his hard-headed, cynical protestations: *"If I had a chance, I'd like to get enough money to bring us all back to Alabama for a visit. Then I could prove it that it may be good down there, a little bit, even if it's not good, either. Like she says, we had to get out of there or we'd be dead by now. I hear say we all may get killed soon, it's so bad here; but I think we did right to get up here, and if we make them listen to us, the white man, maybe he will."*

To which Peter's mother adds: *"We've carried a lot of trouble in us, from way back in the beginning. I have these pains, and so does everyone around here. But you can't just die until you're ready to. And I do believe something is happening. I do believe I see that."*

To which Peter adds: *"Maybe it won't be that we'll win, but if we get killed, everyone will hear about it. Like the minister said, before we used to die real quiet, and no one stopped to pay notice."*

Two years before Peter spoke those words he drew a picture for me, one of many he has done. When he was younger, and when I didn't know him so well as I think I do now, it was easier for us to have something tangible to do and then talk about. I used to visit the alley with him, as I still do, and one day I asked him to draw the alley. That was a good idea, he thought. (Not all of my suggestions were, however.) He started in, then stopped, and finally worked rather longer and harder than usual at the job. I busied myself with my own sketches, which from the start he insisted I do. Suddenly from across the table I heard him say he was through. Ordinarily he would slowly turn the drawing around for me to see; and I would get up and walk over to his side of the table, to see even better. But he didn't move his paper, and I didn't move myself. I saw what he had drawn, and he saw me looking. I was surprised and a bit stunned and more than a bit upset, and surely he saw my face and heard my utter silence. Often I would break the awkward moments when neither of us seemed to have anything to say, but this time it was his turn to do so: *"You know what it is?"* He knew that I liked us to talk about our work. I said no, I didn't — though in fact the vivid power of his

black crayon had come right across to me. *"It's that hole we dug in the alley. I made it bigger here. If you fall into it, you can't get out. You die."*
He had drawn circles within circles, all of them black, and then a center, also black. He had imposed an X on the center. Nearby, strewn across the circles, were fragments of the human body — two faces, an arm, five legs. And after I had taken the scene in, I could only think to myself that I had been shown *"like it is in the alley"* — by an intelligent boy who knew what he saw around him, could give it expression, and, I am convinced, would respond to a different city, a city that is alive and breathing, one that is not for many of its citizens a virtual morgue.

Part Five
Middle Childhood and Adolescence

As the child approaches adolescence, social roles and social systems outside the family play an increasing part in shaping his abilities, motives, and behavior. Thus Bronfenbrenner's research illustrates how social class and family structure interact to produce differing patterns of sex-role differentiation among parents and children within the family. The impact of these same kinds of social factors on the child's motivation and perceived capacity to cope with his environment is documented in the studies by Battle and Rotter, and Rosen and D'Andrade.

Next, Shapira and Madsen's cross-cultural research shows how a new and deliberately contrived life setting, the Israeli kibbutz, creates a distinctive pattern of social interaction among the children who are its products. The power of deliberately constructed social settings to shape behavior is then even more dramatically illustrated in Sherif's "Robber's Cave Experiment," in which the same groups of middle class White Anglo-Saxon boys were transformed in the space of a few weeks first into a gang of unscrupulous and heartless competitors, and then into a group of cooperative and compassionate citizens of the children's community.

The next group of studies records continuities in the impact of the already familiar social contexts of ordinal position, television, and social class. Altus documents the "academic primogeniture" of first-borns who excel, all out of proportion to their numbers, in intellectual

531

motivation and performance. But, as the ingenious experiment by Becker, Lerner, and Carroll demonstrates, this academic achievement is not acquired without some social cost, specifically in the area of social conformity. For their part, Walters and Thomas demonstrate the power of graphic displays to activate aggressive and even sadistic behavior among adolescents and young adults. Nichols' review of the famous Coleman Report then shows how schools, at least as presently constituted, seem unable to alter the developmental trajectories established by class and race in contemporary American society. And the contrast between our own nation and others is illuminated by Kandel and Lesser's comparative study of adolescence in the United States and Denmark.

The section and the book close on a concern for the developing phenomenon of alienation among children and youth in American society. Block, Haan, and Smith focus specifically on student activism, its varying forms, and its origins in patterns of socialization. Looking at the phenomenon even more broadly, Bronfenbrenner probes the "roots of alienation" as revealed in research studies, and offers a series of recommendations for modification of basic social institutions, such as business, industry, transportation, and urban planning, in order to provide "support systems" to the family and other socializing agencies bearing responsibility for children and youth.

5.1 The Changing American Child—A Speculative Analysis

Urie Bronfenbrenner
Cornell University

It is now a matter of scientific record that patterns of child rearing in the United States have changed appreciably over the past twenty-five years (5). At the same time, the gap between social classes in their goals and methods of child rearing appears to be narrowing, with working-class parents beginning to adopt both the values and techniques of the middle class. Finally, there is dramatic correspondence between these observed shifts in parental values and behavior and the changing character of attitudes and practices advocated in successive editions of such widely read manuals as the Children's Bureau bulletin on *Infant Care* and Dr. Spock's *Baby and Child Care*. Such correspondence should not be taken to mean that the expert has now become the principal instigator and instrument of social change, since the ideas of scientists and professional workers themselves reflect in part the operation of deep-rooted cultural processes. Nevertheless, the fact remains that changes in values and practices advocated by prestigeful professional figures can be substantially accelerated by rapid and widespread dissemination through mass media of communication and public discussion.

Given these facts, it becomes especially important to gauge the effect of the changes that are advocated and adopted. We must ask whether the changes that have occurred in the attitudes and actions of parents over the past twenty-five years have been such as to affect the personality development of their children, so that the boys and girls of today are somewhat different in character structure from those of a decade or more ago. Or, to put the question more succinctly: Has the changing American parent produced a changing American child?

A Strategy of Inference

Do we have any basis for answering this intriguing question? Do we have any evidence of changes in the behavior of children in successive decades analogous to the evidence we have already been able to find for parents(5)?

Unfortunately, the present writer has, to date, been unable to locate enough instances in which comparable methods of behavioral assessment have been employed over an extended period of time with different

Reprinted from the *Merrill-Palmer Quarterly*, 1961, **7**, No. 2, 73–84, by permission of the Merrill-Palmer Institute.

groups of children of similar ages. Although the absence of such material precludes any direct and unequivocal approach to the question at hand, it is nevertheless possible, through a series of inferences from facts already known, to arrive at some estimate of the effects on children of changing parental attitudes and actions.

Specifically, although as yet we have no comparable data on the relation between parental and child behavior for different families at successive points in time, we do have facts on the influence of parental treatment on child behavior at a given point in time; that is, we know that certain variations in parental behavior tend to be accompanied by systematic differences in the personality characteristics of children. If we are willing to assume that these same relationships obtain not only at a given moment but across different points in time, we are in a position to infer the possible effects on children of changing patterns of child rearing over the years. It is this strategy that we propose to follow.

The Changing American Parent

In a recent analysis of data reported over a twenty-five-year period(5), we have already noted the major changes in parental behavior. These secular trends may be summarized as follows: (a) greater permissiveness toward the child's spontaneous desires; (b) freer expression of affection; (c) increased reliance on indirect "psychological" techniques of discipline (such as reasoning or appeals to guilt) vs. direct methods (such as physical punishment, scolding, or threats); (d) in consequence of the above shifts in the direction of what are predominantly middle-class values and techniques, a narrowing of the gap between social classes in their patterns of child rearing

Since the above analysis was published, a new study has documented an additional trend. Bronson, Katten, and Livson(7) have compared patterns of paternal and maternal authority and affection in two generations of families from the California Guidance Study. Unfortunately, the time span surveyed in their study overlaps only partially with the twenty-five-year period covered in our own analysis, the first California generation having been raised in the early 1900's and the second in the late 1920's and early 1930's. Accordingly, if we are to consider the California results along with the others cited above, we must make the somewhat risky assumption that a trend discerned in the first three decades of the century has continued in the same direction through the early 1950's.

With this important qualification, an examination of the data cited by Bronson et al. points to a shift over the years in the pattern of parental role differentiation within the family. Specifically, in succeeding generations the relative position of the father vis-a-vis the mother is shifting

with the former becoming increasingly more affectionate and less authoritarian and the latter becoming relatively more important as the agent of
discipline, especially for boys.

"Psychological" Techniques of Discipline and their Effects

In pursuing our analytic strategy, we seek next for evidence of the
effects on the behavior of children of the changes in parental treatment
noted in our inventory. We may begin by noting that the variables involved in the first three secular trends listed above constitute a complex
that has received considerable attention in recent research on parent-
child relations.

Within the last three years, two sets of investigators, working independently, have called attention to the greater efficacy of "love-oriented" or
"psychological" techniques in bringing about desired behavior in the
child(13, 14, 20). The present writer, noting that such methods are especially favored by middle-class parents, has offered the following analysis
of the nature of these techniques and the reasons for their effectiveness.

Such parents are, in the first place, more likely to overlook offenses,
and when they do punish, they are less likely to ridicule or inflict
physical pain. Instead, they reason with the youngster, isolate him,
appeal to guilt, show disappointment — in short, convey in a variety of
ways, on the one hand, the kind of behavior that is expected of the
child; on the other, the realization that transgression means the interruption of a mutually valued relationship. . . .

These findings mean that middle class parents, though in one sense
more lenient in their discipline techniques, are using methods that are
actually more compelling. Moreover, the compelling power of these
practices is probably enhanced by the more permissive treatment accorded to middle class children in the early years of life. The successful use of withdrawal of love as a discipline technique implies the prior
existence of a gratifying relationship; the more love present in the first
instance, the greater the threat implied in its withdrawal (5, p. 419).

It is now a well-established fact that children from middle-class families
tend to excel those from lower-class families in many characteristics
ordinarily regarded as desirable, such as self-control, achievement, responsibility, leadership, popularity, and adjustment in general (15,
pp. 347–352, 429–432). If, as seems plausible, such differences in behavior are attributable at least in part to class-linked variations in parental
treatment, the strategy of inference we have adopted would appear on
first blush to lead to a rather optimistic conclusion.

Since, over the years, increasing numbers of parents have been adopt-

ing the more effective socialization techniques typically employed by the middle class, does it not follow that successive generations of children should show gains in the development of effective behavior and desirable personality characteristics?

Unfortunately, this welcome conclusion, however logical, is premature, for it fails to take into account all of the available facts.

Sex, Socialization, and Social Class

To begin with, the parental behaviors we have been discussing are differentially distributed not only by socioeconomic status but also by sex. As we point out elsewhere(6), girls are exposed to more affection and less punishment than boys but at the same time are more likely to be subjected to love-oriented discipline of the type which encourages the development of internalized controls. And, consistent with our line of reasoning, girls are found repeatedly to be "more obedient, cooperative, and in general better socialized than boys at comparable age levels"(6). But this is not the whole story.

. . . At the same time, the research results indicate the girls tend to be more anxious, timid, dependent, and sensitive to rejection. If these differences are a function of differential treatment by parents, then it would seem that the more "efficient" methods of child rearing employed with girls involve some risk of what might be called "oversocialization" (6, p. 260).

One could argue, of course, that the contrasting behaviors of boys and girls have less to do with differential parental treatment than with genetically based maturational influences. Nevertheless, two independent lines of evidence suggest that socialization techniques do contribute to individual differences, *within the same sex*, precisely in the types of personality characteristics noted above.

In the first place, variations in child behavior and parental treatment strikingly similar to those we have cited for the two sexes are reported in a recent comprehensive study of differences between first- and later-born children(19). Like girls, first children receive more attention, are more likely to be exposed to psychological discipline, and end up more anxious and dependent, whereas later children, like boys, are more aggressive and self-confident.

A second line of evidence comes from our own current research. We have been concerned with the role of parents in the development of such constructive personality characteristics as responsibility and leadership among adolescent boys and girls. Our findings reveal not only the usual differences in adolescents' and parents' behaviors associated with the

sex of the child but also a striking contrast in the relationship between parental and child behaviors for the two sexes.

As we expected, girls were rated by their teachers as more responsible than boys, whereas the latter obtained higher scores on leadership. Expected differences similarly appeared in the realm of parental behavior: Girls received more affection, praise, and companionship; boys were subjected to more physical punishment and achievement demands.

Quite unanticipated, however, at least by us, was the finding that both parental affection and discipline appeared to facilitate effective psychological functioning in boys but to impede the development of such constructive behavior in girls. Closer examination of our data indicated that both extremes of either affection or discipline were deleterious for all children, but that the process of socialization entailed somewhat different risks for the two sexes. Girls were especially susceptible to the detrimental influence of overprotection; boys, to the ill effects of insufficient parental discipline and support. Or, to put it in more colloquial terms: Boys suffered more often from too little taming; girls, from too much.

In an attempt to account for this contrasting pattern of relationships, we proposed the notion of differential optimal levels of affection and authority for the two sexes.

> The qualities of independence, initiative, and self-sufficiency, which are especially valued for boys in our culture, apparently require for their development a somewhat different balance of authority and affection than is found in the "love-oriented" strategy characteristically applied with girls. While an affectional context is important for the socialization of boys, it must evidently be accompanied by and be compatible with a strong component of parental discipline. Otherwise, the boy finds himself in the same situation as the girl, who, having received greater affection, is more sensitive to its withdrawal, with the result that a little discipline goes a long way and strong authority is constricting rather than constructive (6, p. 260).

Class Differences

Available data suggest that this process may already be operating for boys from upper middle-class homes. To begin with, differential treatment of the sexes is at a minimum for these families. Contrasting parental attitudes and behaviors toward boys and girls are pronounced only at lower-class levels and decrease as one moves up the socioeconomic scale (6,10). Our own results show that it is primarily at lower middle-class levels that boys get more punishment than girls, and the latter receive greater warmth and attention. With an increase in the family's social position, direct discipline drops off, especially for boys, and indul-

gence and protectiveness decrease for girls. As a result, patterns of parental treatment for the two sexes begin to converge. In like manner, we find that the differential effects of parental behavior on the two sexes are marked only in the lower middle class. It is here that girls are at special risk of being overprotected and boys of not receiving sufficient discipline and support. In the upper middle class the picture changes. Girls are not as readily debilitated by parental affection and power, nor is parental discipline as effective in fostering the development of responsibility and leadership in boys.

All these trends point to the conclusion that the risks experienced by each sex during the process of socialization tend to be somewhat different at different social class levels. Thus the danger of overprotection for girls is especially great in lower-class families, but less in the upper middle class. Analogously, boys are in greater danger of suffering from inadequate discipline and support in the lower middle than in the upper middle class. But the upper middle-class boy, unlike the girl, exchanges one hazard for another. Since at this upper level the more potent psychological techniques of discipline are likely to be employed with both sexes, the boy presumably now too runs the risk of being oversocialized, of losing some of his capacity for independent aggressive accomplishment.

Accordingly, if our line of reasoning is correct, we should expect a changing pattern of sex differences at successive socioeconomic levels. Specifically, aspects of effective psychological functioning favoring girls should be most pronounced in the upper middle class; those favoring boys, in the lower middle class. A recent analysis of some of our data bears out this expectation. Girls excel boys on such variables as responsibility and social acceptance primarily at the higher socioeconomic levels. In contrast, boys surpass girls on such traits as leadership, level of aspiration, and competitiveness almost exclusively in the lower middle class. Indeed, with a rise in family social position, the differences tend to reverse themselves with girls now excelling boys.

Trends in Personality Development: A First Approximation

The implications for our original line of inquiry are clear. We are suggesting that the love-oriented socialization techniques, which over the past twenty-five years have been employed in increasing degree by American middle-class families, may have negative as well as constructive aspects. While fostering the internalization of adult standards and the development of socialized behavior, they may also have the effect of undermining capacities for initiative and independence, particularly in boys. Males exposed to this "modern" pattern of child rearing might be expected to differ from their counterparts of a quarter century ago in

being somewhat more conforming and anxious, less enterprising and self-sufficient, and, in general, possessing more of the virtues and liabilities commonly associated with feminine character structure.

At long last, then, our strategy of inference has led us to a first major conclusion. The term "major" is appropriate since the conclusion takes as its points of departure and return four of the secular trends which served as the impetus for our inquiry. Specifically, through a series of empirical links and theoretical extrapolations, we have arrived at an estimate of the effects on children of the tendency of successive generations of parents to become progressively more permissive, to express affection more freely, to utilize psychological techniques of discipline, and, by moving in these directions, to narrow the gap between the social classes in their patterns of child rearing.

Family Structure and Personality Development

But one other secular trend remains to be considered: What of the changing pattern of parental role differentiation during the first three decades of the century? If our extrapolation is correct, the balance of power within the family has continued to shift, with fathers yielding parental authority to mothers and taking on some of the nurturant and affectional functions traditionally associated with the maternal role. Again we have no direct evidence of the effects of this change on successive generations of children and must look to analogous data on contemporary relationships.

We may begin by considering the contribution of each parent to the socialization processes we have examined thus far. Our data indicate that it is primarily mothers who tend to employ love-oriented techniques of discipline and fathers who rely on more direct methods like physical punishment. The above statement must be qualified, however, by reference to the sex of the child, for it is only in relation to boys that fathers use direct punishment more than mothers. More generally:

> . . . the results reveal a tendency for each parent to be somewhat more active, firm, and demanding with a child of the same sex, more lenient and indulgent with a child of the opposite sex. The reversal is most complete with respect to discipline, with fathers being stricter with boys, mothers with girls. In the spheres of affection and overprotectiveness, there is no actual shift in preference, but the tendency to be especially warm and solicitous with girls is much more pronounced among fathers than among mothers. in fact, generally speaking, it is the father who is especially likely to treat children of the two sexes differently (6, p. 249).

Consistent with this pattern of results, it is primarily the behavior of fathers that accounts for the differential effects of parental behavior on the two sexes and for the individual differences within each sex. In other words, it is paternal authority and affection that tend especially to be salutary for sons but detrimental for daughters.

But as might be anticipated from what we already know, these trends are pronounced only in the lower middle class; with a rise in the family's social status, both parents tend to have similar effects on their children, both within and across sexes. Such a trend is entirely to be expected since parental role differentiation tends to decrease markedly as one ascends the socio-economic ladder. It is almost exclusively in lower middle-class homes that fathers are stricter with boys, and mothers with girls. To the extent that direct discipline is employed in upper middle-class families, it tends to be exercised by both parents equally. Here again we see a parallelism between shifts in parental behavior across time and social class in the direction of forms (in this instance of family structure) favored by the upper middle-class group.

What kinds of children, then, can we expect to develop in families in which the father plays a predominantly affectionate role, and a relatively low level of discipline is exercised equally by both parents? A tentative answer to this question is supplied by a preliminary analysis of our data in which the relation between parental role structure and adolescent behavior was examined with controls for the family's social position. The results of this analysis are summarized as follows:

> . . . Both responsibility and leadership are fostered by the relatively greater salience of the parent of the same sex. . . . Boys tend to be more responsible when the father rather than the mother is the principal disciplinarian; girls are more dependable when the mother is the major authority figure. . . . In short, boys thrive in a patriarchal context, girls in a matriarchal. . . . The most dependent and least dependable adolescents describe family arrangements that are neither patriarchal nor matriarchal, but equalitarian. To state the issue in more provocative form, our data suggest that the democratic family, which for so many years has been held up and aspired to as a model by professionals and enlightened laymen, tends to produce young people who "do not take initiative," "look to others for direction and decision," and "cannot be counted on to fulfill obligations" (6, p. 267).

In the wake of so sweeping a conclusion, it is important to call attention to the tentative, if not tenuous, character of our findings. The results were based on a single study employing crude questionnaire methods and rating scales. Also, our interpretation is limited by the somewhat attenuated character of most of the families classified as patriarchal or

matriarchal in our sample. Extreme concentrations of power in one or the other parent were comparatively rare. Had they been more frequent, we suspect the data would have shown that such extreme asymmetrical patterns of authority are detrimental rather than salutary for effective psychological development, perhaps even more disorganizing than equalitarian forms.

Nevertheless, our findings do receive some peripheral support in the work of others. A number of investigations, for example, point to the special importance of the father in the socialization of boys(4,16). Further corroborative evidence appears in studies of the effects of paternal absence(1, 12, 21, 23). The absence of the father apparently not only affects the behavior of the child directly but also influences the mother in the direction of greater overprotectiveness. The effect of both these tendencies is especially critical for male children; boys from father-absent homes tend to be markedly more submissive and dependent. Studies dealing explicitly with the influence of parental role structure in intact families are few and far between.

Papanek, in an unpublished doctoral dissertation, reports greater sex role differentiation among children from homes in which the parental roles were differentiated(17). And in a carefully controlled study, Kohn and Clausen find that "schizophrenic patients more frequently than normal persons . . . report that their mothers played a very strong authority role and their fathers a very weak authority role" (11, p. 309).

Finally, what might best be called complementary evidence for our inferences regarding trends in family structure and their effects comes from the work of Miller and Swanson(13) and their associates on the differing patterns of behavior exhibited by families from *bureaucratic* and *entrepreneurial* work settings. These investigators argue that the bureaucratic-entrepreneurial dichotomy represents a new cleavage in American social structure that cuts across and overrides social class influences and carries with it its own characteristic patterns of family structure and socialization. Thus one investigation(8) contrasts the exercise of power in families of husbands employed in two kinds of job situations: (a) those working in large organizations with three or more levels of supervision; and (b) those self-employed or working in small organizations with few levels of supervision. With appropriate controls for social class, equalitarian families were found more frequently in the bureaucratic group; patriarchal and, to a lesser extent, matriarchal, in the entrepreneurial setting.

Miller and Swanson(13) show that parents from these same two groups tend to favor rather different means and ends of socialization, with entrepreneurial families putting considerably more emphasis on the use of psychological techniques of discipline. These differences appear at

both upper and lower middle-class levels but are less pronounced in higher socioeconomic strata. It is Miller and Swanson's belief, however, that the trend is toward the bureaucratic way of life, with its less structured patterns of family organization and child rearing. The evidence we have cited on secular changes in family structure and the inferences we have drawn regarding their possible effects on personality development are on the whole consistent with their views.

Looking Forward

If Miller and Swanson are correct in the prediction that America is moving toward a bureaucratic society that emphasizes, to put it colloquially, "getting along" rather than "getting ahead," then presumably we can look forward to ever increasing numbers of equalitarian families who, in turn, will produce successive generations of ever more adaptable but unaggressive "organization men." But recent signs do not all point in this direction. In our review of secular trends in child-rearing practices(5), we detected in the data from the more recent studies a slowing up in the headlong rush toward greater permissiveness and toward reliance on indirect methods of discipline. We pointed out also that if the most recent editions of well-thumbed guidebooks on child care are as reliable harbingers of the future as they have been in the past, we can anticipate something of a return to the more explicit techniques of an earlier era.

Perhaps the most important forces acting to redirect both the aims and methods of child rearing in America emanate from behind the Iron Curtain. With the firing of the first sputnik, achievement began to replace adjustment as the highest goal of the American way of life. We have become concerned, perhaps even obsessed, with "education for excellence" and the maximal utilization of our intellectual resources. Already, ability grouping and the guidance counselor who is its prophet have moved down from the junior high to the elementary school, and parents can be counted on to do their part in preparing their youngsters for survival in the new competitive world of applications and achievement tests.

But if a new trend in parental behavior is to develop, it must do so in the context of changes already under way. And if the focus of parental authority is shifting from husband to wife, then perhaps we should anticipate that pressures for achievement will be imposed primarily by mothers rather than fathers. Moreover, the mother's continuing strong emotional investment in the child should provide her with a powerful lever for evoking desired performance. It is noteworthy in this connection that recent studies of the familial origins of need-achievement point to the

matriarchy as the optimal context for development of the motive to excel(18, 22).

The prospect of a society in which socialization techniques are directed toward maximizing achievement drive is not altogether a pleasant one. As a number of investigators have shown(2, 3, 9, 18, 24), high achievement motivation appears to flourish in a family atmosphere of "cold democracy" in which initial high levels of maternal involvement are followed by pressures for independence and accomplishment. Nor does the product of this process give ground for reassurance. True, children from achievement-oriented homes excel in planning ability and performance, but they are also more aggressive, tense, domineering, and cruel(2, 3, 9). It would appear that education for excellence, if pursued single-mindedly, may entail some sobering social costs.

But by now we are in danger of having stretched our chain of inference beyond the strength of its weakest link. Our speculative analysis has become far more speculative than analytic and to pursue it further would bring us past the bounds of science into the realms of science fiction. In concluding our discussion, we would re-emphasize that speculations should, by their very nature, be held suspect. It is for good reason that, like "damn Yankees," they too carry their almost inseparable sobriquets: Speculations are either *idle* or *wild*. Given the scientific and social importance of the issues we have raised, we would dismiss the first of these labels out of hand, but the second cannot be disposed of so easily. Like the impetuous child, the wild speculation responds best to the sobering influence of friendly but firm discipline, in this instance from the hand of the behavioral scientist.

As we look ahead to the next twenty-five years of human socialization, let us hope that the optimal levels of involvement and discipline can be achieved not only by the parent who is unavoidably engaged in the process but also by the scientist who attempts to understand its working and who, also unavoidably, contributes to shaping its course.

References

Bach, G. R. Father-fantasies and father-typing in father-separated children. *Child Develpm.*, 1946, **17**, 63–79.

Baldwin, A. L. Socialization and the parent-child relationship. *Child Develpm.*, 1948, **19**, 127–136.

Baldwin, A. L., Kalhorn, J. and Breese, F. H. The appraisal of parent behavior. *Psychol. Monogr.*, 1945, **58**, No. 3 (Whole No. 268).

Bandura, A. and Walters, R. H. *Adolescent aggression.* New York: Ronald Press, 1959.

Bronfenbrenner, U. Socialization and social class through time and

space. In Eleanor E. Maccoby, T. M. Newcomb and E. L. Hartley (Eds.), *Readings in social psychology.* New York: Holt, 1958. Pp. 400–425.

Bronfenbrenner. U. Some familial antecedents of responsibility and leadership in adolescents. In L. Petrullo and B. M. Bass (Eds.), *Leadership and interpersonal behavior.* New York: Holt, Rinehart, and Winston, 1961. Pp. 239–271.

Bronson, W. C., Katten, E. S. and Livson, N. Patterns of authority and affection in two generations. *J. abnorm. soc. Psychol.*, 1959, **58,** 143–152.

Gold, M. and Slater, C. Office, factory, store—and family: a study of integration setting. *Amer. sociol. Rev.*, 1958, **23,** 64–74.

Haggard, E. A. Socialization, personality, and academic achievement in gifted children. *Sch. Rev.*, 1957, **65,** 388–414.

Kohn, M. L. Social class and parental values. *Amer. J. Sociol.*, 1959, **44,** 337–351.

Kohn, M. L. and Clausen, J. A. Parental authority behavior and schizophrenia. *Amer. J. Orthopsychiat.*, 1956, **26,** 297–313.

Lynn, D. B. and Sawrey, W. L. The effects of father-absence on Norwegian boys and girls. *J. abnorm. soc. Psychol.*, 1959, **59,** 258–262.

Miller, D. R. and Swanson, G. E. *The changing American parent.* New York: John Wiley, 1958.

Miller, D. R. and Swanson, G. E. *Inner conflict and defense.* New York: Holt, 1960.

Mussen, P. H. and Conger, J. J. *Child development and personality.* New York: Harper, 1956.

Mussen, P. H. and Distler, L. Masculinity, identification, and father-son relationships. *J. abnorm. soc. Psychol.*, 1959, **59,** 350–356.

Papanek, M. Authority and interpersonal relations in the family. Unpublished doctoral dissertation, Radcliffe College, 1957.

Rosen, B. L. and D'Andrade, R. The psychosocial origins of achievement motivation. *Sociometry,* 1959, **22,** 185–217.

Schachter, S. *The psychology of affiliation.* Stanford, Calif.: Stanford Univ. Press, 1959.

Sears, R. R., Maccoby, Eleanor E. and Levin, H. *Patterns of child rearing.* Evanston, Ill.: Row, Peterson, 1957.

Sears, R. R., Pintler, M. H. and Sears, P. S. Effects of father-separation on preschool children's doll play aggression. *Child Develpm.*, 1946, **17,** 219–243.

Strodtbeck, F. L. Family interaction, values, and achievement. In D. C. McClelland, A. L. Baldwin, U. Bronfenbrenner and F. L. Strodtbeck (Eds.), *Talent and society.* Princeton, N. J.: Van Nostrand, 1958. Pp. 135–194.

Tiller, P.O. Father-absence and personality development of children in
sailor families. *Nordisk Psykologi's Monograph Series* 1958, **9,** 1–48.
Winterbottom, M. R. The relation of need achievement to learning experiences in independence and mastery. In J. W. Atkinson (Ed.), *Motives in fantasy, action, and society.* Princeton, N. J.: Van Nostrand,
1958. Pp. 453-494.

5.2   Social Class and Parent-Child Relationships: an Interpretation

Melvin L. Kohn

This essay is an attempt to interpret, from a sociological perspective.
the effects of social class upon parent-child relationships. Many past discussions of the problem seem somehow to lack this perspective, even though
the problem is one of profound importance for sociology. Because most
investigators have approached the problem from an interest in psychody-
namics, rather than social structure, they have largely limited their attention
to a few specific techniques used by mothers in the rearing of infants and
very young children. They have discovered, *inter alia,* that social class has a
decided bearing on which techniques parents use. But, since they have come
at the problem from this perspective, their interest in social class has not
gone beyond its effects for this very limited aspect of parent-child relationships.

The present analysis conceives the problem of social class and parent-
child relationships as an instance of the more general problem of the effects
of social structure upon behavior. It starts with the assumption that social
class has proved to be so useful a concept because it refers to more than
simply educational level, or occupation, or any of the large number of
correlated variables. It is so useful because it captures the reality that the
intricate interplay of all these variables creates different basic conditions of
life at different levels of the social order. Members of different social classes,
by virtue of enjoying (or suffering) different conditions of life, come to see
the world differently—to develop different conceptions of social reality,
different aspirations and hopes and fears, different conceptions of the
desirable.

Reprinted from the *American Journal of Sociology*, 1963, Vol. LXVIII, No. 4,
471-480, by permission of the author and the University of Chicago Press. Copyright
1963 by the University of Chicago.

The last is particularly important for present purposes, for from people's conceptions of the desirable—and particularly from their conceptions of what characterics are desirable in children—one can discern their objectives in child-rearing. Thus, conceptions of the desirable—that is, values[1]—become the key concept for this analysis, the bridge between position in the larger social structure and the behavior of the individual. The intent of the analysis is to trace the effects of social class position on parental values and the effects of values on behavior.

Since this approach differs from analyses focused on social class differences in the use of particular child-rearing techniques, it will be necessary to re-examine earlier formulations from the present perspective. Then three questions will be discussed, bringing into consideration the limited available data that are relevant: What differences are there in the values held by parents of different social classes? What is there about the conditions of life distinctive of these classes that might explain the differences in their values? What consequences do these differences in values have for parents' relationships with their children?

Social Class

Social classes will be defined as aggregates of individuals who occupy broadly similar positions in the scale of prestige.[2] In dealing with the research literature, we shall treat occupational position (or occupational position as weighted somewhat by education) as a serviceable index of social class for urban American society. And we shall adopt the model of social stratification implicit in most research, that of four relatively discrete classes: a "lower class" of unskilled manual workers, a "working class" of manual workers in semiskilled and skilled occupations, a "middle class" of white-collar workers and professionals, and an "elite," differentiated from the middle class not so much in terms of occupation as of wealth and lineage.

Almost all the empirical evidence, including that from our own research, stems from broad comparisons of the middle and working class. Thus we shall have little to say about the extremes of the class distribution. Furthermore, we shall have to act as if the middle and working classes were each homogeneous. They are not, even in terms of status considerations alone. There is evidence, for example, that within each broad social class, variations in parents' values quite regularly parallel gradations of social status. Moreover, the classes are heterogeneous with respect to other factors that affect parents' values, such as religion and ethnicity. But even when all such considerations are taken into account, the empirical evidence clearly shows that being on one side or the other of the line that divides manual from non-manual workers has profound consequences for how one rears one's children.[3]

Stability and Change

Any analysis of the effects of social class upon parent-child relationships should start with Urie Bronfenbrenner's analytic review of the studies that had been conducted in this country during the twenty-five years up to 1958.[4] From the seemingly contradictory findings of a number of studies, Bronfenbrenner discerned not chaos but orderly change: there have been changes in the child-training techniques employed by middle-class parents in the past quarter-century; similar changes have been taking place in the working class, but working-class parents have consistently lagged behind a few years; thus, while middle-class parents of twenty-five years ago were more "restrictive" than were working-class parents, today the middle-class parents are more "permissive"; and the gap between the classes seems to be narrowing.

It must be noted that these conclusions are limited by the questions Bronfenbrenner's predecessors asked in their research. The studies deal largely with a few particular techniques of child-rearing, especially those involved in caring for infants and very young children, and say very little about parents' over-all relationships with their children, particularly as the children grow older. There is clear evidence that the past quarter-century has seen change, even faddism, with respect to the use of breast-feeding, or bottle-feeding, scheduling or not scheduling, spanking or isolating. But when we generalize from these specifics to talk of a change from "restrictive" to "permissive" practices—or, worse yet, of a change from "restrictive" to "permissive" parent-child relationships—we impute to them a far greater importance than they probably have, either to parents or to children.[5]

There is no evidence that recent faddism in child-training techniques is symptomatic of profound changes in the relations of parents to children in either social class. In fact, as Bronfenbrenner notes, what little evidence we do have points in the opposite direction: the over-all quality of parent-child relationships does not seem to have changed substantially in either class.[6] In all probability, parents have changed techniques in service of much the same values, and the changes have been quite specific. These changes must be explained, but the enduring characteristics are probably even more important.

Why the changes? Bronfenbrenner's interpretation is ingenuously simple. He notes that the changes in techniques employed by middle-class parents have closely paralleled those advocated by presumed experts, and he concludes that middle-class parents have changed their practices *because* they are responsive to changes in what the experts tell them is right and proper. Working-class parents, being less educated and thus less directly responsive to the media of communication, followed behind only later.[7]

Bronfenbrenner is almost undoubtedly right in asserting that middle-class parents have followed the drift of presumably expert opinion. But why have they done so? It is not sufficient to assume that the explanation lies in their

greater degree of education. This might explain why middle-class parents are substantially more likely than are working-class parents to *read* books and articles on child-rearing, as we know they do.[8] But they need not *follow* the experts' advice. We know from various studies of the mass media that people generally search for confirmation of their existing beliefs and practices and tend to ignore what contradicts them.

From all the evidence at our disposal, it looks as if middle-class parents not only read what the experts have to say but also search out a wide variety of other sources of information and advice: they are far more likely than are working-class parents to discuss child-rearing with friends and neighbors, to consult physicians on these matters, to attend Parent-Teacher Association meetings, to discuss the child's behavior with his teacher. Middle-class parents seem to regard child-rearing as more problematic than do working-class parents. This can hardly be a matter of education alone. It must be rooted more deeply in the conditions of life of the two social classes.

Everything about working-class parents' lives—their comparative lack of education, the nature of their jobs, their greater attachment to the extended family—conduces to their retaining familiar methods.[9] Furthermore, even should they be receptive to change, they are less likely than are middle-class parents to find the experts' writings appropriate to their wants, for the experts predicate their advice on middle-class values. Everything about middle-class parents' lives, on the other hand, conduces to their looking for new methods to achieve their goals. They look to the experts, to other sources of relevant information, and to each other not for new values but for more serviceable techniques.[10] And within the limits of our present scanty knowledge about means-ends relationships in child-rearing, the experts have provided practical and useful advice. It is not that educated parents slavishly follow the experts but that the experts have provided what the parents have sought.

To look at the question this way is to put it in a quite different perspective: the focus becomes not specific techniques nor changes in the use of specific techniques but parental values.

Values of Middle- and Working-Class Parents

Of the entire range of values one might examine, it seems particularly strategic to focus on parents' conceptions of what characteristics would be most desirable for boys or girls the age of their own children. From this one can hope to discern the parents' goals in rearing their children. It must be assumed, however, that a parent will choose one characteristic as more desirable than another only if he considers it to be both important, in the sense that failure to develop this characteristic would affect the child adversely, and problematic, in the sense that it is neither to be taken for granted that the child will develop that characteristic nor impossible for him

to do so. In interpreting parents' value choices, we must keep in mind that their choices reflect not simply their goals but the goals whose achievement they regard as problematic.

Few studies, even in recent years, have directly investigated the relationship of social class to parental values. Fortunately, however, the results of these few are in essential agreement. The earliest study was Evelyn Millis Duvall's pioneering inquiry of 1946.[11] Duvall characterized working-class (and lower middle-class) parental values as "traditional"—they want their children to be neat and clean, to obey and respect adults, to please adults. In contrast to this emphasis on how the child comports himself, middle-class parental values are more "developmental"—they want their children to be eager to learn, to love and confide in the parents, to be happy, to share and co-operate, to be healthy and well.

Duvall's traditional-developmental dichotomy does not describe the difference between middle- and working-class parental values quite exactly, but it does point to the essence of the difference: working-class parents want the child to conform to externally imposed standards, while middle-class parents are far more attentive to his internal dynamics.

The few relevant findings of subsequent studies are entirely consistent with this basic point, especially in the repeated indications that working-class parents put far greater stress on obedience to parental commands than do middle-class parents.[12] Our own research, conducted in 1956-57, provides the evidence most directly comparable to Duvall's.[13] We, too, found that working-class parents value obedience, neatness, and cleanliness more highly than do middle-class parents, and that middle-class parents in turn value curiosity, happiness, consideration, and—most importantly—self-control more highly than do working-class parents. We further found that there are characteristic clusters of value choice in the two social classes: working class parental values center on conformity to external proscriptions, middle-class parental values on *self*-direction. To working-class parents, it is the overt act that matters: the child should not transgress externally imposed rules; to middle-class parents, it is the child's motives and feelings that matter: the child should govern himself.

In fairness, it should be noted that middle- and working-class parents share many core values. Both, for example, value honesty very highly—although, characteristically, "honesty" has rather different connotations in the two social classes, implying "trustworthiness" for the working-class and "truthfulness" for the middle-class. The common theme, of course, is that parents of both social classes value a decent respect for the rights of others; middle- and working-class values are but variations on this common theme. The reason for emphasizing the variations rather than the common theme is that they seem to have far-ranging consequences for parents' relationships with their children and thus ought to be taken seriously.

It would be good if there were more evidence about parental values—

data from other studies, in other locales, and especially, data derived from more than one mode of inquiry. But, what evidence we do have is consistent, so that there is at least some basis for believing it is reliable. Furthermore, there is evidence that the value choices made by parents in these inquiries are not simply a reflection of their assessments of their own children's deficiencies or excellences. Thus, we may take the findings of these studies as providing a limited, but probably valid, picture of the parents' generalized conceptions of what behavior would be desirable in their preadolescent children.

Explaining Class Differences in Parental Values

That middle-class parents are more likely to espouse some values, and working-class parents other values, must be a function of differences in their conditions of life. In the present state of our knowledge, it is difficult to disentangle the interacting variables with a sufficient degree of exactness to ascertain which conditions of life are crucial to the differences in values. Nevertheless, it is necessary to examine the principal components of class differences in life conditions to see what each may contribute.

The logical place to begin is with occupational differences, for these are certainly pre-eminently important, not only in defining social classes in urban, industrialized society, but also in determining much else about people's life conditions.[14] There are at least three respects in which middle-class occupations typically differ from working-class occupations, above and beyond their obvious status-linked differences in security, stability of income, and general social prestige. One is that middle-class occupations deal more with the manipulation of interpersonal relations, ideas, and symbols, while working-class occupations deal more with the manipulation of things. The second is that middle-class occupations are more subject to self-direction, while working-class occupations are more subject to standardization and direct supervision. The third is that getting ahead in middle-class occupations is more dependent upon one's own actions, while in working-class occupations it is more dependent upon collective action, particularly in unionized industries. From these differences, one can sketch differences in the characteristics that make for getting along, and getting ahead, in middle- and working-class occupations. Middle-class occupations require a greater degree of self-direction; working-class occupations, in larger measure, require that one follow explicit rules set down by someone in authority.

Obviously, these differences parallel the differences we have found between the two social classes in the characteristics valued by parents for children. At minimum, one can conclude that there is a congruence between occupational requirements and parental values. It is, moreover, a reasonable supposition, although not a necessary conclusion, that middle- and working-class parents value different characteristics in children *because* of these

differences in their occupational circumstances. This supposition does not necessarily assume that parents consciously train their children to meet future occupational requirements; it may simply be that their own occupational experiences have significantly affected parents' conceptions of what is desirable behavior, on or off the job, for adults or for children.[15]

These differences in occupational circumstances are probably basic to the differences we have found between middle- and working-class parental values, but taken alone they do not sufficiently explain them. Parents need not accord pre-eminent importance to occupational requirements in their judgments of what is most desirable. For a sufficient explanation of class differences in values, it is necessary to recognize that other differences in middle- and working-class conditions of life reinforce the differences in occupational circumstances at every turn.

Educational differences, for example, above and beyond their importance as determinants of occupation, probably contribute independently to the differences in middle- and working-class parental values. At minimum, middle-class parents' greater attention to the child's internal dynamics is facilitated by their learned ability to deal with the subjective and the ideational. Furthermore, differences in levels and stability of income undoubtedly contribute to class differences in parental values. That middle-class parents still have somewhat higher levels of income, and much greater stability of income, makes them able to take for granted the respectability that is still problematic for working-class parents. They can afford to concentrate, instead, on motives and feelings—which, in the circumstances of their lives, are more important.

These considerations suggest that the differences between middle- and working-class parental values are probably a function of the entire complex of differences in life conditions characteristic of the two social classes. Consider, for example, the working-class situation. With the end of mass immigration, there has emerged a stable working class, largely derived from the manpower of rural areas, uninterested in mobility into the middle class, but very much interested in security, respectability, and the enjoyment of a decent standard of living.[16] This working class has come to enjoy a standard of living formerly reserved for the middle class, but has not chosen a middle-class style of life. In effect, the working class has striven for, and partially achieved, an American dream distinctly different from the dream of success and achievement. In an affluent society, it is possible for the worker to be the traditionalist—politically, economically, and, most relevant here, in his values for his children.[17] Working-class parents want their children to conform to external authority because the parents themselves are willing to accord respect to authority, in return for security and respectability. Their conservatism in child-rearing is part of a more general conservatism and traditionalism.

Middle-class parental values are a product of a quite different set of

conditions. Much of what the working class values, they can take for granted. Instead, they can—and must—instil in their children a degree of self-direction that would be less appropriate to the conditions of life of the working class.[18] Certainly, there is substantial truth in the characterization of the middle-class way of life as one of great conformity. What must be noted here, however, is that *relative* to the working class, middle-class conditions of life require a more substantial degree of independence of action. Furthermore, the higher levels of education enjoyed by the middle class make possible a degree of internal scrutiny difficult to achieve without the skills in dealing with the abstract that college training sometimes provides. Finally, the economic security of most middle-class occupations, the level of income they provide, the status they confer, allow one to focus his attention on the subjective and the ideational. Middle-class conditions of life both allow and demand a greater degree of self-direction than do those of the working class.

Consequences of Class Differences in Parents' Values

What consequences do the differences between middle- and working-class parents' values have for the ways they raise their children?

Much of the research on techniques of infant- and child-training is of little relevance here. For example, with regard to parents' preferred techniques for disciplining children, a question of major interest to many investigators, Bronfenbrenner summarizes past studies as follows: "In matters of discipline, working-class parents are consistently more likely to employ physical punishment, while middle-class families rely more on reasoning, isolation, appeals to guilt, and other methods involving the threat of loss of love."[19] This, if still true,[20] is consistent with middle-class parents' greater attentiveness to the child's internal dynamics, working-class parents' greater concern about the overt act. For present purposes, however, the crucial question is not *which* disciplinary method parents prefer, but when and why they use one or another method of discipline.

The most directly relevant available data are on the conditions under which middle- and working-class parents use physical punishment. Working-class parents are apt to resort to physical punishment when the direct and immediate consequences of their children's disobedient acts are most extreme, and to refrain from punishing when this might provoke an even greater disturbance.[21] Thus, they will punish a child for wild play when the furniture is damaged or the noise level becomes intolerable, but ignore the same actions when the direct and immediate consequences are not so extreme. Middle-class parents, on the other hand, seem to punish or refrain from punishing on the basis of their interpretation of the child's intent in acting as he does. Thus, they will punish a furious outburst when the context

is such that they interpret it to be a loss of self-control, but will ignore an equally extreme outburst when the context is such that they interpret it to be merely an emotional release.

It is understandable that working-class parents react to the consequences rather than to the intent of their children's actions: the important thing is that the child not transgress externally imposed rules. Correspondingly, if middle-class parents are instead concerned about the child's motives and feelings, they can and must look beyond the overt act to why the child acts as he does. It would seem that middle- and working-class values direct parents to see their children's misbehavior in quite different ways, so that misbehavior which prompts middle-class parents to action does not seem as important to working-class parents, and vice versa.[22] Obviously, parents' values are not the only things that enter into their use of physical punishment. But unless one assumes a complete lack of goal-directedness in parental behavior, he would have to grant that parents' values direct their attention to some facets of their own and their children's behavior, and divert it from other facets.

The consequences of class differences in parental values extend far beyond differences in disciplinary practices. From a knowledge of their values for their children, one would expect middle-class parents to feel a greater obligation to be *supportive* of the children, if only because of their sensitivity to the children's internal dynamics. Working-class values, with their emphasis upon conformity to external rules, should lead to greater emphasis upon the parents' obligation to impose contraints.[23] And this, according to Bronfenbrenner, is precisely what has been shown in those few studies that have concerned themselves with the over-all relationship of parents to child: "Over the entire twenty-five-year period studied, parent-child relationships in the middle-class are consistently reported as more acceptant and equalitarian, while those in the working-class are oriented toward maintaining order and obedience."[24]

This conclusion is based primarily on studies of *mother*-child relationships in middle- and working-class families. Class differences in parental values have further ramifications for the father's role.[25] Mothers in each class would have their husbands play a role facilitative of the child's development of the characteristics valued in that class: Middle-class mothers want their husbands to be supportive of the children (especially of sons), with their responsibility for imposing constraints being of decidedly secondary importance; working-class mothers look to their husbands to be considerably more directive—support is accorded far less importance and constraint far more. Most middle-class fathers agree with their wives and play a role close to what their wives would have them play. Many working-class fathers, on the other hand, do not. It is not that they see the constraining role as less important than do their wives, but that many of

them see no reason why they should have to shoulder the responsibility. From their point of view, the important thing is that the child be taught what limits he must not transgress. It does not much matter who does the teaching, and since mother has primary responsibility for child care, the job should be hers.

The net consequence is a quite different division of parental responsibilities in the two social classes. In middle-class families, mother's and father's roles usually are not sharply differentiated. What differentiation exists is largely a matter of each parent taking special responsibility for being supportive of children of the parent's own sex. In working-class families, mother's and father's roles are more sharply differentiated, with mother almost always being the more supportive parent. In some working-class families, mother specializes in support, father in constraint; in others, perhaps in most, mother raises the children, father provides the wherewithal.[26]

Thus, the differences in middle- and working-class parents' values have wide ramifications for their relationships with their children and with each other. Of course, many class differences in parent-child relationships are not directly attributable to differences in values; undoubtedly the very differences in their conditions of life that make for differences in parental values reinforce, at every juncture, parents' characteristic ways of relating to their children. But one could not account for these consistent differences in parents' avowed values.

Conclusion

This paper serves to show how complex and demanding are the problems of interpreting the effects of social structure on behavior. Our inquiries habitually stop at the point of demonstrating that social position correlates with something, when we should want to pursue the question, "Why?" What are the processes by which position in social structure molds behavior? The present analysis has dealt with this question in one specific form: Why does social class matter for parents' relationships with their children? There is every reason to believe that the problems encountered in trying to deal with that question would recur in any analysis of the effects of social structure on behavior.

In this analysis, the concept of "values" has been used as the principal bridge from social position to behavior. The analysis has endeavored to show that middle-class parental values differ from those of working-class parents; that these differences are rooted in basic differences between middle- and working-class conditions of life; and that the dfferences between middle- and working-class parental values have important consequences for their relationships with their children. The interpretive model, in essence, is: social class—conditions of life—values—behavior.

The specifics of the present characterization of parental values may prove to be inexact; the discussion of the ways in which social class position affects values is undoubtedly partial; and the tracing of the consequences of differences in values for differences in parent-child relationships is certainly tentative and incomplete. I trust, however, that the perspective will prove to be valid and that this formulation will stimulate other investigators to deal more directly with the processes whereby social structure affects behavior.

Notes

1 "A value is a conception, explicit or implicit, distinctive of an individual or characteristic of a group, of the desirable which influences the selection from available modes, means, and ends of action" (Clyde Kluckhohn, "Values and Value Orientations," in Talcott Parsons and Edward A. Shils (eds.), *Toward A General Theory of Action* [Cambridge, Mass.: Harvard University Press, 1951], p. 395). See also the discussion of values in Robin M. Williams, Jr. *American Society: A Sociological Interpretation* (New York: Alfred A. Knopf, Inc., 1951), chap. xi, and his discussion of social class and culture on p. 101.

2Williams, *op. cit.*, p. 89.

3These, and other assertions of fact not referred to published sources, are based on research my colleagues and I have conducted. For the design of this research and the principal substantive findings see my "Social Class and Parental Values," *American Journal of Sociology*, LXIV (January, 1959), 337-51; my "Social Class and the Exercise of Parental Authority," *American Sociological Review*, XXIV (June, 1959), 352-66; and with Eleanor E. Carroll, "Social Class and the Allocation of Parental Responsibilities," *Sociometry*, XXIII (December, 1960), 372-92. I should like to express my appreciation to my principal collaborators in this research, John A. Clausen and Eleanor E. Carroll.

4Urie Bronfenbrenner, "Socialization and Social Class through Time and Space," in Eleanor E. Maccoby, Theodore M. Newcomb, and Eugene L. Hartley (eds.), *Readings in Social Psychology* (New York: Henry Holt & Co., 1958).

5Furthermore, these concepts employ a priori judgments about which the various investigators have disagreed radically. See, e.g., Robert R. Sears, E. Eleanor Maccoby, and Harry Levin, *Patterns of Child Rearing* (Evanston, Ill.: Row, Peterson & Co., 1957), pp. 444-47, and Richard A. Littman, Robert C. A. Moore, and John Pierce-Jones, "Social Class Differences in Child Rearing: A Third Community for Comparison with Chicago and Newton," *American Sociological Review*, XXII (December, 1957), 694-704, esp. p. 703.

6Bronfenbrenner, *op. cit.*, pp. 420-22 and 425.

7Bronfenbrenner gives clearest expression to this interpretation, but it has been adopted by others, too. See, e.g., Martha Sturm White, "Social Class, Child-Rearing Practices, and Child Behavior," *American Sociological Review*, XXII (December, 1957), 704-12.

8This was noted by John E. Anderson in the first major study of social class and family relationships ever conducted, and has repeatedly been confirmed (*The Young Child in the Home: A Survey of Three Thousand American Families* [New York: Appleton-Century, 1936]).

9The differences between middle- and working-class conditions of life will be discussed more fully later in this paper.

10Certainly middle-class parents do not get their values from the experts. In our

research, we compared the values of parents who say they read Spock, Gesell, or other books on child-rearing, to those who read only magazine and newspaper articles, and those who say they read nothing at all on the subject. In the middle class, these three groups have substantially the same values. In the working class, the story is different. Few working-class parents claim to read books or even articles on child-rearing. Those few who do have values much more akin to those of the middle class. But these are atypical working-class parents who are very anxious to attain middle-class status. One suspects that for them the experts provide a sort of handbook to the middle class; even for them, it is unlikely that the values come out of Spock and Gesell.

[11] "Conceptions of Parenthood," *American Journal of Sociology,* LII (November, 1946), 193-203.

[12]Alex Inkeles has shown that this is true not only for the United States but for a number of other industrialized societies as well ("Industrial Man: The Relation of Status to Experience, Perception, and Value," *American Journal of Sociology,* LXVI (July, 1960), 20-21 and Table 9.)

[13]"Social Class and Parental Values," *op. cit.*

[14]For a thoughtful discussion of the influence of occupational role on parental values see David F. Aberle and Kaspar D. Naegele, "Middle Class Fathers' Occupational Role and Attitudes Toward Children," *American Journal of Orthopsychiatry,* XXII (April, 1952), 366-78.

[15]Two objections might be raised here. (1) Occupational experiences may not be important for a mother's values, however crucial they are for her husband's, if she has had little or no work experience. But even those mothers who have had little or no occupational experience know something of occupational life from their husbands and others, and live in a culture in which occupation and career permeate all of life. (2) Parental values may be built not so much out of their own experiences as out of their expectations of the child's future experiences. This might seem particularly plausible in explaining working-class values, for their high valuation of such stereotypically *middle-class* characteristics as obedience, neatness, and cleanliness might imply that they are training their children for a middle-class life they expect the children to achieve. Few working-class parents, however, do expect (or even want) their children to go on to college and the middle-class jobs for which a college education is required. (This is shown in Herbert H. Hyman, "The Value Systems of Different Classes: A Social Psychological Contribution to the Analysis of Stratification," in Reinhard Bendix and Seymour Martin Lipset [eds.], *Class, Status and Powers: A Reader in Social Stratification* [Glencoe, Ill.: Free Press, 1953], and confirmed in unpublished data from our own research.)

[16]See, e.g., S. M. Miller and Frank Riessman, "The Working Class Subculture: A New View," *Social Problems,* IX (Summer, 1961), 86-97.

[17]Relevant here is Seymour Martin Lipset's somewhat disillusioned "Democracy and Working-Class Authoritarianism," *American Sociological Review,* XXIV (August, 1959), 482-501.

[18]It has been argued that as larger and larger proportions of the middle class have become imbedded in a bureaucratic way of life—in distinction to the entrepreneurial way of life of a bygone day—it has become more appropriate to raise children to be accommodative than to be self-reliant. But this point of view is a misreading of the conditions of life faced by the middle-class inhabitants of the bureaucratic world. Their jobs require at least as great a degree of self-reliance as do entrepreneurial enterprises. We tend to forget, nowadays, just how little the small- or medium-sized entrepreneur controlled the conditions of his own existence and just how much he was

subjected to the petty authority of those on whose pleasure depended the survival of his enterprise. And we fail to recognize the degree to which monolithic-seeming bureaucracies allow free play for—in fact, require—individual enterprise of new sorts: in the creation of ideas, the building of empires, the competition for advancement.

At any rate, our data show no substantial differences between the values of parents from bureaucratic and enterpreneurial occupational worlds, in either social class. But see Daniel R. Miller and Guy E. Swanson, *The Changing American Parent: A Study in the Detroit Area* (New York: John Wiley & Sons, 1958).

[19]Bronfenbrenner, *op. cit.*, p. 424.

[20]Later studies, including our own, do not show this difference.

[21]"Social Class and the Exercise of Parental Authority," *op. cit.*

[22]This is not to say that the methods used by parents of either social class are necessarily the most efficacious for achievement of their goals.

[23]The justification for treating support and constraint as the two major dimensions of parent-child relationships lies in the theoretical argument of Talcott Parsons and Robert F. Bales, *Family, Socialization and Interaction Process* (Glencoe, Ill.: Free Press, 1955), esp. p. 45, and the empirical argument of Earl S. Schaefer, "A Circumplex Model for Maternal Behavior," *Journal of Abnormal and Social Psychology*, LIX (September, 1959), 226-34.

[24]Bronfenbrenner, *op. cit.*, p. 425.

[25]From the very limited evidence available at the time of his review, Bronfenbrenner tentatively concluded: "though the middle-class father typically has a warmer relationship with the child, he is also likely to have more authority and status in family affairs" (*ibid*, p. 422). The discussion here is based largely on subsequent research, esp. "Social Class and the Allocation of Parental Responsibilities," *op. cit.*

[26]Fragmentary data suggest sharp class differences in the husband-wife relationship that complement the differences in the division of parental responsibilities discussed above. For example, virtually no working-class wife reports that she and her husband ever go out on an evening or weekend without the children. And few working-class fathers do much to relieve their wives of the burden of caring for the children all the time. By and large, working-class fathers seem to lead a largely separate social life from that of their wives; the wife has full-time responsibility for the children, while the husband is free to go his own way.

5.3   Children's Feelings of Personal Control as Related to Social Class and Ethnic Group

Esther S. Battle
The Ohio State University

Julian B. Rotter
University of Connecticut

Social class and ethnic group membership are generally accepted as important determinants of personality. This study is devoted to an exploration of the interaction of class and ethnic group with one personality variable: "internal versus external" control of reinforcements.

This construct distributes individuals according to the degree to which they accept personal responsibility for what happens to them, in contrast to the attribution of responsibility to forces outside their control. The external forces might be those of chance, fate, an inability to understand the world, or the influence of other, powerful people. In social learning theory (Rotter, 1954), this construct is considered to describe a generalized expectancy, operating across a large number of situations, which relates to whether or not the individual possesses or lacks power (or personal determination) over what happens to him.

The sense of "powerlessness" has been discussed by Seeman (1959) as one meaning of the sociological variable of "alienation." It is thought to relate to the individual's social circumstances (class and ethnic group status) as well as affecting his social learning. An individual who is thus alienated would hold the expectation that his own behavior cannot determine the outcomes he desires. There is some empirical evidence to support this interpretation. Seeman and Evans (1962) used a form of the forced-choice, adult scale of internal-external control (I-E Scale) developed by Liverant, Rotter, Crowne, and Seeman (Gore and Rotter, 1963), to study the behavior of patients in a tuberculosis hospital. Although the I-E scale makes no reference to disease, they found statistical support for their hypotheses that patients scoring as "internals" would know more about their own condition, would be better informed about T.B. in general, and would be regarded by ward personnel as "better" patients.

In another study, Seeman (in press) studied the effect of such alienation on the learning of prison inmates. He found that the alienated inmate (externally controlled) learned significantly less material relevant

From E. S. Battle, J. B. Rotter, *Journal of Personality*, 1963, **31**, 482–490. Reprinted by permission of the Publisher. Copyright 1963, Duke University Press, Durham, North Carolina.

to release than those less alienated. It was in the realm of long-range planning and control that the variable was predictive.

The related attitude of "mastery" was discussed by Strodtbeck (1958) as it is affected by religious, national, and social-class orientations perpetuated within the family. He found that Jewish middle- and upper-class Ss were differentiated from lower-class Italians on the basis of this variable. Most of the variance was attributable to factors of social class. Graves and Jessor adapted the I-E Scale for high school students (Graves, 1961) and studied ethnic differences in an isolated tri-ethnic community. They found whites to be most internal, followed by Spanish Americans. Indians were most external in attitudes. These findings were consistent with their predictions. Although economic factors undoubtedly contributed to differences, Graves felt that "ethnicity" was an important source of variance after other factors were controlled.

The effect of this personality characteristic has been studied by Phares (1957) and James (1957), who were instrumental in the development of the first I-E scales. The latest form of the adult scale has recently been related to the prediction of the type and degree of commitment behavior manifested by Southern Negro students to effect social change in the cause of desegregation (Gore & Rotter, 1963). Crowne and Liverant (1963) showed a relationship between conformity under conditions of high personal involvement and scores on this same scale.

Other approaches to the assessment of this attitude with children have been developed by Crandall, Katkovsky, and Preston (1962), relative to achievement situations, and by Bialer (1961). Bialer's *Locus of Control* questionnaire was developed from the James-Phares (James, 1957) adult scale of internal-external control. Bialer was interested in the developmental aspects of this attitude as well as its relation to the conceptualization of success and failure. He found the more mature child to be more internally controlled and to show greater response to success and failure cues. The Bialer questionnaire was used in the present study.

James (1957) studied the effect of this variable on behavior in angle and line-matching tasks. He demonstrated that externals had more "unusual shifts" in their expectancy for success. That is, they were more likely to expect future success when they had just failed and more likely to expect failure after succeeding. He also found the internals to have a greater increment in expectation for success in a 75 per cent reinforced sequence, substantiating the hypothesis that when one believes he is in control of what happens, positive reinforcement leads to an increasing certainty for future success.

Phares (1957, 1962), James and Rotter (1958), James (1957), Rotter, Liverant, and Crowne (1961), Holden and Rotter (1962), and others have shown that the growth and extinction of expectancies for reward

vary predictively under different experimental conditions if the tasks are perceived by S as chance, luck, or E-controlled, rather than as a matter of personal skill.

The present study involves the development of a projective test of the internal-external control attitude to be used with children; the establishment of the relationship between I-E and several sociological and demographic variables (age, sex, class, ethnic group, and IQ); and the replication of some previous findings with adult I-E scales in a performance task.

The behavioral task was an adaptation of James's line-matching task (James, 1957), which allows E to control success and failure without S's knowledge. The child is required to match a series of lines which vary in length. Before each trial, he states his expectancy for success on an eleven-point scale. Following a ten-trial training sequence (with a 50 per cent reinforcement schedule), his responses to continuous failure are examined over the 30 extinction trials. This task yields three measures which reflect the effect of the experimental variables: (a) Ss mean expectancy for success over the ten training trials; (b) the number of "unusual shifts" in expectancy during training (raised expectation for success after failing or lowered expectancy after succeeding); and (c) the number of trials to extinction (two successive trials at zero or one expectancy on a scale of zero to ten.)

The projective task was a "Children's Picture Test of Internal-External Control" originated by Battle. On the six-item cartoon test, the child states "what he would say" in various "lifelike" situations which involve the attribution of responsibility. The reliability of the scoring procedure was established with an independently scored sample of 40 protocols.[1] The result was a Pearsonian $r = .93$ ($p < .001$).

In the development of the test, 29 cartoon items were eliminated because of strong "picture pull" toward one or the other end of the scale. Six items were selected from a remaining eleven on the basis of correlation with the total scores with that item removed. Thirty-eight school children were used as pretest Ss for this analysis. Table 1 gives the six final items (their correlations with total score given in parenthesis). The

Table 1
Items from the Children's Picture Test of Internal-External Control

1. How come you didn't get what you wanted for Christmas? (.32)
2. Why is she always hurting herself? (.49)
3. When you grow up do you think you could be anything you wanted? (.25)
4. Whenever you're involved something goes wrong! (.22)
5. That's the third game we've lost this year. (.39)
6. Why does her mother always "holler" at her? (.32)

items are scored along a seven-point scale with three degrees of "inter-nality," three of "externality," and a nondiscriminatory midpoint. The *higher* the score, the more external the orientation.

Method

Ss in this study were 80 sixth- and eighth-grade children selected on the basis of sex, social class, and ethnic group membership (Negro-white) from five metropolitan schools.[2] The California Mental Maturity total score was used as a crude measure of "intelligence."

Each child was given the three tasks individually in the same order: (*a*) line matching, (*b*) cartoons, and (*c*) Bialer scale.

The Bialer *Locus of Control* questionnaire was administered to the last 40 Ss primarily to determine its relationship to the projective test being studied. This is a 23-item "yes" or "no" questionnaire in which S attributes the locus of control to himself or others. A *low* score on this scale indicates an external orientation. Since only 40 of the 80 Ss received the Bialer, some analyses made with the picture test were not repeated with the Bialer scale because of insufficient N.

Any child expressing doubt was reassured that there were no punishments or rewards associated with his performance. If the child asked the purpose of the line-matching technique, he was told it was a test to "see how well he could match the length of lines." No child persisted in his questions after this explanation. Each child was thanked and requested not to tell the other children about the tests before a specific day, at which time the testing would be completed. An attempt was made to test all the children in one class and school as rapidly as possible to prevent gossip from contaminating the results.

Demographic characteristics were obtained in the following manner: age, sex, and ethnic group were reported on the cumulative record for each child. IQ also was obtained from the cumulative record and was based, in most cases, on the full score of the California Mental Maturity Test most recently attained. Socioeconomic status was determined on the basis of the father or mother's occupation as given on the cumulative record. These occupations were categorized according to Lloyd Warner's classification (Warner, Meeker, & Eels, 1949). For purposes of analysis, classes one, two, three, and four were grouped together and called "middle class" in contrast to the "lower class" of five, six, and seven.

Results

The means and sigmas of the Children's I-E scale scores for each combination of class and ethnic group are given in Table 2.

Table 2
Means and Sigmas of Children's I-E Scores by Social Class and
Ethnic Group.

| | Middle Class | | | Lower Class | | |
	Mean	Sigma	N	Mean	Sigma	N
White	15.0	4.4	20	16.4	3.5	21
Negro	15.8	3.5	16	18.3	3.4	23

With an analysis of variance for unequal Ns (Walker & Lev, 1953), a significant F ratio was found between social classes ($F = 5.13$; $df = 1$ and 72; $p < .05$); for the interaction of ethnic group and social class ($F = 72.50$; $df = 1$ and 72; $p < .01$); and for the triple interaction of ethnic group, social class, and IQ ($F = 8.12$; $df = 1$ and 72; $p < .01$). The following two-tailed t tests isolate the source of variance for the interaction effects.

A contrast of the middle-class white with the lower-class Negro gives a t of 2.75, $p < .01$. The only other significant comparison was between the lower-class Negro and the middle-class Negro groups ($t = 2.10$, $p < .05$).

It can be seen that the most significant comparison is between the middle-class white as most "internal" and the lower-class Negro as most "external." In addition, it is apparent that it is the lower-class Negro group which differs from all the others.

The means and sigmas of the children's I-E scale scores for each combination of social class, ethnic group, and IQ are given in Table 3.

Table 3
Means and Sigmas of Children's I-E Scores by Social Class, Ethnic
Group, and IQ.

| | Negro | | | | | | White | | | | | |
| | Middle Class | | | Lower Class | | | Middle Class | | | Lower Class | | |
	Mean	Sigma	N	Mean	Sigma	N	Mean	Sigma	N	Mean	Sigma	N
IQ												
High	16.1	2.9	10	19.1	3.2	7	15.4	4.5	16	17.0	.8	4
Low	15.3	5.1	6	18.0	3.8	16	13.8	4.0	4	16.3	4.2	17

The significant comparison is between the lower-class Negro with a high IQ (mean I-E score $= 19.1$) and the middle-class white with low IQ (mean I-E $= 13.8$). For the combined N of 11 Ss the $t = 2.21$, $p < .06$. One interpretation is that it is the externally scoring lower-class Negro whose higher IQ scores reflect a greater need value for academic achievement. When such a person encounters deprivation, due to his

class and ethnic group membership, he defends himself with an "external" attitude. The middle-class white with a low IQ may have incorporated his class values of personal responsibility and when faced with the fact of his low ability, he responds characteristically by blaming himself for the failure.

Of the three line-matching measures, only the mean expectancy for success during the ten training trials was found to relate significantly to the children's I-E test ($r = -.31$, $p < .01$). That is, "internals" were "more certain of success" than "externals."

The Bialer questionnaire (1961) was found to relate significantly to the Children's Picture Test ($r = -.42$, $p < .01$). A high score on the Bialer is similar to a low score on the children's I-E scale. Bialer scores were also found to relate to the "number of unusual shifts" in expectancy during the training trials ($r = -.47$, $p < .01$). That is, "external" Ss raised expectancies after failure and lowered them after success more often than "internals." "Internal control" on the Bialer scale was found to relate significantly to higher social class (r pt. bis. $= .53$, $p < .01$). Since the Bialer scale is a questionnaire test and the children's I-E scale is a projective test, the correlation of these two instruments ($- .42$) lends support to the construct validity of the internal-external control dimension as applied to grade school children.

Neither age (sixth vs. eighth grade) nor sex were found to relate to either children's I-E scale or the Bialer questionnaire.

The most interesting finding in this study is the effect of the interaction of social class and ethnic group on I-E scores. Analysis of the means in Table 2 shows clearly that the combined influence of the two variables is to make the lower-class Negro more external than all other groups. The results suggest that the middle-class Negro in this community might be raised to accept the white cultural beliefs in responsibility and opportunity. These results suggest that one important antecedent of a generalized expectancy that one can control his own destiny is the perception of opportunity to obtain the material rewards offered in a culture. Direct teaching of attitudes of internal vs. external control may also be involved.

Summary

A generalized expectancy for internal vs. external control of reinforcement was examined in 80 Negro and white school children. To assess this characteristic, a newly developed cartoon test was given to all children and a questionnaire scale developed earlier by Bialer was given to half the children. The relationship of test scores to sex, age, social class, ethnic group, and behavior on a line-matching task was investigated. The following findings were obtained.

1. The interaction of social class and ethnic group was highly related to internal-external control attitudes. Lower-class Negroes were significantly more external than middle-class Negroes or whites. Middle-class children, in general, were significantly more internal than lower-class children.

2. Lower-class Negroes with high IQ's were more external than middle-class whites with lower IQ's. Caution must be exercised in interpreting this triple interaction because of the small N involved. The findings suggest, however, that brighter lower-class Negroes may develop extreme external attitudes as a defense reaction to perceived reduced choices for cultural or material rewards.

3. Sex was not a determiner of I-E scores in this study nor was age for the two-year difference investigated. California Mental Maturity Test scores did not relate to I-E scores when class and race were undifferentiated.

4. On a line-matching test, higher children's I-E scores were significantly associated with lower mean expectancy for success but not significantly associated with unusual shifts or trials to extinction.

5. The Bialer questionnaire of internal-external control expectancies correlated significantly (− .42) with the projective measure used in this study. The Bialer scale was also significantly related to social class.

6. For the 40 Ss who had taken the Bialer scale, a significant predicted relationship was found between test scores and number of unusual shifts on line-matching task; but not with mean expectancy or trials to extinction.

7. The overall findings lend support to the construct validity of the internal-external control variable as a generalized personality dimension and suggest some of the developmental conditions involved in the acquisition of such generalized expectancies.

Notes

1. Mr. Forest Ward's help in the development of the scoring manual and in rating responses is gratefully acknowledged.

2. Half of the Ss came from two lower-class, ethnically integrated schools in Columbus, Ohio. The other 40 Ss were obtained from three Dayton, Ohio, schools. Of the latter Ss, most of the middle-class Negro children came from the same elementary school. Most middle-class white students came from a second school. Only seven Ss came from the last school which is situated in a lower-class, ethnically integrated, rooming-house district.

References

Bialer, I. Conceptualization of success and failure in mentally retarded and normal children. *J. Pers.*, 1961, *29*, 303–320.

Crandall, V. J., Katkovsky, W., & Preston, A. Motivational and ability determinants of young children's intellectual achievement behaviors. *Child Develpm.* 1962, **33,** 643–661.

Crowne, D. P., & Liverant, S. Conformity under varying conditions of personal commitment. *J. abnorm. soc. Psychol.,* 1963, **66,** 547–555.

Gore, M. P., & Rotter, J. B. A personality correlate of social action. *J. Pers., 1963,* **31,** 58–64.

Graves, T. D. Time perspective and the deferred gratification pattern in a tri-ethnic community. Research Report No. 5, Tri-Ethnic Research Project, Univer. of Colorado, Institute of Behavioral Science, 1961.

Holden, K. B., & Rotter, J. B. A nonverbal measure of extinction in skill and chance situations. *J. exp. Psychol.,* 1962, **63,** 519–520.

James, W. H. Internal vs. external control of reinforcement as a basic variable in learning theory. Unpublished Ph.D. dissertation, Ohio State Univer., 1957.

James, W. H., & Rotter, J. B. Partial and 100 per cent reinforcement under chance and skill conditions. *J. exp. Psychol.,* 1958, **55,** 397–403.

Phares, E. J. Expectancy changes in skill and chance situations. *J. abnorm. soc. Psychol.,* 1957, **54,** 339–342.

Phares, E. J. Perceptual threshold decrements as a function of skill and chance expectancies. *J. Psychol.,* 1962, **53,** 399–407.

Rotter, J. B. *Social learning and clinical psychology.* Englewood Cliffs, N. J.: Prentice-Hall, 1954.

Rotter, J. B., Liverant, S., & Crowne, D. P., The growth and extinction of expectancies in chance controlled and skilled tasks. *J. Psychol.,* 1961, **52,** 161–177.

Seeman, M. On the meaning of alienation. *Amer. sociol. Rev.,* 1959, **24,** 783–791.

Seeman, M. An experimental study of alienation and social learning. *Amer. J. sociol.,* in press.

Seeman, M., & Evans, J. W. Alienation and learning in a hospital setting. *Amer. sociol. Rev.,* 1962, **27,** 772–782.

Strodtbeck, F. L. Family interaction, values and achievement. In D. McClelland (Ed.), *Talent and society.* New York: Van Nostrand, 1958. Pp. 138–195.

Walker, H. M., & Lev, J. *Statistical inference.* New York: Holt, Rinehart & Winston, 1953.

Warner, W. L., Meeker, M., & Eels, K. *Social class in America.* Science Research Associates, Chicago, 1949. Pp. 140–141.

5.4 The Psycho-Social Origins of Achievement Motivation

Bernard C. Rosen,
University of Connecticut

Roy D'Andrade,
Cambridge, Massachusetts

The purpose of this study is to examine the origins of achievement motivation (*n* Achievement) within the context of the individual's membership in two important groups: family and social class. Specifically, this paper explores, through the observation of family interaction, the relationship between achievement motivation and certain child-training practices, and the relationship between these practices and the parent's social class membership.

The importance of group membership for personality development has been demonstrated many times. Perhaps the most important of these groups is the family, whose strategic role in the socialization process has led investigators to study the nexus between child-rearing practices and motivation formation. Thus, Winterbottom (15) examined the relationship between independence-mastery training and achievement motivation and found that achievement motivation is strongest among boys whose mothers (all of whom were middle class) expected relatively early indications of self-reliance and mastery from them.

Since many socialization practices are known to be dissimilar between social groups (3, 4), it might be expected that independence training practices would also differ. A study by McClelland *et al.* (8), later replicated by Rosen (10), demonstrated this to be the case: middle-class parents place greater stress upon independence training than lower class parents. The deduction from this finding that classes differ in their level of *n* Achievement was shown to be correct by Rosen (9) who found that, on the average, *n* Achievement scores for middle-class adolescents were significantly higher than those for their lower class counterparts.

Significantly, although these studies flow logically from one another, in none of them were all three variables — group membership, child training practices, and *n* Achievement — studied simultaneously. Furthermore, there were certain gaps in these studies which called for theoretical and methodological modifications and additions. The nature of these gaps, and the contributions which it was the research objective of this study to make, are as follows:

Reprinted with abridgment from *Sociometry*, 1959, *22*, 185–195; 215–217, by permission of the senior author and the American Sociological Association.

Theoretical. The keystone around which studies of the origins of achievement motivation have been built is the notion that training in independent mastery is an antecedent condition of *n* Achievement (6, 15). This approach grew out of McClelland's and his associates' theory of the nature and origins of motivation. They argue that all motives are learned, that "they develop out of repeated affective experiences connected with certain types of situations and types of behavior. In the case of achievement motivation, the situation should involve 'standards of excellence,' presumably imposed on the child by the culture, or more particularly by the parents as representatives of the culture, and the behavior should involve either "competition' with those standards of excellence or attempts to meet them which, if successful, produce positive affect or, if unsuccessful, negative affect. It follows that those cultures of families which stress competition with standards of excellence or which insist *that the child be able to perform certain tasks well by himself. . .* should produce children with high achievement motivation" (7).

Two distinctly different kinds of child-training practices are implicit in this theory. The first is the idea that the child is trained to do things "well"; the second, the notion that he is trained to perform tasks "by himself." The former has been called *achievemen training* (2) in that it stresses competition in situations involving standards of excellence; the latter has been called *indpendence training* in that it involves putting the child on his own. The failure to disentangle these two concepts has resulted in a focus of attention upon independence training largely to the exclusion of achievement training, although the former is primarily concerned with developing self-reliance, often in areas involving self-care-taking (e.g., cleaning, dressing, amusing, or defending oneself). Although both kinds of training practices frequently occur together, they are different in content and consequences and needed to be examined separately. We believe that of the two training practices, achievement training is the more effective in generating *n* Achievement.

There is another component of independence training—one which is explicit in the idea of independence—that needed further exploration: *autonomy.* By autonomy, we mean training and permitting the child to exercise a certain amount of freedom of action in decision making. Although a related aspect of autonomy—*power*—was studied by Strodtbeck (13), who examined the relationship between power distribution in the family, *n* Achievement, and academic achievement among a group of Jewish and Italian adolescents, no study had examined simultaneously the self-reliance and autonomy components of independence training. The operation of both components, we believed, tends to increase the power of independence training to generate *n* Achievement, since in it-

self high parental expectations for self-reliance may cause rebellion, feelings of rejection, or of apathy on the part of the child, while autonomy without parental expectations for self-reliance and achievement may be perceived as mere permissiveness or indifference.

In association with parental demands that the child be self-reliant, autonomous, and show evidence of high achievement, there must be sanctions to see that these demands are fulfilled. Winterbottom found that mothers of children with high n Achievement gave somewhat more intense rewards than mothers of children with low n Achievement. Little was known about the role of negative sanctions, or of the relative impact of sanctions from either parent. Further study was required of the degree and kind of sanctions employed by both parents to see that their demands are met.

Methodological. This study departed from two practices common in studies of the origins of n Achievement. The first practice is to derive data exclusively from ethnographic materials; the second, to obtain information through questionnaire-type interviews with mothers. Interviews and ethnographies can be valuable sources of information, but they are often contaminated by interviewer and respondent biases, particularly those of perceptual distortion, inadequate recall, and deliberate inaccuracies. There was a need for data derived from systematic observation of parent-child relations. It is not enough to know what parents *say* their child-rearing practices are; these statements should be checked against more objective data, preferably acquired under controlled experimental conditions, that would permit us to *see* what they do. In this study, experiments were employed which enabled a team of investigators to observe parent-child interaction in problem-solving situations that were standardized for all groups and required no special competence associated with age or sex.

An equally strong objection can be raised against the tendency to ignore the father's role in the development of the child's need to achieve. Apart from an earlier study of father-son power relations, no efforts had been made to determine the father's contribution to achievement and independence training—a surprising omission even granted the mother's importance in socializing the child in American society. Although we were not prepared to take a position on the nature of the role relationships between father, mother, and son with respect to this motive, we deliberately created experimental conditions which would enable us to observe the way in which the three members of the family interacted in a problem-solving situation. Finally, this study incorporated in one design the variables of group membership, child-training practices, and motivation, variables that heretofore had not been studied simultaneously. In

so doing we hoped to establish the nexus among class membership, socialization practices, and achievement motivation.

Hypotheses

This study was designed to provide data that would permit testing two basic hypotheses.

1.   Achievement motivation is a result of the following socialization practices: (a) *achievement training*, in which the parents set high goals for their son to attain, indicate that they have a high evaluation of his competence to do a task well, and impose standards of excellence upon tasks against which he is to compete, even in situations where such standards are not explicit; (b) *independence training*, in which the parents indicate to the child that they expect him to be *self-reliant*, while at the same time permit him relative *autonomy* in situations involving decision making where he is given both freedom of action and responsibility for success or failure; (c) *sanctions*, rewards and punishments employed by parents to ensure that their expectations are met and proper behavior is reinforced. Although each contributes to the development of achievement motivation, achievement training is more important than independence training. Neither are effective without supporting sanctions.

2.   Differences in the mean level of achievement motivation between social classes is in part a function of the differential class emphases upon independence and achievement training: middle-class parents are more likely than lower class parents to stress self-relience, autonomy, and achievement in problem-solving situations, particularly those involving standards of excellence. They are more likely to recognize and reward evidences of achievement, as well as to be more sensitive of and punitive toward indications of failure.

Experimental Procedure

The subjects selected to provide data needed for the testing of these hypotheses about the origins of achievement motivation were 120 persons who made up 40 family groups composed of a father, mother, and their son, aged nine, ten, or eleven. The selection of the family groups began with testing the boy. Seven schools in three northeastern Connecticut towns were visited by the same field worker who administered a Thematic Apperception Test individually and privately to 140 boys, aged nine, ten, or eleven. As is customary in the TAT procedure, the subject was presented with a set of four ambiguous pictures and asked to tell a story about each. His imaginative responses were then scored according to a method developed by McClelland and his associates which

involves identifying and counting the frequency with which imagery about evaluated performance in competition with a standard of excellence appears in the thoughts of a person when he tells a brief story under time pressure. Experience has shown that this imagery can be identified objectively and reliably. It is the assumption of this test that the more the individual shows indications of evaluated performance connected with affect in his fantasy, the greater the degree to which achievement motivation is part of his personality (7). The stories were scored by two judges; the Pearsonian coefficient of correlation between scorers was .87, a level of reliability similar to those reported in earlier studies with this measure.

Subjects with scores of plus 2 to minus 4 (approximately the bottom quartile) were labeled as having low *n* Achievement, those with scores of plus 9 to plus 22 (approximately the top quartile) as having high *n* Achievement. Any boy with an I.Q. score below 98, with physical defects, whose parents were separated, or who had been raised during part of his life by persons or relatives other than his parents (e.g., grandparents) was eliminated from the sample.

Forty boys, matched by age, race, I.Q., and social class were chosen for further study. All were white, native born, and between nine and eleven years of age; the average was ten years. Half of the boys had high *n* Achievement scores, half had low scores. In each achievement motivation category, half of the boys were middle class, half were lower class. Their social class position was determined according to a modified version of the Hollingshead Index of Social Position (5) which uses the occupation and education of the chief wage-earner—usually the father— as the principal criteria of status. The middle-class father (class II or III) held either a professional, managerial, white collar position or was self-employed as an owner of a small- to medium-size business. Often one or both parents in middle-class families were college graduates; all were high-school graduates. The parents of lower class (IV or V) boys were quasi-skilled or skilled workers in local factories, or owners of very small farms—often the farmers held factory jobs as well. Relatively few of these parents had completed high school, none had gone beyond high school.

It can be seen that the study was designed in such a way that the subjects fell into one of four cells, with the achievement motivation level of the boys and the class position of the parents as the classificatory variables. Within each cell there were ten families. This four-cell factorial design was constructed so as to facilitate the use of the analysis of variance technique in the statistical analysis of the data.

After the boy was selected, a letter was sent to his parents from the principal of the school asking their cooperation with the investigators.

Later, appointments were made over the telephone to visit the families. Cooperation was very good; there were only two refusals. A pair of observers visited each family group, usually at night. There were two teams of observers, each composed of a man and woman. Both teams had been trained together to ensure adequate intra- and interteam reliability.

Once in the home, the observers explained that they were interested in studying the factors related to success in school and eventually to a career, and that the son was one of many boys selected from a cross-section of the community. When rapport had been established, the parents and their son were placed at a table—usually in the kitchen—and it was explained that the boy was going to perform certain tasks.

Experimental Tasks

The observers wanted to create an experimental situation from which could be derived objective measures of the parents' response to their son as he engaged in achievement behavior. Tasks were devised which the boy could do and which would involve the parents in their son's task performance. The tasks were constructed so that the subjects were often faced with a choice of giving or refusing help. At times they were permitted to structure the situation according to their own norms; at other times the experimenters set the norms. In some situations they were faced with decision conflicts over various alternatives in the problem-solving process. The observation of the parents' behavior as their son engaged in these experimental tasks provided information about the demands the parents made upon him, the sanctions employed to enforce these demands, and the amount of independence the child had developed in relations with his parents. A category system, similar to the Bales system (1), was devised to permit scoring interaction between parents and son so that the amount and form of each subject's participation could be examined. The investigators were able to learn from these interaction data how self-reliant the parents expected their son to be, how much autonomy they permitted him in decision-making situations, and what kind and amount of affect was generated in a problem-solving situation.

In creating the experimental tasks an effort was made to simulate two conditions normally present when boys are solving problems in the presence of their parents: (1) tasks were constructed to make the boys relatively dependent upon their parents for aid, and (2) the situation was arranged so that the parents either knew the solution to the problem or were in a position to do the task better than their son. In addition, tasks were created which tapped manual skills as well as intellectual capacities, although intelligence is a factor in any problem-solving situation. It was for this reason that the experimenters controlled for I.Q.

In one particular respect the experimental situation was deliberately made atypical. The investigators sought to get the parents involved in the experiment by deliberately building stress into the situation. It was hoped that these *stress experiments* would so involve the parents that they would abandon their protective "company behavior" and generate more authentic action in several hours than could be gained through casual observation over several days. This manoeuvre was generally successful, although it is impossible to evaluate how and in what way the nature of the experiments and the presence of observers affected the subjects. It is a basic assumption of this study that by studying present-time interaction in a controlled situation one can achieve a valid picture of the patterns of interaction between parents and child most likely to have occurred in the child's earlier years. It is recognized, however, that the conflicting evidence about changes in socialization practices as the child grows older leaves the wisdom of this assumption an open question.

Pretesting had shown that no single task would provide sufficient data to test all hypotheses. Hence, five tasks were constructed, each designed to attack the problem from a somewhat different angle and yet provide certain classes of data that could be scored across tasks. The five tasks used in this study are as follows:

1. *Block Stacking.* The boys were asked to build towers out of very irregularly shaped blocks. They were blindfolded and told to use only one hand in order to create a situation in which the boy was relatively dependent upon his parents for help. His parents were told that this was a test of their son's ability to build things, and that they could *say* anything to their son but could not touch the blocks. A performance norm was set for the experiment by telling the parents that the average boy could build a tower of eight blocks; they were asked to write down privately their estimate of how high they thought their son could build his tower. The purposes of this experiment were (a) to see how high were the parents' aspirations for and evaluations of their son, e.g., if they set their estimates at, above, or below the norm; (b) to see how self-reliant they expected or permitted their son to be, e.g., how much help they would give him.

There were three trials for this task. The first provided measures of parental evaluations and aspirations not affected by the boy's performance; the second and third trial estimates provided measures affected by the boy's performance. The procedure for the third trial differed from the first two in that the boy was told that he would be given a nickel for each block he stacked. Each member of the family was asked to estimate privately how high the boy should build his tower. No money would be

given for blocks stacked higher than the estimate nor would the subject receive anything if the stack tumbled before he reached the estimate. Conservative estimates, hence, provided security but little opportunity for gain; high estimates involved more opportunity for gain but greater risk. The private estimates were then revealed to all and the family was asked to reach a group decision. In addition to securing objective measures of parental aspiration-evaluation levels, the observers scored the interaction between subjects, thus obtaining data as to the kind and amount of instructions the parents gave their son, the amount of help the son asked for or rejected, and the amount and kind of affect generated during the experiment.

2. *Anagrams.* In this task the boys were asked to make words of three letters or more out of six prescribed letters: G, H, K, N, O, R. The letters, which could be reused after each word was made, were printed on wooden blocks so that they could be manipulated. The parents were given three additional lettered blocks, T, U, and B, and a list of words that could be built with each new letter. They were informed that they could give the boy a new letter (in the sequence T, U, B) whenever they wished and could say anything to him, short of telling him what word to build. There was a ten-minute time limit for this experiment. Since this is a familiar game, no efforts were made to explain the functions of the task.

The purposes of this experiment were: (a) to see how self-reliant the parents expected their son to be, e.g., how soon they would give him a new letter, how much and what kind of direction they would give him, if they would keep him working until he got all or most of the words on the list or "take him off the hook" when he got stuck. And (b) to obtain, by scoring interaction between the subjects, measures of the affect generated by the problem-solving process, e.g., the amount of tension shown by the subjects, the positive and negative remarks directed toward one another:

3. *Patterns.* In this experiment the parents were shown eight patterns, graduated in difficulty, that could be made with Kohs blocks. The subjects were informed that pattern 1 was easier to make than pattern 2, pattern 3 was more difficult than 2 but easier than 4, and so forth. The subjects were told that this was a test of the boy's ability to remember and reproduce patterns quickly and accurately. Each parent and boy was asked to select privately three patterns which the boy would be asked to make from memory after having seen the pattern for five seconds. All three patterns were chosen *before* the boy began the problem solving so that his performance in this task would not affect the choice of the pat-

terns. Where there were differences of choice, as inevitably there were, the subjects were asked to discuss their differences and make a group decision. Insofar as possible the observers took a verbatim account of the decision-making process, scoring for three kinds of variables: (a) the number of acts each subject contributed to the decision-making process, (b) the number of times each individual initiated a decision, and (c) the number of times each subject was successful in having the group accept his decision or in seeing to it that a decision was made.

The purposes of this experiment were: (a) to obtain another measure of the parents' evaluations of and aspirations for the boy, e.g., whether they would pick easy or difficult tasks for him to do; (b) to get a measure of the autonomy permitted the boy, e.g., whether they would let him choose his own patterns or impose their choices upon him; and (c) to see how much help they would give him and what affect would be generated by the experiment.

4. *Ring Toss.* In this experiment each member of the group was asked to choose privately ten positions, from each of which the boy was to throw three rings at a peg. The distance from the peg was delineated by a tape with 1-foot graduations laid on the floor. The subjects were told that this was a test of discrimination and judgment and that after each set of three tosses they would be asked to make a judgment as to the best distance from which to make the next set of tosses. Group decisions were made as to where the boy should stand. The purposes of this experiment were: (a) to see whether the parents imposed standards of excellence upon a task for which no explicit standard had been set, e.g., whether the parents would treat this as a childish game or see it as a task which could and should be done well. Would they choose easy or difficult positions? (b) To determine how much autonomy they permitted their son, e.g., would they let him choose his own position?

5. *Hatrack.* The Maier Hatrack Problem was used in this experiment. The boy was given two sticks and a C-clamp and instructed to build a rack strong enough to hold a coat and hat. His parents were told that this was a test of the boy's ability to build things. In this task no one was given the solution at the beginning of the experiment. For the first time the parents had no advantage over the boy—a most uncomfortable position for many parents, particularly the fathers. This stress situation was created deliberately to maximize the possibility of the problem generating affect, as was often the case, with some hostility being directed at the observers. After seven minutes the parents were given the solution to the problem. The purposes of this experiment were: (a) to see how self-reliant the parents expected their son to be. After receiving the solu-

tion what kind of clues would the parents give the boy? How hard would they expect him to work on his own? (b) To obtain measures of the affect created in an unusually frustrating situation. How would the parents handle their frustration? Would they turn it against the boy?

Category System

References have been made to the use of a category system for scoring interaction between subjects. A brief description of this system, shown in Diagram 1, is in order. Most of the subjects' verbal and some of their motor behavior (e.g., laughing, hand-clapping, scowling) was scored in one of twelve categories. In eight of these categories were placed acts involving relatively strong affect. Four additional categories were used to distinguish between various kinds of statements — either giving, requesting, or rejecting directions — which contained very little or no affect. A distinction was made between negative and positive affective acts. Affective acts associated with explicit or implicit evaluations of the boy's performance which aimed at motivating or changing his behavior were scored differently from affective acts which involved reactions to the boy and only indirectly to his performance.

Diagram 1
The System of Categories Used in Scoring Parent-Child Interaction

+X	Expresses approval, gives love, comfort, affection
+T	Shows positive tension release, jokes, laughs
+E	Gives explicit positive evaluation of performance, indicates job well done
+P	Attempts to push up performance through expression of enthusiasm, urges cheers on
N	Gives nonspecific directions, gives hints, clues, general suggestions
S	Gives specific directions, gives detailed information about how to do a task
aa	Asks aid, information, or advice
ra	Rejects aid, information, or advice
−P	Attempts to push up performance through expressions of displeasure; urges on indicating disappointment at speed and level of performance
−E	Gives explicit negative evaluation of performance, indicates job poorly done
−T	Shows negative tension release, shows irritation, coughs
−X	Expresses hostility, denigrates, makes sarcastic remarks

Directional acts by the parents were remarks designed to help the boy perform his task. A distinction was made between *specific* directions (S) which were acts instructing the subject to do particular things which would facilitate task completion, and *nonspecific* (N) which were acts aimed at giving the subject some information but not specific enough to enable him to rely entirely upon it. It was believed that nonspecific state-

ments were more likely than specific statements to create self-reliance in the child.

The affective acts were schematized in two sets—one positive, the other negative. The first set was comprised of acts involving direct expressions of emotions toward another person, not necessarily in the context of task performance, either of a positive character (+X), such as expressions of love or approval, or of a negative character (−X), such as indications of hostility and rejection. Another set was of acts involving release of tension, either associated with positive affect (+T) such as grins, laughter, jokes, or negative affect (−T) such as scowls, coughs, or irritated gestures. Tension-release acts differ from acts of direct emotion (X) in that the former were not focused toward any person but were diffused, undirected reactions to the general situation. The next set of acts involved parental evaluation of the boy's performance. Those acts in which the parents stated that the boy was doing the task well were scored as positive evaluations (+E), while statements that the boy was doing poorly were scored as negative evaluations (−E). The last two categories involved acts aimed at urging or pushing the boy to perform more effectively. These "pushing up the performance level acts" were scored in one of two categories. Those acts in which the parents "cheered" the boy on while at the same time indicating that they expected him to do better were scored as positive pushing acts (+P); negative pushing acts (−P) were statements in which the parents sought to improve the boy's performance by indicating in a threatening way that they thought he could do better.

Only four kinds of acts were scored for the boy: whether he asked for aid (aa), rejected aid (ra), showed positive tension (+T) or negative tension (−T). An act was defined as the smallest segment of verbal or motor behavior which could be recognized as belonging to one of the twelve categories in the system. The actor rather than the target of the acts was used as the observer's frame of reference.

This category system involves a good deal of inference on the part of the observer—a factor which can make for low observer reliability. To ensure adequate reliability, the interaction in each family was scored by two observers who had been trained to work as a team. In the early stages of the field work tape recordings were taken of family interaction. After the experiments the observers rescored the interaction protocols and discussed scoring differences in order to increase interobserver reliability. Tape recordings were discontinued when the scorers felt that their scores were substantially the same. Each team of observers visited 20 families. The reliability of observers for the gross number of acts scored is high. The Pearsonian coefficient of correlation between the

first pair of scorers is plus .93, and for the second pair plus .97. No significant differences between pairs of observers has been discovered. . . .

Discussion and Summary

The question of how achievement training, independence training, and sanctions are related to achievement motivation may be rephrased by asking, How does the behavior of parents of boys with high n Achievement differ from the behavior of parents whose sons have low n Achievement?

To begin with, the observers' subjective impressions are that the parents of high n Achievement boys tend to be more competitive, show more involvement, and seem to take more pleasure in the problem-solving experiments. They appear to be more interested and concerned with their son's performance; they tend to give him more things to manipulate rather than fewer; on the average they put out more affective acts. More objective data show that the parents of a boy with high n Achievement tend to have higher aspirations for him to do well at any given task, and they seem to have a higher regard for his competence at problem solving. They set up standards of excellence for the boy even when none is given, or if a standard is given will expect him to do "better than average." As he progresses they tend to react to his performance with warmth and approval, or, in the case of the mothers especially, with disapproval if he performs poorly.

It seems clear that achievement training contributes more to the development of n Achievement than does independence training. Indeed, the role of independence training in generating achievement motivation can only be understood in the context of what appears to be a division of labor between the fathers and mothers of high n Achievement boys.

Fathers and mothers both provide achievement training and independence training, but the fathers seem to contribute much more to the latter than do the mothers. Fathers tend to let their sons develop some self-reliance by giving hints (N) rather than always telling "how to do it" (S). They are less likely to push (P) and more likely to give the boy a greater degree of autonomy in making his own decisions. Fathers of high n Achievement boys often appear to be competent men who are willing to take a back seat while thier sons are performing. They tend to beckon from ahead rather than push from behind.

The mothers of boys with high achievement motivation tend to stress achievement training rather than independence training. In fact, they are likely to be more dominant and to expect less self-reliance than the mothers of boys with low n Achievement. But their aspirations for their

sons are higher and their concern over success greater. Thus, they expect the boys to build higher towers and place them farther away from the peg in the Ring Toss experiment. As a boy works his mother tends to become emotionally involved. Not only is she more likely to reward him with approval (Warmth) but also to punish him with hostility (Rejection). *In a way, it is this factor of involvement that most clearly sets the mothers of high n Achievement boys apart from the mothers of low n Achievement boys:* the former score higher on every variable, expect specific directions. And although these mothers are likely to give their sons more option as to exactly (fewer Specifics) what to do, they give them less option about doing something and doing it well. Observers report that the mothers of high *n* Achievement boys tend to be striving, competent persons. Apparently they expect their sons to be the same.

The different emphasis which the fathers and mothers of high *n* Achievement boys place upon achievement and independence training suggest that the training practices of father and mother affect the boy in different ways. Apparently, the boy can take and perhaps needs achievement training from both parents, but the effects of independence training and sanctions, in particular Autonomy and Rejection, are different depending upon whether they come from the father or mother. In order for high *n* Achievement to develop, the boy appears to need more autonomy from his father than from his mother. The father who gives the boy a relatively high degree of autonomy provides him with an opportunity to compete on his own ground, to test his skill, and to gain a sense of confidence in his own competence. The dominating father may crush his son (and in so doing destroys the boy's achievement motive), perhaps because he views the boy as a competitor and is viewed as such by his son. On the other hand, the mother who dominates the decision-making process does not seem to have the same affect on the boy, possibly because she is perceived as *imposing her standards* on the boy, while a dominating father is perceived as *imposing himself* on the son. It may be that the mother-son relations are typically more secure than those between father and son, so that the boy is better able to accept higher levels of dominance and rejection from his mother than his father without adverse affect on his needs to achieve. Relatively rejecting, dominating fathers, particularly those with less than average warmth—as tended to be the case with the fathers of low *n* Achievement boys—seem to be a threat to the boy and a deterent to the development of *n* Achievement. On the other hand, above-average dominance and rejection, coupled with above-average warmth, as tends to be the case with mothers of high *n* Achievement boys, appear to be a spur to achievement motivation. It will be remembered that the fathers of high *n* Achievement boys are on

the average less Rejecting, less Pushing, and less Dominant—all of which points to their general hands-off policy.

It is unlikely that these variables operate separately, but the way in which they interact in the development of achievement motivation is not clear. Possibly the variables interact in a manner which produces cyclical effects roughly approximating the interaction that characterized the experimental task situations of this study. The cycle begins with the parents imposing standards of excellence upon a task and setting a high goal for the boy to achieve (e.g., Ring Toss, estimates and choices in Block Stacking and Patterns). As the boy engages in the task, they reinforce acceptable behavior by expressions of warmth (both parents) or by evidences of disapproval (primarily mother). The boy's performance improves, in part because of previous experience and in part because of the greater concern shown by his parents and expressed through affective reaction to his performance and greater attention to his training. With improved performance, the parents grant the boy greater autonomy and interfere less with his performance (primarily father). Goals are then reset at a higher level and the cycle continues.

References

Bales, R. F., *Interaction Process Analysis*, Cambridge, Mass.: Addison-Wesley, 1951.

Child, I. L., T. Storm, and J. Veroff, "Achievement Themes in Folk Tales Related to Socialization Practice," in J. W. Atkinson, *Motives in Fantasy, Action and Society*, Princeton, N. J.: Van Nostrand, 1958.

Erickson, M. C., "Social Status and Child-rearing Practices," in T. Newcomb and E. Hartley, *Readings in Social Psychology*, New York: Holt, 1947.

Havighurst, R. J., and A. Davis, "Social Class Differences in Child-rearing," *American Sociological Review*, 1955, **20**, 438–442.

Hollingshead, A., and F. C. Redlick, "Social Stratification and Psychiatric Disorders," *American Sociological Review*, 1953, **18**, 163–169.

McClelland, D. C., and G. A. Friedman, "A Cross-Cultural Study of the Relationship between Child-Training Practices and Achievement Motivation, appearing in Folk Tales," in G. E. Swanson, T. M. Newcomb, and E. L. Harley, eds., *Readings in Social Psychology*, New York: Holt, 1952.

McClelland, D. C., J. W. Atkinson, R. Clark, and E. Lowell, *The Achievement Motive*, New York: Appleton-Century-Crofts, 1953.

McClelland, D. C., A. Rindlisbacher, and R. deCharms, "Religious and Other Sources of Parental Attitudes toward Independence Training,"

in D. C. McClelland, ed., *Studies in Motivation*, New York: Appleton-Century-Crofts, 1955.

Rosen, B. C., "The Achievement Syndrome: a Psychocultural Dimension of Social Stratification," *American Sociological Review*, 1956, **21**, 203 – 211.

Rosen, B. C., "Race, Ethnicity, and the Achievement Syndrome," *American Sociological Review*, 1959, **24**, 47 – 60.

Sakoda, J. M., "Directions for a Multiple-Group Method of Factor Analysis," mimeographed paper, University of Connecticut, June, 1955.

Sears, R. R., E. E. Maccoby, and H. Levin in collaboration with E. L. Lowell, P. S. Sears, and J. W. M. Whiting, *Patterns of Child Rearing*, Evanston, Ill.: Row, Peterson, 1957.

Strodtbeck, F. L., "Family Interaction, Values, and Achievement," in D. C. McClelland, A. L. Baldwin, U. Bronfenbrenner, and F. L. Strodtbeck, *Talent and Society*, Princeton, N. J.: Van Nostrand, 1958.

Tryon, R. C., *Cluster Analysis*, Ann Arbor, Mich.: Edwards Brothers, 1939.

Winterbottom, M. R., "The Relation of Need for Achievement to Learning Experiences in Independence and Mastery," in J. W. Atkinson, *Motives in Fantasy, Action, and Society*, Princeton, N. J.: Van Nostrand, 1958.

5.5   Cooperative and Competitive Behavior of Kibbutz and Urban Children in Israel

Ariella Shapira
Millard C. Madsen
University of California, Los Angeles

Several researchers have attempted to determine the extend of subcultural differences in the cooperative and competitive behavior of children in the United States. McKee and Leader (1955) found preschool children of low socioeconomic level to be more competitive than chil-

Reprinted from *Child Development*, June 1969, **40**, No. 2, 609 – 617, by permission of the author and The Society for Research in Child Development, Inc. Copyright © 1969 by The Society for Research in Child Development, Inc.

dren of middle-class families. Goodman (1952) found Negro children (age 4) to be more competitive than white children, while Sampson and Kardush (1965) found the opposite to be true with older children (age 7 – 11). Nelson and Madsen (in press) found no differences in cooperation and competition between Negro and white lower-class and white middle-class 4-year-olds. There are many methodological differences between the above studies, as well as differences of time and place. It is also probably true that subcultural groups in the United States cannot be as rigidly differentiated, with respect to social values and child-rearing practices that give rise to differential interdependent behavior, then is possible in other settings.

In an experimental study of subcultural differences in competitive and cooperative behavior, Madsen (1967) found that both rural and urban poor children in Mexico were dramaticaly more cooperative than Mexican urban middle-class children. An attempt was made to account for these differences in performance on experimental tasks by reference to the environmental milieu in which the different subcultural groups had developed. The study reported here was carried out in Israel and used the same techniques to compare two other subcultural groups: children from agricultural social communes (kibbutzim) and those from an urban environment.

Children in an Israeli urban middle-class community are encouraged by parents and teachers to achieve and succeed. Competition is an acceptable means of arriving at this goal. In the kibbutz, on the other hand, children are prepared from an early age to cooperate and work as a group, in keeping with the objectives of communal living. Spiro (1965) found, through questionnaires given to parents in the kibbutz, that generosity and cooperation were the most frequently rewarded behaviors, while selfishness and failure to cooperate were among the behaviors most frequently punished.

The formal teaching methods in the kibbutz are also noted for their minimal emphasis on competitive goals and techniques. Grades and examinations are viewed as unnecessary or even undesirable. Competition, with all its punitive aspects, is far less intense in the classroom of the kibbutz than in that of the city. Not only do the agents of socialization avoid inducing a favorable set toward competition, but also the children themselves develop an attitude against competition. Spiro found that only one out of 28 students saw himself or his peers as being competitively motivated. By far the majority of the students said that their desire was primarily to become equal to their peers or, as Rabin (1965) observed, to raise the achievement level of their group as a whole. Generally, kibbutz children do not accept competition as a socially desirable norm and dislike those who try to excel over members of their own

group. This anti-competition attitude is so strong that, according to some teachers, students are ashamed of being consistently at the top of the class. Spiro also found that these cooperative attitudes and behaviors increase with age concomitant with a decrease in competitive motivation.

In line with these basic differences in child-rearing practices and values, it was hypothesized that kibbutz children would be more cooperative than urban middle-class children when playing a social interaction game with their peers.

Method

Subjects

The kibbutz sample included 40 children, 20 boys and 20 girls, ages ranging from 6 to 10 years, with a mean age of 8 years. Children from three different kibbutzim were included: Beit Zerah (in the Jordan valley), Beit Hashita (in the Yisrael valley), and Ein Hahoresh (in the Sharon). Both Ein Hahoresh and Beit Zerah belong to the Hashomer Hatzair, a radical socialist movement which is idealogically the most puritanical of all kibbutz movements in Israel. Beit Hashita belongs to Hakibbutz Hameuhad, a relatively more moderate ideological movement. All of the kibbutz children who played the experimental game knew the children with whom they participated. They were usually from the same *kvutza*, a group within a kibbutz comprised of children who spend almost all their time together.

The city sample consisted of 40 children, 20 boys and 20 girls, ages ranging from 6 to 10 years, with a mean age of 8 years. These children were from Mount Carmel, an upper-middle-class community in which most people have a relatively high income. The children, who were spending their vacation at a summer day camp, had already been together for several weeks and therefore knew each other quite well. This particular group of urban children was chosen because they were quite similar to kibbutz children in intelligence and opportunities for development.

In both samples, by far the majority of the children had been born in Israel.

Apparatus

The Madsen Cooperation Board was used. This board is 18 inches square with an eyelet fastened to each of the four corners. Strings strung through each eyelet are connected to a metal weight which serves as a holder for a ball-point pen filler. A sheet of paper is placed on the board for each trial, thus recording the movement of the pen as Ss pull their

strings. Because the string passes through the eyelets, any individual child can pull the pen only toward himself. In order to draw a line through the circles, the children must work together. The essential features of the apparatus and position of circles to be crossed can be seen in Figure 1.

Experiment 1

The purpose of this experiment was to train the Ss in playing the game in a cooperative manner so the children would know how to play cooperatively under the individual reward condition, if motivated to do so. It

Figure 1
Madsen Cooperation Board

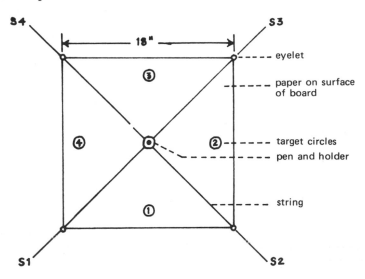

would also reveal whether there was any pre-existing tendency to behave competitively or cooperatively.

Procedure

Two treatment conditions, Group Reward (GR) and Individual Reward (IR), were compared over three trials. In trials 1–3 (GR), all four children received a prize as soon as the group was able to draw a line through the four circles within the time allowed. In trials 4–6 (IR), each of the four players had his own circle and would receive a prize only when his circle was crossed.

Four children of the same sex and approximately the same age were

taken from the group (either kibbutz or city) into a separate room. The experimental board was set on a low table. The four children were seated at the four corners of the board and told that they were going to play a game. The children were instructed to hold on to the handles, one in each hand, and to listen to the instructions of the game.

Instructions for Trials 1 – 3

> As you can see, when we pull the strings, the pen draws lines. In this game we are going to pull the strings and draw lines, but in a special way. The aim of the game is for you to draw a line over the four circle within 1 minute. If you succeed in doing this, each one of you will get a prize. If you cover the four circles twice, everyone will get two prizes, and so on. But if you cover less than four circles no one will get a prize. You may talk to each other but are not allowed to touch another child's string or handle. Are there any questions?

While the children were playing the game, E announced the number of circles crossed and also announced when a round of four circles was completed. When 1 minute was up, the children were stopped and E announced and recorded the number of rounds and extra circles the children had crossed.

At this point each child was given a paper bag with his name on it, and the prizes were given out in accordance with the number of rounds completed. Trial 1 was completed and a new sheet of paper was attached to the board. The procedure was repeated for the second and third trials.

Instructions for Trials 4 – 6

> Now the game is going to be somewhat different. Now every one of you gets his own circle. This is David's circle [E writes name on a circle to the right of David]. This is Ron's circle [etc.]. Now, when the pen draws a line across one of the circles, the child whose name is in the circle gets a prize. When it crosses David's circle, David gets a prize; when it crosses Ron's circle, Ron gets a prize, and so on. You will have 1 minute to play before I stop you. Are there any questions?

During this trial, E announced every time a circle was crossed. When the trial was over, E announced and recorded, for each child, the number of times his circle had been crossed. Prizes were given out accordingly. Trials 5 and 6 followed the same procedure as trial 4.

Results

Figure 2 shows the mean number of circles crossed by the two subcultural samples under the group and individual reward conditions. It was

indicated by t tests that there were no significant differences between city and kibbutz groups for any of the three GR trials or for the three trials combined. Similar tests indicated significant differences between these groups after the introduction of individual reward (trial 4, $p < .01$; trials 5 and 6, $p < .05$). Both groups crossed fewer circles on trial 4 than on trial 3. While the average drop from trial 3 to trial 4 for city groups was 10.1 circles, the average drop in the kibbutz was 5.6 circles. This difference in the amount of decrease was significant at the .05 level (t test).

Observation indicated that this lowered performance occurred for different reasons. On trial 4, most city groups began competing, thus reducing drastically the number of circles crossed. The kibbutz groups, on the other hand, simply slowed down. The reason for this could have been either because they made an effort to avoid competition or because they were adjusting to the new rules as if it were a different game. It can also be seen from Figure 2 that the kibbutz groups recovered on trials 5

Figure 2
Mean Number of Circles Crossed Per Trial by Kibbutz and Urban Children.

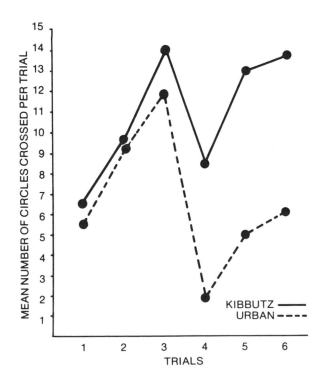

and 6, whereas the city groups never regained the level of performance attained under the GR condition.

The same pattern of results occurred for both sexes. The mean circles crossed by boys and girls under GR within both groups was nearly identical. However, the difference between kibbutz and city groups under the IR condition was greater for the boys. The mean circles crossed by urban boys was 30.6 fewer than by kibbutz boys, whereas the urban girls crossed a mean of 12.8 fewer circles than the kibbutz girls (trials ans Ss collapsed).

Experiment II

The purpose of this experiment was to compare the behavior of kibbutz and city children in a situation where competition is an adaptive behavior. Since in this situation the circles were at the corners of the page, it was possible for a competitive child to win more prizes than the others by pulling the string sharply toward himself and drawing a line through his own circle.

Procedure

The circles were drawn at the corners of the page so that each child had a circle directly in front of him. The following instructions were given:

> As you see, the circles are now at the corners of the page. This time the game is somewhat different so listen carefully. Again everyone has his own circle. [*E* writes each child's name in the circle closest to him.] Now, when the pen draws a line across the circle of one of the children, that child will get a prize. At this point, we shall stop the game and return the pen to the center of the page and begin again. We will do this four times without changing the page. Are there any questions?

When a line was drawn across one of the circles, *E* stopped the game and recorded the time of the trial and the order. The child whose circle was crossed received a prize. The same procedure was carried out for trials 2, 3, and 4. If no circle was crossed within a minute, *E* stopped the game and began a new trial.

When the experiment was over, *E* gave prizes to those children who had not won many during the game, so that all children received about the same number of prizes. Although the prizes were of little value (candy, gum, and small plastic charms) they were effective reinforcers, as demonstrated by the children's eagerness to work for them.

Results

Any line which passed through an individual circle without deviating

more than 1 inch from the direct path from the center starting point to the circle, and which did not reverse directions within those limits, was considered a noncompetitive response. Lines which violated these criteria were considered competition in that they indicated that children were pulling against each other.

Table 1 gives the mean number of noncompetitive responses for four trials for the two groups, by sex.

Table 1
Mean Noncompetitive Responses for Kibbutz and Urban Children by Sex

Group	Female	Male
Kibbutz	2.8	2.4
Urban	2.2	0.6

Kibbutz groups had more noncompetitive responses than urban groups (mean 2.6 vs. 1.4, respectively), but this difference only approaches significance ($t = 1.70$ $p < .05 < .10$).

Most of the differences between kibbutz and city groups can be attributed to the fact that the city boys were more competitive than city girls as well as both boys and girls from the kibbutzim.

Discussion

The hypothesis that kibbutz children would show more cooperative behavior than city children in Israel was confirmed. Under the individual reward condition in Experiment I, the kibbutz children showed performance superior to that of the city children. Since both groups had learned the task equally well, as evidenced by their similar performances under the group reward condition, differences in performance under the individual reward condition can be attributed to different types of motivational stress in urban and kibbutz environments. Thus, changes in instructions produced different behaviors in city children but not in kibbutz children. The slight improvement in performance for kibbutz groups under the individual reward condition probably reflects the effect of practice as the children continue to follow the cooperative techniques adopted under the group reward condition. Once reward was given out on an individual basis, city children changed the tactics they had used to obtain group rewards and began pulling toward themselves. Even though they obviously realized, after trials 4 and 5, that these competitive procedures were not paying off for any of them, they were unable to stop their irrational competition.

Perhaps of greater interest is the fact that the children themselves did not enjoy the competition and wanted to change the rules. A number of

children kept asking *E* not to write names on the circles, evidently realizing that as long as there were names on the circles they would continue to compete.

At times a child would suggest that they take turns, or help each other, but usually the other children refused. In some isolated cases, the children agreed to cooperate, but the instant one child pulled a little harder, cooperation broke down completely and they all started pulling toward themselves.

Among the kibbutz groups the picture was entirely different. When individual reward instructions were introduced, the first response of most of the groups was to set up rules for cooperation. Some examples of these responses were: "OK gang, let's go in turns," or "Let's help each other," or "We'll start here, then here," etc. Some groups asked *E* if they were allowed to help each other or whether they could go in rounds like before. When *E* said they could do as they wished, they always decided upon cooperation. These children were very organized in their performance. They usually had decided the order before the trial began. During the game they were also very active in directing one another.

The kibbutz children were very eager to do well as a group and tried their best to improve their performance on every subsequent trial. Some of the groups asked to compare their results with other groups and wanted to know what the best score had ever been. Such responses indicate that a desire to achieve and to do well characterizes these children, who do compete with other groups on the kibbutz but not within their group. At the group level, they cooperate and work together as a team.

In most of the kibbutz groups there was a great concern about equality in prizes ("Every one should get the same"). They were so concerned about this that, in many cases, they rotated the starting point so that if they were stopped before a round was completed a different child would get the extra prize on each trial. When, in some isolated cases, one of the children tried to compete against the others, the group usually restrained him.

In general, the results and observations indicate that, when cooperative behavior was adaptive, children of the kibbutz were generally able to cooperate successfully for maximum performance, whereas urban children were usually not able to do so.

Many aspects of kibbutz life and collective education are potentially competitive. The children of the kibbutz, more than those of the city, must compete for the nurses' attention and affection, must compete for the toys they play with, etc. It is possible that because of this, the development of cooperative tendencies is so instrumental to proper functioning of the group and that, without such a development, conflict would be exceptionally severe.

References

Goodman, M. E. *Race awareness in young children*. Cambridge, Mass.: Addison-Wesley, 1952.

McKee, J. P., & Leader, F. The relationship of socioeconomic status and aggression to the competitive behavior of preschool children. *Child Development*, 1955, **26**, 175–182.

Madsen M. C. Cooperative and competitive motivation of children in three Mexican subcultures. *Psychological Reports,* 1967, 20, 1307–1320.

Nelson, L., & Madsen, M. C. Cooperation and competition in four-year-olds as a function of availability of reward and subculture. *Developmental Psychology,* in press.

Rabin, A. I. *Growing up in the kibbutz*. New York: Springer, 1965.

Sampson, E. E., & Kardush, M. Age, sex, class, and race differences in response to a two-person non-zero-sum game. *Journal of Conflict Resolution,* 1965, **9**, 212–220.

Spiro, M. E. *Children of the kibbutz*. Cambridge, Mass.: Harvard University Press, 1965.

5.6   Superordinate Goals in the Reduction of Intergroup Conflict

Muzafer Sherif

In the past, measures to combat the problems of intergroup conflicts, proposed by social scientists as well as by such people as administrators, policy-makers, municipal officials, and educators, have included the following: introduction of legal sanctions; creation of opportunities for social and other contacts among members of conflicting groups; dissemination of correct information to break down false prejudices and unfavorable stereotypes; appeals to the moral ideals of fair play and brotherhood; and even the introduction of rigorous physical activity to produce catharsis by releasing pent-up frustrations and aggressive complexes in the unconscious. Other measures proposed include the encouragement of co-operative habits in

Reprinted from the *American Journal of Sociology*, 1958, LXIII, no. 4, 349-356, by permission of the author and the University of Chicago Press. Copyright 1958 by the University of Chicago.

one's own community, and bringing together in the cozy atmosphere of a meeting room the leaders of antagonistic groups.

Many of these measures may have some value in the reduction of intergroup conflicts, but, to date, very few generalizations have been established concerning the circumstances and kinds of intergroup conflict in which these measures are effective. Today measures are applied in a somewhat trial-and-error fashion. Finding measures that have wide validity in practice can come only through clarification of the nature of intergroup conflict and analysis of the factors conducive to harmony and conflict between groups under given conditions.

The task of defining and analyzing the natue of the problem was undertaken in a previous publication.[1] One of our major statements was the effectiveness of superordinate goals for the reduction of intergroup conflict. "Superordinate goals" we defined as goals which are compelling and highly appealing to members of two or more groups in conflict but which cannot be attained by the resources and energies of the groups separately. In effect, they are goals attained only when groups pull together.

Intergroup Relations and The Behavior of Group Members

Not every friendly or unfriendly act toward another person is related to the group membership of the individuals involved. Accordingly, we must select those actions relevant to relations between groups.

Let us start by defining the main concepts involved. Obviously, we must begin with an adequate conception of the key term—"group." A group is a social unit (1) which consists of a number of individuals who, at a given time, stand in more or less definite interdependent status and role relationships with one another and (2) which explicitly or implicitly possesses a set of values or norms regulating the behavior of individual members, at least in matters of consequence to the group. Thus, shared attitudes, sentiments, aspirations, and goals are related to and implicit in the common values or norms of the group.

The term "intergroup relations" refers to the relations between two or more groups and their respective members. In the present context we are interested in the acts that occur when individuals belonging to one group interact, collectively or individually, with members of another in terms of their group identification. The appropriate frame of reference for studying such behavior includes the functional relations between the groups. Intergroup situations are not voids. Though not independent of relationships within the groups in question, *the characteristics of relations between groups cannot be deduced or extrapolated from the properties of in-group relations.*

Prevalent modes of behavior within a group, in the way of co-operativeness and solidarity or competitiveness and rivalry among members, need not be typical of actions involving members of an out-group. At times, hostility

toward out-groups may be proportional to the degree of solidarity within the group. In this connection, results presented by the British statistician L. F. Richardson are instructive. His analysis of the number of wars conducted by the major nations of the world from 1850 to 1941 reveals that Great Britain heads the list with twenty wars—more than the Japanese (nine wars), the Germans (eight wars), or the United States (seven wars). We think that this significantly larger number of wars engaged in by a leading European democracy has more to do with the intergroup relations involved in perpetuating a far-flung empire than with dominant practices at home or with personal frustrations of individual Britishers who participated in these wars.[2]

In recent years relationships between groups have sometimes been explained through analysis of individuals who have endured unusual degrees of frustration or extensive authoritarian treatment in their life-histories. There is good reason to believe that some people growing up in unfortunate life-circumstances may become more intense in their prejudices and hostilities. But at best these cases explain the intensity of behavior in a given dimension.[3] In a conflict between two groups—a strike or a war—opinion within the groups is crystallized, slogans are formulated, and effective measures are organized by members recognized as the most responsible in their respective groups. The prejudice scale and the slogans are not usually imposed on the others by the deviate or neurotic members. Such individuals ordinarily exhibit their intense reactions within the reference scales of prejudice, hostility, or sacrifice established in their respective settings.

The behavior by members of any group toward another group is not primarily a problem of deviate behavior. If it were, intergroup behavior would not be the issue of vital consequence that it is today. The crux of the problem is the participation by group members in established practices and social-distance norms of their group and their response to new trends developing in relationships between their own group and other groups.

On the basis of his UNESCO studies in India, Gardner Murphy concludes that to be a good Hindu or a good Moslem implies belief in all the nasty qualities and practices attributed by one's own group—Hindu or Moslem—to the other. Good members remain deaf and dumb to favorable information concerning the adversary. Social contacts and avenues of communication serve, on the whole, as vehicles for further conflicts not merely for neurotic individuals but for the bulk of the membership.[4]

In the process of interaction among members, an in-group is endowed with positive qualities which tend to be praiseworthy, self-justifying, and even self-glorifying. Individual members tend to develop these qualities through internalizing group norms and through example by high-status members, verbal dicta, and a set of correctives standardized to deal with cases of deviation. Hence, possession of these qualities, which reflect their particular brand of ethnocentrism, is not essentially a problem of deviation or personal frustration. It is a question of participation in in-group values and

trends by good members, who constitute the majority of membership as long as group solidarity and morale are maintained.

To out-groups and their respective members are attributed positive or negative qualities, depending on the nature of functional relations between the groups in question. The character of functional relations between groups may result from actual harmony and interdependence or from actual incompatibility between the aspirations and directions of the groups. A number of field studies and experiments indicate that, if the functional relations between groups are positive, favorable attitudes are formed toward the out-group. If the functional relations between groups are negative, they give rise to hostile attitudes and unfavorable stereotypes in relation to the out-group. Of course, in large group units the picture of the out-group and relations with it depend very heavily on communication, particularly from the mass media.

Examples of these processes are recurrent in studies of small groups. For example, when a gang "appropriates" certain blocks in a city, it is considered "indecent" and a violation of its "rights" for another group to carry on its feats in that area. Intrusion by another group is conducive to conflict, at times with grim consequences, as Thrasher showed over three decades ago.[5]

When a workers' group declares a strike, existing group lines are drawn more sharply. Those who are not actually for the strike are regarded as against it. There is no creature more lowly than the man who works while the strike is on.[6] The same type of behavior is found in management groups under similar circumstances.

In time, the adjectives attributed to out-groups take their places in the repertory of group norms. The lasting, derogatory stereotypes attributed to groups low on the social-distance scale are particular cases of group norms pertaining to out-groups.

As studies by Bogardus show, the social-distance scale of a group, once established, continues over generations, despite changes of constituent individuals, who can hardly be said to have prejudices because of the same severe personal frustrations or authoritarian treatment.[7]

Literature on the formation of prejudice by growing children shows that it is not even necessary for the individual to have actual unfavorable experiences with out-groups to form attitudes of prejudice toward them. In the very process of becoming an in-group member, the intergroup delineations and corresponding norms prevailing in the group are internalized by the individual.[8]

A Research Program

A program of research has been under way since 1948 to test experimentally some hypotheses derived from the literature of intergroup relations.

The first large-scale intergroup experiment was carried out in 1949, the second in 1953, and the third in 1954.[9] The conclusions reported here briefly are based on the 1949 and 1954 experiments and on a series of laboratory studies carried out as co-ordinate parts of the program.[10]

The methodology, techniques, and criteria for subject selection in the experiments must be summarized here very briefly. The experiments were carried out in successive stages: (1) groups were formed experimentally; (2) tension and conflict were produced between these groups by introducing conditions conducive to competitive and reciprocally frustrating relations between them; and (3) the attempt was made toward reduction of the intergroup conflict. This stage of reducing tension through introduction of superordinate goals was attempted in the 1954 study on the basis of lessons learned in the two previous studies.

At every stage the subjects interacted in activities which appeared natural to them at a specially arranged camp site completely under our experimental control. They were not aware of the fact that their behavior was under observation. No observation or recording was made in the subjects' presence in a way likely to arouse the suspicion that they were being observed. There is empirical and experimental evidence contrary to the contention that individuals cease to be mindful when they know they are being observed and that their words are being recorded.[11]

In order to insure validity of conclusions, results obtained through observational methods were cross-checked with results obtained through sociometric technique, stereotype ratings of in-groups and out-groups, and through data obtained by techniques adapted from the laboratory. Unfortunately, these procedures cannot be elaborated here. The conclusions summarized briefly are based on results crosschecked by two or more techniques.

The production of groups, the production of conflict between them, and the reduction of conflict in successive stages were brought about through the introduction of problem situations that were real and could not be ignored by individuals in the situation. Special "lecture methods" or "discussion methods" were not used. For example, the problem of getting a meal through their own initiative and planning was introduced when participating individuals were hungry.

Facing a problem situation which is immediate and compelling and which embodies a goal that cannot be ignored, group members *do* initiate discussion and *do* plan and carry through these plans until the objective is achieved. In this process the discussion becomes *their* discussion, the plan *their* plan, the action *their* action. In this process discussion, planning, and action have their place, and, when occasion arises, lecture or information has its place, too. The sequence of these related activities need not be the same in all cases.

The subjects were selected by rigorous criteria. They were healthy,

normal boys around the age of eleven and twelve, socially well adjusted in school and neighborhood, and academically successful. They came from a homogeneous sociocultural background and from settled, well-adjusted families of middle or lower-middle class and Protestant affiliations. No subject came from a broken home. The mean I.Q. was above average. The subjects were not personally acquainted with one another prior to the experiment. Thus, explanation of results on the basis of background differences, social maladjustment, undue childhood frustrations, or previous interpersonal relations was ruled out at the beginning by the criteria for selecting subjects.

The first stage of the experiments was designed to produce groups with distinct structure (organization) and a set of norms which could be confronted with intergroup problems. The method for producing groups from unacquainted individuals with similar background was to introduce problem situations in which the attainment of the goal depended on the co-ordinated activity of all individuals. After a series of such activities, definite group structures or organizations developed.

The results warrant the following conclusions for the stage of group formation: When individuals interact in a series of situations toward goals which appeal to all and which require that they co-ordinate their activities, group structures arise having hierarchical status arrangements and a set of norms regulating behavior in matters of consequence to the activities of the group.

Once we had groups that satisfied our definition of "group," relations between groups could be studied. Specified conditions conducive to friction or conflict between groups were introduced. This negative aspect was deliberately undertaken because the major problem in intergroup relations today is the reduction of existing intergroup frictions (Increasingly, friendly relations between groups is not nearly so great an issue.) The factors conducive to intergroup conflict give us realistic leads for reducing conflict.

A series of situations was introduced in which one group could achieve its goal only at the expense of the other group—through a tournament of competitive events with desirable prizes for the winning group. The results of the stage of intergroup conflict supported our main hypotheses. During interaction between groups in experimentally introduced activities which were competitive and mutually frustrating, members of each group developed hostile attitudes and highly unfavorable stereotypes toward the other group and its members. In fact, attitudes of social distance between the groups became so definite that they wanted to have nothing further to do with each other. This we take as a case of experimentally produced "social distance" in miniature. Conflict was manifested in derogatory name-calling and invectives, flare-ups of physical conflict, and raids on each other's cabins and territory. Over a period of time, negative stereotypes and unfavorable attitudes developed.

At the same time there was an increase in in-group solidarity and co-operativeness. This finding indicates that co-operation and democracy within groups do not necessarily lead to democracy and co-operation with out-groups, if the directions and interests of the groups are conflicting.

Increased solidarity forged in hostile encounters, in rallies from defeat, and in victories over the out-group is one instance of a more general finding: Intergroup relations, both conflicting and harmonious, *affected the nature of relations within the groups involved.* Altered relations between groups produced significant changes in the status arrangements *within* groups, in some instances resulting in shifts at the upper status levels or even a change in leadership. Always, consequential intergroup relations were reflected in new group values or norms which signified changes in practice, word, and deed within the group. Counterparts of this finding are not difficult to see in actual and consequential human relations. Probably many of our major preoccupations, anxieties, and activities in the past decade are incomprehensible without reference to the problems created by the prevailing "cold war" on an international scale.

Reduction of Intergroup Friction

A number of the measures proposed today for reducing intergroup friction could have been tried in this third stage. A few will be mentioned here, with a brief explanation of why they were discarded or were included in our experimental design.

1. Disseminating favorable information in regard to the out-group was not included. Information that is not related to the goals currently in focus in the activities of groups is relatively ineffective, as many studies on attitude change have shown.[12]

2. In small groups it is possible to devise sufficiently attractive rewards to make individual achievement supreme. This may reduce tension between groups by splitting the membership on an "every-man-for-himself" basis. However, this measure has little relevance for actual intergroup tensions, which are in terms of group membership and group alignments.

3. The resolution of conflict through leaders alone was not utilized. Even when group leaders meet apart from their groups around a conference table, they cannot be considered independent of the dominant trends and prevailing attitudes of their membership. If a leader is too much out of step in his negotiations and agreements with out-groups, he will cease to be followed. It seemed more realistic, therefore, to study the influence of leadership within the framework of prevailing trends in the groups involved. Such results will give us leads concerning the conditions under which leadership can be effective in reducing intergroup tensions.

4. The "common-enemy" approach is effective in pulling two or more

groups together against another group. This approach was utilized in the 1949 experiment as an expedient measure and yielded effective results. But bringing some groups together against others means larger and more devastatinf conflicts in the long run. For this reason, the measure was not used in the 1954 experiment.

5. Another measure, advanced both in theoretical and in practical work, centers around social contacts among members of antagonistic groups in activities which are pleasant in themselves. This measure was tried out in 1954 in the first phase of the integration stage.

6. As the second phase of the integration stage, we introduced a series of superordinate goals which necessitated co-operative interaction between groups.

The social contact situations consisted of activities which were satisfying in themselves—eating together in the same dining room, watching a movie in the same hall, or engaging in an entertainment in close physical proximity. These activities, which were satisfying to each group, but which did not involve a state of interdependence and co-operation for the attainment of goals, were not effective in reducing inter-group tension. On the contrary, such occasions of contact were utilized as opportunities to engage in name-calling and in abuse of each other to the point of physical manifestations of hostility.

The ineffective, even deleterious, results of intergroup contact without superordinate goals have implications for certain contemporary learning theories and for practice in intergroup relations. Contiguity in pleasant activities with members of an out-group does not necessarily lead to a pleasurable image of the out-group if relations between the groups are unfriendly. Intergroup contact without superordinate goals is not likely to produce lasting reduction of inter-group hostility. John Gunther, for instance, in his survey of contemporary Africa, concluded that, when the intergroup relationship is exploitation of one group by a "superior" group, intergroup contact inevitably breeds hostility and conflict.[13]

Introduction of Superordinate Goals

After establishing the ineffectiveness, even the harm, in intergroup contacts which did not involve superordinate goals, we introduced a series of superordinate goals. Since the characteristics of the problem situations used as superordinate goals are implicit in the two main hypotheses for this stage, we shall present these hypotheses:

1. When groups in a state of conflict are brought into contact under conditions embodying superordinate goals, which are compelling but cannot be achieved by the efforts of one group alone, they will tend to co-operate toward the common goals.

2. Co-operation between groups, necessitated by a series of situations embodying superordinate goals, will have a cumulative effect in the direction of reducing existing conflict between groups.

The problem situations were varied in nature, but all had an essential feature in common—they involved goals that could not be attained by the efforts and energies of one group alone and thus created a state of interdependence between groups: combating a water shortage that affected all and could not help being "compelling"; securing a much-desired film, which could not be obtained by either group alone but required putting their resources together; putting into working shape, when everyone was hungry and the food was some distance away, the only means of transportation available to carry food.

The introduction of a series of such superordinate goals was indeed effective in reducing intergroup conflict: (1) when the groups in a state of friction interacted in conditions involving superordinate goals, they did co-operate in activities leading toward the common goal and (2) a series of joint activities leading toward superordinate goals had the cumulative effect of reducing the prevailing friction between groups and unfavorable stereotypes toward the out-group.

These major conclusions were reached on the basis of observational data and were confirmed by sociometric choices and sterotype ratings administered first during intergroup conflict and again after the introduction of a series of superordinate goals. Comparison of the sociometric choices during intergroup conflict and following the series of superordinate goals shows clearly the changed attitudes toward members of the out-group. Friendship preferences shifted from almost exclusive preference for in-group members toward increased inclusion of members from the "antagonists." Since the groups were still intact following co-operative efforts to gain superordinate goals, friends were found largely within one's group. However, choices of out-group members grew, in one group, from practically none during intergroup conflict to 23 per cent. Using chi square, this difference is significant ($P < .05$). In the other group, choices of the out-group increased to 36 per cent, and the difference is significant ($P < .001$). The findings confirm observations that the series of superordinate goals produced increasingly friendly associations and attitudes pertaining to out-group members.

Observations made after several superordinate goals were introduced showed a sharp decrease in the name-calling and derogation of the out-group common during intergroup friction and in the contact situations without superordinate goals. At the same time the blatant glorification and bragging about the in-group, observed during the period of conflict, diminished. These observations were confirmed by comparison of ratings of stereotypes (adjectives) the subjects had actually used in referring to their

own group and the out-group during conflict with ratings made after the series of superordinate goals. Ratings of the out-group changed significantly from largely unfavorable ratings to largely favorable ratings. The proportions of the most unfavorable ratings found appropriate for the out-group —that is, the categorical verdicts that "all of them are stinkers" or ". . . smart alecks" or ". . . sneaky"—fell, in one group, from 21 percent at the end of the friction stage to 1.5 per cent after interaction oriented toward superordinate goals. The corresponding reduction in these highly unfavorable verdicts by the other group was from 36.5 to 6 per cent. The over-all differences between the frequencies of stereotype ratings made in relation to the out-group during intergroup conflict and following the series of superordinate goals are significant for both groups at the .001 level (using chi-square test).

Ratings of the in-group were not so exclusively favorable, in line with observed decreases in self-glorification. But the differences in ratings of the in-group were not statistically significant, as were the differences in ratings of the out-group.

Our findings demonstrate the effectiveness of a series of superordinate goals in the reduction of intergroup conflict, hostility, and their by-products. They also have implications for other measures proposed for reducing intergroup tensions.

It is true that lines of communication between groups must be opened before prevailing hostility can be reduced. But, if contact between hostile groups, takes place without superordinate goals, the communication channels serve as media for further accusations and recriminations. When contact situations involve superordinate goals, communications is utilized in the direction of reducing conflict in order to attain the common goals.

Favorable information about a disliked out-group tends to be ignored, rejected. or reinterpreted to fit prevailing stereotypes. But, when groups are pulling together toward superordinate goals, true and even favorable information about the out-group is seen in a new light. The probability of information being effective in eliminating unfavorable stereotypes is enormously enhanced.

When groups co-operate in the attainment of superordinate goals, leaders are in a position to take bolder steps toward bringing about understanding and harmonious relations. When groups are directed toward incompatible goals, genuine moves by a leader to reduce intergroup tension may be seen by the membership as out of step and ill advised. The leader may be subjected to severe criticism and even loss of faith and status in his own group. When compelling superordinate goals are introduced, the leader can make moves to further co-operative efforts, and his decisions receive support from other group members.

In short, various measures suggested for the reduction of intergroup

conflict—disseminating information, increasing social contact, conferences of leaders—acquire new significance and effectiveness when they become part and parcel of interaction processes between groups oriented toward superordinate goals which have real and compelling value for all groups concerned.

INSTITUTE OF GROUP RELATIONS

UNIVERSITY OF OKLAHOMA

Notes

1 Muzafer Sherif and Carolyn W. Sherif, *Groups in Harmony and Tension* (New York: Harper & Bros. 1953).

2 T. H. Pear, *Psychological Factors of Peace and War* (New York: Philosophical Library, 1950), p. 126.

3 William R. Hood and Muzafer Sherif, "Personality Oriented Approaches to Prejudice," *Sociology and Social Research,* XL (1955), 79—85.

4 Gardner Murphy, *In the Minds of Men* (New York: Basic Books, 1953).

5 F. M. Thrasher, *The Gang* (Chicago: University of Chicago Press, 1927).

6 E. T. Hiller, *The Strike* (Chicago: University of Chicago Press, 1928).

7 E. S. Bogardus, "Changes in Racial Distances," *International Journal of Opinion and Attitude Research,* I (1947), 55-62.

8 E. L. Horowitz, " 'Race Attitudes,' " in Otto Klineberg (ed.), *Characteristics of the American Negro,* Part IV (New York: Harper & Bros., 1944).

9 The experimental work in 1949 was jointly supported by the Yale Attitude Change Project and the American Jewish Committee. It is summarized in Sherif and Sherif, *op. cit.,* chaps. ix and x. Both the writing of that book and the experiments in 1953-54 were made possible by a grant from the Rockefeller Foundation. The 1953 research is summarized in Muzafer Sherif, B. Jack White, and O. J. Harvey, "Status in Experimentally Produced Groups," *American Journal of Sociology,* LX (1955), 370-79. The 1954 experiment was summarized in Muzafer Sherif, O. J. Harvey, B. Jack White, William R. Hood, and Carolyn W. Sherif, "Experimental Study of Positive and Negative Intergroup Attitudes between Experimentally Produced Groups: Robbers Cave Study" (Norman, Okla.: University of Oklahoma, 1954). (Multilithed.) For a summary of the three experiments see chaps. vi and ix in Muzafer Sherif and Carolyn W. Sherif, *An Outline of Social Psychology* (rev. ed.; New York: Harper & Bros., 1956).

10 For an overview of this program see Muzafer Sherif, "Integrating Field Work and Laboratory in Small Group Research," *American Sociological Review,* XIX (1954), 759-71.

11 E.g., see F. B. Miller, " 'Resistentialism' in Applied Social Research," *Human Organization,* XII (1954), 5-8; S. Wapner and T. G. Alper, "The Effect of an Audience on Behavior in a Choice Situation," *Journal of Abnormal and Social Psychology,* XLVII (1952), 222-29.

12 E.g., see R. M. Williams, *The Reduction of Intergroup Tensions* (Social Science Research Council Bull. 57 [New York, 1947]).

13 John Gunther, *Inside Africa* (New York: Harper & Bros., 1955).

5.7 Birth Order and its Sequelae

William D. Altus

The relation of order of birth to achievement has been investigated for nearly a hundred years. The first known data appear in Sir Francis Galton's *English Men of Science*, published in 1874. Galton selected his scientists according to objective criteria, such as being a Fellow of the Royal Society, and then asked them for biographical data, including their order of birth. He found more only sons and first-born sons among them than his calculations showed chance should have allowed. This finding he thought easy to interpret: Through the law of primogeniture, the eldest son was likely to become possessed of independent means and to be able to follow his own tastes and inclinations. Further, Galton argued, parents treated an only child and a first-born child (who is an only child for a period of time) as a companion and accorded him more responsibility than other children were given. Thus first arrivals on the family scene were favored from the start.

A generation later Havelock Ellis (*1*) published *A Study of British Genius*, based on 975 eminent men and 55 eminent women selected from the 66 volumes of the *Dictionary of National Biography*. In the main, he chose those to whom three or more pages were devoted in this dictionary, but excluded those who were of nobility and also those whom he judged to be notorious rather than famous. Among those eminent people, Ellis found some striking linkages to order of birth: The probability of appearance was much greater for a first-born than for an intermediate child, and the youngest likewise was favored over the intermediate child, though not to the same degree. Ellis does not interpret his finding; he merely reports that it is congruent with an American study (*2*) published a decade earlier:

> This predominance of eldest and youngest children among persons of genius accords with the results reached by Yoder in studying an international group of 50 eminent men; he found that youngest sons occurred oftener than intermediate sons and eldest sons than youngest.

About the time Ellis published his survey of eminent Britishers, the American psychologist Cattell (*3*) published data based on 855 American scientists, which showed the same relation between birth order and eminence, the eldest and then the youngest being favored.

Reprinted from *Science*, 7 Jan. 1966, *151*, No. 3706, 44–49, by permission of the author and the American Association for the Advancement of Science. Copyright 1972 by the American Association for the Advancement of Science.

In 1915, Corrado Gini (4) showed a linkage between order of birth and being a university professor. From 445 replies to a questionnaire he sent to his fellow professors in Italian universities, he found that twice as many were first-born as would have been expected from chance, and that all the other birth orders were below expectancy or no higher than expectancy. Gini's published data do not allow comparisons between the youngest and the in-between. I report these data with considerable diffidence, since most of us have had personal experience with university professors who would not qualify as eminent people, no matter how lax a criterion one employed. Still, it is of some interest to know that the first-born also takes precedence in the academic milieu, if data gathered a half century ago in Italy have generality beyond that time and place.

In his dissertation, on the nature and nurture of American men of letters, E. L. Clarke (5) reported that eldest and youngest sons appeared in greater than chance numbers. He rationalized his findings in a somewhat different way from his predecessors:

> First-born and last-born children frequently enjoy greater educational opportunity than do their intermediate brothers and sisters. First borns often succeed in getting a start before adversity befalls the family, or before the expense of caring for an increasing family of young children becomes so great that it is necessary to curtail the education of some of the older children.

He also notes that the youngest comes along when older brothers may be grown up and in a position to help the youngest through school.

In 1938, the American geographer Ellsworth Huntington published a book (6) primarily concerned with what he felt were sequelae of one's season of birth. He collected data on 1210 Americans whom he thought to be the most distinguished of those vitae he found in genealogical works. Of those who came from two-child families, 59 were first-born and 33 were second-born. While his finding is typical of all those reported thus far, his explanation of the linkage is not typical: He argued that the first-born probably tend to be physically stronger and healthier. The more vigorous eminent, he claimed, tended to be born early in the year (perhaps, though he doesn't say so, as the first fruits of the traditional June wedding). One may safely accept his data on the birth order of the eminent without accepting his explanation.

In a study of the birth order on Rhodes Scholars, mainly those from the United States, Apperly (7) found the first-born to be overrepresented. Among two-child family representatives, 144 were first-born, 91 second-born. He also found the youngest child to take precedence over the in-between one.

Jones (8) gives some statistics on birth order of persons listed in *Who's Who*. Some of 64 percent of the representatives of two-child fam-

ilies were first-born; if inclusion in *Who's Who* were a strictly chance affair, one would expect, of course, a 50–50 distribution on the older and the younger from two-child families. Of the three-child family representatives 52 percent were first-born, instead of the 33 percent to be expected.

The last of the studies relating to eminence to be reviewed here, though it is by no means the lates, it that by Anne Roe (9), who published in 1953 her researches on 64 eminent scientists, selected for their distinguished contributions by the elder statesmen in their respective specialties. Thirty-nine, of 61 percent, were first-born. But the evidence for primogeniture of talent is even more overwhelming, according to Roe:

> Of the 25 scientists in my groups who were not first born, five are oldest sons, and two of the second born were effectively the oldest during their childhood because of the death of older sibs, one at birth, one at age two.

Therefore, Roe concludes, some 46 of the 64 – 72 percent – were actually or effectively the oldest sons in their respective families. Roe's data corroborate in an accentuated way all the evidence which has been marshalled on the topic of birth order and eminence, beginning with Galton's study in 1874. I have found no study that shows trends divergent from those here reported.

Birth Order and Intelligence

Forty years ago Lewis Madison Terman published the first volume (*10*) of his studies of 1000 "gifted" school children – that is, children with IQ's of 140 or higher, which is the IQ of the top 1 percent of the general population. Most of these children came from small families; only a few came from families of five or more children. Among those from families of two, three, and four children, Terman found the eldest the most numerous, followed by the youngest, and then by the in-between children. Terman noted that the breakdown was quite similar to the one Cattell had found for eminent American scientists some 20 years before, but he did not attempt to bind these separate studies together by theory.

Terman's findings, which indicate that – at least among the very bright – birth order may be of some significance, have to my knowledge never been checked on a large sample until quite recently. In June 1964, Robert C. Nichols, of the National Merit Scholarship Corporation, sent me some data (*11*) on 1618 high school students who were finalists in the National Merit competition and who earned exceptionally high scores among this restricted group. Nichols reports the average score of this

selected group of finalists to be "almost three standard deviations above the mean of the general population," which would imply an aptitude at least in the top 0.5 percent of the general population. This level of aptitude is superior to that of Terman's gifted group. Nichols reported that of the 568 representatives of the two-child family, 66 percent were first-born. Of the 414 from three child families, 52 percent were first-born; the other two ranks obviously contributed 48 percent. Of the 244 students from four-child families, 59 percent were first born, the other three ranks contributing 41 percent. Of the 85 representatives of the five-child family, 52 percent were first-born, the other *four* birth ranks contributing 48 percent. In summary, nearly 60 percent of the Merit Finalists who came from families of two, three, four, and five children were first-born. Here is intellectual primogeniture with a vengeance! But Nichols shows that birth order is effectively linked to aptitude *only at the top level.* In the very large number of high school students who took the first round of tests before any were eliminated, birth order does not appear to be related to the scores earned. In one respect Nichols' data do not corroborate the findings on eminence: Youngest children are less numerous among his restricted Merit Finalists than the in-betweens. In fact, Nichols' data show a stairstep progression downward, from the first-born to the last in each family group, whether of two children, three children, four children, or five children.

I have found birth-order linkages to aptitude-test data among students in the University of California (*12*), about whom I have been collecting statistics since 1959. Students at this university are a select group, since in general only those applicants who rank in the top 10 to 15 percent with respect to high school grades are eligible for admission. In two samples, one consisting of 1800 undergraduates and another of 2500, the first-born scored higher to a small though statistically significant degree than did the later-born on tests of verbal intelligence, which measure such things as the size of general vocabulary and the ability to infer correctly the right words to make sense of statements from which key words have been omitted. On the other hand, measures of quantitative ability were not found to be associated with birth order per se. However, when birth order is linked to another parameter, the sex of the sibling, certain correlations are noted. First-born students, either male or female, from two-child families earned a significantly (.05 level of confidence) higher mean score on a test of quantitative ability if their siblings were male. This finding corroborates in part an earlier study by Helen Koch (*13*), who found that 5- and 6-year-old boys and girls in two-child families earned higher scores on the Primary Mental Abilities Test if the other child in the family was a boy rather than a girl. Koch's finding is independent of birth order: Having a brother for a sibling helped both the younger and

the older in the two-child family. My data on college students show a facilitating effect only for the first-born with a brother and only in a measure of quantitative ability.

Nichols' data on the National Merit Scholarship contestants suggest that there may be hierarchies of aptitude related to birth order and family size. For instance, the first-born with three siblings had the highest mean aptitude scores of all birth ranks among those who came from families of two, three, four, and five children. The mean score of contestants with two older siblings was the lowest of all these ranks, significantly lower (.01 level of confidence) than that of the first-born from four child families. My data from the University of California confirm these findings: The first-born in the four-child family is significantly brighter (.01 level of confidence) in verbal aptitude than the youngest from the three-child family; he has the highest verbal aptitude among all students who come from families of two, three, and four children—a group which accounts for four-fifths of the student population. The only child scores even higher, but he is eliminated from these comparisons because Nichols did not include the only child in his reported data. Schachter (*14*) shows the only child to be markedly overrepresented among graduate students at the University of Minnesota. These two items of data may be related: The only child may be the ablest and thus persist longer as a student.

It seems reasonable to infer from the foregoing that order of birth may well be associated with aptitude if the population is quite bright. Terman's findings, Nichols', and mine all point in this direction. The data are obviously neither conclusive nor definitive, but they are consistent and compelling. There is, additionally, some evidence that the sex of the sibling, where there is only one, may affect one's aptitude score. Finally there is a suggestion that there may be hierarchies of aptitude levels among the intellectually able related to birth order and family size.

Birth Order and College Attendance

Given the data on birth order and eminence and birth order and aptitude, one would expect to find some degree of correspondence between birth order and college attendance. I first became aware of the correspondence in tabulating the birth ranks of certain of the students on the Santa Barbara campus in 1959. During the next 4 years, 1960 through 1963, I gathered annual data for all—or nearly all—students who matriculated there for the first time. Of the 1817 representatives of the two-child family, 63 percent were first-born. The figures for men and women are almost exactly alike. During the same period, 1299 representatives of the three-child family matriculated; 50.5 percent of these were first-born; 30.8 percent were second-born, 18.7 percent were third-born.

Matriculants from four-child families numbered 538, of whom 50.5 percent were first-born, 25.8 percent second-born, 14 percent third-born, 9.7 percent fourth-born. We noted this downward progression by birth order also in Nichols' data for Merit Finalists. Here the data on college attendance and Merit Finalists part company with the data on eminence: The youngest is not favored over the intermediate sibling; he is at the bottom step in the progression.

Are the data on college attendance and birth order thus far reported merely a parochial accident? Sufficient data are not at hand for a definitive answer, but there is some evidence that it would be no. At Yale, 61 percent of an undergraduate sample proved to be first-born (15); at Reed College (16), 66 percent; at the University of Minnesota, slightly over 50 percent (14). The differences in percentages may be a function of the degree of selectivity exercised by the various institutions—the more stringent the standards for admission, the higher the percentage of first-borns. This inference is based, of course, upon what has been found in the realm of aptitude testing. If the inference proves to be correct, then public junior colleges should have the lowest percentage of first-borns, since in most states, if not all, their entrance requirements are least stringent. Cal Tech, Rice University, and Harvard should, according to this hypothesis, enroll a very high percentage of first-borns. It does not seem likely, however, that in any college the percentage should much exceed the 66 percent of the Reed College sample.

Mary Steward, in 1962, reported (17) a study of 7000 boys and girls in grammar and modern secondary schools in a London borough. The grammar school is mainly college preparatory and is entered by virtue of passing a state examination, the "11 plus." Those who do not pass may attend the modern school. Stewart found the first-born to be overrepresented in the grammar school, and the later-born in the modern school. However, of those who remain in school after the legal attendance requirements have been met at age 15, roughly the same proportion of first-borns is found in both schools, when the ratio of the first- to the later-borns becomes slightly greater than two to one. It seems clear that birth-order influences on schooling are present in England and are just as sharp as they are here.

Schachter (14) reported data from colleges and certain professional schools in the United States which show that at the graduate level, also, the first-born is overrepresented. This overrepresentation holds not only for the ratio of all first-born to all later-born, but also for families of any given size.

Several studies (18) in the psychological journals show that birth-order linkages to college attendance goes back at least to the '20's. Bender (19) reported some data in 1928 which show that the first-born were

clearly in excess at Dartmouth at that time. His focus was on something other than the relation of birth order to college attendance; consequently, he missed the significance of this aspect of his data. In this he was like all others who reported birth-order data for college students, until Schacter, in 1963. (14) finally noted the connection between order of birth and going to college.

The evidence is of course not all in. The reports are fairly numerous by now, and they are consistent in their findings. Since the evidence is congruent with what has been consistently found for various degrees of eminence for nearly 100 years, and also with what has recently been found concerning the linkage of verbal aptitude and birth order among the very bright, it seems a fairly safe assumption that there is a kind of academic primogeniture operating at the college level.

Birth Order and Personality

Alfred Adler believed that order of birth was influential in the channeling of the socially very significant power drives. The first-born, he said (20), is a "power-hungry conservative." The foregoing data suggest that the later-born may come out poorly in competition for position in our technological society, but it does not necessarily follow that industrial or professional achievement derives from a hunger for power. As to the allegation that the first-born is a conservative, I have been unable to find convincing evidence on the college campus. I have found at Santa Barbara that the first-born is somewhat more likely to say he attends church services than is the later-born, but this bit of evidence is about all I have found linking the first-born with conservatism. None of the measure of liberalism-conservatism I have tried out thus far show consistent trends related to birth order.

Sears, Maccoby, and Levin (21) came to the conclusion that the first-born shows greater "conscience" development than does the later-born. They thought that the differences they found in children were probably due to differences in handling of the first-born by parents, that the first-born had more metes and bounds set to his behavior and was more likely to be pubished for transgressions. The father, it was noted, often participated in the disciplining of the first-born, a practice he did not usually continue with the later children. Dean (22) found the first-born to be more cooperative and more given to curiosity, the later-born to be more pugnacious and also more affectionate. This latter finding—that the later born are more affectionate—may have a sequel in a recent report by Schachter (23) that first-born were not so well liked as later-born by their fraternity brothers in the University of Minnesota.

Koch (24) found in her study of 5- and 6-year-old boys and girls from

two-child families that the sex of their siblings together with birth order could influence their social behavior. For instance, a boy who is junior to a sister close to him in age (within 30 months, say) will often be rather "sissy" in comparison with a boy who has an older brother. The boy with the not-much-older sister will more commonly admit to liking to play with girls and with dolls than will boys reared in other sibling relationships. Recently I have found some similar evidence among college students. Male students with older sisters close to their own age were significantly less masculine on two measures of masculinity-feminity than were other males from two-child families.

Schachter (25) in 1959 concluded from a series of studies conducted over several years that the first-born is more driven by "affiliative needs" than is the later-born, especially when danger threatens. If the first-born feels that danger or pain lurks in the offing, he wants to share his anxiety by being with others; the later-born shows considerably less need to be with other people under similar circumstances. In this sense, the first born is more dependent on others. These generalizations of Schacter's derive largely from studies of undergraduates at the University of Minnesota.

Capra and Dittes (15) have reported that among Yale undergraduates first-borns were more likely to volunteer for a psychological experiment than were later-borns. I have also found, in a study recently concluded (May, 1965), that first-born males showed up for voluntary experimental testing in somewhat greater proportion than did later-borns. The differences among the female undergraduates were in the same direction but were not statistically significant. It may be that there is a sex factor here; it is also plausible that the nature of the experiment influences the ratio of volunteers. More research is certainly necessary to determine the significant parameters, if any, relating to birth order and volunteering for experimentation. If first-born do tend, even though only under certain circumstances, to offer themselves as subjects with greater alacrity, this would have great significance for those who base research on samples drawn from college students, especially where the first-born is already considerably overrepresented. Social scientists, in particular, who often use college populations in their studies, would have to control another parameter in their experimental designs.

It seems a reasonable hypothesis that birth-order effects are seldom unitary, but are mixtures involving other family aspects, such as the sex of the siblings and their difference in age. It has already been mentioned that a boy whose only sibling is an older sister, especially a close-up older sister, tends to be somewhat more effeminate than a boy with an older brother. I have found at Santa Barbara that on self-rating tests a girl from a two-child family tends to check more disparaging adjectives

about herself if she has an older brother than if she has an older sister. The same girl with an older brother tends to check more unfavorable adjectives about her sibling and about their father than does the second-born of two sisters. What lends interest to this datum is that there are more girls here who have older brothers than who have older sisters. One may conjecture that such a girl's academic motivation might be at the expense of self-esteem and esteem for her brother and father. In any event, there is some tentative evidence that the junior member of either sex in the two-child family has some unfortunate attitudinal residuals if the older sibling is of the opposite sex.

There have been many studies of the relation of mental disorder to birth order. Since the data reported tend to be confusing and generally rather contradictory the will not be introduced here, except for those of Schooler (26), who has done two studies on birth order and schizophrenia. He found that females who were among the younger in large families, that is, of five or more children, were overrepresented in his two samples of schizophrenics. Schooler believes that the difference in incidence is probably social in origin rather than biological, but he does not attempt to explain the presumed social genesis. In students at the University of California I have been unable to find any relation between birth order or family size and maladjustment, as measured by such a standard device as the Minnesota Multiphasic Personality Inventory. There are differences, to be sure, in the way certain items in this test are answered by first-borns as compared with later-borns, but generally these differentiating items bear no relation to symptoms of a neurotic or psychotic nature. This is not to say that personality differences do not obtain, as both family size and birth order are varied, for they do; but the differences in this admittedly parochial population seem not to be related to deviant adjustment to any significant degree.

An Attempt at a Synthesis

In England and in the United States, there appears to be an indubitable relation of birth order to the achievement of eminence, however it has been defined. The dice are loaded in favor of the first-born. There is also some evidence that in the *quite bright* segment of our population the first-born are not only present in greater numbers, but are also somewhat more verbally able. The first-born is overrepresented among college populations, and there is some indication that the more selective the college, the greater the overrepresentation. It seems reasonable to believe that the aptitude data and the college attendance figures must be interrelated, and it seems equally reasonable that both sets of data are linked, quite possibly in a causal way, to the numerous data on eminence that have been presented.

Cattell observed (*3*) that the preeminence of the first-born was "probably due to social rather than to physiological causes." In my opinion the most prominent of the presumed social "causes" is likely to be the differential parental treatment accorded children of different ordinal positions, to greater "conscience" development, greater dependence on adult norms, and higher expectations of achievement falling to the lot of the first-born. I have already mentioned the report of Sears *et al.* (*21*) that parents tend to be stricter with the first-born child. Lasko (*27*) noted that later-born children tend to be treated in a more relaxed, permissive way. This difference in rearing practices may explain why Dean (*22*) found the first-born to be more dependent upon adults and the later-born more physically aggressive — that is, less hampered by social restraint. She also reported that the first-born showed more curiosity — that is, he asked more questions — and that he sought adult attention more frequently. Finally, one further difference which sets the first-born apart is that he is the only child who has access for an indeterminate period of time to parental interaction which he does not have to share with a sibling.

The foregoing data suggest fairly strongly, I think, why the first-born may do better in school. His curiosity, dependence upon adults, and greater conscience development doubtless make him respond more affirmatively to the teacher and to the school. He should thus more frequently win the teacher's approval, which should serve to augment further his tendencies to do that which is expected of him as a student. If this inference is correct, it is easy to understand why the colleges attract such a high proportion of the first-born.

Schachter argues (*14*) that the greater predilection of the first-born for college explains his greater eminence: His superior educational attainments make the achievement of eminence easier for him when he competes for place and position with the less well-trained later-born. This would appear to be unquestionable today, at least as regards eminence in science and technology. I would suspect, however, that in creative writing, sculpture, painting, music — the arts generally — the dependence on college training is not nearly so marked. I would also suspect that a century ago it was easier to achieve eminence, however defined, without having gone to college. Still, the greater incidence of the first-born among the eminent must have somewhere its origin: Educational attainment cannot be discounted as an important source of the observed differences in eminence among the birth orders.

The intellectual superiority of the first-born noted by Terman, by Altus, and by Nichols among the very bright segment of the population deserves further comment. Hunt (*28*), who has summarized the literature on the development of intelligence, leaves room to believe that the child can increase his intelligence by hard intellectual work. If the first-born, by virtue of his different treatment in the home, takes to school

more readily, works harder, persists longer (as the college attendance figures attest), then it might be expected that he may well increase his intellectual stature in the process. The first-born who arrives at college has given himself a boost, as it were, by hard tugging at his intellectual bootstraps.

Finally, one must grapple with this problem: If differential treatment of the first-born by his parents makes him a better prospect for higher aptitude, for college training, and for eminence, why does it affect relatively few of the total available first-borns? McClelland (29), who has given two decades to research on motivation and achievement, has generalized his findings on optimal home influences thus: " . . . what is desirable . . . is a stress on meeting certain achievement standards between the ages of six and eight." The child is given, he continues, training in independence and mastery, and he is held in warm regard by both parents, who are ambitious for him but not too dominating, and who have a strong, positive attitude toward education.

Not many parents would fill this bill of particulars in all details. Even when they do, their offspring must have an initial aptitude for learning that places them in the upper half of the total pool of children, if the parental impetus toward achievement is to have the desired result. It seems to me that the preceding considerations impose sufficient restrictions to ensure that only a minor portion even of the relatively fortunate first-born will attain a college degree. And to the extent that aptitude and eminence are a product, even partially, of the educational process, they would tend to vary with education.

In conclusion, the viewpoint embodied in this paper may be fairly summarized by a single sentence: Ordinal position at birth has been shown to be related to significant social parameters, though the reasons behind the relations are as yet unknown or at best dimly apprehended.

Notes

1. H. Ellis, *A Study of British Genius* (Houghton Mifflin, Boston, 1926, new rev. ed.), p. 103. Originally published in 1904 by Hurst and Blackett, London.

2. A. H. Yoder, *Pedag. Seminary* **3**, 146 (1894).

3. J. M. Cattell, *Sci. Monthly* **5**, 371 (1917). Cattell had been concerned, according to his own admission, with eminence and eminent men since the 1880's, probably owing to the writings and personal influence of Galton. Cattell first published on eminent men in the 1890's and continued to do so for 30 years thereafter. His *American Men of Science*, in its various editions, bears testimony to this early interest.

4. C. Gini, *J. Heredity* **6**, 37 (1915).

5. E. L. Clarke, *American Men of Letters, Their Nature and Nurture* (Columbia Univ. Press, New York, 1916), p. 84.

6. E. Huntington. *Season of Birth* (Wiley, New York, 1938), p. 292.

7. F. L. Apperly, *J. Heredity* **30**, 493 (1939).

8. H. E. Jones, "The environment and mental development," in *Manual of Child Psychology*, L. Carmichael, Ed. (Wiley, New York, 1954), p. 668.

9. A. Roe, *Psychol. Monograph No. 352* (1953), p. 3.

10. L. M. Terman, *Genetic Studies of Genius*, vol. 1. *The Mental and Physical Traits of a Thousand Gifted Children* (Stanford Univ. Press, Stanford, Calif., 1925), p. 121.

11. R. C. Nichols, "Birth Order and Intelligence," unpublished.

12. W. D. Altus, *Amer. Psychologist* **17**, 304 (1962); *ibid.* **18**, 361 (1963); *ibid.* **19**, 506 (1964); *J. Consult. Psychol.* **29**, 202 (1965).

13. H. L. Koch, *Child Develop*, **25**, 209 (1954).

14. S. Schachter, *Amer. Sociol. Rev.* **28**, 760 (1963).

15. P. C. Capra and J. E. Dittes, *J. Abnorm. Soc. Psychol.* **64**, 203 (1962).

16. Private communication from Reed College, April 1964.

17. M. Stewart, *The Success of the First Born Child* (Workers Educational Association, London, 1962), 19-page pamphlet.

18. W. D. Altus, *J. Consult. Psychol.* **29**, 202 (1965); *J. Personality and Soc. Psychol.* **2**, 872 (1965).

19. I. E. Bender, *J. Abnormal Soc. Psychol.* **23**, 137 (1928).

20. A. Adler, *Children* **3**, 14 (1928).

21. R. R. Sears, E. Maccoby, H. Levin, *Patterns of Child Rearing* (Row Peterson, Evanston, Ill., 1957), p. 418.

22. D. A. Dean, thesis, State Univ. of Iowa (1947), p. 21.

23. S. Schachter, *J. Abnormal Soc. Psychol.* **68**, 453 (1964).

24. H. L. Koch, *J. Genet. Psychol.* **88**, 231 (1956).

25. S. Schachter, *The Psychology of Affiliation* (Stanford Univ. Press, Stanford, Calif., 1959).

26. C. Schooler, *J. Abnormal Soc. Psychol.* **69**, 576 (1964); *Arch. Gen. Psychiatr.* **4**, 120 (1961).

27. J. K. Lasko, *Genet. Psychol.* Monographs **49**, 97 (1954).

28. J. M. Hunt, *Intelligence and Experience* (Ronald, New York, 1961).

29. D. C. McClelland, *The Achieving Society* (Van Nostrand, New York, 1961), p. 345.

5.8   Conformity as a Function of Birth Order and Type of Group Pressure: A Verification

Selwyn W. Becker
Jean Carroll
University of Chicago

Melvin J. Lerner
University of Kentucky

In a recent experiment (Becker, Lerner, & Carroll, 1964) first-born and later-born adolescents were tested in an Asch (1956) situation. By introducing the anticipation of a small or large "payoff" for each correct judgment the amount of yielding was significantly affected. A small payoff greatly decreased conforming errors in the first-born group, and somewhat decreased conforming errors in later-born subjects. A large payoff, however, led to increased yielding only for the later-born subjects. These findings were interpreted as confirming the hypothesis that first-born persons were more dependent on others for social support while later-born persons rely more on others for validation of their beliefs.

Confidence in the validity and generality of this interpretation is somewhat limited because of two aspects in the experimental situation. The first is based on the characteristics of the subjects, all of whom were golf caddies from the same country club. It is probably safe to suggest that they were from the lower middle class and were somewhat special within that class in terms of the kind of employment they sought and achieved.

The second, more serious problem derives from the line of reasoning concerning the effect of a small versus a large payoff as a technique for manipulating the normative and informational influence (Deutsch & Gerard, 1955) operating in the Asch situation. A small payoff was assumed to provide motivation to resist the normative influence in the situation and a large payoff was supposed to enhance the informational value of the unamimous majority's judgments. Though perhaps it was a logical manipulation, there was very little historical precedent for using payoffs in this manner.

The study reported here was designed to validate the original hypotheses by testing them under different experimental conditions. It differs from the initial study in several important respects. First, the sub-

Reprinted from Becker, S. W., Lerner, M. J. and Carroll, J. Conformity as a function of birth order and type of group pressure: A verification. *Journal of Personality and Social Psychology*, 1966, *3*, No. 2, 242–244. Copyright 1966 by the American Psychological Association, and reproduced by permission.

jects were all students in a high school located in an upper income community. Second, the techniques for manipulating normative and informational influences were changed. Instead of a control and two payoff conditions the design included a control condition, a "memory" condition which was expected to increase the informational influence, and a "group-reward" condition which was intended to heighten normative influence. The specific techniques employed to create the "memory" and "group" conditions were similar to those used by Deutsch and Gerard when they initially made the distinction between these two sources of influence. Third, in the initial study a small payoff reduced normative influence while a large payoff increased informational influence. In this study the selected manipulations operated so as to increase both normative and informational influences.

Despite the contrasting experimental conditions, we expected to confirm the original hypotheses that first-born persons will appear more dependent on other people when normative influence is operating in a situation, whereas later-born persons will appear to be more dependent to the extent that informational influence is present in the situation.

Procedure

Subjects were 48 male volunteers from a large high school located in an upper-middle-class suburb north of Chicago. Twenty-three of the subjects were the first-born or only children in their families and 25 were later-born children. Subjects were recruited and scheduled for the experiment during their study (or free) periods.

As each subject appeared he was asked to identify himself and then he was informally questioned as to the number and age of his siblings, if any. The subjects were assigned randomly to a control group, a group-reward group, and a memory group with the restriction that half the subjects run under each condition be the first- or only-born child in their family, while the remaining subjects in the three groups each had at least one older sibling. (One error in the assignment was made by the experimenter so that in the memory condition the first-born group included seven rather than eight subjects and the later-born group contained nine subjects.) Accomplices were recruited from the same pool of volunteers from which the subjects were selected. The school was large enough, with enough simultaneous study periods, so that in no case was the naive subject acquainted with any of the accomplices.

The control condition was an exact replication of the control condition used in our earlier study and also of Deutsch and Gerard's face-to-face (visual series) solution. That is, three accomplices were employed with each naive subject, all of whom were required to make 18 judgments of

which 12 were "critical trials," that is, those where the accomplices unanimously gave incorrect answers. The subjects were instructed to match accurately the length of the standard line with one of three companion lines. The memory condition was like the control condition except that the lines were removed before any of the choices were announced. Just as Deutsch and Gerard did in their memory series, we allowed approximately 3 seconds to elapse before asking for the first judgment.

The group-reward condition was similar to Deutsch and Gerard's group situation. The subjects were told that several groups were taking part in the experiment and that the group which made the fewest number of total errors would be rewarded with tickets to a Chicago Black Hawk hockey game. The judgments were made with the lines physically present.

These procedures allowed us to make the following predictions. In the control condition we expected to replicate the finding of Becker and Carroll (1962) and Becker et al. (1964) that first borns yield more than later borns in an Asch situation. Compared to control-group subjects we predicted that first-born subjects under group-reward conditions would exhibit a significant increase in yielding while later-born subjects under group-reward conditions would be relatively unchanged. We also predicted that later-born subjects would exhibit a significant increase in yielding in the memory condition compared with the control condition while the first borns would remain relatively unaffected.

Results

From an inspection of Table 1 it can be seen that the predictions were upheld by the data. In the control condition the first-born subjects yielded more than the later borns ($p = .058$). However, when the subjects were led to believe that their responses would affect the likelihood of their fellow respondents winning a prize (group-reward condition) the first-born subjects showed a significantly greater degree of yielding than in the control condition ($p = .058$). The later-born subjects exhibited no comparable increase in yielding behavior ($p > .41$). The difference between the yielding of the first borns in the control versus the group-reward condition was not significantly greater than the differences in yielding for the later-born subjects ($t = .90$, $df = 28$).

In the memory condition the pattern of yielding was different than in either the control or group-reward conditions. The later-born subjects made significantly more errors in the memory condition than in the control condition ($p = .05$) while the first-born subjects made fewer errors than in the control condition ($p = .05$) or in the group-reward condition

Table 1
Birth Order and Conformity under Varying Conditions

Condition	Number of errors	
	First born	Later born
Control	0	0
	2	0
	2	0
	2	2
	2	2
	3	2
	4	2
	4	2
Group reward	0	0
	2	0
	4	0
	4	1
	4	2
	4	2
	6	3
	6	5
Memory	0	0
	0	1
	1	2
	1	2
	1	2
	2	3
	6	3
		4
		12

($p = .03$). All p values were based on Mann-Whitney U tests (Siegel, 1956). An additional test was performed to determine if the difference in errors made by the later borns in the control versus the memory condition was greater than the differences exhibited between the first-born subjects in these conditions. This comparison yielded a $t = 2.365$, $df = 28$, $p < .05$.

Discussion

The present study differed from the initial one in certain essential respects. The subjects, although approximately the same age as the golf caddies were from families living in an extremely different social environment—a suburban upper-middle-class community versus an urban lower-class neighborhood. The experimental procedures used to manipulate the normative and informational influences were also relatively dis-

tinct in the two studies. In the first study normative influence was reduced by a small payoff and informational influence enhanced by a large payoff. In this study normative influence was increased by a group reward and informational influence increased by compelling the subjects to respond from their memory of the stimuli.

Given these differences between the two experiments the findings can be considered remarkably similar. Later-born subjects were most influenced when they had reason to believe that the other people in the situation were providing them with valid information about the common "reality" which confronted them. The first-born subjects remained relatively unaffected by the informational value of the responses of their peers. Their yielding behavior was significantly altered by the motivation induced in them to go along with or resist the expectations of the unanimous majority. In the initial experiment the first-born subjects were induced to resist going along with the majority by offering them a reward for a correct answer. In this second experiment they were led to greater conforming behavior by increasing the apparent need of the majority to have the subject go along with their choice.

Although most of the predictions in this study were confirmed at marginal levels of significance, when the findings are considered in conjunction with those of Becker et al. (1964) they present a rather clear picture. Either the first- or the later-born person will appear more or less dependent upon other people as a function of the type of influence operating in the situation. To the extent that normative influence is present the first born will appear more dependent. If informational influence predominates the later-born person will be more affected.

References

Asch, S. E. Studies of independence and conformity: I. A minority of one against a unanimous majority. *Psychological Monographs*, 1956, 70(9, Whole No. 416).

Becker, S. W., & Carroll, Jean. Ordinal position and conformity. *Journal of Abnormal and Social Psychology*, 1962, **65**, 129–131.

Becker, S. W., Lerner, M. J., & Carroll, Jean. Conformity as a function of birth order, payoff, and type of group pressure. *Journal of Abnormal and Social Psychology*, 1964, **69**, 318–323.

Deutsch, M., & Gerard, H. B. A study of normative and informational social influences upon individual judgment. *Journal of Abnormal and Social Psychology*, 1955, **51**, 629–636.

Siegel, S. *Nonparametric statistics for the behavioral sciences.* New York: McGraw-Hill, 1956.

5.9   Enhancement of Punitiveness by Visual and Audiovisual Displays

Richard H. Walters
University of Toronto

Edward Llewellyn Thomas
Ontario Hospital, New Toronto

Studies in which children or adolescents have been exposed to film-mediated aggressive models (Bandura, 1962; Lövaas, 1961; Mussen & Rutherford, 1961; Siegel, 1959) have uniformly indicated that *vicarious* participation in aggressive activity increases, rather than decreases, the frequency and intensity of aggressive responses. In contrast, Feshbach (1961), in a careful study with college students, claims to have provided evidence that vicarious participation in film-mediated aggression has a cathartic effect on subjects who have been previously angered. Fifty-two students were subjected to "unwarranted and extremely critical remarks" (Insult group), while another fifty-two students (Non-insult group) were given standard tests instructions. Half the Insult and half the Non-insult subjects then witnessed a film clip of a prize fight; the remainder of the subjects in both groups saw a "neutral" movie depicting the effects of the spread of rumours in a factory. Subjects in the Insult group who saw the fight gave fewer aggressive responses to a word-association test (Gellerman, 1960) and to a questionnaire (Feshbach, 1955) than did the insulted subjects who saw the "neutral" movie. There was no significant difference between the two subgroups of non-insulted subjects. As Feshbach points out, the relatively low level of aggression of the Insult subjects who saw the prize fight could be due to the arousal of revulsion or guilt stimulated by the fight theme, an explanation of apparent cathartic effects which has been favoured by Berkowitz (1958, 1962). Moreover, one may question the "neutrality" of a film depicting the effects of the spread of rumours. Indeed, for college students, socially disruptive rumour and gossip may represent highly aggressive responses. Inappropriateness of stimulus material may account also for Feshbach's failure to confirm his hypothesis that Non-insult subjects exposed to the prize fight would show a greater increase in aggression than Non-insult subjects exposed to the rumour movie.

In other catharsis studies experimental subjects have been *themselves* permitted to express aggression in fantasy, play, or real life and then

Reprinted from the *Canadian Journal of Psychology*, 1963, *17*, 2, 245–255, by permission of the author and the Canadian Psychological Association.

tested for aggression in the same or a different stimulus situation. Again, studies in which children have served as subjects (Feshbach, 1956; Kenny, 1952) have failed to support the catharsis hypothesis, while findings from studies with adults (for example, Feshbach, 1955; Rosenbaum & de Charms, 1960; Thibaut & Coules, 1952) have been open, generally speaking, to alternative interpretations (Buss, 1961; Berkowitz, 1958, 1962; Rosenbaum & de Charms, 1960).

The discrepancy in findings yielded by the child and the adult studies and the conflicting results from experiments based on adult subjects may be partly attributable to variations in criterion measures. The child studies have without exception employed measures of overt aggression. In contrast, the adult studies have generally relied on questionnaire responses, self-ratings, and ambiguous measures obtained from ratings of the experiment and the experimenter, all of which are subject to response sets which may seriously affect results.

This paper reports results from a three-phase study of the influence of film-mediated aggressive models in which the primary measure of aggression was behavioural, while questionnaires provided only supplementary data. The aggressive film sequence was the knife-fight scene from the motion picture, *Rebel Without a Cause*. The control movie was an educational film depicting adolescents engaged in art work. This latter stimulus differed from Feshbach's (1961) supposedly neutral movie in that it displayed constructive co-operative activities.

Some of the data obtained from the first phase of the study have already been reported by Walters, Llewellyn Thomas, and Acker (1962). For comparison, these data are included in the present paper. With only minor variations, the same procedures were used throughout all phases of the study. Consequently, only the procedure used in the second phase is reported in detail.

The following hypothesis was advanced: Subjects who watch an aggressive movie sequence depicting physical aggression will subsequently display more physically aggressive responses, delivered in the form of punitive electric shocks, than subjects who watch a movie sequence depicting constructive activities.

Method

Subjects (Ss)

In the first phase of the study 28 hospital attendants, with a median age of 34 years, were randomly assigned in equal number to the experimental and control conditions. Ss were unpaid, but were permitted to participate during work hours. In the second phase, 24 Grade 9 and

Grade 10 boys, with a median age of 15 years, 3 months, served as Ss. All were paid volunteers who attended a single high school in the vicinity of the hospital at which they were tested. Ss were randomly assigned to the experimental and control conditions, with 12 Ss in each group. In Phase III, Ss were 32 females, with a median age of 20 years, from a hostel for working girls. All were unpaid volunteers.

Confederates (Cs)

When hospital attendants served as Ss, Cs were University of Toronto students who were brought to the hospital for a half-day each. It was not possible to use a single confederate throughout this phase of the study, since his continued presence at the hospital would have caused Ss to become suspicious of his role. In Phase II, C was a Grade 10 boy, who attended a different high school from Ss, and was consequently unknown to them. In Phase III, Cs were undergraduate students who were assigned to an equal number of experimental and control Ss in a 2 × 2 factorial design. Half the experimental and half the control Ss administered shock to a male C, while the remaining Ss administered shock to a female C.

Apparatus

The equipment was a modified version of a "conditioning" apparatus described by Buss (1961). It consisted of three panels: S's panel, C's panel, and E's. S, who served as "E's assistant," was provided with a panel which contained four switches controlling stimulus lights on C's panel, a rotary switch for selecting shock intensities with settings from zero to ten, a red and green signal light operated from E's panel, a pair of electrodes, and a spring-loaded toggle-switch which S depressed to administer shocks to C and raised to signal that C had made a correct response.

E's panel contained stimulus keys to activate the green and red lights on S's panel, four lights which registered S's selection of light switches, a row of eleven lights to indicate the intensity of shock chosen by S, and an outlet to a Standard Electric Timer for recording the duration, in $\frac{1}{10}$-sec. intervals, of the shock administered.

C's panel was a dummy "unit" with no electrical connections to the other units. In order to deceive S, dead cables which appeared to provide such connections were led across the laboratory floor.

Tables holding the panels were arranged in such a way that E could observe S and C, both of whom faced away from E. C was seated behind a buttress 15 ft. to the rear of S so that he was not visible to S during testing.

Procedure (Phase II)

E first met *S* in the laboratory and explained to him that he and another subject (in fact, *E*'s confederate) would be required to watch a scene in a film and then, after a lapse of a few minutes, to answer some questions concerning the events they had witnessed. The experiment was presented as a test for memory for witnessed events which would provide comparative data concerning the attention and memory of persons of different ages.

The experimenter then explained that he was also collecting some data on the effects of punishment on learning and would need an assistant to help operate the equipment used for this purpose, a service which *S* was requested to perform. The "assistance" provided by *S* was ostensibly to administer punishment, in the form of electric shocks, for errors made by *C* in the learning task.

After *S* had consented to act as an assistant, he was shown how to operate the equipment and was given a few shocks, not exceeding the level of 4, to familiarize him with the pain levels corresponding to sample settings on the dial. He was told that shock intensities became increasingly more painful as shock levels were increased from zero to ten.

S was then given a programme of settings for the signal switches on his panel, each setting consisting of a pairing of two of the numbers 1 through 4. He was told that on each trial he must depress two of the four stimulus keys in the order indicated by his programme and that these would light up two of the lights on the "subject's" (i.e., *C*'s) panel. He was informed that if the "subject" responded correctly, the green panel would go on and that he should signal to the "subject" that he was correct by raising the spring-loaded toggle-switch. However, if the red light came on, indicating that the "subject" had made an incorrect response, he was told to punish him by selecting one of the shock intensities and depressing the switch. A few practice trials were given to familiarize *S* with the equipment.

At this point *E* remarked that "the other fellow" should have arrived by this time and telephoned to "ask if he were there." The telephone call was, in fact, taken by *C*, who was waiting in *E*'s office and for whom it was a signal to come to the laboratory.

On his arrival *C* was also told, in front of *S*, that this was a study of memory for events in a movie but that, during the break between the movie and the recall test, *E* wished to gather additional data concerning the effects of punishment on learning. *C*'s consent to serve as a "subject" was then obtained.

E explained that he wished to have the interval between the showing of the movie and the recall test rather precise and that therefore he would like *S* and *C* to have a "practice run" on the learning equipment

before seeing the movie to ensure that there would be no undue hold-ups on the later series of trials. *S* was given a programme of 30 settings to present to *C*. The latter was seated at the "receiving" end of the punishment equipment with an electrode strap placed around his wrist. During this "practice" session, which supplied the *pre-test* measures, *S* was required to punish *C* 15 times, that is, *E* illuminated the red button on fifteen occasions. Since *E* had surreptitiously removed one of the electrodes from the strap, *C* in fact received no shocks.

Immediately after the "trial" run, experimental *S*s and *C* were shown the knife-fight scene, while control *S*s and *C* were shown the art scene.

The *post-test* series of trials on the learning task followed. Another programme of 30 settings was handed to *S* and again he was required to punish *C* 15 times during the run.

Modification of Procedure for Adult Ss

Except for minor changes in the wording of instructions to make them appropriate to the ages of *S*s and *C*s, the procedures used in Phases I and II of the study were identical. Phase III of the study was conducted at the University of Toronto in two adjoining rooms, separated by a one-way vision mirror. The movie sequences were shown in the observation room, where *E*'s panel was located. The "conditioning" procedure was conducted in the adjoining room with *S* and *C* separated by a partition. The movie sequences were the same as in the other phases, except that *no sound was used*, that is, *the displays were purely visual in character*. The procedure was otherwise, except for minor necessary changes in instructions, identical with that used in Phases I and II.

Measures

The average of the shock-level settings selected by each *S* was obtained for both the pre-test and the post-test series of trials. The effects of exposure to film-mediated aggression was assessed primarily from pre-test – to – post-test changes in this behavioural index of punitiveness.

The Buss-Durkee Hostility-Aggression Inventory (Buss & Durkee, 1957) was utilized as a supplementary measure. The hospital attendants and young females were given this inventory immediately after the post-test session of the conditioning task. In the case of the adolescents it proved possible to administer the inventory about ten days before the experimental session and again after completion of the conditioning task.

All three sets of subjects were also required to fill out, at the very end of the testing session, a multiple-choice questionnaire concerning the film they had watched. This questionnaire was administered only to preserve the impression that the study was primarily one of memory for events; no analysis of the data was attempted.

Results

Results for adult male subjects. As reported elsewhere (Walters, Llewellyn Thomas, & Acker, 1962), experimental and control male adults did not differ significantly in respect to pre-test shock levels ($p >$ .05). There was a significant difference ($t = 2.37$; $p < .05$) between the two groups for the index of change in punitiveness, with experimental subjects showing a quite marked mean increase in punitiveness and control subjects a slight mean decrease.

Results for adolescent subjects. Adolescent experimental and control subjects did not differ in respect to pre-test shock levels ($p > .05$). Both adolescent groups showed a pre-test–to–post-test increase in shock level, with experimental subjects showing a greater increase than controls ($t = 2.04$; $p = .05$, approx.). A supplementary t-test was performed in order to ascertain whether the control group's scores had increased significantly beyond zero. The obtained value for t was 2.18, which for 11 df is again significant approximately at the .05 level.

Comparison of adult male and adolescent subjects. Although the conditions for testing adult and adolescent males were somewhat different, in that the adults delivered shocks to students who were generally somewhat younger than themselves while the adolescents delivered shocks to a confederate of approximately their own age, it was decided to compare these adult and adolescent subjects in respect to initial selection of shock levels and in a 2 × 2 analysis of variance of changes in shock level. The pre-test shock-level means of adult and adolescent subjects were compared by means of a t-test, which showed that the difference between the two groups was not significant ($p > .05$). When the results of both the experimental and control groups were taken into account, adolescents showed a significantly greater increase in shock level than did adults ($p < .05$). The significance of the difference between the combined experimental and combined control groups was < .005. The interaction effect was not significant.

Results for female subjects. Females who watched the aggressive film sequence showed a significant increase in punitiveness ($p < .01$). The sex of the confederate did not influence results and there was no interaction effect.

Inventory Data

The Buss-Durkee inventory was administered to the adults, male and female, only at the end of the testing session. On all four of the scales with high loadings on Buss's aggression factor, the experimental group

scored significantly higher than the control group. In contrast, results for female subjects were all non-significant. Pre-test – to – post-test change scores were available for adolescent subjects. There was no significant difference in change scores for experimental and control subjects on any of the individual scales. On the total aggression-hostility index, obtained by combining scores on Scales 1 through 7, experimental subjects showed a mean increase of 2.83, while the controls' mean increase was only 1.42. This difference, however, was not great enough to reach an acceptable level of significance ($t = 1.58$; $p > .05$).

Discussion

The results of this study in general lend considerable support to the hypothesis that subjects exposed to an aggressive movie sequence show a significant increment in aggressive pain-producing responses in comparison to a control group who watch a movie showing constructive activities. This finding is consistent with those obtained from studies in which children have served as subjects.

In the third phase of the study the auditory components of the stimuli were omitted and at the same time subjects were of a different sex from the aggressive model presented on film. Nevertheless, the results for the behavioural index were similar to those obtained for male subjects with the audiovisual display. A direct comparison of the effects of aggressive audiovisual, auditory, and visual stimuli on both male and female subjects is clearly indicated. It would also be of interest to investigate the influence of aggressive material which is presented in other media, for example, in still pictures or in print.

In contrast to the behavioural measure of punitiveness, the inventory data failed to provide consistent findings. Buss has pointed out that the pattern of results obtained with the male adults might have been expected, since only the aggression scales should be influenced by situational factors.[1] Possibly the inventory was not suitable for use with the adolescents, whose scores tended to be very high even on the first administration. The negative findings for the adult females cannot, however, be attributed to the unsuitability of the instrument. One problem with the inventory is that it is quite evidently asking questions concerning socially disapproved hostility and aggression in a variety of contexts, all different from the one provided by the experiment. In contrast, the administration of shocks was sanctioned in the experimental setting and had no apparent relation to the presentation of the filmed material.

When both experimental and control scores were taken into account, the adolescent subjects were found to have increased shock levels during testing to a greater extent than the adults. This finding is not too sur-

prising, in view of the fact that inhibition of aggression is a gradual process that probably, for most individuals, continues into young adult life. Indeed, a significant interaction between the experimental treatments and the age of subjects might have been expected. *Rebel Without a Cause* portrayed adolescents engaged in aggressive activities; consequently, greater "identification" on the part of the adolescent subjects could have led to a greater pre-test–to–post-test increment in punitiveness (Maccoby & Wilson, 1957). However, the over-all findings suggest that neither sex nor age similarity between observer and model is necessary in order to produce an increment in punitive pain-producing responses.

The *control* group of adolescents showed a significant increment of aggression from pre-test to post-test. Two explanations suggest themselves. In the first place, as the adolescent confederate observed, the control movie may have been boring and therefore frustrating for the adolescent subjects. It is more likely, however, that most adolescents were initially somewhat timid of using shock, but tended to increase the shock level under conditions in which no serious consequences to the confederate were observed. Support for the latter interpretation is provided by the experimenter's observation that nearly every individual adolescent record sheet showed a pattern of gradually ascending shock level even during the pre-test trials.

The study thus suggests two ways in which disinhibition of aggression may occur. In the first place, mere observation of an aggressive model who is not punished for his aggression may lead to the lessening of inhibitions on the expression of aggression. Secondly, for some groups of subjects, aggression may increase, even in the absence of anger, positive reinforcement, or the example set by a model, if no untoward social consequences of their previous aggression are apparent. It is probably only the continual expectation of retaliation by the recipient or by other members of society that prevents many individuals from more freely expressing aggression.

The authors were astonished at the shock-levels selected by some adolescents who, even near the commencement of the pre-test period, gave long shocks at levels between 8 and 10. The sample shocks provided at the commencement of the session clearly indicated that such levels, even if only briefly administered, were very painful. A few adolescents even made remarks, such as "I bet I made that fellow jump," which reflected enjoyment with the task of administering pain.

Perhaps such responses are to be expected from adolescent males who live in a society in which they are constantly exposed to aggressive sports, such as boxing, and to T.V. and motion-picture scenes of violence, warfare, and destruction. Schramm, Lyle, and Parker (1961) not-

ed that Grade 10 students who were fantasy-oriented (high T.V. users, low users of print) scored significantly higher on a self-report measure of antisocial aggression (Sears, 1961) than did reality-oriented Grade 10 children (low T.V. users, high users of print). Under the influence of the catharsis hypothesis these authors interpret their findings as indicating that frustrated (high-fantasy) children "tend to try to work out some of their aggression vicariously through television fantasy" (p. 121). In this instance, as with most field study findings, it is impossible to determine the direction of the cause-effect relationship if such a relationship is indeed involved. Indeed, it is just as reasonable to interpret the finding of Schramm, *et al.* as indicating that high T.V.-viewing predisposes an adolescent to express antisocial aggression. While it is quite evident that all children are not similarly influenced by T.V. scenes of violence (Himmelweit, Oppenheim, & Vince, 1958; Maccoby, 1955; Schramm, Lyle, & Parker, 1961), the bulk of evidence from controlled experimental studies suggests that the immediate effect of audiovisually presented violence is to increase the social aggression of the viewers.

It is possible, of course, that T.V.- or film-viewers who are emotionally disturbed either through temporary or long-term situational factors will be more adversely influenced by the presentation of violence than viewers who are not thus aroused. The field studies of television (Himmelweit, *et al.*, 1958; Schramm, *et al.*, 1961) certainly seem to indicate that, contrary to Feshbach's (1955, 1961) contention, the angry or hostile viewer is more likely than the non-angry viewer to behave aggressively as a result of viewing T.V. or filmed aggression. Moreover, previous studies by Walters and his collaborators (McNulty & Walters, 1961; Walters, Marshall, & Shooter, 1960) suggest that the influence of social models may be enhanced when observers are in an emotionally aroused state. While further studies of the manner in which "personality" and situational factors modify viewers' reactions to televised and filmed violence are undoubtedly necessary, mounting evidence against the catharsis hypothesis must raise questions concerning the social wisdom of the sponsors of such productions.

Notes

1. Personal communication.

References

Bandura, A. Social learning through imitation. In M. R. Jones, Ed., *Nebraska symposium on motivation.* Lincoln: University of Nebraska Press, 1962, pp. 211–69.

Bandura, A., & Walters, R. H. Aggression. In *Child psychology: The sixty-second yearbook of the National Society for the Study of Education*, part I. Chicago: National Society for the Study of Education, 1963, pp. 364–415.

Berkowitz, L. The expression and reduction of hostility. *Psychol. Bull.*, 1958, **55**, 257–83.

_____ *Aggression: a social psychological analysis*. New York: Mc-Graw-Hill, 1962.

Buss, A. H. *The psychology of aggression*. New York: Wiley, 1961.

Buss, A. H., & Durkee, Ann. An inventory for assessing different kinds of hostility. *J. consult. Psychol.*, 1957, **21**, 343–8.

Feshbach, S. The drive-reducing function of fantasy behavior. *J. abnorm. soc. Psychol.*, 1955, **50**, 3–11.

_____ The catharsis hypothesis and some consequences of interaction with aggressive and neutral play objects. *J. Pers.*, 1956, **24**, 449–62.

_____ The stimulating vs. cathartic effects of a vicarious aggressive activity. *J. abnorm. soc. Psychol.*, 1961, **63**, 381–5.

Ferguson, G. A. *Statistical analysis in psychology and education*. New York: McGraw-Hill, 1959.

Gellerman, S. The effects of experimentally induced aggression and inhibition on word association response sequences. Unpublished doctoral dissertation, University of Pennsylvania, 1960.

Himmelweit, Hilde T., Oppenheim, A. N., & Vince, Pamela. *Television and the child: an empirical study of the effect of television on the young*. Toronto: Oxford University Press, 1958.

Kenny, D. T. An experimental test of the catharsis theory of aggression. Unpublished doctoral thesis, University of Washington, 1952.

Lövaas, O. I. Effect of exposure to symbolic aggression on aggressive behavior. *Child Develpm.*, 1961, **32**, 37–44.

Maccoby, Eleanor E., & Wilson, W. C. Identification and observational learning from films. *J. abnorm. soc. Psychol.*, 1957, **55**, 76–87.

Maccoby, Eleanor E. Testimony before the Subcommittee to investigate juvenile delinquency of the Committee on the Judiciary, United States Senate, Eighty-Fourth Congress, *S. Res. 62*. Washington, D.C.: U.S. Government Printing Office, 1955.

McNulty, J. A., & Walters, R. H. Emotional arousal, conflict, and susceptibility to social influence. *Canad. J. Psychol.*, 1962, **16**, 211–20.

Mussen, P. H., & Rutherford, E. Effects of aggressive cartoons on children's aggressive play. *J. abnorm. soc. Psychol.*, 1961, **62**, 461–4.

Rosenbaum, M. E., & de Charms, R. Direct and vicarious reduction of hostility. *J. abnorm. soc. Psychol.*, 1960, **60**, 105–11.

Schramm, W., Lyle, J., & Parker, E. B. *Television in the lives of our children*. Toronto: University of Toronto Press, 1961.

Sears, R. R. Relation of early socialization experiences to aggression in middle childhood. *J. abnorm. soc. Psychol.*, 1961, **63**, 466 – 92.

Siegel, Alberta E. Film-mediated fantasy aggression and strength of aggressive drive. *Child Develpm.*, 1956, **27**, 365 – 78.

Thibaut, J. W., & Coules J. The role of communication in the reduction of interpersonal hostility. *J. abnorm. soc. Psychol.*, 1952, **47**, 770 – 7.

Walters, R. H., Llewellyn Thomas, E., & Acker, C. W. Enhancement of punitive behavior by audiovisual displays. *Science*, 1962, **136**, 872 – 3.

Walters, R. H., Marshall, W. E., & Shooter, J. R. Anxiety, isolation, and susceptibility to social influence. *J. Pers.*, 1960, **28**, 518 – 29.

5.10 Schools and the Disadvantaged (A Summary of the Coleman Report)

Robert C. Nichols

The recent spate of federally financed education programs intended to improve the performance of racial minorities and other disadvantaged groups rests on a foundation of plausible assumptions and commendable intentions but with essentially no data to indicate their probable effectiveness. Will Head Start improve the school performance of deprived children? Will excellent teachers for the poor help break the "cycle of poverty"? Will Negro students learn more in integrated schools? Will the performance of middle-class children suffer if they attend school with predominantly lower-class children? Will increased expenditures for education result in greater student achievement? There are currently no firm answers to these questions.

Apparently as a reaction to the dearth of information, Section 402 of the Civil Rights Act of 1964 directed the Commissioner of Education to conduct a survey of inequalities in educational opportunities for all groups in the United States. What seemed to be called for was a tabulation of the physical facilities, teachers, and expenditures in schools attended by various minority groups; but at a more fundamental level answers to such questions as those posed above are necessary, since equality of educational opportunity is ultimately defined not by dollars,

Reprinted from *Science*, 9 Dec. 1966, *154*, No. 3754, 1312 – 1314, by permission of the author and the American Association for the Advancement of Science. Copyright 1966 by the American Association for the Advancement of Science.

teachers, and buildings, but by the effects of these facilities on student achievement. Fortunately, the congressional directive was interpreted as including the more basic questions.

Several studies were initiated by the U.S. Office of Education's National Center for Educational Statistics, directed by Assistant Commissioner Alexander M. Mood, a statistician of some note and author of *Introduction to the Theory of Statistics*. The studies were directed by two consultants: James S. Coleman, professor of social relations at Johns Hopkins and author of *The Adolescent Society* and *Introduction to Mathematical Sociology*, among other books; and Ernest Q. Campbell, chairman of the Department of Sociology and Anthropology at Vanderbilt and author of *Christians in Racial Crisis*.

The results of these studies are reported by Coleman, Campbell, Mood, and four USOE staff members—Carol J. Hobson, James McPartland, Frederic D. Weinfeld, and Robert L. York—in **Equality of Educational Opportunity** (Government Printing Office, Washington, D.C. 1966. 743 pp. $4.25), a thick, paperbound volume filled with tables and charts and accompanied by a separately bound **Supplemental Appendix** ($3) containing 548 pages of computer-printed correlations. The report shows signs of being hastily put together to meet the two-year congressional deadline. The major findings are imbedded in a mass of trivial detail, and the summary (available as a separate 33-page booklet, $0.30), which appears to have been guided by a desire to avoid disturbing public opinion, is actually misleading. The survey itself, however, was carefully planned and skillfully analyzed. Conducted at a cost of $1.25 million— about half the cost of an F-4 Phantom Jet—it is one of the largest studies yet completed in the field of education, and its startling findings assure it the status of a landmark in educational research.

The principal study was a survey of over 600,000 children enrolled in grades 1, 3, 6, 9, and 12 of about 4000 schools generally representative of all U.S. public schools, but with some intentional overrepresentation of schools enrolling minority children. The children answered questionnaires about their attitudes and home backgrounds and took tests of educational achievement and verbal and nonverbal ability. Teachers, principals, and superintendents also answered questionnaires, and the teachers took a brief verbal-ability test. A survey of such scope would have been nearly impossible just 15 years ago; but, through the magic of optical scanners, computers, and probably Benzedrine, the current report was released an unbelievable ten months after data collection was started. The survey was met with suspicion and slander in many communities, and school systems in several major cities refused to participate. Complete data were available for only 59 percent of the sampled schools, which shortcoming detracts from the survey's value as a census.

Analyses of the data were concerned with four major questions:

1) *Are minority groups segregated in public schools?* To no one's surprise, it was found that segregation prevails. Nationwide, 65 percent of Negroes attended schools in which over 90 percent of the students were Negro, and 80 percent of whites attended schools in which over 90 percent of the students were white. There was greater segregation in the South than in the North. Mexican Americans, American Indians, Puerto Ricans, and Oriental Americans were also segregated, but to a lesser extent than Negroes and whites.

2) *Are the school facilities for minority children inferior to those for the majority?* On the basis of such indicators of school quality as class size, educational programs, physical facilities, and teacher qualifications, no consistent advantage was found for any one group, and the differences in the quality of education available to the various racial and ethnic groups were small when compared with differences between regions of the country and between metropolitan and nonmetropolitan areas. In terms of these indicators, the educationally deprived groups in the U.S. are not racial or ethnic minorities, but children — regardless of race — living in the South and in the nonmetropolitan North.

3) *Do the various racial and ethnic groups perform differently from each other on tests of school achievement and of verbal and nonverbal ability?* The substantial differences between the average test scores of the different racial and ethnic groups were quite similar on the various tests and at the various grade levels. Whites obtained the highest average scores, followed, in order, by Oriental Americans, American Indians, Mexican Americans, Puerto Ricans, and Negroes. "The Negroes' averages tend to be about one standard deviation below those of the whites, which means that about 85 percent of the Negro scores are below the white average" (p. 219). The differences between regions for Negroes followed the pattern for whites, but the regional variation tended to be greater for Negroes. The highest scores were obtained in the metropolitan North and the lowest in the nonmetropolitan South. The highest regional average score for Negroes was below the lowest for whites. . . .

This survey suffers from problems common to all nonexperimental studies in attempting to assess the effects of natural experiments, which are so messy that one can never be certain that all relevant variables have been taken into account or that the correlations observed in the natural setting would continue to hold if the variables were artificially manipulated. Two uncontrolled variables that come to mind as possible distorting influences in this study are student dropout and migration. If there are differential dropout rates for the various groups, loss of the less able minority students at higher grades may obscure an increasing decrement in group performance. Because of student migration, the student's

present school may not be a good indicator of the quality of education to which he has been exposed, and this clouding of the independent variable may make the regression analysis less sensitive to whatever school effects may exist.

It is unfortunate that the sensitivity of the racial issue made it necessary to collect the data from the students anonymously. If each student's name could have been associated with his test scores, a retesting of the same grades in the same schools three years later would have yielded data for a longitudinal study in four segments stretching from the first through the 12th grade.

The study would also have been improved if Jews and possibly Catholics had been identified as additional minority groups, since both are probably subject to some *de facto* segregation in public schools. The higher average performance usually found among Jews would have provided a useful contrast in the attempt to understand the lower average performance of the other minorities.

In view of these shortcomings it is obvious that this is not a good study of the effects of education on minority-group performance; it is just the best that has ever been done. Moreover, it provides the best evidence available concerning the differential effects – or rather the lack of such effects – of schools. AAAS members may find it hard to believe that the $28-billion-a-year public education industry has not produced abundant evidence to show the differential effects of different kinds of schools, but it has not. That students learn more in "good" schools than in "poor" schools has long been accepted as a self-evident fact not requiring verification. Thus, the finding that schools with widely varying characteristics differ very little in their effects is literally of revolutionary significance.

It is not customary for educational practice in the U.S. to be based on research, and these results will likely have little influence on educational policy. The conservatism may be adaptive in this instance, because the findings are too astonishing to be accepted on the basis of one imperfect study. What seems to be required is additional study of differential school effects with better controls for input. However, until these findings are clarified by further research they stand like a spear pointed at the heart of the cherished American belief that equality of educational opportunity will increase the equality of intellectual achievement.

5.11 Parent-Adolescent Relationships and Adolescent Independence in the United States and Denmark

Denise Kandel
Gerald S. Lesser

This paper examines patterns of interactions between adolescents and their parents in two cultures, the United States and Denmark. We focus in particular on factors within the family which promote the development of independence, clearly the major task facing both adolescents and parents during the adolescent period.

The data come from a larger study concerned with the internal structure and relative influence of families and peer groups in the United States and Denmark.[1]

Method

A. Sample

In the spring and summer of 1965, data were collected from all students in three high schools in the United States (N = 2,327) and 12 secondary schools in Denmark (N = 1,552) through the use of structured questionnaires. In addition, the students' mothers were asked to complete self-administered, structured mailed questionnaires containing many questions identical to those included in the students' instrument: 70 percent of the mothers in the United States and 75 percent in Denmark returned their questionnaires. The findings to be discussed in this chapter are based on data from students of matched adolescent-mother pairs from intact families; there are 1,141 such pairs in the American sample and 977 in the Danish. The proportion of boys in these pairs is 51 percent in the United States and 48 percent in Denmark.

The samples in this study were not selected to be representative of the total adolescent population in each country, but rather to include schools in different ecological settings, such as rural and urban. While an attempt was made to match Danish and American schools on that basis, differences appear in the demographic characteristics of the American and Danish families sampled.[2] The American families are larger than the Danish ones. Because of differences in the secondary school system of the two countries, the Danish students in the sample are slightly younger than the Americans. The median age of the Americans is 16 years as compared to 15 years for the Danes. There are also large differences in

Reprinted from the *Journal of Marriage and the Family*, 1969, *31*, 348–358, by permission of the author and the National Council of Family Relations.

the occupational distribution of the two samples. The Danish sample contains a much larger proportion of farmers (24 percent) and managers and officials (28 percent) and a smaller proportion of skilled (15 percent) and unskilled workers (20 percent) than the American sample where these groups amount to two percent, 11 percent, 36 percent, and 34 percent, respectively.

We were concerned, therefore, that the differences in family patterns observed between the Danish and American samples might reflect structural or occupational characteristics of each sample rather than true cultural differences. However, we examined the effect of each of these factors, and in particular father's occupation, on the patterns of family interaction to be described below and found no significant or consistent differences among the different occupational groups in the two countries. Therefore, while the cross-cultural comparisons to be presented do not control for father's occupation, this probably does not affect the cross-cultural differences that appear.

Overall, in both countries, the patterns of family life reported by the mothers are similar to those reported by the adolescents. This paper is based upon the adolescents' answers.

B. Questionnaires

Data from respondents were collected through self-administered structured questionaires. The topics included, among others, adolescents' values and attitudes and patterns of family interaction. Identical forms of the questionnaire were used in both countries.

Great care was taken to insure that the questions asked, which had been developed in the United States, would be relevant in Denmark. In the effort to establish conceptual as well as linguistic equivalence of the questionnaire items, the pretesting of instruments combined back translation with both individual and group field interviewing in the following sequence:

1. The original questionnaires were translated into Danish; then another translator independently translated this Danish version back into English (back translation).
2. Original and retranslated English versions were then compared and discrepancies clarified and corrected.
3. A second Danish version was then pretested in interviews with individual adolescents, with probes used to assess the meaning of the questions to them.
4. Based upon this pretest information, the Danish questionnaire was again revised and then back translated into English and then once again into Danish.
5. Field interviewing in small groups constituted the next trial phase.

6. A final back translation was performed.

In these successive cycles of translation, back translation, individual field testing, back translation, group field testing, and additional translation, the back translation steps attempted to reach linguistic equivalence, while the interspersed field interviewing attempted to approach conceptual equivalence in the meaning of the questions.

Results

The analysis that follows is divided into three sections and examines the following points: (1) the distribution of patterns of parent-adolescent interaction in the United States and Denmark, (2) the independence which adolescents experience in both countries, and (3) the association between family patterns and feelings of independence.

1. *Patterns of Parent-Adolescent Interaction in the United States and Denmark*

A. *Parental authority.*   As an index of parental power structure, patterns of decision-making between parent and adolescent were used. These patterns were measured by two five-response category items, one for the mother and one for the father. These items were modified from Bowerman and Elder, and Elder.[3]

Three types of power were defined:

Authoritarian: The parent makes all decisions relavant to the adolescent.

Democratic: Decisions are made jointly by the child and his parent.

Permissive: The adolescent has more influence in making decisions than his parent.

Striking differences exist between Danish and American families in the distribution of these patterns of parental authority. Some of these differences have been discussed elsewhere[4] and they will only be reviewed briefly here.

In both countries, the father relates in a more authoritarian manner to his children than the mother.[5] However, the Danes report democratic and equalitarian patterns between parents and adolescents to a much greater extent than the Americans. The relative predominance of one pattern of parental authority over the other in the two countries is illustrated even more vividly when one considers simultaneously the authority patterns of mother and father in the same family. The predominant family combination in Denmark is the joint democratic (41 percent); the predominant American pattern is the joint authoritarian (32 percent).[6]

Consistent with their more autocratic control, American parents insist

on many more specific rules than do the Danes. Respondents were presented with a list of eight rules and asked to check which ones the parents had for their teen-age children in the family: 55 percent of the American adolescents indicate that their parents have three or more rules for them as compared to only 29 percent of the Danes.

The differences in prevalence of the democratic pattern in both countries do not explain the differences in number of rules. While the number of rules in a family is directly related to the amount of power which parents exercise toward their children in the decision-making process, the cross-cultural differences in number of rules persist even when type of power is held constant. Within each pattern, Danish mothers and fathers have fewer rules for their children than the Americans. (Data are not presented.)

B. *Communication between parents and adolescents.* Danish parents and their adolescents also communicate with each other more extensively than do American parents and their children. Danish parents provide more explanations for their decisions and rules than the American parents. (In both countries, fathers provide fewer explanations than mothers.) In addition, Danish adolescents are more likely than Americans to discuss their personal problems with their parents.

Although a strong relationship exists between type of parental authority and the frequency of parental explanations for rules, the cross-cultural differences in frequency of explanations are reduced only slightly when type of parental authority is controlled for. Within each pattern, the Danish parent is more likely to provide explanations than the American.

C. *Other patterns.* With respect to the other patterns investigated— reliance, affective behavior, and modeling—in both countries adolescents have close relationships with their parents. However, the Danes are somewhat less likely than the Americans to rely upon the mother for advice; they are also less close to the mother and less likely than the Americans to want to be the kind of person the mother is. By contrast, they are closer to the father and are more likely than the Americans to rely upon the father for advice, to enjoy doing things with him, and to want to be the kind of person he is.

It is against the background of the Danish data that the relative importance of the mother in the American family assumes its full significance.[7]

2. Adolescent Independence

A. *When are rules instituted?* American and Danish parents differ not only with respect to the number of rules they insist upon, but also

with respect to the conditions under which they apply these rules. The patterns of socialization of adolescents by their parents—the need for rules and the specific ways in which rules function—appear to be completely the opposite in the United States and Denmark. For three areas for which the adolescent has been asked about parental rules, information is also available about the adolescent's corresponding behavior. These areas are television watching, number of hours on homework, and going steady. . . .

For each area, it has been assumed that the following behaviors on the part of the adolescent represent the kind of behavior which parents try to enforce with their rule: watching television as little as possible (one hour or less), doing homework for two hours or more, and not going steady. The association between rules and (assumed) preferred behavior operates in opposite directions in the two countries. In the United States the proportion of adolescents showing the behavior favored by parents is *highest* when the parents have a *specific* rule about it. In Denmark it is *highest* when there is *no* rule. For instance, the proportion of adolescents watching TV for one hour or less every day in the United States is 41 percent when the parents have a rule about number of hours spent watching television as against only 27 percent when they have no rule. In Denmark the corresponding percentages are 39 and 66. Similar differences appear with respect to the other two areas.

Those associations throw some light on the functioning of the family in the United States and Denmark. The data suggest the existence of two different patterns of adolescent socialization in the two countries: external constraints in the United States versus internalized norms in Denmark. In the United States, parents apparently need to enforce specific rules in order to insure that the adolescent does what is expected of him. If there are no rules, the adolescent is likely to engage in the disapproved behavior. In Denmark the adolescents appear to have internalized their parents' wishes and to behave in the approved fashion without any further external constraints. Rules are instituted in those cases in which Danish adolescents do not yet do what is expected of them. Thus, the Danish adolescent appears better able to act in a self-governing and independent fashion than the American.

These findings suggest also that the different socialization patterns during adolescence may be a consequence of different socialization practices during childhood. We would suggest that the American parent fails to limit the behavior of the child adequately so as to lead him to acquire some self-discipline early in life, while the Danish parent exercises greater control in childhood leading to greater self-direction in adolescence. If the speculation is correct, there would thus be early permissiveness and later constraint in the United States versus early control

and later independence in Denmark. Data are not currently available to test these hypotheses. But the early permissiveness of American parents has been amply documented in existing American parent-child studies and has been one of the aspects of American life most frequently commented upon by foreigners.[8] No data are available about early child-rearing practices in Denmark.

B. *The independence of Danish adolescents.* A series of additional findings provide evidence that the Danish adolescent is not only treated more like an adult by his parents but also that he feels *subjectively* more independent from his parents than does the American.

The feeling of independence from parents expresses itself in a variety of ways. For example, in case of a conflict with parents, Danes are more likely than the Americans to act according to their own rather than their parents' wishes. When asked what they would do if their parents were to object to their friends, more Danes than Americans say they would continue to see these friends. More Danish than American adolescents also believe (1) that they hold opinions different from their parents' and (2) are granted the freedom from both parents which they, the adolescents, think they should have.[9] Similarly, about twice as many Americans as Danes believe that their parents should treat them more like an adult than they do at present. The last two items are very highly correlated: students who experience freedom are less likely to wish their parents would treat them more like adults. However, among American adolescents who feel they get enough freedom, almost half feel it is given to them in such a way that nevertheless they do not feel they are being treated as adults. (Data are not presented.)

It can be argued that the adolescent's satisfaction with the degree of freedom granted to him by his parents depends as much upon his *subjective* definition of how much freedom is enough freedom as upon the *actual* amount of liberty granted him. The American adolescent's relative dissatisfaction with the amount of freedom granted him by his parents could reflect greater absolute demands on his part as compared to the Danes. However, the data indicate that the subjective feeling of freedom is based upon reality. The smaller the number of rules, the stronger the feeling of satisfaction with the amount of freedom granted by parents.[10] The satisfaction expressed by the child therefore appears to be an accurate indicator of the independence with which he is being raised. Greater freedom and independence are being granted the adolescent in Denmark than in the United States.

That American parents treat their children as children for a longer period of time than the Danes becomes even more apparent when one examines adolescents of different ages. In both countries, as adolescents

grow older, the number of rules decreases and the proportion of adolescents experiencing adequate freedom increases. But the American adolescent is still subject to more rules at the age of 18 than the Dane at 14 years. The proportion of adolescents satisfied with the amount of freedom granted them by both parents is at the same level among the 14-year-old Danes as among the 17-year-old Americans; and while at 18 years of age 59 percent of Americans say that their parents should treat them more like adults than they presently do, only 18 percent of Danes feel this way. Furthermore, the proportion of children desiring more adult status remains at a constant level in the United States at ages 15 through 18, while in Denmark this proportion decreases consistently with age.

Thus, the pattern of adolescent socialization seems to be different in the United States and Denmark, the Danish adolescents experiencing an increasing degree of independence through his teens while the American appears to remain at a stationary and less emancipated level.

3. Family Patterns and Independence

In both countries, feelings of independence from parents are associated with certain family patterns. It was noted earlier that the fewer the rules in the family, the greater the feelings of independence experienced by adolescents. However, permissiveness in decision-making, as such, does not lead to most intense feelings of being granted independence. Most freedom and most satisfaction with adult status granted by parents are experienced by children of democratic mothers and fathers who engage their children actively in the decision-making process. Similarly, the adolescents' subjective feelings of independence are enhanced when parents provide many explanations for their rules and decisions.

The patterns of parent-adolescent interaction which are associated with feelings of independence were noted above to be more characteristic of Danish families than of the American. However, the cross-cultural differences in the frequency of these family patterns do not account entirely for the cross-cultural difference in adolescents' feelings of independence, especially with respect to feeling that one is being granted adequate adult status. With respect to feelings of freedom, when type of parental authority is held constant, cross-cultural differences have completely disappeared among the authoritarian families and are very much reduced in the other two patterns. When frequency of parental explanations is held constant, cross-cultural differences in feeling of freedom are reduced only when parents provide frequent explanations. And even when they are subject to the same number of rules, more Danes than Americans are satisfied with the amount of freedom granted them.

The cross-cultural differences in satisfaction with adult status granted

by parents are not much affected when family patterns are held constant, except for frequency of parental explanations.

The family patterns examined so far pertain to the parents' interactions toward their children. As regards the child's interaction with his parents, in both countries, the feeling of being granted adequate independence from parents is associated with positive interactions with parents. Far from leading to estrangement from parents, the enhanced feeling of independence is associated with closeness to parents and positive feelings toward them. Thus, many of the adolescents in the sample are able to develop a sense of autonomy while maintaining close relationships with their parents.[11]

Students who feel they get enough freedom from their parents are more likely to feel extremely close to them, to enjoy doing many things with them, to talk most problems over with them, to depend upon their parents for advice, to want to be like their parents in many ways. A strong positive association exists between the adolescents' satisfaction with the freedom granted them by their parents and their attitudes toward their parents. In both countries, adolescents who experience sufficient freedom less frequently see their parents as old-fashioned, less frequently report that it is harder to get along with them than it used to be, or report conflicts with their mother or their father than adolescents who yearn for greater freedom.

It is clear that in contrast to the strong cross-cultural differences observed in the distribution of family patterns, the relationship of family patterns to other variables follows *identical* trends in both the United States and Denmark. The fact that some cross-cultural differences in feelings of independence still persist when relevant family patterns are held constant shows that adolescents and their families exist within a larger social and cultural context which exercises its influence beyond that of the family itself.

Discussion and Conclusion

Contrary to the commonly held belief that adolescents are estranged from their parents, the present data suggest that in the United States and Denmark adolescents are close to their parents,[12] in particular to their mothers.

Five general areas of interaction were examined: authority, communication, reliance, affective behavior, and modeling.

The patterns reported by adolescents in the two countries differ most dramatically in the areas of parental authority and communication. Families where the parent alone makes decisions have been characterized as "authoritarian"; where both parent and child decide jointly, as "democratic"; and where the child alone decides, as "permissive." The author-

itarian pattern is the one most frequently observed in the United States, whether the practice of mothers alone, of fathers alone, or of the two jointly are considered. The authoritarian pattern is infrequent in Denmark, and the modal family pattern is the democratic. American families have more rules and provide fewer explanations for their rules and decisions than do Danish families. Danish adolescents are more likely than the Americans to discuss their problems with their parents. The prominence of the mother in the American family is revealed in the cross-cultural distribution of adolescent dependence for advice on his mother, closeness to her, and desire to be the same kind of person she is.

A most striking cross-cultural difference appears around the issue of independence. Danish adolescents have a strong subjective sense of their independence from parental influence: they feel more frequently than the Americans that they would disregard their parents' wishes about not seeing friends, that their opinions are different from those of their parents, that they are being treated like adults by their parents and get sufficient freedom from their parents.[13] Furthermore, in contrast to the Danes, American adolescents appear unable to behave according to their parents' wishes unless their parents have clear and specific rules for them. These findings, thus, do not support the widespread belief that American adolescents act independently and are encouraged by their parents to be independent at an earlier age than Europeans.[14]

In both countries, feelings of independence are enhanced when parents have few rules, when they provide explanations for their rules, and when they are democratic and engage the child actively in the decision-making process. Furthermore, feelings of independence from parents in both countries, far from leading to rebelliousness, are associated with closeness to parents and positive attitudes toward them.

Thus, while the two countries are characterized by different distributions of family patterns, the interrelationships among these patterns and the consequences for adolescent socialization follow similar trends in both countries.[15] For example, the implications of authority structure for independence are the same in the United States and Denmark. Parental authority, which is defined along a continuum involving the child's participation in the decision-making process, is related in a curvilinear fashion to the feeling of independence. Children with democratic parents experience most freedom. Similarly, Devereaux and his collaborators[16] found differences in socialization practices of parents in England, Germany, and the United States, but great uniformities in the interrelationships among different variables within each country. These cross-cultural data suggest that, while socialization practices of families in the Western world differ somewhat, the consequences of particular practice for the child are similar within each culture.

The overall similarity in the interrelationships among variables in both

countries should not conceal the possibility that differences in the distribution of the items and the preponderance of particular patterns in one culture as compared to the other may lead to great differences in adolescent behavior in the two countries. For example, extrapolations from Elder's[17] findings suggest that the greater prevalence of the democratic authority pattern in combination with the more frequent explanations of rules in Denmark than in the United States may have particular implications for the issue of adolescent independence. Danish adolescents would not only be more independent than the Americans, but they would also experience a more complete type of autonomy vis-à-vis their parents. The combination of authoritarian parental authority and frequent explanations, which is common in the American situation, would indeed lead to feelings of dependency.

An inescapable conclusion from these results is that in the United States, parents treat their adolescents as children longer than in Denmark. Danish adolescents are expected to be self-governing; American adolescents are not. One can speculate about conditions in the two countries which lead to these differences in family structure. For example, children in the United States remain in school longer than in Denmark. They are not expected to make adult decisions as quickly as the Danes. Yet, at the same time American children have more money and experience greater pressure to spend in adult ways than the Danes. Having delayed the adulthood training—that is, teaching the children self-discipline—the parents are faced in the United States with adolescents who are in fact more dependent on them psychologically yet have the greater economic opportunity to do things independently. We would suggest that children in the United States are subject to a delayed socialization pattern, both in terms of autonomy from parental control as an adolescent and perhaps discipline as an earlier child. We would speculate that, as young children, Danes are subject to stronger discipline than the Americans. If this were indeed true, the discipline exercised at an early age would create a child who as an adolescent is far more disciplined and one to whom, as a consequence, the parent can afford to give freedom.

Notes

1. Denise B. Kandel, Gerald S. Lesser, Gail Roberts, and Robert S. Weiss, *Adolescents in Two Societies: Peers, School, and Family in the United States and Denmark,* Final Report, Office of Education: Contract No. OE-4-10-069, 1968.

2. Kandel *et al., op. cit.*

3. Charles E. Bowerman and Glen H. Elder, "Variations in Adolescent Perception of Family Power Structure," *American Sociological Review,* 29 (1964), pp. 551-567; Elder, *op. cit.*

4. Denise B. Kandel and Gerald S. Lesser, "Parental Relationships of Adolescents in the United States and Denmark," *Transactions of the 6th World Congress of Sociology,* 4, Louvain: Editions Nauwelaerts, 1968.

5. The greater authoritarianism of the adolescent's father as compared to the mother is also reported by Elder (*op. cit.*) for the United States.

6. Kandel and Lesser, *op. cit.*

7. In this discussion of cross-cultural differences, within-family differences which result from the sex of the child have been purposely ignored. The same general cross-cultural differences appear among both boys and girls, and the same intrafamily variations appear in both countries. Overall, one can observe in both countries a somewhat warmer and more intimate contact between children and parents of the same sex than of the opposite sex. The differences in many instances are small. Furthermore, while girls are consistently closer to their mothers than to their fathers, boys are not always closer to their fathers than to their mothers.

8. Geoffrey Gorer, *The American People*, New York: W. W. Norton & Company, 1948. ms. pp. 258-260
10:11

9. The exact text of the question is: "Do your parents give you as much freedom as you think you *should* have?" Responses are: yes, both do; mother does; father does; neither does.

10. The same findings obtain on the mother's report of number of rules in the family.

11. Elizabeth B. Murphey, Earle Silber, George V. Coelho, David A. Hamburg, and Irwin Greenberg, "Development of Autonomy and Parent-Child Interaction in Late Adolescence," *American Journal of Orthopsychiatry,* 33 (1963), pp. 643–652.

12. A recently completed study, based on a representative sample of American adolescents, now provides supporting evidence for this conclusion (IRS National Survey of Youth, 1967, A Report to Participants).

13. This independence may express itself in a variety of ways, including the sexual sphere. For example, Harold T. Christensen and George R. Carpenter, "Value-Behavior Discrepancies Regarding Premarital Coitus," *American Sociological Review,* 27 (1962), pp. 66–74, found a greater permissiveness in attitudes and behaviors regarding premarital secual intimacy among university students in Denmark than in the United States.

14. Lenore Boehm, "The Development of Independence: A Comparative Study," *Child Development,* 28 (1957), pp. 85–92; Lawrence Wylie, "Youth in France and the United States," *Daedalus,* 91 (1962), pp. 198–215.

15. This finding provides confirmatory evidence for Bronfenbrenner's theoretical concept of "optimal level" in the influence of parental behavior upon the child (Urie Bronfenbrenner, "Toward a Theoretical Model for the Analysis of Parent-Child Relationships in a Social Context," in *Parental Attitudes and Child Behavior,* ed. by John Glidewell, Springfield, Illinois: Charles C. Thomas, 1961, pp. 90–109).

16. Edward C. Devereaux, *Socialization in Cross-Cultural Perspective: A Comparative Study of England, Germany, and the United States,* paper presented at the 9th International Seminar on Family Research, Tokyo, Japan, September 1965.

17. Elder, *op. cit.,* "Parental Power Legitimation and Its Effects on the Adolescent."

5.12 Socialization Correlates of Student Activism

Jeanne H. Block
Norma Haan
M. Brewster Smith

Studies assessing the intellectual dispositions, academic careers, value systems, and personality characteristics of student activists are amassing. In the studies completed to date, activist students have been defined variously as members of the Students for a Democratic Society (Braungart, 1966), marchers in peace parades (Soloman and Fishman, 1964), protestors against university compliance with ranking students for the draft (Flacks, 1967), dissenters against university cooperation with the House unAmerican Activities Committee (Gamson, Goodman & Gurin, 1967), organizers of the Vietnam Summer Project (Keniston, 1968) and participants in the Berkeley Free Speech Movement (FSM) (Watts and Whittaker, 1966; Heist, 1966; Lyonns, 1965; Somers, 1965; Block, Haan & Smith, 1968; Haan, Smith, & Block, 1968; Smith, Haan, & Block, 1967). Despite these differing selective criteria for student activism, the results across studies have been remarkably coherent. Activists are found to be intellectually gifted, academically superior, and politically radical young people from advantaged homes in which the parents are successful in their careers, comfortable in their economic position, and liberal in their political orientations.

The positions taken by youth vis-a-vis contemporary issues provide a social laboratory in which commitment, rebellion, apathy, and disengagement can be studied. The present paper is concerned with (a) extending our understanding of the antecedents of activism as they may be inferred from students' retrospective descriptions of the child-rearing orientations and values of their parents, and (b) identifying socialization practices differentially associated with diverging orientations toward political-social activism that could be identified in 1965 – 1966.

The assessment of socialization practices and their relationship to student activism gains importance in the present social climate. The recent change in the character of student activism has tried society's patience and increased its hostility toward activists, resulting in demands for repressive action on the part of societal institutions to control student behavior. Furthermore, the child-rearing doctrines of the recent past, based on differentiated responsiveness to the legitimate needs of the child, are being repudiated in the popular press, perhaps in reaction to the indictment of Dr. Benjamin Spock who provided the blueprint for

Excerpted and reprinted from the *Journal of Social Issues*, 1969, *XXV*, No. 4, 143 – 177, by permission of the Society for the Psychological Study of Social Issues.

contemporary child-rearing practices. Parents are being implicated for their "permissiveness" and their failure to establish limits for their children. Fundamental to the arguments for "law and order" and restoration of "respect for authority" is the assumption that contemporary youth are lacking in internal controls because they were not disciplined sufficiently in their malleable years. Our data speak directly to these questions.

Additionally, this paper seeks to demonstrate that, despite the constancies noted among studies of student activists, a more articulated definition of activism conjoined with more differentiated analyses reveals important differences among activists heretofore obscured by the broad criteria used in studies to date.

Two dimensions seem helpful to us in considering activism in young adults (Block, et al., 1968). First is the *degree of involvement* with contemporary political-social issues. At one extreme of this dimension are the uninvolved or apathetic youth unconcerned with political or social matters; at the opposite pole are the active, politically and socially involved young people, who feel a sense of instrumentality lacking in apathetic youth.

The quality of activism is determined in large part by a second dimension relating to the *acceptance or rejection of institutional authority and traditional societal values*. At one end of this continuum we find the conforming young person who accepts the prevailing values of society, while the opposite pole is defined by young people who categorically reject traditional societal values and repudiate both personal and institutional authority.

In accruing samples of young people to participate in this research, we attempted to recruit subjects representing different degrees of commitment, varying attitudes about institutional authority, and divergent ideological positions. Approaching activism in this more differentiated way, we studied the nature, scope, and patterns of political-social activity, moral orientations, and socialization antecedents in samples of students recruited during 1965–66 from the University of California at Berkeley and from San Francisco State College, plus several groups of Peace Corps trainees (Block et al., 1968; Haan et al., 1968; Smith et al., 1967).

The Contact Samples

Sampling strategies were designed (*a*) to identify activist students by virtue of criterion behaviors (arrest in the FSM sit-in, tutoring in the ghetto, participation in demonstrations, joining the Peace Corps) rather than solely by organizational affiliations, (*b*) to include activists varying in the degree to which their activities involve overt rejection of institutional authority (those arrested in sit-ins vs. those working in the ghetto or joining the Peace Corps), and (*c*) to replicate findings and extend the

generalizations possible by conducting the study on two campuses differing in academic selectivity and in the prevalent socio-economic levels from which their students are drawn.

Student activists were recruited from those arrested in the 1964 Free Speech Movement sit-in at Berkeley and from participants in the Experimental College, Tutorial Project, and Community Development Program at San Francisco State College. Three political groups from Berkeley representing different ideological positions (members of the campus Democratic and Republican groups as well as the California Conservatives for Political Action) were included to extend the definition of activism to include explicitly political behaviors. Both at Berkeley and at San Francisco State College, students were selected randomly from the registration files to constitute contrast samples against which the activist samples could be compared. All student samples were restricted to sophomores, juniors, and seniors. Finally, a sample of Peace Corps volunteers was included, anticipating that their commitments did not involve a challenge of institutional authority. In all, 1033 young people participated in this research. Demographic description of the various contact samples can be found in Smith et al., 1967.

The Activism Samples

From the total pool of subjects, relatively homogeneous subgroups were identified to permit a more differentiated analysis of activism. It was apparent that neither formal membership, informal commitment to an ad hoc movement, or even arrest in the FSM sit-in provided an unambiguous indication of a student's characteristic orientation to political-social action. The Berkeley random sample, for example, included a number of students who had sat in at Sproul Hall, but who left before arrests were made. Larger numbers had been active in the FSM crisis — picketing, attending FSM rallies, raising money for bail and other purposes. Also, among the FSM participants differences existed in their previous involvements with political-social issues. Accordingly, using the information available about the political-social *behaviors* of our participants, we defined five sub-groups according to the following criteria:

Inactives: young people who reported no participation in political or social organizations or activities. They may be either socially isolated or career-oriented young people who have not involved themselves with campus organizations or ad hoc movements.

Conventionalists: young people who were fraternity or sorority members but who fell below the mean in their participation in protest

activities (sit-ins, picketing, demonstrating, etc.) and in social service activities (tutoring, social agency or hospital volunteer work, helping the handicapped, etc.). The Conventionalists tend in these respects to follow the traditional college student stereotype, more concerned with social functions than with social action.

Constructivists: young people whose scores on social service were above the mean of the total sample but whose scores on protest activities fell below the mean. The Constructivists tend to commit themselves to restitutive work aimed at relieving social ills and are infrequently involved in organized protest.

Dissenters: young people whose scores on protest activities were above the mean but whose scores on social service activities were below the mean of the total sample. The Dissenters tend to devote their energies to protesting the policies of Establishment-oriented institutions.

Activists: young people whose scores on both social action and protest action fell above the means of the total sample. Note that we make a distinction between the Activist and the Dissenter. The Activist, according to our definition, is concerned about the plight of his fellow human beings and works to alleviate pain and poverty and injustice. At the same time, he is disillusioned with the status quo and involves himself in protest against policies and institutions that do not accord with his image of a just society. . . .

The Inactives

Overall, the Inactives characterized their parents rather neutrally with respect to the affective quality of the parent-child relationship. The parents were seen as being both most worried about the health of their children and, relative to the other groups, least emotionally involved. Inactives' parents tended to suppress sex, emphasize self-control, and inhibit self-expressiveness, according to the CRPR descriptions by their young. These parents were adjudged relatively high in their concerns about conformity but were only moderate in their emphasis on achievement and independence. They were described as using anxiety arousal to control the behavior of their children; and this psychological mechanism, coupled with intrusive supervision, augmented other techniques of discipline in the socialization of the Inactives. The parents of Inactives appeared to be somewhat anxious, suppressive, and concerned with obedience and conformity to parental demands. They seemed to value docility and to discourage steps toward individuation in their children.

The suppressive control attributed to the parents of Inactives appears to be more true for males where the mothers emphasized early training and self-control for their sons and tended to discourage both self-assertiveness and independence. Fathers of the male Inactives were oriented toward punishments and discipline and concerned about conformity, according to the CRPR descriptions by their sons. These fathers were also most anxious about the health status of their sons.

In summary, the parents of Inactives were depicted as being concerned about conformity, obedience, and docility. Their demands were primarily for "good" behavior rather than for achievement or independence as shown by the rank ordering or the standardized factor scores in terms of their salience for the Inactives. The five factors ranked highest in terms of the overall means are: *Worry about Child's Health, Emphasis on Conformity, Control by Anxiety Induction, Prohibition of Self-expression*, and *Suppression of Sex*. The five factors ranked lowest in terms of their overall means are: *Prohibition of Teasing, Emotional Involvement, Emphasis on Early Achievement of Physiological Controls, Encouragement of Independence*, and *Emphasis on Achievement*.

The Conventionalists

The Conventionalists described relationships with their parents most positively and felt their parents were emotionally involved in their parental roles. The child-rearing orientation of Conventionalists' parents emphasizes (according to their young) socially-appropriate behavior, independence, achievement, and obedience. These parental demands were invoked with clarity (see scores on *Structuring of Responsibilities*) and enforced with a variety of disciplinary techniques, ranging from physical punishment to psychological mechanisms of control. The Conventionalists' parents scored highest on *Punishment Orientation, Intrusive Control, Guilt Induction* as well as the selective use of rewards and punishments (although the last factor was not significant). The parents of Conventionalists were described as suppressing sex but were more tolerant of aggression—physical aggression in males and verbal aggression in both sexes. Despite the circumscription of behavior in many areas, the parents of Conventionalists were seen as moderately accepting of self-assertiveness, and as recognizing the needs of their children for privacy. More than any other group, these parents were described as demanding—both in terms of insistence on socially-appropriate behavior and in their emphasis on achievement and assumption of responsibility.

The pattern of factor scores for the two sexes suggests that the child-rearing orientations of Conventionalists' parents may be most differentiated in terms of sex role. For male Conventionalists, parental socializa-

tion seems most focused upon the development of assertive masculinity. Males were encouraged to be independent; self-expression and aggression were accepted more often than was true of female Conventionalists. Both mothers and fathers of the Conventionalist males scored highest on the dimension of *Suppression of Sex* and the various factors reflecting disciplinary practices were somewhat more salient for males than for females in the Conventionalist group.

The parents of female Conventionalists appear to emphasize sex-typed behavior in their daughters as reflected in their highest scores on the dimensions of *Suppression of Aggression* and *Prohibition of Self-expression*. The parents also emphasize achievement and encourage competition in their daughters, an unexpected departure from the traditional definition of the feminine role but explainable, perhaps, if one recalls the sorority affiliations of these young women, possibly an expression of social ambition in these families.

In summary, the conventional orientation of students in this group seems to have been achieved through identification with parents who themselves adhere to traditional societal values. The socialization of the Conventionalists emphasizes classical Protestant virtues — responsibility, conformity, achievement, obedience as shown by the five factors ranked highest in terms of salience by the Conventionalists: *Control by Guilt Induction, Punishment Orientation, Emphasis on Achievement, Suppression of Sex*, and *Emphasis on Sex-appropriate Behavior*. The factors with the lowest mean scores for the Conventionalists are: *Prohibition of Teasing, Opposition to Child's Secrecy Needs, Worry about Child's Health, Control by Anxiety Induction*, and *Emphasis on Self-control*. The child training of the Conventionalists appears to have been accomplished more be precept than by percept within a learning context that was described as caring and consistent.

The Constructivists

The Constructivists — like the Conventionalists — evaluated the parent-child relationship positively, but differed from the Conventionalists in that they described their parents as somewhat lower in their emotional involvement in their parental roles. They also appeared to share with the Conventionalists a coherent child-rearing philosophy that values obedience and inhibits self expression. The parents of Constructivists, like the Conventionalists, were perceived as emphasizing discipline, but diverged in their greater (although not significantly so) use of non-physical punishments. Prohibition of self-expression was characteristic of both Constructivists' and Conventionalists' parents, but the former differed in that they tended to place less emphasis on achievement and competition.

Constructivists' parents were seen as controlling the child by the use of anxiety induction; however, they were low on the dimension of guilt induction relative to the other groups.

Parental restrictions of spontaneity seemed to be related more to self-assertive behaviors than to physical aggression where Conventionalists' parents were rated as least suppressive. Again the results are most readily summarized by listing the five factors ranked in terms of salience for the Constructivists: *Punishment Orientation, Positive Evaluation of the Parent-child Relationship, Prohibition of Self-expression, Control by Anxiety Induction*, and *Emphasis on Conformity*. The five factors which the Constructivists placed lowest are: *Control by Guilt Induction, Emphasis on Achievement, Worry about Child's Health, Suppression of Aggression*, and *Naive Faith in Child's Dependability*. The relatively high positive evaluation of the parental relationships despite the restrictiveness noted in parental practices indicates that little overt rebellion has been directed against these parents, at least not at this time in the life histories of the Constructivist young people. The altruistic volunteer activities in which the Constructivists engage seem to be consistent with the parental values according to which they have been raised.

The Activists

Affectively, the Activists are not reliably distinguished from the other groups: they describe the parent-child relationship in somewhat negative terms, admitting to conflict with parents and feeling that they may have disappointed their parents. At the same time, however, they describe their parents as moderately involved in their parental roles.

In their maturity demands, the Activists' parents are similar to the Conventionalists' in that both tend to empahsize independence, responsibility, and early maturity. However, the parents of Activists diverged from the Conventionalists (and were more like the Constructivists) in their de-emphasis of achievement and competition. As might be expected, the parents of Activists were low in their demands for conformity, tending rather to encourage the individuation and independent judgment of the child.

The parents of Activists were described as most suppressing of aggression and as most prohibiting of teasing, although differences in teasing behavior did not reliably distinguish among the groups. Activists' parents were seen as accepting of sexual curiosity and encouraging of self-expressiveness. They were perceived as most tolerant of the child's secrecy and privacy needs.

In terms of discipline, the Activists' parents were portrayed as low on Punishment Orientation with its emphasis on obedience, docility, and

use of physical punishments. Psychological mechanisms of control, *Anxiety Induction and Intrusive Control*, were also significantly less often relied upon. Rather, there is a tendency, although not significant, for Activists' parents to be more oriented to non-physical punishments (isolation, withdrawal of privileges, etc.) for enforcing their demands.

Differential training emphases ascribed to parents by male and female Activists indicate that less pressure is characteristic of the upbringing of girls. Activist women described the parent-child relationship as less emotionally involved, less oriented to discipline, less concerned with achievement and competition, and less inhibiting of self-assertiveness than did the males. Parents of women were seen, however, as more suppressive of sex, and opposed to secrecy and privacy needs. For male Activists, the parents appeared to be relatively more oriented to the suppression of aggressive behaviors.

In summary, the parents of Activists encourage their children to be independent and responsible, qualities shared to some degree with parents of Conventionalists. Diverging from the Conventionalists, the parents of Activists were described as encouraging the child's differentiation and self-expressiveness, with discipline per se being less critical. Activists' parents tended to be unaccepting of aggression. The factors accorded most salience in the socialization of Activists are: *Suppression of Aggression, Encouragement of Independence, Emphasis on Early Achievement of Physiological Controls, Emotional Involvement, Prohibition of Teasing.* The factor scores with the lowest ranked means are: *Punishment Orientation, Intrusive Control, Suppression of Sex, Control by Anxiety Induction,* and *Opposition to Child's Secrecy Needs.* Like the parents of Conventionalists, the Activists' parents appear to be preparing their young to lead responsible, autonomous lives, but in accordance with inner-directed goals and values rather than externally defined roles.

Dissenters

Dissenters evaluate their parents most negatively in terms of the affective quality of the parent-child relationship. This factor includes items dealing with admitted conflict, anger, expressions of criticism and disappointment, authoritarianism, tension, lack of respect for the child, absence of intimacy, warmth, and appreciation. The negative evaluation given by Dissenters may relate to the inconsistency attributed to these parents by their young. The pattern of factor scores shows Dissenters' parents to be permissive, even laissez-faire, in many areas of child training, but controlling in others. Although not significant, Dissenters' parents are described as placing the least emphasis on independence and early maturity relative to the other groups, while pressing at the same

time for achievement and encouraging competition. They appear to stress self-expression and individuation of the young, while opposing the secrecy and privacy needs of their children. Dissenters described their parents as low in their emphasis on discipline and punishment, and neither were they said to control the child by invoking anxiety.

The Dissenters' parents diverge most markedly from the parents of Activists in their opposition to the child's secrecy and privacy needs. Although not significant, the means of the two groups were at opposite extremes on *Encouraging Independence* and *Emphasis on the Early Achievement of Physiological Controls*, with Dissenters' parents de-emphasizing these dimensions. The descriptions of Activist and Dissenter parents converged on the dimensions of conformity where both are low relative to other sub-groups, in their encouragement of self-expression, in their lesser use of psychological mechanisms to control the child, and in the negative evaluation ascribed to parent-child relationships, particularly by the Dissenters.

Male and female Dissenters characterized their parents' child-rearing attitudes in rather similar ways. Dissenting women said their fathers were more involved emotionally in the parent-child relationship, and indicated that self-expression was more acceptable than for the males. Male Dissenters were most negative in their affective evaluations of the parent-child relationship, and saw their mothers as more permissive relative to punishments and self-control while also being most opposed to secrecy in their sons.

In summary, the child-rearing of the Dissenters' parents appeared somewhat lacking in coherence. The most salient child-rearing dimensions for the Dissenters, judged by the rank ordering of the factors are: *Opposition to Child's Secrecy Needs, Prohibition of Teasing, Emphasis on Achievement, Suppression of Aggression*, and *Emotional Involvement*. The least salient factors for the Dissenters are: *Positive Parent-child Relationship, Control by Anxiety Induction, Punishment Orientation, Emphasis on Self-control*, and *Worry about Child's Health*. It is perhaps not surprising that this pattern of indulgence and permissiveness—conjoined with an interest in achievement, encouragement of competition, and opposition to the child's privacy needs—results in the conflicted, unsatisfying parental relationship described by the Dissenting young. . . .

Comparison with Other Studies

The results of this study, based on the perceptions of parental child-rearing practices by their young, are consistent with those gained from studies of parents themselves (Flacks, 1967; Schedler, 1966). Flacks

found that parents of student activists "place greater stress . . . on opportunity for self-expression, and tend to de-emphasize or positively disvalue personal achievement, conventional morality and conventional religiosity (p. 68)." Parents of non-activists expressed "conventional orientations toward achievement, material success, sexual morality, and religion," according to Flacks (1967, p. 68). Schedler (1966) found activists' parents to be significantly more tolerant of unconventional behavior and more permissive, as defined by allowing the child autonomy in decision making, than were parents of non-activists. Mothers of activists were less strict while fathers of activists were not differentiated by strictness in Schedler's study.

In the study of parents of Berkeley students recently completed and cited earlier, Block has replicated many of the essential findings reported here: Parents of Activists described greater parent-child conflict while a more positive evaluation was given by Constructivists. Suppression of aggression, a rational (rather than punitive) approach to discipline, de-emphasis of conformity and competition, encouragement of independence and expectations for responsible, mature behavior were found to characterize the child-rearing orientations of the parents of Activist students. In addition, the parents of Activists described their child-rearing in ways that differed from the descriptions offered by parents of Dissenters and that paralleled results reported here: Dissenters' parents were more inconsistent in their demands, were less rational in their disciplinary practices, were less restrictive of the child, and placed less emphasis on independence and maturity.

Methodologically, the confluence of findings from direct studies of parents with those reported here based on student appraisals of parental child-rearing practices offers justification for using this approach when parent samples cannot be assessed directly. The obtained replication for the several activism groups of salient distinguishing features derived from the student perceptions to the results obtained from samples of parents argues for the validity of young adults' evaluations of parental socialization practices.

Psychological vs. Sociological Antecedents

Reassured by the convergence of the findings, we can now confront issues regarding the interpretation of the relationships found between constellations of socialization practices and political-social protest. The sociologist Lipset (1968) has suggested that the attempts by psychologists to relate activism and parental child-rearing practices are unconvincing because "the extant studies do not hold constant the sociological and politically relevant factors in the backgrounds of the students. For

example, they report that leftist activists tend to be the offspring of permissive families characterized by a strong mother who dominates family life and decisions. Conversely, conservative activists tend to come from families with more strict relationships between parents and children, and in which the father plays a dominant controlling role. But to a considerable extent these differences correspond to little more than the variations reported in studies of Jewish and Protestant families. Childhood rearing practices tend to be linked to social-cultural-political outlooks. To prove that such factors play an independent role in determining the political choices of students, it will first be necessary to compare students *within* similar ethnic, religious, and political-cultural environments. This has not yet been done (pp. 49–50)."

Lipset is, of course, correct in reminding us of a confounding of psychological and sociological sources of explanation in much previous research. What is necessary in order to clarify matters is to disentangle the competing explanatory variables.

If Lipset's contentions are correct, the differences found between activist and non-activist groups should wash out when these samples are matched on relevant demographic variables. In the present study, separating particular demographic variables from activism is possible because of the relatively large sample size and the articulated definitions used to compose activist and non-activist sub-groups.

The "unconfounding" analysis to be reported used only the non-activist Conventionalist and the Activist sub-groups since analyses of variance had demonstrated that these two groups were not significantly different with respect either to occupational or educational levels of the parents. There was, however, a disproportionately higher number of Jews in the Activist group. In order to match these two sub-groups as closely as possible, *all* Jews were excluded from the analyses in order to evaluate Lipset's assertions that the permissive, maternally-dominated environment found to characterize the homes of protest-oriented students was a manifestation of child-rearing practices that are basically and uniquely Jewish.

The non-Jewish students in the Conventionalist and Activist sub-groups were compared with respect to the child-rearing attitudes attributed to parents, using t-tests to evaluate the reliability of differences. The results of this analysis are presented in Table 7.

These results in which religious, educational, and occupational differences between the Conventionalists and Activists have been controlled reproduce the essential findings reported earlier characterizing the differences between these two groups as a whole.[1] The parents of the Conventionalists are portrayed as more concerned with achievement, competition, docility, and obedience. The parents of non-Jewish Activists

are revealed as less controlling, less punishing (with the exception of the fathers of females who are more punishing), and less concerned with achievement. They are more suppressive of both verbal and physical aggression, and they emphasize early maturity.

It is instructive, also, to examine the dimensions on which the parents were described similarly by the Activist and Conventional students. The factors on which no differences were found—despite respectable N's (35 and 38, respectively)—in any of the four analyses of the two matched groups include: *Encouragement of Independence and Responsibility; Emotional Involvement with Child; Socialization via Explicit Rewards and Punishments; Control by Anxiety Induction; Naive Faith in Child's Dependability;* and *Subservience to Spouse.* In addition, no differences were found on the following factors in three of the four analyses: *Emphasis on Self-control, Emphasis on Sex-appropriate Behavior, Emphasis on Conformity vs. Differentiation,* and *Opposition to Child's Secrecy Needs.* Clearly, both the Conventionalists and the Activists see their parents as emphasizing maturity, dependability, and the need for behavioral limits.

These results based on samples that are comparable with respect to educational, occupational, and religious variables undermine Lipset's contentions about the explanatory power of ethnic and other demographic variables. A second line of evidence against the causal significance of demographic variables *per se* (granted as we do not, that demographic variables can *ever* have direct, theoretically interpretable causal significance) is provided by the results of the within-activism group comparisons presented earlier. Although differences in child-rearing orientations were found to exist, the Activists and Dissenters did *not* differ significantly with respect to socio-economic or educational levels. The religious backgrounds of students in the two protest-prone categories were not significantly different, and the average ratings of parents' radicalism-conservatism were also similar. Despite these similaritees on the usual demographic indices, significant differences on the CRPR were found between the Activist and Dissenter groups. Again, it follows that differences in religion, education, socio-economic status, or political ideology *cannot* be invoked to explain the divergences in child-rearing orientations that were found to discriminate the two activist sub-groups.

These results suggest that demographic characteristics may not be as potent as Lipset (together with other sociologists) has assumed in determining the differences in socialization practices found to distinguish activists' parents. Certainly socio-economic and educational levels, religious orientations, together with ecological variables, personality dispositions, and parental value orientations conjoin to pattern the parental socialization practices and so to define the learning matrix in which the

child develops and matures. Alone, however, these indices cannot be considered determinative.

Differentiating among Activists

The classification of the sample into sub-groups representing different political-social orientations has not only helped to demonstrate the independent role of socialization variables, as shown above, but has resulted, also, in more discriminating descriptions of students with different political-social orientations. The divergence between the Activist and Dissenter sub-groups is perhaps the most interesting, not only because this distinction has not been made previously in the literature but also because the change in the character of student protest in the years since the inception of this study stresses the outer limits of dissent as measured here. The present study may be only tangentially relevant for an understanding of the new student generation. The differences between the Activists and Dissenters presented here may, however, provide a basis for extrapolation to the new "Confrontationist" generation. Developing such extrapolations is beyond the scope of the present paper but the adventurous reader so inclined may find some help for his predictions in some additional comparisons of the two activist sub-groups with respect to family background variables.

Rebellion vs Concordance with Parents

Perhaps not surprisingly, the Dissenters were found to be more frequently in rebellion against the political-social ideologies of their parents than were the Activists . . . Significantly more mothers ($P < .05$) and fathers ($P < .10$) of the Dissenters were rated as conservatives in their political ideologies. Block (1968) found that, within the political spectrum of the Left, gross disjunction between the political-social attitudes of young people and those of their parents is associated with less integrated personality functioning, particularly for women. Among the Dissenting women, 20 % of their fathers and 15 % of their mothers were rated in the conservative category whereas the comparable figures for Activist women are 9 and 4 percent, respectively. This divergence in political attitudes between Dissenter and parents is not an isolated finding since the Dissenters were found to score uniformly lowest on the dimensions reflecting overall agreement with mother and with father on six contemporary political-social issues (Smith et al., 1967).

This set of findings suggests thtat Dissenters are in greater rebellion against parental attitudes than Activists who exhibit concordance across

generational boundaries. It might be anticipated that studies of today's student demonstrators, more extreme now on the dimension of protest, would reveal even greater disjunction between parent and student attitudes than was found here.

Parental Permissiveness

The second distinction to be made between the Activists and Dissenters involves the notion of permissiveness and its applicability to the parental child-rearing orientations of activists. When the descriptions of student protesters' parents are compared with the stereotype of permissiveness ascribed to these parents by the lay press, it is apparent that the newspaper interpretation is reasonably correct in regard to the *Dissenters*' origins but is quite wrong regarding the *Activists*.

The data from this study indicate that permissiveness, with its corollary laissez-faire attitudes, is more characteristic of the parents of Dissenters. Dissenters' parents were described as making relatively minimal demands upon the child for independent mature behavior, being laissez-faire with respect to limits and discipline, being tolerant of self assertiveness, and de-emphasizing self-control. These parental practices have been subsumed under the permissive label as it has been popularly understood and, accordingly, permissiveness does seem an appropriate description of the socialization practices experienced by the Dissenters. The departures from permissiveness for these parents are in the areas of aggression, opposition to secrecy, and concern with competition and achievement.

In contrast, the parents of Activists make more demands upon their children, particularly for independence, for responsible and mature behaviors. They are unaccepting of aggression, both physical and verbal. Although low in punishment orientation, Activists' parents tend to respond to misbehaviors – but with non-physical rather than physical punishments. These perceived parental behaviors are not consistent with permissiveness. Rather these parents seem to have imparted to their young a reasonably coherent set of expectations, consistent with parental values, in a manner that maintains parental dignity. Activists' parents may be considered permissive in the sense that they encourage the individuation and self-expression of the child, are more accepting of sexuality, and reject harsh punitive disciplinary methods. Although these latter parental practices and policies embody the concept of permissiveness in the circumscribed definition (and re-definition) provided by Benjamin Spock, they diverge importantly from the concept as more generally, loosely, and incriminatingly used today. The Activists, like the non-activist Conventionalists, see their parents as attempting to prepare them

to lead responsible, independent lives. This coherent set of expectations seems lacking in the Dissenters' perceptions of their parents.

These aggregated results, conjoined with the differences in ego functioning of Activist and Dissenter parents noted in the previous section, offer rather convincing evidence that parents of Activists (using the restricted definition of Activist given here) are seen as more differentiated with respect to ego functioning than are parents of Dissenting (and Nonactivist) students. Their relatively more mature ego functioning appears to be manifested in a more coherent child-rearing philosophy that is involved with respect for both self and child. The learning context established by Activists' parents appears to rely on rational, cognitive principles of learning, and the perceived goals of socialization appear to be an independent, mature, self-knowing child. Were it not for the independent confirmation of these results found in Block's study of parents themselves, it might be argued that the less charitable picture of parents portrayed by the Dissenters might be an attempt to retrospectively justify their own rebellion. This interpretation does not appear to be warranted on the basis of the external validation of these results that has been offered.

These findings taken *in toto* imply that generalizations about activists are not valid for all student demonstrators. Participants in student protests have been shown to be heterogeneous, and distinctions of consequence have been found between Activists and Dissenters. Similarly, heterogencities have been found to characterize non-active students as documented by the differences between the Inactives and the Conventionalists. Respect for these diversities should result in better understanding and more articulated predictions.

Notes

1. After excluding students with Jewish backgrounds from the two samples, t-tests of socio-economic status and educational achievement were completed to determine if the samples remained comparable after being redefined. For the female sample, no differences were found; for the male sample, the only significant finding was that the mothers of Activists tended to be better educated ($p < .05$) than were the mothers of Conventionalists.

References

Block, J. H. The child-rearing practices report. Institute of Human Development, University of California, 1965. (Mimeo)

Block, J. H. Rebellion re-examined: The role of identification and alienation. Paper presented at the Foundations' Fund for Research in Psychiatry conference on Adaptation to change, Puerto Rico, June, 1968.

Block, J. H., Haan, N., & Smith, M. B. Activism and apathy in contemporary adolescents. In J. F. Adams (Ed.), *Understanding adolescence: Current developments in adolescent psychology.* Boston: Allyn & Bacon, 1968.

Braungart, R. G. SDS and YAF: Backgrounds of student political activists. Paper presented at the annual meeting of the American Sociological Association, Miami, Florida, August, 1966.

Flacks, R. The liberated generation: An exploration of the roots of student protest. *Journal of Social Issues,* 1967, **23** (3), 52–75.

Gamson, Z. F., Goodman, J., & Gurin, G. Radicals, moderates and bystanders during a university protest. Paper presented at the annual meeting of the American Sociological Association, San Francisco, August, 1967.

Haan, N., Smith, M. B., & Block, J. The moral reasoning of young adults: Political-social behavior, family background and personality correlates. *Journal of Personality and Social Psychology,* 1968, **10**, 183–201.

Heist, P. The dynamics of student discontent and protest. Paper presented at the SPSSI Symposium of the annual meeting of the American Psychological Association, New York, September, 1966.

Keniston, K. *Young radicals: Notes on committed youth.* New York: Harcourt, Brace & World, 1968.

Lipset, S. M. The activists: A profile. *The Public Interest,* Fall, 1968, 39–51.

Loevinger, J. The meaning and measurement of ego development. *American Psychologist,* 1966, **21**, 195–206.

Lyonns, G. The police car demonstration: A survey of participants. In S. M. Lipset & S. S. Wolin (Eds.), *The Berkeley student revolt: Facts and interpretations.* Garden City, N.Y.: Anchor Books, 1965.

Schedler, P. Parental attitudes and political activism of college students. Unpublished master's thesis, University of Chicago, 1966.

Smith, M. B., Haan, N., & Block, J. Social-psychological aspects of student activism. Paper presented to the annual meeting of the American Sociological Association, San Francisco, California, August 28–31, 1967.

Soloman, F. & Fishman, J. R. Youth and peace: A psychological study of student peace demonstrators in Washington, D.C. *The Journal of Social Issues,* 1964, **20** (4), 54–73.

Somers, R. H. The mainsprings of the rebellion: A survey of Berkeley students in November, 1964. In S. M. Lipset & S. S. Wolin (Eds.), *The Berkeley student revolt: Facts and interpretations.* Garden City, N.Y.: Anchor Books, 1965.

Watts, W. A., & Whittaker, D. N. E. Free speech advocates at Berkeley. *Journal of Applied Behavioral Science,* 1966, **2** (1), 41–62.

5.13 The Roots of Alienation

Urie Bronfenbrenner
Cornell University

I. Alienation vs. Idealism

American college students in the 1970's are clearly a different breed from their predecessors of previous decades, but the distinctive characteristics of the new breed are both complex and paradoxical. Perhaps the most salient difference appears with respect to the attitudes of young people toward their own society. As is documented in the recent survey conducted by Daniel Yankelovich (1972) for the John D. Rockefeller, 3rd Fund, there is widespread disillusionment among youth with what they call "the system" — the major political, economic, and social institutions of the country. This rejection is not limited to the raucous, radical left; it is shared by the great majority of the nation's college students. "They believe that the country's major institutions — the political parties, the military, the penal system, and business — stand in need of drastic reform." (*New York Times* editorial on Yankelovich report, April 17, 1972.)

But those who would infer from this rejection of the system a clash in fundamental values between the generations, and who are thereby quickened to the fear — or hope — of social revolution, are probably misled. In the light of the evidence, the present generation of college students, in the absence of constructive moves from the rest of the society, are not likely as a group to achieve major social changes either through revolution or reform. Yet, the prospect offers no ground for complacency to those of conservative persuasion. For what we can anticipate from the coming generations of college students, so long as the rest of us continue to tolerate things as they are, is pervasive disaffection, erupting from time to time in pointless disruption, destruction, and tragic violence. It will not be a climate conducive to higher learning, or to the development of responsible leadership for our society.

The immediate and pressing reasons for this pervasive discontent lie, of course, in the genuine ills of contemporary society — notably poverty, racism, violence, and war. But the alienation of youth has deeper roots as well, that derive from psychological characteristics acquired through the curiously dissonant course of development through which these young people have passed.

To begin with, contrary to popular impression, the present generation of students — the same ones who are so critical of contemporary American institutions — hold personal, social, and political values that are almost indistinguishable from those of their parents. In the Yankelovich

survey, youthful respondents answered in much the same way as their elders to questions concerned with what they deemed to be morally right or personally desirable. In the political realm, the profile of youth was strikingly similar to that for the nation as a whole: 70 percent of the students held what were referred to as "mainstream" views, and, among the rest, conservatives outnumbered radicals two-to-one. Where youth parted company with their elders was in their sharply negative evaluation of contemporary society and its institutions. But the values in the name of which these institutions were found wanting were precisely those which the young people shared with their elders. The paradox is nicely summarized in the aforementioned editorial from *The New York Times*: "The overwhelming majority of youth's moderate center are [sic] losing hope in the workability of the system to which they seem so eager to remain loyal." They are losing hope because the system did not respond.

Unfortunately, even this more balanced and sobering formulation is probably too optimistic, for it suggests, or at least permits the interpretation, that it is only the system which is at fault, that basically the students themselves are fine; they are "eager to remain loyal;" just make the system "workable," and they will respond.

Regrettably, the reality is not quite so reassuring. First of all, there are some students who are not so "eager to remain loyal." Although they represent but a small minority, the damage and destruction to human institutions and human lives that they can ultimately precipitate are incalculable

But, from the point of view both of the fundamental responsibilities of the university and the welfare of the society, even more significant and disturbing than the destructive action of the minority of students is the social and political apathy of the majority. While perceiving gross injustice in the major institutions of their society, most students are apparently not motivated to do very much about it. Unlike their predecessors in the 1960's, who actively sought to bring about social and political changes within the system, the present generation of college students, as revealed in recent surveys and special studies, feels powerless and already defeated.

What accounts for this change over less than a decade? From the perspective of human development, the roots of the process lie farther back in the history both of the society and of the individual. They relate to the general breakdown, since World War II, of the major institutions that carry responsibility for the development of the young—namely, the family, school, neighborhood, and the community.

II. The Roots of Alienation

To consider first what has been happening to the family; in the words

of a report prepared for the White House Conference on Children (*Report to the President*),

> America's families and their children are in trouble, trouble so deep and pervasive as to threaten the future of the nation. The source of the trouble is nothing less than a national neglect of children and those primarily engaged in their care — America's parents (P. 252).

If the statement just quoted is correct, it speaks directly to our concern, for it identifies childhood as the period in which the origins of alienation are to be sought and counteracted. What then are the facts? To quote again from the foregoing report:

> The neglect begins even before the child is born. America, the richest and most powerful country in the world, stands thirteenth among the nations in combating infant mortality; even East Germany does better (*Profiles of Children*, P. 61). Moreover, our ranking has dropped steadily in recent decades.[1]. A similar situation obtains with respect to maternal and child health, day care, children's allowances, and other basic services to children and families.
>
> But the figures for the nation as a whole, dismaying as they are, mask even greater inequities. For example, infant mortality for non-Whites in the United States is almost twice that for Whites, and there are a number of Southern states, and Northern metropolitan areas, in which the ratios are considerably higher (*Profiles of Children*, Pp. 90 – 92).
>
> Ironically, of even greater cost to the society than infants who die are the many more who sustain injury but survive with disability. Many of these suffer impaired intellectual function and behavioral dis turbance including hyperactivity, distractability, and low attention span, all factors contributing to school retardation and problem behavior. Again, the destructive impact is greatest on the poorest segments of the population, especially non-Whites. It is all the more tragic that this massive damage and its subsequent cost in reduced productivity, lower income, unemployability, welfare payments, and institutionalization are avoidable if adequate nutrition, prenatal care, and other family and child services are provided, as they are in a number of countries less prosperous than ours (*Report to the President*, Pp. 252 – 253).

But it is not only children from disadvantaged families who show signs of progressive neglect. For example, an analysis carried out a few years ago (Bronfenbrenner, 1958) of data on child rearing practices in the United States over a twenty-five year period reveals a decrease in all spheres of interaction between parents and children. A similar conclu-

sion is indicated by results of cross-cultural studies comparing American parents with those from Western and Eastern Europe (Bronfenbrenner, 1970; Devereux, Bronfenbrenner & Rodgers, 1969; Rodgers, 1971). Moreover, as parents and other adults have moved out of the lives of children, the vacuum has been filled by the age-segregated peer group. Recently, two of my colleagues (Condry & Siman, in press) have completed a study showing that, at every age and grade level, children today show a greater dependency on their peers than they did a decade ago. A parallel study (Condry & Siman, in press) indicates that such susceptibility to group influence is higher among children from homes in which one or both parents are frequently absent. In addition, "peer oriented" youngsters describe their parents as less affectionate and less firm in discipline. Attachment to age-mates appears to be influenced more by a lack of attention and concern at home than by any positive attraction of the peer group itself. In fact, these children have a rather negative view of their friends and of themselves as well. They are pessimistic about the future, rate lower in responsibility and leadership, and are more likely to engage in such antisocial behavior as lying, teasing other children, "playing hooky", or "doing something illegal".

More recent evidence comes from a dissertation currently being completed by Mr. Michael Siman. Siman did something which, so far as I know, has never been done before. Working with a large sample of teenagers (ages 12 to 17), most of them from middle and lower middle-class homes in New York City, he went to a great deal of trouble to identify and study the actual peer groups in which these adolescents spend so much of their time. There were 41 such peer groups in all. Siman was interested in determining the relative influence of parents versus peers on the behavior of the teenager. Three classes of behavior were studied:

1. *Socially constructive activities* such as taking part in sports, helping someone who needs help, telling the truth, doing useful work for the neighborhood or community without pay, etc.
2. *Neutral activities* such as listening to records, spending time with the family, etc.
3. *Anti-social activities* such as "playing hooky", "doing something illegal", hurting people, etc.

Siman also obtained information on the extent to which each teenager perceived these activities to be approved or disapproved by his parents and by the members of his peer group. The results are instructive. In the case of boys, for example, he finds that for all three classes of behavior, peers are substantially more influential than parents. In fact, in most cases, once the attitudes of the peer group are taken into account, the

attitudes of the parents make no difference whatsoever. The only exceptions are in the area of constructive behavior, where the parent does have some secondary influence in addition to the peer group. But in the neutral, and, especially, the anti-social sphere the peer group is all determining. When it comes to such behaviors as doing something illegal, smoking, or aggression, once the attitude of the peer group is taken into account, the parents' disapproval carries no weight.

What we are seeing here, of course, are the roots of alienation and its milder consequences. The more serious manifestations are reflected in the rising rates of youthful drug abuse, delinquency, and violence documented in charts and tables specially prepared for the White House Conference on Children (*Profiles of Children*, Pp. 78, 79, 108, 179, 180). According to these data the proportion of youngsters between the ages of 10 and 18 arrested for drug abuse doubled between 1964; since 1963, juvenile delinquency has been increasing at a faster rate than the juvenile population; over half the crimes involve vandalism, theft, or breaking and entry; and, if the present trends continue, one out of every nine youngsters will appear in juvenile court before age 18. These figures index only detected and prosecuted offenses.

Why is it that the parents have so little influence? There are those who are quick to put the blame on the parents themselves, charging them with willful neglect and inadequate discipline. But to take this view is to disregard the social context in which families live, and thereby to do injustice to parents as human beings. Although there is no systematic evidence on the question, there are grounds for believing that parents today, far from not caring about their children, are more worried about them than they have ever been in the course of recent history. The crux of the problem, as indicated by Siman's data, is that many parents have become powerless as forces in the lives of their children. The nature of the problem has been spelled out in the previously mentioned report for the White House Conference. The following excerpts convey the thrust of the argument:

> In today's world parents find themselves at the mercy of a society which imposes pressures and priorities that allow neither time nor place for meaningful activities and relations between children and adults, which downgrade the role of parents and the functions of parenthood, and which prevent the parent from doing things he wants to do as a guide, friend, and companion to his children . . .
>
> The frustrations are greatest for the family of poverty where the capacity for human response is crippled by hunger, cold, filth, sickness, and despair. For families who can get along, the rats are gone, but the rat race remains. The demands of a job, or often two jobs, that claim mealtimes, evenings, and weekends as well as days; the trips

and moves necessary to get ahead or simply hold one's own; the ever increasing time spent in commuting, evenings out, social and community obligations — all the things one has to do to meet so-called primary responsibilities — produce a situation in which a child often spends more time with a passive babysitter than a participating parent.

The family is changing not only in its function, but also in its structure. For example, in 1971, 43 percent of the nation's mothers worked outside the home; in 1948, the figure was only 18 percent. In 1971, 10 percent of all mothers of children under six were single parents bringing up children without a husband; half of these mothers also held down a job. Among families classified as living under poverty, 45 percent of all children under six are living in female-headed households. Fifty years ago, in the state of Massachusetts, half of all families had at least one other adult besides the parents living in the household; that figure today is less than 2.5 percent. (Bronfenbrenner and Bruner 1972)

And even when the parent is at home, a compelling force cuts off communication and response among family members. To quote again from the White House Report:

> Although television could, if used creatively, enrich the activities of children and families, it now only undermines them. . . . The primary danger of the television screen lies not so much in the behavior it produces as the behavior it prevents — the talks, the games, the family festivities and arguments through which much of the child's learning takes place and his character is formed. Turning on the television set can turn off the process that transforms children into people.

In our modern way of life, children are deprived not only of parents but of people in general. A host of factors conspire to isolate children from the rest of society. The fragmentation of the extended family, the separation of residential and business areas, the disappearance of neighborhoods, zoning ordinances, occupational mobility, child labor laws, the abolishment of the apprentice system, consolidated schools, television, separate patterns of social life for different age groups, the working mother, the delegation of child care to specialists — all these manifestations of progress operate to decrease opportunity and incentive for meaningful contact between children and persons older, or younger, than themselves.

And here we confront a fundamental and disturbing fact: *Children need people in order to become human.* The fact is fundamental because it is firmly grounded both in scientific research and in human experience. It is disturbing because the isolation of children from adults simultaneously threatens the growth of the individual and the survival of the society. Child rearing is not something children can do for themselves. It

is primarily through observing, playing, and working with others older and younger than himself that a child discovers both what he can do and who he can become — that he develops both his ability and his identity. It is primarily through exposure and interaction with adults and children of different ages that a child acquires new interests and skills and learns the meaning of tolerance, cooperation, and compassion. Hence to relegate children to a world of their own is to deprive them of their humanity, and ourselves as well.

Yet, this is what is happening in America today. *We are experiencing a breakdown in the process of making human beings human.* By isolating our children from the rest of society, we abandon them to a world devoid of adults and ruled by the destructive impulses and compelling pressures both of the age-segregated peer group and the aggressive and exploitive television screen, we leave our children bereft of standards and support and our own lives impoverished and corrupted.

This reversal of priorities, which amounts to a betrayal of our children, underlies the growing disillusionment and alienation among young people in all segments of American society. Those who grew up in settings where children, families, still counted are able to react to their frustration in positive ways — through constructive protest, participation, and public service. Those who come from circumstances in which the family could not function, be it in slum or suburb, can only strike out against an environment they have experienced as indifferent, callous, cruel, and unresponsive. This report . . . points to the roots of a process which, if not reversed, . . . can have only one result: the far more rapid and pervasive growth of alienation, apathy, drugs, delinquency, and violence among the young, and not so young, in all segments of our national life. We face the prospect of a society which resents its own children and fears its youth. . . . What is needed is a change in our patterns of living which will once again bring people back into the lives of children and children back into the lives of people (*Report to the President*, Pp. 241 – 243).

Stripped of their rhetoric, the foregoing passages can be seen as spelling out the consequence of a breakdown in social process at two levels: first a failure in the primary institution of the society for making human beings human — the family; second, a "withering away" of the support systems in the larger society that in fact enable the family to function. In the last analysis, therefore, the roots of alienation are found to lie in the institutions of our society as they are presently structured and as they currently function. Specifically, urbanization, modern technological development, and their sequellae (extremes of affluence and poverty, mechanization of labor, bureaucritization of services, occupational specialization, geographic mobility) have had the effect of removing adults from

the lives of children, while placing a premium on the development of cognitive and technical skills at the expense of behavior in accord with humanistic and social values. In the past, such behavior was a primary and joint concern of family, church, and neighborhood, but with the progressive breakdown of these institutions, they have been less able to perform their socializing functions. This is particularly true for children of school age and beyond. As a result, by the time of junior high school, a discontinuity becomes apparent between values and behavior. In the preschool and primary years, when associations with adults are still frequent and intense, the child internalizes parental and community values, but many of them only at a verbal level. For previous generations, such values were then translated into corresponding patterns of action in a community which permitted and invited the involvement of children and adults in each other's lives at school, in the neighborhood, and in the world of work. In recent decades, however, these institutions have become technologized, dehumanized, and, in effect, discharged from their child-rearing responsibilities. In consequence, the child has been deprived of experience precisely in those social contexts in which values learned within the family can be translated into concrete social actions outside the family. Instead, the vacuum created by the absence of adults has been filled by the age-segregated peer groups, and the television screen, both of which provide simplistic verbalization but highly sophisticated implementation of aggressive and exploitive behaviors, which are often in direct conflict with the social values the child has learned to know, but not yet to act upon, during his formative years.

To be sure, these early humanistic values are often invoked later on by teachers and books in school, but again this occurs only at the verbal level. Moreover, especially in recent years, when presented in the classroom, these values have been recognized more in the breach than in the observance. In counter-reaction against the myths perpetuated in the teaching and texts of earlier generations, social science courses in today's schools emphasize the yawning gulf between American ideals and American reality. In foreign and domestic policy, in economic policy, in economic practice and social mores, the young person is repeatedly shown how the presumed values of the society are violated to insure the maintenance and aggrandizement of those already in power.

Thus, as he emerges from adolescence, the young person in America finds himself in a profound and crippling moral dilemma. By and large, he identifies with the ideals and values of his society, but he has been taught to recognize the widespread betrayal of these ideals and values in every day life, and has been given only minimal exposure to the substantial, if only occasional, achievements of the ideal, and — even more critically — to the concrete courses of action through which the ideal might

be pursued. Neither in school, nor in the university, is he given much information or, above all, experience in how to use the institutions of his society—both public and private—to remedy social and political ills. In terms of social action, all he knows is the simplistic, one-shot [demand or destroy] so characteristic of the context in which he has spent so much of his time—the age-segregated peer group and the commercial television screen. For those coming from environments in which the family was still strong, the aggressive impulse is inhibited by early-internalized humanistic values, but there is little knowledge or experience with an alternative course of action for resolving human problems by institutionalized means.

This brings us both to the crux of the problem and the possible strategy for its solution. We must institute changes in the education of the young so that they are exposed not only to social values but to experiences in which these values are implemented through example and personal participation.

The crucial question becomes, can our social institutions be changed, can old ones be modified and new ones introduced in such a way as to rebuild and revitalize the social context which families and children require for their effective function and growth. It is to this question that we turn as our final and most important concern.

III. Support Systems for Children and Families

To counteract the forces of alienation in contemporary American society will require the involvement of all our social institutions—not only those having direct and acknowledged impact on children and families— such as schools, churches, health and welfare services, and recreation programs—but also other organizations and enterprises.

We begin our discussion with those institutions on the contemporary American scene, which, in our judgment, will have the greatest impact in affecting, for better or for worse, the welfare of America's children and youth.

The role of day care in counteracting alienation depends on the extent to which day care programs are so located and so organized as to encourage rather than to discourage the involvement of parents and other non-professionals in the development and operation of the program both at the center and in the home. Like Project Head Start, day care programs can have no lasting constructive impact on the development of the child unless they affect not only the child himself but the people who constitute his enduring day-to-day environment in the family, neighborhood, and community. This means not only that parents must play a prominent part in the planning and administration of day care programs,

but that they must also actively participate in the execution of the program as volunteers and aides. It means that the program cannot be confined to the center, but must reach out into the home and the community so that the whole neighborhood is caught up in activities in behalf of its children. From this point of view, we need to experiment in location of day care centers in places that are within reach of the significant people in the child's life. For some families this means neighborhood centers; for others, centers at the place of work. A great deal of variation and innovation will be required to find the appropriate solutions for different groups in different settings.

Availability of part-time employment. But all of these solutions confront a critical obstacle in contemporary American society. The keystone of an effective day care program as here outlined is *parent participation.* But how can a mother, let alone a father, participate if she works full time, (which is one of the main reasons why the family needs day care in the first place)? I see only one possible solution to this problem — *increased opportunities and rewards for part-time employment.* It was in the light of this consideration that the aforementioned Report to the White House Conference urged business, industry, and government as employers to increase the number and status of part-time positions. In addition the Report recommended that state legislatures enact a "Fair Part-Time Employment Practices Act", which would prohibit discrimination in job opportunity, rate of pay, fringe benefits, and status for parents who sought or engaged in part-time employment.

Modification of work schedules and obligations. Along the same line, the Report also urged employers to re-examine and modify present policies and practices of the organization as they affected family life, especially in the following areas: out of town, weekend and overnight obligations; frequency and timing of geographical moves; flexibility of work schedule; leave and rest privileges for maternal and child care; and job-related social obligations.

The role of women in American society. These concerns bring us to a consideration of a factor which, in my judgment, profoundly affects the welfare of the nation's children. I refer to the place and status of women in American society. Setting aside the thorny but important issue of whether women are more gifted and effective in the care of young children than are men, the fact remains that in our society today, it is overwhelmingly on the women, and especially on mothers, that the care of our children depends. Moreover, with the withdrawal of the social supports for the family to which I alluded earlier, women and mothers have

become increasingly isolated. With the breakdown of community, neighborhood, and the extended family, an increasingly greater responsibility for the care and upbringing of children has fallen on the young mother. Under these circumstances, it is not surprising that many young women in America are in the process of revolting. I for one understand and share their sense of rage, but I fear the consequences of the solutions they advocate, which will have the effect of isolating children still further from the kind of care and attention they need. There is, of course, a constructive implication to this line of thought; namely, *a major route to the rehabilitation of children and youth in American society lies in the enhancement of the status and power of women in all walks of life — both on the job and in the home.* As I read the research literature, the ideal arrangement for the development of the young child is one in which his mother — and father for that matter — works part-time, for only in this way can she be the full person that being an effective parent requires.

Reacquainting children with adults as participants in the world of work. One of the most significant effects of age-segregation in our society has been the isolation of children from the world of work. Whereas in the past children not only saw what their parents did for a living but even shared substantially in the task, many children nowadays have only a vague notion of the nature of the parent's job, and have had little or no opportunity to observe the parent, or for that matter any other adult, when he is fully engaged in his work. Although there is no systematic research evidence on this subject, it appears likely that the absence of such exposure contributes significantly to the growing alienation among children and youth that we have already described. Yet, as experience in other modern urban societies indicates, such isolation of children from adults in the world of work is not inevitable, since it may be countered by creative social innovations. Perhaps the most imaginative and pervasive of these is the pattern universally employed in the Soviet Union (Bronfenbrenner, 1970), in which a place of work — such as a shop in a factory, an office, institute, or business enterprise — adopts a group of children as their "wards." The children's group is typically a school classroom, but may also include a nursery hospital ward, or any other setting in which children are dealt with collectively. The workers not only visit the children's group wherever it may be, but also invite the youngsters to the place of work in order to familiarize the child with the nature of their own activities and with themselves as people. The aim is not vocational education, but rather acquaintance with adults as participants in the world of work.

There seems to be nothing in such an approach that would be incompatible with the values and aims of her own society, and this writer has

urged its adaptation to the American scene. Acting on this suggestion, Dr. Ðavid Goslin of the Russell Sage Foundation persuaded one of America's great newspapers, the *Detroit Free Press*, to participate in an unusual experiment as a prelude to the White House Conference on Children. By the time it was over, two groups of twelve-year-old children, one from a slum area, the other predominantly middle class, had spent six to seven hours a day for three days in virtually every department of the newspaper, not just observing, but actively participating in the department's activities. There were boys and girls in the press room, the city room, the composing room, the advertising department, and the dispatch department. The employees of the *Free Press* entered into the experiment with serious misgivings. "This is a busy place; we have a newspaper to get out every day. What are those kids going to do, just sit around? And besides, the language that's used around here isn't exactly what you'd want a kid to hear!" What actually happened is recorded in a documentary film that was made of the experiment.[2] The children were not bored; nor were the adults. And the paper did get out every day. Here are some of the spontaneous comments recorded in the film.

"Adults should talk more with children and pay more attention to them instead of leaving them in the dark — because you can't really get to know much about each other unless you talk." — Gian, age 11

"It's sad to see her leaving. In three days she became part of the group up there." — Tony, age 53

"This is a place to meet, a way to understand people." — Megan, age 11

"It's been fun, it really has . . . I talked to him about having him out to our house to meet my sons and visit with us." — Joe, age 36

"If every kid in Detroit and all around the United States got to do this — I don't think there would be as many problems in the world." — Collette, age 11

Of course, the adults at work whom the children got to know at the *Detroit Free Press* were not their own parents. Remarking on this fact, a group of leading businessmen and industrialists at a conference convened by the Johnson Foundation in follow-up of the White House recommendations came up with a modification which they proposed to try in their own companies; namely, having the employees invite their own children to spend an extended period at the parent's place of work. At first, the notion was that the parents would take time off, so that they could be free to be with their children, but one of the participants correctly pointed out that this would defeat the entire purpose of the under-

taking, which was to enable children to see their parents engaged in responsible and demanding tasks.

It should be clear that if these kinds of innovations are to accomplish their objective, they cannot be confined to a single experience, even of three days, but must be continued, at intermittent intervals, over an extended period of time. Nor is it yet established what the effect of such innovations will be on the behavior and development of children. Indeed we do not even know whether American society will find such innovations acceptable and feasible. But there is some hope that experiments of this kind will be tried. As this is being written, the *Detroit Free Press* film has just become available for distribution to the public, and already the word has come back that a variety of innovations are being initiated. In one community, for example, the city government has decided to "adopt" groups of children in order to acquaint them with the people and activities involved in that enterprise. In another area, advertisements have been placed in the local newspaper asking persons engaged in a wide variety of occupations (e.g. carpenter, insurance salesman, garage mechanic, social worker, etc.) whether they would be willing to have one child accompany them as they go through the day's work. As such innovations are introduced, they should be evaluated not only in terms of their impact on the child, but also on the adult who, perhaps for the first time, is being asked to relate to a young child in the context of his life's occupation.

The involvement of children in genuine responsibilities. If the child is to become a responsible person, he must not only be exposed to adults engaged in demanding tasks, but himself, from early on, begin to participate in such activities. In the perspective of cross-cultural research, one of the characteristics that emerges most saliently for our nation is what Nicholas Hobbs has called "the inutility of childhood" in American society. To quote again from the White House Report:

> Our children are not entrusted with any real responsibilities in their family, neighborhood, or community. Little that they do really matters. When they do participate, it is in some inconsequential undertaking. They are given duties rather than responsibilities; that is, the ends and means have been determined by someone else, and their job is to fulfill an assignment involving little judgment, decision making, or risk. The latter remain within the purvay of supervising adults. Although this policy is deemed to serve the interest of the children themselves by protecting them from burdens beyond their years, there is reason to believe that it has been carried too far in contemporary American society and has contributed to the alienation and alleged incapacity of young people to deal constructively with personal and social prob-

lems. The evidence indicates that children acquire the capacity to cope with difficult situations when they have been given opportunity to take on consequential responsibilities in relation to others, *and are held acountable for them* (*Report to the President*, P. 247).

The role of the school. While training for responsibility by giving responsibility clearly begins in the family, the institution which has probably done the most to keep children insulated from challenging social tasks is the American school system. For historical reasons rooted in the separation of church and state, this system has been isolated from responsible social concern both substantively and spatially. In terms of content, education in America, when viewed from a cross-cultural perspective, seems peculiarly one-sided; it emphasizes subject matter to the exclusion of another molar aspect of the child's development. The neglect of this second area is reflected by the absence of any generally accepted term for it in our educational vocabulary. What the Germans call *Erziehung*, the Russians *vospitanie*, and the French *education* has no common counterpart in English. Perhaps the best equivalents are "upbringing" or "character education"—terms which, to the extent that they have any meaning to us at all, sound outmoded and irrelevant. In many countries of Western and Eastern Europe, however, the corresponding terms are not only current, but constitute what is regarded as the core of the educational process—the development of the child's qualities as a person—his values, motives, and patterns of social response. The last mentioned category underscores the point that these are matters not only of educational philosophy, as they are sometimes with us, but of concrete educational practice both within the classroom and without—in home, neighborhood, and larger community.

The preceding statement highlights the second insular aspect of the American educational process; our schools, and thereby our children, are kept insulated from the immediate social environment, from the life of the community, neighborhood, and the families that the schools purport to serve, and the life for which they are supposedly preparing the children under their charge.

Moreover, the insularity characterizing the relation of the American school to the outside world is repeated within the school system itself, where children are segregated into classrooms that have little social connection to each other or to the school as a common community, for which members might take active responsibility both as individuals and groups.

During the past decade, the trend toward segregation of the school from the rest of the society has been rapidly accelerated by the other forces of social disorganization that we have discussed. *As a result, the*

*schools have become one of the most potent breeding grounds of aliena-
tion in American society.* For this reason, it is of crucial importance for
the welfare and development of school age children that schools be rein-
tegrated into the life of the community. Above all, we must reverse the
present trend toward the construction and administration of schools as
isolated compounds divorced from the rest of the community. Many
such schools are becoming quasi-penal institutions in which teachers are
increasingly forced to function as detectives and guards with pupils being treated as suspects or prisoners for whom liberty is a special privilege.

As studies of other contemporary societies show (Bronfenbrenner,
1970; Jarus, Marcus, Oren, & Rapaport, 1970) educational programs do
not have to be carried out in isolation from the rest of the society. We
have already described the Soviet institution of "group adoption" which
provides a bridge between the school and the world of working adults.
The Russians apply this same pattern within the school itself. Here it is
groups of children who do the "adopting". Thus each class takes on responsibility for the care of a group of children at a lower grade level. For
example, a third grade class "adopts" a first grade class in the same
school, or a kindergarten in the immediate neighborhood. The older children escort the younger ones to the school or center, play with them on
the playground, teach them new games, read to them, help them learn.
Moreover, the manner in which they fulfill this civic responsibility enters
into the evaluation of their school performance as a regular part of the
curriculum.

Again, there is nothing in this pattern which would be incompatible
with the values and objectives of our own society. Indeed, some of its
elements are already present in the cross-age tutoring programs which
have begun to spring up around the country (Cloward, 1967; National
Commission on Resources for Youth, Inc., 1969; Parke, 1969). But here
again the focus tends to be on the development of skills and subject matter rather than concern for the total child as an individual and a member
of his own and the larger community.

One way of translating this broader concept in concrete terms would
be to establish in the school, beginning even at the elementary level,
what might be called *functional courses in human development.* These
would be distinguished in a number of important ways from courses or
units on "family life", as they are now taught in the junior high school,
chiefly for girls who do not plan to go on to college. The material is typically presented in vicarious form; that is, through reading, discussion, or
at most, through role playing, rather than actual role taking. In contrast,
the approach being proposed here would have as its core responsible
and active concern for the lives of young children and their families.
Such an experience could be facilitated by locating day care centers and

Head Start Programs in or near schools, so that they could be utilized as an integral part of the curriculum. The older children would be working with the younger ones on a regular basis. In addition, they would escort the little ones to and from school or center, and spend some time with them out of school. In this way, they would have an opportunity to become acquainted with the younger children's families, and the circumstances in which they live. This in turn would provide a vitalizing context for the study of services and facilities available to children and families in the community, such as health care, social services, recreation facilities, and of course, the schools themselves. Obviously, the scope of responsibility would increase with the age of the child, but throughout there would have to be adequate supervision and clear delineation of the limits of responsibility carried by older children in relation to the young.

The same pattern of responsible involvement could also be applied in relation to other groups such as the aged, the sick, the disadvantaged, and those living alone.

Finally, within a broader perspective, the children should be given an active part in defining what the problems are in their school and their community, and what their responsibility is or should become in contributing to a solution to these problems. Within the school, this implies greater involvement of children in the formulation and enforcement of codes of behavior and in the planning and development of activities of the classroom, so that the burden of maintaining discipline does not fall solely or even primarily on the shoulders of the teacher, who would then be left free to perform the primary function of expanding the children's horizon and range of competence.

Neighborhoods and communities as support systems. It has been the central thesis of this paper that the power of parents, and other adults, to function as constructive forces in the lives of children depends in substantial measure on the degree to which the surrounding community provides the place, time, example, and encouragement for persons to engage in activities with the young. This, in turn, implies the existence, and, where need be, the establishment in the community of institutions which address themselves primarily to these concerns. It is significant that, at the present time, few such institutions do in fact exist. As matters now stand, the needs of children are parceled out among a hopeless confusion of agencies with diverse objectives, conflicting jurisdictions, and imperfect channels of communication. The school, the health department, churches, welfare services, youth organizations, the medical profession, libraries, the police, recreation programs — all of these see the children and parents of the community at one time or another, but no one of them is concerned with the total pattern of life for children and families in the community. If such child and family oriented institutions

and activities were to be established, what might they be like? Here are some possibilities:

1. *Commission for Children and Families.* Such a Commission, established at the community or neighborhood level, would have as its initial charge finding out what the community is doing, or not doing, for its children and their families. The Commission would examine the adequacy of existing programs such as maternal and child health services, day care facilities, and recreational opportunities. It would also investigate what places and people are available to children when they are not in school, what opportunities they have for play, challenging activities, or useful work, and to whom they can turn for guidance or assistance. The Commission would also assess the existing and needed resources in the community that provide families with opportunities for learning, living, and leisure that involve common activity across levels of age, ability, knowledge, and skill.

In order to accomplish its task, the Commission would need to include representatives of the major institutions concerned with children and families, as well as other segments of community life such as business, industry, and labor. Especially important is inclusion on the Commission of teenagers and older children who can speak directly from their own experiences. The Commission would be expected to report its findings and recommendations to appropriate executive bodies and to the public at large through mass media. After completing the initial assessment phase, the Commission would assume continued responsibility for developing and monitoring programs to implement its recommendations.

2. *Neighborhood Family Centers.* Families are strengthened through association with each other in common activities and responsibilities. For this to occur, there must be places where families can meet in order to work and play together. The Neighborhood Family Center is such a place. Located in the school, church, or other community building, it provides a focal point for leisure and learning and community problem solving to all family members. The Center offers facilities for games and creative activities that could be engaged in by persons of all ages with space for those who prefer merely to "watch the fun". To eliminate fragmentation of services, the Center can also serve as the local "one door" entry point for obtaining family services in the areas of health, child care, legal aid, welfare, etc. The Center differs from the traditional community center in emphasizing cross-age rather than age-segregated activities.

3. *Community and Neighborhood Projects.* Community organizations should be encouraged to provide a variety of activities which ena-

ble different generations to have contact and become a significant part of each other's lives. Through community sponsored projects, individuals of all ages can grow in their appreciation of each other as they learn to give to one another through a sharing of their talents and skills. The growing interest in ecology—cleaning up the environment—provides an excellent focus for such common endeavors, since it requires a variety of knowledges, skills, and services. Concern for the aged, the sick, and the lonely provide similar challenges. In the organization and execution of such projects, young people should participate not as subordinates but as active collaborators who can contribute ideas and direction as well as service. In addition to work projects, there is a need for recreational facilities and programs in which cross-age activities can take place (for example, family camps, fairs, games, picnics, etc.).

4. *Participation of Youth in Local Policy Bodies.*   In keeping with the principle that young people become responsible by being given and held accountable for responsibilities that really matter, every community organization having jurisdiction over activities affecting children and youth should include some teenagers and older children as voting members. This would include such organizations as school boards, welfare commissions, recreation commissions, and hospital boards.

5. *Community and Neighborhood Planning.*   Much of what happens to children and families in a community is determined by the ecology of the neighborhood in which the family lives. The implication of this principle for our own times is illustrated in a recent research report on the effect of the so-called "new towns" on the lives of children. It is perhaps characteristic that the question was raised not within our own society but in West Germany. The study compared the actions of children living in 18 new "model communities" with those from youngsters living in older German cities. The research was conducted by the Urban and Planning Institute in Nuremberg in collaboration with the Institute of Psychology at the University of Erlangen-Nuremberg. As of this writing, copies of the technical report are not yet available in this country; the following are excerpts from a special bulletin to the *New York Times* (May 9, 1971):

> In the new towns of West Germany, amid soaring rectangular shapes of apartment houses with shaded walks, big lawns and fenced-in play areas, the children for whom much of this has been designed apparently feel isolated, regimented and bored . . .
>
> The study finds that the children gauge their freedom not by the extent of open areas around them, but by the liberty they have to be among people and things that excite them and fire their imaginations . . .

Children in the older cities seemed enthusiastic about their surroundings, painting a great amount of detail into a variety of things they found exciting around them, according to those who interpreted their art.

The children in the model communities often painted what were considered despairing pictures of the world the adults had fashioned for them, depicting an uninviting, concrete fortress of cleanliness and order and boredom.

The implications of the research are self evident. In the planning and design of new communities, housing projects, and urban renewal, the planners, both public and private, need to give explicit consideration to the kind of world that is being created for the children who will be growing up in these settings. Particular attention should be given to the opportunities which the environment presents or precludes for involvement of children with persons both older and younger than themselves. Among the specific factors to be considered are the location of shops and businesses where children could have contact with adults at work, recreational and day care facilities readily accessible to parents as well as children, provision for a Family Neighborhood Center and family oriented facilities and services, availability of public transportation, and, perhaps most important of all, places to walk, sit, and talk in common company.

It is perhaps most fitting to end this discussion with a proposal for nothing more radical than providing a setting in which young and old can simply set and talk. The fact that such settings are disappearing and have to be deliberately recreated points both to the roots of the problem and its remedy. The evil, and the cure, lie not with the victims of alienation but in the social institutions which produce it, and their failure to be responsive to the most human needs and values of our democratic society.

Notes

1. Except as otherwise noted, the comparative data cited in this statement are documented in Bronfenbrenner, U., *Two Worlds of Childhood: U. S. and U.S.S.R.* (New York: Russell Sage Foundation, 1970). See especially pages 95 – 124.

2. "A Place to Meet, a Way to Understand". The National Audiovisual Center (GSA), Washington, D. C. 0409.

References

Bronfenbrenner, U. Socialization and social class through time and space. In E. E. Maccoby, T. M. Newcomb, and E. Hartley (Eds.),

Readings in Social Psychology, 3rd edition. New York: Holt, 1958, 400–425.

Brofenbrenner, U. and Bruner J. The President and the children. *The New York Times*, January 31, 1972, p. 41.

Bronfenbrenner, U. Socialization and social class through time and space. In E. E. Maccoby, T. M. Newcomb, and E. Hartley (Eds.), *Readings in Social Psychology*, 3rd edition. New York: Holt, 1958, 400–425.

Bronfenbrenner, U. *Two Worlds of Childhood: U.S. and U.S.S.R.* New York: Russell Sage Foundation, 1970.

Cloward, R. D. Studies in tutoring. *Journal of Experimental Education*, Fall 1967, **36,** 14–25.

Condry, J. C. & Siman, M. A. Characteristics of peer- and adult-oriented children. Unpublished manuscript, Cornell University, 1968.

Condry, J. C. & Siman, M. A. An experimental study of adult versus peer orientation. Unpublished manuscript, Cornell University, 1968.

Devereux, E. C., Jr., Bronfenbrenner, U., & Rodgers, R. R. Child rearing in England and the United States: A cross-national comparison. *Journal of Marriage and the Family*, May 1969, **31,** 257–270.

Garbarino, J. A note on the effects of television. In Bronfenbrenner, U. (ed.), *Influences on human development*. Hinsdale, Illinois: The Dryden Press, 1972.

Jarus, A., Marcus, J., Oren, J., & Rapaport, Ch. *Children and Families in Israel.* New York: Gordon and Breach, 1970.

National Commission on Resources for Youth, Inc. *Youth tutoring youth—it worked.* A final report, January 31, 1969. 36 West 44th St., New York, N. Y. 10036.

Parke, B. K. Towards a new rationale for cross-age tutoring. Unpublished manuscript, Cornell University, November 1969.

Profiles of Children: White House Conference on Children. Washington, D. C.: U. S. Government Printing Office, 1970.

Report to the President: White House Conference on Children. Washington, D. C.: U. S. Government Printing Office, 1970. 240–255.

Rodgers, R. R. Changes in parental behavior reported by children in West Germany and the United States. *Human Development*, 1971, **14,** 208–224.

Yankelovich, D. *The changing values on campus: Political and personal attitudes of today's college students.* New York: Washington Square Press, 1972.

Dr. Spitz wishes to add the following statement, clarifying certain theoretical points omitted in the present condensed version of his articles:

I.   This research supports the proposition that ego formation is an adaptive process, leading to the inception and establishment of a coherent psychic system by the end of the first year.

II.   Consequently so-called "psychiatric disturbances" *before* the establishment of a psychic system cannot be due to genuine *psychic* conflict. Therefore infantile behavior disturbances are not comparable to adult psychiatric disease. They originate actually in disturbances of the survival-ensuring adaptive process of reciprocal affective exchanges between mother and child.

III.   These findings disprove also the Kleinian hypothesis on earliest psychic development and infantile fantasies; the latter cannot be postulated before the establishment of a coherent psychic system. Nor can developmental propositions like the so-called "depressive position" be entertained at an age level at which cognition, volition, representation and even perception is not yet established in a coherent form.

R. A. SPITZ, M.D.
September 6, 1972

Influences on Human Development

Edited by
Urie Bronfenbrenner
Cornell University

With the assistance of Maureen A. Mahoney

The Dryden Press Inc.
Hinsdale, Illinois

Influences
on Human
Development